Modula-2 Reference Chart (cont.)

Program Composition (Page in Text)	Exa...

Procedure section
  Proper procedure
    definition (27ff)

```
PROCEDURE ReadInfo(VAR Dept : CHAR,
                   VAR Id : CARDINAL);
  (* Read department code & employee id *)
  BEGIN
    WriteString('Enter dept. code & employee id: ');
    Read(Dept);
    ReadCard(Id)
  END ReadInfo;
```

  Function procedure
    definition (27ff)

```
PROCEDURE RoundCents(Amount : REAL) : REAL;
  (* Returns Amount rounded to the nearest cent *)
  BEGIN
    RETURN TRUNC(100.00 * Amount + 0.05) / 100.0
  END RoundCents;
```

Module section
  Local module format (103ff)
    Local module heading
      Opening documentation
      Import-export part

      Declaration part

      Statement part.

```
MODULE ReportGenerator;
(* Procedures to generate special reports *)
  FROM SpecialInOut IMPORT FWriteReal;
  EXPORT PrintReport, PrintSummary, WrapUp;
  PROCEDURE PrintReport(TotalSales, . . .);
    .
    .
    .
END ReportGenerator;
```

Statement part (5)

```
BEGIN
  statement-1;
    .
    .
    .
  statement-n
END Demo.
```

Definition module format (30ff, 152ff)
  Definition module heading
    Opening documentation
    Import part
    Declaration part
  END module-name;

```
DEFINITION MODULE BooleanInOut;
  (* Procedures for boolean input/output *)
  PROCEDURE WriteBoolean(BVal : BOOLEAN);
    (* Displays value of BVal *)
  PROCEDURE ReadBoolean(VAR BVal : BOOLEAN);
    (* Reads a value for BVal *)
END BooleanInOut.
```

Implementation module format
(31ff, 154ff)
  Implementation module heading
  Opening documentation
  Import part
  Declaration part
  Statement part.

```
IMPLEMENTATION MODULE BooleanInOut;
  (* Procedures for boolean input/output *)
  FROM InOut IMPORT ReadString, WriteString;
  PROCEDURE WriteBoolean(BVal : BOOLEAN);
    (* Displays value of BVal *)
    BEGIN
      IF BVal THEN WriteString('TRUE')
      ELSE WriteString('FALSE')
      END (* IF *)
    END WriteBoolean;
      .
      .
END BooleanInOut.
```

Data Structures and
Program Design
in Modula-2

LARRY NYHOFF
SANFORD LEESTMA
Department of Mathematics and Computer Science
Calvin College, Grand Rapids, Michigan

Data Structures and Program Design in Modula-2

Macmillan Publishing Company
NEW YORK

Collier Macmillan Publishers
LONDON

Editor(s): David Johnstone, Ed Moura
Production Supervisor: Ron Harris
Production Manager: Nicholas Sklitsis
Text Designer: Eileen Burke
Cover Designer: Jody Ouellette
Cover photograph: Dick Brown
Photo Researcher: John Schultz

This book was set in 10½/12 Times Roman by Waldman Graphics Inc., printed and bound by Halliday Lithograph.
The cover was printed by Phoenix Color Corp.

Macmillan Publishing Company
866 Third Avenue, New York, New York 10022

Collier Macmillan Canada, Inc.

Library of Congress Cataloging in Publication Data

Nyhoff, Larry R.
    Data structures and program design in Modula-2 / Larry
Nyhoff, Sanford Leestma.
        p. cm.
    A portion of this book is reprinted from PASCAL, programming and
problem solving, 2nd ed.
    Includes index.
    ISBN 0-02-388621-8
    1. Modula-2 (Computer program language) 2. Data structures
(Computer science) I. Leestma, Sanford. II. Leestma, Sanford.
Pascal. 1990. III. Title.
QA76.73.M63N94 1990
005.13'3--dc20   89-12370
                                                                          CIP

Printing: 2 3 4 5 6 7 8   Year: 0 1 2 3 4 5 6 7 8 9

PREFACE

In the early 1980s the Curriculum Task Force of the ACM (Association of Computing Machinery) was given the task of producing an updated syllabus for the first two courses in computer science, CS1: *Introduction to Programming Methodology* and CS2: *Program Design and Implementations*. In their report "Recommended Curriculum for CS, 1984," which appeared in the August, 1985 issue of the *Communications of the ACM*, the following objectives for CS2 were presented:

- To continue developing a disciplined approach to the design, coding, and testing of programs written in a block-structured high-level language.
- To teach the use of data abstraction using as examples data structures other than those normally provided as basic types in current programming languages—for example, linked lists, stacks, queues, and trees.
- To provide an understanding of the different implementations of these data structures.
- To introduce searching and sorting algorithms and their analysis.
- To provide a foundation for further studies in computer science.

This text is designed to meet these course objectives. It continues to emphasize the application of software engineering principles to the design of structured algorithms and programs begun in our texts *Programming and Problem Solving in Modula-2* and *Pascal: Programming and Problem Solving,* Third Edition, which were written to meet the objectives for CS1. More than thirty examples consisting of algorithms, complete programs, and sample runs illustrate the application of these basic principles. In this text the simple data structures introduced in CS1 are used as building blocks for the more complex data structures listed in the preceding objectives, emphasizing the distinction between an abstract data type and its implementation. Separate chapters are devoted to searching and sorting algorithms, and techniques for measuring the efficiency of these and other algorithms and for verifying their correctness are introduced. Examples and exercises are carefully selected to provide an introduction to a number of areas in computer science—for example,

- Reverse Polish Notation and generation of machine code
- Indirect recursion and parsing
- Symmetric linked lists and large integer arithmetic

- String processing and data encryption schemes (DES and public key)
- Random number generation and simulation
- Concurrent programming

A solid base is thus established on which later courses in theoretical and/or applied computer science can build.

We assume that the reader has completed a first course in programming that presented the basic features of Modula-2 or Pascal. Chapter 0 is included to provide a transition to Modula-2 for those whose background is in Pascal. Arrays, records, sets, and modules are presented in separate sections of Chapter 2, allowing the instructor to omit or assign for reading and review those sections dealing with topics already familiar to the student. A summary of the main features of Modula-2 is given in Appendixes B, C, D, and F and on the front and back covers.

A solutions manual for the text is available from the publisher. It contains solutions to nearly all the written exercises together with complete programs, program segments, or algorithms for many of the programming exercises. Disks containing all the sample programs and data files used in the text are also available.

Acknowledgments

We express our sincere appreciation to all those who were involved in the preparation of this text. We especially thank David Johnstone, who initiated this project, and Ed Moura, Ron Harris, and other Macmillan personnel who guided it to completion. The work of Jon Cremer and Andy Bass in the preparation of some of the programs and supplementary materials is also much appreciated. We also wish to thank the following reviewers for their valuable comments and suggestions: Kulbir Arora, SUNY at Buffalo; Larre Egbert, Utah State University; Richard Hunkler, Slippery Rock State University; Abe Kandel, Florida State University; John Kuhl, University of Iowa; Robert Little, Mississippi State University; Brent Murrill, Virginia Commonwealth University; Edwin Reilly, SUNY at Albany; Paul Sand, University of New Hampshire; Nancy Weigand, University of Wisconsin; Laurie White, Eckerd College; and Richard Wiener, University of Colorado at Colorado Springs. We thank our families—Shar, Jeff, Dawn, Jim, Julie, Joan, Marge, Michelle, Sandy, and Michael—for their support and encouragement, for being more understanding, patient, loving, and long-suffering than we have any right to expect. We thank God for them and we thank Him too for giving us the opportunity to write this text and for allowing us to see it through to completion.

L. N.
S. L.

CONTENTS

Data Structures and Program Design in Modula-2

0

From Pascal to Modula-2

The purpose of this text is to study some advanced techniques of program design and to introduce several basic data structures. The programming language used to implement these techniques and structures is Modula-2. The book assumes that the reader has completed a first course in programming that presented the basic features of either Modula-2 or Pascal. This opening chapter summarizes those topics in Modula-2 that are normally covered in a first course and is intended to provide an easy transition from Pascal to Modula-2. It assumes familiarity with the basic features of Pascal, including functions, procedures, text files, arrays, and records. Readers who have already studied the Modula-2 topics covered in this chapter may proceed directly to Chapter 1.

Modula-2, like Pascal, was developed by the Swiss computer scientist Niklaus Wirth. It was introduced in the late 1970s, and although no official standard has yet appeared, Wirth's text *Programming in Modula-2* has served as the de facto standard for the language.[1] It is the version of Modula-2 described in the fourth edition of Wirth's book that serves as the basis for this text. It should be noted, however, that several Modula-2 systems have appeared in recent years and that some of these do not support the language exactly as Wirth described it.

0.1 Program Composition

There are many similarities between Pascal programs and Modula-2 programs. To illustrate some of these, consider the following Pascal program that reads integers, counts them, and calculates their range, that is, the difference between the largest and smallest integers.

[1] Niklaus Wirth, *Programming in Modula-2*, 4th ed. (New York: Springer-Verlag, 1989). The third and fourth editions of this book include a number of changes in and extensions to earlier descriptions of the language.

```
program CalculateRange (input,output);

(* This program calculates the range of a set of integers
   entered by the user. *)

const
    EndOfData = -9999;

var
    Number,                 (* current number *)
    Largest,                (* largest number in the set *)
    Smallest,               (* smallest number in the set *)
    Count : integer;        (* a count of the numbers *)

begin
    write ('Enter the integers, using ', EndOfData:1);
    writeln ('to signal the end of data.');

    (* Read the first integer and initialize Largest, Smallest, and Count *)
    write ('Number?  ');
    readln (Number);
    Count := 1;
    Largest := Number;
    Smallest := Number;

    (* Read remaining integers until user signals the end of data *)
    write ('Number?  ');
    readln (Number);
    while Number <> EndOfData do
        begin
            Count := Count + 1;
            if Number > Largest then
                Largest := Number
            else if Number < Smallest then
                Smallest := Number;
            write ('Number?  ');
            readln (Number)
        end (* while *);

    (* Display count of values and their range *)
    writeln (Count:1, ' numbers');
    writeln ('Range = ', Largest - Smallest:1)
end (* Calculate Range *).
```

The corresponding program in Modula-2 is

```
MODULE CalculateRange;

(* This program calculates the range of a set of integers
    entered by the user. *)

    FROM InOut IMPORT ReadInt, WriteInt, WriteCard,
                    WriteString, WriteLn, Done;

    VAR
        Number,                 (* current number *)
        Largest,                (* largest number in the set *)
        Smallest : INTEGER;     (* smallest number in the set *)
        Count : CARDINAL;       (* a count of the numbers *)

BEGIN
    WriteString('Enter the integers; enter any non-digit');
    WriteLn;
    WriteString('character to signal the end of data.');
    WriteLn;

    (* Read the first integer and initialize Largest, Smallest, and Count *)

    WriteString('Number?  ');
    ReadInt(Number);
    Count := 1;
    Largest := Number;
    Smallest := Number;

    (* Read remaining integers until user signals the end of data *)
    WriteString('Number?  ');
    ReadInt(Number);
    WHILE Done DO
        WriteLn;
        INC(Count);
        IF Number > Largest THEN
            Largest := Number
        ELSIF Number < Smallest THEN
            Smallest := Number
        END (* IF *);
        WriteString('Number?  ');
        ReadInt(Number)
    END (* WHILE *);

(* Display count of values and their range *)
    WriteLn;
    WriteCard(Count, 1);
    WriteString(' numbers');
    WriteLn;
    WriteString('Range = ');
    WriteInt(Largest - Smallest, 1);
    WriteLn
END CalculateRange.
```

This example illustrates that the general structure of a Modula-2 program is quite similar to that of a Pascal program. There are a number of differences, however, and we now list several of these. Others will be described in the sections that follow.

1. Both Pascal and Modula-2 programs include a heading, a declaration part, and a statement part, but a Modula-2 program also includes an import part.

Pascal	Modula-2
program heading	program heading
declaration part	import part
statement part.	declaration part
	statement part.

2. The ***program heading*** in Modula-2 begins with the reserved word MODULE and does not include a file list.

Pascal	Modula-2
program *program-name* (*file-list*);	MODULE *program-name*;

3. Comments in Modula-2 must be enclosed between (* and *); { and } are used to denote set constants. Also, comments may be nested; that is, one comment may be included within another.

Pascal	Modula-2
(* *comment* *)	(* *comment* *)
{ *comment* }	(* *comment* (* *comment* *) *comment* *)

4. An ***import part*** must be used in a Modula-2 program to import input/output procedures and various other items into a program from standard library modules such as *InOut* and other user-developed library modules.

Pascal	Modula-2
	FROM *library-module-name* IMPORT *list*;
	IMPORT *library-module-name*;

5. The ***declaration part*** of a Modula-2 program may not have a label section, but it may have a module section in which local modules are defined:

Pascal	Modula-2
label section	constant section;
constant section;	type section;
type section;	variable section;
variable section;	procedure section;
subprogram section;	module section;

Also, unlike Pascal, the sections in a Modula-2 declaration part may appear any number of times and in any order, subject to the usual restriction that an item must be defined before it can be used to declare another item.

6. *Type sections* and *variable sections* have the same forms in Modula-2 as in Pascal, but constant expressions are allowed in *constant sections*.

Pascal	Modula-2
const	CONST
identifier-1 = constant-1;	*identifier-1 = constant-expression-1*;
⋮	⋮
identifier-k = constant-k;	*identifier-k = constant-expression-k*;
type	TYPE
identifier-1 = type-1;	*identifier-1 = type-1*;
⋮	⋮
identifier-m = type-m;	*identifier-m = type-m*;
var	VAR
identifier-1 : type-1;	*identifier-1 : type-1*;
⋮	⋮
identifier-n : type-n;	*identifier-n : type-n*;

7. In the *statement part* of a Modula-2 program, the program name that appears in the program heading must appear in the END clause that closes the statement part.

Pascal	Modula-2
begin	BEGIN
statement-1;	*statement-1*;
⋮	⋮
statement-s	*statement-s*
end.	END *program-name*.

8. Unlike Pascal, Modula-2 is *case sensitive*. For example, *MoreData*, *Moredata*, *MOREDATA*, and *moredata* are different identifiers.

9. Pascal and Modula-2 have many *reserved words* in common. However, all reserved words in Modula-2 must be in upper case.

Pascal	Modula-2
and	AND
array	ARRAY
begin	BEGIN
	BY
case	CASE
const	CONST
	DEFINITION
div	DIV
do	DO
downto	
else	ELSE
	ELSIF
end	END
	EXIT
	EXPORT
file	
for	FOR
	FROM
function	
goto	
if	IF
	IMPLEMENTATION
	IMPORT
in	IN
label	
	LOOP
mod	MOD
	MODULE
nil	(NIL is a standard identifier)
not	NOT
of	OF
or	OR
packed	
	POINTER
procedure	PROCEDURE
program	
	QUALIFIED
record	RECORD
repeat	REPEAT
	RETURN
set	SET
then	THEN
to	TO
type	TYPE
until	UNTIL
var	VAR
while	WHILE
with	WITH

0.2 Data Types

Pascal and Modula-2 provide essentially the same simple data types, and both provide the structured data types arrays, records, and sets.

Pascal	Modula-2
	CARDINAL
integer	INTEGER
real	REAL
char	CHAR
boolean	BOOLEAN
array [*index-type*] **of** *comp-type*	ARRAY *index-type* OF *comp-type*
packed array [*index-type*] **of** *comp-type*	
record *field-list* **end**	RECORD *field-list* END
	BITSET
set of *element-type*	SET OF *element-type*
text	
file of *comp-type*	*File* (imported from a library module)
enumerated: (*id-1, id-2, . . . , id-n*)	enumeration: (*id-1, id-2, . . . , id-n*)
subrange: *first .. last*	subrange: [*first .. last*]

In this section we summarize the simple data types of Modula-2 and arrays and records. Sets are described in Section 2.6.

Simple Data Types. A simple data type is a type whose values consist of single items. Modula-2 provides five standard simple data types[2]—CARDINAL, INTEGER, REAL, CHAR, and BOOLEAN—and two user-defined simple types—enumeration types and subrange types.

Values of type **CARDINAL** are nonnegative integers that usually range from 0 through $2^w - 1$, where w is the word length of the computer being used. In addition to the usual unsigned base-10 representation, an octal representation consisting of a base-8 numeral followed by the letter B may be used. A hexadecimal representation consisting of a base-16 numeral whose first digit must be one of 0, 1, . . . , 9 and that must be followed by the letter H is also allowed.

---

[2] In *Programming in Modula-2*, Wirth mentions three other data types, LONGCARD, LONGINT, and LONGREAL, that may be used to process large cardinal, integer, and real values, respectively. But because descriptions of these types are not complete and implementations vary widely among Modula-2 systems, we will not use them in this text.

Values of type **INTEGER** are usually restricted to the range -2^{w-1} through $2^{w-1} - 1$, where w is the word length. Decimal, octal, and hexadecimal representations of values of type INTEGER are allowed.

As in Pascal, **REAL** values may be in either decimal or scientific form. The decimal representation of a real constant must include at least one digit before the decimal point but need not have a digit after the decimal point. Scientific or floating-point representation consists of a real constant in decimal form (but not an integer) followed by E (but not e) followed by an integer constant.

A value of type **CHAR** consists of a character enclosed within single quotes (apostrophes) or within double quotes. If this character is an apostrophe, it must be enclosed within double quotes; if it is a double quote, it must be enclosed within single quotes. A character constant may also be represented by its numeric code written in octal and followed by the letter C. Thus, if ASCII is assumed, 'Z', "Z", and 132C all denote the same character constant.

Although there is no predefined string type in Modula-2, string constants may be displayed by the *WriteString* procedure. String constants consist of strings enclosed within single or double quotes. If the string contains an apostrophe, it must be enclosed in double quotes; if it contains a double quote, single quotes must be used to enclose it.

There are two **BOOLEAN** values in Modula-2: TRUE and FALSE. Since these are reserved words, they must be written in upper case.

Types CARDINAL, INTEGER, and BOOLEAN are predefined *ordinal types*. Like Pascal, Modula-2 also provides user-defined ordinal types: enumeration and subrange. *Enumeration types* are defined just as they are in Pascal, by simply listing the values of that data type, separated by commas and enclosed in parentheses; for example,

```
TYPE
    DaysOfWeek = (Sunday, Monday, Tuesday, Wednesday,
                  Thursday, Friday, Saturday);
```

Definitions of *subrange types* are similar to those in Pascal except that they must be enclosed within brackets; for example,

```
TYPE
    Digit = [0..9];
```

For integer subranges such as this, the base type is CARDINAL if the first value is nonnegative, INTEGER if it is negative. Subrange declarations of the form

type-identifier[first-value .. last-value]

in which the base type is specified explicitly are also allowed.

Arrays.   Like Pascal, Modula-2 supports both one-dimensional and multidimensional arrays. In this section we confine our attention to one-dimensional arrays; arrays of higher dimension are described in Section 2.3.

Declarations of one-dimensional arrays in Modula-2 have the same form as declarations in Pascal:

ARRAY *index-type* OF *component-type*

where *index-type* may be BOOLEAN, CHAR, an enumeration type, or a subrange type and *component-type* may be any type. Arrays may not be declared to be packed arrays, however.

One-dimensional arrays are processed in Modula-2 programs in essentially the same way as they are processed in Pascal. One difference is in the way that arrays of type CHAR are used to process strings. In Pascal, a declaration of a string type has the form **packed array**[1..*MaxString*] **of** *char*, but in Modula-2, string types are zero based; that is, a string declaration has the form ARRAY [0..*MaxString*] OF CHAR. Strings are considered in detail in Chapter 3. Another difference between Pascal and Modula-2 is in the use of open array parameters, which are described in Section 0.6.

Records. Records in Modula-2 may have several fixed parts and several variant parts. In this chapter we confine our attention to fixed records, those that have no variant parts; variant records are described in detail in Section 2.4. Declarations of fixed records in Modula-2 have a form that is almost identical to such declarations in Pascal:

RECORD
    list-1 : *type-1*;
        :
    list-n : *type-n*
END

where each *list-i* is a single indentifier or a list of identifiers that name the fields of the record, and *type-i* specifies the type of each of these fields. The fields in a record are accessed in the usual way by using *field-designated variables* of the form

record-name.field-name

Records are processed in Modula-2 in essentially the same way as in Pascal. In particular, a WITH statement may be used to attach a record name as a prefix to field names. The differences between the Modula-2 WITH statement and the Pascal **with** statement are described in Section 0.4.

0.3 Predefined Operations, Functions, and Procedures

The basic arithmetic operators in Modula-2 are denoted by the same symbols and identifiers as in Pascal:

Pascal	Modula-2
+	+
−	−
*	*
/	/
div	DIV
mod	MOD

However, the rules governing the use of these operators in Modula-2 are stricter than those for Pascal:

1. For +, −, and *, the operands must be of the same type, both CARDINAL, both INTEGER, or both REAL, and the result is the same type as the operands.[3]
2. The division operator / requires operands of type REAL and produces a real result.
3. For DIV and MOD, both the operands must be of type CARDINAL, or both must be of type INTEGER; the result has the same type as that of the operands. Moreover, in an expression of the form x MOD y, x must be nonnegative, and y must be positive.

The six relational operators are =, <, >, <=, >=, and # (or <>) and may be used with any of the simple data types. Both operands must have the same type when compared with one of these operators.

The three boolean operators are NOT (or ~), AND (or &), and OR. Boolean expressions of the form p AND q and p OR q are evaluated from left to right using *short-circuit evaluation* in which no more of the boolean expression is evaluated than is necessary to determine its value. For example, in evaluating the expression (N # 0) AND (M DIV N < 4), no division-by-zero error will occur, for if N is 0, the first expression N # 0 is false, and so the entire expression is false; the second expression is not evaluated.

Modula-2 also provides a number of predefined functions, as described in the following table:

Predefined function procedures

Procedure	Description	Type of Parameter(s)	Type of Value
ABS(x)	Absolute value of x	any numeric type	same as parameter
CAP(ch)	The uppercase letter corresponding to ch, if ch is a lowercase letter; ch, if ch is an uppercase letter	CHAR	CHAR
CHR(c)	Character whose ordinal number is c	CARDINAL	CHAR
FLOAT(c)	Real number equivalent to c	CARDINAL	REAL

[3]Unless noted otherwise, subranges of CARDINAL may be substituted for the type CARDINAL and subranges of INTEGER for the type INTEGER in any of the rules of this section.

Predefined function procedures (cont.)

Procedure	Description	Type of Parameter(s)	Type of Value
HIGH(a)	Maximum index (in first dimension) of a	any open array type	CARDINAL
MAX(T)	Maximum value of type T	name of any ordinal type	T
MIN(T)	Minimum value of type T	name of any ordinal type	T
ODD(x)	TRUE if x is odd, FALSE otherwise	CARDINAL or INTEGER	BOOLEAN
ORD(x)	Ordinal number of x	any ordinal type	CARDINAL
SIZE(T)	Size of a value of a variable T or of a variable of type T	any variable or any type identifier	CARDINAL
TRUNC(r)	Integer part of r	REAL	CARDINAL
VAL(T, c)	The value of type T whose ordinal number is c	T is any ordinal type; c is of type CARDINAL	T

It also provides the following predefined procedures:

Predefined proper procedures

Procedure	Description	Type of Parameter(s)
DEC(x)	Decrement x by 1; replace x by its predecessor	any ordinal type
DEC(x, c)	Decrement x by c; replace x by its cth predecessor	any ordinal type
EXCL(S, x)	Remove x from set S	S is a set of some type T (or BITSET); x is of type T
HALT	Terminate execution	none
INC(x)	Increment x by 1; replace x by its successor	any ordinal type
INC(x, c)	Increment x by c; replace x by its cth successor	any ordinal type
INCL(S, x)	Add x to set S	S is a set of some type T (or BITSET); x is of type T

Because Modula-2 is **strongly typed**, it is often necessary to convert values of one type to another. The functions FLOAT and TRUNC are especially useful for this. For example, if *Num* is of type CARDINAL, the expression

FLOAT(*Num*) / 3.0

can be used to calculate the real quotient of *Num* divided by 3.0. Similarly, if X is a positive real value, the expression

Num + TRUNC(X)

can be used to add the value of the integer part of the nonnegative real value X to the cardinal value *Num*. There is no rounding function provided in Modula-2.

VAL is another type conversion function; it can be used to convert a value of one ordinal type into the corresponding value of another ordinal type. For example, if *Num* is a variable of type CARDINAL with value 4, the value of the expression

   VAL(INTEGER, *Num*)

is the integer 4; thus, the expression

   -3 * VAL(INTEGER, *Num*)

is valid, since both operands are of type INTEGER. Similarly, if *Temp* is a variable of type INTEGER whose value is 13, the value of the expression

   VAL(CARDINAL, *Temp*)

is the cardinal number 13. If *Colors* is the enumeration type defined by

   TYPE
      Colors = (*red, white, blue, green, yellow, black*);

and *Num* is of type CARDINAL with value 4, the value of

   VAL(*Colors, Num*)

is *yellow*. Note, however, that an error occurs if the value being converted does not fall within the range of the type of the result; for example, an error results in evaluating the last expression if *Num* is negative or is greater than 5.

There are other useful type conversion and arithmetic functions, but they are not part of the Modula-2 language itself. Rather, they must be imported from the standard library module *MathLib0* (or *MathLib1* in some versions). The functions available in *MathLib0* may vary somewhat from one version of Modula-2 to another, but in all cases they should include at least the following:

Functions in *MathLib0*

Function	Description	Type of Parameter	Type of Value
arctan(x)	Inverse tangent of x (value in radians)	REAL	REAL
cos(x)	Cosine of x (in radians)	REAL	REAL
entier(x)	x truncated to its integer part	REAL	INTEGER
exp(x)	Exponential function e^x	REAL	REAL
ln(x)	Natural logarithm of x	REAL	REAL
real(n)	n converted to a real number	INTEGER	REAL
sin(x)	Sine of x (in radians)	REAL	REAL
sqrt(x)	Square root of x	REAL	REAL

If any of these functions are to be used in a program, they must appear in an import declaration of the form

FROM *MathLib0* IMPORT *list*

in the import part of the program, where *list* is a list of the functions to be used. Note that *entier* and *real* are the INTEGER ↔ REAL type conversion function analogous to the CARDINAL ↔ REAL type conversion functions TRUNC and FLOAT.

0.4   Statements

Modula-2 has basically the same statements as Pascal, although the syntax is different in many cases. The following table lists the basic statements in the two languages, showing the syntax for each; in each case, *var* denotes a variable, *exp* an expression, *stat* a statement, and *stat-seq* a sequence of statements separated by semicolons:

Statement	Pascal	Modula-2
assignment	*var* := *exp*	*var* := *exp*

case	**case** *exp* **of**
	    list-1 : *stat-1*;
	    list-2 : *stat-2*;
	        ⋮
	    list-n : *stat-n*
	end
		CASE *exp* OF
		    list-1 : *stat-seq-1*
		        |
		    list-2 : *stat-seq-2*
		        |
		        ⋮
		        |
		    list-n : *stat-seq-n*
		ELSE
		            stat-seq-n + 1
		END

compound	**begin** *stat-seq* **end**	not provided
exit	not provided	EXIT

for	**for** *var* := *exp-1*
	        to *exp-2* **do**
	    stat
	
	for *var* := *exp-1*
	        downto *exp-2* **do**
	    stat
		FOR *var* := *exp-1* TO *exp-2*
		            BY *constant-exp* DO
		    stat-seq
		END

goto	**goto** *label*	not provided

if	**if** *exp* **then**
	    stat
		IF *exp* THEN
		    stat-seq
		END

(cont.)

Statement	Pascal	Modula-2

	if *exp-1* **then**
	   stat-1
	else if *exp-2* **then**
	   stat-2
	    ⋮
	else
	   stat-n
		IF *exp-1* THEN
		   stat-seq-1
		ELSIF *exp-2* THEN
		   stat-seq-2
		    ⋮
		ELSE
		   state-seq-n
		END

loop	not provided	LOOP *stat-seq* END
procedure reference	*name*($a_1, a_2, \ldots, a_n$)	*name*($a_1, a_2, \ldots, a_n$)

repeat	**repeat**
	   stat-seq
	until *exp*
		REPEAT
		   stat-seq
		UNTIL *exp*

return	not provided	RETURN

while	**while** *exp* **do**
	   stat
		WHILE *exp* DO
		   stat-seq
		END

with	**with** *list-of-variables* **do**
	   stat
		WITH *var* DO
		   state-seq
		END

Assignment Statement.   In a Modula-2 assignment statement, the variable and expression must be of the same type; the only exceptions to this rule are that an expression of type CARDINAL may be assigned to a variable of type INTEGER, and an expression of type INTEGER may be assigned to a variable of type CARDINAL. However, in such mixed-mode assignments, an error results if the value of the expression is not in the range allowed for the variable. Unlike Pascal, Modula-2 does not allow assignment of a cardinal or integer value to a real variable. Instead, the value must first be converted to REAL type using the FLOAT and *real* functions described in the preceding section. Modula-2 also provides two predefined procedures, INC and DEC (see Section 0.3), for incrementing and decrementing the value of an ordinal variable, respectively. For example, a procedure reference of the form

    INC(*var*)

where the type of *var* is some ordinal type, is equivalent to the assignment statement

    var := *var* + 1

Case Statement.   The main difference between the **case** statement in Pascal and the CASE statement in Modula-2 is that an optional ELSE clause is provided in the Modula-2 statement. The statement sequence in this ELSE part is executed if the value of the selector does not appear in any label list. For example, a CASE statement to classify class codes might be

```
CASE Class OF
        1 : INC(Freshman);
            WriteString('Freshman');
            WriteLn
          |
        2..4 : INC(UpperClassPersons)
        ELSE
            WriteString('Illegal class code');
            WriteLn
END (* CASE *)
```

This example shows that sequences of statements are allowed in the various parts of a CASE statement and that these are separated by vertical bars (with none preceding the ELSE part). It also shows that ranges of values of the form *first-value .. last-value* may be included in the label lists.

Compound Statements—Statement Sequences. Pascal's compound statement is not needed in Modula-2 because the syntax of the basic control statements has been changed to allow statement sequences rather than single statements. The only use of BEGIN and END is to enclose the statements that comprise the statement part of a program, module, or procedure.

For Loops. The Pascal **for** statement allows only changes of $+1$ or -1 in the index variable (as specified by the use of **to** or **downto**, respectively), and the loop body must consist of a single (possibly compound) statement. The default step-size in a Modula-2 FOR statement is $+1$, and other step-sizes are specified by using a BY clause containing a constant expression of type CARDINAL or INTEGER. The loop body may be a single statement or a statement sequence but must be followed by an END to mark the end of the for loop.

Goto Statement. The **goto** statement of Pascal is not a part of Modula-2. It is not needed, since the control structures provided are adequate.

If Statement. Each form of the Pascal **if** statement has an analogue in Modula-2. The major differences in the Modula-2 IF statements are that (1) each alternative may be either a single statement or a statement sequence; (2) the reserved word ELSIF replaces Pascal's **else if**; and (3) each IF statement must have a closing END.

LOOP and EXIT Statements. The LOOP statement is new to Modula-2. When it is executed, the body of the loop is executed repeatedly; and since there is no mechanism for terminating this repetition in the LOOP statement itself, the loop is infinite. Although such infinite loops may be useful in some special applications, most programs are not intended to execute forever. For this reason, Modula-2 provides the EXIT statement, whose sole purpose is to terminate repetition in a LOOP statement. When it is encountered, it immediately terminates execution of the (innermost) LOOP statement in which it is contained, and execution continues with the statement following the reserved word END that marks the end of the loop. Typically this EXIT statement is used as part of an IF statement so that the loop is exited when some boolean expression is true. For example, the following loop might be used to read and process a set of scores in the range 0 though 100; an EXIT statement is used to terminate the loop if some illegal value is read:

```
LOOP
    INC(NumScores);
    ReadCard(Score);
    IF (Score < 0) OR (Score > 100) THEN
        Error := TRUE;
        EXIT
    END (* IF *);
    (* statements to process Score are placed here *)
END (* LOOP *);
IF Error THEN
    WriteString('Illegal value for score #');
    WriteCard(NumScores, 1)
ELSE
    .
    .
    .
```

Procedure Reference Statements.   Procedure reference statements have the same form in both Pascal and Modula-2. They are described in more detail in the next section.

Repeat-Until Loops.   Repeat-until loops have the same form in both Pascal and Modula-2. The only difference is the requirement in Modula-2 that the reserved words REPEAT and UNTIL (like all reserved words) must be in uppercase.

RETURN Statement.   The RETURN statement is used in Modula-2 to return a value from a function procedure (see Section 0.6) or to provide a return from a proper procedure before the end of the procedure is reached. It is described in more detail in the next section.

WHILE Statement.   While loops in Modula-2 have almost the same form as while loops in Pascal. The main differences in that in Modula-2, the body of a while loop may be a single statement or a statement sequence, and the end of a while loop must be marked with the reserved word END.

WITH Statement.   The Modula-2 WITH statement is the analogue of the Pascal **with** statement. One difference between these statements is in their syntax. The Pascal **with** statement allows a list of record variables in the **with** clause, whereas the Modula-2 WITH statement allows only a single record name. If several record names are required, nested WITH statements must be used. Also, Modula-2 allows either a single statement or a sequence of statements within a WITH statement, and each WITH statement must be closed with an END.

Another difference between the Pascal and Modula-2 with statements is that the record referenced in a WITH clause is "evaluated" only once, before the statement sequence in the WITH statement is executed. This means, for example, that a WITH statement of the form

WITH *array-name*[*i*] DO
        .
        .
        .
    statement that changes the value of *i*
        .
        .
        .
END (* WITH *)

will not do what is intended. Although the specified statement will change the value of *i*, the record referenced in the WITH clause will not be changed.

0.5 Input/Output

Input and output are carried out in Pascal by the predefined procedures *read*, *readln*, *write*, and *writeln*, which are part of the language itself, and these procedures can be used to read and write values of various data types. For example, *writeln* can be used to display single characters, strings, integers, real values, and boolean values, and after each, it advances to a new output line by writing an end-of-line character. Modula-2, however, does not provide such general-purpose input/output procedures. In fact, the language Modula-2 itself does not include any input/output procedures. Instead, such procedures must be imported into a program from special library modules. The number and contents of these libraries vary from one Modula-2 system to another, but most of them include the two standard modules *InOut* and *RealInOut* described by Wirth in *Programming in Modula-2*. In this section we describe the contents of these modules.

InOut. Although the contents of library module *InOut* may vary from one Modula-2 system to another, almost all versions contain at least the following items:

Item	Description
Write	Procedure to display a single character
WriteString	Procedure to display a string of characters
WriteCard	Procedure to display a cardinal value
WriteInt	Procedure to display an integer value
WriteLn	Procedure to terminate the current output line
WriteOct	Procedure to display a cardinal value in octal format
WriteHex	Procedure to display a cardinal value in hexadecimal format
Read	Procedure to read a single character
ReadCard	Procedure to read a cardinal value
ReadInt	Procedure to read an integer value
ReadString	Procedure to read a string
Done	A boolean variable used to indicate whether an input operation has been completed successfully.

(cont.)

Item	Description
EOL	A constant equal to the end-of-line character
termCH	A character variable that stores the character used to terminate an input value
OpenInput	Procedure to open an input file
OpenOutput	Procedure to open an output file
CloseInput	Procedure to close an input file
CloseOutput	Procedure to close an output file

The procedure **Write** is called with a statement of the form

Write(char-expression)

where *char-expression* is an expression of type CHAR. When this statement is executed, the single character that is the value of the specified expression is displayed in the next position of the current output line.

The procedure **WriteString** is used to display string expressions and is called with a statement of the form

WriteString(string-expression)

For example, the statement

WriteString('Hello world');

displays the string constant 'Hello world' in the next eleven spaces of the current output line.

The procedures **WriteCard** and **WriteInt** are used to display values of type CARDINAL and type INTEGER, respectively. *WriteCard* is called with a statement of the form

WriteCard(cardinal-expression, field-width)

and *WriteInt* with a statement of the form

WriteInt(integer-expression, field-width)

where *field-width* is an expression of type CARDINAL whose value specifies the number of spaces to be used to display the specified expression. In both cases, if the field width is larger than necessary, the value will be right-justified in the field. If the value is too large for the specified field, the field will be automatically enlarged to accommodate it.

Values of type CARDINAL can also be displayed in octal or hexadecimal form, using procedures **WriteOct** and **WriteHex**, respectively. They are called with statements of the form

WriteOct(cardinal-expression, field-width)

and

WriteHex(cardinal-expression, field-width)

Each of the preceding output procedures displays the output on the current line. For example, if *Num1* and *Num2* are variables of type CARDINAL with values 10 and 27, respectively, the statements

WriteString('The value of the product');
WriteCard(Num1, 3);
Write('*');
WriteCard(Num2, 1);
WriteString(' is');
WriteCard(Num1*Num2, 5);

produce the output

```
The value of the product 10*27 is   270
```

The procedure **WriteLn** can be used in a statement of the form

WriteLn

to terminate output to the current line so that subsequent output will begin on a new line. Thus, for example, the statements

WriteLn;
WriteString('Num1 = ');
WriteCard(Num1, 1);
WriteLn;
WriteString('Num2 = ');
WriteCard(Num2, 1);
WriteLn;

produce two lines of output,

```
Num1 = 10
Num2 = 27
```

followed by an advance to a new line.

The procedure **Read** is used to read a single character and assign it to a variable of type CHAR. When called with a statement of the form

Read(char-variable)

it reads a character from the standard input device and assigns it to the specified variable of type CHAR.

A value for a variable of type CARDINAL can be read by calling the procedure **ReadCard** with a statement of the form

ReadCard(cardinal-variable)

When this statement is executed, it reads a string of characters terminated by a blank or some other control character (such as a RETURN), ignoring leading blanks, converts it to a cardinal value if possible, and assigns it to the specified cardinal variable. Similarly, an integer value for a variable of type INTEGER can be read by calling the procedure **ReadInt** with a statement of the form

ReadInt(integer-variable)

The procedure **ReadString** can be used to read a string not containing blanks or control characters and assign it to a string variable. It is called with a statement of the form

ReadString(string-variable)

When executed, this statement ignores leading blanks and reads characters until a blank or any (control) character preceding a blank in the collating sequence is encountered; this termination character is not part of the string assigned to the specified variable.

The constant **EOL** exported by *InOut* is a special control character that signals the **E**nd **O**f a **L**ine. In most Modula-2 systems this *end-of-line character* is the character 36C generated when the return key is depressed. It can be used to detect the end of an input line, for example, in a program segment like the following that counts the characters in a line:

```
Count := 0;
Read(Ch);
WHILE Ch # EOL DO
    INC(Count);
    Read(Ch)
END (* WHILE *);
```

Note that the boolean expression *Ch* # EOL plays a role similar to that of the *eoln* function in Pascal. However, *eoln* returns true when the *next* character in the input stream is an end-of-line character; *Ch* # EOL becomes TRUE when the character *just read* for *Ch* is an end-of-line character.

EOL can also be used in a statement of the form

Write(EOL)

to terminate the current output line. This statement is equivalent, therefore, to the statement

WriteLn

The boolean variable ***Done*** is used to indicate whether an input operation was successfully carried out. When the input statement

Read(Ch)

(where *Ch* is of type CHAR) is executed, *Done* is always set to TRUE unless the end-of-file condition is encountered. In an interactive mode, the end-of-file condition is usually signaled by entering some system-dependent control character such as *control-c, control-z,* or the ESC character.

When the *ReadCard* or *ReadInt* procedure is called, execution of the program is interrupted while the user enters a string of characters, terminating it with a blank or some other control character such as the RETURN character. Execution then resumes, and this string is converted to a cardinal or integer value, respectively, provided such conversion is possible. If conversion is successful, the resulting value is assigned to the variable, and *Done* is set to TRUE. If it is not successful, *Done* is set to FALSE, and the value of the variable is uncertain; in some Modula-2 systems it has a ''garbage'' value, whereas in others it may be assigned the value 0. For example, if the string

$-1234\bullet$

is entered in response to the input statement

ReadInt(Number)

where $\bullet$ denotes the end-of-line character generated by depressing the return key (or a blank or some other control character) and *Number* is an integer variable, the string $'-1234'$ is converted to the integer value -1234 and assigned to *Number*, and *Done* is assigned the value TRUE. If, however, the string

$-12.34\bullet$

or

$-1234ABC\bullet$

is entered, *Done* is set to FALSE, and the status of *Number* is uncertain. If the input string contains leading blanks, they are ignored. Also, backspacing may be used in interactive input to erase characters in the input string.

Procedures *ReadString*, *ReadCard*, and *ReadInt* read characters until a blank or some other control character is encountered. This character terminates the input string and is assigned to the character variable ***termCH*** which, like *Done*, is exported from *InOut*.

The procedure ***OpenInput*** is used to redirect input so that values are read from a previously prepared data file rather than from the keyboard (or some other standard input device). *OpenInput* is called with a statement of the form

OpenInput(string)

where *string* represents an extension that will be attached to the name of the data file entered by the user if this name ends with a period. If no extension is necessary, *OpenInput* may be called with an empty extension:

OpenInput('')

When this procedure is called, execution of the program is interrupted, and the user is requested to enter the name of the file to be used for input. If this file is successfully opened, the variable *Done* is set to TRUE, and *all* subsequent input is obtained from this file rather than from the standard input device. *Done* is set to FALSE if the file cannot be opened.

Data values are read from the specified file until the procedure *CloseInput* is called with a statement of the form

CloseInput

Execution of this statement terminates input from the file so that subsequent input is once again obtained from the standard input device. *CloseInput* should always be called before execution of a program is terminated.

Input may be redirected several times within the same program, but no more than one file can be open for input at one time. Note also that if the same file is closed and then reopened, input will begin at the beginning of the file again.

As an illustration of redirecting input, suppose that we have prepared a data file named ''SCORES'' that contains a collection of test scores:

```
99
87
55
100
65
77

 .
 .
 .
84
```

The program in Section 0.1 can be easily modified to read values from this file rather than from the keyboard. We need only import the procedures *OpenInput* and *CloseInput* from *InOut*, call *OpenInput* at the beginning of the statement part, and call *CloseInput* at the end, giving the following program. Also shown is a listing of a small test file and a sample run using this file. When the program was executed, the prompt

in>

was displayed to the user, who responded with the name of the file from which input values were to be obtained.

```
MODULE CalculateRange;

    (* This program calculates the range of a set of integers
       read from a file using input redirection. *)

    FROM InOut IMPORT ReadInt, WriteInt, WriteCard, WriteString,
                      WriteLn, Done, OpenInput, CloseInput;

    VAR
        Number,                     (* current number *)
        Largest,                    (* largest number in the set *)
        Smallest : INTEGER;         (* smallest number in the set *)
        Count : CARDINAL;           (* a count of the numbers *)

BEGIN
    WriteString('Enter name of input file.'); WriteLn;
    OpenInput('');

    (* Read the first integer and intialize Largest, Smallest, and Count *)
    ReadInt(Number);
    Count := 1;
    Largest := Number;
    Smallest := Number;

    (* Read rest of integers until the end of the file is reached *)
    ReadInt(Number);
    WHILE Done DO
        INC(Count);
        IF Number > Largest THEN
            Largest := Number
        ELSIF Number < Smallest THEN
            Smallest := Number
        END (* IF *);
        ReadInt(Number)
    END (* WHILE *);
    CloseInput;

    (* Display count of values and their range *)
    WriteLn;
    WriteCard(Count, 1);
    WriteString(' numbers');
    WriteLn;
    WriteString('Range = ');
    WriteInt(Largest - Smallest, 1);
    WriteLn
END CalculateRange.
```

(cont.)

Listing of file SCORES used in sample run:

```
 99
 87
 55
100
 65
 77
 79
 68
 92
 95
 84
```

Sample run:

```
Enter name of input file:
in>SCORES

11 numbers
Range = 45
```

Output redirection is also possible and is carried out by using the **OpenOutput** and **CloseOutput** procedures in module *InOut*. *OpenOutput* is called with a statement of the form

OpenOutput(string)

where, as before, *string* denotes an extension to be attached to the name of the output file if the file name entered by the user ends with a period. Once again an empty extension is allowed:

OpenOutput('')

When *OpenOutput* is called, the user is asked to enter the name of the file to which output is to be written. If this file is successfully opened, the variable *Done* is set to TRUE, and *all* subsequent output is written to this file. Output continues to be directed to this file until the procedure *CloseOutput* is called with a statement of the form

CloseOutput

Execution of this statement terminates output to the file so that subsequent output will once again be directed to the standard output device. *CloseOutput* should always be called before execution of a program is terminated. Failure to do so may result in the loss of some or all of the output redirected to the file.

Output, like input, may be redirected several times within the same program, but no more than one file can be open for output at any one time. If a file that already exists is opened for output, most systems will replace its contents with the new output. If the file does not exist, usually a new empty file is created, and output is directed to it.

RealInOut. The constants, variables, and procedures exported from the library module *InOut* are used for the input and output of character, string, cardinal, and integer values. Input and output of real values uses the following items exported from the library module *RealInOut*, another of the library modules described by Wirth (but whose contents may vary from one Modula-2 system to another):

Item	Description
WriteReal	Procedure to display a real value
WriteRealOct	Procedure to display a real value in octal format
ReadReal	Procedure to read a real value
Done	A boolean variable used to indicate whether an input operation has been completed successfully

These procedures can be imported from *RealInOut* by using an import declaration of the form

> FROM *RealInOut* IMPORT *list*;

in the import part of the program.

The ***WriteReal*** procedure is used in a statement of the form

> WriteReal(*real-expression*, *field-width*)

where *field-width* is a cardinal-valued expression whose value represents the number of spaces to be used in displaying the value of the specified real expression. As with *WriteCard* and *WriteInt*, the displayed value will be right-justified in this field, which will be enlarged if necessary. For example, if *RealNum1*, *RealNum2*, and *RealNum3* are values of type REAL, with values 9.6, 595.0, and .0001234, respectively, the statements

> WriteReal(*RealNum1*, 1);
> WriteLn;
> WriteReal(*RealNum2*, 15);
> WriteReal(*RealNum3*, 15);
> WriteLn;

produce output like the following:

```
9.6E+00
------------------------------
    5.950000E+02    1.234000E-04
------------------------------
```

The exact format of the output—the number of significant digits, the number of digits in the exponent, and so on—will differ from one implementation of Modula-2 to another, but in most versions, real values will be displayed in scientific notation similar to that shown here. Procedures to display real output in a decimal format may also be provided in *RealInOut* or in some other library module.[4]

The procedure **WriteRealOct** is used in a statement of the form

WriteRealOct(real-expression, field-width)

which displays in octal form the *internal* representation of the value of the specified real expression.

Real values can be read using procedure **ReadReal** in a statement of the form

ReadReal(real-variable)

where *real-variable* is a variable of type REAL for which a real value is to be read. Real data values may be entered in either decimal or scientific form and are read and assigned in a manner analogous to that described earlier for *ReadCard* and *ReadInt*.

Note that like *InOut*, this module also exports a boolean variable *Done*. When the procedure *ReadReal* is executed, *Done* is set to TRUE if a real value in either decimal or scientific form is read successfully; otherwise, it is set to FALSE.

If a program requires the use of both the variable *Done* from module *InOut* and the variable *Done* from *RealInOut*, it is necessary to use a special form of import declaration and to qualify one of the identifiers. For example, one might use the import declarations

FROM *InOut* IMPORT *Done*, *WriteString*, *WriteLn*, *WriteCard*,
                               ReadCard;
IMPORT *RealInOut*;

The unqualified identifier *Done* will then refer to the variable *Done* from *InOut*, and the **qualified identifier** *RealInOut.Done* must be used for the variable *Done* from *RealInOut*.

0.6   Procedures

Both Pascal and Modula-2 provide two kinds of subprograms. In Pascal these are called *procedures* and *functions*, and in Modula-2 they are called *proper procedures* and *function procedures*. In this section we describe each of these

---

[4]In some Modula-2 systems, *WriteReal* is called with three parameters,

WriteReal(real-expression, field-width, num-dec-places)

where *num-dec-places* is the number of places to which the value of *real-expression* is to be rounded. Also, some Modula-2 systems do not have a separate library module for real input/output procedures but simply include *WriteReal*, *WriteRealOct*, and *ReadReal* in the module *InOut*.

kinds of subprograms and a special Modula-2 feature for using arrays as parameters.

Proper Procedures.   Pascal procedures and proper procedures in Modula-2 have nearly identical syntaxes:

Pascal	Modula-2
procedure *name(parameter-list)*;	PROCEDURE *name(parameter-list)*;
Declarations	Declarations
begin	BEGIN
statement-sequence	*statement-sequence*
end;	END *name*;

The main differences between them are the following:

1. The end of the statement part of a Modula-2 procedure must have the form END *procedure-name*.
2. In Modula-2, procedures may be declared in any order. In particular, it is not necessary to declare a procedure before all other procedures that reference it. Thus, there is no need for the **forward** directive of Pascal.[5]
3. The statement part of a Modula-2 procedure may contain RETURN statements. A RETURN statement causes an immediate return from the procedure to the calling program unit.
4. In the heading of a parameterless procedure in Modula-2, the parentheses normally used to enclose the formal parameter list may either be used or be omitted. In any case, it makes no difference whether or not parentheses are used in a reference to such a procedure.

Function Procedures.   The syntax of a function procedure in Modula-2 is very similar to that of a proper procedure and is therefore rather different from that of a function in Pascal:

Pascal	Modula-2
function *name(param-list)* : *type*;	PROCEDURE *name(param-list)* : *type*;
Declarations	Declarations
begin	BEGIN
statement-1;	*statement-1*;
.	.
.	.
.	.
name := *expression*;	RETURN *expression*;
.	.
.	.
.	.
statement-n	*statement-n*
end;	END *name*;

---

[5] Some versions of Modula-2 do require that procedures be defined before being used. These versions require the use of forward declarations, as in Pascal.

In this table, *param-list* denotes the list of formal parameters (which may be empty), and *type* is a type identifier specifying the type of the function's value.

The major differences between Modula-2 function procedures and Pascal functions are the following:

1. As with proper procedures, the name of the function procedure in Modula-2 must follow the reserved word END in the statement part.
2. In Modula-2, function procedures may be declared in any order and may be intermingled with declarations of proper procedures. As with proper procedures, a function procedure may be referenced by another procedure before it has been declared.
3. The value returned by a function procedure in Modula-2 is specified by a RETURN statement of the form

    RETURN *expression*

    rather than by assigning a value to the function name. This statement causes an immediate return from the function procedure and returns the value of the specified expression as the value of the function. The RETURN statement may also be used without an expression to cause a premature return, as described for proper procedures.[6]
4. In the heading of a parameterless function procedure in Modula-2, the parentheses normally used to enclose the formal parameter list *must* be present,

    PROCEDURE *name*( ) : *type;*

    and any reference to such a function *must* contain empty parentheses.

Open Array Parameters.   In a Modula-2 procedure, a formal parameter that is a one-dimensional array may be declared to be an open array parameter using an **open array** declaration of the form

   ARRAY OF *type*

where *type* is a type identifier specifying the type of the array elements. For example, a procedure to zero out an array of cardinal numbers might have the following heading:

   PROCEDURE *ZeroOut*(*CardArray* : ARRAY OF CARDINAL);

When an open array parameter is used, the type of its elements and the type of the elements in the corresponding actual array must be the same, but the index type of the formal array is "left open." Any index type is allowed for the actual array.

Within a procedure that uses an open array parameter, *the index type of the open array is always taken to be a subrange of type* CARDINAL *with first value 0, regardless of the index type of an actual array parameter.* The largest index of this open array can be obtained using the predefined function **HIGH**, which is referenced with an expression of the form

   HIGH(*array-name*)

---

[6] Some versions of Modula-2 require that the last statement of every function procedure be a RETURN statement.

Thus, the complete procedure *ZeroOut* may be written as

PROCEDURE *ZeroOut*(VAR *CardArray* : ARRAY OF CARDINAL);

(∗ Procedure to set all elements of the open array *CardArray* of cardinal numbers to zero ∗)

VAR
    i : CARDINAL;   (∗ index ∗)

BEGIN
    FOR i := 0 TO HIGH(*CardArray*) DO
        CardArray[*i*] := 0
    END (∗ FOR ∗)
END *ZeroOut*;

Modula-2 also allows procedures to be used as parameters in other procedures. As an illustration, consider the problem of approximating the area under the graph of a nonnegative function $y = f(x)$ from $x = a$ to $x = b$. An appropriate procedure for calculating this approximation would have the function f as one of its parameters together with the endpoints a and b and perhaps also the number of subintervals of $[a, b]$ to use in the approximation:

PROCEDURE *ApproxArea* (*f* : *RealFunction*;
                                        a, *b* : REAL;
                                        n : CARDINAL) : REAL;

(∗ Returns the approximate area under the graph of function f from $x = a$ to $x = b$ using n subintervals. ∗)

The type identifier *RealFunction* used to declare the formal parameter f must be defined in a type section of the program unit that contains this procedure; for example,

TYPE
    RealFunction = PROCEDURE(REAL) : REAL;

It can then be used to specify that the value of the formal parameter f (or any other identifier) is a function procedure having one parameter of type REAL and whose value is of type REAL.

Modula-2 does provide one predefined procedure type **PROC** that can be used to declare that an identifier is the name of a parameterless procedure. It is equivalent, therefore, to the type specification PROCEDURE( ).

0.7 User-Defined Library Modules

Procedures or comparable constructs are part of almost every high-level language, but in designing Modula-2, Wirth also introduced an even more powerful tool for designing modular programs, the *module*. There are two kinds of modules—library or external modules and local or internal modules. In this section we consider only library modules; local modules are described in Section 2.7.

A *library* or *external module* consists of two parts, a definition part and an implementation part. Simply stated, the definition part specifies what processing the items in the library module do and the corresponding implementation part specifies how the processing is carried out.

The definition part of a library module is called a *definition module* and has the following form:

DEFINITION MODULE *name*;
Import part
Declaration part (modified)
END *name*.

Since a definition module only specifies *what* the library module is to do (not how it does it), its statement part is trivial; it contains no statements but consists only of the reserved word END followed by the module name. This is also the reason that the declaration part has a modified structure. Although its constant and variable sections have the usual forms, its procedure sections contain *only procedure headings* that specify *what* the procedures in this library module are to do (not how they do it). The import part may not be used to import procedures or variables from other modules, but it may be used to import constants or types.

The definition part of a library module serves as an *interface* between the user and the module. It contains all the information necessary to understand what the module does and how to use it. To illustrate, suppose we wish to develop a special library module for processing the enumeration type

DaysOfWeek = (*Sunday, Monday, Tuesday, Wednesday,*
Thursday, Friday, Saturday)

We might write a definition module like the following, which defines this enumeration type and declares input/output procedures for this data type:

```
DEFINITION MODULE DaysInOut;

(*********************************************************************

   Define the enumeration type DaysOfWeek and procedures for the
   input and output of values of this type.

   *******************************************************************)

   TYPE
       DaysOfWeek = (Sunday, Monday, Tuesday, Wednesday,
                     Thursday, Friday, Saturday);

   PROCEDURE PrintDay(Day : DaysOfWeek);

       (* Display the string corresponding to Day of type DaysOfWeek *)
```

(cont.)

```
    PROCEDURE ReadDay(VAR Day : DaysOfWeek);

        (* Read a day number and convert it to the corresponding
           value Day of the enumeration type DaysOfWeek *)

END DaysInOut.
```

A definition module can be compiled, and once this has been done, programs or other modules can import items from it. These programs and modules can then be compiled, but they cannot be executed until the associated implementation part of the library module has been written and compiled, because it is this part that actually implements the procedures (and opaque types) specified in the definition module.

The implementation part of a library module is called an ***implementation module***. Its form is the same as that of a program module, except that the heading is preceded by the reserved word IMPLEMENTATION:

IMPLEMENTATION MODULE *name*;
Import part
Declaration part
Statement part.

Here the name given in the module heading must be the same as the name of the corresponding definition module.[7]

All constants and variables (and types) defined in the definition module are available in the corresponding implementation module and need not be imported into it. However, any items imported into the definition module must again be imported into the implementation module if they are needed there. The statement part of an implementation module may be trivial, consisting simply of the reserved word END followed by the module name. If it does contain statements, however, then these are executed before the statements of any program unit into which items from this library module are imported.

As an example, one possible implementation module for the library module *DaysInOut* is the following:

```
IMPLEMENTATION MODULE DaysInOut;

    (*****************************************************************

        Export input/output procedures for enumeration type DaysOfWeek

    *****************************************************************)
```

---

[7] Many Modula-2 systems also require that the name under which a definition module is saved be *name*.DEF and that for the corresponding implementation module be *name*.MOD, where *name* is that which appears in the module headings.

(cont.)

```
    FROM InOut IMPORT WriteString, WriteLn, ReadCard;

    PROCEDURE PrintDay(Day : DaysOfWeek);

        (* Display the string corresponding to Day of type DaysOfWeek *)

        BEGIN
            CASE Day OF
                Sunday    : WriteString ('Sunday')
                          |
                Monday    : WriteString ('Monday')
                          |
                Tuesday   : WriteString ('Tuesday')
                          |
                Wednesday : WriteString ('Wednesday')
                          |
                Thursday  : WriteString ('Thursday')
                          |
                Friday    : WriteString ('Friday')
                          |
                Saturday  : WriteString ('Saturday')
            END  (* CASE *)
        END PrintDay;

    PROCEDURE ReadDay(VAR Day : DaysOfWeek);

        (* Read a day number and convert it to the corresponding
           value Day of the enumeration type DaysOfWeek *)

        VAR
            DayNum : CARDINAL;

        BEGIN
            WriteString('Enter the day number (1 - 7): ');
            ReadCard(DayNum);
            IF (1 <= DayNum) AND (DayNum <= 7) THEN
                Day := VAL(DaysOfWeek, DayNum - 1)
            ELSE
                WriteString('*** Illegal day number ***')
            END  (* IF *);
            WriteLn
        END ReadDay;

END DaysInOut.
```

Once the definition part of a library module has been compiled, the corresponding implementation part can be compiled (and linked in some systems). The library module is then ready for use. Its constants, variables, and procedures (and types) are ready to be *exported* to programs and other modules. They must be imported into these programs and modules by using an ***import declaration*** of the form

FROM *library-module-name* IMPORT *list-of-items*;

or

    IMPORT *library-module-name*;

The first form imports only those items in the specified list, whereas the second imports *all* of the items from the specified library module. However, in the case of the second form, each item must be **qualified** whenever it is used. That is, each reference to this item must be by means of a **qualified identifier** of the form

    library-module-name.item-name

Thus, for example, if a program contains the import declaration

    IMPORT *InOut*;

then qualified identifiers such as *InOut.WriteCard*, *InOut.ReadCard*, and *InOut.Done* must be used to reference the procedures *WriteCard* and *ReadCard* and the variable *Done*.

    The first form of import declaration in which the FROM clause is used requires no such qualification and is the form most commonly used. Thus, for example, we can import the type *DaysOfWeek* and procedures *PrintDay* and *ReadDay* from the library module *DaysInOut* with the import declaration

    FROM *DaysInOut* IMPORT *DaysOfWeek, PrintDay, ReadDay*;

These items can then be referenced by their unqualified names; the qualified identifiers *DaysInOut.DaysOfWeek*, *DaysInOut.PrintDay*, and *DaysInOut.ReadDay* need not be used (but they may be). The following program for calculating the average high temperature for a given week uses this import declaration:

```
MODULE AverageTemperature;

(*************************************************************************

   Program to read the high temperature for each day of the week and
   calculate the average high temperature for the week.

*************************************************************************)

   FROM InOut IMPORT WriteString, WriteLn, Read, ReadReal,WriteReal;

   FROM DaysInOut IMPORT DaysOfWeek, PrintDay;

   VAR
       Day : DaysOfWeek;        (* index *)
       Temperature,             (* high temperature for a given day *)
       Sum : REAL;              (* sum of temperatures *)
       Response : CHAR;         (* user response *)
```

(cont.)

```
BEGIN
    REPEAT
        Sum := 0.0;
        FOR Day := Sunday TO Saturday DO
            WriteLn;
            WriteString('High temperature for ');
            PrintDay(Day);
            WriteString('?  ');
            ReadReal(Temperature);
            Sum := Sum + Temperature
        END (* FOR *);
        WriteLn; WriteLn;
        WriteString('Average high temperature for the week: ');
        WriteReal(Sum / 7.0, 10);
        WriteLn; WriteLn;
        WriteString('More temperatures to process (Y or N)? ');
        Read(Response)
    UNTIL CAP(Response) # 'Y'
END AverageTemperature.
```

<u>Sample run:</u>

```
High temperature for Sunday?  80
High temperature for Monday?  90
High temperature for Tuesday?  85
High temperature for Wednesday?  80
High temperature for Thursday?  90
High temperature for Friday?  100
High temperature for Saturday?  88

Average high temperature for the week:   8.767E+01

More temperatures to process (Y or N)? N
```

The library module *DaysInOut* provides special input/output procedures to supplement those in the standard modules *InOut* and *RealInOut*. Many Modula-2 systems include similar nonstandard modules for reading and displaying boolean values, for formatting the output of real values, and so on. In this text we assume that the module *SpecialInOut* is available, which contains procedures *ReadBoole*, *WriteBoole*, and *FWriteReal* (and others) for these input/output operations. Complete definition and implementation modules are given in Appendix F.

Library modules like *DaysInOut* and *SpecialInOut* are designed to extend the input/output facilities of the modules described by Wirth in *Programming in Modula-2*. Many Modula-2 systems also extend the collection of mathematical functions contained in Wirth's *MathLib0*. One important mathematical function that may be provided is a ***random number generator***, which is a procedure that produces a number selected from some fixed range in such a way that a sequence of these numbers tends to be uniformly distributed over the given range. Such random numbers are used in programs that simulate random processes. Although a random number generator is not included in any of Wirth's library modules, it is convenient to have such a generator available.

The first step in developing a library module *Random* is to design its definition part, that is, to design a definition module whose name is *Random*.

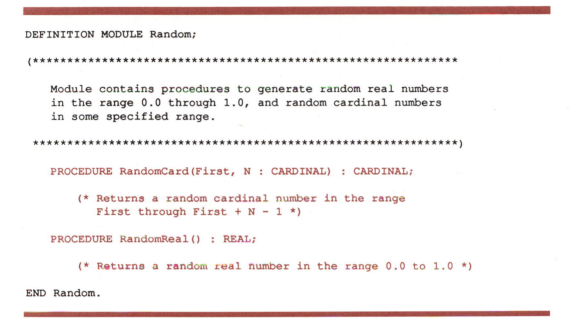

```
DEFINITION MODULE Random;

(***************************************************************

    Module contains procedures to generate random real numbers
    in the range 0.0 through 1.0, and random cardinal numbers
    in some specified range.

 ***************************************************************)

    PROCEDURE RandomCard(First, N : CARDINAL) : CARDINAL;

        (* Returns a random cardinal number in the range
           First through First + N - 1 *)

    PROCEDURE RandomReal() : REAL;

        (* Returns a random real number in the range 0.0 to 1.0 *)

END Random.
```

One possible implementation module is

```
IMPLEMENTATION MODULE Random;

(******************************************************************

    Module contains procedures to generate random real numbers
    in the range 0.0 through 1.0, and random cardinal numbers in
    some specified range.  It also uses a local procedure to read
    a seed for the random number generator. NOTE:  The global
    constants Mult = 29, Addend = 431, and Modulus = 2048 used to
    generate random numbers are appropriate for a machine having
    16-bit words.  After 2048 random numbers have been generated by
    the linear congruential method used here, repetition will begin.
    For other techniques of generating random numbers, see THE ART
    OF COMPUTER PROGRAMMING: SEMINUMERICAL ALGORITHMS, vol. 2,
    by Donald Knuth.

 ******************************************************************)
```

(cont.)

```
FROM InOut IMPORT WriteString, WriteLn, ReadCard;

CONST
    Mult = 29;
    Modulus = 2048;
    Addend = 431;

VAR
    Seed : CARDINAL;

PROCEDURE RandomReal() : REAL;

    (* This function procedure generates a random real number in
       the interval 0 to 1.  It uses the global constants Mult and
       Modulus and the global variable Seed which is initialized
       by procedure GetSeed; thereafter, Seed is the cardinal
       number generated on the preceding reference to RandomReal. *)

    BEGIN
        Seed := Seed * Mult + Addend;
        Seed := Seed MOD Modulus;
        RETURN FLOAT(Seed) / FLOAT(Modulus)
    END RandomReal;

PROCEDURE RandomCard(First, N : CARDINAL) : CARDINAL;

    (* Returns a random cardinal number in the range
       First through First + N - 1 *)

    BEGIN
        RETURN First + TRUNC(FLOAT(N) * RandomReal())
    END RandomCard;

PROCEDURE GetSeed;

    (* Reads a seed for the random number generator *)

    BEGIN
        WriteLn;
        WriteString('Enter a seed for the random number generator');
        WriteLn;
        WriteString('(preferably a prime number): ');
        ReadCard(Seed);
        Seed := Seed MOD Modulus
    END GetSeed;

BEGIN (* body of module Random *)
    GetSeed
END Random.
```

When these definition and implementation modules have been compiled, the library module *Random* is ready for use, and its procedures can be imported into a simulation program. Since the statement part of the implementation module *Random* is executed before the statement part of such a program, the user will be prompted to enter a seed to initialize the random number generator before the simulation actually begins.

As these examples illustrate, there are several benefits that result from using library modules. One benefit is that a library module extends the language by making additional procedures, constants, variables and types available to any program or other module. For example, procedures for generating random numbers in the module *Random* may be used in a program simply by importing them into that program. There is no need for the programmer to "reinvent the wheel" each time random numbers are required.

Several other benefits result from separating library modules from the programs that use them and from separating a library module itself into a definition module and an implementation module. Because all the information that one needs to know to use the items in a library module is given in the definition part, the implementation details can be hidden in the implementation part. This *information hiding* makes it possible to use the library module without being concerned about these details. For example, one can use the library module *Random* without understanding the details of the particular method used to generate random numbers. This is especially true of the standard library modules. We have used the items provided in *InOut* and *RealInOut* without giving the slightest thought as to how they are actually implemented.

Another benefit that results from this separation of programs, definition modules, and implementation modules is that they can be compiled separately. *Separate compilation* makes it possible to change the implementation module and recompile it without changing or recompiling the corresponding definition module or the programs that use the module. For example, if procedure *RandomReal* (but not its heading) in the library module *Random* were changed so that it used some other scheme for generating random real numbers, then only the implementation module *Random* would require recompilation. (It may be necessary, however, to relink programs and other modules that use this module.) It should be noted, however, that if the definition module is changed, both it and the corresponding implementation module as well as all programs that use this library module must be recompiled.

A final benefit of using library modules is that they introduce another level of modularity into software design. Procedures are designed to perform particular tasks, and modules allow procedures (and other items) that perform related tasks to be grouped together into independent units. This is especially useful in large programming projects. Separate library modules can be developed and tested independently, perhaps by different programmers or teams of programmers. The definition parts of these modules provide a well-defined *interface* between the modules, their developers, and users of these modules.

Exercises

1. Determine which of the following are valid constants of type (i) CARDINAL, (ii) INTEGER, (iii) REAL:

(a) 12	**(b)** 12.	**(c)** 12.0	**(d)** .12
(e) '12'	**(f)** 8 + 4	**(g)** −3.7	**(h)** 3.7−
(i) 1,024	**(j)** +1	**(k)** $3.98	**(l)** 0.357E4

(m) 24E0	(n) E3	(o) 2.7E0.5	(p) five
(q) .00001	(r) 1.2×10	(s) $-(-1)$	(t) 0E0
(u) 1/2	(v) 23B	(w) 18B	(x) 23H
(y) ABH	(z) 127C		

2. Which of the following are legal string constants?

(a) 'X'	(b) "123"	(c) IS'	(d) 'Hello"
(e) 'too yet'	(f) 'DOESN'T'	(g) "isn't"	(h) 'constant'
(i) '$1.98"	(j) '12 + 34'	(k) " 'twas"	(l) 'A"B"C"D'
(m) " ' ' ' "	(n) " " " " " "	(o) '130C'	(p) 130C

3. Write a variable section to declare *Alpha* and *Beta* to be of type CARDINAL, *Gamma* to be of type INTEGER, *Code* to be of type CHAR, *Root* to be of type REAL, and *RootExists* to be of type BOOLEAN.

4. Assume that *Card1* and *Card2* are variables of type CARDINAL with values 12 and 34, respectively; that *Num1* and *Num2* are variables of type INTEGER with values 567 and −89, respectively; and that *Ch* is a variable of type CHAR with value F. For each of the following, write a set of output statements that use these variables to produce the given output:

(a) ```
1234567

F89

```

(b) ```
12 + 34 = 567?
--------------
F
--------------
```

(c) ```
Numbers are −89 and 567

```

(d) ```
Absolute value of −89 is 89
---------------------------
Digits of 34 are 3 and 4
------------------------
```

5. Assume that *Card1* and *Card2* are variables of type CARDINAL, that *Num1* and *Num2* are variables of type INTEGER, that *RNum1* and *RNum2* are variables of type REAL, and that *Ch1* and *Ch2* are variables of type CHAR. For each of the following, write a set of input statements to read the specified values for the specified variables in the order given. Also show how the data can be entered so that the values assigned to *Card1*, *Card2*, *Num1*, *Num2*, *RNum1*, *RNum2*, *Ch1*, and *Ch2* will be 12, 34, 567, −89, 1.234, 56.789E − 1, E, and *, respectively.

(a) *Card1, Num1, RNum1, Ch1*
(b) *Card1, Card2, Ch1, Ch2, RNum1*
(c) *Ch1, Ch2, RNum1, RNum2, Num1, Num2*

6. Write a program heading for a program named *FinancialReport*; an import part that will enable it to display strings, read cardinal values,

display cardinal, integer, and real values, and advance to new lines of output; a constant section that names 1900 with the name *Year*, 0.18 with *InterestRate*, and the name of the bank, People's Bank, with *BankName*; and a variable section that declares cardinal variables *AccountNumber* and *TransCode*, the integer variable *GainOrLoss*, and real variables *Transaction*, *Interest*, and *Balance*.

7. Assuming that *Month1* and *Month2* are variables of type *MonthAbbrev* = (*Jan, Feb, Mar, Apr, May, Jun, Jul, Aug, Sep, Oct, Nov, Dec*) with values *Apr* and *Sep*, respectively, find the value of the expression or the value assigned to *Month1* or *Month2* by the statement, for each of the following.

(a) INC(*Month1*)
(b) DEC(*Month2*)
(c) INC(*Month1*, 3)
(d) DEC(*Month1*, 3)
(e) INC(*Month2*, ORD(*Month1*))
(f) DEC(*Month2*, ORD(*Month2*))
(g) ORD(*Jun*)
(h) ORD(*Sep*) − ORD(*Jan*)
(i) VAL(*MonthAbbrev*, 5)
(j) VAL(*MonthAbbrev*, 0)
(k) ORD(VAL(*MonthAbbrev*, 3))
(l) VAL(*MonthAbbrev*, ORD(*May*))
(m) INC(*Month1*, ORD(*Month1*))
(n) DEC(*Month2*, ORD(*Month2*))
(o) ORD('5') − ORD('0')
(p) CHR(5 + ORD('0'))

8. Describe the syntax errors in the following program:

```
(*  1 *)   MODULE Error
(*  2 *)      (* "Example BEGIN END" *)
(*  3 *)      FROM InOut IMPORT Write, WriteString, WriteCard;
(*  4 *)                        WriteLn, ReadCard, ReadCard
(*  5 *)      CONST Year = 1776;
(*  6 *)      VAR
(*  7 *)          Alpha, Beta, Rho
(*  8 *)            : REAL;
(*  9 *)          ADD, SUB, MULT, DIV : cardinal;
(* 10 *)   BEGIN
(* 11 *)      MULT := 3.14;
(* 12 *)      ReadCard(DIV);
(* 13 *)      ALPha := 3.0;
(* 14 *)      ADD := MULT MOD 3;
(* 15 *)      Beta := Alpha + 1;
(* 16 *)      WriteString('Value is:);
(* 17 *)      WriteCard(ADD);
(* 18 *)      WriteString(' isn't negative');
(* 19 *)      INC(Year);
(* 20 *)      WriteReal(Rho); WriteLn
(* 21 *)   END Error
```

9. Given that *Cost* is of type REAL and *Distance* is of type CARDINAL, write

   (a) an IF statement
   (b) a CASE statement

   to assign the value to *Cost* corresponding to the value of *Distance* given in the following table:

Distance	Cost
0 through 100	5.00
More than 100 but not more than 500	8.00
More than 500 but less than 1000	10.00
1000 or more	12.00

10. Assuming that I, J, and K are variables of type INTEGER, describe the output produced by each of the following program segments:

    (a)
    ```
    I := 0;
    J := 0;
    LOOP
        K := 2 * I + J;
        IF K > 10 THEN EXIT END;
        WriteInt(I, 2);
        WriteInt(J, 2);
        WriteInt(K, 2);
        WriteLn;
        INC(I);
        INC(J)
    END (* LOOP *);
    WriteInt(K, 2);
    WriteLn;
    ```

    (b)
    ```
    I := 0;
    J := 0;
    LOOP
        K := 2 * I + J;
        IF K > 10 THEN EXIT END;
        WriteInt(I, 2);
        WriteInt(J, 2);
        WriteInt(K, 2);
        WriteLn;
        IF (I + J > 5) THEN EXIT END;
        INC(I);
        INC(J)
    END (* LOOP *);
    WriteInt(K, 2);
    WriteLn;
    ```

(c) $I := 5;$
LOOP
    WriteInt(I, 3);
    DEC(I, 2));
    IF $I < 1$ THEN EXIT END;
    $J := 0;$
    LOOP
        INC(J);
        WriteInt(J, 3);
        IF $(J >= I)$ THEN EXIT END
    END (* LOOP *);
    WriteString('###');
    WriteLn
END (* LOOP *);
WriteString('***');
WriteLn;

11. Write a function procedure *GPA* that accepts a letter grade and returns the corresponding numeric value (A = 4.0, B = 3.0, C = 2.0, D = 1.0, F = 0.0).

12. Write a character-valued function procedure *LetterGrade* that assigns a letter grade to an integer score using the following grading scale:

    90–100: A
    80–89: B
    70–79: C
    60–69: D
    0–59: F

Use the procedure in a program that reads several scores and displays the corresponding letter grades.

13. Write a program that reads text from a file and counts the occurrences of a specified character entered during execution of the program.

14. Design a library module for converting various units of measurement. Include, at least, procedures for converting minutes to hours, feet to meters, and degrees Fahrenheit to degrees Celsius.

15. Create a library module that defines the enumeration type *Month-Abbrev* (see Exercise 7) and input/output procedures for values of this type. The input procedure should allow the user to enter the number of a month in the range 1 through 12 and then should return the corresponding month abbreviation. The output procedure should accept a month abbreviation and display the name of that month.

16. Write a program to count the occurrences of each of the letters A, B, . . . , Z or their lowercase equivalents a, b, . . . , z in a file of text.

17. The local chapter of the Know-Nothing party maintains a file of names and addresses of its contributors. Each line of the file contains the following items of information in the order indicated:

Last name : a string of length at most 12
First name : a string of length at most 10
Middle initial: a character
Street address: a string of length at most 25
City and state: a string of length at most 25
Zip code: a string of 5 digits

The strings are separated by a single blank and none of them contains a blank; for example,

Doe⌷John⌷Q⌷123SomeStreet⌷AnyTown,AnyState⌷12345●

(where ● denotes an end-of-line mark). Write a program that reads each line of the file, storing the items in a record, and produces a mailing label having the format

John Q. Doe
123SomeStreet
AnyTown,AnyState 12345

18. Repeat Exercise 17, but assume that the strings may contain blanks and are separated by some delimiter such as #; for example,

Doe#John#Q#123⌷Some⌷Street#Any⌷Town,⌷Any⌷State#12345●

1

Programming Methodology Revisited

Problem solving with a computer requires the use of both hardware and software. The **hardware** of a computing system consists of the actual physical components, such as the central processing unit (CPU), memory, and input/output devices that make up the system. **Software** refers to programs used to control the operation of the hardware in order to solve problems. Software design is a complex process that is both an art and a science. It is an art in that it involves a good deal of imagination, creativity, and ingenuity. But it is also a science in that certain standard techniques and methodologies are used. The term **software engineering** has come to be applied to the study and use of these techniques.

Although the problems themselves and the techniques used in their solution vary, there are several common phases or steps in software development:

1. Problem analysis and specification.
2. Data structure selection and algorithm development.
3. Program coding.
4. Program execution and testing.
5. Program maintenance.

In this chapter we briefly review and illustrate by means of a case study each of the phases of this **software life cycle**, describing some of the questions and complications that face professional programmers and some of the software engineering techniques they use in dealing with them.

1.1 Problem Analysis and Specification

```
            CPSC 152—Assignment 4

Due: Wednesday, March 11


One method of calculating depreciation is the
sum-of-the-years digits method. It is illus-
trated by the following example. Suppose that
$15,000 is to be depreciated over a five-year
period. We first calculate the "sum-of-the-
years digits," 1 + 2 + 3 + 4 + 5 = 15. Then 5/15
of $15,000 ($5,000) is depreciated the first
year, 4/15 of $15,000 ($4,000) is depreciated
the second year, 3/15 the third year, and so on.

Write a program that reads the amount to be
depreciated and the number of years over which
it is to be depreciated. Then for each year from
1 through the specified number of years, print
the year number and the amount to be depre-
ciated for that year under appropriate
headings. Run the program with the following
data: $15,000 for 3 years: $7,000 for 10 years;
$500 for 20 years; $100 for 1 year.
```

```
                DISPATCH UNIVERSITY

To:     Bob Byte, Director of Computer Center

From:   Chuck Cash, V.P. of Scholarships and
        Financial Aid

Date:   Wednesday, March 11



Because of new government regulations, we must
keep more accurate records of all students
currently receiving financial aid and submit
regular reports to FFAO (Federal Financial Aid
Office). Could we get the computer to do this
for us?
```

The above assignment sheet is typical of the programming problems given in an introductory programming course. The exercises and problems in such courses are usually quite simple and are clearly stated. But as illustrated in the memo, this is usually not the case in most real-world problems. The initial descriptions of such problems are often vague and imprecise. The person posing the problem often does not understand it well. Neither does he or she understand how to solve it nor what the capabilities and limitations of a computer are. The first step in solving such a problem is to analyze the problem and formulate a precise specification of it. This analysis typically requires determining, first of all, what *output* is required, that is, what information must be produced to solve the problem. It may be necessary to answer many questions to determine this. For example, what must be included in the reports to be submitted to the FFAO? Is there a special format that these reports must take? Must similar reports be generated for any other government agencies or university departments? Must reports be prepared for mailing to individual students? Must computer files of student records be updated?

Once the output of the problem has been specified, one must then analyze the problem to determine its *input*, that is, what information is available for solving the problem. Often the problem's statement includes irrelevant items of information, and one must determine which items will be useful in solving the problem. Usually additional questions must be answered. For example, what information is available for each student? How is the program to access this information? What data will be entered during execution by the user?

Besides the input and output specifications, additional information will be required before the specification of the problem is complete and the development of algorithms and programs can begin. What hardware and software are available? What performance requirements are there? For example, what response time is necessary? How often will the program be used? Will users of the program be sophisticated, or will they be novices so that the program will have to be extra user friendly and robust?

Once a complete specification of the problem has been obtained, a decision must be made regarding the feasibility of a computer solution. Is it possible to design a program to carry out the processing required to obtain the desired output from the given input? If so, is it economically feasible? Could the problem be solved better manually? How soon must the software be available? What is the expected lifetime of the program? If it is determined that a computer-aided solution is possible and is cost effective, the next phase is to select suitable structures to organize the data and develop the algorithms required to do the necessary processing.

1.2   Data Structure Selection and Algorithm Development

Once the specification of a problem is complete, appropriate data structures must be selected to organize the input data, and algorithms must be designed to process this data and produce the output required to solve the problem. Because the computer has no inherent problem-solving capabilities, this phase of the problem-solving process requires ingenuity and creativity and is the most difficult. In this section we take a quick look at this phase, reviewing some of the basic concepts introduced in a first programming course. Data structures and algorithms are central themes of this text, however, and thus are studied in detail in the chapters that follow.

The structures used to organize the data in a given problem often are *predefined data structures*, or as they are called in Modula-2, *structured data types*. The most common of these, and one with which you should already be familiar, is the *array*. Nearly every high-level programming language provides arrays as predefined structures. Arrays are used to organize data items that are all of the same type, for example, a collection of test scores (integers) or a collection of names (strings). They may be *one-dimensional*, in which case each item in the array is accessed by specifying its location in the array, usually by enclosing it in brackets or parentheses and attaching it as an index to the array name. Arrays may also be *multidimensional*, in which case access to an element requires using more than one index to specify its location. For example, in Modula-2, if *Score* is a one-dimensional array of integers and *Mat* is a two-dimensional array of reals declared by

```
CONST
    MaxScores = 100;
    MaxRows = 10;
    MaxColumns = 10;

TYPE
    ListOfScores = ARRAY [1..MaxScores] OF CARDINAL;
    Matrix = ARRAY [1..MaxRows], [1..MaxColumns] OF REAL;

VAR
    Score : ListOfScores;
    Mat : Matrix;
```

then the fifth score can be accessed with the array reference *Score*[5], and the entry in the first row and third column of the matrix with *Mat*[1,3].

Another predefined data structure that you may have already studied is a *record*. It differs from an array in that the items in a record need not be of the same type. For example, a student record might consist of an identification number that is some positive integer; a name that is itself a (*nested*) record consisting of a last name (string of length 16), a first name (string of length 12), and a middle initial (character); an address that might also be a record consisting of strings of various lengths; a grade point average that is a real number; and other items of information of various types.

Records are thus useful in organizing nonhomogeneous collections of data items. However, some high-level languages do not provide records as predefined data structures, and in such languages it is necessary to simulate them. For example, in FORTRAN 77, to process a collection of student records like the one just described, one might use nine *parallel arrays* IDNUMB, LNAME, FNAME, INIT, STREET, CITY, STATE, ZIP, GPA (and others as necessary) in which IDNUMB(I) is the identification number for the Ith student; LNAME(I), FNAME(I), and INIT(I) are his or her last name, first name, and middle initial, respectively; and so on.

Even though the language in which you do most of your programming is rich in predefined data structures, situations will arise in which it is necessary to organize the data into a structure that is not provided in the language. For example, *strings, stacks,* and *queues* are user-defined structures that may have been introduced in an earlier course. A large part of this text is devoted to studying these and other data structures in detail.

In addition to organizing a problem's data into structures, algorithms must be designed to process this data and to produce the required output. The selection of data structures and the design of algorithms that are correct, well structured, and efficient are at the heart of software design. These two aspects of software development are equally important and, in fact, are inextricably linked; neither can be carried out independently of the other. Indeed, as Niklaus Wirth, the originator of the Pascal and Modula-2 languages, has entitled one of his texts

Algorithms + Data Structures = Programs

The word *algorithm* is derived from the name of an Arab mathematician Abu Ja'far Mohammed ibn Musa al Khowarizmi (c. 825 A.D.), who wrote a book describing procedures for calculating with Hindu numerals. In modern parlance, the word has come to mean a "step-by-step procedure for solving a problem or accomplishing some end." In computer science, however, the term *algorithm* refers to a procedure that can be executed by a computer, and this requirement imposes additional limitations on the instructions that comprise these procedures:

1. They must be *definite* and *unambiguous* so that it is clear what each instruction is meant to accomplish.
2. They must be *simple* enough so that they can be carried out by a computer.
3. They must satisfy a *finiteness* property; that is, the algorithm must terminate after a finite number of operations.

In view of the first two requirements, clarity and simplicity, algorithms are usually described in a form that resembles a computer program so that it is easy to implement each step of the algorithm as a computer instruction or as a sequence of instructions. Consequently, algorithms are commonly described in *pseudocode*, a pseudoprogramming language that is a mixture of natural language and symbols, terms, and other features commonly used in one or more high-level programming languages. Because it has no standard syntax, it varies from one programmer to another, but it typically includes the following features:

1. The usual computer symbols $+$, $-$, $*$, and $/$ are used for the basic arithmetic operations.
2. Symbolic names (identifiers) are used to represent the quantities being processed by the algorithm.
3. Some provision is made for indicating comments, for example, using the Modula-2 convention of enclosing them between a pair of special symbols such as (* and *).
4. Key words that are commmon in high-level languages are allowed, for example, *read* or *enter* for input operations, and *display, print* or *write* for output operations, *if* and *else* for selection structures, *while, for, repeat,* and *until* for repetition structures.
5. Indentation is used to set off blocks of instructions.

The finiteness property requires that an algorithm will eventually terminate, that is, that it will terminate after a finite number of steps. In particular, this means that the algorithm may not contain any infinite loops. For example, if an algorithm includes a set of statements that are to be executed repeatedly while some boolean expression is true, then these statements must eventually cause that boolean expression to become false so that repetition is terminated. Also, when an algorithm terminates, we obviously expect that it has produced the required results. Thus, in addition to demonstrating that a given algorithm will terminate, it is also necessary to verify its correctness.

As a practical matter, simply knowing that an algorithm terminates may not be sufficient. For example, an algorithm for playing a winning game of chess that at each stage of the game examines every possible move to determine whether or not it is a winning move will terminate but will require so much time that is has no practical value. In other words, useful algorithms must terminate in some *reasonable* amount of time. In Chapter 5 we consider some techniques that are useful in estimating the computing time of an algorithm.

The analysis and verification of algorithms and of programs that implement them are greatly facilitated if they are well structured. Recall that *structured algorithms* and *programs* are designed using three basic control structures:

1. *Sequence:* Steps are performed in a strictly sequential manner, each step being executed exactly once.
2. *Selection:* One of several alternative actions is selected and executed.
3. *Repetition:* One or more steps is performed repeatedly.

These three control mechanisms are individually quite simple, but in fact they are sufficiently powerful that any algorithm can be constructed using them.

Algorithms that are carefully designed using only these control structures are much more readable and understandable and hence can be analyzed and verified much more easily than can unstructured ones. To illustrate, consider the following unstructured algorithm:

ALGORITHM (UNSTRUCTURED VERSION)

(* Algorithm to read and count several triples of numbers and print the largest number in each triple. *)

1. Initialize *Count* to 0.
2. Read a triple x, y, z.
3. If x = end-of-data-flag then go to Step 14.
4. Increment *Count* by 1.
5. If $x > y$ then go to Step 9.
6. If $y > z$ then go to Step 12.
7. Display z.
8. Go to Step 2.
9. If $x < z$ then go to Step 7.
10. Display x.
11. Go to Step 2.
12. Display y.
13. Go to Step 2.
14. Display *Count*.

The "spaghetti logic" of this algorithm is vividly displayed in the first diagram in Figure 1.1.

In contrast, consider the following structured algorithm. The clarity and the simple elegance of its logical flow are shown in the second diagram in Figure 1.1.

ALGORITHM (STRUCTURED VERSION)

(* Algorithm to read and count several triples of numbers and print the largest number in each triple. *)

1. Initialize *Count* to 0.
2. Read the first triple of numbers x, y, z.
3. While $x \neq$ end-of-data-flag do the following:
   a. Increment *Count* by 1.
   b. If $x > y$ and $x > z$ then
         Display x.
      Else if $y > x$ and $y > z$ then
         Display y.
      Else
         Display z.
   c. Read next triple x, y, z.
4. Display *Count*.

Whereas programs written in introductory programming courses rarely exceed a few hundred lines in length, those in real-world applications often consist of several thousand lines of code. In developing such programs, it is usually not possible to visualize or anticipate at the outset all the details of a single algorithm or program to solve the entire problem. Instead, a ***divide-and-conquer strategy*** is used, in which the original problem is divided into a sequence

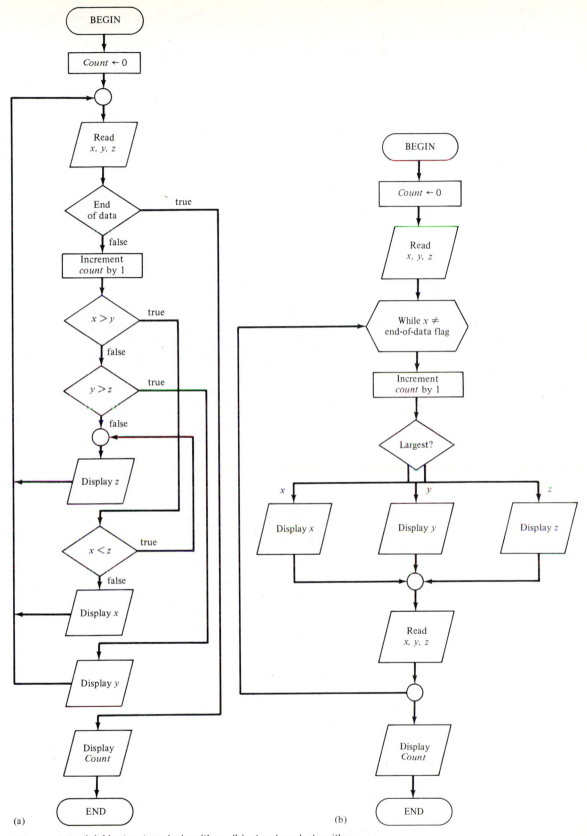

Figure 1.1 (a) Unstructured algorithm, (b) structured algorithm

of simpler subproblems, each of which can be attacked independently. Some or all of these subproblems may still be fairly complicated, and this divide-and-conquer approach can be repeated for them, continuing until subproblems are obtained that are sufficiently simple so that complete structured (sub)algorithms can be written for them. This *top-down approach* to program development is reviewed and illustrated in the case study in Section 1.6.

1.3 Program Coding

The first decision that must be made when one is translating algorithms into programs is what programming language to use. This obviously depends on the languages available to the programmer and those that he or she is able to use. Also, there may be characteristics of the problem that make one language more appropriate than another. For example, if the problem requires scientific computing with extended precision and/or complex numbers, FORTRAN may be the most suitable language. Problems that involve extensive file manipulation and report generation may perhaps best be done with COBOL. Structured algorithms, especially those developed as a collection of subalgorithms in a top-down manner, can best be implemented in a structured language such as Pascal, Modula-2, or Ada.

Regardless of the language in which they are written, *programs must be correct, readable, and understandable.* Correctness is obviously the most important property. No matter what other qualities a program has—whether it is well structured, is well documented, looks nice, and so on—it is worthless if it does not produce correct results. Program testing and validation are thus important steps in program development and are reviewed in more detail in the next section.

It is often difficult for beginning programmers to appreciate the importance of the other program characteristics and of practicing good programming habits that lead to the design of programs that are readable and understandable. This happens because programs developed in an academic environment are often quite different from those developed in real-world situations, where programming style and form are critical. Student programs are usually quite small (more than a few hundred lines of code are uncommon); are executed and modified only a few times (almost never, once they have been handed in); are rarely examined in detail by anyone other than the student and the instructor; and are not developed within the context of severe budget restraints. Real-world programs, on the other hand, may be very large (several thousand lines of code); are developed by teams of programmers; are commonly used for long periods of time and thus require maintenance if they are to be kept current and correct; and are often maintained by someone other than the original programmer. As hardware costs continue to decrease and programmer costs increase, the importance of reducing programming and maintenance costs, and the corresponding importance of writing programs that can be easily read and understood by others, continues to increase.

There are a number of programming practices that contribute to the development of correct, readable, and understandable programs. Because good programming habits are essential, we review some of these guidelines once again.

One principle is that *programs and modules should be well structured.* The following guidelines are helpful in this regard:

- *Use a top-down approach in developing a program for a complex problem.* Divide the problem into simpler subproblems and write individual procedures to solve these subproblems. These procedures should be relatively short and as self-contained as possible.
- *Use the basic control structures, sequence, selection, and repetition, in developing programs and modules.*
- *Use local variables within procedures.* Variables used only within a procedure should be declared within that procedure.
- *Use parameters to pass information to and from procedures.* Using **global variables** to share information among procedures should be avoided because it destroys their independence. Determining the value of a global variable at some point in the program can be very difficult because it may have been changed by any of the program units.
- *To protect parameters that should not be modified by a procedure, declare them to be value parameters rather than variable parameters.* Otherwise, the procedure may unexpectedly change the value of an actual parameter in some other program unit. One common exception is for arrays; declaring them to be variable parameters saves memory and makes it unnecessary to copy the elements of the actual array into the formal array.
- *Use variable "status" parameters to signal error conditions or other special conditions encountered during execution of a procedure.* For example, a procedure for searching a list should return a value for a boolean parameter that indicates whether the search was successful; it might also return a list-empty indicator. A procedure to insert an item into a list might return a value for a parameter *ListFull*, and a delete procedure might return a value for *ListEmpty*.
- *Use constant identifiers to improve readability, flexibility, and portability.* For example, the "magic numbers" that suddenly arise without explanation in the statement

$$PopChange := (0.1758 - 0.1257) * Population;$$

should be replaced by constant identifiers (or variables whose values are read during execution) as in

CONST
     BirthRate = 0.1758;
     DeathRate = 0.1257;

and the preceding assignment statement rewritten as

$$PopChange := (BirthRate - DeathRate) * Population;$$

The second assignment statement is more readable than the first. Also, if these numbers must be changed, one need only change the definitions of *BirthRate* and *DeathRate* in the constant section rather than conduct an exhaustive search of the program to locate all their occurrences.

- *Strive for simplicity and clarity.* Clever programming tricks intended only to demonstrate the programmer's ingenuity or to produce code that executes only slightly more efficiently should be avoided.

A second principle is that *each program and module should be documented.* In particular:

- *Each program and module should include opening documentation.* Comments should be included at the beginning of the program to explain what it does, how it works, any special algorithms it implements, and so on and may also include such items of information as the name of the programmer, the date the program was written, when it was last modified, and references to books and manuals that give additional information about the program. In addition, it is a good practice to explain the use of each identifier declared in the constant and variable declaration sections.
- *Each procedure should be documented.* One important component of this documentation is a description of the information passed to the procedure and the information returned by it.
- *Comments should be used to explain key program segments and/or segments whose purpose or design is not obvious.* However, don't clutter the program with needless comments as in

  INC(*Count*); (* Increment *Count* *)

- *Meaningful identifiers should be used.* For example,

  Wages : = *HoursWorked* * *HourlyRate*;

  is more meaningful than

  W : = *H* * *R*;

  Don't use "skimpy" abbreviations just to save a few keystrokes when entering the program. Also, avoid "cute" identifiers, as in

  BaconBroughtHome : = *SlaveLabor* * *LessThanImWorth*;

A third principle has to do with a program's appearance: *Programs and modules should be formatted in a style that enhances their readability.* In particular, the following are some guidelines for good programming style:

- *Put each statement on a separate line.* One exception made by some Modula-2 programmers is to allow more than one input/output statement per line.
- *Use uppercase and lowercase letters in a way that contributes to readability.* For example, capitalize the first letter of each user-defined identifier and each part of a "compound" identifier, as in *TotalHonorPoints*.
- *Use spaces between the items in a statement to make it more readable,* for example, before and after each operator (+, −, <, : =, etc.).
- *Insert a blank line before each section of the program and wherever appropriate in a sequence of statements to set off blocks of statements.*

- *When a statement is continued from one line to another, indent the continuation line(s).*
- *Adhere rigorously to alignment and indentation guidelines to emphasize the relationship between reserved words, clauses, and statements that comprise control structures, program sections, and so on.*

1.4 Program Execution and Testing

Only in the rarest cases is a program written without errors. **Syntax errors** (caused by incorrect punctuation, misspelled reserved words, and so on) and **run-time errors** such as division by zero and integer overflow that occur during program execution are usually quite easy to detect and correct, since system-generated error messages help locate and explain these errors. **Logical errors**, however, are far more difficult to detect, because the program executes but does not produce the correct results. The error may be due to inaccurate coding of the algorithm or in the design of the algorithm itself.

To illustrate how such errors can be detected and corrected, let us consider a program to perform a binary search for some item in an ordered array. It has been estimated that 80 percent of all beginning programmers, when asked to write this program, do not write it correctly. One common attempt is the following:

BINARY SEARCH ALGORITHM (∗ INCORRECT VERSION ∗)

(∗ Algorithm to perform a binary search of the list $A[1], \ldots , A[n]$, ordered in ascending order, for *Item*. *Found* is set to true and *Mid* to the position of *Item* if the search is successful; otherwise, *Found* is set to false. ∗)

1. Set *Found* equal to false.
2. Set *First* equal to 1.
3. Set *Last* equal to *n*.
4. While *First* ≤ *Last* and not *Found* do the following:
   a. Calculate *Mid* = (*First* + *Last*) / 2.
   b. If *Item* < *A[Mid]* then
        Set *Last* equal to *Mid*.
      Else if *Item* > *A[Mid]* then
        Set *First* equal to *Mid*.
      Else
        Set *Found* equal to true.

The corresponding Modula-2 procedure is

```
PROCEDURE BinarySearch(VAR A : NumberArray; n : CARDINAL
                            Item : ElementType;
                       VAR Found : BOOLEAN;
                       VAR Mid : CARDINAL):
```

(* **INCORRECT PROCEDURE** to perform a binary search of array *A* having *n* elements for *Item*. If search is successful, *Found* is returned as TRUE, and *Mid* is the location of *Item*; otherwise, *Found* is FALSE. *)

```
VAR
     First,                    (* First and last positions in *)
     Last : CARDINAL;    (* sublist currently being searched *)
BEGIN
     Found := FALSE;
     First := 1;
     Last := n;
     WHILE (First <= Last) AND NOT Found DO
          Mid := (First + Last) DIV 2;
          IF Item < A[Mid] THEN
               Last := Mid
          ELSIF Item > A[Mid] THEN
               First := Mid
          ELSE
               Found := TRUE
          END (* IF *)
     END (* WHILE *)
END BinarySearch;
```

This procedure was tested with the following array of integers:

$$A[1] = 45$$
$$A[2] = 62$$
$$A[3] = 68$$
$$A[4] = 77$$
$$A[5] = 84$$
$$A[6] = 90$$
$$A[7] = 96$$

A search for *Item* = 77 was successful and returned 4 as its location in the array. A search for *Item* = 96 failed, however, because the search procedure did not terminate; it was necessary for the programmer to terminate execution using the "break" key on the keyboard.

One technique that may prove useful in locating a logical error is to trace the execution of a program segment by inserting temporary output statements to display values of key variables at various stages of program execution. For example, inserting the statements

```
WriteString('DEBUG: At top of while loop in BinarySearch');
WriteLn;
WriteString('First = ');
WriteCard(First, 1);
WriteString(', Last = ');
WriteCard(Last, 1);
```

WriteString(', Mid = ');
WriteCard(Mid, 1);
WriteLn;

after the statement that assigns a value to *Mid* at the beginning of the while loop in the preceding procedure *BinarySearch* results in the following output in a search for 96:

```
DEBUG: At top of while loop in BinarySearch
First = 1, Last = 7, Mid = 4
DEBUG: At top of while loop in BinarySearch
First = 4, Last = 7, Mid = 5
DEBUG: At top of while loop in BinarySearch
First = 5, Last = 7, Mid = 6
DEBUG: At top of while loop in BinarySearch
First = 6, Last = 7, Mid = 6
DEBUG: At top of while loop in BinarySearch
First = 6, Last = 7, Mid = 6
                    .
                    .
                    .
```

One must be careful, however, to put such temporary output statements in places that are helpful in locating the source of the error and not to use so many of these statements that the volume of output hinders the search for the error.

One can also trace an algorithm or program segment manually by working through it step by step, recording the values of certain key variables in a **trace table**. This technique is also known as **walking through the code** or **desk checking** the algorithm/program segment. For example, tracing the while loop in the binary search algorithm using the array *A* given above and with *Item* = 96, recording the values of *First*, *Last*, and *Mid*, gives the following trace table:

Step	First	Last	Mid
Initially	1	7	—
4a	1	7	4
4b	4	7	4
4a	4	7	5
4b	5	7	5
4a	5	7	6
4b	6	7	6
4a	6	7	6
4b	6	7	6
4a	6	7	6
4b	6	7	6
⋮	⋮	⋮	⋮

Using either manual or automatic tracing of this procedure reveals that when *Item* = 96, the last array element, *First* eventually becomes 6, and *Last* becomes 7, and *Mid* is then always computed as 6, so that *First* and *Last* never change. Because the algorithm does locate each of the other array elements, the beginning programmer might "patch" it by treating this special case separately and inserting the statement

```
IF Item = A[n] THEN
    Mid := n;
        Found := TRUE
END (* IF *);
```

before the while loop. The procedure now correctly locates each of the array elements, but it is still not correct. Searching for any item greater than $A[7]$ still results in an infinite loop.

"Quick and dirty patches" like that attempted here are not recommended because they fail to address the real source of the problem and make the program unnecessarily complicated and "messy." The real source of difficulty in the preceding example is not that the last element of the array requires special consideration but that the updating of *First* and *Last* within the while loop is not correct. If $Item < A[Mid]$, then the part of the array *preceding* location *Mid*, that is, $A[First], \ldots, A[Mid - 1]$ should be searched, not $A[First],$ $\ldots, A[Mid]$. Thus, in this case, *Last* should be set equal to $Mid - 1$, not *Mid*. Similarly, if $Item > A[Mid]$, then *First* should be set equal to $Mid + 1$ rather than *Mid*.

Once an error has been found, the program must be corrected and tested again. This cycle of testing, tracing, and correcting may have to be repeated many times before one is reasonably confident that the program is correct. The program should be executed with data values entered in several different orders, with large data sets and small data sets, with extreme values, with "bad" data, and with test data carefully selected so that each part of the program is checked. It must be realized, however, that because it is usually not possible to test a program with every possible set of test data, obscure "bugs" will often remain and will not be detected until some time later, perhaps after the program has been released for public use. As these bugs turn up, the cycle of testing, tracing, and correction must be repeated and a "fix" or "patch" or a new release sent to the users.

In some applications, such as defense systems and spacecraft guidance systems, program errors are more than just a nuisance and cannot be tolerated. In such cases, relying on the results of test runs may not be sufficient. It may be necessary to give a deductive proof that the program is correct and that it will *always* produce the correct results (assuming no system malfunction). But even in less critical applications, the techniques used in correctness proofs are still helpful in uncovering errors that might otherwise be overlooked.

To prove that an algorithm for solving a given problem is correct, we must prove deductively that the steps of the algorithm process the input correctly so that the required output is obtained. Thus, a ***proof of correctness*** of an algorithm begins with an **assertion** (assumption) *I* about its input data and provides a logical argument demonstrating that execution of the algorithm will yield some specified assertion (conclusion) *O* about the output. To illustrate, consider the following algorithm to find the mean of a set of numbers stored in an array:

ALGORITHM TO CALCULATE MEAN

(* Algorithm that accepts an array of n real numbers ($n \geq 1$), $X[1], \ldots, X[n]$, and returns their mean. *)

1. Initialize *Sum* to 0.
2. Initialize index variable i to 0.
3. While $i < n$ do the following:
   a. Increment i by 1.
   b. Add $X[i]$ to *Sum*.
4. Calculate and return *Mean* = *Sum* / n.

Here the input assumption might be stated as

I: Input consists of an integer $n \geq 1$ and an array X of n real numbers.

The output conclusion is

O: The algorithm terminates, and when it does, the value of the variable *Mean* is the mean (average) of $X[1], \ldots, X[n]$.

To demonstate that the output assertion O follows from the input assertion I, one usually introduces intermediate assertions at several points in the algorithm, which describe the state of processing when execution reaches these points. The following diagram displays the algorithm we are considering with three points—1, 2, and 3—at which assertions are attached. The input assertion is attached to point 1, the output assertion to point 3, and we have attached one intermediate assertion, called a ***loop invariant***, at point 2, the bottom of the while loop.

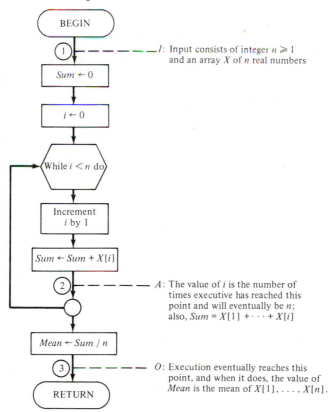

I: Input consists of integer $n \geq 1$ and an array X of n real numbers

A: The value of i is the number of times executive has reached this point and will eventually be n; also, $Sum = X[1] + \cdots + X[i]$

O: Execution eventually reaches this point, and when it does, the value of *Mean* is the mean of $X[1], \ldots, X[n]$.

The proof then consists of showing that assertion A follows from the input assertion I and then showing that the output assertion O follows from A.

Mathematical induction can be used to establish the loop invariant A. To see this, suppose we let k denote the number of times execution has reached point 2, and let i_k and Sum_k denote the values of i and Sum, respectively, at this time. When $k = 1$, that is, when execution reaches point 2 for the first time, the value of i will be 1, since it was initially 0 and has been incremented by 1. Sum will be equal to $X[1]$, since it was initially 0, i has the value 1, and $X[i]$ has been added to Sum. Thus i and Sum have the values asserted in A when $k = 1$.

Now assume that when execution reaches point 2 for the kth time, the loop invariant A holds:

$$i_k = k \text{ and } Sum_k = X[1] + \cdots + X[k]$$

We must prove that A is also true when execution continues around the loop and reaches point 2 for the $k + 1$-st time, that is,

$$i_{k+1} = k + 1 \text{ and } Sum_{k+1} = X[1] + \cdots + X[k + 1]$$

On this $k + 1$-st pass through the loop, the value of i will be incremented by 1 so that

$$i_{k+1} = i_k + 1 = k + 1$$

Thus i will have the correct value; also,

$$Sum_{k+1} = Sum_k + X[k + 1] = X[1] + \cdots + X[k] + X[k + 1]$$

It now follows by induction that each time execution reaches point 2, i and Sum will have the values asserted in the loop invariant A. In particular, when point 2 is reached for the nth time, Sum will equal $X[1] + \cdots + X[n]$ and i will become equal to n.

Since i will eventually have the value n, the boolean expression $i < n$ that controls repetition will become false, and the while loop will terminate. Execution will then continue with Statement 4 in the algorithm. This statement correctly calculates the mean of the array elements, and execution will reach point 3, the end of the algorithm. Thus the output assertion is established, and the correctness proof is complete.

This simple example of a correctness proof has been rather informal. It could be formalized, however, by using some special notation to state the assertions (such as the predicate calculus or some other formal notation) and a formal deductive system that spells out the rules that can be used to reason from one assertion to the next. For example, a rule governing an assignment statement S of the form $v := e$ might be stated symbolically as

$$P \xrightarrow{\ \ S\ \ } \{Q = P(v,e)\}$$

an abbreviation for "If **precondition** P holds before an assignment statement S of the form $v := e$ is executed, then the **postcondition** Q is obtained from P by replacing each occurrence of the variable v by the expression e." Such formalization is necessary in the design of mechanized "theorem provers," and we leave it to more advanced courses in theoretical computer science where it more properly belongs.

Also, this example was very simple in that only one intermediate assertion A was used, so that the form of the proof is

$$I \Rightarrow A \Rightarrow O$$

that is, the input assertion I implies the intermediate assertion A, and A implies the output assertion O. For more complex algorithms it is usually necessary to introduce several intermediate assertions $A_1, A_2, \ldots, A_n$. The algorithm/program is broken down into small segments, each having one of the A_i (or I) as a "preassertion" and A_{i+1} (or O) as a "postassertion":

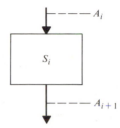

One must show that A_{i+1} follows logically from A_i for each $i = 1, \ldots, n$, and thus, the structure of the correctness proof is

$$I \Rightarrow A_1 \Rightarrow A_2 \Rightarrow \cdots \Rightarrow A_n \Rightarrow O$$

If one of these program segments is or contains a selection structure, there may be a large number of paths that execution may follow, and because it is necessary to examine *all* such paths, the correctness proof can become quite complex.

Algorithm/program verification is an important part of program development, and ideally, the correctness of each program should be formally proved. In practice, however, the time and effort required to write out carefully and completely all the details of a correctness proof of a complicated algorithm are usually prohibitive. Nevertheless, it is still a good programming practice to formulate the major assertions that would be used in a correctness proof and to "walk through" the algorithm/program, tracing each possible execution path, following the pattern of a deductive proof. This is a more formal and systematic way of desk checking that every good programmer uses in testing algorithms and programs. Although it does not ensure that the algorithm/program is absolutely correct, it does increase one's confidence in the program's correctness and one's understanding of the program, and it may uncover logical errors that might otherwise go undetected. As programmers gain experience, it is important that they accumulate ***toolboxes*** of constructs and algorithms whose correctness has already been established and that can therefore be used with confidence.

1.5 Program Maintenance

Once a program has been tested and debugged, it begins its useful life and will, in many cases, be used for several years. It is likely, however, that it will eventually require some modification. As we noted in the previous section, some programs, especially large software packages developed for complex projects, often have obscure bugs that have not been detected during testing and that surface after the programs are released for public use. One important aspect of program maintenance is fixing such flaws in the software.

It may also be necessary to modify software to improve its performance, to add new features, and so on. Other modifications may be required because of changes in the computer hardware and/or the system software such as the operating system. External factors such as changes in government rules and regulations and changes in the organizational structure of the company may also force program modification. These changes are easier to make in programs that are written in a modular fashion than in poorly structured ones, because the changes can often be made by modifying only a few of the modules or by the addition of new modules.

Software maintenance is a major component of the life cycle of a program. A 1985 report estimated that 50 percent of computer center budgets and more than 50 percent of programmer time were devoted to program maintenance, and that worldwide, more than $30 billion was spent on program maintenance. A major factor that contributes to this high cost in money and time is that many programs are originally written with poor structure, documentation, and style. The problem is complicated by the fact that most program maintenance is done by someone not involved in the original design. Thus it is mandatory that each programmer do his or her utmost to design programs that are readable, well documented, and well structured so they are easy to understand and modify and are thus easy to maintain.

1.6 Case Study: The Financial Aid Problem

To illustrate the ideas and techniques reviewed in the preceding sections, we will develop a program to solve the financial aid problem introduced in Section 1.1. Recall that the statement of the problem as posed by the vice-president of scholarships and financial aid was quite vague, stating only that accurate records of all students currently receiving financial aid must be maintained and that regular reports must be submitted to the FFAO (Federal Financial Aid Office).

The first step in solving this problem is to formulate a precise statement of it, in particular, to identify its input and output. In this example we might determine that the program must make it possible for the user to do any of the following:

1. Retrieve and display at the user's terminal the record for any specified student.
2. Update the record for a particular student by changing his or her cumulative grade-point average (gpa) and/or credits and/or amount of financial aid received.
3. Print a report showing the current (updated) information—student number, name, gpa, credits, and financial aid—for all students.

The input data consists of information about students receiving financial aid at Dispatch University. However, before detailed algorithms to process this information can be developed, we must decide what data structures to use to organize the data. The information for each student consists of his or her student number, name, grade-point average, current credits, and amount of financial aid received. Since these five items of information all are related (they all pertain to one student) but are of different types (integer, string, real, real, real), it seems natural to organize this information into a record. These records are stored on a disk, and thus the input data is organized as a *file of records*. The basic processing operations that must be performed on this data are

1. Retrieve the information for a particular student given his or her number.
2. Modify a student's record by updating the grade-point average, current credits, or amount of financial aid.
3. Traverse the set of records so that a report can be generated and also so that an updated file of records can be created.

The first two basic operations, retrieval and modification, both require searching the collection of records to locate a particular record. One possibility would be to use a *sequential file* and to search it from its beginning each time a record must be retrieved or modified. In the case of modification, we would copy the records into another file as they are examined until the desired record is located, then write the updated record for that student into the new file, and then copy the remainder of the original file into the new file. The contents of this new file would then be copied back into the original file so that more searches could be performed. File input/output is slow, however, so if a large number of retrievals and/or modifications are to be performed, the response time using this approach may not be acceptable.

Another possibility would be to use a *direct access file*, in which a given record can be located directly without processing all those that precede it, and this record in the file can then be read and/or written; thus modification of a record in the file can be carried out "in place" without an excessive amount of file input/output. However, some programming languages do not support direct access files.

A third alternative would be to make direct access to the records possible by first copying them from the file into an array (or into several arrays), assuming of course that the number of records is not so large that they cannot be stored in main memory. Because storing data in and retrieving data from main memory is considerably faster than for secondary memory, this would appear to be the most attractive option and is the one we adopt in this example.

Using a top-down strategy to solve this problem, we begin by identifying three main tasks needed to solve it, describing them in fairly general terms:

1. An initialization task in which the student information in the file stored on disk must be copied into main memory so that it can be processed.
2. A processing task that processes this information to produce the required output.
3. A wrap-up task in which the updated information is copied back into the disk file, where it can be saved for later processing.

It is helpful to display these tasks and their relationship to each other in a *structure diagram* like the following:

Typically, one or more of these first-level tasks are still quite complex and so must be divided into subtasks. In this example, the description of the task *ProcessRecords* is very general, and further analysis shows that this task consists of servicing the three main types of requests identified earlier:

1. Retrieve the record for a given student.
2. Update the information in a student's record.
3. Generate a report displaying information for all students.

Also, the task *ReadFile* requires reading records having a special structure, and we might thus consider input of these records as a special subtask *ReadRecord*. These subtasks are displayed in the second level of the following refined structure diagram:

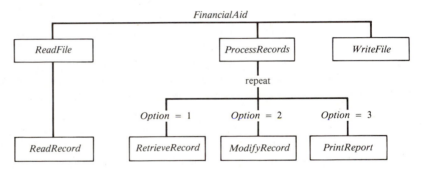

These subtasks may require further division into still smaller subtasks, producing additional levels of refinement, for example:

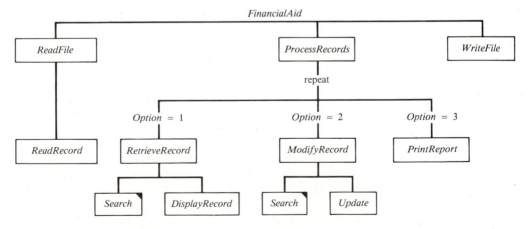

(The shaded corner indicates a subalgorithm or procedure that is shared by two or more [sub]algorithms.) This ***top-down design*** process continues until each subtask is sufficiently simple so that designing an algorithm for it is quite straightforward.

Given this general description of the algorithm and the data structures to be used, we can now give more detailed descriptions of the required subalgorithms. The main part of the program will call three separate subprograms to perform the three top-level tasks:

MAIN ALGORITHM

1. Use the subprogram *ReadFile* to copy the records from a given input file into an array.
2. If this file load was not successful then
    display an unsuccessful load message.
   Else do the following:
       a. Call the subprogram *ProcessRecords* to carry out processing as requested by the user.
       b. After processing is completed, use subprogram *WriteFile* to copy the array of updated records back into the file.

FIRST-LEVEL ALGORITHMS

ReadFile
1. Open the file for input.
2. Initialize a counter *NumRecs* to 0 and a boolean variable *ArrayFull* to false.
3. Read the first student record.
4. While there are more records and not *ArrayFull* do the following:
   a. Increment *NumRecs* by 1.
   b. If *NumRecs* ≤ *ArrayLimit* then:
       i. Store the student record in location *NumRecs* of the array *Student*.
       ii. Read the next student record.
      Otherwise
         Display an appropriate array-full message and set *ArrayFull* to true to signal the file load was not successful.
5. Close the input file.

ProcessRecords
Repeat the following:
   a. Get an *Option*—R(etrieve), Modify, P(rint report), or Q(uit).
   b. If the option selected is legal, then call an appropriate subprogram to carry out the required action or quit processing records:
       ′R′: *RetrieveRecord*;
       ′M′: *ModifyRecord*;
       ′P′: *PrintReport*;
       ′Q′: Terminate repetition

WriteFile
1. Open the file for output.
2. For an index *i* ranging from 1 to *NumRecs* do the following:
    Write the *i*th element of array *Student* into the file.
3. Close the output file.

SECOND-LEVEL ALGORITHMS

ReadRecord
A custom-designed procedure to read a student record.

RetrieveRecord
1. Enter student's number.
2. Call subprogram *Search* to search array *Student* for a record containing this number.
3. If student's record is found then
        Call subprogram *DisplayRecord* to display it
    Else
        Display a 'Not Found' message.

ModifyRecord
1. Enter student's number.
2. Call subprogram *Search* to search array *Student* for record containing this number.
3. If student's record is found, then
        Call subprogram *Update* to update it.
    Else
        Display a 'Not Found' message.

PrintReport
For an index *i* ranging from 1 to *NumRecs* do the following:
        Display the *i*th record in array *Student*.

THIRD-LEVEL ALGORITHMS

Search
A standard binary search algorithm that every programmer should have in his or her toolbox.

DisplayRecord
A custom-designed output procedure to display the fields in a student's record in an acceptable format.

UpdateRecord
1. Get the first *SubOption*— G(PA change), C(redits change), F(inancial aid change), or D(one updating).
2. While *SubOption* ≠ 'D' do the following:
    a. Read a new value for grade-point average, current credits, or

financial aid in this record according to whether the *SubOption* is G, C, or F.

b. Get the next *SubOption*.

A program can be coded and tested using the same top-down approach that is used in developing the algorithm and subalgorithms. To illustrate, a first version of the program to solve the financial aid problem is shown in Figure 1.2. Here only one of the first-level algorithms, namely, *ReadFile*, and the second-level algorithm *ReadRecord* have been implemented as procedures. The other first-level algorithms are represented by **program stubs**; *ProcessRecords* produces a temporary printout of the number of records and the student numbers in the first and last records of the array as a check that *ReadFile* and *ReadRecord* have performed correctly; and *WriteFile* simply displays a message indicating that it has been called.

```
MODULE FinancialAid;

(****************************************************************

   Program that reads student records from a file, allows the user to
   retrieve the record of a given student, to update the information in
   a record, or to generate a report for all students.  After processing
   is done, the updated list of records is copied into a new file.

****************************************************************)

FROM InOut IMPORT Write, WriteString, WriteCard, WriteLn,
                  Read, ReadCard, ReadString, Done,
                  OpenInput, OpenOutput, CloseInput, CloseOutput;
FROM RealInOut IMPORT WriteReal, ReadReal;
FROM SpecialInOut IMPORT FWriteReal;

CONST
    StringLimit = 20;      (* limit on number of characters in string *)
    ArrayLimit = 100;      (* limit on number of student records *)

TYPE
    StringType = ARRAY [0..StringLimit] OF CHAR;
    StudentRecord = RECORD
                        Number : CARDINAL;
                        FirstName,
                        LastName : StringType;
                        GPA,
                        Credits : REAL;
                        FinAid : CARDINAL
                    END;
    ArrayOfRecords = ARRAY [1..ArrayLimit] OF StudentRecord;

VAR
    Student : ArrayOfRecords;   (* array of student records read *)
    NumRecs : CARDINAL;         (* number of records *)
    ArrayFull : BOOLEAN;        (* signals if array becomes full *)
```

Figure 1.2

Figure 1.2 (cont.)

```
PROCEDURE ReadFile (VAR Student : ArrayOfRecords;
                    VAR NumRecs : CARDINAL;
                    VAR ArrayFull : BOOLEAN);

(*******************************************************************

    Procedure that reads records from a file and constructs
    the array Student of these records;  NumRecs is the actual
    number of records read.  ArrayFull is returned as TRUE if
    there are too many records to store in the array.

 ******************************************************************)

VAR
    i : CARDINAL;            (* index *)
    StuRec:  StudentRecord; (* record read from file *)
    MoreRecords : BOOLEAN;  (* indicates if record was read *)

PROCEDURE ReadRecord(VAR StuRec : StudentRecord;
                     VAR MoreRecords : BOOLEAN);

    (***************************************************************

        Procedure that reads and returns a student record StuRec if
        there are more records in the file.  A value of TRUE is
        returned for MoreRecords if a record was read successfully;
        FALSE signals end of file.

     **************************************************************)

    BEGIN
        WITH StuRec DO
            ReadCard(Number);
            ReadString(FirstName);
            ReadString(LastName);
            ReadReal(GPA);
            ReadReal(Credits);
            ReadCard(FinAid)
        END (* WITH *);
        MoreRecords := Done
    END ReadRecord;

BEGIN (* ReadFile *)
    WriteString('Enter name of input file: '); WriteLn;
    OpenInput('');
    NumRecs := 0;
    ArrayFull := FALSE;
    ReadRecord(StuRec, MoreRecords);
    WHILE MoreRecords AND NOT ArrayFull DO
        INC(NumRecs);
        IF (NumRecs <= ArrayLimit) THEN
            Student[NumRecs] := StuRec;
            ReadRecord(StuRec, MoreRecords)
        ELSE
            ArrayFull := TRUE
        END (* IF *)
    END (* WHILE *);
    CloseInput
END ReadFile;
```

Figure 1.2 (cont.)

```
PROCEDURE ProcessRecords (VAR Student : ArrayOfRecords;
                              NumRecs : CARDINAL);

    (*******************************************************************

        Procedure that allows the user to process any of the NumRecs
        records in array Student by retrieving a record, modifying it,
        or printing a list of the updated records.

    *******************************************************************)

    BEGIN
        WriteLn;
        WriteString('***** In ProcessRecords *****');
        WriteLn;
        WriteCard(NumRecs, 1);
        WriteString(' records read');
        WriteLn;
        WriteString('Student numbers in first and last records:');
        WriteLn;
        WriteCard(Student[1].Number,6);
        WriteCard(Student[NumRecs].Number, 6);
        WriteLn
    END ProcessRecords;

PROCEDURE WriteFile (VAR Student : ArrayOfRecords; NumRecs : CARDINAL);

    (*******************************************************************

        Procedure to copy the NumRecs updated records in array
        Student into a new file.

    *******************************************************************)

    BEGIN
        WriteString('***** In WriteFile *****');
        WriteLn
    END WriteFile;

BEGIN (* main program *)
    ReadFile (Student, NumRecs, ArrayFull);
    IF ArrayFull THEN
        WriteString('Error in reading student records from file');
        WriteLn
    ELSE
        ProcessRecords (Student, NumRecs);
        WriteFile(Student, NumRecs)
    END (* IF *)
END FinancialAid.
```

Figure 1.2   (cont.)

<u>Listing of STUFILE used in sample run:</u>

```
1234 John Smith
3.35 22.0 5000
1237 Mary Doe
2.94 16.5 2500
1355 Fred Jones
2.00 28.5 6250
```

<u>Sample run:</u>

```
Enter name of input file:
in>STUFILE

***** In ProcessRecords *****
3 records read
Student numbers in first and last records:
  1234  1355
***** In WriteFile *****
```

The sample run indicates that procedures *ReadFile* and *ReadRecord* appear
to be working correctly. Thus one might now begin developing the next first-
level algorithm *ProcessRecords*. It might be coded and tested as shown in
Figure 1.3, where the second-level procedures *RetrieveRecord*, *ModifyRecord*,
and *PrintReport* are program stubs that simply signal their execution.

```
MODULE FinancialAid;

(************************************************************************

    Program that reads student records from a file, allows the user to
    retrieve the record of a given student, to update the information in
    a record, or to generate a report for all students.  After processing
    is done, the updated list of records is copied into a new file.

************************************************************************)

    FROM InOut IMPORT Write, WriteString, WriteCard, WriteLn,
                    Read, ReadCard, ReadString, Done,
                    OpenInput, OpenOutput, CloseInput, CloseOutput;
    FROM RealInOut IMPORT WriteReal, ReadReal;
    FROM SpecialInOut IMPORT FWriteReal;

    CONST
        StringLimit = 20;      (* limit on number of characters in string *)
        ArrayLimit = 100;      (* limit on number of student records *)
```

Figure 1.3

Figure 1.3   (cont.)

```
TYPE
    StringType = ARRAY[0..StringLimit] OF CHAR;
    StudentRecord = RECORD
                        Number : CARDINAL;
                        FirstName,
                        LastName : StringType;
                        GPA,
                        Credits : REAL;
                        FinAid : CARDINAL
                    END;
    ArrayOfRecords = ARRAY [1..ArrayLimit] OF StudentRecord;

VAR
    Student : ArrayOfRecords;    (* array of student records read *)
    NumRecs : CARDINAL;          (* number of records *)
    ArrayFull : BOOLEAN;         (* signals if array becomes full *)

PROCEDURE ReadFile (VAR Student : ArrayOfRecords;
                    VAR NumRecs : CARDINAL;
                    VAR ArrayFull : BOOLEAN);

(*******************************************************************

    Procedure that reads records from a file and constructs
    the array Student of these records;  NumRecs is the actual
    number of records read.  ArrayFull is returned as TRUE if
    there are too many records to store in the array.

    *****************************************************************)
                                 •
                                 •
                                 •
PROCEDURE ProcessRecords (VAR Student : ArrayOfRecords;
                          NumRecs : CARDINAL);

(*******************************************************************

    Procedure that allows the user to process any of the NumRecs
    records in array Student by retrieving a record, modifying it,
    or printing a listing of the updated records.

    *****************************************************************)

    VAR
        Option : CHAR;        (* User option *)


    PROCEDURE RetrieveRecord (VAR Student : ArrayOfRecords;
                              NumRecs : CARDINAL);

    (***************************************************************

        Procedure to retrieve a specified record from the array
        Student of NumRecs records.

        *************************************************************)
```

Figure 1.3 (cont.)

```
        BEGIN
            WriteLn;
            WriteString('*** In RetrieveRecord ***')
        END RetrieveRecord;

    PROCEDURE ModifyRecord (VAR Student : ArrayOfRecords;
                                NumRecs : CARDINAL);

        (*****************************************************************

            Procedure to modify a specified record in the array
            Student of NumRecs records.

         ****************************************************************)

        BEGIN
            WriteLn;
            WriteString('*** In ModifyRecord ***')
        END ModifyRecord;

    PROCEDURE PrintReport (VAR Student : ArrayOfRecords;
                               NumRecs : CARDINAL);

        (*****************************************************************

            Procedure to display the NumRecs records in the array Student.

         ****************************************************************)

        BEGIN
            WriteLn;
            WriteString('*** In PrintReport ***')
        END PrintReport;

BEGIN (* ProcessRecords *)
    LOOP
        WriteLn;
        WriteString('Option:  R(etrieve), M(odify), P(rint report), ');
        WriteString('Q(uit)?  ');
        Read(Option);
        CASE CAP(Option) OF
            'R' : RetrieveRecord (Student, NumRecs)
                |
            'M' : ModifyRecord (Student, NumRecs)
                |
            'P' : PrintReport (Student, NumRecs)
                |
            'Q' : EXIT
            ELSE
                    WriteLn;
                    Write(Option);
                    WriteString(' is not a legal option')
        END (* CASE *)
    END (* LOOP *)
END ProcessRecords;
```

Figure 1.3 (cont.)

```
    PROCEDURE WriteFile (VAR Student : ArrayOfRecords; NumRecs : CARDINAL);

       (*************************************************************

           Procedure to copy the NumRecs updated records in array
           Student into a new file.

           *********************************************************)

       BEGIN
           WriteLn;
           WriteString('***** In WriteFile *****')
       END WriteFile;

BEGIN (* main program *)
    ReadFile (Student, NumRecs, ArrayFull);
    IF ArrayFull THEN
        WriteString('Error in reading student records from file');
        WriteLn
    ELSE
    ProcessRecords (Student, NumRecs);
    WriteFile(Student, NumRecs)
    END (* IF *)
END FinancialAid.
```

Listing of STUFILE used in sample run:

```
1234 John Smith
3.35 22.0 5000
1237 Mary Doe
2.94 16.5 2500
1355 Fred Jones
2.00 28.5 6250
```

Sample run:

```
Enter name of input file:
in>STUFILE

Option:  R(etrieve), M(odify), P(rint report), Q(uit)?  R
*** In RetrieveRecord ***
Option:  R(etrieve), M(odify), P(rint report), Q(uit)?  N
N is not a legal option
Option:  R(etrieve), M(odify), P(rint report), Q(uit)?  M
*** In ModifyRecord ***
Option:  R(etrieve), M(odify), P(rint report), Q(uit)?  P
*** In PrintReport ***
Option:  R(etrieve), M(odify), P(rint report), Q(uit)?  Q
***** In WriteFile *****
```

This process of successive *stepwise refinement* continues until eventually the complete program in Figure 1.4 results. Once a program unit has been developed and tested, it normally will not require change in later phases of this development proces. Also, when an error is detected at some stage, it will usually be in one of the new subprograms written or refined since the preceding phase.

```
MODULE FinancialAid;

(*************************************************************************

   Program that reads student records from a file, allows the user to
   retrieve the record of a given student, to update the information in
   a record, or to generate a report for all students.  After processing
   is done, the updated list of records is copied into a new file.

*************************************************************************)

   FROM InOut IMPORT Write, WriteString, WriteCard, WriteLn,
                     Read, ReadCard, ReadString, Done,
                     OpenInput, OpenOutput, CloseInput, CloseOutput;
   FROM RealInOut IMPORT WriteReal, ReadReal;
   FROM SpecialInOut IMPORT FWriteReal;

CONST
     StringLimit = 20;      (* limit on number of characters in string *)
     ArrayLimit = 100;      (* limit on number of student records *)

TYPE
     StringType = ARRAY[0..StringLimit] OF CHAR;
     StudentRecord = RECORD
                         Number : CARDINAL;
                         FirstName,
                         LastName : StringType;
                         GPA,
                         Credits : REAL;
                         FinAid : CARDINAL
                     END;
     ArrayOfRecords = ARRAY [1..ArrayLimit] OF StudentRecord;

VAR
     Student : ArrayOfRecords;   (* array of student records read *)
     NumRecs : CARDINAL;         (* number of records *)
     ArrayFull : BOOLEAN;        (* signals if array becomes full *)
```

Figure 1.4

Figure 1.4 (cont.)

```
PROCEDURE ReadFile (VAR Student : ArrayOfRecords;
                    VAR NumRecs : CARDINAL;
                    VAR ArrayFull : BOOLEAN);


(*******************************************************************

    Procedure that reads records from a file and constructs
    the array Student of these records;  NumRecs is the actual
    number of records read.  ArrayFull is returned as TRUE if
    there are too many records to store in the array.

********************************************************************)


VAR
    i : CARDINAL;             (* index *)
    StuRec:  StudentRecord; (* record read from file *)
    MoreRecords : BOOLEAN;  (* indicates if record was read *)


PROCEDURE ReadRecord(VAR StuRec : StudentRecord;
                     VAR MoreRecords : BOOLEAN);


    (*******************************************************************

        Procedure that reads and returns a student record StuRec if
        there are more records in the file.  A value of TRUE is
        returned for MoreRecords if a record was read successfully;
        FALSE signals end of file.

    ********************************************************************)


    BEGIN
        WITH StuRec DO
            ReadCard(Number);
            ReadString(FirstName);
            ReadString(LastName);
            ReadReal(GPA);
            ReadReal(Credits);
            ReadCard(FinAid)
        END (* WITH *);
        MoreRecords := Done
    END ReadRecord;

BEGIN (* ReadFile *)
    WriteString('Enter name of input file: '); WriteLn;
    OpenIhput('');
    NumRecs := 0;
    ArrayFull := FALSE;
    ReadRecord(StuRec, MoreRecords);
    WHILE MoreRecords AND NOT ArrayFull DO
        INC(NumRecs);
        IF (NumRecs <= ArrayLimit) THEN
            Student[NumRecs] := StuRec;
            ReadRecord(StuRec, MoreRecords)
        ELSE
            ArrayFull := TRUE
        END (* IF *)
    END (* WHILE *);
    CloseInput
END ReadFile;
```

Figure 1.4   (cont.)

```
PROCEDURE ProcessRecords (VAR Student : ArrayOfRecords;
                               NumRecs : CARDINAL);

   (**********************************************************************

     Procedure that allows the user to process any of the NumRecs
     records in array Student by retrieving a record, modifying it,
     or printing a list of the updated records.

   **********************************************************************)

   VAR
       Option : CHAR;        (* User option *)

   PROCEDURE Search (VAR Student : ArrayOfRecords;
                         NumRecs, Snumb : CARDINAL;
                     VAR Found : BOOLEAN; VAR Location : CARDINAL);

       (**********************************************************************

         Procedure to search the array Student of NumRecs records for a
         record having Snumb in its Number field using the binary search
         algorithm.  If such a record is found, a value of TRUE is
         returned for Found and the Location of the record is returned;
         otherwise, FALSE is returned for Found and 0 for Location.

       **********************************************************************)

       VAR
           First,             (* first item in sublist being searched *)
           Last,              (* last item in sublist *)
           Middle : CARDINAL; (* middle item in sublist *)

       BEGIN
           First := 1;
           Last := NumRecs;
           Found := FALSE;
           Location := 0;
           WHILE (First <= Last) AND NOT Found DO
               Middle := (First + Last) DIV 2;
               IF Snumb < Student[Middle].Number THEN
                   Last := Middle - 1  (* item in first half of sublist *)
               ELSIF Snumb > Student[Middle].Number THEN
                   First := Middle + 1 (* item in last half of sublist *)
               ELSE                      (* item found *)
                   Found := TRUE;
                   Location := Middle
               END (* IF *)
           END (* WHILE *)
       END Search;

   PROCEDURE RetrieveRecord(VAR Student : ArrayOfRecords;
                                NumRecs : CARDINAL);

       (**********************************************************************

         Procedure to retrieve a specified record from the array
         Student of NumRecs records.

       **********************************************************************)
```

Figure 1.4   (cont.)

```
    VAR
        Snumb,                   (* student number in record to retrieve *)
        Location : CARDINAL;     (* location of record in array Student *)
        Found : BOOLEAN;         (* indicates if search is successful *)

    PROCEDURE DisplayRecord(StuRec : StudentRecord);

        (***************************************************************

            Procedure to display the fields of record StuRec.

        ***************************************************************).

        BEGIN
            WITH StuRec DO
                WriteLn;
                WriteString(FirstName);
                Write(' ');
                WriteString(LastName);
                WriteLn;
                WriteString('GPA  - - - - - - - -');
                FWriteReal(GPA, 8, 2);
                WriteLn;
                WriteString('Credits  - - - - - - -');
                FWriteReal(Credits, 8, 1);
                WriteLn;
                WriteString('Financial Aid  - - - - $');
                WriteCard(FinAid, 6)
            END (* WITH *);
            WriteLn
        END DisplayRecord;

    BEGIN (* RetrieveRecord *)
        WriteLn;
        WriteString("Enter Student's number:  ");
        ReadCard(Snumb);
        Search(Student, NumRecs, Snumb, Found, Location);
        IF Found THEN
            DisplayRecord(Student[Location])
        ELSE
            WriteLn;
            WriteString('*** Student ');
            WriteCard(Snumb, 1);
            WriteString(' not found ***')
        END (* IF *)
    END RetrieveRecord;

PROCEDURE ModifyRecord(VAR Student : ArrayOfRecords;
                           NumRecs : CARDINAL);

    (*****************************************************************

        Procedure to modify a specified record in the array
        Student of NumRecs records.

    *****************************************************************)
```

Figure 1.4   (cont.)

```
VAR
    Snumb,                  (* student number in record to modify *)
    Location : CARDINAL;    (* location of record in array Student *)
    Found : BOOLEAN;        (* indicates if search is successful *)

PROCEDURE Update(VAR StuRec : StudentRecord);

    (*************************************************************

        Procedure to update the student record StuRec.

    *************************************************************)

    VAR
        SubOption : CHAR; (* option selected from submenu for updating *)

    BEGIN
        LOOP
            WriteLn;
            WriteString('Option:  G(pa), C(redits), F(in. aid), D(one)? ');
            Read(SubOption);
            CASE CAP(SubOption) OF
                'C' : WriteLn;
                    WriteString('Enter new credits:  ');
                    ReadReal(StuRec.Credits)
                |
                'G' : WriteLn;
                    WriteString('Enter new GPA:  ');
                    ReadReal(StuRec.GPA)
                |
                'F' : WriteLn;
                    WriteString('Enter new financial aid:  ');
                    ReadCard(StuRec.FinAid)
                |
                'D' : EXIT
                ELSE
                    WriteLn;
                    Write(SubOption);
                    WriteString(' is not a legal option')
            END (* CASE *)
        END (* LOOP *)
    END Update;

BEGIN (* ModifyRecord *)
    WriteLn;
    WriteString("Enter Student's number:  ");
    ReadCard(Snumb);
    Search(Student, NumRecs, Snumb, Found, Location);
    IF Found THEN
        Update(Student[Location])
    ELSE
        WriteLn;
        WriteString('*** Student ');
        WriteCard(Snumb, 1);
        WriteString(' not found ***')
    END (* IF *)
END ModifyRecord;
```

Figure 1.4   (cont.)

```
PROCEDURE PrintReport (VAR Student : ArrayOfRecords;
                           NumRecs : CARDINAL);

(*****************************************************************

    Procedure to display the NumRecs records in the array Student.

*****************************************************************)

VAR
    i : CARDINAL;        (* index *)

BEGIN
    WriteLn;
    FOR i := 1 TO NumRecs DO
        WITH Student[i] DO
            WriteLn;
            WriteCard(Number, 4);
            WriteString(' ');
            WriteString(FirstName);
            Write(' ');
            WriteString(LastName);
            WriteLn;
            WriteString(' GPA:');
            FWriteReal(GPA, 6, 2);
            WriteString('    Credits:');
            FWriteReal(Credits, 6, 1);
            WriteString('    Fin. Aid:  $');
            WriteCard(FinAid,1)
        END (* WITH *)
    END (* FOR *);
    WriteLn
END PrintReport;

BEGIN (* ProcessRecords *)
    REPEAT
        WriteLn;
        WriteString('Option:  R(etrieve), M(odify), P(rint list),');
        WriteString('Q(uit)?  ');
        Read(Option);
        CASE CAP(Option) OF
            'R' : RetrieveRecord (Student, NumRecs)
                |
            'M' : ModifyRecord (Student, NumRecs)
                |
            'P' : PrintReport (Student, NumRecs)
                |
            'Q' : (* no action -- processing terminated *)
            ELSE
                WriteLn;
                Write(Option);
                WriteString(' is not a legal option')
        END (* CASE *)
    UNTIL CAP(Option) ='Q'
END ProcessRecords;
```

Figure 1.4   (cont.)

```
PROCEDURE WriteFile (VAR Student : ArrayOfRecords; NumRecs : CARDINAL);

    (****************************************************************

        Procedure to copy the NumRecs updated records in array
        Student into a new file.

        ***************************************************************)

    VAR
        i : CARDINAL;   (* index *)
    BEGIN
        WriteLn; WriteLn;
        WriteString('Enter name of output file.'); WriteLn;
        OpenOutput('');
        FOR i := 1 TO NumRecs DO
            WITH Student[i] DO
                WriteCard(Number, 5);
                Write(' ');
                WriteString(FirstName);
                Write(' ');
                WriteString(LastName);
                WriteLn;
                FWriteReal(GPA, 5, 2);
                FWriteReal(Credits, 5, 1);
                WriteCard(FinAid, 5);
                WriteLn
            END (* WITH *)
        END (* FOR *);
        CloseOutput
    END WriteFile;

BEGIN (* main program *)
    ReadFile (Student, NumRecs, ArrayFull);
    IF ArrayFull THEN
        WriteString('Error in reading student records from file');
        WriteLn
    ELSE
        ProcessRecords (Student, NumRecs);
        WriteFile(Student, NumRecs)
    END (* IF *)
END FinancialAid.
```

Listing of STUFILE used in sample run:

```
1234 John Smith
3.35 22.0 5000
1237 Mary Doe
2.94 16.5 2500
1355 Fred Jones
2.00 28.5 6250
```

Figure 1.4   (cont.)

<u>Sample run:</u>

```
Enter name of input file:
in>STUFILE

Option:  R(etrieve),  M(odify),  P(rint report),  Q(uit)?  R
Enter Student's number:  1237
Mary Doe
GPA  - - - - - - - - -    2.94
Credits  - - - - - - -    16.5
Financial Aid  - - - - $  2500

Option:  R(etrieve), M(odify), P(rint report), Q(uit)?  M
Enter Student's number:  1244
*** Student 1244 not found ***
Option:  R(etrieve), M(odify), P(rint report), Q(uit)?  M
Enter Student's number:  1234
Option:  G(pa), C(redits), F(in. aid), D(one)?  G
Enter new GPA:  3.6
Option:  G(pa), C(redits), F(in. aid), D(one)?  F
Enter new financial aid:  7000
Option:  G(pa), C(redits), F(in. aid), D(one)?  D
Option:  R(etrieve), M(odify), P(rint report), Q(uit)?  P

 1234  John Smith
 GPA:  3.60     Credits:  22.0     Fin. Aid  $7000
 1237  Mary Doe
 GPA:  2.94     Credits:  16.5     Fin. Aid  $2000
 1355  Fred Jones
 GPA:  2.00     Credits:  28.5     Fin. Aid  $6250

Option:  R(etrieve), M(odify), P(rint report), Q(uit)?  Q

Enter name of output file.
out>NEWSTUFILE
```

<u>Listing of updated NEWSTUFILE produced:</u>

```
1234 John Smith
3.60 22.0 7000
1237 Mary Doe
2.94 16.5 2500
1355 Fred Jones
2.00 28.5 6250
```

Exercises

1. List and briefly describe the five phases of the software life cycle.

2. What are some ways in which problems in introductory programming courses differ from real-world problems?

3. What are structured data types? Give some examples from Modula-2.

4. Give some examples of user-defined data structures.

5. Define an algorithm, naming and describing the properties it must possess.

6. What is pseudocode?

7. Name and describe the three control structures used in developing structured algorithms.

8. Describe the top-down approach to algorithm design.

9. What are some of the ways in which student programs differ from real-world programs?

10. Name three kinds of programming errors and give examples of each. When during program development is each likely to be detected?

11. Describe the general pattern of a proof of the correctness of an algorithm.

12. What are some situations in which program maintenance may be required?

13. Write the following unstructured algorithm as a structured program segment (but different from those given in Exercises 14 and 15):

    (* Search the entries of the $n \times n$ matrix *Mat* in rowwise order for an entry equal to *Item*. *)

    1. Set *Row* equal to 0.
    2. Set *Col* equal to 0.
    3. Increment *Row* by 1.
    4. Increment *Col* by 1.
    5. If *Col* $<=$ n then
            Jump ahead to Step 7.
    6. Jump back to Step 2.
    7. If *Row* $<=$ n then
            Jump ahead to Step 9.
    8. Jump ahead to Step 13.
    9. If *Mat*[*Row*, *Col*] = *Item* then
            Jump ahead to step 11.
    10. Jump back to Step 4.
    11. Write a message indicating that *Item* was found.
    12. Skip over the next instruction and exit from this algorithm.
    13. Write a message indicating that *Item* was not found.

14. Although the following program segment is structured, it is not a correct solution to Exercise 13. Explain.

(∗ Search the entries of the $n \times n$ matrix *Mat* in rowwise order for an entry equal to *Item*. ∗)

```
FOR Row := 1 TO n DO
    FOR Col := 1 TO n DO
        IF Mat[Row, Col] = Item THEN
            Found := TRUE
        ELSE
            Found := FALSE
        END (∗ IF ∗)
    END (∗ FOR Col ∗)
END (∗ FOR Row ∗);
IF Found THEN
    WriteString('Item found')
ELSE
    WriteString('Item not found')
END (∗ IF ∗);
WriteLn;
```

15. The following program segment is structured, but it is not a good solution to Exercise 13. Why isn't it? (Consider its efficiency.)

(∗ Search the entries of the $n \times n$ matrix *Mat* in rowwise order for an entry equal to *Item*. ∗)

```
Found := FALSE;
FOR Row := 1 TO n DO
    FOR Col := 1 TO n DO
        IF Mat[Row, Col] = Item THEN
            Found := TRUE
        END (∗ IF ∗)
    END (∗ FOR Col ∗)
END (∗ FOR Row ∗);
IF Found THEN
    WriteString('Item found')
ELSE
    WriteString('Item not found')
END (∗ IF ∗);
WriteLn;
```

16. Consider the following algorithm:

ScanAndCount

(∗ Algorithm returns a count of those elements in an array X with n elements that exceed some specified *Cutoff* value. ∗)

1. Initialize *Count* to 0.
2. Initialize i to 0.

3. While $i < n$ do the following:
  a. Increment i by 1.
  b. If $X[i] > Cutoff$ then
        Add 1 to *Count*.

Using the input, intermediate, and output assertions shown in the following diagram, use mathematical induction to give an informal correctness proof of this algorithm. Note that there are two possible initial execution paths from point 1 to point 4 that must be considered: $1 \rightarrow 2 \rightarrow 4$ and $1 \rightarrow 2 \rightarrow 3 \rightarrow 4$. Similarly, on each pass through the loop there are two possible paths from point 4 to point 4: $4 \rightarrow 5 \rightarrow 4$ and $4 \rightarrow 5 \rightarrow 3 \rightarrow 4$.

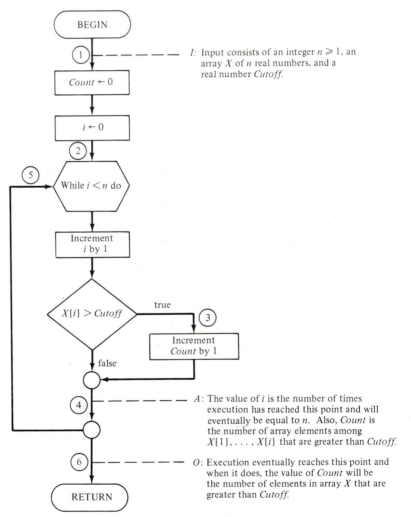

I: Input consists of an integer $n \geq 1$, an array X of n real numbers, and a real number *Cutoff.*

A: The value of i is the number of times execution has reached this point and will eventually be equal to n. Also, *Count* is the number of array elements among $X[1], \ldots, X[i]$ that are greater than *Cutoff.*

O: Execution eventually reaches this point and when it does, the value of *Count* will be the number of elements in array X that are greater than *Cutoff.*

17. The *factorial* of a nonnegative integer n, denoted by $n!$, is defined by

$$0! = 1$$
$$n! = 1 \times 2 \times \cdots \times n \text{ for } n > 0$$

Give an algorithm that calculates $n!$ iteratively (nonrecursively), and prove its correctness.

18. Give an algorithm that finds and returns the largest element in an array X of n elements, and prove its correctness.

19. Mathematical induction is a natural tool to use in proving the correctness of recursive algorithms. Use it to prove the correctness of the following recursive Modula-2 function procedure for calculating factorials (see Exercise 17):

PROCEDURE *Factorial*(n : CARDINAL) : CARDINAL;

(* Recursive function procedure to calculate the factorial $n!$ *)

```
BEGIN
    IF n = 0 THEN
        RETURN 1
    ELSE
        RETURN n * Factorial(n − 1)
    END (* IF *)
END Factorial;
```

2

Introduction to Data Structures and Abstract Data Types

The second phase of the software life cycle described in Chapter 1 is the selection of structures to organize the data and the design of algorithms to solve the problem, and the main purpose of this text is to explore these two aspects of program development. The data to be processed by a program must be organized using some structure that reflects the relationships between the data items and that allows the data to be processed efficiently. As we have already noted, the selection of these structures and the design of algorithms cannot be separated; they must be done in parallel.

Because these structures and algorithms must be implemented in some programming language, they must be designed to take advantage of the features of that language. This means that when possible, they should be based on the predefined data types, operations, and procedures available in the language. In this chapter we define and illustrate data structures and their implementations and describe how some of the predefined Modula-2 data types are implemented in computer systems.

2.1 Data Structures, Abstract Data Types, and Implementations

To illustrate the process of organizing and structuring data in a given problem, let us consider the following example: Suppose that Trans-Fryslan Airlines operates a single ten-passenger airplane. TFA would like to modernize its operation and, as a first step, needs a program that will determine for each flight which seats are unoccupied so that seat assignments can be made.

In this problem, it is clear that the input information is a collection of ten seats and, for each seat, some indication of whether it is occupied. We must be able to perform the following operations: (1) examine the collection of seats to determine which of them are unoccupied; (2) reserve a seat; and (3) cancel a seat assignment. To perform these operations, it is convenient to think of the seats as organized in a list.

After organizing the data as a list of ten seats and identifying the basic operations to be performed, we can consider possible ways to implement this structure. A variety of implementations are possible. For example, we might define an enumeration type

TYPE
   SeatStatus = (*Occupied, Unoccupied*);

and represent the list of seats by ten simple variables of type *SeatStatus*:

VAR
   Seat1, Seat2, . . . , Seat10 : *SeatStatus*;

Although this is a simple representation of the list of seats, the algorithms to perform the required operations are somewhat awkward. For example, the algorithm to scan the list of seats and to produce a listing of those seats that are unoccupied might be as follows:

ALGORITHM TO LIST UNOCCUPIED SEATS

1. If *Seat1* = *Unoccupied* then
   Display 1.
2. If *Seat2* = *Unoccupied* then
   Display 2.
3. If *Seat3* = *Unoccupied* then
   Display 3.

   $\vdots$

10. If *Seat10* = *Unoccupied* then
    Display 10.

An algorithm for reserving a seat is even more awkward and, in fact, is completely unreasonable!

ALGORITHM TO RESERVE A SEAT

1. Set *Done* to false.
2. If *Seat1* = *Unoccupied* then do the following:
   a. Display 'Do you wish to assign Seat # 1?'.
   b. Read *Response* from user.
   c. If *Response* = 'Y' then do the following:
      i. Set *Seat1* equal to *Occupied*.
      ii. Set *Done* equal to true.
3. If not *Done* and *Seat2* = *Unoccupied* then do the following:
   a. Display 'Do you wish to assign Seat # 2?'.
   b. Read *Response* from user.
   c. If *Response* = 'Y' then do the following:
      i. Set *Seat2* equal to *Occupied*.
      ii. Set *Done* equal to true.

      $\vdots$

An algorithm for canceling a seat assignment would be equally ridiculous.

Modula-2 procedures could be written to implement these algorithms, but they would be clumsy and horribly inelegant. They would be inflexible and difficult to modify and would become even more awkward if TFA replaced its ten-seat airliner with a larger aircraft having more seats.

These difficulties certainly suggest that it may be appropriate to consider other ways to represent the data of this problem. One viable alternative is to represent the list of seats as an array whose elments are of type *SeatStatus*:

```
CONST
    MaxSeats = 10; (* upper limit on the number of seats *)

TYPE
    SeatStatus = (Occupied, Unoccupied);
    SeatList = ARRAY [1..MaxSeats] OF SeatStatus;

VAR
    Seat : SeatList;
```

Because the elements of an array can be easily accessed by using an indexed variable, the algorithms to implement the required operations are much simpler:

ALGORITHM TO LIST UNOCCUPIED SEATS

1. For *Number* ranging from 1 to *MaxSeats* do the following:
   If *Seat[Number]* = *Unoccupied* then
      Display *Number*.

ALGORITHM TO RESERVE A SEAT

1. Read *Number* of seat to be reserved.
2. If *Seat[Number]* = *Unoccupied* then
      Set *Seat[Number]* equal to *Occupied*.
   Else
      Display a message that seat having this *Number* has already been assigned.

The algorithm for canceling a seat assignment is similar to that for reserving a seat.

Although this is a very simple example, it does illustrate several general concepts. One is that solving a problem involves the manipulation of data and that an important part of the solution is the careful organization of the data. This requires that we identify the collection of data items and possible relationships between them and the basic operations that must be performed on these data items. Such a collection together with the relevant operations and relations is called an ***abstract data structure*** (or simply a ***data structure***) or an ***abstract data type*** (sometimes abbreviated as ***ADT***). In this example, the data structure consists of a list of seats or some representation of them (for example, a seating chart of the plane), together with the basic operations: (1) scan the list to determine which seats are unoccupied and (2) change a seat's status from unoccupied to occupied or from occupied to unoccupied.

The terms *abstract data structure* and *abstract data type* are often used interchangeably. However, the term *data structure* is more appropriate when data is being studied at a logical or conceptual level, independent of any programming considerations. The term *abstract data type* is appropriate when the structure is being viewed as an object to be processed in a program. In both cases, the word *abstract* refers to the fact that the data and the basic operations and relations defined on it are being studied independently of any implementation.

An ***implementation*** of a data structure consists of ***storage structures*** to store the data items and ***algorithms*** for the basic operations and relations. In the preceding example, two implementations are given. In the first, the storage structure consists of ten simple variables, and in the second implementation, it is an array. In both cases, algorithms for the basic operations are given, but those in the second implementation are considerably better than those in the first.

This idea of ***data abstraction***, in which the definition of the data structure is separated from its implementation, is an important concept that is a natural part of a top-down approach to program development. It makes it possible to study and use the structure without being concerned about the details of its implementation. In fact, this is usually the approach used for predefined data types such as CARDINAL, INTEGER, and CHAR and arrays; a programmer uses these data types without knowing how they are implemented. Nevertheless, these data types can be used more effectively and efficiently if the programmer has some understanding of the implementation used. Consequently, in the next several sections we review the predefined data types of Modula-2 and examine some of their implementations.

2.2   Simple Data Types

As we indicated in the preceding section, problem solving invariably involves manipulating some kind of data. In its most basic form, data values (as well as instructions) are encoded in the memory of a computer as sequences of 0s and 1s. This is because the devices that make up the memory unit are two-state devices and hence are ideally suited for storing information that is coded using only two symbols. If one of the states is interpreted as 0 and the other as 1, then a natural scheme for representing information is one that uses only the two binary digits, or ***bits***, 0 and 1. The two-state devices used in computer memory are organized into groups called ***words***, each of which contains a fixed number of these devices. Each of these words can thus store a fixed number of bits. Word sizes vary with computers, but common sizes are 16 and 32 bits. These words are ordinarily numbered beginning with zero, and the number associated with a memory word is called its ***address***. Thus any memory word can be accessed by means of its address.

Words are the basic storage structures in which all data values are stored. Basic data types such as CARDINAL, INTEGER, REAL, CHAR, and BOOL-EAN in Modula-2 are called ***simple data types*** because a value of one of these types is atomic; that is, it is a single entity that cannot be subdivided. Nevertheless, each can be viewed as an abstract data type because it consists of a set of values and one or more basic operations and relations defined on these values. Their implementations use words as storage structures, and the algorithms for the basic operations and relations are implemented by the hardware and/or software of the computer system. In this section we examine the implementations of these Modula-2 simple data types.

CARDINAL Data.   *Cardinal numbers* are the whole numbers 0, 1, 2, 3, ... The number system that we are accustomed to using to represent such values is a *decimal* or *base-ten number system*, which uses the digits 0, 1, 2, 3, 4, 5, 6, 7, 8, and 9. The significance of these digits in a numeral depends on the positions they occupy in that numeral. For example, in the numeral 427, the digit 4 is interpreted as 4 hundreds, the digit 2 as 2 tens, and the digit 7 as 7 ones. Thus, the numeral 427 represents the number four-hundred twenty-seven and can be written in *expanded form* as

$$4 \cdot 100 \, + \, 2 \cdot 10 \, + \, 7 \cdot 1$$

or

$$4 \cdot 10^2 \, + \, 2 \cdot 10^1 \, + \, 7 \cdot 10^0$$

The digits that appear in the various positions of the base-ten numeral thus represent coefficients of powers of 10.

Similar positional systems can be devised with numbers other than 10 as a base. The *base-two number system* uses 2 as the base and has only two digits, 0 and 1. As in a decimal system, the significance of a binary digit (or *bit*) in a base-two numeral is determined by its position in that numeral. For example, the base-two numeral 101 can be written in expanded form (in decimal notation) as

$$1 \cdot 2^2 \, + \, 0 \cdot 2^1 \, + \, 1 \cdot 2^0$$

that is, the base-two numeral 101 has the decimal value

$$4 \, + \, 0 \, + \, 1 \, = \, 5$$

Thus the cardinal number 5 can be stored in a 16-bit word as

0	0	0	0	0	0	0	0	0	0	0	0	0	1	0	1

Similarly, 427 can be written in base-two as 110101011 and can be stored as

0	0	0	0	0	0	0	1	1	0	1	0	1	0	1	1

The algorithms to implement the usual arithmetic operations on cardinal numbers are similar to the familiar algorithms for carrying out these operations on base-ten numbers. The basic addition and multiplication tables are

+	0	1
0	0	1
1	1	10

×	0	1
0	0	0
1	0	1

Thus, for example, the sum $5 + 7$ is calculated by adding, bit by bit, the base-two representations 101 and 111 of these numbers, carrying when necessary:

$$111 \longleftarrow \text{carries}$$
$$101$$
$$+ \ 111$$
$$\overline{1100}$$

Although the details of how cardinal numbers are represented internally in a computer may be of little concern to a programmer because they are automatically handled by the compiler, one aspect that is important is that the word length limits the size of cardinal numbers that can be stored. The largest cardinal number that can be stored in an 8-bit word is $2^8 - 1 = 255$; in a 16-bit word, $2^{16} - 1 = 65535$; and in a 32-bit word, $2^{32} - 1 = 4294967295$. An attempt to store a value greater than the maximum allowed will result in the loss of some of the bits of its binary representation; this phenomenon is known as *overflow*. This limitation can be partially overcome by using more than one word to store a number. This is the way that some Modula-2 systems implement the predefined data type LONGCARD used to process cardinal values larger than those allowed by type CARDINAL. Although this approach enlarges the range of cardinal numbers that can be stored, it does not resolve the problem of overflow, as the range of representable cardinal numbers is still finite. Thus the data type CARDINAL in Modula-2 is not a perfect representation of the mathematical concept of cardinal number because in mathematics, the set of cardinal numbers $\{0, 1, 2, 3, \ldots\}$ is infinite.

This base-two representation is not the only way to represent cardinal numbers as bit strings. The ***binary coded decimal (BCD)*** scheme represents a number with the bit string obtained by concatenating the 4-bit base-two representations of the decimal digits in the number. Thus the BCD representation of 427 in a 16-bit word would be

| 0 0 0 0 | 0 1 0 0 | 0 0 1 0 | 0 1 1 1 |

INTEGER Data. The set of integers consists of the whole numbers and their negatives $\{\ldots, -3, -2, -1, 0, 1, 2, 3 \ldots\}$. Most schemes for representing integers use one of the bits of a memory word to indicate the sign of a number. One simple way to do this is to set the leftmost bit to 1 if the number is negative, 0 if it is not, and to use the remaining bits to store the magnitude of the number, using the base-two representation described earlier. This representation is called the ***sign-magnitude*** representation for integers. For example, the 8-bit sign-magnitude representation of 6 is

$$6 \rightarrow 00000110$$
$$\uparrow$$
$$\text{sign bit}$$

and the sign-magnitude representation of -6 is

$$-6 \rightarrow 10000110$$
$$\uparrow$$
$$\text{sign bit}$$

Although this is a very simple scheme for representing integers, the algorithms for the basic arithmetic operations are not as easy as they are in some other representations. In particular, the addition of numbers of opposite signs is rather difficult.

A commonly used scheme to represent integers for which the algorithms are simpler is called *two's complement* notation. In this scheme, nonnegative integers are represented as in the sign-magnitude notation. The representation of a negative integer $-n$ is obtained by first finding the base-two representation for n, complementing it (that is, changing each 0 to 1 and each 1 to 0), and then adding 1 to the result. Thus the two's complement representation of -6 using a string of 8 bits is obtained as follows:

1. Represent 6 as an 8-bit base-two number:

$$00000110$$

2. Complement this bit string:

$$11111001$$

3. Add 1:

$$11111010$$

Since 2^n different patterns can be formed with n bits, it follows that there are 2^n different integers that can be represented by a string of n bits. For example, using $n = 4$ bits, we can represent $2^4 = 16$ different integers. If the two's complement scheme is used, the integers in the range from -8 through 7 can be represented as follows:

Two's Complement	Decimal
1000	-8
1001	-7
1010	-6
1011	-5
1100	-4
1101	-3
1110	-2
1111	-1
0000	0
0001	1
0010	2
0011	3
0100	4
0101	5
0110	6
0111	7

Note that the leftmost bit of the two's complement representation of each of the negative integers -1 through -8 is 1, whereas the leftmost bit of the two's complement representation of the nonnegative integers 0 through 7 is 0. Thus the leftmost bit is the sign bit, with 0 indicating a nonnegative value and 1 indicating a negative value.

Addition and multiplication of signed integers can still be carried out as described earlier for the base-two representation of nonnegative integers. For example, the sum $3 + (-4)$ is calculated as

$$
\begin{array}{r}
0011 \\
+ \ 1100 \\
\hline
1111
\end{array}
$$

Comparison of two integers in two's complement notation to determine which is larger is somewhat awkward, however, since the representation of negative numbers seems to indicate that these values are greater than positive values.

Another useful scheme for representing integers is the *excess* or *biased notation*. In this scheme, the representation of an integer as a string of n bits is formed by adding the bias 2^{n-1} to the integer and representing the result in base-two. Thus, the 8-bit biased representation of -6 is obtained as follows:

1. Add the bias $2^7 = 128$ to -6, giving 122.
2. Represent the result in base-two notation:

$$01111010$$

The integers in the range from -8 through 7 can be represented using 4 bits (and thus a bias of $2^3 = 8$) as follows:

Biased	Decimal
0000	-8
0001	-7
0010	-6
0011	-5
0100	-4
0101	-3
0110	-2
0111	-1
1000	0
1001	1
1010	2
1011	3
1100	4
1101	5
1110	6
1111	7

Note that the leftmost bit is again a sign bit, with 0 indicating a negative value and 1 a nonnegative value.

Although algorithms for the basic arithmetic operations are more complicated in this scheme than in two's complement notation, comparison of two integers can be carried out more easily. This is one reason that the biased representation is typically used for the exponent in the floating-point representation of real numbers to be described momentarily.

As was true for cardinal numbers, the length of a memory word limits the range of integers that can be stored. Because one of the bits is reserved for the sign, the largest positive integer that can be stored in a given word is approximately one-half of the largest cardinal number that can be stored in that word: $2^7 - 1 = 127$ for an 8-bit word, $2^{15} - 1 = 32767$ for a 16-bit word, and $2^{31} - 1 = 2147483647$ for a 32-bit word. If two's complement representation is used, the smallest integer that can be stored is $-2^7 = -128$ for an 8-bit word, $-2^{15} = -32768$ for a 16-bit word, and $-2^{31} = 2147483648$ for a 32-bit word. Once again, an attempt to store a number outside the allowed range leads to overflow. And using more than one word to store a number (as might be done in implementing the data type LONGINT) does enlarge the range of representable integers but does not eliminate the problem of overflow.

REAL Data.   In a decimal numeral representing a fraction, the digits to the right of the decimal point are also coefficients of powers of 10. In this case, however, the exponents are negative integers. For example, the numeral 0.317 can be written in expanded form as

$$3 \cdot 10^{-1} + 1 \cdot 10^{-2} + 7 \cdot 10^{-3}$$

The point in a base-two numeral representing a fraction is called a ***binary point***, and the positions to the right of the binary point represent negative powers of the base 2. For example, the expanded form of 110.101 is

$$1 \cdot 2^2 + 1 \cdot 2^1 + 0 \cdot 2^0 + 1 \cdot 2^{-1} + 0 \cdot 2^{-2} + 1 \cdot 2^{-3}$$

and thus it has the decimal value

$$4 + 2 + 0 + \tfrac{1}{2} + 0 + \tfrac{1}{8} = 6.625$$

There are a number of schemes used to store real numbers as bit strings, but nearly all of them use a ***scientific*** or ***floating-point form***. For example, the base-two representation

$$110.101$$

of the real value 6.625 is equivalent to

$$0.110101 \times 2^3$$

Typically, one part of a memory word (or words) is used to store a fixed number of bits of the ***mantissa*** or ***fractional part*** 0.110101 in ***normalized*** form—that is, so that the first bit is nonzero (unless the value is 0)—and another part to store the ***exponent*** 3. For example, suppose this value is stored in a 32-bit word in which the first 24 bits store the mantissa and the last 8 bits store the exponent. If two's complement representation is used for the mantissa and biased notation is used for the exponent, 6.625 can be stored as

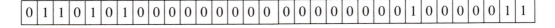

mantissa	exponent

Thus we see that the ***overflow*** problem discussed in connection with integer representation also occurs in the storage of a real number when the exponent is too large; a negative exponent that is too small results in ***underflow***.

Another problem that results from the fixed word length occurs when the

mantissa requires more than the alloted number of bits. For example, the base-two representation of 0.7 is

$$0.10110011001100110 \ldots$$

where the block 0110 is repeated indefinitely. Since only a finite number of these bits can be stored, the stored value is not exactly 0.7. To illustrate, suppose that in a 16-bit word, 11 bits are used to store the mantissa and 5 bits to store the exponent. If the first eleven bits of the mantissa are stored and all remaining bits are truncated, then the stored representation of 0.7 is

$$0.1011001100$$

which has the decimal value 0.69921875. If the binary representation is rounded to eleven bits, then the stored representation for 0.7 is

$$0.1011001101$$

which has the decimal value 0.700195312. In either case, the stored value is not exactly 0.7. This error, called ***roundoff error*** (in both cases), can be reduced, but not eliminated, by using a larger number of bits to store the mantissa (as might be done in implementing the data type LONGREAL).

    This approximation error may be compounded when real numbers are combined in arithmetic expressions. To illustrate, consider adding the three real numbers 0.4104, 1.0, and 0.2204; for simplicity, assume that the computations are done using decimal representation with four-digit precision. The normalized floating-point representations of these values are 0.4104×10^0, 0.100×10^1, and 0.2204×10^0. The first step in the addition of two values is to "align the decimal point" by increasing the smaller of the two exponents and shifting the mantissa. Thus the sum of the first two values is obtained by adding 0.0410×10^1 and 0.1000×10^1, which gives 0.1410×10^1. Adding the third number again requires adjusting the exponent and shifting the mantissa, 0.0220×10^1, and the final result is 0.1630×10^1, or 1.630. On the other hand, if the two smaller values are added first, giving 0.6308×10^0, and then the larger number is added, the result is 0.1631×10^1 or 1.631 (assuming rounding). In a long chain of such calculations, these small errors can accumulate so that the error in the final result may be very large. This example also illustrates that two real quantities that are algebraically equal, such as $(A + B) + C$ and $(A + C) + B$, may have computed values that are not equal. Consequently, some care must be taken when one compares two real quantities with the relational operators = and # or <>.

    It should now be clear that, as with cardinal numbers and integers, only a finite range of real numbers can be stored because of the fixed word length. Unlike cardinal numbers and integers, however, not all real numbers within this range can be stored because of the fixed length of the mantissa. In fact, only a finite subset of these real numbers can be stored exactly, and this means that there are infinitely many real numbers that cannot be stored exactly.

Character Data. Computers store and process not only numeric data but also character data and other types of nonnumeric information. The schemes used for storing character data are based on the assignment of a numeric code to each of the characters in the character set. Several standard coding schemes have been developed, such as ASCII (American Standard Code for Information Interchange) and EBCDIC (Extended Binary Coded Decimal Interchange Code). A complete table of ASCII and EBCDIC codes for all characters is given in Appendix B.

Characters are represented internally by these binary codes. A 16-bit memory word is usually divided into two 8-bit segments called **bytes**, each of which can store the binary representation of a single character. For example, the character string HI would be stored in a single 16-bit word with the code for H in one byte and the code for I in the other byte; with ASCII code, the result would be as follows:

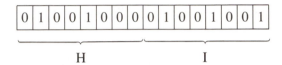

An 8-bit memory word can store one character; 32-bit words are usually divided into four bytes and thus can store four characters. A character string whose length is greater than the number of bytes in a word can be stored in two or more consecutive memory words.

The most common operation involving character values is comparison to determine whether two characters are equal or to determine whether one is less than another. This comparison is carried out using the numeric codes that represent the characters; two characters are equal if their codes are equal, and one character is less than another if the code of the first is less than the code of the second. The ordering defined in this way is called the **collating sequence** for the character set.

Boolean Data. There are only two boolean values, TRUE and FALSE. These values can be represented by single bits, with 0 representing FALSE and 1 representing TRUE. In some systems, boolean values are stored one per word with a bit string of all zeros representing FALSE and any other bit string representing TRUE.

Three boolean operations are defined in Modula-2: AND (or &), OR, and NOT (or ~). Because a boolean expression of the form p AND q is true only in the case that both p and q are true, the bit operation that implements AND is defined by the following table:

AND	0	1
0	0	0
1	0	1

Similarly, a boolean expression of the form p OR q is false only in the case that both p and q are false, and so the corresponding bit operation is defined by

OR	0	1
0	0	1
1	1	1

The boolean operation NOT is implemented simply by bit complementation.

Summary. We have seen that each of the simple data types CARDINAL, INTEGER, REAL, CHAR, and BOOLEAN can be represented by bit strings. It is the *interpretation* of a bit string and the operations that may be applied to it that determine the data type of the value represented by that bit string. A given bit string may represent a cardinal, integer, real, character, or boolean value, depending on the interpretation used. For example, the bit string

$$0\ 1\ 0\ 0\ 1\ 0\ 0\ 1\ 0\ 1\ 0\ 1\ 0\ 0\ 0\ 1$$

can be interpreted as the cardinal or integer value

$$2^{14} + 2^{11} + 2^8 + 2^6 + 2^4 + 2^0 = 18769$$

or as the real value (using an 11-bit mantissa and a biased 5-bit exponent)

$$(\tfrac{1}{2} + \tfrac{1}{16} + \tfrac{1}{128} + \tfrac{1}{512}) \times 2^1 = 1.154453124$$

or as the pair of characters (if ASCII code is used)

IQ

or as the single boolean value

FALSE

or as a sequence of sixteen boolean values

FALSE, TRUE, FALSE, FALSE, TRUE, . . . , TRUE

Exercises

1. Find the cardinal number (base-ten value) represented by each of the following bit strings of length 16:

   (a) 0000000010000000 (b) 0000000010101010
   (c) 0001000010001001 (d) 0000011110001110
   (e) 0100000000000001 (f) 0100100010000100
   (g) 1000000000000001 (h) 1010101000000000

2. Find the integer (base-ten value) represented by each of the following bit strings of length 16, assuming sign-magnitude representation:

   (a) 0100000001000000 (b) 0110111001101111
   (c) 1011111111111110 (d) 1100000000000001
   (e) 1001100110011001 (f) 1010101010101010

3. Find the integer represented by each of the bit strings in Exercise 2, assuming two's complement representation.

4. Find the integer represented by each of the bit strings in Exercise 2, assuming BCD representation, or explain why it cannot be interpreted as a BCD integer.

5. Find the integer represented by each of the bit strings in Exercise 2, assuming biased notation.

6. Find the real value represented by each of the bit strings in Exercise 2, assuming an 11-bit mantissa for which two's complement notation is used, and a 5-bit exponent for which biased notation is used.

7. Indicate how each of the bit strings in Exercise 2 can be interpreted as (i) a boolean value or (ii) a sequence of boolean values.

8. Interpret each of the bit strings in (a) and (b) of Exercise 2 as a pair of characters assuming (i) ASCII and (ii) EBCDIC representation.

9. Another useful and important number system in computer science is an *octal* number system, which uses a base of 8 and the digits 0, 1, 2, 3, 4, 5, 6, and 7. In the octal representation of a positive integer such as 1703_8, the digits represent coefficients of powers of 8.[1] Thus this numeral is an abbreviation for the expanded form

$$(1 \times 8^3) + (7 \times 8^2) + (0 \times 8^1) + (3 \times 8^0)$$

which has the decimal value

$$512 + 448 + 0 + 3 = 963$$

Find the decimal value represented by each of the following octal numerals:

(a) 321_8 (b) 2607_8 (c) 100000_8
(d) 7777_8 (e) 6.6_8 (f) 432.234_8

10. Besides an octal system (see Exercise 9), a *hexadecimal* number system is also useful. This is a base-sixteen system that uses the digits 0, 1, 2, 3, 4, 5, 6, 7, 8, 9, A (ten), B (eleven), C (twelve), D (thirteen), E (fourteen), and F (fifteen). The hexadecimal numeral $7E3_{16}$ has the expanded form

$$(7 \times 16^2) + (14 \times 16^1) + (3 \times 16^0)$$

which has the decimal value

$$1792 + 224 + 3 = 2019$$

---

[1] When numerals are written in bases other than ten, the number base is sometimes written as a subscript to prevent confusion.

Find the decimal value represented by each of the following hexadecimal numerals:

(a) 45_{16} **(b)** $3A0_{16}$ **(c)** ABC_{16}
(d) FFF_{16} **(e)** $7.C_{16}$ **(f)** $FE.DC_{16}$

11. Conversion from octal to binary (base-two) is easy; we need only replace each octal digit by its three-bit binary equivalent. For example, to convert 714_8 to binary, replace 7 by 111, 1 by 001, and 4 by 100 to obtain 111001100_2. Convert each of the octal numerals in Exercise 9 to binary numerals.

12. Imitating the conversion scheme in Exercise 11, convert each of the hexadecimal numerals in Exercise 10 to binary numerals.

13. To convert a binary numeral to octal, one can group the digits in groups of three, starting from the binary point (or from the right end if there is no binary point), and replace each group with the corresponding octal digit. For example,

$$11110101_2 = (11\ 110\ 101)_2 = 365_8$$

Convert each of the following binary numerals to octal numerals:

(a) 101010   **(b)** 1011
(c) 10000000000   **(d)** 0111111111111111111111
(e) 11.1   **(f)** 10101.10101

14. Imitating the conversion scheme in Exercise 13, convert each of the binary numerals given there to hexadecimal numerals.

15. One method for finding the **base-b representation** of a positive integer represented in base-ten notation is to repeatedly divide the number by b until a quotient of zero results. The successive remainders are the digits from right to left of the base-b representation. For example, the base-two representation of 26 is 11010_2, as the following computation shows:

$$
\begin{array}{r}
0 \text{ R } 1 \\
2\overline{)\,1}\ \text{R } 1 \\
2\overline{)\,3}\ \text{R } 0 \\
2\overline{)\,6}\ \text{R } 1 \\
2\overline{)13}\ \text{R } 0 \\
2\overline{)26}
\end{array}
$$

Convert the following base-ten numerals to base (i) two; (ii) eight; (iii) sixteen:

(a) 99   **(b)** 2571   **(c)** 5280

16. To convert a decimal fraction to its base-b equivalent, one can repeatedly multiply the fractional part of the number by b. The integer parts are the digits from left to right of the base-b representation. For example, the decimal numeral .6875 corresponds to the base-two numeral .1011_2, as the following computation shows:

$$
\begin{array}{r|l}
 & .6875 \\
 & \times\ 2 \\
\hline
1 & .375 \\
 & \times\ 2 \\
\hline
0 & .75 \\
 & \times 2 \\
\hline
1 & .5 \\
 & \times 2 \\
\hline
1 & .0 \\
\end{array}
$$

Convert the following base-ten numerals to base (i) two; (ii) eight; (iii) sixteen:

(a) .5   **(b)** .6875   **(c)** 13.828125

17. As noted in the text, even though the base-ten representation of a fraction may terminate, its representation in some other base need not terminate; for example, $0.7 = (0.1011001100110011001100110\cdots)_2 = 0.1\overline{0110}_2$, where the "overline" in the last notation indicates that the bit string 0110 is repeated indefinitely.

$$
\begin{array}{r|l}
 & .7 \\
 & \times\ 2 \\
\hline
1 & .4 \\
 & \times\ 2 \\
\hline
0 & .8 \\
 & \times\ 2 \\
\hline
1 & .6 \\
 & \times\ 2 \\
\hline
1 & .2 \\
 & \times\ 2 \\
\hline
0 & .4 \\
\end{array}
$$

Convert the following base-ten numerals to base (i) two; (ii) eight; (iii) sixteen:

(a) 0.6   **(b)** 0.05   **(c)** $0.\overline{3} = 0.33333\cdots = \frac{1}{3}$

18. Find the 16-bit two's complement representation for each of the following integers:

(a) 99   **(b)** 5280   **(c)** 255
(d) -255 **(e)** 1024   **(f)** -1024

19. Assuming an 11-bit mantissa for which two's complement notation is used and a 5-bit exponent for which biased notation is used, indicate how each of the following real numbers will be stored in a 16-bit word if extra bits in the mantissa are (i) truncated or (ii) rounded:

    (a) 0.625   **(b)** 25.625   **(c)** 14.78125
    (d) 0.015625   **(e)** 0.1   **(f)** 2.01

20. Indicate how each of the following character strings will be stored in two-byte words using ASCII:

    (a) BE   **(b)** be   **(c)** ABLE
    (d) Mr. Doe   **(e)** 1234   **(f)** 12.34

21. Write Modula-2 procedures to add and multiply nonnegative integers in base-two. Use these procedures in a program that reads two bit strings representing nonnegative integers, calls these procedures to find their sum and product, and then displays the corresponding bit strings.

22. The "successive division" method for converting from base-two to base-b described in Exercise 15 generates the base-b digits in reverse order, from right to left. Describe a data structure that could be used to store these digits as they are generated so that they can be displayed in correct order when the conversion is complete.

23. Write a program to carry out the conversion described in Exercise 22 for $0 \leq b \leq 10$.

24. Proceed as in Exercise 23, but for $0 \leq b \leq 16$. Use A, B, C, D, E, and F for digits as necessary.

25. Proceed as in Exercise 23, but for $b = 26$; use as "digits" A for 1, B for 2, . . . , Y for 25, and Z for 0.

2.3 Arrays

In addition to simple data types, most high-level programming languages also provide **structured data types**. Values of variables of these types consist of collections of data items. In this section we consider the most common of these data types, the array.

As a data structure, an **array** may be defined as a finite sequence or ordered set of elements, all of the same type, for which the basic operation is direct access to each position in the array so that the element in this position can be retrieved or so that a data item can be stored in this position. Thus an array must have a specific fixed number of elements, also called *components*, and these must be ordered so that there is a first element, a second element, and so on. All the array components must be of the same type; thus we might have an array of integers, an array of characters, or even an array of arrays.

Direct or *random access* means that each array element can be accessed directly by specifying its location in the array, so that the time required to access each element in the array is the same for all elements, regardless of their positions in the array. For example, in an array of 100 elements, the time required to access the seventy-fifth component is the same as that for the fifth. This is quite different from a *sequential access* structure in which one can access an element only by first processing all those that precede it. Clearly, the time required to access the seventy-fifth element would be considerably greater than that needed for the fifth.

In most high-level languages, an array is denoted by a variable whose value is the collection of elements that comprise the array. A particular component of the array is then accessed by attaching to the array name one or more *indices* (also called *subscripts*) that specify the position of that component in the array. If only one index is used, the array is said to be *one-dimensional*; arrays involving more than one index are called *multidimensional arrays*.

One-Dimensional Arrays.   An array declaration must specify two features of the array: the type of the array components and the index type. Declarations of one-dimensional arrays in Modula-2 have the general form

ARRAY *index-type* OF *component-type*

where *index-type* specifies the type of values for the index and may be BOOLEAN, CHAR, an enumeration type, or a subrange type; *component-type* specifies the type of the array elements and may be any type. For example, an array *A* to store a collection of twenty integers could be declared by

    CONST
        ArrayLimit = 20;

    TYPE
        NumberArray = ARRAY [1..*ArrayLimit*] OF INTEGER;

    VAR
        A : *NumberArray*;

This array declaration instructs the compiler to reserve a block of consecutive memory locations that is large enough to store the components of the array. The address of the first memory word used to store the components is called the *base address* of the array, denoted base(*A*), and the address of any other array component can be calculated by the system in terms of this base address. For example, if an integer can be stored in a single memory word, then the address of the fifth component *A*[5] of *A* is base(*A*) + 4; and in general, as the following diagram indicates, *A*[*i*] is stored in location

$$\text{base}(A) + (i - 1)$$

When an array element is to be accessed, the computer first performs this *address translation*; the bit string stored in the word whose address is calculated is then retrieved and interpreted as an integer, since the array declaration specifies that the data type of each component of *A* is INTEGER.

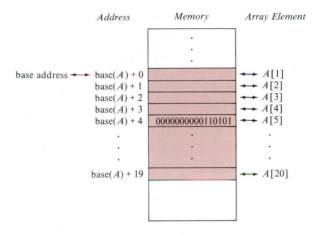

As another example, consider the array *Alpha* declared by

TYPE
    RealArray = ARRAY [−3..3] OF REAL;

VAR
    Alpha : *RealArray*;

and suppose that each real value requires two memory words for storage; then the fifth array component *Alpha*[1] is stored in memory words base(*Alpha*) + 8 and base(*Alpha*) + 9. Since the data type of the components of *Alpha* is declared as REAL, the bit string formed by concatenating the bit strings in these two words is interpreted as a real number when a reference is made to *Alpha*[1].

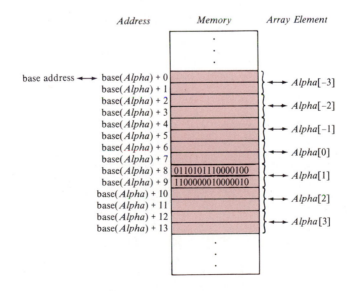

In general, if w words are required to store each component of an array A, the ith array component is stored in w consecutive memory words, beginning at the word with address base$(A) + (i - 1)w$. This means that if the subscripts of A are integers ranging from l through u, then the address of the memory word where $A[k]$ begins is

$$\text{base}(A) + (k - l)w$$

since $A[k]$ is in position $i = k - l + 1$ of the array.

The components of the arrays considered thus far have been numeric, and the values of these types are usually stored in one or more memory words. For other types of components, such as CHAR and BOOLEAN, it may be possible to store several values in a single memory word. For example, the standard coding schemes ASCII and EBCDIC use only 8 bits (1 byte) to store a single character. Thus, using an entire memory word to store a single character may be an inefficient use of memory. For example, in a 32-bit word machine, only 8 bits of a 32-bit word would be used to store a character, and thus three-fourths of each such word would be wasted. Memory utilization in such machines can be improved by packing several characters in a single word. Similarly, since a boolean value can be represented by a single bit, it may also be possible to pack several components of an array of type BOOLEAN into a single word.

To illustrate, consider the string variable S declared by

CONST
    MaxString = 30;

TYPE
    String = ARRAY [0 .. *MaxString*] OF CHAR;

VAR
    S : *String*;

and suppose that four characters are packed in a single memory word. The array elements $S[0]$, $S[1]$, $S[2]$, and $S[3]$ are then stored in bytes 1, 2, 3, and 4, respectively, of the memory word with address base(S); $S[4]$, $S[5]$, $S[6]$, and $S[7]$ are stored in the four bytes of the word with address base$(S) + 1$; and so on.

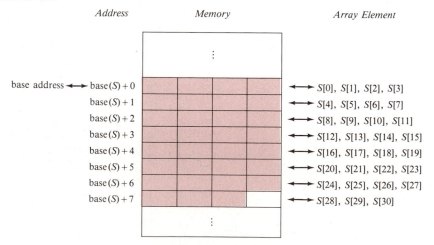

In general, array element $S[i]$ is stored in one of the bytes of the word with address

$$\text{base}(S) + i \text{ DIV } 4$$

The number of the byte in which it is stored is given by

$$1 + i \text{ MOD } 4$$

For example, $S[26]$ is stored in byte

$$1 + 26 \text{ MOD } 4 = 3$$

of the memory word having address

$$\text{base}(S) + 26 \text{ DIV } 4 = \text{base}(S) + 6$$

and the bit string stored in this byte is interpreted as a character when $S[26]$ is referenced.

As this illustration shows, accessing elements in packed arrays is more complicated than for unpacked arrays, because the address translation formulas are more complex and a portion of a memory word must be extracted and interpreted. Consequently, processing packed arrays may be more time-consuming than for unpacked arrays.

Multidimensional Arrays. In addition to one-dimensional arrays, most high-level languages also support arrays of more than one dimension. Two-dimensional arrays are particularly useful when the data being processed can be arranged in rows and columns. Similarly, a three-dimensional array is appropriate when the data can be arranged in rows, columns, and ranks. When several characteristics are associated with the data, still higher dimensions may be appropriate, with each dimension corresponding to one of these characteristics.

As an illustration of the use of two-dimensional arrays, consider the problem of recording and processing the daily sales of four different items at each of three different stores. These sales figures can be arranged naturally in a table having 4 rows and 3 columns

	Store		
Item	1	2	3
1	15	20	7
2	5	0	3
3	12	14	29
4	1	1	2

and a two-dimensional array is therefore an appropriate data structure to use to store these values. Such an array can be declared in Modula-2 as follows:

```
CONST
    MaxItems = 4;
    MaxStores = 3;
```

TYPE
    SalesTable = ARRAY [1..*MaxItems*], [1..*MaxStores*] OF CARDINAL;

VAR
    SalesTab : *SalesTable*;

The doubly-indexed variable *SalesTab*[3,2] can then be used to access the number of sales (14) of item 3 (row 3) at store 2 (column 2).

Now suppose that the sales figures are collected for a six-day week so that six such tables are collected:

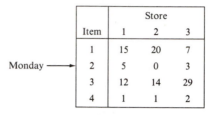

		Store		
Item	1	2	3
1	15	20	7
Monday → 2	5	0	3
3	12	14	29
4	1	1	2

		Store		
Item	1	2	3
1	6	2	9
Tuesday → 2	10	5	4
3	15	17	22
4	0	2	3

⋮

		Store		
Item	1	2	3
1	8	5	1
Saturday → 2	7	11	0
3	34	28	17
4	2	1	0

A three-dimensional array *Sales* declared by

CONST
    MaxItems = 4;
    MaxStores = 3;

TYPE
    Days = (*Monday, Tuesday, Wednesday, Thursday, Friday, Saturday*);
    ListOfSalesTable =
        ARRAY *Days*, [1..*MaxItems*], [1..*MaxStores*] OF CARDINAL;

VAR
    Sales : *ListOfSalesTable*;

might be used to store and organize these 72 sales figures. Access to the array element in the table for Monday, third row, and second column—that is, to the number representing sales (14) on Monday of item 3 at store 2—is provided by the triply indexed variable *Sales*[*Monday*, 3, 2].

As an illustration of an array with more than three dimensions, consider the 5-dimensional array *Inv* declared by

TYPE
    Make = (*Chrysler, Dodge, Plymouth*);
    Style = (*TwoDoor, FourDoor, StationWagon, Van*);
    Color = (*blue, green, brown, red, yellow, charcoal*);
    Year = [1975..1990];
    ModelCode = [1..5];
    InventoryArray =
        ARRAY *Make, Style, Color, Year, ModelCode* OF CARDINAL;

VAR
    Inv : *InventoryArray*;

Such an array might be used in a program to maintain an inventory at an automobile dealership;

    DEC(*Inv*[*Chrysler, TwoDoor, red*, 1989, 4])

would record the sale of one red two-door Model-4 1989 Chrysler.

Unlike some other high-level languages, Modula-2 places no limit on the number of dimensions that an array may have. For any positive integer *n*, an *n*-dimensional array can be defined with a declaration of the form

    ARRAY *index-type-1, index-type-2, . . . , index-type-n*
        OF *component-type*

where *index-type-i* specifies the type of the *i*th index and may be BOOLEAN, CHAR, an enumeration type, or a subrange type.

An alternative approach to multidimensional arrays is to define them as **arrays of arrays**, that is, arrays whose components are arrays. For example, the array declaration

TYPE
    SalesTable = ARRAY [1..*MaxItems*], [1..*MaxStores*] OF CARDINAL;

used to declare the earlier two-dimensional array *SalesTab* could equivalently be given as

TYPE
    StoreList = ARRAY [1..*MaxStores*] OF CARDINAL;
    SalesTable = ARRAY [1..*MaxItems*] OF *StoreList*;

or

TYPE
    SalesTable = ARRAY [1..*MaxItems*] OF
        ARRAY [1..*MaxStores*] OF CARDINAL;

In any case, *SalesTab* can be viewed as an array whose components are one-dimensional arrays. For example, *SalesTab*[3] is a one-dimensional array whose value is the third row of the sales table

12	14	29

and either *SalesTable*[3][2] or *SalesTab*[3,2] refers to the second entry (14) in this array.

Similarly, the three-dimensional array *Sales* declared using

TYPE
    Days = (*Monday, Tuesday, Wednesday, Thursday, Friday, Saturday*);
    ListOfSalesTable =
        ARRAY *Days*, [1..*MaxItems*], [1..*MaxStores*] OF CARDINAL;

can equivalently be declared using

TYPE
    Days = (*Monday, Tuesday, Wednesday, Thursday, Friday, Saturday*);
    StoreList = ARRAY [1..*MaxStores*] OF CARDINAL;
    SalesTable = ARRAY [1..*MaxItems*] OF *StoreList*;
    ListOfSalesTable = ARRAY *Days* OF *SalesTable*;

In either case, *Sales*[*Tuesday*] refers to the sales table for Tuesday:

		Store	
Item	1	2	3
1	6	2	9
2	10	5	4
3	15	17	22
4	0	2	3

Sales[*Tuesday*][1] or *Sales*[*Tuesday*,1] is the list of sales on Tuesday of item 1:

6	2	9

And any of *Sales*[*Tuesday*][1][3], *Sales*[*Tuesday*,1,3], *Sales*[*Tuesday*][1,3], or *Sales*[*Tuesday*,1][3] is the sales on Tuesday of item 1 at store 3:

Implementation of multidimensional arrays is somewhat more complicated than for one-dimensional arrays. Memory is organized as a sequence of memory words and thus is one-dimensional in nature. Consequently we must determine how to use a one-dimensional structure to store a higher-dimensional one.

To illustrate, suppose that M is a 3 $\times$ 4 array of integers declared by

TYPE
    Table = ARRAY [1..3], [1..4] OF INTEGER;

VAR
    M : *Table*;

or equivalently,

TYPE
    Row = ARRAY [1..4] OF INTEGER;
    Table = ARRAY [1..3] OF *Row*;

VAR
    M : *Table*;

in which the following table is to be stored:

$$\begin{bmatrix} 37 & 45 & 82 & 75 \\ 61 & 50 & 0 & 27 \\ 17 & 9 & 62 & 91 \end{bmatrix}$$

If an integer can be stored in a single memory word, then this array declaration instructs the compiler to reserve twelve consecutive words to store the array components. These components might be stored in a ***rowwise*** order (also called ***row major*** order), with the first four words beginning at base(M) used to store the elements in the first row of M, the next four words for the second row, and so on.

Address	Memory	Array Element
	. . .	
base(M) + 0	37	$\longleftrightarrow M[1,1]$
base(M) + 1	45	$\longleftrightarrow M[1,2]$
base(M) + 2	82	$\longleftrightarrow M[1,3]$
base(M) + 3	75	$\longleftrightarrow M[1,4]$
base(M) + 4	61	$\longleftrightarrow M[2,1]$
base(M) + 5	50	$\longleftrightarrow M[2,2]$
base(M) + 6	0	$\longleftrightarrow M[2,3]$
base(M) + 7	27	$\longleftrightarrow M[2,4]$
base(M) + 8	17	$\longleftrightarrow M[3,1]$
base(M) + 9	9	$\longleftrightarrow M[3,2]$
base(M) + 10	62	$\longleftrightarrow M[3,3]$
base(M) + 11	91	$\longleftrightarrow M[3,4]$
	. . .	

It would also be possible to store the components in ***columnwise*** (or ***column major***) order, with the first three words storing the elements in the first column of M, the next three words storing the elements in the second column, and so on.

Address	Memory	Array Element
	⋮	
base(M) + 0	37	⟷ $M[1,1]$
base(M) + 1	61	⟷ $M[2,1]$
base(M) + 2	17	⟷ $M[3,1]$
base(M) + 3	45	⟷ $M[1,2]$
base(M) + 4	50	⟷ $M[2,2]$
base(M) + 5	9	⟷ $M[3,2]$
base(M) + 6	82	⟷ $M[1,3]$
base(M) + 7	0	⟷ $M[2,3]$
base(M) + 8	62	⟷ $M[3,3]$
base(M) + 9	75	⟷ $M[1,4]$
base(M) + 10	27	⟷ $M[2,4]$
base(M) + 11	91	⟷ $M[3,4]$
	⋮	

In either case, an address translation must be carried out to determine the memory word in which a given array element $M[i,j]$ is stored.

The formulas for this address translation can be derived from those given earlier for one-dimensional arrays if a two-dimensional array is viewed as a one-dimensional array whose components are also one-dimensional arrays. To see this, suppose that rowwise storage is used for M. M can then be viewed as a one-dimensional array having three components (the rows of M), each of which requires four memory words for storage. Thus, by the address translation formula for one-dimensional arrays, the ith row of M, $M[i]$, is stored at the word with address

$$\text{base}(M[i]) = \text{base}(M) + 4(i - 1)$$

Since this ith row of M is itself a one-dimensional array with base address base($M[i]$), the jth element in this row, $M[i,j]$, is stored in memory word

$$\text{base}(M[i]) + (j - 1)$$

that is, $M[i,j]$ is stored in word

$$\text{base}(M) + 4(i - 1) + (j - 1)$$

In general, consider rowwise storage of a two-dimensional array M declared using an array declaration of the form

ARRAY $[l_1..u_1]$, $[l_2..u_2]$ OF *component-type*

where l_1, u_1, l_2 and u_2 are integers, and suppose that each array component requires w memory words for storage. Each row of M has $n = u_2 - l_2 + 1$ elements, each of which requires w words for storage so that $\overline{w} = n \cdot w$ consecutive words are needed to store one row of M. Since M is a one-dimensional array whose components are these rows, the address translation formulas of the preceding section given the beginning address of the ith row of M, $M[i]$, as

$$\text{base}(M[i]) = \text{base}(M) + (i - l_1)\overline{w} = \text{base}(M) + (i - l_1)nw$$

Because this row of M is itself a one-dimensional array with base address $\text{base}(M[i])$, where each component requires w words of storage, we find, using these same formulas, that the jth element of this row, $M[i,j]$, is stored in the w consecutive words beginning at

$$\begin{aligned}
\text{base}(M[i]) + (j - l_2)w &= \text{base}(M) + (i - l_1)nw + (j - l_2)w \\
&= \text{base}(M) + [(i - l_1)n + (j - l_2)]w
\end{aligned}$$

Similarly, the address translation formulas for one- and two-dimensional arrays can be used to derive formulas for three-dimensional arrays if they are thought of as one-dimensional arrays whose components are two-dimensional arrays (or as two-dimensional arrays whose components are one-dimensional arrays). For example, consider the three-dimensional array B declared by

    TYPE
        ThreeDimArray = ARRAY [1..3], [0..3], [2..4] OF REAL;

    VAR
        B : *ThreeDimArray*;

or equivalently,

    TYPE
        TwoDimArray = ARRAY [0..3], [2..4] OF REAL;
        ThreeDimArray = ARRAY [1..3] OF *TwoDimArray*;

    VAR
        B : *ThreeDimArray*;

B can thus be viewed as a one-dimensional array having three components, $B[1]$, $B[2]$, and $B[3]$, each of which is a two-dimensional array with twelve elements.

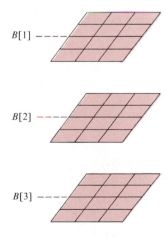

$B[1]$ ----

$B[2]$ ----

$B[3]$ ----

If each real number requires two words of storage, then twenty-four words are needed to store each of the tables $B[1]$, $B[2]$, $B[3]$. Thus, $B[i]$ is stored beginning at the word with address

$$\text{base}(B[i]) = \text{base}(B) + 24(i - 1)$$

Since each $B[i]$ is a two-dimensional array, the address translation formulas for two-dimensional arrays give as the beginning address for $B[i,j,k]$

$$\begin{aligned}
&\text{base}(B[i]) + 6(j - 0) + 2(k - 2) \\
&= \text{base}(B) + 24(i - 1) + 6(j - 0) + 2(k - 2)
\end{aligned}$$

In general, for a three-dimensional array B declared with an array declaration of the form

ARRAY $[l_1..u_1]$, $[l_2..u_2]$, $[l_3..u_3]$ OF *component-type*

in which each component requires w words of storage, the beginning address of $B[i,j,k]$ using this storage scheme would be

$$\text{base}(B) + [(i - l_1)n_2 n_3 + (j - l_2)n_3 + (k - l_3)]w$$

where $n_2 = u_2 - l_2 + 1$ and $n_3 = u_3 - l_3 + 1$. Address translation formulas for arrays having more than three dimensions can be derived similarly, but their complexity increases as the number of dimensions increases.

Exercises

1. Assuming that values of type CARDINAL and INTEGER are stored in one memory word, that reals require two memory words, and that strings (arrays of the form ARRAY $[0..L]$ OF CHAR) are packed two characters per word, find where the indicated components of an array A of the specified type are stored, if the base address of A is 100:

   (a) ARRAY $[1..10]$ OF REAL; $A[4]$ and $A[10]$
   (b) ARRAY $[-5..5]$ OF INTEGER; $A[-3]$ and $A[4]$
   (c) ARRAY $[0..7]$ OF CHAR; $A[4]$ and $A[5]$
   (d) ARRAY $['A'..'Z']$ OF CARDINAL; $A['B']$ and $A['X']$

2. Assuming the storage requirements and array declarations of a one-dimensional array A given in Exercise 1, indicate with diagrams like those in the text, where each component of A is stored if the base address of A is b; also, give the general address translation formula for $A[i]$.

3. Assuming the storage requirements given in Exercise 1, find where the indicated components of a two-dimensional array M of the specified type are stored, if the base address of M is 100 and storage is rowwise:

   (a) ARRAY $[0..3]$, $[1..10]$ OF REAL; $M[0,9]$ and $M[3,3]$
   (b) ARRAY $[2..9]$, $[-3..3]$ OF INTEGER; $M[5,-1]$ and $M[3,3]$

(c) ARRAY $['A'..'J']$, $[1..5]$ OF REAL; $M['F',1]$ and $M['C',3]$

(d) ARRAY $[1..6]$ OF *String*, where *String* = ARRAY $[0..7]$ OF CHAR; $M[4,2]$ and $M[3,3]$

(e) ARRAY $['W'..'Z']$ of *String*, where *String* = ARRAY $[0..7]$ OF CHAR; $M['X',2]$ and $M['Y',6]$

4. Repeat parts (a) through (c) of Exercise 3, but for columnwise storage.

5. In the text, a general address translation formula for $M[i,j]$ was derived for a two-dimensional array M of type *Table* = ARRAY $[1..3]$, $[1..4]$ OF INTEGER, assuming rowwise storage and that integers can be stored in one memory word. Find the corresponding formula if the array elements are stored columnwise.

6. Find the general address translation formula for a component $M[i,j]$ of a two-dimensional array M of type

ARRAY $[l_1..u_1]$, $[l_2..u_2]$ OF *component-type*

assuming columnwise storage.

7. In the text, a general address translation formula for $B[i,j,k]$ was derived for a three-dimensional array B of type *ThreeDimArray* = ARRAY $[1..3]$, $[0..3]$, $[2..4]$ OF REAL by viewing B as a one-dimensional array whose components were two-dimensional arrays. Alternatively, we could have viewed B as a two-dimensional array whose components are one-dimensional arrays, that is, as though *ThreeDimArray* was defined by

TYPE
    OneDimArray = ARRAY $[2..4]$ OF REAL;
    ThreeDimArray = ARRAY $[1..3]$, $[0..3]$ OF *OneDimArray*;

Carry out the derivation of the address translation formula for $B[i,j,k]$ in this case, assuming that real values require two words for storage.

8. Derive the address translation formula for $F[i,j,k,l]$, where F is a four-dimensional array of type

ARRAY $[l_1..u_1]$, $[l_2..u_2]$, $[l_3..u_3]$, $[l_4..u_4]$ OF *component-type*

by viewing F as a one-dimensional array indexed by $[l_1..u_1]$ of three dimensional arrays indexed by $[l_2..u_2]$, $[l_3..u_3]$, $[l_4..u_4]$. Assume that three-dimensional arrays are allocated storage as described in the text.

9. Give one possible address translation formula for a component $H[i_1, i_2, \ldots, i_n]$ of an n-dimensional array of type

ARRAY $[l_1..u_1]$, $[l_2..u_2]$, $\ldots$, $[l_n..u_n]$ OF *component-type*

assuming that each component requires w words of storage.

10. A *lower triangular* matrix M is a square matrix in which the only positions where nonzero entries may appear are on and below the main diagonal from the upper left corner to the lower right corner; all entries above this diagonal are zero:

That is, M is a two-dimensional array in which $M[i,j] = 0$ if $i < j$. Memory would be used more efficiently if instead of storing all the entries of M, only those on and below the diagonal were stored in consecutive memory words. Derive an address translation formula in this case for $M[i,j]$ where $i \geq j$, assuming that each entry of M can be stored in one memory word and rowwise storage is used beginning at the word with address b.

11. Proceed as in Exercise 10 but for an *upper triangular* matrix in which the only positions where nonzero entries may appear are on and above the diagonal; all entries below the diagonal are zero:

12. A *tridiagonal* matrix is a square matrix M in which the only positions where nonzero entries may appear is in the "band" consisting of locations on the diagonal, immediately above the diagonal (on the "superdiagonal"), and immediately below it (on the "subdiagonal"); all entries not in this band are zero:

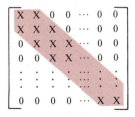

That is, $M[i,j] = 0$ if $|i - j| \geq 1$. Devise an efficient storage scheme for such matrices and derive an address translation formula.

13. Letter grades are sometimes assigned to numeric scores by using the grading scheme commonly known as *grading on the curve*. In this

scheme, a letter grade is assigned to a numeric score according to the following table:

x = Numeric Score	Letter Grade
$x < m - \dfrac{3}{2}\sigma$	F
$m - \dfrac{3}{2}\sigma \le x < m - \dfrac{1}{2}\sigma$	D
$m - \dfrac{1}{2}\sigma \le x < m + \dfrac{1}{2}\sigma$	C
$m + \dfrac{1}{2}\sigma \le x < m + \dfrac{3}{2}\sigma$	B
$m + \dfrac{3}{2}\sigma \le x$	A

Here m is the mean score and σ is the standard deviation; for a set of n numbers $x_1, x_2, \ldots, x_n$, these are defined as follows:

$$m = \frac{1}{n}\sum_{i=1}^{n} x_i, \qquad \sigma = \sqrt{\frac{1}{n}\sum_{i=1}^{n}(x_i - m)^2}$$

Write a program to read a list of real numbers representing numeric scores, calculate their mean and standard deviation, and then determine and display the letter grade corresponding to each numeric score.

14. Peter the postman became bored one night, and to break the monotony of the night shift, he carried out the following experiment with a row of mailboxes in the post office. These mailboxes were numbered 1 through 150, and beginning with mailbox 2, he opened the doors of all the even-numbered mailboxes. Next, beginning with mailbox 3, he went to every third mail box, opening its door if it was closed, closing it if it was open. Then he repeated this procedure with every fourth mailbox, then every fifth mailbox, and so on. When he finished, he was surprised at the distribution of closed mailboxes. Write a program to determine which mailboxes these were.

15. Write a program to add two large integers of length up to 300 digits. One approach is to treat each number as a list, each of whose elements is a block of digits of the number. For example, the integer 179,534,672,198 might be stored with $Block[1] = 198$, $Block[2] = 672$, $Block[3] = 534$, $Block[4] = 179$. Then add the two integers (lists) element by element, carrying from one element to the next when necessary.

16. Proceeding as in Exercise 15, write a program to multiply two large integers of length up to 300 digits.

17. A demographic study of the metropolitan area around Dogpatch divided it into three regions—urban, suburban, and exurban—and published the following table showing the annual migration from one region to another (the numbers represent percentages):

↱	Urban	Suburban	Exurban
Urban	1.1	0.3	0.7
Suburban	0.1	1.2	0.3
Exurban	0.2	0.6	1.3

For example, 0.3 percent of the urbanites (0.003 times the current population) move to the suburbs each year. The diagonal entries represent internal growth rates. Using a two-dimensional array with an enumeration type for the indices to store this table, write a program to determine the population of each region after 10, 20, 30, 40, and 50 years. Assume that the initial populations of the urban, suburban, and exurban regions are 2.1 million, 1.4 million, and 0.9 million, respectively.

18. If A and B are two $m \times n$ matrices, their **sum** is defined as follows: If A_{ij} and B_{ij} are the entries in the ith row and jth column of A and B, respectively, then $A_{ij} + B_{ij}$ is the entry in the ith row and jth column of their sum, which will also be an $m \times n$ matrix. Write a program to read two $m \times n$ matrices, display them, and calculate and display their sum.

19. The **product** or an $m \times n$ matrix A with an $n \times p$ matrix B is the $m \times p$ matrix $C = A * B$ whose entry C_{ij} in the ith row and jth column is given by

$$C_{ij} = \text{the sum of the products of the entries in row } i \text{ of } A$$
$$\text{with the entries in column } j \text{ of } B$$
$$= A_{i1} * B_{1j} + A_{i2} * B_{2j} + \cdots + A_{in} * B_{nj}$$

Write a program that will read two matrices A and B, display them, and calculate and display their product (or a message indicating that it is not defined).

20. A **magic square** is an $n \times n$ matrix in which each of the integers 1, 2, 3, . . . , n^2 appears exactly once and all column sums, row sums, and diagonal sums are equal. For example, the following is a 5×5 magic square in which all the rows, columns, and diagonals add up to 65:

17	24	1	8	15
23	5	7	14	16
4	6	13	20	22
10	12	19	21	3
11	18	25	2	9

The following is a procedure for constructing an $n \times n$ magic square for any odd integer n. Place 1 in the middle of the top row. Then after integer k has been placed, move up one row and one column to the right to place the next integer $k + 1$, unless one of the following occurs:

a. If a move takes you above the top row in the jth column, move to the bottom of the jth column and place the integer there.

b. If a move takes you outside to the right of the square in the ith row, place the integer in the ith row at the left side.

c. If a move takes you to an already-filled square or if you move out of the square at the upper right-hand corner, place $k + 1$ immediately below k.

Write a program to construct an $n \times n$ magic square for any odd value of n.

21. Suppose that each of the four edges of a thin square metal plate is maintained at a constant temperature and that we wish to determine the steady-state temperature at each interior point of the plate. To do this, we divide the plate into squares (the corners of which are called *nodes*) and find the temperature at each interior node by averaging the four neighboring temperatures; that is, if T_{ij} denotes the old temperature at the node in row i and column j, then

$$\frac{T_{i-1,j} + T_{i,j-1} + T_{i,j+1} + T_{i+1,j}}{4}$$

will be the new temperature.

To model the plate, we can use a two-dimensional array, with each array element representing the temperature at one of the nodes. Write a program that first reads the four constant temperatures (possibly different) along the edges of the plate, and some guess of the temperature at the interior points, and uses these values to initialize the elements of the array. Then determine the steady-state temperature at each interior node by repeatedly averaging the temperatures at its four neighbors, as just described. Repeat this procedure until the new temperature at each interior node differs from the old temperature at that node by no more than some specified small amount. Then print the array and the number of iterations used to produce the final result. (It may also be of interest to print the array at each stage of the iteration.)

22. The game of *Life*, invented by the mathematician John H. Conway, is intended to model life in a society of organisms. Consider a rectangular array of cells, each of which may contain an organism. If the array is viewed as extending indefinitely in both directions, then each cell has eight neighbors, the eight cells surrounding it. In each generation, births and deaths occur according to the following rules:

a. An organism is born in any empty cell having exactly three neighbors.

   b. An organism dies from isolation if it has less than two neighbors.

   c. An organism dies from overcrowding if it has more than three neighbors.

   d. All other organisms survive.

To illustrate, the following shows the first five generations of a particular configuration of organisms:

Write a program to play the game of *Life* and investigate the patterns produced by various initial configurations. Some configurations die off rather rapidly; others repeat after a certain number of generations; others change shape and size and may move across the array; and still others may produce ''gliders'' that detach themselves from the society and sail off into space.

2.4 Records

Like an array, a **record** is a finite sequence of elements; however, these elements may be of different types and are called the **fields** of the record. As for arrays, the basic operation is direct access to each field in the record so that an item can be stored in that field or retrieved from it.

The declaration of this structured data type in Modula-2 specifies the name of the record and the type of each of its fields. It has the form

RECORD
    field-list
END;

where a simple form of *field-list* is

   list-1 : *type-1*;
   list-2 : *type-2*;
      .
      .
   list-k : *type-k*

Each *list-i* is a single identifier or a list of identifiers that name the fields of the record, and *type-i* specifies the type of each of these fields.

To illustrate, records maintained for users of a computer system might contain a user identification number, a password, a resource limit, and the resources used to date. Such records could be declared by

```
TYPE
    String = ARRAY [0..9] OF CHAR;
    UserRecord = RECORD
                    IdNumber : CARDINAL;
                    Password : String;
                    ResourceLimit,
                    ResourcesUsed : REAL
                 END;

VAR
    User : UserRecord;
```

The variable *User* may have as a value any record of type *UserRecord*. The first field of the record is of type CARDINAL and is named with the field identifier *IdNumber*; the second field is of type *String* and has the name *Password*; the third and fourth fields, named *ResourceLimit* and *ResourcesUsed* both are of type REAL. A typical value for *User* might be pictured as follows:

IdNumber	Password	ResourceLimit	ResourcesUsed
12345	EPSILON	100.00	37.45

Each field of a record can be accessed directly by using a **field-designated variable**, or simply **fielded variable**, of the form

record-name.field-name

Thus *User.IdNumber* specifies the first field of the value of record variable *User* and can be assigned a value by the statement

    User.IdNumber := 12345;

or

    ReadCard(User.IdNumber);

Similarly, *User.Password*, *User.ResourceLimit*, and *User.ResourcesUsed* refer to the second, third, and fourth fields, and they can be accessed in statements such as

    WriteString(User.Password);

and

```
IF User.ResourcesUsed > User.ResourceLimit THEN
    WriteString('*** Resource limit exceeded ***')
END (* IF *);
```

or equivalently,

        WITH *User* DO
             WriteString(Password)
        END (* WITH *);

and

        WITH *User* DO
            IF *ResourcesUsed* > *ResourceLimit* THEN
                 WriteString('*** Resource limit exceeded ***')
            END (* IF *)
        END (* WITH *);

We have seen that to store an array, sufficient memory is allocated to store all the array elements, and that each array reference involves two steps: first, an address translation must be performed to locate the memory word(s) in which that array element is stored, and second, the bit string stored there must be interpreted in the manner prescribed by the type specification for the array components in the array declaration. Similarly, the implementation of a record structure also requires sufficient memory to store all of the fields that comprise the record. Address translation is again required to determine the location in which a particular field is stored, but this address translation is slightly more complex than for arrays, because different fields usually require a different number of words for storage. Also, unlike arrays, different interpretations of the bit strings are usually required for different fields, since the fields of a record need not be of the same type.

To illustrate, suppose that cardinal numbers can be stored in one memory word, that characters in a string are packed two per word, and that real values require two memory words for storage. The preceding declaration for *User-Record* instructs the compiler to reserve a block of ten consecutive memory words to store such a record, the first of which, as for arrays, is called the **base address**. The field *User.IdNumber* is then stored in the word with address base(*User*); *User.Password* is stored in words base(*User*) + 1 through base(*User*) + 5; *User.ResourceLimit*, in words base(*User*) + 6 and base(*User*) + 7; and *User.ResourcesUsed*, in words base(*User*) + 8 and base(*User*) + 9:

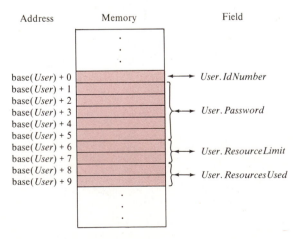

When one of these fields is accessed, the bit string stored in the associated word or words is interpreted according to the type specified for that field in the record declaration.

In general, for a record R with fields F_1 of type T_1, F_2 of type T_2, . . . , F_n of type T_n, which require $w_1, w_2, \ldots, w_n$ words for storage, respectively, the field $R.F_i$ is stored in the block of w_i consecutive words beginning with

$$\text{base}(R) + \sum_{j=1}^{i-1} w_j = \text{base}(R) + w_1 + w_2 + \cdots + w_{i-1}$$

and the bit string stored in this block is interpreted as a value of data type T_i.

Examples of records considered thus far have consisted of a fixed number of fields, each of which has a fixed type. In Modula-2 it is also possible to declare **variant records**, in which some of the fields are fixed, but the number and types of other fields may vary, so that a record may have both **fixed parts** and **variant parts**. The number and types of the fields in a fixed part do not change during program execution, but those in a variant part may change in number and/or in type.

To illustrate variant records, consider the computer–user records described by

```
UserRecord1 = RECORD
                    IdNumber : CARDINAL;
                    Password : String;
                    ResourceLimit,
                    ResourcesUsed : REAL;
                    Department : CHAR
              END;
```

where *String* is defined as ARRAY [0..9] of CHAR. Such records are suitable for the support staff who use the computer system at an engineering laboratory. For research personnel, records might have the following structure:

```
UserRecord2 = RECORD
                    IdNumber : CARDINAL;
                    Password : String;
                    Account : CARDINAL;
                    SecurityClearance : [1..10]
              END;
```

and for administrators, an appropriate record structure might be

```
UserRecord3 = RECORD
                    IdNumber : CARDINAL;
                    Password : String;
                    Division : CHAR
              END;
```

All of these record structures can be incorporated into a single record by using a record with a variant part:

```
UserRecord = RECORD
                 IdNumber : CARDINAL;
                 Password : String;
                 CASE UserCode : CHAR OF
                     'S' : (* support staff *)
                         ResourceLimit,
                         ResourcesUsed : REAL;
                         Department : CHAR
                         |
                       'R' : (* research personnel *)
                             Account : CARDINAL;
                             SecurityClearance : [1..10]
                             |
                       'A' : (* administration *)
                             Division : CHAR
                 END
             END;
```

This record has a fixed part that is the same for all values of type *UserRecord*, and this fixed part consists of the fields *IdNumber* and *Password*. In addition to these two fields, some values have *ResourceLimit*, *ResourcesUsed*, and *Department* fields; others have *Account* and *Security-Clearance* fields; and still others have only a *Division* field. If *UserCode* has the value S, the fields *ResourceLimit, ResourcesUsed,* and *Department* are in effect; if *UserCode* has the value R, the fields *Account* and *SecurityClearance* are in effect; and if the value of *UserCode* is A, the field *Division* is in effect.

The field *UserCode* in this record is called a **tag field**. The values it may have are used to label the variant fields of the record and to determine the structure of a particular value of type *UserRecord*. Thus, if the value of *UserCode* is S, which labels the variant for a member of the support staff, the structure of the record is the same as one of type *UserRecord1*, except that it has one additional field, the tag field *UserCode*. If the value of *UserCode* is R, which labels the variant for research personnel, the structure of the record is basically that of type *UserRecord2*. Finally, if the value of *UserCode* is A, which labels the variant for an administrator, the structure is essentially the same as that of type *UserRecord3*.

In a variant record, several tag field values may label the same variant field list. For example, suppose that research personnel are classified according to their areas of specialization and these areas are coded as C, D, E, and M, so that the code for these employees may be any of these letters rather than simply R. In this situation an appropriate record declaration might be

```
UserRecord = RECORD
                IdNumber : CARDINAL;
                Password : String;
                CASE UserCode : CHAR OF
                        'S' : (* support staff *)
                                ResourceLimit,
                                ResourcesUsed : REAL;
                                Department : CHAR
                                    |
                    'C'..'E',
                        'M' : (* research personnel *)
                                Account : CARDINAL;
                                SecurityClearance : [1..10]
                                    |
                        'A' : (* administration *)
                                Division : CHAR
                END
             END;
```

It is also permissible for tag field values to label empty variant field lists. To illustrate, suppose that in addition to support staff, researchers, and administrators, records of computer use are maintained for several other groups of individuals who are not currently on the payroll, for example, student interns, visiting researchers, and people on leave. These groups could be individually coded, I, V, and L, and so on, and an empty variant field used for them:

```
UserRecord = RECORD
                IdNumber : CARDINAL;
                Password : String;
                CASE UserCode : CHAR OF
                        'S' : (* support staff *)
                                ResourceLimit,
                                ResourcesUsed : REAL;
                                Department : CHAR
                                    |
                    'C'..'E',
                        'M' : (* research personnel *)
                                Account : CARDINAL;
                                SecurityClearance : [1..10]
                                    |
                        'A' : (* administration *)
                                Division : CHAR
                                    |
                'I', 'V', 'L' : (* currently not on payroll *)
                                (* no information stored *)
                END
             END;
```

An alternative approach is to use a default variant, which can be implemented by using an ELSE clause:

```
UserRecord = RECORD
                 IdNumber : CARDINAL;
                 Password : String;
                 CASE UserCode : CHAR OF
                         'S' : (* support staff *)
                             ResourceLimit,
                             ResourcesUsed : REAL;
                             Department : CHAR
                                 |
                    'C'..'E',
                         'M' : (* research personnel *)
                             Account : CARDINAL;
                             SecurityClearance : [1..10]
                                 |
                         'A' : (* administration *)
                             Division : CHAR
                                 |
                     ELSE    (* currently not on payroll *)
                             (* no information stored *)
             END
         END;
```

Records may have any number of fixed parts and/or variant parts, and these may appear in any order. For example, in the preceding user record we might wish to add a field to keep track of the number of logins and a variant part that records additional accounting information. For example, users may have access to one of two systems, A or B, and for System A, the terminal connect time must be recorded, whereas for System B, an amount is charged for disk space used. The following record structure might be used:

```
UserRecord = RECORD
                 IdNumber : CARDINAL;
                 Password : String;
                 CASE UserCode : CHAR OF
                         'S' : (* support staff *)
                             ResourceLimit,
                             ResourcesUsed : REAL;
                             Department : CHAR
                                 |
                    'C'..'E',
                         'M' : (* research personnel *)
                             Account : CARDINAL;
                             SecurityClearance : [1..10]
                                 |
                         'A' : (* administration *)
                             Division : CHAR
                                 |
                    'I','V','M' : (* currently not on payroll *)
                             (* no information stored *)
             END;
```

Logins : CARDINAL;
CASE *System* : CHAR OF
    'A' : *ConnectTime* : CARDINAL
      |
    'B' : *DiskStorage* : CARDINAL
  END
END;

Records are frequently used in problems involving the storage and retrieval of information because in many such applications, not all the items of information are of the same type. Typically, one of the fields within the record serves as a *key field*, which uniquely identifies the record.

To illustrate, suppose that a file contains records for computer usage by the three kinds of users described earlier: support staff (S), research personnel (R), and administrators (A):

```
11395
DINGALING
S 500.00 329.74 A
12274
SANTACLAUS
R 1135 17
12556
HELLOTHERE
S 300.00 53.25 C
12690
SECRET
AC
13007
BINGO
R 225 9
13234
XXYYZZ
S 400.00 399.55 B
        .
        .
        .
```

Each record contains the id number (which serves as a key field), the password, and the user code of a computer user, together with other information determined by the user code. The program in Figure 2.1 is an information retrieval program similar to that in Figure 1.1. It calls the procedure *ReadFile*, which reads these records from the file, using procedure *ReadRecord*, counts them, and stores them in the array *User*, whose components are variant records of type *UserRecord*. We assume that the records in this file have been sorted so that the id numbers are in ascending order. Thus the array *User* will also be sorted so that the procedure *BinarySearch* can be used to locate the record for a given user. If this record is found, the procedure *DisplayRecord* is called to display the information in it. The program thus has the following structure:

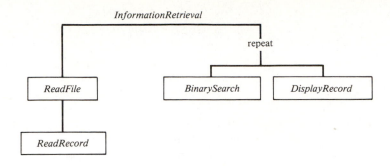

```
MODULE InformationRetrieval;

(**********************************************************************

   Program to copy the information in a computer usage file into an
   array of variant records and then search this array to retrieve
   information about a given user. The file and thus the array also
   are assumed to be sorted so id numbers are in ascending order;
   a binary search is then used to retrieve a user's record.

**********************************************************************)

   FROM InOut IMPORT Write, WriteString, WriteLn, WriteCard, Read,
                     ReadCard, ReadString, Done, OpenInput, CloseInput;
   FROM RealInOut IMPORT ReadReal, WriteReal;
   FROM SpecialInOut IMPORT FWriteReal;

   CONST
       MaxString = 10;        (* limit on length of string *)
       ArrayLimit = 100;      (* limit on size of array *)

   TYPE
       String = ARRAY [0..MaxString] OF CHAR;
       UserRecord = RECORD
                        IdNumber : CARDINAL;
                        Password: String;
                        CASE UserCode : CHAR OF
                          'S' : (* support staff *)
                                ResourceLimit,
                                ResourcesUsed : REAL;
                                Department : CHAR
                              |
                          'R' : (* research personnel *)
                                Account : CARDINAL;
                                SecurityClearance: CARDINAL
                              |
                          'A' : (* administration *)
                                Division : CHAR
                        END (* CASE *)
                    END;
       ArrayOfRecords = ARRAY [1..ArrayLimit] OF UserRecord;
```

Figure 2.1

Figure 2.1   (cont.)

```
VAR
    User : ArrayOfRecords;      (* array of user records *)
    Count,                      (* number of records *)
    Location,                   (* location of specified record in the array *)

    IdSought : CARDINAL;        (* id number of user to be searched for *)
    Found : BOOLEAN;            (* indicates if record is found *)

PROCEDURE ReadFile(VAR User: ArrayOfRecords;
                   VAR Count : CARDINAL);

    (****************************************************************

        Procedure to read and Count records from a computer usage file
        and store them in the array User of user records.

    ****************************************************************)

    VAR
        i,                      (* index *)
        UserRec : UserRecord;   (* user's id-number *)
        MoreRecords : BOOLEAN;  (* indicates if there are more records *)

    PROCEDURE ReadRecord(VAR UserRec : UserRecord;
                         VAR MoreRecords : BOOLEAN);

        (************************************************************

            Procedure to read a user record UserRec.  MoreRecords is
            returned as TRUE or FALSE according to whether or not
            there is another record to be read.

        ************************************************************)

    BEGIN
        MoreRecords := TRUE;
        WITH UserRec DO
            ReadCard(IdNumber);
            IF NOT Done THEN
                MoreRecords := FALSE;
                RETURN
            END (* IF *);
            ReadString(Password);
            Read(UserCode);
            CASE UserCode OF
                'S' : (* support staff*)
                        ReadReal(ResourceLimit);
                        ReadReal(ResourcesUsed);
                        Read(Department)
                    |
                'R' : (* research personnel *)
                        ReadCard(Account);
                        ReadCard(SecurityClearance)
                    |
                'A' : (* administration *)
                        Read(Division)
            END (* CASE *)
        END (* WITH *)
    END ReadRecord;
```

Figure 2.1   (cont.)

```
BEGIN (* ReadFile *)
    WriteString('Enter name of input file.'); WriteLn;
    OpenInput('');
    Count := 0;
    ReadRecord(UserRec, MoreRecords);
    WHILE MoreRecords AND (Count <= ArrayLimit) DO
        INC(Count);
        IF Count > ArrayLimit THEN
            WriteLn;
            WriteString('*** Too many records ***');
            RETURN
        ELSE
            User[Count] := UserRec
        END (* IF *);
        ReadRecord(UserRec, MoreRecords)
    END (* WHILE *);
    CloseInput
END ReadFile;

PROCEDURE BinarySearch (VAR User : ArrayOfRecords; n : CARDINAL;
                            IdSought : CARDINAL;
                        VAR Mid : CARDINAL; VAR Found : BOOLEAN);

    (****************************************************************

        Procedure to binary search the array User of size n for the
        record containing a specified user-id.  TRUE is returned
        for Found if the search is successful and Mid is then the
        location of this record; else Found is set to FALSE

    ****************************************************************)

    VAR
        First, Last : CARDINAL; (* first and last positions of
                                    the sublist being searched *)
    BEGIN
        First := 1;
        Last := n;
        Found := FALSE;
        WHILE (First <= Last) AND NOT Found DO
            Mid := (First + Last) DIV 2;
            WITH User[Mid] DO
                IF IdSought < IdNumber THEN
                    Last := Mid - 1
                ELSIF IdSought > IdNumber THEN
                    First := Mid + 1
                ELSE
                    Found := TRUE
                END (* IF *)
            END (* WITH *)
        END (* WHILE *)
    END BinarySearch;
```

Figure 2.1 (cont.)

```
PROCEDURE DisplayRecord (UserRec : UserRecord);

    (*****************************************************************

              Procedure to print the record of a user

     ****************************************************************)
BEGIN
    WITH UserRec DO
        WriteLn;
        WriteString('Password:  ');
        WriteString(Password);
        CASE UserCode OF
            'S' : WriteLn;
                  WriteString('*** Support staff ***');
                  WriteLn;
                  WriteString('Resource Limit . .');
                  FWriteReal(ResourceLimit, 8, 2);
                  WriteLn;
                  WriteString('Resources Used . .');
                  FWriteReal(ResourcesUsed, 8, 2);
                  WriteLn;
                  WriteString('Department . . . . . . . ');
                  Write(Department)
                |
            'R' : WriteLn;
                  WriteString('*** Research personnel ***');
                  WriteLn;
                  WriteString('Account  . . . . .');
                  WriteCard(Account,8);
                  WriteLn;
                  WriteString('Sec. Clearance . .')
                |
            'A' : WriteLn;
                  WriteString('*** Administration ***');
                  WriteLn;
                  WriteString('Division . . . . . . . . ');
                  Write(Division)
        END (* CASE *)
    END (* WITH *)
END DisplayRecord;
```

Figure 2.1   (cont.)

```
BEGIN (* main program *)
    ReadFile(User, Count);
    WriteString('Enter 0 for user-id to quit.');
    WriteLn; WriteLn;
    WriteString("User's id-number?  ");
    ReadCard(IdSought);
    WHILE IdSought # 0 DO
        BinarySearch (User, Count, IdSought, Location, Found);
        IF Found THEN
            DisplayRecord (User[Location])
        ELSE
            WriteLn;
            WriteString("User's record not found")
        END (* IF *);
        WriteLn; WriteLn;
        WriteString("User's id-number?  ");
        ReadCard(IdSought)
    END (* WHILE *)
END InformationRetrieval.
```

<u>Listing of USERSFILE used in sample run:</u>

```
11395
DINGALING
S 500.00 329.74 A
12274
SANTACLAUS
R 1135 7
12556
HELLOTHERE
S 300.00 53.25 C
12690
SECRET
AC
13007
BINGO
R 225 9
13234
XXYYZZ
S 400.00 399.55 B
```

<u>Sample run:</u>

```
Enter name of input file.
in> USERSFILE

Enter 0 for user-id to quit.

User's id-number?  11395
Password:  DINGALING
*** Support staff ***
Resource Limit . .  500.00
Resources Used . .  329.74
Department . . . . . . . A
```

Figure 2.1   (cont.)

```
User's id-number?  12699
User's record not found

User's id-number?  12690
Password:  SECRET
*** Administration ***
Division . . . . . . . . C

User's id-number?  13007
Password:  BINGO
*** Research personnel ***
Account  . . . . .     225
Sec. Clearance . .       9

User's id-number?  0
```

In summary, the general form of a record structure is

RECORD
    field-list
END

where *field-list* contains any number (possibly none) of fixed parts and/or variant parts arranged in any order. Each fixed part has the form

    list-1 : type-1;
    list-2 : type-2;
         $\vdots$
    list-m : type-m;

where each *list-i* is a single identifier or a list or identifiers separated by commas, which name the fields of the record and where *type-i* specifies the type of these fields. Each variant part has the form

CASE *tag-field : tag-type* OF
    tag-list-1 : variant-1
        |
    tag-list-2 : variant-2
        |
        $\vdots$
    tag-list-n : variant-n
    ELSE
        variant-n + 1
END

where each *variant-i* is a field list of the form previous described (or is empty), and the ELSE clause is optional.

It might also be noted that the tag field identifier, but not the colon following it or its type identifier, may be omitted. In this case, access to the items in a variant field list is still possible, even though no tag field exists. Such records might be used when it is possible to determine by some other means which variant field list is in effect, for example, when the first fifty records in an array of one hundred records all use the same variant field list and the remaining fifty records involve some other variant field list. Omitting the tag field identifier, however, can easily lead to subtle errors and should normally be avoided.

For a variant record, sufficient memory is ordinarily allocated to store the fixed parts together with the largest variants in each variant part. To illustrate, consider the record declaration

```
TYPE
    String  =  ARRAY [0..5] OF CHAR;
    RecordType  =  RECORD
                    A : String;
                    B : INTEGER;
                    CASE T : CARDINAL OF
                        1 : C1 : String;
                            C2 : CARDINAL;
                            C3 : BOOLEAN;
                            C4 : INTEGER
                          |
                        2 : D1 : BOOLEAN;
                            D2 : String;
                            D3 : INTEGER
                          |
                        3 :
                    END
                END;

    VAR
        R : RecordType;
```

and suppose that characters in a string are packed two per word and that values of type CARDINAL, INTEGER, and BOOLEAN require one word for storage. This record has one fixed part and it requires 4 memory words, the tag field requires one word, and it has only one variant part in which the first variant is the largest and requires six words for storage. Thus, a block of eleven consecutive memory words would be allocated for *R*. If one of the other variants is in effect, this same block is used to store the record. The following diagram illustrates this storage scheme and indicates the locations of the fields in different variants in the block of memory words allocated to *R*:

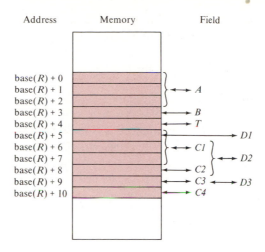

Now suppose that a value is assigned to R using the second variant:

```
WITH R DO
    A := 'ABCDEF';
    B := 16392;
    T := 2;
    D1 := TRUE;
    D2 := 'GHIJKL';
    D3 := 0
END(* WITH *);
```

The bit strings stored in the eleven memory words allocated to R might then be as follows:

base(R) + 0	0100000101000010
base(R) + 1	0100001101000100
base(R) + 2	0100010101000110
base(R) + 3	0100000000001000
base(R) + 4	0000000000000010
base(R) + 5	0000000000000001
base(R) + 6	0100011101001000
base(R) + 7	0100100101001010
base(R) + 8	0100101101001100
base(R) + 9	0000000000000000
base(R) + 10	0000000000001111

base(R) + 10 ← "Garbage"

The last word in this block has been indicated as containing "garbage" because this bit string was not stored there by this assignment of a value to R; it is a carryover from some previous computation when this memory word was used, perhaps in a reference to R using the first (largest) variant.

If now $R.D3$ is referenced, the address base(R) + 3 + 1 + 1 + 1 + 3 = base(R) + 9 is calculated, and the bit string 0000000000000000 stored in this memory word is interpreted as the integer 0. Similarly, if $R.D2[3]$ is referenced, the beginning address base(R) + 3 + 1 + 1 + 1 = base(R) + 6 of the field $R.D2$ is computed, the location of the third element of this array is determined to be the first byte of word base$(R) + 6 + 1 =$ base$(R) + 7$ (using the address translation formulas of section 2.3), and the bit string 01001001 stored in this byte is interpreted as the character I.

If a reference is made to a field in a variant part different from that used to assign a value to a record variable, the address translation and interpretation appropriate for the referenced field are carried out. Thus, if $R.C1[5]$ is referenced, its location, the first byte of word (base $(R) + 3 + 1 + 1) + 2 =$ base$(R) + 7$, is computed, and the bit string stored in this byte is interpreted as the character I. A reference to $R.C3$ locates the memory word base$(R) +$ 9, and the bit string composed of all zeros that is stored there is interpreted as the boolean value FALSE, even though it was created as a representation of the integer constant 0 when this value was assigned to $R.D3$. Had the value 6 been assigned to $R.D3$ so this memory word stored 0000000000000110, a reference to $R.C3$ produces the boolean value FALSE if only the rightmost bit is used, the boolean value TRUE if any nonzero bit string represents true, or an error if interpretation is not possible.

Exercises

1. For each of the following, design a variant record structure to store the given information, writing appropriate type declarations for the records:

   (a) Time in either civilian or military format as specified by the tag field in the record.

   (b) Information about a person: name; birthday; age; sex; social security number; height; weight; hair color; eye color; marital status; and, if married, number of children.

   (c) Statistics about a baseball player: name; age; birthdate; position (pitcher, catcher, infielder, outfielder); for a pitcher: won-lost record, earned-run average, number of strikeouts, number of walks; if a starting pitcher, number of complete games; and if a relief pitcher, number of innings pitched and number of saves; for the other positions, batting average; slugging average; bats right, left, or is a switch hitter; fielding percentage; also, for an infielder, the positions he can play; for a catcher, whether he can catch a knuckleball.

   (d) Weather statistics: date; city and state, province, or country; time of day; temperature; barometric pressure; weather conditions (clear skies, partly cloudy, cloudy, stormy); if cloudy conditions prevail, cloud level and type of clouds; for partly cloudy, percentage of cloud cover; for stormy conditions, snow depth if it is snowing, amount of rainfall if it is rainy, size of hail if it is hailing.

2. Write a declaration of a record having only a variant part for four geometric figures: a circle, a square, a rectangle, a triangle. For a circle, the record should store its radius; for a square, the length of a side; for a rectangle, the length of two adjacent sides; and for a triangle, the lengths of the three sides. Then write a program that reads one

of the letters C (circle), S (square), R (rectangle), T (triangle), and the appropriate numeric quantity or quantities for a figure of that type and then calculates its area. For example, the input R 7.2 3.5 represents a rectangle with length 7.2 and width 3.5, and T 3 4 6.1 represents a triangle having sides of lengths 3, 4, and 6.1 (For a triangle, the area can be found with **Hero's formula**: area $= \sqrt{s(s-a)(s-b)(s-c)}$, where a, b, and c are the lengths of the sides, and s is one half of the perimeter.

3. Modify the program of Figure 2.1 by making it a menu-driven program that allows at least the following options:

GET: Get the records from the file and store them in the array *User*.

INS: Insert the record for a new person, keeping the array sorted so the name fields are in alphabetical order.

RET: Retrieve and display the record for a specified person.

UPD: Update the information in the record for a specified person.

DEL: Delete the record for some person.

LIS: List the records (or perhaps selected items in the records) in order. This option should allow suboptions

U—to list for all users
S—to list for only support staff
R—to list for only research personnel
A—to list for only administrators.

SAV: Copy the records from the array into a permanent file.

4. Suppose that values of type CARDINAL, INTEGER, CHAR, and BOOLEAN are stored in one memory word, that values of type REAL require two words for storage, and that strings are packed two characters per word. Give diagrams like those in the text showing where each field of the following record types would be stored:

(a) *Point* = RECORD
        X, Y : REAL
    END;

(b) *Date* = RECORD
        Month : ARRAY [0..7] of CHAR;
        Day, Year : CARDINAL
    END;

(c) *StudentRecord* = RECORD
        Snumb : CARDINAL;
        Name : ARRAY [0..15] OF CHAR;
        Scores : RECORD
                Homework, Tests, Exam : REAL;
            END;
        FinalNumScore : REAL;
        LetterGrade : CHAR
    END;

    (d) *ClassRecord* = RECORD
                    Snumb : CARDINAL;
                    Name : ARRAY [0..15] OF CHAR;
                    Sex : CHAR;
                    TestScore : ARRAY[1..5] OF CARDINAL
        END;

    (e) A record of type *UserRecord* as defined in Figure 2.1.

    (f) *Transaction* = RECORD
                    CustomerName : ARRAY [0..20] OF CHAR;
                    AccountNumber : CARDINAL;
                    CASE *TransType* : CHAR OF
                        'D', 'W' : *Amount* : REAL
                                |
                        'L' : *LoanNumber* : CARDINAL;
                             Payment, Interest,
                             NewBalance : REAL
                                  |
                        'T' : *TransferAccount* : CARDINAL;
                             AmountOfTransfer : REAL;
                             Code : CHAR
                                  |
                      ELSE
                          (* void transaction *)
                END;
                    TransDate : RECORD
                             Month, Day, Year : CARDINAL;
                    END
        END;

5. Consider the student records in the financial aid program of Figure 1.4. Suppose that Modula-2 did not provide records as a predefined structured data type. Write a program that reads such records and stores them in **parallel arrays**, one containing the students' names, another their student numbers, and so on. Then implement the *Retrieve* option.

6. Proceed as in Exercise 5, but sort the arrays and print the student records so that the amounts of financial aid are in descending order.

7. Describe how an array of variant records might be implemented in Modula-2 if it did not provide records as a predefined data type. Illustrate using the records of type *UserRecord* in the program of Figure 2.1, and write procedures *BinarySearch* and *DisplayRecord* in this implementation.

2.5   Sets in Modula-2

In mathematics and computer science, the term **set** refers to an unordered collection of objects called the **elements** or **members** of the set. A set is commonly denoted by listing the elements enclosed in braces, { and }. For example, the set of decimal digits contains the elements 0, 1, 2, 3, 4, 5, 6, 7, 8, and 9 and is denoted {0, 1, 2, 3, 4, 5, 6, 7, 8, 9}. The set of uppercase letters is {A, B, C, . . . , Z}. The set of even prime numbers {2} contains the single element 2; and the set of even prime numbers greater than 2 is the empty set, denoted ∅ or { }, that is, the set containing no elements.

In a problem involving sets, the elements are selected from some given set called the **universal set** for that problem. For example, if the set of vowels or the set {X, Y, Z} is being considered, the universal set might be the set of all letters. If the universal set is the set of names of months of the year, then one might use the set of summer months, {June, July, August}; the set of months whose names do not contain the letter *r*, {May, June, July, August}; or the set of all months having fewer than thirty days, {February}.

The basic relation in defining a set is the **membership** relation. Given a set S and any object x in the universal set, one must be able to determine that x belongs to S, denoted by $x \in S$, or that it does not belong to S, denoted by $x \notin S$.

Three basic set operations are intersection, union, and set difference. The **intersection** of two sets S and T, denoted in mathematics by $S \cap T$, is the set of elements that are in both sets. The **union** of S and T, $S \cup T$, is the set of the elements that are in S or in T or in both. The set **difference** $S - T$ consists of those elements of S that are not in T. The following **Venn diagrams** illustrate these basic set operations:

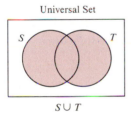

Universal Set

$S \cup T$

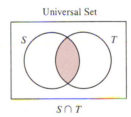

Universal Set

$S \cap T$

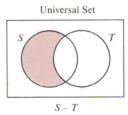

Universal Set

$S - T$

Viewed as a data structure, a set is an unordered collection of objects on which are defined the basic operations of membership, union, intersection, and difference. Since the elements of a set are not ordered, it does not make sense to speak of a first element, a second element, and so on. For example, the set whose elements are the odd digits 1, 3, 5, 7, and 9 is the same as the set {3, 1, 9, 5, 7} or {9, 7, 5, 3, 1}. Thus, the elements of a set are not directly accessible, as they are in an array.

Sets differ from records in two important ways. Data items stored in a record are directly accessible and may be of different types. In Modula-2, however, the elements of a set must be of the same type, and as we have noted, they are not directly accessible. In this section we describe how sets can be processed in Modula-2.

Set Declarations. In Modula-2, all of the elements of a set must be of the same type, called the **base type** of the set, and a **set declaration** has the form

SET OF *base-type*

Such a declaration specifies the type of elements in a universal set from which elements of sets of this type will be chosen. The base type must be an enumeration type, a subrange of an enumeration type, or a subrange of type CARDINAL; thus sets with base type CARDINAL, INTEGER, REAL, or CHAR or sets of arrays, strings, or records are not allowed.

The number of elements that a set may have varies from one compiler to another, however, so that subrange or enumeration base types that are allowed in one system may not be allowed in another. A limit of 16 or 32 elements of an enumeration base type and a maximum value of 15 or 31 on a cardinal subrange used as a base type are common. However, some compilers allow much larger sets and may allow CHAR as a base type. In some cases, a special library module for handling large sets is provided. In the next section we develop one such module.

Modula-2 does provide one predefined set type, **BITSET**. It is equivalent to a set declaration of the form

$$\text{BITSET} = \text{SET OF } [0..W - 1]$$

where W is the word length of the particular computer being used. For example, on a 16-bit machine, BITSET is equivalent to the set declaration

SET OF [0..15]

As we will see, sets of this type can be stored in a single memory word and consequently can be processed more efficiently than larger sets can.

To illustrate set declarations, consider the following:

TYPE
    Digits = [0..9];
    Months = (*January, February, March, April, May, June, July,*
                August, September, October, November, December);
    DigitSet = SET OF *Digits*;
    MonthSet = SET OF *Months*;
    MonthArray = ARRAY [1..4] OF *MonthSet*;

VAR
    Numbers : BITSET;
    Evens, Odds : *DigitSet*;
    Winter : *MonthSet*;
    Season : *MonthArray*;

The variable *Numbers* may have as a value any set of elements chosen from $0, 1, 2, \ldots, W - 1$, where W is the word length of the computer being used; *Evens* and *Odds* may have as values any sets of elements chosen from 0, 1, 2, . . . , 9; and the value of *Winter* may be any set of elements selected from *January, February, . . . , December*. The array *Season* has four components, each of which is a set of months.

Set Constants. A *set constant* in Modula-2 has the form

set-type{element-list}

where *element-list* is a list (possibly empty) of constant expressions, separated by commas, and the type identifier *set-type* is the name of the set type. Thus, for the base types just defined,

DigitSet{0, 2, 4, 6, 8}

is a valid constant of type *DigitSet* that might be the value of *Evens*. The same set constant can also be written

DigitSet{4, 0, 8, 2, 6}

or

DigitSet{8, 6, 4, 2, 0}

or by using any other arrangement of the elements.

When some or all of the elements of a set are consecutive values of the base type, it is permissible to use subrange notation to specify them. For example, the set constant

DigitSet{0, 1, 2, 3, 4}

can also be expressed as

DigitSet{0..4}

and the set constant

DigitSet{0, 1, 2, 5, 7, 8, 9}

can be expressed as

DigitSet{0..2, 5, 7..9}

Set constants of type BITSET need not be preceded by the type identifier BITSET; thus,

{0, 4, 6, 7}

is equivalent to

BITSET*{0, 4, 6, 7}*

and

{1..3, 7}

is equivalent to

> BITSET{1..3, 7}

Set Assignment.   To assign a value to a variable of set type, an assignment statement of the form

> *set-variable* := *set-value*

may be used. The base type of *set-value* must be **compatible** with the base type of *set-variable*; that is, they are the same type, one is a subrange of the other, or both are subranges of the same type. Thus, for the base types defined earlier, the statement

> *Evens* := *DigitSet*{0, 2, 4, 6, 8}

is a valid assignment statement and assigns the set consisting of the cardinal numbers 0, 2, 4, 6, and 8 to *Evens*. Similarly, the statement

> *Numbers* := {0};

is a valid assignment statement and assigns the singleton set {0} to *Numbers*.
The **empty set** is denoted in Modula-2 by a set constant of the form

> *set-type*{ }

and may be assigned to a set variable whose base type is compatible with *set-type*. Thus

> *Numbers* := { };
> *Evens* := *DigitSet*{ };
> *Winter* := *MonthSet*{ };

are valid assignment statements.

Set Membership.   The test for set membership is implemented in Modula-2 by the relational operator IN. Boolean expressions used to test set membership have the form

> *element* IN *set*

where *set* is a set constant, a set variable, or a set expression, and the type of *element* and the base type of *set* are compatible. For example, if $N = 4$,

> 2 IN *Evens*
> 3 IN *Evens*
> $N + 1$ IN *Evens*

are valid boolean expressions and have the values TRUE, FALSE, and FALSE, respectively.

Sometimes it is necessary to determine whether all of the elements of some set *set1* are also members of another set *set2*, that is, to determine whether *set1* is a **subset** of *set2*. This can be done in Modula-2 by using the relational operators $<=$ and $>=$ to construct boolean expressions of the form

$$set1 <= set2$$

or equivalently

$$set2 >= set1$$

where *set1* and *set2* are set constants, variables, or expressions of the same type. These expressions are true if *set1* is a subset of *set2* and are false otherwise. For example, the value of the boolean expression

$$DigitSet\{2, 6\} <= Evens$$

is true.

Two sets are said to be **equal** if they contain exactly the same elements. Set equality can be checked in Modula-2 with a boolean expression of the form

$$set1 = set2$$

where again *set1* and *set2* must be of the same type. The relational operators # and $<>$ can be used to check set inequality:

$$set1 \ \# \ set2 \qquad \text{or} \qquad set1 <> set2$$

These are equivalent to the boolean expression

$$\text{NOT } (set1 = set2)$$

Set Operations. In addition to the relational operations IN, $<=$, $>=$, $=$, #, and $<>$, there are several set operations that may be used to combine two sets to form another set. The **union** of *set1* and *set2* is denoted by a set expression of the form

$$set1 \ + \ set2$$

and the **intersection** of *set1* and *set2* by

$$set1 * set2$$

The **set difference**

$$set1 \ - \ set2$$

is the set of elements that are in *set1* but are not in *set2*. For each of these expressions, *set1* and *set2* must have the same type.

In addition to these basic operations, Modula-2 provides another set operation called symmetric difference. The **symmetric difference** of *set1* and *set2* is the set of elements that are in either *set1* or *set2* but not in both, and is denoted by a set expression of the form

$$set1 \; / \; set2$$

which is equivalent to

$$(set1 \; + \; set2) \; - \; (set1 \; * \; set2)$$

When a set expression contains two or more of these operators, it is evaluated according to the following priorities:

$$*, / \quad \longleftrightarrow \text{high priority}$$
$$+, \; - \longleftrightarrow \text{low priority}$$

Thus in the expression

$$\{2,3,5\} \; + \; \{2,4,7\} \; * \; \{2,4,6,8\}$$

the intersection operation is performed first, giving the set {2,4}, and

$$\{2,3,5\} \; + \; \{2,4\}$$

is then evaluated, yielding

$$\{2,3,4,5\}$$

Operations having the same priority are evaluated in the order in which they appear in the expression, from left to right. Parentheses may be used in the usual way to alter the standard order of evaluation.

Input/Output of Sets.   To construct a set by reading its elements, we first initialize it to the empty set and then read each element and add it to the set. This process is described in the following algorithm:

ALGORITHM TO CONSTRUCT A SET

(* Algorithm to construct a set *S* by repeatedly reading an element *x* of *S* and adding it to *S*. *)

1. Initialize *S* to the empty set.
2. While there is more data, do the following:
   a. Read a value for a variable *x* whose type is the base type of *S*.
   b. Add *x* to *S*.

The predefined procedure **INCL** can be used to implement the operation in Step 2-b. It is called with a statement of the form

$$INCL(S, \, x)$$

and includes the element x in S; that is, it adds x to S. Here x is an expression whose type is the same as the base type of set variable S.

To display the elements of a set S, we must consider elements of the base type and display those that are members of S. This could be done as follows:

> FOR x ranging from the first element of the base type
> to the last element do the following:
>
> If x is in S then
> Display x.

With this algorithm, however, each element of the base type must be checked, and this may be inefficient for some sets. For example, if S contains only the first element of the base type, its single element would be displayed on the first pass through the loop, and all subsequent passes would accomplish nothing.

An alternative approach is to remove an element from the set S after it is displayed and to terminate repetition when S becomes empty. An algorithm for displaying a set using this technique is

ALGORITHM TO DISPLAY A SET

(* Algorithm to display a set S by repeatedly finding an element x of S, displaying it, and removing it from S. Note that the set S is destroyed, since it is reduced to the empty set. *)

1. Let x be a variable whose type is the base type of S and initialize x to be the first element of this base type.
2. While S is not empty, do the following:
   a. While x is not in S, replace x with its successor.
   b. Display x.
   c. Remove x from S.

If the set to be displayed with this algorithm is to be preserved, it should first be copied into some temporary set

$TempSet := S;$

whose elements are then displayed.

The predefined procedure **EXCL** can be used to exclude an element from a set, as required in Step 2-c. It is called with a statement of the form

EXCL(S, x)

where the type of expression x must be the same as the base type of set variable S.

To illustrate the use of sets, consider the following problem. Suppose that at a certain university, students are required to complete a certain set of courses as part of their major program in computer science. A file is maintained that records the computer science courses taken each semester by each of the current majors and that is updated at the end of each semester.

```
John Doe
1  2  5  8  #
Mary Smith
1  2  5  6  9  10  12  #
Peter Van
1  2  3  4  5  7  8  9  10  11  13  14  15  #
            .
            .
            .
```

Each student record in this file consists of two lines; the first contains the student's name, and the second is a list of the computer science courses (encoded as positive integers) that the student has taken, followed by a closing delimiter (#) to mark the end of the list.

To solve this problem we must read these student records and determine which courses (if any) are in the set of required core courses but not in the set of courses that a student has completed. If there are no such courses, the student has satisfied the requirements. This approach is used in the following algorithm:

ALGORITHM TO CHECK MAJOR PROGRAM REQUIREMENTS

1. Read first student record.
2. While there are more student records do the following:
   a. If the set of courses completed contains the set of required core courses, then do the following:
      Display a message that all required courses have been taken.

      Otherwise do the following:
         i. Calculate the set of courses yet to be taken as the set difference
            {required courses} − {courses completed}.
         ii. Display this set of courses.
   b. Read the next student record.

The program in Figure 2.2 implements this algorithm. It uses three sets, each having the enumeration type *Courses* as its base type: the set constant *CoreCourses*, which is the set of courses required of each major, the set *Major.Courses* of courses taken by a given major, and *RemainingCourses*, which is the set *CoreCourses* − *Major.Courses* of courses yet to be taken by that major. The boolean expression *CoreCourses* $<=$ *Major.Courses* is used to check whether the major has taken all of the required core courses.

```
MODULE   MajorRequirementChecker;

(**********************************************************************

     Program that reads a file of computer science courses taken by
     majors in the computer science department and determines which of
     them have taken all of the required core courses.

 **********************************************************************)

     FROM InOut IMPORT WriteString, WriteLn, WriteCard, ReadCard,
                       ReadString, Done, OpenInput, CloseInput;
     FROM SpecialInOut IMPORT ReadAString;

     CONST
         StringLimit = 30;

     TYPE
         Courses = (Programming1, Programming2, AssemblyLanguage,
                    OperatingSystems, DataStructures, CompilerDesign,
                    DataBase, ArtificialIntelligence, Graphics,
                    TheoryOfComputation, ProgLanguages, AdvDataStructures,
                    ComputerArchitecture, AlgorithmAnalysis, SoftwareDesign);

         String = ARRAY [0..StringLimit] OF CHAR;
         CourseSet = SET OF Courses;
         MajorRecord = RECORD
                           Name : String;
                           CoursesTaken : CourseSet
                       END;

     CONST
         (* Set of required core courses *)
         CoreCourses = CourseSet{Programming1, Programming2,
                                 AssemblyLanguage, OperatingSystems,
                                 DataStructures, ProgLanguages,
                                 ComputerArchitecture};


     VAR
         Major : MajorRecord;            (* record for one major *)
         NumMajors : CARDINAL;           (* number of majors *)
         RemainingCourses : CourseSet;   (* set of courses not taken *)
         MoreRecords : BOOLEAN;          (* signals end of file *)

PROCEDURE ReadCourseSet(VAR S : CourseSet);

     (*************************************************************

         Procedure to read the numbers of courses taken by a student
         and add the corresponding enumeration constants to the set
         of courses already taken by him/her.

      *************************************************************)
```

Figure 2.2

Figure 2.2   (cont.)

```
    VAR
        x : CARDINAL;

    BEGIN
        S := CourseSet{};
        ReadCard(x);
        WHILE Done DO
            INCL(S, VAL(Courses, x - 1));
            ReadCard(x)
        END (* WHILE *)
    END ReadCourseSet;

PROCEDURE PrintCourseSet (S : CourseSet);

    (***************************************************************

        Procedure to display the numbers of the courses in set S

    ***************************************************************)

    VAR
        x : Courses;

    BEGIN
        x := MIN(Courses);
        WHILE S # CourseSet{} DO
            WHILE NOT (x IN S) DO
                INC(x)
            END (* WHILE *);
            WriteCard(1 + ORD(x), 3);
            EXCL(S, x)
        END (* WHILE *)
    END PrintCourseSet;

PROCEDURE ReadARecord(VAR Major : MajorRecord;
                      VAR MoreRecords : BOOLEAN);

    (***************************************************************

        Procedure to read and return a major's record; MoreRecords
        is retured as TRUE if the end-of-file is encountered.

    ***************************************************************)

    BEGIN
        ReadAString(Major.Name);
        MoreRecords := Done;
        IF MoreRecords THEN
            ReadCourseSet(Major.CoursesTaken)
        END (* IF *);
    END ReadARecord;
```

Figure 2.2   (cont.)

```
BEGIN (* main program *)
    WriteString('Enter name of input file.'); WriteLn;
    OpenInput('');
    ReadARecord(Major, MoreRecords);
    WHILE MoreRecords DO
        WITH Major DO
            WriteLn;
            WriteString(Name);
            IF CoreCourses <= CoursesTaken THEN
                WriteString(' has completed all required core courses.')
            ELSE
                RemainingCourses := CoreCourses - CoursesTaken;
                WriteString(' must still complete courses: ');
                PrintCourseSet(RemainingCourses)
            END (* IF *);
            WriteLn
        END (* WITH *);
        ReadARecord(Major, MoreRecords)
    END (* WHILE *)
END MajorRequirementChecker.
```

Listing of MAJORSFILE used in sample run:

```
John Doe
1 2 5 8 #
Mary Smith
1 2 5 6 9 10 12 #
Peter Van
1 2 3 4 5 7 8 9 10 11 13 14 15 #
Fred Johnson
1 2 4 5 7 8 10 11 13 15 #
Jane Jones
1 2 3 4 5 6 7 8 9 11 #
Ann Van
1 2 3 4 6 7 8 10 12 13 14 15 #
Joe Blow
1 2 4 5 #
Jon Boy
1 2 3 5 6 #
Alice Girl
1 2 3 4 5 6 7 8 9 10 11 12 13 14 15 #
Gloria Bee
1 3 5 7 9 #
Dick Moby
2 4 6 8 10 #
```

Sample run:

```
Enter name of input file.
in>MAJORSFILE

John Doe must yet complete courses:   3  4 11 13

Mary Smith must still complete courses:   3  4 11 13

Peter Van has completed all required core courses.
```

Figure 2.2 (cont.)

```
Fred Johnson must still complete courses:    3

Jane Jones must still complete courses:   13

Ann Van must still complete courses:    5 11

Joe Blow must still complete courses:    3 11 13

Jon Boy must still complete courses:    4 11 13

Alice Girl has completed all required core courses.

Gloria Bee must still complete courses:   2  4 11 13

Dick Moby must still complete courses:   1  3  5 11 13
```

Sets whose elements are selected from a *finite* universal set can be represented in computer memory by bit strings in which the number of bits is equal to the number of elements in this universal set. Each bit corresponds to exactly one element of the universal set. A given set is then represented by a bit string in which the bits corresponding to the elements of that set are 1 and all other bits are 0.

To illustrate, suppose the universal set is the set of cardinal numbers 0, 1, 2, . . . , 15. Then any set of cardinal numbers in this range can be represented by a string of sixteen bits, with the first bit corresponding to the number 0, the second bit corresponding to the number 1, and so on. Thus, the set of even cardinal numbers less than 15 can be represented by the bit string

```
1  0  1  0  1  0  1  0  1  0  1  0  1  0  1  0
|  |  |  |  |  |  |  |  |  |  |  |  |  |  |  |
0  1  2  3  4  5  6  7  8  9 10 11 12 13 14 15  ← bit numbers
```

and the empty set by

```
0  0  0  0  0  0  0  0  0  0  0  0  0  0  0  0
|  |  |  |  |  |  |  |  |  |  |  |  |  |  |  |
0  1  2  3  4  5  6  7  8  9 10 11 12 13 14 15
```

The bit operations corresponding to the boolean operations AND, OR, and NOT described in Section 2.2 can be used to implement the basic set operations. Applying the AND operation bitwise to the bit string representing two sets yields a bit string representing the intersection of these sets. For example, consider the sets $S = \{0, 1, 2, 3\}$ and $T = \{0, 2, 4, 6, 8\}$, where the universal set is the set of cardinal numbers in the range 0 through 15. The bit string representations of these sets are as follows:

```
S:  1  1  1  1  0  0  0  0  0  0  0  0  0  0  0  0
T:  1  0  1  0  1  0  1  0  1  0  0  0  0  0  0  0
    |  |  |  |  |  |  |  |  |  |  |  |  |  |  |  |
    0  1  2  3  4  5  6  7  8  9 10 11 12 13 14 15
```

Performing the AND operation bitwise gives the bit string

```
1  0  1  0  0  0  0  0  0  0  0  0  0  0  0  0
|  |  |  |  |  |  |  |  |  |  |  |  |  |  |  |
0  1  2  3  4  5  6  7  8  9  10 11 12 13 14 15
```

which represents the set {0, 2}, the intersection of S and T.

Bitwise application of the OR operation to the bit strings representing two sets S and T yields the representation of $S \cup T$. For these sets, this gives the bit string

```
1  1  1  1  1  0  1  0  1  0  0  0  0  0  0  0
|  |  |  |  |  |  |  |  |  |  |  |  |  |  |  |
0  1  2  3  4  5  6  7  8  9  10 11 12 13 14 15
```

which represents {0, 1, 2, 3, 4, 6, 8}, the union of S and T.

Complementing each bit in the representation of a set T gives a bit string representing T', the **complement** of T, that is, the set of elements of the universal set which are not in T. Applying the AND operation to the bit string for a set S and this string for T' yields a bit string for $S \cap T'$, which is clearly equal to $S - T$. For the preceding set, bitwise complementation of the string for T gives

```
0  1  0  1  0  1  0  1  0  1  1  1  1  1  1  1
|  |  |  |  |  |  |  |  |  |  |  |  |  |  |  |
0  1  2  3  4  5  6  7  8  9  10 11 12 13 14 15
```

and performing bitwise AND with S gives

```
0  1  0  1  0  0  0  0  0  0  0  0  0  0  0  0
|  |  |  |  |  |  |  |  |  |  |  |  |  |  |  |
0  1  2  3  4  5  6  7  8  9  10 11 12 13 14 15
```

which represents $S - T = \{1, 3\}$.

This method of representing sets by bit strings is the approach used in most Modula-2 systems for implementing sets. In many of these systems, these bit strings are stored in a single word, which limits their size and thus limits the size of the sets they represent. In the next section we show how this approach can be extended to represent larger sets.

Exercises

1. Given that A, B, C, and D are variables of type BITSET whose values are assigned by

   A := {2, 4..8, 11};
   B := {1..7, 11, 12};
   C := {1, 3, 5, 7, 9};
   D := {5..9};

calculate the following:

(a) $A * B$ (b) $A + B$ (c) A / B
(d) $A - B$ (e) $B - A$ (f) $A + D$
(g) A / D (h) $A - D$ (i) $A * D$
(j) $D - A$ (k) $C + C$ (l) $C * C$
(m) C / C (n) $C - C$ (o) $C - \{\}$
(p) $A + B + C + D$ (q) $(A - B) - C$ (r) $A - (B - C)$
(s) $A * B * C * D$ (t) $A + B * C$ (u) $A * B + C$
(v) $A * B - C * D$ (w) $(A - (B + C)) * D$ (x) $A * B - (A + B)$
(y) $A - B / C - D$ (z) $B - B - C$

2. Write appropriate declarations for the following set type identifiers:

(a) *SmallIntegers* : set of integers from 1 through 9.
(b) *MonthAbbrevs*: the set of three-letter abbreviations of the names of the months.
(c) *Suit*: the set of thirteen cards in a suit.

3. Write appropriate variable declarations for the following set variables, and write statements to assign to each the specified value:

(a) *Evens*: the set of all even integers from 1 though N and *Odd*: the set of all odd integers in the range from 1 through N for some CARDINAL number N.
(b) *OneModThree*: the set of all numbers of the form $3k + 1$ in the range 1 though N for some CARDINAL number N, where k is an integer.
(c) *EvenPrimes*: the set of all even primes. (A **prime number** is an integer n greater than 1 whose only divisors are 1 and n itself.)
(d) *LargeEvenPrimes*: the set of all even primes greater than 3.
(e) *JMonths*: the set of months whose names begin with the letter "J" (assuming the base type *MonthSet* given in the text).
(f) *UDays*: the set of months whose names begin with the letter "U" (assuming the base type *MonthSet* given in the text).
(g) *FaceCards*: the set of all face cards in a suit; and *NumberCards*: the set of all number cards in a suit (see Exercise 2).

4. Write a procedure to print a set of type BITSET using the usual mathematical notation in which the elements are enclosed in braces { and } and are separated by commas. For example, the set {2, 5, 7} should be displayed as {2, 5, 7}, the set {3..6} as {3, 4, 5, 6}, the set whose only element is 4 as {4}, and the empty set as { }.

5. (a) Write a procedure that returns the complement of a set A.
   (b) Suppose that $+$ and $*$ are predefined set procedures, but $-$ is not. Rewriting the procedure in (a) if necessary (so it does not use $-$), explain how it could be used to calculate $A - B$.

6. Write a function procedure to determine the number of elements in the set.

7. Write a program that reads a CARDINAL number and finds the set of all digits that occur in that number.

8. Repeat Exercise 7 for a REAL number.

9. Write a program that reads two CARDINAL numbers and finds all digits that appear in both numbers.

10. The following algorithm describes a method for finding prime numbers developed by the Greek mathematician Eratosthenes (c. 276–c. 194 B.C.) and known as the **Sieve Method of Eratosthenes**.

ALGORITHM FOR THE SIEVE METHOD OF ERATOSTHENES

(* When this algorithm terminates, the elements remaining in the set *Sieve* are the primes in the range 2 through n. *)

1. Initialize the set *Sieve* to contain the integers from 2 through n.
2. Select the smallest element *Prime* in *Sieve*.
3. While $Prime^2 \leq n$, do the following:
   a. Remove from *Sieve* all elements of the form $Prime * k$ for $k > 1$.
   b. Replace *Prime* with the smallest element in *Sieve* that is greater than *Prime*.

The following diagram illustrates this algorithm for $n = 30$.

Sieve
$\{2,3,4,5,6,7,8,9,10,11,12,13,14,15,16,17,18,19,20,21,22,23,24,25,26,27,28,29,30\}$
↓
$Prime = 2$
↓
$\{2,3,5,7,9,11,13,15,17,19,21,23,25,27,29\}$
↓
$Prime = 3$
↓
$\{2,3,5,7,11,13,17,19,23,25,29\}$
↓
$Prime = 5$
↓
$\{2,3,5,7,11,13,17,19,23,29\}$
↓
$Prime = 7$; terminate, since $Prime^2 > 30$

Write a program using sets and this sieve method to find prime numbers.

11. Since some Modula-2 systems only allow very small sets, the Sieve Method of Eratosthenes for finding prime numbers described in Exercise 10 cannot be used to find large primes. Write a program that can. (*Hint*: Use an array *Sieve* of sets *Sieve*[0], *Sieve*[1], *Sieve*[2], . . . whose elements are integers in the range 0 through 9. Each element of *Sieve*[1] must be interpreted as 10 plus its value, each element of *Sieve*[2] as 20 plus its value, and so on.)

12. Write a program for a computer dating service similar to that in Figure 2.2. It should allow the user to enter a set of characteristics that he or she desires and then should search a file of names and characteristics to find all those persons in the file who have these traits.

13. Proceed as in Exercise 12, but search the file to find the best match(es) in case there are no persons who have all of the desired traits.

14. Write a program for a real estate firm similar to that in Figure 2.2. It should allow the user to enter a set of features that he or she is looking for in a home and then should search a file of addresses and features of homes on the market to find all those homes in the file that have these features.

15. Proceed as in Exercise 14, but search the file to find the best match(es) in case there are no homes that have all of the desired features.

16. Suppose that the components of an inventory file are records whose fields are the following:

> Stock number: a cardinal number
> Item name: a string with at most 25 characters
> Number currently in stock: a cardinal number
> Unit price: a real value

The first digit of each stock number represents a brand, and the second represents a model. Write a program in which the user enters two sets of digits and that then displays the records in this file of all parts for which the first digit of the stock number is in the first set and the second digit is in the second set.

17. Assuming a universal set with base type [0..15], give the bit string representations of the following sets:

(a) The set of odd integers.
(b) The set of prime integers.
(c) The intersection of the set of prime integers and the set of even integers.
(d) The union of the set of prime integers and the set of odd integers.
(e) The set of odd integers that are not prime integers.
(f) The set of integers divisible by 1.
(g) The set of integers not divisible by 1.

18. For the base type *Months* given in the text, describe bit strings for the following sets:

(a) The set of months whose names begin with the letter J.
(b) *MonthSet{January..May, October, November, December}*.
(c) The set of months that have 31 days.
(d) The set of months that have 28 or more days.
(e) The set of months that have 32 days.

2.6 Abstract Data Types and Library Modules; the Module *ExtendedSets*

Data abstraction is the process of separating the definition of an abstract data type from its implementation. The definition of an abstract data type is a description of the values of this type, together with descriptions of the basic operations and relations defined on this set of values. An implementation consists of storage structures for these values together with algorithms for the operations and relations. Data abstraction can be achieved in Modula-2 by using library modules, and in this section we illustrate how this is done by developing a module for processing sets.

In the preceding section we observed that there are two limitations on sets in many Modula-2 systems: (1) The size of a set is often limited by the length of a memory word, typically 16 or 32, and (2) the type of the set elements must be an enumeration type, a subrange of an enumeration type, or a subrange of type CARDINAL. These limitations are quite stringent and reduce the usefulness of sets. Consequently, it is desirable to define a new data type that can be used to process larger sets and sets whose elements may be any ordinal type.

The values of this new data type will be sets of elements from a subrange [*FirstElement .. LastElement*] of any ordinal type. The basic operations obviously must include union, intersection, set difference, and perhaps symmetric difference as well, since it is provided in Modula-2. The basic relations are the membership relation, set equality, and set inclusion. To construct and display sets we also need a procedure to create an empty set, as well as analogues of the predefined Modula-2 procedure INCL to add an element to a set and procedure EXCL to remove an element from a set.

In the implementation of sets described in the preceding section, the basic storage structure is a bit string in which each bit corresponds to one element of the universal set. To store a subset *S* of the universal set, a particular bit is set to 1 if that element belongs to *S* and is set to 0 otherwise. If 0 is interpreted as false and 1 as true, each such bit string can be interpreted as a string of boolean values, and this suggests that an alternative way of representing sets is to use boolean arrays. It is this storage structure that we use to implement the abstract data type *SetType*.

Suppose, for example, that we wish to store sets of cardinal numbers in the range 0 through 99. If *S* is an array of type ARRAY [0..99] OF BOOLEAN, then the set of even numbers in this range can be assigned to *S* by setting the values of $S[0], S[2], S[4], \ldots S[98]$ to TRUE (T) and the other array elements to FALSE (F):

i	0	1	2	3	4	5	6	7	8	9	$\cdots$	98	99
$S[i]$	T	F	T	F	T	F	T	F	T	F	$\cdots$	T	F

This implementation of sets can also be used to represent sets of other ordinal types. For example, to represent sets of uppercase letters, we might use boolean arrays indexed by ['A'..'Z']. Thus, if S is an array of type ARRAY ['A'..'Z'] OF BOOLEAN, the set of vowels can be represented by

Ch	A	B	C	D	E	F	G	H	I	J	K	L	M	N	O	P	Q	R	S	T	U	V	W	X	Y	Z
$S[Ch]$	T	F	F	F	T	F	F	F	T	F	F	F	F	F	T	F	F	F	F	F	T	F	F	F	F	F

and the empty set by

Ch	A	B	C	D	E	F	G	H	I	J	K	L	M	N	O	P	Q	R	S	T	U	V	W	X	Y	Z
$S[Ch]$	F	F	F	F	F	F	F	F	F	F	F	F	F	F	F	F	F	F	F	F	F	F	F	F	F	F

The basic storage structure in implementing this new data type for processing sets is therefore a boolean array indexed by the base type of the universal set. The declarations needed to establish these arrays have the form

```
CONST
    FirstElement = ...; (* first element of base type *)
    LastElement = ...; (* last element of base type *)

TYPE
    ElementType = [FirstElement .. LastElement];
    SetType = ARRAY ElementType OF BOOLEAN;
```

Procedures to implement the basic operations and relations can then be written and packaged with these declarations in a library module to provide an implementation of the abstract data type.

Recall that a **library module** has two parts, a **definition part** and an **implementation part**. The definition part defines what items are in the module and specifies what they are designed to do, but it does not carry out any actual processing. The definition part of a *generic library module* for implementing the abstract data type *SetType* contains the declarations to establish the storage structure and the headings of the procedures that implement the basic operations listed earlier:

```
DEFINITION MODULE ExtendedSets;

(*****************************************************************
    Module to implement the abstract data type SetType whose values are sets
    of elements selected from any subrange [FirstElement .. LastElement]
    of an ordinal type.  Boolean arrays are used as the basic storage
    structures and procedures implement the basic set operations and
    relations of union, intersection, difference, symmetric difference,
    membership, inclusion, equality, inclusion of an element in a set, and
    exclusion of an element from a set.
    EXPORTED:  Constants FirstElement and LastElement, which define
                  the base type
               Types ElementType and SetType
               Variable EmptySet, which is initialized by this module
                  to the empty set.
*****************************************************************)

    CONST
        FirstElement = ...;   (* first element of base type *)
        LastElement =  ...;   (* last element of base type *)

    TYPE
        ElementType = [FirstElement .. LastElement];
        SetType = ARRAY ElementType OF BOOLEAN;

    VAR
        EmptySet : SetType;

    PROCEDURE Union(    A, B : SetType;
                    VAR C : SetType);

        (* Procedure returns C = the union of A and B. *)

    PROCEDURE Intersection(    A, B : SetType;
                           VAR C : SetType);

        (* Procedure returns C = the intersection of A and B. *)

    PROCEDURE Difference(    A, B : SetType;
                         VAR C : SetType);

        (* Procedure returns C = the set difference A - B. *)

    PROCEDURE SymmetricDifference(    A, B : SetType;
                                  VAR C : SetType);

        (* Procedure returns C = the symmetric difference of A and B. *)

    PROCEDURE IsAMember(x : ElementType; A : SetType) : BOOLEAN;

        (* Function procedure that returns TRUE or FALSE depending
           on whether or not x is an element of set A. *)
```

(cont.)

```
    PROCEDURE Equal(A, B : SetType) : BOOLEAN;

        (* Function procedure that returns TRUE or FALSE depending
           on whether or not sets A and B are equal. *)

    PROCEDURE Subset(A, B : SetType) : BOOLEAN;

        (* Function procedure that returns TRUE or FALSE depending
           on whether or not A is a subset of B. *)

    PROCEDURE Include(    x : ElementType;
                      VAR A : SetType);

        (* Procedure to add element x to set A. *)

    PROCEDURE Exclude(    x : ElementType;
                      VAR A : SetType);

        (* Procedure to remove element x from set A. *)

END ExtendedSets.
```

A definition module can be compiled, and once this has been done, programs or other modules can import items from it. These programs and modules can then be compiled, but they cannot be executed until the associated implementation part of the library module has been written and compiled, since it is this part that contains the actual procedures (and opaque types) specified in the definition module.

The implementation part of a library module is called an ***implementation module***. Its form is the same as that of a program module, except that the heading is preceded by the reserved word IMPLEMENTATION. It may use any constants, variables, and types defined in the definition module of the same name without importing them, but any items imported into the definition module must also be imported into the implementation module if they are needed there. Thus, the constants *FirstElement* and *LastElement* together with the types *ElementType* and *SetType* and the variable *EmptySet* declared in the definition module *ExtendedSets* may be used in the following implementation module that contains the complete procedures to carry out the basic operations and relations:

```
IMPLEMENTATION MODULE ExtendedSets;

(***********************************************************************

    Module that gives the complete procedures needed to implement
    the basic operations of the abstract data type SetType: union,
    intersection, difference, symmetric difference, membership,
    inclusion, equality, inclusion of an element in a set, and
    exclusion of an element from a set whose values are sets of
    elements selected from any subrange of an ordinal type.
    The basic storage structure is defined in the corresponding
    definition module and is a boolean array whose index type is
    ElementType = [FirstElement .. LastElement].

 ***********************************************************************)

    PROCEDURE Union(    A, B : SetType;
                    VAR C : SetType);

        (* Procedure returns C = the union of A and B. *)

        VAR
            Elm : ElementType;      (* index *)

        BEGIN
            FOR Elm := FirstElement TO LastElement DO
                C[Elm] := A[Elm] OR B[Elm]
            END (* FOR *)
        END Union;

    PROCEDURE Intersection(    A, B : SetType;
                           VAR C : SetType);

        (* Procedure returns C = the intersection of A and B. *)

        VAR
            Elm : ElementType;      (* index *)

        BEGIN
            FOR Elm := FirstElement TO LastElement DO
                C[Elm] := A[Elm] AND B[Elm]
            END (* FOR *)
        END Intersection;

    PROCEDURE Difference(    A, B : SetType;
                         VAR C : SetType);

    (* Procedure returns C = the set difference A - B. *)

        VAR
            Elm : ElementType;      (* index *)

        BEGIN
            FOR Elm := FirstElement TO LastElement DO
                C[Elm] := A[Elm] AND NOT B[Elm]
            END (* FOR *)
        END Difference;
```

(cont.)

```
PROCEDURE SymmetricDifference(    A, B : SetType;
                              VAR C : SetType);

    (* Procedure returns C = the symmetric difference of A and B. *)

    VAR
        Elm : ElementType;      (* index *)

    BEGIN
        FOR Elm := FirstElement TO LastElement DO
            C[Elm]:= A[Elm] # B[Elm]
        END (* FOR *)
    END SymmetricDifference;

PROCEDURE IsAMember(x : ElementType; A : SetType) : BOOLEAN;

    (* Function procedure that returns TRUE or FALSE depending
       on whether or not x is an element of set A. *)

    BEGIN
        RETURN (A[x])
    END IsAMember;

PROCEDURE Equal(A, B : SetType) : BOOLEAN;

    (* Function procedure that returns TRUE or FALSE depending
       on whether or not sets A and B are equal. *)

    VAR
        Elm : ElementType;

        BEGIN
            FOR Elm := FirstElement TO LastElement DO
                IF A[Elm] # B[Elm] THEN
                    RETURN FALSE
                END (* IF *)
            END (* FOR *);
            RETURN TRUE
        END Equal;

PROCEDURE Subset(A, B : SetType) : BOOLEAN;

    (* Function procedure that returns TRUE or FALSE depending
       on whether or not A is a subset of B. *)

    VAR
        Elm : ElementType;

    BEGIN
        FOR Elm := FirstElement TO LastElement DO
            IF A[Elm] AND NOT B[Elm] THEN
                RETURN FALSE
            END (* IF *)
        END (* FOR *);
        RETURN TRUE
    END Subset;
```

(cont.)

```
    PROCEDURE Include(    x : ElementType;
                     VAR A : SetType);

      (* Procedure to add element x to set A. *)

      BEGIN
          A[x] := TRUE
      END Include;

    PROCEDURE Exclude(    x : ElementType;
                     VAR A : SetType);

      (* Procedure to remove element x from set A. *)

      BEGIN
          A[x] := FALSE
      END Exclude;

BEGIN
    (* Initialize the empty set *)
    FOR Elm := FirstElement TO LastElement DO
        EmptySet[Elm] := FALSE
    END (* FOR *)
END ExtendedSets.
```

Once the definition part of a library module has been compiled, the corresponding implementation part can be compiled. The library module is then ready for use. Its constants, variables, procedures, and types are ready to be *exported* to programs and other modules. To illustrate how this is done, we consider the problem of reading a file and determining the set of distinct letters that appear in it. An algorithm for solving this problem is straightforward:

ALGORITHM TO FIND LETTERS IN A FILE

1. Initialize the set *LetterSet* to the empty set.
2. Read the first character from the file.
3. While there are more characters in the file, do the following:
   a. If the character is a letter then convert it to upper case and add it to *LetterSet*.
   b. Read the next character.
4. Display *LetterSet* using the algorithm in the preceding section.

The program in Figure 2.3 implements this algorithm. It imports the new data type *SetType* and the type *ElementType* from the library module *CHARSets* obtained by defining the constants *FirstElement* and *LastElement* in the module *ExtendedSets* by

FirstElement = 0C;
LastElement = 377C;

It also imports the set constant *FirstElement*, the set variable *EmptySet*, and the procedures *Include*, *Exclude*, *Equal* and *IsAMember*.

```
MODULE FindLetters;

(**********************************************************************

    Program to read characters from a file and construct the set of
    distinct letters that appear in this file.

  **********************************************************************)

    FROM InOut IMPORT Read, Write, WriteLn, WriteString, Done,
                      OpenInput, CloseInput;

    FROM CHARSets IMPORT LastElement, EmptySet, ElementType,
                         SetType, Include, Exclude, Equal, IsAMember;

    VAR
        LetterSet : SetType;

    PROCEDURE ConstructSet (VAR LetterSet : SetType);

        (*****************************************************************

            Procedure to read characters from a file and construct
            the set LetterSet of distinct letters in the file.

          *****************************************************************)

        VAR
            Ch : CHAR;       (* character read from file *)

        BEGIN
            WriteString('Enter name of input file.'); WriteLn;
            OpenInput('');
            LetterSet := EmptySet;
            Read(Ch);
            WHILE Done DO
                IF ('a' <= Ch) AND (Ch <= 'z') OR
                   ('A' <= Ch) AND (Ch <= 'Z') THEN
                    Include(LetterSet, CAP(Ch))
                END (* IF *);
                Read(Ch)
            END (* WHILE *);
            CloseInput
        END ConstructSet;
```

Figure 2.3

Figure 2.3   (cont.)

```
PROCEDURE PrintCHARSet (S : SetType);

    (*********************************************************************

        Procedure to display the characters in set S

    *******************************************************************)

    VAR
        x : ElementType;

    BEGIN
        x := FirstElement;
        WHILE NOT Equal(S, EmptySet) DO
            WHILE NOT IsAMember(x, S) DO
                INC(x)
            END (* WHILE *);
            Write(x);
            Write(' ');
            Exclude(S, x)
        END (* WHILE *);
        WriteLn
    END PrintCHARSet;

BEGIN
    ConstructSet(LetterSet);
    WriteString('Set of letters found in file:');
    WriteLn;
    PrintCHARSet(LetterSet)
END FindLetters.
```

Listing of CHARFile used in sample run:

```
Fourscore and seven years ago, our fathers brought forth on
this continent a new nation, conceived in liberty and dedicated
to the proposition that all men are created equal.
```

Sample run:

```
Enter name of input file.
in>CHARFile

Set of letters found in file:
A B C D E F G H I L M N O P Q R S T U V W Y
```

The library module *ExtendedSets* can be used to process any sets whose base type is a subrange of some ordinal type, simply by defining the constants *FirstElement* and *LastElement* in the definition part of the module. For example, to process sets of cardinal numbers, we might set *FirstElement* = 0 and *LastElement* = 999. However, one must remember that any such changes in the definition part of a library module require that both the definition module and the implementation module, as well as any program or other module that imports items from this module, must be recompiled before they can be executed. Of course, such recompilation could be avoided by having separate modules for each of several base types. For example, the library module *CHAR-Sets* for processing sets of characters used in the program in Figure 2.3 was obtained by defining *FirstElement* = 0C and *LastElement* = 377C; a library module *CARDINALSets* for processing sets of large cardinal numbers might have *FirstElement* = 0 and *LastElement* = 999; and still another library module *INTEGERSets* might set *FirstElement* = −999 and *LastElement* = 999 so that sets of integers can be processed.

An alternative to changing the definitions of *FirstElement* and *LastElement*, in the definition module that allows *ExtendedSets* to stand alone as a generic extended set module is to remove these definitions and place them in a separate module whose only function is to define the base type of the sets to be processed. The definition part of such a "declaration module" has the form

```
DEFINITION MODULE SetBaseType;

(* Module to define the base type for sets
   processed by the library module ExtendedSets *)

   CONST
       FirstElement = ...;   (* first element of base type *)
       LastElement = ...;    (* last element of base type *)

   TYPE
       ElementType = [FirstElement .. LastElement];

END SetBaseType.
```

Although the corresponding implementation module is trivial, it is nevertheless required in most Modula-2 systems:

```
IMPLEMENTATION MODULE SetBaseType;

END SetBaseType.
```

The module *ExtendedSets* must then import *FirstElement*, *LastElement*, and *ElementType* from the module *SetBaseType*:

```
DEFINITION MODULE ExtendedSets;
    .
    .
    .
    FROM SetBaseType IMPORT ElementType;

    TYPE
        SetType = ARRAY ElementType of BOOLEAN;

    PROCEDURE Union (    A,B : SetType;
                      VAR C : SetType);

        (* Procedure returns C = the union of A and B. *)
        .
        .
        .
END ExtendedSets.
```

```
IMPLEMENTATION MODULE ExtendedSets;
    .
    .
    .

   FROM SetBaseType IMPORT FirstElement, LastElement, ElementType;

   PROCEDURE Union (    A, B : SetType;
                    VAR C : SetType):

      (* Procedure returns C = the union of A and B. *)

      VAR
         Elm : ElementType;   (* index *)

      BEGIN
         FOR Elm := FirstElement TO LastElement DO
             C[Elm] := A[Elm] OR B[Elm]
         END (* FOR *)
      END Union;
         .
         .
END ExtendedSets.
```

Since a library module exports only those items defined in it, the module *ExtendedSets* does not export the constants *FirstElement* and *LastElement* or the type *ElementType*. Consequently, any program that uses these constants or this type must import them from the module *SetBaseType*.

In summary, the steps required to use this generic library module for processing sets are as follows:

1. Assign the constants *FirstElement* and *LastElement* in the module *SetBaseType*.
2. Recompile both the definition and implementation parts of *SetBaseType*.
3. Import *FirstElement*, *LastElement*, and *ElementType* from the module *SetBaseType* into the program or module in which they needed.
4. Import the type *SetType* together with other necessary items from the module *ExtendedSets* into the program or module.
5. Recompile and/or relink these programs and modules as required by your system.

In this section we showed how library modules can be used to implement abstract data types. In the approach illustrated here, the storage structures in the implementation are defined in the definition part of the module, and although headings of the procedures that carry out the basic operations and relations appear there as well, the actual procedures themselves are in the implementation part of the module. The separation of an abstract data type from its implementation would be sharper if the definition part of the module contained only a description of the data type and all of the implementation details were hidden in the implementation part. That is, the definition module contains only the *name* of the data type and headings of procedures for the basic operations and relations; the implementation module contains all of the details of the storage structure used to represent values of this type and the actual procedures used to perform the basic operations and relations. This ***information hiding*** is possible in Modula-2 by using pointers and opaque types, as described in Chapter 7.

Exercises

1. Write a program to find the set of all vowels and the set of all consonants that appear in a given line of text.

2. Write a program to read two lines of text and find all characters that appear in both lines.

3. Write a program to find all letters that are not present in a given line of text and display them in alphabetical order.

4. A real number in Modula-2 has one of the forms $m.$, $+m.$, $-m.$, $m.n$, $+m.n$, or $-m.n$, where m and n are cardinal numbers; or it may be expressed in exponential form xEe, $xE+e$, $xE-e$, where x is a real number not in exponential form and e is a cardinal number. Write a program that accepts a string of characters and then checks to see if it represents a valid real constant.

5. Write a program like that in Exercise 16 of Section 2.5, but suppose that the stock numbers are strings consisting of three letters followed by three digits, in which the first letter represents a brand and the second letter represents a model.

6. Write a program to find large prime numbers using the Sieve Method of Eratosthenes described in Exercise 10 of Section 2.5. Use the library module *ExtendedSets* to process sets of large cardinal numbers.

7. The implementation of sets as boolean arrays described in this section can be extended to universal sets whose elements are not ordinal types, provided the elements are fixed in some specific order, and $S[i]$ is then true or false according to whether or not the ith element of this ordered universal set is in S. Consider the universal set $U = \{0.0, 0.1, 0.2, \ldots, 9.9, 10.0\}$ consisting of all real numbers in the range 0 through 10 that can be expressed in decimal form with one digit to the right of the decimal point; assume that these real numbers are fixed in increasing order. Describe how each of the following sets would be represented:

    (a) $\{x \in U \mid 3 \le x \le 4\}$ (b) $\{x \in U \mid 3x - 1.1 = 4.7\}$
    (c) $\{x \in U \mid x < 8.8\}$ (d) $\{x \in U \mid x^2 - 5x + 6 = 0\}$

8. Proceed as in Exercise 7, but for a universal set consisting of a set of names (strings), Alan, Alice, Barb, Ben, Bob, Carl, Cora, Dick, Don, Dora, Dot, and Fred, arranged in alphabetical order. Show how the following sets would be represented:

    (a) Set of names that begin with B.

(b) Set of names that begin with E.

(c) Set of names that begin with D and have fewer than three letters.

(d) Set of names that have fewer than six letters.

9. Write a program like that described in Exercise 5, but have the user enter a set of three-letter strings and display the records of all parts whose stock numbers begin with one of these three-letter combinations. Use the implementation of sets described in Exercise 7.

*2.7 Local Modules

In the preceding section we showed how abstract data types can be implemented using library modules that are physically and logically separate from programs and other modules that use these data types. This method of implementing data types is most appropriate when the data type is one that can be used in a variety of different applications, because the items in the library module can be used by simply importing them into a program. There are times, however, when a collection of variables, constants, types, and procedures are related and thus should be grouped together, but they will be used in only one program and so there is no real advantage in separating them from this program. One example of this is a data type that is designed for a particular application, such as the enumeration type *DaysOfWeek* and the special input/output procedures described in Section 0.7. In this section we describe how related items can be grouped together in a module that is contained within a program that uses that module. Such modules are called **internal** or **local modules** to distinguish them from library (external) modules.

To illustrate the use of local modules, we consider again the problem of checking major program requirements described in Section 2.5. In the program in Figure 2.2 developed to solve this problem, sets were used whose elements were of type

> *Courses* = (*Programming1, Programming2, AssemblyLanguage,*
> *OperatingSystems, DataStructures, CompilerDesign,*
> *DataBase, ArtificialIntelligence, Graphics,*
> *TheoryOfComputation, ProgLanguages, AdvDataStructures,*
> *ComputerArchitecture, AlgorithmAnalysis, SoftwareDesign*);

Because values of an enumeration type cannot be read or written, special input/ output procedures for sets of type

> *CourseSet* = SET OF *Courses*;

had to be developed. Since these are not directly related to the problem of checking major program requirements, it would have been nice to hide the details of these procedures. This could be done using library modules, as described in the preceding section, but this set type is closely tied to this particular application. Consequently, the development of a separate library module with its definition part and implementation part is not warranted. This situation is, therefore, precisely the kind described earlier, in which a local module can be used to achieve logical separation of the details of procedures for reading and writing items of a special type from the real purpose of a program.

Local modules are defined in the module section of a program's declaration part. The form of a local module is almost the same as that of a program except that the import part is replaced with an import–export part and a semicolon follows its statement part:

> Module heading
> Import–export part
> Declaration part
> Statement part;

The module heading has exactly the same form as the program heading. For example, a local module for defining and processing sets of type *CourseSet* might begin

> MODULE *CourseSetType*;
>
> (∗ Module to define the abstract data type *CourseSet* whose elements have the enumeration type *Courses*. This type is an extension to the set type provided in Modula-2; to supplement the usual Modula-2 features for processing sets, special input/output procedures *ReadCourseSet* and *PrintCourseSet* are defined in and exported from this module. ∗)

The ***import–export part*** contains any number (possibly none) of import declarations followed by at most one export declaration. ***Import declarations*** specify items to be imported from the main program module or from other modules internal to the main program. *If an item (constant, variable, or procedure) defined outside an internal module is needed within that module, it must be imported into it from the immediately surrounding program, module, or procedure.* For example, the procedure *ReadCourseSet* uses procedure *ReadCard* from library module *InOut* to read course numbers, and *PrintCourseSet* uses *WriteCard* to display course numbers. *ReadCard* and *WriteCard* thus must be imported into the local module *CourseSetType* by using an import declaration:

> FROM *InOut* IMPORT *ReadCard*, *WriteCard*;

Since items can be imported only from the *immediately surrounding program unit*, which in this case is the main program itself, these input/output procedures must first be imported into the main program. This is accomplished by including the statement

> IMPORT *InOut*;

in the import part of the main program. This ***import declaration*** imports the *complete* library module *InOut* into the main program. It makes all of the items exported from *InOut* available to the main program. However, using these items requires *qualified identifiers* such as *InOut.WriteString* and *InOut.WriteCard* in which the module name is attached as a prefix to the item name. Adding an import declaration of the form

FROM *module-name* IMPORT *list*;

makes it possible to use the listed items without qualification.

The import–export part may also include one **export declaration** of the form

EXPORT *list*;

where *list* is a list of items such as constants, variables, and procedures to be made available to the immediately surrounding program unit. This export declaration, if present, must follow all of the import declarations. *Items that appear in such export lists are the only items declared in a local module that are accessible outside the module. All other items remain hidden in the module and are not accessible outside it.* For example, the data types *Courses* and *CourseSet* and the procedures *ReadCourseSet* and *PrintCourseSet* are defined in the local module *CourseSetType*, but they are needed in the program to declare variables and to read and display sets of courses. Thus they must be exported from the local module by listing them in an export list:

EXPORT *Courses, CourseSet, ReadCourseSet, PrintCourseSet*;

These data types and procedures then become accessible throughout the program (and can be imported into other local modules within the program).

The declaration part of a local module has the same form as that for a program module. It may contain constant sections, type sections, and procedure sections. Thus, the declaration part of the module *CourseSetType* contains a type section to define the enumeration type *Courses* and the data type *CourseSet*, as well as definitions of the procedures *ReadCourseSet* and *PrintCourseSet*. Note, however, that a local module does not have a module section and thus may not itself contain other local modules.

Figure 2.4 shows the program that results when the program in Figure 2.2 is modified to contain the local module *CourseSet*. Note that all of the details pertaining to the extended set type *CourseSet* are grouped together into a separate unit within the program, and thus, though not physically separate from it, they are logically separated from the program.

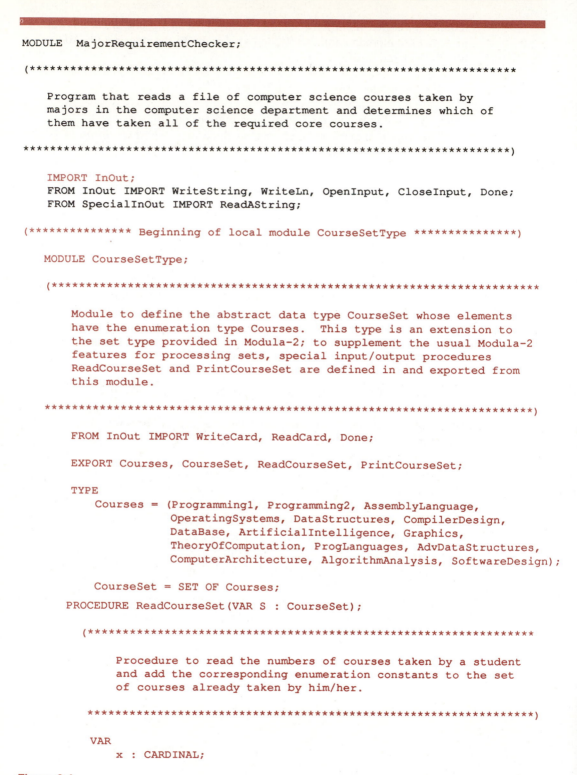

```
MODULE  MajorRequirementChecker;

(***********************************************************************

    Program that reads a file of computer science courses taken by
    majors in the computer science department and determines which of
    them have taken all of the required core courses.

***********************************************************************)

    IMPORT InOut;
    FROM InOut IMPORT WriteString, WriteLn, OpenInput, CloseInput, Done;
    FROM SpecialInOut IMPORT ReadAString;

(*************** Beginning of local module CourseSetType ***************)

    MODULE CourseSetType;

    (***********************************************************************

        Module to define the abstract data type CourseSet whose elements
        have the enumeration type Courses.  This type is an extension to
        the set type provided in Modula-2; to supplement the usual Modula-2
        features for processing sets, special input/output procedures
        ReadCourseSet and PrintCourseSet are defined in and exported from
        this module.

    ***********************************************************************)

    FROM InOut IMPORT WriteCard, ReadCard, Done;

    EXPORT Courses, CourseSet, ReadCourseSet, PrintCourseSet;

    TYPE
        Courses = (Programming1, Programming2, AssemblyLanguage,
                   OperatingSystems, DataStructures, CompilerDesign,
                   DataBase, ArtificialIntelligence, Graphics,
                   TheoryOfComputation, ProgLanguages, AdvDataStructures,
                   ComputerArchitecture, AlgorithmAnalysis, SoftwareDesign);

        CourseSet = SET OF Courses;

    PROCEDURE ReadCourseSet(VAR S : CourseSet);

        (***********************************************************************

            Procedure to read the numbers of courses taken by a student
            and add the corresponding enumeration constants to the set
            of courses already taken by him/her.

        ***********************************************************************)

        VAR
            x : CARDINAL;
```

Figure 2.4

Figure 2.4   (cont.)

```
        BEGIN
            S := CourseSet{};
            ReadCard(x);
            WHILE Done DO
                INCL(S, VAL(Courses, x - 1));
                ReadCard(x)
            END (* WHILE *);
        END ReadCourseSet;


    PROCEDURE PrintCourseSet (S : CourseSet);

        (*************************************************************

            Procedure to display the numbers of the courses in set S

         ************************************************************)

        VAR
            x : Courses;

        BEGIN
            x :=  MIN(Courses);
            WHILE S # CourseSet{} DO
                WHILE NOT (x IN S) DO
                    INC(x)
                END (* WHILE *);
                WriteCard(1 + ORD(x), 3);
                EXCL(S, x)
            END (* WHILE *)
        END PrintCourseSet;

        BEGIN
        END CourseSetType;

(************** End of local module CourseSetType **************)


    CONST
        StringLimit = 30;

    TYPE
        String = ARRAY [0..StringLimit] OF CHAR;
        MajorRecord = RECORD
                        Name : String;
                        CoursesTaken : CourseSet
                      END;

    CONST
        (* Set of required core courses *)
        CoreCourses = CourseSet{Programming1, Programming2,
                        AssemblyLanguage, OperatingSystems,
                        DataStructures, ProgLanguage,
                        ComputerArchitecture};
```

Figure 2.4   (cont.)

```
    VAR
        Major : MajorRecord;             (* record for one major *)
        NumMajors : CARDINAL;            (* number of majors *)
        RemainingCourses : CourseSet;    (* set of courses not taken *)
        MoreRecords : BOOLEAN;           (* signals end of file *)

    PROCEDURE ReadARecord(VAR Major : MajorRecord;
                          VAR MoreRecords : BOOLEAN);

        (*****************************************************************

            Procedure to read and return a major's record; MoreRecords
            is retured as TRUE if the end-of-file is encountered.

        *****************************************************************)

    BEGIN
        ReadAString(Major.Name);
        MoreRecords := Done;
        IF MoreRecords THEN
            ReadCourseSet(Major.CoursesTaken)
        END (* IF *)
    END ReadARecord;
BEGIN (* main program *)
    WriteString('Enter name of input file.');
    OpenInput('');
    ReadARecord(Major, MoreRecords);
    WHILE MoreRecords DO
        WITH Major DO
            WriteLn;
            WriteString(Name);
            IF CoreCourses <= CoursesTaken THEN
                WriteString(' has completed all required core courses.'
            ELSE
                RemainingCourses := CoreCourses - CoursesTaken;
                WriteString(' must still complete courses: ');
                PrintCourseSet(RemainingCourses)
            END (* IF *);
            WriteLn
        END (* WITH *);
        ReadARecord(Major, MoreRecords);
    END (* WHILE *);
    CloseInput
END MajorRequirementChecker.
```

Although the local module in this example contains an empty statement part, this need not be the case. If the statement part of a local module is nonempty, then it will be executed before the statement part of the containing program or library module is executed. If a program or module contains several internal modules, then all of their statement parts will be executed first, in the order in which the modules appear.

Exercises

1. Modify the program in Section 0.7 so that it contains a local module that defines the special enumeration type *DaysOfWeek* and provides input/output procedures for values of this type.

2. Write a menu-driven program that allows the user to convert measurements from either minutes to hours or feet to meters (1 foot = 0.3048 meters), or from degrees Fahrenheit to degrees Celsius (C = $\frac{5}{9}$(F − 32)). Use a local module to carry out the conversions of these units of measurement.

3. Write a menu-driven program to help balance a checkbook with a monthly bank statement. It should allow the following three kinds of processing:

   (1) Add a deposit to the current balance.
   (2) Subtract the amount of a check written and a check-processing charge from the current balance.
   (3) Print a statement of the month's activity. This statement should include the initial balance, number of checks written, total amount of checks, number of deposits, total deposits, total service charges, and the final balance.

   Use two local modules in the program: an initialization module to display instructions to the user and initialize key variables, and a processing module that displays the menu of options and carries out the processing required by these options.

3

Strings

Some data structures such as arrays and records are implemented directly with corresponding predefined data types provided in the programming language being used. For such structures the programmer usually need not be concerned with the details of the storage structures and algorithms used in their implementations because these are handled by the compiler and other system software. In many applications, however, new data types must be designed and implemented by the programmer. In these cases, the implementation can usually be done most efficiently by using data types that have been previously defined and implemented. The remaining chapters of this text describe a number of the more common of these ''higher-level'' data structures.

In this chapter we consider the string data type. This data type is useful in processing sequences of characters such as words and sentences in text-editing and word-processing applications. The string data type is implemented directly by a predefined string data type in many programming languages such as BASIC, FORTRAN 77, and SNOBOL. This is not the case for Modula-2, however, and thus we also consider how strings can be implemented with the data types that are provided in Modula-2.

3.1 Strings As Abstract Data Types

A *string* is a finite sequence of characters drawn from some character set. The basic operations on strings depend on the particular application, but in most text-editing and word-processing applications, they include the following:

Length: The length of a string is the number of characters in it.

Concat(enate): The concatenation of string *str1* with *str2* is obtained by appending *str2* to *str1*.

Copy: The copy operation copies a substring of a specified length from a given string, beginning at some specified position.

170

Position: The position operation determines the *index* of one string *str1* in another string *str2*; this is the starting position of the first occurrence (if any) of *str1* in *str2*.

Insert: This insert operation inserts one string *str1* into another string *str2* at a specified position in *str2*.

Delete: The delete operation removes a specified number of characters from a given string *str*, starting at some specified position in *str*.

The preparation of textual material such as letters, books, and computer programs often involves the insertion, deletion, and replacement of parts of the text. The software of most computer systems includes an **editor** that makes it easy to carry out these operations. These and other text-editing operations are often implemented using the basic string operations. To illustrate, we consider the problem of implementing the change or replacement text-editing function. More precisely, we consider how to replace a specified substring in a given line of text with another string.

A level-1 algorithm for solving this problem is

TEXT-EDITING ALGORITHM

1. Open the file of text to be edited and read the lines of text into an array of strings, each of which is one line of text.
2. Edit the lines of text.
3. Open an output file and copy the edited text from the array into it.

The heart of this algorithm is the editing task in Step 2, and so we concentrate on developing an algorithm for it.

Editing commands that the user enters have the form

old-string/new-string/

where *old-string* is the part of the current text line that is to be replaced by *new-string*. An algorithm for processing such editing commands is

Edit

For each text line do the following:

1. Display the line.
2. While more editing is required, do the following:
   a. Read an edit command and extract *OldString* and *NewString*.
   b. Locate the position *Loc* of *OldString* in the current text line.
   c. If *OldString* is not found in this line, then
      Display a message indicating this fact.
   Otherwise
      Replace the first occurrence of *OldString* in the line with *NewString*.

The processing of edit commands required in Step 2-a of this algorithm can be carried out using the basic string operations length, position, copy, and delete. An algorithm for this is

GetEditCommand

1. Read an *EditCommand* of the form *OldString/NewString/*.
2. Calculate the length of *OldString* by determining the position of the first slash (/) in *EditCommand*.
3. Use the copy operation to extract *OldString* from *EditCommand*.
4. Delete *OldString* and the first / from *EditCommand*.
5. Find the length of *NewString*.
6. Use the copy operation to extract *NewString* from *EditCommand*.

The string operations length, insert, delete, and concat can be used to carry out the replacement operation required in Step 2-c of the editing algorithm, as follows:

Replace

1. Delete the first occurrence of *OldString* from *TextLine*.
2. If this occurrence was not at the end of *TextLine* then
       Use the insert operation to insert *NewString* in *TextLine*.
   Otherwise
       Use the concat operation to append *NewString* to *TextLine*.
3. Display the edited line to the user.

The program in Figure 3.1 uses these algorithms to solve the text-editing problem. Its organization is given by the structure diagram

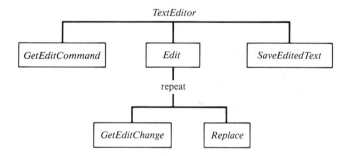

It assumes the availability of a library module of string-processing functions and procedures like *StringsLib* described in the next section. Also, it uses the procedure *ReadAString* from the library module *SpecialInOut* to read the lines of text (see Appendix F). *ReadAString* reads strings of characters, including blanks, into a character array until an end of line is encountered or the array is full and then inserts the null character 0C at the end of the string, if there is room in the array. The boolean variable *ReadOkay*, also exported from *SpecialInOut*, is set to TRUE by *ReadAString* unless an end-of-file condition is encountered.

The sample run shows that in addition to string replacements, the program can be used to make insertions and deletions. For example, changing the substring

A N

in the line of text

A NATION CONCEIVED IN LIBERTY AND AND DEDICATED

to

A NEW N

yields the edited line

A NEW NATION CONCEIVED IN LIBERTY AND AND DEDICATED

Entering the edit change

AND //

changes the substring

AND∅

(where ∅ denotes a blank) in the line of text to an empty string containing no characters, and so the edited result is

A NEW NATION CONCEIVED IN LIBERTY AND DEDICATED

```
MODULE TextEditor;

(*********************************************************************

  Program to perform some basic text-editing functions on lines of
  text.  The basic operation is that of replacing a substring of
  the text by another string.  This replacement is accomplished
  by a command of the form
                 OldString/NewString/
  where OldString specifies the substring in the text to be replaced
  by the specified string NewString; NewString may be an empty
  string which then causes the substring OldString (if found) to be
  deleted.  The text lines are read from TextFile, and after editing
  has been completed, the edited lines are written to NewTextFile.

*********************************************************************)
```

Figure 3.1

Figure 3.1 (cont.)

```
FROM InOut IMPORT Write, WriteString, WriteLn, Read,
                  OpenInput, CloseInput, OpenOutput, CloseOutput;
FROM StringsLib IMPORT Length, Concat, Copy, Position, Insert,
                  Delete, Assign, Compare;
FROM SpecialInOut IMPORT ReadAString, ReadOkay;

CONST
    StringLimit = 60;      (* limit on number of characters in string *)
    MaxLines = 100;        (* maximum number of lines in document *)

TYPE
    String = ARRAY [0..StringLimit] OF CHAR;
    ArrayOfLines = ARRAY[1..MaxLines] OF String;

VAR
    Line : ArrayOfLines;  (* lines of text to be edited *)
    NumLines : CARDINAL;  (* number of lines of text *)

PROCEDURE GetLinesOfText(VAR Line : ArrayOfLines;
                         VAR NumLines : CARDINAL);

    (*****************************************************************

        Procedure to read lines of text from a file and store them
        in the array Line.  NumLInes is the number of lines read.

        ****************************************************************)

    VAR
        NextLine : String;    (* next line from the file *)

    BEGIN
        WriteString('Enter name of input file.'); WriteLn;
        OpenInput('');
        NumLines := 0;
        ReadAString(NextLine);
        WHILE ReadOkay DO
            IF (NumLines < MaxLines) THEN
                INC(NumLines);
                Line[NumLines] := NextLine
            ELSE
                WriteString('*** Array full -- too many lines *');
                RETURN
            END (* IF *);
            ReadAString(NextLine);
        END (* WHILE *);
        CloseInput
    END GetLinesOfText;

PROCEDURE Edit(VAR Line : ArrayOfLines; NumLines : CARDINAL);

    (*****************************************************************

        Procedure to carry out the editing operations on the NumLines
        lines of text stored in array Line.

        ****************************************************************)
```

Figure 3.1 (cont.)

```
VAR
    OldString,              (* old string in edit change *)
    NewString : String;     (* new string in edit change *)
    i,                      (* index *)
    Location : CARDINAL;    (* location of OldString in TextLine *)
    Response : String;      (* user response *)

PROCEDURE GetEditCommand (VAR OldString, NewString : String);

    (**************************************************************

        Procedure to read the edit change of the form
                    OldString/NewString/
        It returns OldString and NewString.

    *************************************************************)

    VAR
        Ch : CHAR;                 (* a character entered by user *)
        EditChange : String;       (* editing change *)
        i,                         (* index *)
        OldLength,                 (* length of OldString *)
        NewLength : CARDINAL;      (* length of NewString *)

    BEGIN
        WriteString('Edit change:  ');
        WriteLn;
        ReadAString(EditChange);
        OldLength := Position('/', EditChange);
        Copy(EditChange, 0, OldLength, OldString);
        Delete(EditChange, 0, OldLength + 1);
        NewLength := Length(EditChange) - 1;
        Copy(EditChange, 0, NewLength, NewString)
    END GetEditCommand;

PROCEDURE Replace(VAR TextLine: String;
                      OldString, NewString : String;
                      Start : CARDINAL);

    (**************************************************************

        Procedure to replace a substring OldString beginning at
        position Start of TextLine with NewString.

    *************************************************************)

    BEGIN
        Delete(TextLine, Start, Length(OldString));
        IF Start < Length(TextLine) THEN
            Insert(NewString, Start, TextLine)
        ELSE
            Concat(TextLine, NewString, TextLine)
        END (* IF *);
        WriteLn;
        WriteString(TextLine)
    END Replace;
```

Figure 3.1 (cont.)

```
        BEGIN (* Edit *)
            FOR i := 1 TO NumLines DO
                WriteLn;
                WriteString(Line[i]);
                WriteLn;
                WriteString('Edit this line? ');
                ReadAString(Response);
                WHILE CAP(Response[0]) = 'Y' DO
                    GetEditCommand(OldString, NewString);
                    Location := Position(OldString, Line[i]);
                    IF Location > Length(Line[i]) THEN
                        WriteString(OldString);
                        WriteString(' not found');
                        WriteLn
                    ELSE
                        Replace (Line[i], OldString, NewString, Location)
                    END (* IF *);
                    WriteLn;
                    WriteString('More editing (Y or N)? ');
                    ReadAString(Response)
                END (* WHILE *)
            END (* FOR *)
        END Edit;

    PROCEDURE SaveEditedText(Line : ArrayOfLines; NumLines : CARDINAL);

        (****************************************************************

            Procedure to write the NumLines edited lines of text
            stored in array Line to an output file.

            ****************************************************************)


        VAR
            i : CARDINAL;        (* index *)

        BEGIN
            WriteLn;
            WriteString('Enter name of output file.'); WriteLn;
            OpenOutput('');
            FOR i := 1 TO NumLines DO
                WriteString(Line[i]);
                WriteLn
            END (* FOR *);
            CloseOutput
        END SaveEditedText;

BEGIN (* main program *)
    GetLinesOfText(Line, NumLines);
    Edit(Line, NumLines);
    SaveEditedText(Line, NumLines)
END TextEditor.
```

Figure 3.1   (cont.)

Listing of file LINCOLN used in sample run:

FOURSCORE AND FIVE YEARS AGO, OUR MOTHERS
BROUGHT FORTH ON CONTINENT
A NATION CONCEIVED IN LIBERTY AND AND DEDICATED
TO THE PREPOSITION THAT ALL MEN
ARE CREATED EQUAL.

Sample run:

Enter name of input file.
in> LINCOLN

FOURSCORE AND FIVE YEARS AGO, OUR MOTHERS
Edit this line? Y
Edit change:
FIVE/SEVEN/
FOURSCORE AND SEVEN YEARS AGO, OUR MOTHERS
More editing (Y or N)? Y
Edit change:
MOTH/FATH/
FOURSCORE AND SEVEN YEARS AGO, OUR FATHERS
More editing (Y or N)? N

BROUGHT FORTH ON CONTINENT
Edit this line? Y
Edit change:
ONC/ON THIS C/
ONC not found
More editing (Y or N)? Y
Edit change:
ON/ON THIS/
BROUGHT FORTH ON THIS CONTINENT
More editing (Y or N)? N

A NATION CONCEIVED IN LIBERTY AND AND DEDICATED
Edit this line? Y
Edit change:
A/A NEW/
A NEW NATION CONCEIVED IN LIBERTY AND AND DEDICATED
More editing (Y or N)? Y
Edit change:
AND //
A NEW NATION CONCEIVED IN LIBERTY AND DEDICATED
More editing (Y or N)? N

TO THE PREPOSITION THAT ALL MEN
Edit this line? Y
Edit change:
RE/RO/
TO THE PROPOSITION THAT ALL MEN
More editing (Y or N)? N

ARE CREATED EQUAL.
Edit this line? N

Figure 3.1 (cont.)

```
Enter name of output file.
out> EDITED
```

Listing of file EDITED:

```
FOURSCORE AND SEVEN YEARS AGO, OUR FATHERS
BROUGHT FORTH ON THIS CONTINENT
A NEW NATION CONCEIVED IN LIBERTY AND DEDICATED
TO THE PROPOSITION THAT ALL MEN
ARE CREATED EQUAL.
```

3.2 Implementing Strings in Modula-2; the Module *StringsLib*

Recall that implementing a data structure requires (1) choosing appropriate storage structures to store the data items and (2) designing algorithms for the basic operations and relations. Thus we begin our implementation of the string data type by describing an appropriate storage structure.

Because strings are finite sequences of characters, it seems natural to use arrays of characters to store strings. And as we noted in Section 0.2, this is the approach used in Modula-2. More precisely, a *string type* in Modula-2 is any zero-based array of characters. Thus strings are implemented in Modula-2 using declarations of the form

```
CONST
    StringLimit = . . . ;   (* limit on number of characters in string *)

TYPE
    String = ARRAY [0..StringLimit] OF CHAR;

VAR
    Str : String;
```

A string constant may then be assigned to the string variable *Str*, provided that it does not contain too many characters. These characters are copied into the array positions, beginning with position 0, and the *null character* (0C) is placed in the position following the last character unless the array is full. For example, if $StringLimit = 10$, the assignment statement

$Str := $ 'ABC';

assigns A to $Str[0]$, B to $Str[1]$, C to $Str[2]$, and the null character to $Str[3]$:

i	0	1	2	3	4	5	6	7	8	9	10
$Str[i]$	A	B	C	†	?	?	?	?	?	?	?

(Here, the symbol † denotes the null character and ? denotes an undefined value.)

Strings can be input and output using procedures *ReadString* and *Write-String* provided in the library module *InOut*. But none of the basic string operations described in the preceding section is provided in Modula-2. However, many Modula-2 systems do include a library module that does contain procedures that implement these operations. The definition parts of these string library modules are similar to the following:

DEFINITION MODULE *StringsLib*;

(∗ Library module of string processing procedures. If a string variable intended to store the result of a string operation is not large enough, the rightmost characters are truncated. ∗)

    PROCEDURE *Length*(*Str* : ARRAY OF CHAR) : CARDINAL;

        (∗ This function procedure returns the number of characters in string *Str*, excluding the end-of-string character 0C if it is present. ∗)

    PROCEDURE *Concat*(*Str1*, *Str2* : ARRAY OF CHAR;
                VAR *Str* : ARRAY OF CHAR);

        (∗ Returns the string *Str* obtained by concatenating *Str2* onto the end of *Str1* ∗)

    PROCEDURE *Copy*(*Str* : ARRAY OF CHAR;
              Index, *Size* : CARDINAL;
            VAR *Substr* : ARRAY OF CHAR);

        (∗ Returns the substring *Substr* of the specified *Size* from string *Str*, beginning at position *Index* ∗)

    PROCEDURE *Position*(*Str1*, *Str2* : ARRAY OF CHAR) : CARDINAL;

        (∗ This function procedure returns the position of the first character of the first occurrence of string *Str1* within the string *Str2* or 1 + HIGH(*Str2*) if *Str1* is not found in *Str2*. ∗)

    PROCEDURE *Insert*(*Str1* : ARRAY OF CHAR;
              Index : CARDINAL;
            VAR *Str2* : ARRAY OF CHAR);

        (∗ Modifies string *Str2* by inserting the string *Str1* at position *Index* ∗)

    PROCEDURE *Delete*(VAR *Str* : ARRAY OF CHAR;
              Index, *Size* : CARDINAL);

        (∗ Modifies string *Str* by removing a substring of the specified *Size*, starting at position *Index* ∗)

    PROCEDURE *Assign*(*Str1* : ARRAY OF CHAR;
              VAR *Str2* : ARRAY OF CHAR);

        (∗ Assigns *Str1* to *Str2*; i.e., implements *Str2* := *Str1* ∗)

PROCEDURE *Compare(Str1, Str2* : ARRAY OF CHAR) : INTEGER;

(* Returns − 1, 0, or 1 according to whether *Str1* is less than
Str2, Str1 is equal to *Str2*, or *Str1* is greater than *Str2* *)

END *StringsLib.*

Implementation of the length operation is straightforward. The following procedure for this operation simply counts characters in the string *Str* until the end-of-string mark in *Str* or the end of *Str* is reached:

PROCEDURE *Length(Str* : ARRAY OF CHAR) : CARDINAL;

(* This function procedure returns the number of characters in string
Str, excluding the end-of-string character 0C if it is present. *)

CONST
    EOS = 0C;   (* end-of-string character *)

VAR
    MaxIndex,   (* maximum index in *Str* *)
    i : CARDINAL;   (* index *)

BEGIN
    i := 0;
    MaxIndex := HIGH(*Str*);
    WHILE ($i <= MaxIndex$) AND (*Str*[*i*] # *EOS*) DO
        INC(*i*)
    END (* WHILE *);
    RETURN *i*
END *Length*;

Two strings *Str1* and *Str2* can be concatenated by copying the characters in *Str1* into a third string *Str* and then following these with as many characters in *Str2* as will fit in *Str*. This is the approach used in the following procedure *Concat*:

PROCEDURE *Concat*(*Str1, Str2* : ARRAY OF CHAR;
             VAR *Str* : ARRAY OF CHAR);

(* Returns the string *Str* obtained by concatenating *Str2*
  onto the end of *Str1* *)

CONST
    EOS = 0C;   (* end-of-string mark *)

VAR
    Max1, Max2, Max,   (* maximum indices in *Str1, Str2, Str* *)
    i, j : CARDINAL;   (* indices *)

BEGIN
    Max1 := HIGH(*Str1*);
    Max2 := HIGH(*Str2*);
    Max := HIGH(*Str*);

```
(* Copy Str1 to Str *)
i := 0;
WHILE (i <= Max1) AND (i <= Max) AND
        (Str1[i] # EOS) DO
    Str[i] := Str1[i];
    INC(i)
END (* WHILE *);
```

```
(* Copy as many characters of Str2 into the last positions of Str as
    will fit *)
j := 0;
WHILE (j <= Max2) AND (i <= Max) AND
        (Str2[j] # EOS) DO
    Str[i] := Str2[j];
    INC(j);
    INC(i)
END (* WHILE *);
```

```
(* Add end-of-string mark to Str if there is room *)
IF i <= Max THEN
    Str[i] := EOS
END (* IF *)
END Concat;
```

The position operation determines the *index* of one string *Str1* in another string *Str2*; this index is the starting location of the first occurrence of *Str1* (if any) in *Str2*. As an illustration of a "brute-force" implementation of this operation, suppose we wish to find the index of *Str1* = 'abcabd' in *Str2* = 'abcabcabdabba'. The search for *Str1* in *Str2* begins at position 0 of each. The first five characters match, but a mismatch occurs when the next characters are compared:

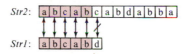

We then backtrack and start the search over again at the character in position 1 of *Str2*:

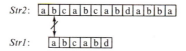

A mismatch occurs immediately, and so we must backtrack again and restart the search with the character in position 2 of *Str2*:

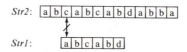

Once again a mismatch occurs, and so we backtrack again and restart at the character in position 3 of *Str2*:

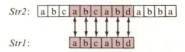

Now the six characters in *Str1* match the corresponding characters in positions 3 through 8 in *Str2*, and thus the index of *Str1* in *Str2* is 3.

The following function procedure implements this brute-force approach:

```
PROCEDURE Position(Str1, Str2 : ARRAY OF CHAR) : CARDINAL;

   (* This function procedure returns the position of the first
      character of the first occurrence of string Str1 within the
      string Str2 or 1 + HIGH(Str2) if Str1 is not found in Str2. *)

   VAR
      Len1,               (* length of Str1 *)
      Len2,               (* length of Str2 *)
      i, j,               (* indices running through Str1, Str2 *)
      Index : CARDINAL;   (* index of Str1 in Str2 *)

   BEGIN
      Len1 := Length(Str1);
      Len2 := Length(Str2);

      (* First take care of special case *)
      IF Len1 > Len2 THEN   (* Str1 longer than Str2 *)
         RETURN 1 + HIGH(Str2)
      END (* IF *);

      (* Otherwise, use brute-force approach to find the index *)
      i := 0;
      j := 0;
      Index := 0;
      WHILE (i < Len1) AND (j < Len2) DO
         IF (Str1[i] = Str2[j]) THEN   (* continue searching *)
            INC(i);
            INC(j)
         ELSE   (* backtrack and start over at next position in Str2 *)
            INC(Index);
            j := Index;
            i := 0
         END (* IF *)
      END (* WHILE *);
      IF (Len1 = 0) OR (i = Len1) THEN (* Str1 found in Str2 *)
         RETURN Index
```

ELSE   (* *Str1* not found in *Str2* *)
            RETURN 1 + HIGH(*Str2*)
        END (* IF *)
    END *Position*;

Similar procedures can be written for the other string operations. They all can be found in Appendix F, which gives a complete listing of the library module *StringsLib* used in this text.

Exercises

1. In some languages, strings are stored in arrays of characters with no special end-of-string symbol to mark the end of the string. If there are fewer characters to be stored than there are array positions, they are stored at the beginning of the array, and any remaining positions are filled with blanks. When such blank padding occurs, it is not possible to distinguish trailing blanks that are part of the string from those used to fill unused array positions. One solution to the problem is simply not to allow trailing blanks in a string.

    (a) Write procedures for the basic string operations in this implementation.
    (b) Write input and output procedures for this implementation.

2. An alternative solution to the problem described in Exercise 1 that allows trailing blanks in strings is to store both the length of the string and the characters that comprise the string. One simple way to do this is to store the characters in array positions 1 and following and to store CHR(*len*) in position 0, where *len* is the length of the string. Redo Exercise 1 using this implementation.

3. The solution to the trailing-blank problem in Exercise 2 imposes an upper limit of 255 on the length of strings, since CHR(*n*) is defined only on the subrange [0..255]. An alternative approach is to use a record with two fields as a storage structure for strings, one field of type CARDINAL to store the length of a string and the other an array to store the characters that make up the string. Redo Exercise 1 using this implementation.

4. Using the string operations provided in the library module *StringsLib* and only the input procedure *Read* from module *InOut*, write a procedure *ReadCard* that reads a string of digits and converts this string to the cardinal number it represents. Be sure that your program checks whether the string is well formed, that is, whether it represents a valid cardinal number.

5. Proceed as in Exercise 4, but write procedure *ReadInt* to read and convert strings representing integers.

6. Proceed as in Exercise 4, but write procedure *ReadReal* to read and convert strings representing real numbers in either decimal or scientific form.

7. A string is said to be a ***palindrome*** if it does not change when the order of characters in the string is reversed. For example,

   MADAM
   45811854
   ABLE WAS I ERE I SAW ELBA

   are palindromes. Write a program to read a string and determine whether it is a palindrome.

8. Write a program that accepts two strings and determines whether one string is an ***anagram*** of the other, that is, whether one string is a permutation of the characters in the other string. For example, *dear* is an anagram of *read*, as is *dare*.

9. The implementation of strings described in the text suffers from wasted space in applications using strings whose lengths vary considerably. An alternative implementation is to establish some ''work space'' array *Storage* of characters to store the characters to be processed, and to represent each string as a record whose fields *Start* and *Length* determine where in *Storage* the string is stored. For example, if *S* is a string variable with $S.Start = 11$ and $S.Length = 8$, the string of characters for *S*, 'JOHN DOE', can be found in positions 11 through $11 + 8 - 1 = 18$ of *Storage*:

   Storage: | F | R | E | D | | S | M | I | T | H | J | O | H | N | | D | O | E | | | | $\cdots$ |

   Assuming this implementation of strings, write procedures to:

   (a) Display the string of characters corresponding to a string variable *S*.
   (b) Implement the length operation.
   (c) Implement the index operation.
   (d) Implement the substring operation.

10. For the string implementation described in Exercise 9, the work space must be managed in some appropriate way. Devise a scheme for doing this, and then write procedures to

    (a) Read a string of characters, store them in *Storage*, and return the appropriate record for a string variable.
    (b) Implement the concatenate operation.

11. Write a program that reads a Modula-2 program and strips all comments from it.

12. Write a program that analyzes text contained in a file by finding the number of nonblank characters, the number of nonblank lines, the

number of words, and the number of sentences, and that calculates the average number of characters per word and the average number of words per sentence.

13. Write a simple *text-formatting* program that reads a text file and produces another text file in which no lines are longer than some given length. Put as many words as possible on the same line. You will have to break some lines of the given file, but do not break any words or put punctuation marks at the beginning of a new line.

14. Extend the text-formatting program of Exercise 13 to right-justify each line in the new text file by adding evenly distributed blanks in lines where necessary. Also, preserve all indentations of lines in the given text file that begin a new paragraph.

15. (Project) Most system text formatters also allow command lines to be placed within the unformatted text. These command lines might have forms like the following:

.P *m n*   Insert *m* blank lines before each paragraph and indent each paragraph *n* spaces.
.W *n*   Width of page (line length) is *n*.
.L *n*   Page length (number of lines per page) is *n*.
.I *n*   Indent all lines following this command line *n* spaces.
.U   Undent all following lines and reset to previous left margin.

Extend the program of Exercises 13 and 14 to implement command lines.

16. (Project) A *pretty-printer* is a special kind of text formatter that reads a text file containing a program and then prints in it a "pretty" format. For example, a pretty-printer for Modula-2 programs might insert blank lines between procedures and indent and align statements within other statements, such as IF statements, type declarations, variable declarations, and the like to produce a format similar to that used in the sample programs of this text. Write a pretty-print program for Modula-2 programs to indent and align statements in a pleasing format.

*3.3 Data Encryption

The basic string operations *length, position, concat, copy, insert,* and *delete* introduced in the preceding section are the operations most useful in text-editing applications. There are, however, some important types of string processing that require other basic operations. In this section we consider one such application, data encryption, and the basic operations of **substitution** and **permutation** that are important in this application.

Encryption refers to the coding of information in order to keep it secret. This encryption is accomplished by transforming the string of characters comprising the information to produce a new string that is a coded form of the information. This is called a **cryptogram** or **ciphertext** and may be safely stored or transmitted. At a later time one can decipher it by reversing the encrypting process to recover the original information, which is called **plaintext**.

Data encryption has been used to send secret messages for military and political reasons from the days of Julius Caesar to the present. Recent applications include the Washington–Moscow hotline, electronic funds transfer, electronic mail, database security, and many other situations in which the transmission of secret data is crucial. Less profound applications have included Captain Midnight secret decoder rings that could be obtained in the 1950s for twenty-five cents and two Ovaltine labels, puzzles appearing in the daily newspaper, and a number of other frivolous applications. In this section we describe some encryption schemes ranging from the Caesar cipher scheme of the first century B.C. to the Data Encryption Standard and the public key encryption schemes of the twentieth century.

The simplest encryption schemes are based on the string operation of **substitution**, in which the plaintext string is traversed and each character is replaced by some other character according to a fixed rule. For example, the **Caesar cipher** scheme consisted of replacing each letter by the letter that appears k positions later in the alphabet for some integer k. (The alphabet is thought of as being arranged in a circle, with A following Z.) In the original Caesar cipher, k was 3, so that each occurrence of A in the plaintext was replaced by D, each B by E, . . . , each Y by B, and each Z by C. For example, using the character set

A B C D E F G H I J K L M N O P Q R S T U V W X Y Z

we would encrypt the string 'IDESOFMARCH' as follows:

Plaintext:	I D E S O F M A R C H
	↓ ↓ ↓ ↓ ↓ ↓ ↓ ↓ ↓ ↓ ↓
Ciphertext:	L G H V R I P D U F K

To decode the message, the receiver uses the same **key** k and recovers the plaintext by applying the inverse transformation, that is, by traversing the ciphertext string and replacing each character by the character k positions earlier in the alphabet. This is obviously not a very secure scheme, since it is possible to "break the code" by simply trying the twenty-six possible values for the key k.

An improved substitution operation can be obtained by the use of a **keyword** to specify several different displacements of letters rather than the single offset k of the Caesar cipher. In this **Vignère cipher** scheme, a repeated keyword is added character by character to the plaintext string, where each character is represented by its position in the character set and addition is carried out mod 26. For example, suppose the character set and positions of characters are given by

Position	0	1	2	3	4	5	6	7	8	9	10	11	12
Character	A	B	C	D	E	F	G	H	I	J	K	L	M

	13	14	15	16	17	18	19	20	21	22	23	24	25
	N	O	P	Q	R	S	T	U	V	W	X	Y	Z

and that the keyword is DAGGER. The plaintext IDESOFMARCH is then encrypted as follows:

```
       Plaintext:   I D E S O F M A R C H
                    ↓ ↓ ↓ ↓ ↓ ↓ ↓ ↓ ↓ ↓ ↓
Repeated keyword:   D A G G E R D A G G E
                    ↓ ↓ ↓ ↓ ↓ ↓ ↓ ↓ ↓ ↓ ↓
      Ciphertext:   L D K Y S W P A X I L
```

Again the receiver must know the key and recovers the plaintext by subtracting the characters in this keyword from those in the ciphertext.

A different substitution operation is obtained by using a *substitution table*, for example:

Original character:	A	B	C	D	E	F	G	H	I	J	K	L	M
Substitute character:	Q	W	E	R	T	Y	U	I	O	P	A	S	D

	N	O	P	Q	R	S	T	U	V	W	X	Y	Z
	F	G	H	J	K	L	Z	X	C	V	B	N	M

The string IDESOFMARCH would then be encoded as follows:

```
 Plaintext:   I D E S O F M A R C H
             ↓ ↓ ↓ ↓ ↓ ↓ ↓ ↓ ↓ ↓ ↓
Ciphertext:   O R T L G Y D Q K E I
```

To decode the ciphertext string, the receiver must again know the key, that is, the substitution table.

Since there are 26! (approximately 10^{28}) possible substitution tables, this scheme is considerably more secure than the simple Caesar cipher scheme. Experienced cryptographers can easily break the code, however, by analyzing frequency counts of certain letters and combinations of letters.

Another basic string operation in some encryption schemes is *permutation*, in which the characters in the plaintext or in blocks of the plaintext are rearranged. For example, we might divide the plaintext string into blocks (substrings) of size 3 and permute the characters in each block as follows:

```
 Original position:   1 2 3
 Permuted position:   3 1 2
```

Thus the message IDESOFMARCH is encrypted (after the addition of a randomly selected character X so the string length is a multiple of the block length) as:

Plaintext: I D E S O F M A R C H X

Ciphertext: D E I O F S A R M H X C

To decode the ciphertext string, the receiver must know the key permutation and uses its inverse:

Original position: 1 2 3
Permuted position: 2 3 1

Data Encryption Standard.   Most modern encryption schemes use both of these techniques, by combining several substitution and permutation operations. Perhaps the best known is the ***Data Encryption Standard (DES)*** developed in the early 1970s by the federal government and the IBM corporation. The scheme is described in *Federal Information Processing Standards Publication 46* (FIPS Pub 46).[1] It is outlined in Figure 3.2, which is a diagram from this government publication.

The input is a bit string of length 64 representing a block of characters in the plaintext string (for example, the concatenation of the ASCII codes of 8 characters), and the output is a 64-bit string which is the ciphertext. The encryption is carried out as a series of permutations and substitutions. The substitution operations used are similar to those in earlier examples; some are obtained by the addition of keywords, and others use a substitution table.

The first operation applied to the 64-bit input string is an initial permutation (*IP*) given by the following table:

IP							
58	50	42	34	26	18	10	2
60	52	44	36	28	20	12	4
62	54	46	38	30	22	14	6
64	56	48	40	32	24	16	8
57	49	41	33	25	17	9	1
59	51	43	35	27	19	11	3
61	53	45	37	29	21	13	5
63	55	47	39	31	23	15	7

For example, the first bit in the permuted result is the 58th bit in the original string, the second bit is the 50th, and so on. This permuted string is then split into two 32-bit substrings: a left substring, denoted by L_0 in the diagram in Figure 3.2, and a right substring, denoted by R_0. A *cipher function* denoted by f uses substitutions and a key K_1 to transform R_0 into a new 32-bit string denoted by $f(R_0,K_1)$. This string is then added to L_0 using bit-by-bit addition modulo 2 (that is, they are combined using the exclusive or operation $\oplus$) to produce the right substring R_1 at the next stage. The original R_0 becomes the left substring L_1.

---

[1] Copies of this publication can be purchased from the National Technical Information Service, U.S. Department of Commerce, 5285 Port Royal Road, Springfield, Virginia 22161.

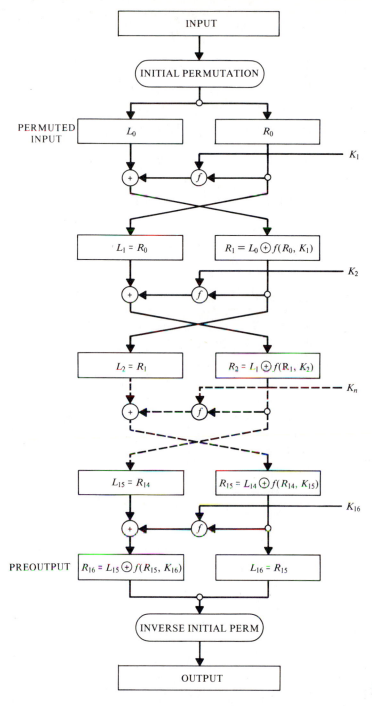

Figure 3.2 DES encryption

This basic sequence of operations is performed sixteen times with sixteen different key strings $K_1, \ldots, K_{16}$, except that no "crossover" is performed at the last stage. These operations produce a 64-bit string $R_{16}L_{16}$ labeled "PREOUTPUT" in the diagram. The inverse of the initial permutation (IP^{-1}) is applied to this preoutput string to yield the final ciphertext.

IP^{-1}							
40	8	48	16	56	24	64	32
39	7	47	15	55	23	63	31
38	6	46	14	54	22	62	30
37	5	45	13	53	21	61	29
36	4	44	12	52	20	60	28
35	3	43	11	51	19	59	27
34	2	42	10	50	18	58	26
33	1	41	9	49	17	57	25

The details of the operation f are shown in Figure 3.3. The right substring denoted by R is first expanded into a 48-bit string using the following bit-selection table E:

E					
32	1	2	3	4	5
4	5	6	7	8	9
8	9	10	11	12	13
12	13	14	15	16	17
16	17	18	19	20	21
20	21	22	23	24	25
24	25	26	27	28	29
28	29	30	31	32	1

Thus the first 6-bit block consists of bits 32, 1, 2, 3, 4, and 5 of R; the second block consists of bits 4, 5, 6, 7, 8, and 9; and so on. A substitution operation

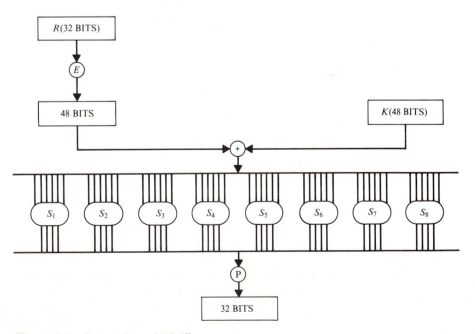

Figure 3.3 Calculation of $f(R,K)$

is then applied to this 48-bit string by combining it with a 48-bit key string K using the exclusive or operation. Another substitution using a different table is then applied to each of the 6-bit blocks to produce 4-bit blocks so that the final result is again a 32-bit string. For example, the substitution table for S_1 is

								S_1								
							Column Number								
Row No.	**0**	**1**	**2**	**3**	**4**	**5**	**6**	**7**	**8**	**9**	**10**	**11**	**12**	**13**	**14**	**15**
0	14	4	13	1	2	15	11	8	3	10	6	12	5	9	0	7
1	0	15	7	4	14	2	13	1	10	6	12	11	9	5	3	8
2	4	1	14	8	13	6	2	11	15	12	9	7	3	10	5	0
3	15	12	8	2	4	9	1	7	5	11	3	14	10	0	6	13

To illustrate how it is used, suppose that the first 6-bit block is 101000. The binary numeral 10 consisting of the first and last bits determines a row in this table, namely, row 2, and the middle four bits 0100 determine a column, namely, column 4. The 4-bit binary representation 1101 of the entry 13 in the second row and the fourth column of this table is the replacement for this 6-bit block. Similar substitution tables $S_2, \ldots, S_8$ are used to transform the other seven 6-bit blocks.

One final permutation P is applied to the resulting 32-bit string to yield $f(R, K)$:

	P		
16	7	20	21
29	12	28	17
1	15	23	26
5	18	31	10
2	8	24	14
32	27	3	9
19	13	30	6
22	11	4	25

The sixteen different keys used in DES are extracted in a carefully prescribed way from a single 64-bit key. Thus the user need supply only one key string to be used for encryption and decryption rather than sixteen different keys. The algorithm for decrypting ciphertext is the same as that for encryption, except that the sixteen keys are applied in reverse order.

DES has been proposed by the National Bureau of Standards as the "standard" encryption scheme. It has been the subject of some controversy, however, because questions have been raised about whether the 48-bit keys used in the substitutions are long enough and the substitution schemes sophisticated enough to provide the necessary security.

Public Key Encryption. Each of the encryption schemes considered thus far requires that both the sender and the receiver know the key or keys used in encrypting the plaintext. This means that although the cryptogram may be transmitted through some public channel such as a telephone line that is not secure, the keys must be transmitted in some secure manner, for example, by a courier. This problem of maintaining secrecy of the key is compounded when it must be shared by several persons.

Recently developed encryption schemes eliminate this problem by using two keys, one for encryption and one for decryption. These schemes are called *public key encryption systems* because the encryption key need not be kept secret. The keys used in these systems have the following properties:

1. For each encryption key there is exactly one corresponding decryption key, and it is distinct from the encryption key.
2. There are many such pairs of keys, and they are relatively easy to compute.
3. It is almost impossible to determine the decryption key if one knows only the encryption key.
4. The encryption key is made public by the receiver to all those who will transmit messages to him or her, but only the receiver knows the decryption key.

In 1978, Rivest, Shamir, and Adelman, proposed one method of implementing a public key encryption scheme.[2] The public key is a pair (e,n) of integers, and one encrypts a message string M by first dividing M into blocks $M_1, M_2, \ldots, M_k$ and converting each block of characters to an integer in the range 0 through $n - 1$ (for example, by concatenating the ASCII codes of the characters). M is then encrypted by raising each block to the power e and reducing modulo n:

$$\text{Plaintext:} \quad M = M_1 M_2 \cdots M_k$$
$$\text{Ciphertext:} \quad C = C_1 C_2 \cdots C_k, \; C_i = M_i^e \text{ MOD } n$$

The ciphertext C is decrypted by raising each block C_i to the power d and reducing modulo n, where d is a secret decryption key. Clearly, to recover the plaintext, we need

$$M_i = C_i^d \text{ MOD } n = (M_i^e)^d \text{ MOD } n = M_i^{e \cdot d} \text{ MOD } n$$

for each block M_i. Thus e and d must be chosen so that

$$x^{e \cdot d} \text{ MOD } n = x$$

for each nonnegative integer x.

The following algorithms summarize this Rivest–Shamir–Adelman (RSA) public key encryption system:

RSA ENCRYPTION ALGORITHM

($*$ To encrypt plaintext M using public encrypting code (e, n) $*$)

1. Pad M with some randomly selected character if necessary so that length(M) is a multiple of *BlockLength*.

----

[2]R. L. Rivest, A. Shamir, and L. Adleman (1978). A Method for Obtaining Digital Signatures and Public-Key Cryptosystems, *Communications of the ACM* 21:2 (February), 120–126.

2. Calculate *NumberOfBlocks* = *length(M)* / *BlockLength*.
3. Initialize index *j* to 1.
4. For *i* = 1 to *NumberOfBlocks* do the following:
   a. Extract the substring M_i from *M* consisting of the *BlockLength* characters beginning at position *j*.
   b. Convert M_i to numeric form to give C_i.
   c. Calculate $C_i = C_i^e$ MOD *n*.
   d. Increment *j* by *BlockLength*.

RSA DECRYPTION ALGORITHM

(* To decrypt the ciphertext consisting of numeric blocks C_i, *i* = 1, . . . , *NumberOfBlocks*, using secret decryption key *d* *)

1. Initialize *M* to the empty string.
2. For *i* = 1 to *NumberOfBlocks* do the following:
   a. Calculate $C_i = C_i^d$ MOD *n*.
   b. Convert C_i to a string of characters M_i.
   c. Concatenate M_i onto *M*.

To illustrate, suppose that (17, 2773) is the public encrypting code and that characters are converted to numeric values using the following table:

Character:	A	B	C	D	E	F	G	H	I	J	K	L	M
Code:	00	01	02	03	04	05	06	07	08	09	10	11	12
Character:	N	O	P	Q	R	S	T	U	V	W	X	Y	Z
Code:	13	14	15	16	17	18	19	20	21	22	23	24	25

To encrypt a string such as *M* = 'IDESOFMARCH' using the RSA algorithm, we divide *M* into two-character blocks (after appending the randomly selected character X) and represent each block as an integer in the range 0 through 2773 − 1 = 2772 by concatenating the numeric codes of the characters that comprise the block:

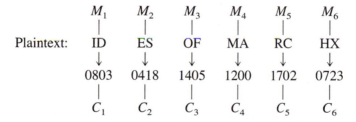

	M_1	M_2	M_3	M_4	M_5	M_6
Plaintext:	ID	ES	OF	MA	RC	HX
	↓	↓	↓	↓	↓	↓
	0803	0418	1405	1200	1702	0723
	C_1	C_2	C_3	C_4	C_5	C_6

Each of these blocks is then raised to the seventeenth power and reduced mod 2773:

Ciphertext:	0779	1983	2641	1444	0052	1400
	C_1	C_2	C_3	C_4	C_5	C_6

For this encryption key, the corresponding decrypting key is $d = 157$. Thus, we decrypt the ciphertext by calculating C_i^{157} MOD 2773 for each block C_i. For the preceding ciphertext this gives

Decrypted ciphertext: 0803 0418 1405 1200 1702 0723

which is the numeric form of the original message.

Two points in the preceding discussion of the RSA encryption scheme require further discussion: (1) How are n, e, and d chosen? (2) How can the exponentiation be performed efficiently?

The number n is the product of two large "random" primes p and q,

$$n = p \cdot q$$

In the preceding example, we used the small primes 47 and 59 to simplify the computations, but Rivest, Shamir, and Adelman suggest that p and q have at least 100 digits. The decrypting key d is then selected to be some large random integer that is relatively prime to both $p - 1$ and $q - 1$, that is, one that has no factors in common with either number. In our example, $d = 157$ has this property. The number e is then selected to have the property that

$$e \cdot d \text{ MOD } ((p - 1) \cdot (q - 1)) \text{ is equal to } 1$$

A result from number theory then guarantees that e and d will have the required property described earlier, namely, that

$$M_i^{e \cdot d} \text{ MOD } n = M_i$$

for each message block M_i.

We can efficiently carry out the exponentiations required in encryption and decryption by repeatedly squaring and multiplying, as follows:

EXPONENTIATION ALGORITHM

(* Algorithm to calculate $y = x^k$ MOD n *)

1. Find the base-two representation $b_t \cdots b_1 b_0$ of the exponent k.
2. Initialize y to 1.
3. For $i = t$ down to 0 do the following:
   a. Set $y = y^2$ MOD n.
   b. If $b_i = 1$ then
        set $y = (y * x)$ MOD n.

Recall that the encrypting key (e, n) is a public key, so that no attempt is made to keep it secret; the decrypting key d is a private key, however, and must be kept secret. To break this code, one would need to be able to determine the value of d from the values of n and e. By the manner in which d and e are selected, this is possible if n can be factored into a product of primes. The security of the RSA encryption scheme is based on the difficulty of determining the prime factors of a large integer. Even with the best factorization algorithms known today, this is a prohibitively time-consuming task. Thus, the public key encryption scheme appears to be quite secure. Although research on factorization algorithms continues, no efficient algorithms have yet been found.

Exercises

1. A pure permutation encryption scheme is very insecure. Explain why by describing how an encrypting scheme that merely permutes the bits in an n-bit string can easily be cracked by studying how certain basic bit strings are encrypted; illustrate for $n = 4$.

2. Consider a simplified DES scheme that encrypts messages using the DES approach pictured in Figure 3.2 but with only two keys K_1 and K_2 instead of sixteen keys $K_1, \ldots, K_{16}$ and, in the calculation of $f(R,K)$ pictured in Figure 3.3, uses the same substitution table S_1 for each of the 6-bit blocks instead of eight different tables $S_1, \ldots, S_8$. Encrypt the string 'AARDVARK' using this simplified DES scheme with keys $K_1 =$ 'ABCDEF' and $K_2 =$ 'SECRET' and assuming that strings are converted into bit strings by replacing each character by its binary ASCII code.

3. Using the character codes $00, 01, \ldots, 25$ given in the text:

   (a) Find the RSA ciphertext produced by the key $(e,n) = (5, 2881)$ for the plaintext 'PUBLIC'.
   (b) Verify that $d = 1109$ is a decrypting key for the RSA scheme in (a).

4. If the RSA ciphertext produced by a key $(e,n) = (13, 2537)$ is 0095 and the character codes $00, 01, \ldots, 25$ given in the text are used, find the plaintext.

5. A public key encryption scheme can be used to provide positive identification of the sender of a message by incorporating a *digital signature* in it. To illustrate, suppose that Al wishes to send a message M to Bob. Al first "signs" M by encrypting it, using his secret decrypting key; we might indicate this by:

$$S = D_{A1}(M)$$

He then encrypts S using Bob's public encryption key and sends the result C to Bob:

$$C = E_{Bob}(S)$$

Bob first decrypts the ciphertext C with his secret decrypting key to obtain the signature S,

$$D_{Bob}(C) = D_{Bob}(E_{Bob}(S)) = S$$

and then extracts the message M by using Al's public encryption key:

$$E_{A1}(S) = E_{A1}(D_{A1}(M)) = M$$

The pair (M, S) possessed by Bob is similar to a paper document signed by Al, since only Al could have created S. For the message $M = $ "HI" and using the character codes $00, 01, \ldots, 25$ given in the text, find C if Al and Bob have published RSA encryption keys (3, 1081) and (1243, 1829), respectively.

6. Write a program to implement the Caesar cipher scheme.

7. Write a program to implement the Vignère cipher scheme.

8. Write a program to encrypt/decrypt a message by using a substitution table.

9. Write a program to encrypt/decrypt a message by using a permutation scheme.

10. Write a program to encrypt/decrypt messages using the simplified DES scheme described in Exercise 2.

11. Write a procedure to implement the algorithm given in the text for calculating $y = x^k$ MOD n by repeated squaring and multiplication.

12. Use the procedure of Exercise 11 in a program that implements the RSA scheme (with integer values in the range allowed by your version of Modula-2).

13. A simple ''probabilistic'' algorithm for testing whether a number is prime that is similar to that recommended for finding the large primes needed in the RSA scheme is based on the following result due to the mathematician Fermat: If n is a prime, then x^{n-1} MOD $n = 1$ for all positive integers x less than n. Thus, to test whether a given number n is prime, one might proceed as follows: Randomly select a positive integer $x < n$ and compute $y = x^{n-1}$ MOD n. If $y \neq 1$, n is not prime; but if $y = 1$, n *may be prime*, and further testing is required, so we repeat the test with another value of x. If $y = 1$ for many different values of x, n is *probably* prime. Write a program that implements this method of testing primality.

*3.4 Pattern Matching

In Section 3.2 we presented algorithms for some of the basic string operations, but as we noted, the brute-force algorithm for the position operation, which finds the index of one string in another, is not the best possible. Because the index operation is a special case of the more general pattern-matching problem that occurs in many applications, such as text editing and text processing, a good deal of work has gone into designing more efficient algorithms. In this section we describe one such algorithm, called the *Knuth–Morris–Pratt algorithm*.

To review the brute-force method and to discover how it can be improved, consider again the example of finding the first occurrence of the pattern ′abcabd′ in the line of text ′abcabcabdabba′:

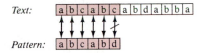

We begin matching characters in *Pattern* with those in *Text* and find that the first five characters match but that the next characters do not:

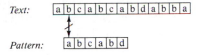

When such a mismatch occurs, we must backtrack to the beginning of *Pattern*, shift one position to the right in *Text*, and start the search over again:

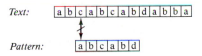

This time a mismatch occurs immediately, and so we backtrack once more to the beginning of *Pattern*, shift another position to the right in *Text*, and try again:

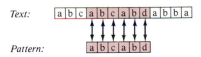

Another mismatch of the first characters occurs, so we backtrack and shift once again:

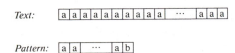

On the next search, all of the characters in *Pattern* match the corresponding characters in *Text*, and the pattern has thus been located in the line of text.

In this example, only three backtracks were required, and two of these required backing up only one character. The situation may be much worse, however. To illustrate, suppose that the text to be searched consists of 100 characters, each of which is the same, and the pattern consists of 49 of these same characters followed by a different character, for example,

Text: a a a a a a a a a   ⋯   a a a

Pattern: a a   ⋯   a b

In beginning our search for *Pattern* in *Text*, we find that the first 49 characters match but that the last character in *Pattern* does not match the corresponding character in *Text*:

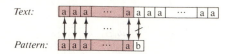

We must therefore backtrack to the beginning of *Pattern*, shift one position to the right in *Text*, and restart the search. As before, 49 successful comparisons of characters in *Pattern* with characters in *Text* are made before a mismatch occurs:

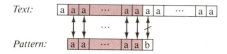

This same phenomenon happens again and again until eventually we reach the end of *Text* and are able to determine that *Pattern* is not found in *Text*. After each unsuccessful scan, we must backtrack from the last character of *Pattern* way back to the first character and restart the search one position to the right in *Text*.

The source of inefficiency in this algorithm is the backtracking required whenever a mismatch occurs. To illustrate how it can be avoided, consider again the first example in which *Pattern* = 'abcabd' and *Text* = 'abcabcab-dabba':

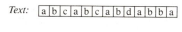

In the first scan, we find that *Pattern*[0] = *Text*[0], *Pattern*[1], = *Text*[1], *Pattern*[2] = *Text*[2], *Pattern*[3] = *Text*[3], *Pattern*[4] = *Text*[4], but *Pattern*[5] ≠ *Text*[5]:

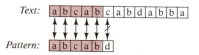

Examining *Pattern*, we see that *Pattern*[0] ≠ *Pattern*[1]; thus *Pattern*[0] cannot possibly match *Text*[1] because *Pattern*[1] did. Similarly, because *Pattern*[0] is different from *Pattern*[2], which matched *Text*[2], neither can *Pattern*[0] match *Text*[2]. Consequently, we can "slide" *Pattern* three positions to the right immediately, eliminating the backtracks to positions 2 and 3 in *Text*. Moreover, examining the part of *Pattern* that has matched a substring of *Text*,

$$a \; b \; c \; a \; b$$

we see that we need not check *Pattern*[0] and *Pattern*[1] again, since they are the same as *Pattern*[3] and *Pattern*[4], respectively, which already matched characters in *Text*:

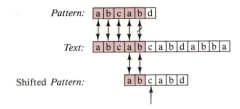

This partial match means that we can continue our search at position 5 in *Text* and position 2 in *Pattern*; no backtracking to examine characters before that in the position where a mismatch occurred is necessary at all!

Now consider the general problem of finding the index of a pattern $p_0 p_1 \cdots p_m$ in a text $t_0 t_1 \cdots t_n$, and suppose that these strings are stored in the arrays *Pattern* and *Text* so that $Pattern[i] = p_i$ and $Text[j] = t_j$. Also suppose that in attempting to locate *Pattern* in *Text* we have come to a point where the first i characters in *Pattern* match characters in *Text* but a mismatch occurs when $Pattern[i]$ is compared with $Text[j]$:

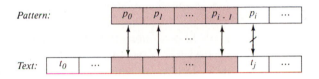

To avoid backtracking, we must shift *Pattern* to the right so that the search can continue with $Text[j]$ and $Pattern[k]$, for some $k < i$:

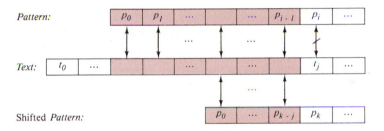

It is clear from this diagram that in order to do this, the first k characters of *Pattern* must be identical to the k characters that precede $Pattern[i]$ and that $Pattern[k]$ must be different from $Pattern[i]$ so that $Pattern[k]$ has a chance of matching $Text[j]$:

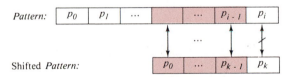

Let us denote this value k by $Next[i]$. Thus, as we have just observed, $Next[i]$ is the position in *Pattern* at which the search can continue by comparing $Pattern[Next[i]]$ with the character $Text[j]$ that did not match $Pattern[i]$; that is, we slide *Pattern* to the right to align $Pattern[Next[i]]$ with $Text[j]$ and continue searching at this point. If no such k exists, we take $Next[i] = -1$ to indicate that the search is to resume with $Pattern[0]$ and $Text[j + 1]$. (In this case, we can think of sliding $Pattern$ to the right to align the nonexistent character in position -1 with $Text[j]$ and resume the search.)

KNUTH–MORRIS–PRATT PATTERN-MATCHING ALGORITHM

(* Algorithm to determine the index of a pattern in a piece of text. The pattern is stored in positions 0 through m of the array $Pattern$, and the text is stored in positions 0 through n of the array $Text$. *)

1. Initialize each of $Index$, i, and j to 0.
   (* $Index$ is the beginning position of the substring of $Text$ being compared with $Pattern$, and indices i and j run through $Pattern$ and $Text$, respectively. *)
2. While $i \leq m$ and $j \leq n$ do the following:
   If $Pattern[i] = Text[j]$ then   (* match *)
      Increment each of i and j by 1.
   Else do the following: (* mismatch *)
      a. (* Slide $Pattern$ to the right the appropriate distance *)
         Add $i - Next[i]$ to $Index$.
      b. (* Determine where the search is to continue *)
         If $Next[i] \neq -1$ then
            Set i equal to $Next[i]$.
         Else
            Set i equal to 0 and increment j by 1.
3. If $i > m$ then $Index$ is the index of $Pattern$ in $Text$; otherwise, $Pattern$ does not appear in $Text$.

To illustrate, consider the following pattern:

$Pattern$ = a b c a a b a b c

and assume that we are given the following table of $Next$ values for this pattern:

i	0	1	2	3	4	5	6	7	8
$Pattern[i]$	a	b	c	a	a	b	a	b	c
$Next[i]$	-1	0	0	-1	1	0	2	0	0

Now suppose that we wish to determine the index of $Pattern$ in

$Text$ = aabcbabcaabcaababcba

Initially, $Index$, i, and j are 0. Both $Text[0]$ and $Pattern[0]$ are 'a', and so both i and j are incremented to 1. A mismatch now occurs;

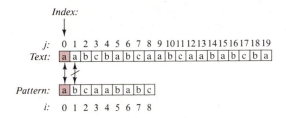

Since *Next*[1] = 0, *Index* is set to *Index* + (1 − *Next*[1]) = *Index* + (1 − 0) = 1; *i* is set to *Next*[1] = 0; *j* retains the value 1; and the search continues by comparing *Pattern*[*Next*[1]] = *Pattern*[0] with *Text*[1]. The next mismatch occurs when *i* = 3 and *j* = 4:

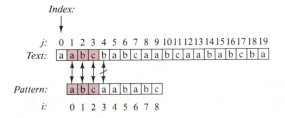

Since *Next*[3] = −1, *Index* is set to *Index* + (3 − (−1)) = 5; *i* is set to 0; and *j* is incremented to 5. The search then resumes by comparing *Pattern*[0] with *Text*[5] and continues until the next mismatch, when *j* = 11 and *i* = 6:

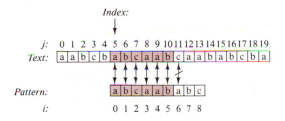

Next[6] = 2, and so *Index* is updated to *Index* + (6 − 2) = 9; *i* is set equal to *Next*[6] = 2; *j* remains at 11; and the search resumes by comparing *Pattern*[2] with *Text*[11]. This search locates a substring of *Text* that matches *Pattern*:

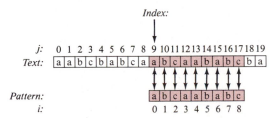

and so the algorithm terminates with *Index* = 9 as the index of *Pattern* in *Text*.

To complete our discussion of the Knuth–Morris–Pratt algorithm, we must describe how the table of *Next* values is computed. Recall that *Next*[*i*] is the length *k* of the longest prefix *Pattern*[0], *Pattern*[1], . . . , *Pattern*[*k* − 1] of

Pattern that matches the *k* characters preceding *Pattern[i]* but *Pattern[k]* ≠ *Pattern[i]*. For example, consider again the pattern 'abcaababc':

i	0	1	2	3	4	5	6	7	8
Pattern[i]	a	b	c	a	a	b	a	b	c

Next[6] = 2, since the characters a and b in positions 0 and 1 match those in positions 4 and 5, and *Pattern*[2] = c is different from *Pattern*[6] = a. The following diagram shows this matching prefix and suffix in abcaaba but that the characters that follow these in positions 2 and 6 do not match:

This property of *Pattern* quarantees that if a mismatch occurs when comparing some character in *Text* with *Pattern*[6], the search can continue by comparing *Pattern[Next*[6]] = *Pattern*[2] with this character:

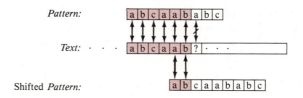

The determination that *Next*[4] = 1 is similar to that for *Next*[6]; the following diagram diaplays the matching prefix and suffix in abca and the fact that *Pattern*[1] ≠ *Pattern*[4]:

The calculation of *Next*[5] requires a bit more care. In looking for a matching prefix and suffix in abcaa, we find one of length 1; that is, *Pattern*[0] = *Pattern*[4]; however, the characters that follow these matching substrings, *Pattern*[1] and *Pattern*[5], are not different. Thus *Next*[5] is not 1. Since an empty prefix always matches an empty suffix, and since *Pattern*[0] = a differs from *Pattern*[5] = b, we obtain *Next*[6] = 0:

By similar analyses, the remaining values of the *Next* table can be verified.

An algorithm for calculating *Next* values using this method is essentially the same as the pattern-matching algorithm, except that the pattern is matched against itself. To see this, consider again a general pattern $p_0 p_1 \cdots p_m$. Clearly, *Next*[0] must have the value -1, since there are no characters that precede *Pattern*[0]. Now, if *Next*[0], . . . , *Next*[$j - 1$] have been determined, these values can be used to calculate *Next*[j], as follows: We "slide" a copy of *Pattern* across itself until we find a prefix (possibly empty) that matches the characters preceding *Pattern*[j]:

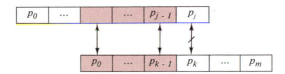

If this prefix has length k (possibly 0) and *Pattern*[k] $\neq$ *Pattern*[j], then *Next*[j] $= k$ by definition. However, if *Pattern*[k] $=$ *Pattern*[j], then clearly *Next*[j] has the same value as *Next*[k], which has already been calculated. This method of calculating *Next* values is used in the following algorithm:

ALGORITHM FOR NEXT TABLE

($*$ Algorithm to compute *Next* values for a pattern stored in positions 0 through m of the array *Pattern*. $*$)

1. Initialize *Next*[0] to -1, k to -1, and j to 0.
2. While $j < m$ do the following:
   a. While ($k \neq -1$) and *Pattern*[k] $\neq$ *Pattern*[j]
        Set k equal to *Next*[k].
   b. Increment k and j by 1.
   c. If *Pattern*[j] $=$ *Pattern*[k] then
        Set *Next*[j] equal to *Next*[k].
      Else
        Set *Next*[j] equal to k.

To illustrate, consider the pattern used earlier:

$$Pattern = \text{abcaababc}$$

The following table traces the execution of this algorithm as it calculates the *Next* table for this pattern:

Instruction	k	j	Next Value Computed
Initially	−1	0	Next[0] = −1
2a	−1	0	
2b	0	1	
2c	0	1	Next[1] = 0
2a	Next[0] = −1	1	
2b	0	2	
2c	0	2	Next[2] = 0
2a	Next[0] = −1	2	
2b	0	3	
2c	0	3	Next[3] = Next[0] = −1
2a	0	3	
2b	1	4	
2c	1	4	Next[4] = 1
2a	Next[1] = 0	4	
	0	4	
2b	1	5	
2c	1	5	Next[5] = Next[1] = 0
2a	1	5	
2b	2	6	
2c	2	6	Next[6] = 2
2a	Next[2] = 0	6	
	0	6	
2b	1	7	
2c	1	7	Next[7] = Next[1] = 0
2a	1	7	
2b	2	8	
2c	2	8	Next[8] = Next[2] = 0

The Knuth–Morris–Pratt solution to the pattern-matching problem has an interesting history. A theorem proved by S. A. Cook in 1970 states that any problem that can be solved using an abstract model of a computer called a *pushdown automation* can be solved in time proportional to the size of the problem using an actual computer (more precisely, using a random access machine). In particular, this theorem implies the existence of an algorithm for solving the pattern-matching problem in time proportional to $m + n$, where m and n are the maximum indices in arrays that store the pattern and text, respectively. Donald Knuth and Vaughn R. Pratt painstakingly reconstructed the proof of Cook's theorem and so constructed the pattern-matching algorithm described in this section. At approximately the same time, James H. Morris, Jr. constructed essentially the same algorithm while considering the practical problem of designing a text editor. Thus we see that not all algorithms are discovered by a "flash of insight" and that theoretical computer science does indeed sometimes lead to practical applications.

Exercises

1. Compute *Next* tables for the following patterns:

(a) A B R A C A D A B R A   (b) A A A A A
(c) M I S S I S S I P P I   (d) I S S I S S I P P I
(e) B A B B A B A B   (f) 1 0 1 0 0 1 1
(g) 1 0 0 1 0 1 1 1   (h) 1 0 0 1 0 0 1 0 0 1

2. Construct tables tracing the action of the *Next* table algorithm for the patterns in Exercise 1.

3. Write a program to implement a CHANGE editor command that is used in the form

    CHANGE(*string1, string2, string3*)

to replace the first occurrence (if there is one) of *string2* in *string1* by *string3*. Use the Knuth–Morris–Pratt method to determine the index of *string2* in *string1*.

4. Write a program that generates a random bit string *Text* of some specified length, say 1000, and a shorter random bit string *Pattern* of length 10 or so and that then uses the Knuth–Morris–Pratt method to locate all occurrences of *Pattern* in *Text*. (See Section 0.7 if your version of Modula-2 does not provide a random number generator.)

5. Many versions of Modula-2 provide some procedure that returns the elapsed CPU time since execution of the program began. If we use it to determine a value *Time1* before some procedure *P* is referenced and then use it again to determine a value for *Time2* after execution of *P* is complete, then *Time2* − *Time1* measures the execution time of *P*. If such a timing procedure is available in your version of Modula-2, use it in a program that implements the index operation, first using the brute-force approach and then using the Knuth–Morris–Pratt scheme and compare the computing times of these two implementations. You might generate test strings *Text* and *Pat* randomly as described in Exercise 4.

4

Stacks

In the preceding chapter we considered the string data type and its implementation using an array to store the characters that comprise the string. There are several other simple but important data structures that can be implemented using arrays as the basic storage structure. In this chapter we consider one such data structure, the stack, and some of its applications. This structure is often implemented using an array because most programming languages provide a predefined array data type, and such an implementation is therefore quite easy. In this chapter we also discuss the strengths and weaknesses of such an array-based implementation.

4.1 Introduction

Data items are stored in computer memory using a binary representation. In particular, cardinal numbers are commonly stored using the base-two representation described in Section 2.2. This means that the base-ten representation of a cardinal number that appears in a program statement or in a data file must be converted to a base-two representation. One algorithm for carrying out this conversion uses repeated division by 2, with the successive remainders giving the binary digits in the base-two representation from right to left. For example, the base-two representation of 26 is 11010, as the following computation shows:

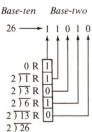

Note that the bits that comprise the base-two representation of 26 have been generated in reverse order, from right to left. Thus, in order for this base-two representation to be displayed in the usual left-to-right sequence, these bits must be displayed in a "last-generated–first-displayed" order. This means that the bits must be retrieved from the "stack" of remainders in the diagram in a "last-in–first-out" order.

Thus an algorithm to carry out this conversion from base-ten to base-two and to display the result is

BASE-CONVERSION ALGORITHM

(* Algorithm to convert the base-ten representation of a positive integer *Number* to base two and display the base-two representation *)

1. While *Number* ≠ 0 do the following:
   a. Calculate the *Remainder* that results when *Number* is divided by 2.
   b. Put *Remainder* on the top of the stack of remainders.
   c. Replace *Number* by the integer quotient of *Number* divided by 2.
2. While the stack of remainders is not empty do the following:
   a. Remove the *Remainder* from the top of the stack of remainders.
   b. Display *Remainder*.

The following diagram traces this algorithm for the integer 26:

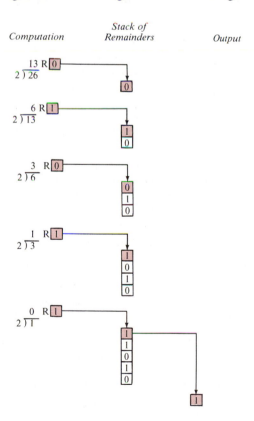

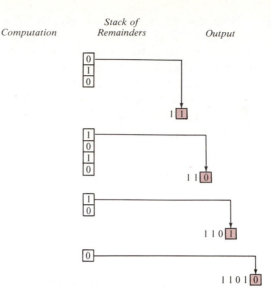

This type of last-in–first-out processing occurs in a wide variety of applications; consequently, an abstract data type that embodies this idea is a very useful one. This **Last-In–First-Out (LIFO)** structure is called a **stack**. It consists of a list or sequence of data items in which all insertions and deletions are made at one end, called the **top** of the stack. More precisely, the basic operations for a stack include

1. *CreateStack*:   Creates an empty stack.
2. *EmptyStack*:   Determines if a stack is empty.
3. *Pop*:   Retrieves and removes the item at the top of the stack.
4. *Push*:   Inserts a new element at the top of the stack.

The reason for the terminology used to describe this data structure should be obvious: The structure functions in the same manner as does an ordinary stack of objects such as a spring-loaded stack of plates or trays used in a cafeteria. One adds plates to the stack by *pushing* them onto the *top* of the stack. When a plate is removed from the top of the stack, the spring causes the next plate to *pop* up.

If we assume that a data type *StackType* is provided together with procedures *CreateStack*, *Pop,* and *Push* referenced with statements of the form

      CreateStack(*Stack*);   (∗ creates an empty stack ∗)
      Pop(*Stack, Item*);   (∗ pops *Item* from *Stack*, assuming the stack is
                                                  nonempty ∗)
      Push(*Stack, Item*);   (∗ pushes *Item* onto *Stack* ∗)

and a boolean-valued function procedure referenced by

      EmptyStack(*Stack*);   (∗ determines if *Stack* is empty ∗)

to implement the basic stack operations, then a program segment to implement the base-conversion algorithm is easy to write:

CreateStack(StackOfRemainders);
WHILE *Number* # 0 DO
    Remainder := *Number* MOD 2;
    Push(StackOfRemainders, Remainder);
    Number := *Number* DIV 2
END (* WHILE *);
WriteLn;
WriteString('Base-two representation is ');
WHILE NOT *EmptyStack(StackOfRemainders)* DO
    Pop(StackOfRemainders, Remainder);
    WriteCard(Remainder, 1)
END (* WHILE *);
WriteLn;

Once again we have an illustration of one of the benefits of data abstraction, that is, of separating the definition of a data structure at a logical or abstract level from its actual physical implementation. Regarding a stack as an abstract data type allows us to use it in a solution of the base-conversion problem without being distracted by implementation details. In the next section we consider how arrays and records can be used to implement stacks, and in Chapter 8 we consider a linked implementation.

4.2 Implementing Stacks with Arrays and Records; the Module *StacksLib*

The first step in implementing a stack data type is to select a storage structure to store the stack elements. Because a stack is a sequence of data items, we might use an array to store these items, with each stack element occupying one position in the array and position 1 serving as the top of the stack. For example, in the base-two conversion problem of the preceding section, if the first three remainders 0, 1, and 0 have already been pushed onto the stack, the stack would be pictured as follows:

```
Stack[1]  ---  | 0 |
Stack[2]  ---  | 1 |
Stack[3]  ---  | 0 |
Stack[4]  ---  | ? |
               | . |
               | . |
               | . |
Stack[MaxSize] ---  | ? |
```

Pushing the next remainder 1 onto the stack, however, would require shifting the array elements in positions 1, 2, and 3 to positions 2, 3, and 4, respectively, so that 1 can be stored in the first position:

```
Stack[1]  ---  | 1 |
Stack[2]  ---  | 0 |
Stack[3]  ---  | 1 |
Stack[4]  ---  | 0 |
               | . |
               | . |
               | . |
Stack[MaxSize] ---  | ? |
```

Similarly, when an item is popped from the stack, all the array elements must be shifted up by one so that the top item is in position 1.

The shifting of array elements in this implementation is time-consuming and unnecessary and can be avoided very simply. We need only "flip the stack over" and let it grow from position 1 toward position *MaxSize*, and use a variable *Top*, which is the index of the current top of the stack, pushing and popping at this location:

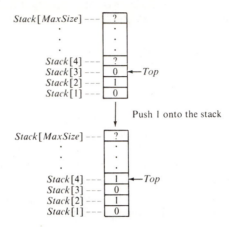

In this implementation, the storage structure for a stack consists of an array that stores the stack elements and a variable *Top* that stores the position of the top element in this array. This structure suggests using a record for storage:

CONST
    MaxSize = . . . ; (* maximum size of the stack *)

TYPE
    ElementType = . . . ; (* type of elements in the stack *)
    StackArray = ARRAY [1..*MaxSize*] OF *ElementType*;
    StackType = RECORD
                        Top : [0..*MaxSize*];
                        Element : *StackArray*
                  END;

VAR
    Stack : *StackType*;

To complete this implementation of a stack, procedures must be written to perform the basic stack operations. The operation of creating an empty stack consists simply of setting *Stack.Top* to 0, and a stack will be empty when the boolean expression *Stack.Top* = 0 is true.

An algorithm for the pop operation is

Pop

(* Algorithm to pop *Item* from the top of *Stack*. *)

If the stack is empty then
    Display a stack-empty message and terminate execution.

Otherwise do the following:
  a. Set *Item* equal to the element *Stack.Element*[*Stack.Top*] at
     the top of the stack
  b. Decrement *Stack.Top* by 1.

And an algorithm for the push operation is

Push

(∗ Algorithm to push *Item* onto the *Stack*. ∗)

If *Stack.Top* is equal to the array limit, then
    Display a stack-full message and terminate execution.
Otherwise do the following:
  a. Increment *Stack.Top* by 1.
  b. Set the element *Stack.Element*[*Stack.Top*] equal to *Item*.

It is important to note that the possibility of a stack-empty condition is inherent in the definition of a stack and does not arise because of the way in which the stack is implemented. However, a stack-full condition is not inherent in this data structure, as there is theoretically no limit on the number of elements that a stack may have. Any implementation of a stack that uses an array to store the stack elements is thus not a completely faithful representation, because an array has a fixed size, which places an upper limit on the size of the stack. This implementation requires, therefore, that the push algorithm include a check to determine if the stack is full before an attempt is made to push an element onto it. In Chapter 8 we consider an alternative implementation using linked lists in which no a priori size limit is imposed and that thus implements stacks more faithfully.

Since stacks are useful in solving many different problems, it would be convenient to have this abstract data type encapsulated in a library module so that it can be used in a variety of programs. The definition part of such a library module for processing stacks of cardinal numbers might be

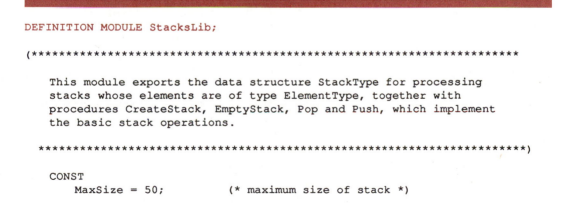

```
DEFINITION MODULE StacksLib;

(**********************************************************************

    This module exports the data structure StackType for processing
    stacks whose elements are of type ElementType, together with
    procedures CreateStack, EmptyStack, Pop and Push, which implement
    the basic stack operations.

**********************************************************************)

    CONST
        MaxSize = 50;           (* maximum size of stack *)
```

(cont.)

```
TYPE
    ElementType = ...;
    StackArray = ARRAY [1..MaxSize] OF ElementType;
    StackType = RECORD
                    Top : [0..MaxSize];
                    Element : StackArray
                END;

PROCEDURE CreateStack(VAR Stack : StackType );

    (****************************************************

            Procedure to create an empty stack

     ***************************************************)

PROCEDURE EmptyStack(Stack : StackType) : BOOLEAN;

    (****************************************************

        Returns TRUE if Stack is empty, FALSE otherwise

     ***************************************************)

PROCEDURE Pop(VAR Stack :StackType; VAR Item : ElementType);

    (****************************************************

        Procedure to pop Item from the top of Stack.
        Execution is terminated if an attempt is made
        to pop from an empty stack.

     ***************************************************)

PROCEDURE Push(VAR Stack : StackType; Item : ElementType);

    (****************************************************

        Procedure to push Item onto Stack.  Execution is
        terminated if an attempt is made to push an item
        onto a full stack.

     ***************************************************)

END StacksLib.
```

The corresponding implementation module might be the following:

```
IMPLEMENTATION MODULE StacksLib;

(***********************************************************************

    This module exports the data structure StackType for processing
    stacks whose elements are of type ElementType, together with
    procedures CreateStack, EmptyStack, Pop and Push, which implement
    the basic stack operations.

 ***********************************************************************)

    FROM InOut IMPORT WriteString, WriteLn;

    PROCEDURE CreateStack(VAR Stack : StackType );

        (****************************************************

                Procedure to create an empty stack

         ****************************************************)

    BEGIN
        Stack.Top := 0
    END CreateStack;

    PROCEDURE EmptyStack(Stack : StackType) : BOOLEAN;

        (****************************************************

            Returns TRUE if Stack is empty, FALSE otherwise

         ****************************************************)

    BEGIN
        RETURN Stack.Top = 0
    END EmptyStack;

    PROCEDURE Pop(VAR Stack :StackType; VAR Item : ElementType);

        (****************************************************

            Procedure to pop Item from the top of Stack.
            Execution is terminated if an attempt is made
            to pop from an empty stack.

         ****************************************************)
```

(cont.)

```
    BEGIN
        IF EmptyStack(Stack) THEN
            WriteString('*** Attempt to pop from an empty stack ***');
            WriteLn;
            HALT
        ELSE
            WITH Stack DO
                Item := Element[Top];
                DEC(Top)
            END (* WITH *)
        END (* IF *)
    END Pop;

    PROCEDURE Push(VAR Stack : StackType; Item : ElementType);

        (********************************************************

        Procedure to push Item onto Stack.  Execution is
        terminated if an attempt is made to push an item
        onto a full stack.

        ********************************************************)

    BEGIN
        IF Stack.Top = MaxSize THEN
            WriteString('*** Attempt to push onto a full stack ***');
            WriteLn;
            HALT
        ELSE
            WITH Stack DO
                INC(Top);
                Element[Top] := Item
            END (* WITH *)
        END (* IF *)
    END Push;

END StacksLib.
```

Note that in this library module, a message is displayed and execution is terminated if a stack error occurs. An alternative approach is to export a boolean variable *StackError*, which is set to TRUE if a push operation is applied to a full stack or if a pop operation is applied to an empty stack:

```
DEFINITION MODULE StacksLib2;

(*****************************************************************

    This module exports the data structure StackType for processing
    stacks whose elements are of type ElementType, together with
    procedures CreateStack, EmptyStack, Pop and Push, which implement
    the basic stack operations. The boolean variable StackError is
    also exported; it is set to TRUE if a push operation is applied to
    a full stack or if a pop operation is applied to an empty stack.

*****************************************************************)

    CONST
        MaxSize = 50;              (* maximum size of stack *)

    TYPE
        ElementType = ...;
        StackArray = ARRAY [1..MaxSize] OF ElementType;
        StackType = RECORD
                        Top : [0..MaxSize];
                        Element : StackArray
                    END;
    VAR
        StackError : BOOLEAN;  (* TRUE if a stack error occurs *)
                    .
                    .
                    .
    PROCEDURE Pop(VAR Stack :StackType; VAR Item : ElementType);

        (***************************************************

            Procedure to pop Item from the top of Stack.
            It sets StackError to TRUE if an attempt is
            made to pop from an empty stack, FALSE if the
            operation is carried out successfully.

        ***************************************************)

    PROCEDURE Push(VAR Stack : StackType; Item : ElementType);

        (***************************************************

            Procedure to push Item onto Stack.  It sets
            StackError to TRUE if an attempt is made to
            push onto a full stack, FALSE if the operation
            is carried out successfully.

        ***************************************************)

END StacksLib2.
```

(cont.)

```
IMPLEMENTATION MODULE StacksLib2;

(*************************************************************

    This module exports the data structure StackType for processing
    stacks of cardinal numbers.  Procedures CreateStack, EmptyStack,
    Pop and Push implement the basic stack operations.  The boolean
    variable StackError is also exported; it is set to TRUE if a push
    operation is applied to a full stack or if a pop operation is
    applied to an empty stack.

*************************************************************)

    FROM InOut IMPORT WriteString, WriteLn;
        .
        .
        .
    PROCEDURE Pop(VAR Stack :StackType; VAR Item : ElementType);

        (*****************************************************

            Procedure to pop Item from the top of Stack.
            It sets StackError to TRUE if an attempt is
            made to pop from an empty stack, FALSE if the
            operation is carried out successfully.

        *****************************************************)

        BEGIN
            StackError := EmptyStack(Stack);
            IF NOT StackError THEN
                WITH Stack DO
                    Item := Element[Top];
                    DEC(Top)
                END (* WITH *)
            END (* IF *)
        END Pop;

    PROCEDURE Push(VAR Stack : StackType; Item : ElementType);

        (*****************************************************

            Procedure to push Item onto Stack.  It sets
            StackError to TRUE if an attempt is made to
            push onto a full stack, FALSE if the operation
            is carried out successfully.

        *****************************************************)

        BEGIN
            StackError := (Stack.Top = MaxSize);
            IF NOT StackError THEN
                WITH Stack DO
                    INC(Top);
                    Element[Top] := Item
                END (* WITH *)
            END (* IF *)
        END Push;

END StacksLib2.
```

In this second version of this library module, the appropriate action to take if a stack error occurs is specified by the programmer rather than in the module itself. There are advantages and disadvantages to both approaches. But in this text we will normally take the first approach in which an error in using an abstract data type—like an error in using a predefined data type—causes program execution to terminate.

Figure 4.1 is a complete program for the base-ten to base-two conversion problem of the preceding section. It imports *StackType* and the procedures *CreateStack*, *EmptyStack*, *Pop*, and *Push* from the library module *CARDINAL-Stacks*. This module is obtained by setting *ElementType* = CARDINAL in the module *StacksLib*.

```
MODULE BaseTenToBaseTwo;

(*************************************************************************

    Program that uses a stack to convert the base-ten representation
    of a positive integer to base two and display this base-two
    representation.

*************************************************************************)

    FROM InOut IMPORT Write, WriteString, WriteLn, WriteCard,
                      Read, ReadCard;
    FROM CARDINALStacks IMPORT StackType, CreateStack, EmptyStack,
                               Push, Pop;

    VAR
        Number,                       (* the number to be converted *)
        Remainder : CARDINAL;         (* remainder when Number is
                                         divided by 2 *)

        StackOfRemainders: StackType;  (* stack of remainders *)
        Response : CHAR;               (* user response *)

BEGIN (* main program *)
    REPEAT
        WriteLn;
        WriteString('Enter positive integer to convert:  ');
        ReadCard(Number);
        CreateStack(StackOfRemainders);
        WHILE Number # 0 DO
            Remainder := Number MOD 2;
            Push (StackOfRemainders, Remainder);
            Number := Number DIV 2
        END (* WHILE *);
```

Figure 4.1

Figure 4.1   (cont.)

```
    WriteLn;
    WriteString('Base two representation is ');
    WHILE NOT EmptyStack(StackOfRemainders) DO
        Pop (StackOfRemainders, Remainder);
        WriteCard(Remainder, 1)
    END (* WHILE *);
    WriteLn; WriteLn;
    WriteString('More (Y or N)?  ');
    Read(Response)
  UNTIL CAP(Response) # 'Y'
END BaseTenToBaseTwo.
```

<u>Sample run:</u>

```
Enter positive integer to convert:  2
Base two representation:   10

More (Y or N)?  Y
Enter positive integer to convert:  127
Base two representation:  1111111

More (Y or N)?  Y
Enter positive integer to convert:  128
Base two representation:  10000000

More (Y or N)?  N
```

Exercises

1. Write algorithms that use the basic stack operations *CreateStack*, *EmptyStack*, *Push*, and *Pop* to

   (a) Retrieve the top stack element, but do not delete it from the stack.
   (b) Retrieve the bottom stack element, leaving the stack empty.
   (c) Retrieve the *n*th stack element, leaving the stack without its top *n* elements.
   (d) Retrieve the bottom stack element, but leaving the stack contents unchanged.
   (e) Retrieve the *n*th stack element, but leaving the stack contents unchanged.

2. Consider the following railroad-switching network:

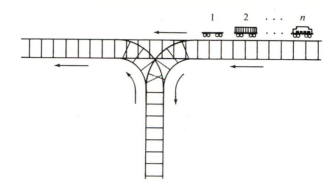

Railroad cars numbered 1, 2, . . . , n on the right track are to be rearranged and moved along on the left track. As the diagram suggests, a car may be moved directly onto the left track, or it may be shunted onto the siding to be removed at a later time and placed on the left track. The siding operates the way a stack does, a push operation moving a car from the right track onto the siding and a pop operation moving the "top" car from the siding onto the left track.

(a) For $n = 3$, find all possible permutations of cars that can be obtained (on the left track) by a sequence of these operations. For example, push 1, push 2, move 3, pop 2, pop 1 arranges them in the order 3, 2, 1. Are any permutations not possible?

(b) Find all possible permutations for $n = 4$. What permutations (if any) are not possible?

(c) Repeat (b) for $n = 5$.

(d) Challenge: In general, what permutations of the sequence 1, 2, . . . , n can be obtained when a stack is used in this manner?

3. Suppose that some application requires using two stacks whose elements are of the same type. A natural implementation of such a two-stack data structure would be to use two arrays and two top pointers. Explain why this may not be a space-efficient implementation.

4. A better implementation of a two-stack data structure than that described in Exercise 3 is to use a single array in the storage structure and to let the stacks grow toward each other:

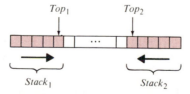

Write appropriate declarations for this implementation and write procedures for the basic stack operations in which the number of the stack to be processed, 1 or 2, is passed as a parameter. The procedure implementing the push operation should not fail because of a stack-full condition until *all* locations in the storage array have been used.

5. Storing the elements of more than two stacks in a single one-dimensional array in such a way that no stack-full condition occurs for any of the stacks until all the array locations have been used cannot be done as efficiently as in Exercise 4 because some shifting of array elements will be necessary. Nevertheless, design such an implementation for *n* stacks, *n* > 2. Write the appropriate declarations and write procedures for the basic stack operations in which the stack number is passed as a parameter. (*Hint:* You might partition the storage array into *n* equal subarrays, one for each stack, and use two arrays of "pointers" *Bottom* and *Top* to keep track of where the bottoms and tops of the stacks are located in the storage array. When one of these stacks becomes full, search to find the nearest empty locations(s) in the array, and then move intervening stacks to enlarge the storage space for this stack.)

6. Empirical evidence suggests that any program that comes close to using all available space will eventually run out of space. Consequently, shifting stacks around in an array as described in Exercise 5 so that all possible array locations are used seems rather futile. Redesign the implementation so that no push operations are attempted if there are fewer than *LowerLimit* unused locations left in the array.

7. Set *ElementType* = CHAR in *StacksLib* or *StacksLib2* to give a module *CHARStacks* for processing stacks of characters. Use the items exported from this module in a program that reads a string, one character at a time, and determines whether the string contains balanced parentheses; that is, for each left parenthesis (if there are any), there is exactly one matching right parenthesis that appears later in the string.

8. For a given integer *n* > 1, the smallest integer *d* > 1 that divides *n* is a prime factor. We can find the prime factorization of *n* if we find *d* and then replace *n* with the quotient of *n* divided by *d*, repeating this procedure until *n* becomes 1. Write a program that determines the prime factorization of *n* in this manner but that displays the prime factors in descending order. For example, for *n* = 3960, your program should produce

$$11 * 5 * 3 * 3 * 2 * 2 * 2$$

9. A program is to be written to find a path from one point in a maze to another.

   (a) Describe how a two-dimensional array could be used to model the maze.
   (b) Describe how a stack could be used in an algorithm for finding a path.
   (c) Write the program.

4.3   Application of Stacks: Reverse Polish Notation

The task of a compiler is to generate the machine language instructions required to carry out the instructions of the source program written in a high-level language. One part of this task is to generate the machine instructions for evaluating arithmetic expressions like that in the assignment statement

$$X := A * B + C$$

The compiler must generate machine instructions like the following:

1. LOA A: Retrieve the value of A from the memory location where it is stored and load it into the accumulator register.
2. MUL B: Retrieve the value of B and multiply the value in the accumulator by it.
3. ADD C: Retrieve the value of C and add it to the value in the accumulator.
4. STO X: Store the value in the accumulator in the memory location associated with X.

   In most programming languages, arithmetic expressions are written in *infix* notation like that above in which the symbol for each binary operation is placed between the operands. Many compilers first transform these infix expressions into *postfix* notation (or prefix notation, see the exercises) in which the operator follows the operands and then generates machine instructions to evaluate this postfix expression. This two-step process is used because the transformation from infix to postfix is straightforward and postfix expressions are, in general, easier to evaluate mechanically than infix expressions.

   When infix notation is used for arithmetic expressions, parentheses are often needed to indicate the order in which operations are to be carried out. For example, parentheses are placed in the expression 2 * (3 + 4) to indicate that the addition is to be performed before the multiplication. If the parentheses were omitted, giving 2 * 3 + 4, the standard priority rules would dictate that the multiplication is to be performed before the addition.

   In the early 1950s, the Polish logician Jan Lukasiewicz observed that parentheses are not necessary in postfix notation, also called *Reverse Polish Notation (RPN)*. For example, the infix expression 2 * (3 + 4) can be written in RPN as

$$2\ 3\ 4\ +\ *$$

   As an illustration of how RPN expressions are evaluated, consider the expression

$$1\ 5\ +\ 8\ 4\ 1\ -\ -\ *$$

which corresponds to the infix expression (1 + 5) * (8 − (4 − 1)). This expression is scanned from left to right until an operator is found. At that point, the last two preceding operands are combined using this operator. For our example, the first operator encountered is +, and its operands are 1 and 5, as indicated by the underline in the following:

$$\underline{1\ 5\ +}\ 8\ 4\ 1\ -\ -\ *$$

Replacing this subexpression with its value 6 yields the reduced RPN expression

$$6\ 8\ 4\ 1\ -\ -\ *$$

Resuming the left-to-right scan, we next encounter the operator $-$ and determine its two operands:

$$6\ 8\ \underline{4\ 1\ -}\ -\ *$$

Applying this operator then yields

$$6\ 8\ 3\ -\ *$$

The next operator encountered is another $-$ and its two operands are 8 and 3:

$$6\ \underline{8\ 3\ -}\ *$$

Evaluating this difference gives

$$6\ 5\ *$$

The final operator is $*$

$$\underline{6\ 5\ *}$$

and the value 30 is obtained for this expression.

This method of evaluating an RPN expression requires that the operands be stored until an operator is encountered in the left-to-right scan; at this point, the last two operands must be retrieved and combined using this operation. This suggests that a last-in–first-out structure—that is, a stack—should be used to store the operands. Each time an operand is encountered, it is pushed onto the stack. Then, when an operator is encountered, the top two values are popped from the stack, the operation is applied to them, and the result is pushed back onto the stack. The following algorithm summarizes this procedure:

ALGORITHM TO EVALUATE RPN EXPRESSIONS

1. Initialize an empty stack.
2. Repeat the following until the end of the expression is encountered:
   a. Get the next token (constant, variable, arithmetic operator) in the RPN expression.
   b. If the token is an operand, push it onto the stack. If it is an operator, then do the following:
      (i) Pop the top two values from the stack. (If the stack does not contain two items, an error due to a malformed RPN expression has occurred, and evaluation is terminated.)
      (ii) Apply the operator to these two values.
      (iii) Push the resulting value back onto the stack.
3. When the end of the expression is encountered, its value is on top of the stack (and, in fact, must be the only value in the stack).

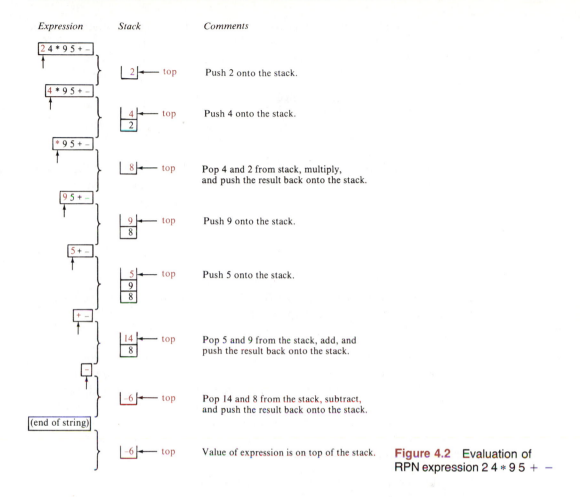

Figure 4.2 Evaluation of RPN expression 2 4 * 9 5 + −

Figure 4.2 illustrates this algorithm for the RPN expression

$$2\,4 * 9\,5 + -$$

The up-arrow (↑) indicates the current token being considered.

As an illustration of how a stack is also used in the conversion from infix to RPN, consider the infix expression

$$7 + 2 * 3$$

In a left-to-right scan of this expression, 7 is encountered and may be immediately displayed. Next, the operator + is encountered, but as its right operand has not yet been displayed, it must be stored and thus is pushed onto a stack of operators:

Output | Stack

7 | +

Next, the operand 2 is encountered and displayed. At this point it must be determined whether 2 is the right operand for the preceding operator + or is the left operand for the next operator. We determine this by comparing the operator $+$ on the top of the stack with the next operator $*$. Since $*$ was higher priority than $+$, the preceding operand 2 that was displayed is the left operand for $*$; thus we push $*$ onto the stack and search for its right operand:

Output	Stack
7 2	$\begin{array}{c} * \\ + \end{array}$

The operand 3 is encountered next and displayed. Since the end of the expression has now been reached, the right operand for the operator $*$ on the top of the stack has been found, and so $*$ can now be popped and displayed:

Output	Stack
7 2 3 $*$	$+$

The end of the expression also signals that the right operand for the remaining operator $+$ in the stack has been found, and so it, too, can be popped and displayed, yielding the RPN expression

$$7 \; 2 \; 3 * +$$

Parentheses within infix expressions present no real difficulties. A left parenthesis indicates the beginning of a subexpression, and when encountered, it is pushed onto the stack. When a right parenthesis is encountered, operators are popped from the stack until the matching left parenthesis rises to the top. At this point, the subexpression originally enclosed by the parentheses has been converted to RPN, and so the parentheses may be discarded and conversion continues. All of this is contained in the following algorithm:

ALGORITHM TO CONVERT FROM INFIX TO RPN

1. Initialize an empty stack of operators.
2. While no error has occurred and the end of the infix expression has not been reached, do the following:
   a. Get the next input *Token* (constant, variable, arithmetic operator, left parenthesis, right parenthesis) in the infix expression.
   b. If *Token* is

(i) a left parenthesis:	Push it onto the stack.
(ii) a right parenthesis:	Pop and display stack elements until a left parenthesis is encountered, but do not display it. (It is an error if the stack becomes empty with no left parenthesis found.)
(iii) an operator:	If the stack is empty or *Token* has higher priority than the top stack element, push *Token* onto the stack. Otherwise, pop and display the top stack element; then repeat the comparison of *Token* with the new top stack item.

Note: A left parenthesis in the stack is assumed to have a lower priority than that of operators.

(iv) an operand: Display it.

3. When the end of the infix expression is reached, pop and display stack items until the stack is empty.

Figure 4.3 illustrates this algorithm for the infix expression

$$7 * 8 - (2 + 3)$$

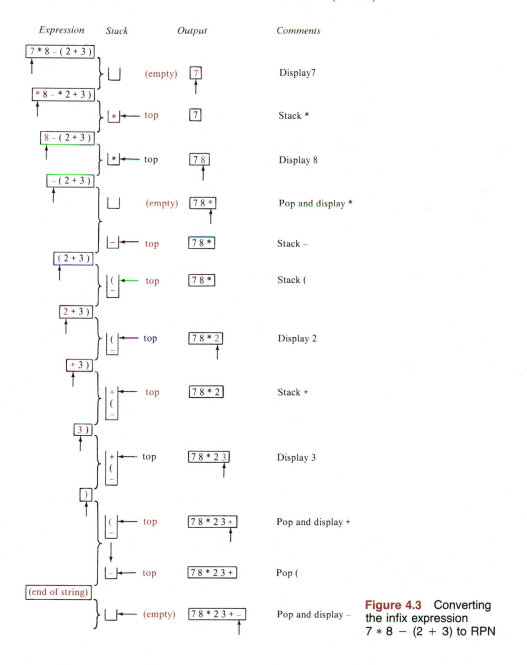

Figure 4.3 Converting the infix expression $7 * 8 - (2 + 3)$ to RPN

An up-arrow (↑) is used to indicate the current input symbol and the symbol displayed by the algorithm.

The program in Figure 4.4 implements this algorithm for converting an infix expression to RPN. It imports the data type *StackType* and modules *CreateStack*, *EmptyStack*, *Push*, and *Pop* from a library module *CHARStacks* for processing stacks of characters. Such a module can be obtained by simply setting *ElementType* = CHAR in the module *StacksLib* given in the preceding section. The program assumes that the input is a valid infix expression and does very little checking to verify that it is well formed. The problem of checking the syntax of an infix expression is considered in the parsing example of Section 5.4.

```
MODULE InfixToRPN;

(***********************************************************************

    Program to convert an infix expression to Reverse Polish Notation.

    **********************************************************************)

    FROM InOut IMPORT Write, WriteString, WriteLn, Read, Done, EOL;
    FROM SpecialInOut IMPORT ReadAString;
    FROM CHARStacks IMPORT StackType, CreateStack, EmptyStack, Push, Pop;

    CONST
        MaxExpression = 50;    (* limit on expression length *)
        EOS = 0C;              (* end-of-string character *)

    TYPE
        Expression = ARRAY[0..MaxExpression] OF CHAR;

    VAR
        Exp : Expression;      (* infix expression *)
        i : CARDINAL;          (* index of a token in Exp *)
        Response : CHAR;       (* user response *)

    PROCEDURE ConvertToRPN(Exp : Expression);

        (***********************************************************

                Procedure to convert infix expression Exp to RPN.

            **********************************************************)

        VAR
            OpStack : StackType;  (* stack of operands *)
            i : CARDINAL;         (* index *)
            Error : BOOLEAN;      (* signals error in expression *)
            Token : CHAR;         (* a character in the expression *)
```

Figure 4.4

Figure 4.4 (cont.)

```
PROCEDURE Priority(Operator : CHAR) : CARDINAL;

(*****************************************************************

    Function to find the priority of an arithmetic operator or (.

*****************************************************************)

BEGIN
    CASE Operator OF
            '(' : RETURN 0
                |
        '+', '-' : RETURN 1
                |
        '*', '/' : RETURN 2
    END (* CASE *)
END Priority;

PROCEDURE ProcessRightParen(VAR OpStack : StackType;
                           VAR Error : BOOLEAN);

    (*****************************************************************

        Procedure to pop and display operators from OpStack until
        a left parenthesis is on top of the stack; it too is popped,
        but not displayed.  Error is returned as TRUE if the stack
        becomes empty with no left parenthesis being found.

    *****************************************************************)

VAR
    TopToken : CHAR;        (* token at top of stack *)

BEGIN
    REPEAT
        Error := EmptyStack(OpStack);
        IF NOT Error THEN
            Pop (OpStack, TopToken);
            IF TopToken # '(' THEN
                Write(TopToken);
                Write(' ')
            END (* IF *)
        END (* IF *)
    UNTIL (TopToken = '(') OR Error
END ProcessRightParen;

PROCEDURE ProcessOperator(Operator : CHAR; VAR OpStack : StackType);

    (*****************************************************************

        Procedure to process an arithmetic operator.  Operators
        are popped from OpStack until the stack becomes empty or
        an operator appears on the top of the stack whose priority
        is less than or equal to that of Operator.  Operator is
        then pushed onto the stack.

    *****************************************************************)
```

Figure 4.4 (cont.)

```
        VAR
            TopOperator : CHAR;      (* operator on top of stack *)
            DonePopping : BOOLEAN; (* signals when stack-popping is
                                        completed *)

        BEGIN
            DonePopping := FALSE;
            REPEAT
                IF EmptyStack(OpStack) THEN
                    DonePopping := TRUE
                ELSE
                    Pop (OpStack, TopOperator);
                    IF (Priority(Operator) <= Priority(TopOperator)) THEN
                        Write(TopOperator);
                        Write(' ')
                    ELSE
                        Push (OpStack, TopOperator);
                        DonePopping := TRUE
                    END (* IF *)
                END (* IF *)
            UNTIL DonePopping;
            Push (OpStack, Operator)
        END ProcessOperator;

    BEGIN (* ConvertToRPN *)

        (* Initialize an empty stack *)
        CreateStack(OpStack);
        Error := FALSE;

        (* Begin the conversion to RPN *)
        i := 0;
        Token := Exp[0];

        WHILE (Token # EOS) AND NOT Error DO
            CASE Token OF
                    ' ' : (* skip blanks *)
                          (* do nothing *)
                        |
                    '(' : (* left parenthesis *)
                          Push(OpStack, Token)
                        |
                    ')' : (* right parenthesis *)
                          ProcessRightParen(OpStack, Error)
                        |
                '+','-',
                '*','/' : (* arithmetic operator *)
                          ProcessOperator(Token, OpStack)
                ELSE
                          (* operand *)
                          Write(Token);
                          Write(' ')
            END (* CASE *);
```

Figure 4.4   (cont.)

```
            (* Now get next Token and process it *)
            INC(i);
            Token := Exp[i]
        END (* WHILE *);

        (* If no error detected, pop and display
           any operands on the stack *)
        IF NOT Error THEN
            WHILE NOT EmptyStack(OpStack) DO
                Pop (OpStack, Token);
                Write(Token);
                Write(' ')
            END (* WHILE *);
            WriteLn
        ELSE
            WriteString('*** Error in infix expression ***');
            WriteLn
        END (* IF *)
    END ConvertToRPN;

BEGIN (* main program *)
    REPEAT
        (* read infix expression *)

        WriteLn;
        WriteString('Enter infix expression: ');
        ReadAString(Exp);

        (* convert to RPN *)

        WriteLn; WriteLn;
        WriteString('RPN Expression:            ');
        ConvertToRPN (Exp);
        WriteLn;
        WriteString('More (Y or N)?  ');
        Read(Response)
    UNTIL CAP(Response) # 'Y'
END InfixToRPN.
```

Sample run:

```
Enter infix expression: A + B

RPN Expression:         A B +

More (Y or N)?  Y
Enter infix expression: A - B - C

RPN Expression:         A B - C -

More (Y or N)?  Y
Enter infix expression: A * B + C

RPN Expression:         A B * C +

More (Y or N)?  Y
Enter infix expression: A + B * C
```

Figure 4.4   (cont.)

```
RPN Expression:          A B C * +

More (Y or N)?   Y
Enter infix expression: A - (B - C)

RPN Expression:          A B C - -

More (Y or N)?   Y
Enter infix expression: ((A + 5)/B - 2)*C

RPN Expression:          A 5 + B / 2 - C *

More (Y or N)?   N
```

Exercises

1. Suppose that $A = 7.0, B = 4.0, C = 3.0, D = -2.0$. Evaluate the following RPN expressions:

(a) $A \ B \ + \ C \ / \ D \ *$ **(b)** $A \ B \ C \ + \ / \ D \ *$
(c) $A \ B \ C \ D \ + \ / \ *$ **(d)** $A \ B \ + \ C \ + \ D \ +$
(e) $A \ B \ + \ C \ D \ + \ +$ **(f)** $A \ B \ C \ + \ + \ D \ +$
(g) $A \ B \ C \ D \ + \ + \ +$ **(h)** $A \ B \ - \ C \ - \ D \ -$
(i) $A \ B \ - \ C \ D \ - \ -$ **(j)** $A \ B \ C \ - \ - \ D \ -$
(k) $A \ B \ C \ D \ - \ - \ -$

2. Convert the following infix expressions to RPN:

(a) $A * B + C - D$ **(b)** $A + B / C + D$
(c) $(A + B) / C + D$ **(d)** $A + B / (C + D)$
(e) $(A + B) / (C + D)$ **(f)** $(A - B) * (C - (D + E))$
(g) $(((A - B) - C) - D) - E$ **(h)** $A - (B - (C - (D - E)))$

3. Convert the following RPN expressions to infix notation:

(a) $A \ B \ C \ + \ - \ D \ *$ **(b)** $A \ B \ + \ C \ D \ - \ *$
(c) $A \ B \ C \ D \ + \ - \ *$ **(d)** $A \ B \ + \ C \ - \ D \ E \ * \ /$
(e) $A \ B \ / \ C \ / \ D \ /$ **(f)** $A \ B \ / \ C \ D \ / \ /$
(g) $A \ B \ C \ / \ D \ / \ /$ **(h)** $A \ B \ C \ D \ / \ / \ /$

4. The symbol $-$ cannot be used for the unary minus operation in postfix notation because ambiguous expressions result. For example, $5 \ 3 \ - \ -$ could be interpreted as either $5 - (-3) = 8$ or $-(5 - 3) = -2$. Suppose instead that $\sim$ is used for unary minus.

(a) Evaluate the following RPN expressions if $A = 7, B = 5$, and $C = 3$:

   (i) $A \sim B \ C \ + \ -$ (ii) $A \ B \sim C \ + \ -$
   (iii) $A \ B \ C \sim + \ -$ (iv) $A \ B \ C \ + \sim -$
   (v) $A \ B \ C \ + \ - \sim$ (vi) $A \ B \ C \ - \ - \sim \sim \sim$

    (b) Convert the following infix expressions to RPN:
        (i) $A * (B + {\sim}C)$ (ii) ${\sim} (A + B / (C - D))$
        (iii) $({\sim}A) * ({\sim}B)$ (iv) ${\sim}(A - ({\sim}B * (C + {\sim}D)))$

5. Convert the following boolean expressions to RPN:

    (a) A AND B OR C
    (b) A AND (B OR NOT C)
    (c) NOT (A AND B)
    (d) (A OR B) AND (C OR (D AND NOT E))
    (e) ($A = B$) OR ($C = D$)
    (f) (($A < 3$) AND ($A > 9$)) OR NOT ($A > 0$)
    (g) (($B * B - 4 * A * C$) $>= 0$) AND (($A > 0$) OR ($A < 0$))

6. An alternative to postfix notation is *prefix* notation, in which the symbol for each operation precedes its operands. For example, the infix expression $2 * 3 + 4$ is written in prefix notation as $+ * 2\ 3\ 4$, and $2 * (3 + 4)$ is written as $* 2 + 3\ 4$. Convert each of the infix expressions in Exercise 2 to prefix notation.

7. Suppose that $A = 7.0, B = 4.0, C = 3.0$, and $D = -2.0$. Evaluate the following prefix expressions (see Exercise 6):

    (a) $* A / + B C D$ **(b)** $* / + A B C D$
    (c) $- A - B - C D$ **(d)** $- - A B - C D$
    (e) $- A - - B C D$ **(f)** $- - - A B C D$
    (g) $+ A B * - C D$ **(h)** $+ * A B - C D$

8. Convert the following prefix expressions to infix notation (see Exercise 6)

    (a) $* + A B - C D$ **(b)** $+ * A B - C D$
    (c) $- - A B - C D$ **(d)** $- - A - B C D$
    (e) $- - - A B C D$ **(f)** $/ + * A B - C D E$
    (g) $/ + * A B C - D E$ **(h)** $/ + A * B C - D E$

9. Write a procedure that implements the algorithm for evaluating RPN expressions that involve only nonnegative integers and the binary operators $+$, $-$, and $*$.

10. Proceed as in Exercise 9, but also allow the binary operators DIV and MOD.

11. Proceed as in Exercise 10, but also allow the unary operator $\sim$ (see Exercise 4).

12. Write a procedure that determines whether an RPN expression is well formed, that is, whether each binary operator has two operands and the unary operator $\sim$ has one (see Exercise 4).

13. The algorithm given in the text for converting from infix to RPN assumes **left associativity**; that is, when two or more consecutive operators of the same priority occur, they are to be evaluated from left to right. For example, $6 - 3 - 1$ is evaluated as $(6 - 3) - 1$ and not as $6 - (3 - 1)$. **Right associativity**, however, is normally used for the exponentiation operator; for example, in FORTRAN 77, exponentiation is denoted by $**$, and the expression $2 ** 3 ** 4$ is evaluated as $2 ** (3 ** 4) = 2^{(3^4)} = 2^{81}$, not as $(2 ** 3) ** 4 = (2^3)^4 = 8^4$. Extend the algorithm in the text to allow $**$ as an additional binary operator with highest priority. (*Hint*: One approach is to use two different priorities for each operator, one when it is in the infix expression and another when it is in the stack.)

14. Extend the program in Figure 4.4 so that it can also convert infix expressions that contain the binary operators DIV and MOD in addition to $+$, $-$, and $*$.

15. Proceed as in Exercise 14, but also allow the exponentiation operator $**$ (see Exercise 13).

16. Proceed as in Exercise 14 or 15, but also allow the unary operator $\sim$ (see Exercise 4).

17. Write a program to evaluate RPN expressions of the form described in Exercise 9, 10, 11, or 13.

18. Write a program that reads a postfix expression containing single-letter variables and the binary operators $+$, $-$, and $*$ and that generates machine instructions in assembly code for evaluating the expression using one accumulator register and the following instructions:

    LOA X—Place the value of X in the accumulator register.
    STO X—Store the contents of the accumulator register into variable X
    ADD X—Add the value of X to the contents of the accumulator.
    SUB X—Subtract the value of X from the contents of the accumulator.
    MUL X—Multiply the contents of the accumulator by the value of X.

    For example, the postfix expression $ABC + *DE* -$ should give the following sequence of instructions:

    LOA B
    ADD C
    STO *TEMP1*
    LOA A
    MUL *TEMP1*
    STO *TEMP2*
    LOA D

MUL E
STO $TEMP3$
LOA $TEMP2$
SUB $TEMP3$
STO $TEMP4$

where each $TEMPi$ is a temporary variable.

19. Write a program that converts a postfix expression into the corresponding fully parenthesized infix expression. For example, $AB+$ and $AB+CD-*$ should give $(A + B)$ and $((A + B) * (C - D))$, respectively.

5

Algorithms and Recursion

As we know, one of the most important parts of problem solving and programming is the design of algorithms. For a given problem, there may be several different algorithms for performing the same task, and in these situations, it is important that some means of comparing algorithms be available. Thus, in this chapter we consider more carefully the design and analysis of algorithms and introduce some techniques for measuring their efficiency.

The algorithms we have considered thus far and the procedures that implement them all have been nonrecursive; that is, they do not reference themselves, either directly or indirectly. There are some problems, however, for which the most appropriate algorithms are recursive. Thus, in this chapter we also review recursion and how recursive procedures are written in Modula-2, and we illustrate recursion with several examples. We also consider how recursive algorithms are proved to be correct and how to compare their efficiency with that of nonrecursive algorithms. Finally, we describe the role that stacks play in supporting recursion.

5.1 Algorithm Efficiency

An algorithm's efficiency is usually measured according to two criteria. The first is *space utilization*, the amount of memory required to store the data, and the second is *time efficiency*, the amount of time required to process the data. Unfortunately, it is usually not possible to minimize both the space and time requirements. Algorithms that require the least memory are often slower than those that use more memory. Thus the programmer is usually faced with a trade-off between space efficiency and time efficiency. An algorithm's time efficiency is usually considered the more important of the two, and in this section we consider how it can be measured.

The execution time of an algorithm is influenced by several factors. Obviously, one factor is the size of the input, since the number of input items usually affects the time required to process these items. For example, the time it takes to sort a list of items surely depends on the number of items in the list. Thus the execution time T of an algorithm must be expressed as a function $T(n)$ of the size n of the input.

The kind of instructions and the speed with which the machine can execute them also influence execution time. These factors, however, depend on the particular computer being used; consequently, we cannot expect to express the value of $T(n)$ meaningfully in real time units such as seconds. Instead, $T(n)$ will be an approximate count of the number of instructions executed.

Another factor that influences computing time is the quality of the source code that implements the algorithm and the quality of the machine code generated from this source code by a compiler. Some languages are better suited than others for certain algorithms; some programmers write better programs than others; and some compilers generate more efficient code than others. This means, in particular, that $T(n)$ cannot be computed as the number of machine instructions executed. Thus, it is taken to be the number of times the instructions in the *algorithm* are executed.

As an illustration, consider the following algorithm for finding the mean of a set of n numbers. (The statements have been numbered for easy reference.)

ALGORITHM TO CALCULATE MEAN

(* Algorithm to read a set of n numbers and calculate their mean *)

1. Read n.
2. Initialize *Sum* to 0.
3. Initialize i to 0.
4. While $i < n$ do the following:
5.   a. Read *Number*.
6.   b. Add *Number* to *Sum*.
7.   c. Increment i by 1.
8. Calculate *Mean* = *Sum* / n.

Statements 1, 2, and 3 each are executed one time. Statements 5, 6, and 7, which comprise the body of the while loop, each are executed n times, and Statement 4, which controls repetition, is executed $n + 1$ times, since one additional check is required to determine that the control variable i is no longer less than the value n. After repetition terminates, Statement 8 is then executed one time. This analysis is summarized in the following table:

Statement	# of times executed
1	1
2	1
3	1
4	$n + 1$
5	n
6	n
7	n
8	1
Total:	$4n + 5$

Thus we see that the computing time for this algorithm is given by

$$T(n) = 4n + 5$$

As the number n of inputs increases, the value of this expression for $T(n)$ grows linearly. We say that $T(n)$ has "order of magnitude n," which is usually denoted using the "big Oh notation" as

$$T(n) = O(n)$$

In general, the computing time $T(n)$ of an algorithm is said have **order of magnitude** $f(n)$, denoted

$$T(n) = O(f(n))$$

if there is some constant C such that

$$T(n) \leq C \cdot f(n) \text{ for all sufficiently large values of } n$$

That is, $T(n)$ is bounded above by some constant times $f(n)$ for all values of n from some point on. The **computational complexity** of the algorithm is said to be $O(f(n))$. For example, the complexity of the preceding algorithm is $O(n)$, since the computing time was found to be

$$T(n) = 4n + 5$$

and since

$$4n + 5 \leq 4n + n \text{ for } n \geq 5$$

we see that

$$T(n) \leq 5n \text{ for all } n \geq 5$$

Thus, taking $f(n) = n$ and $C = 5$, we may write

$$T(n) = O(n)$$

Of course, it would also be correct to write $T(n) = O(5280n)$ or $T(n) = O(4n + 5)$ or $T(n) = O(3.1416n + 2.71828)$, but we prefer a *simple* function like n, n^2, or $\log_2 n$ to express an algorithm's complexity. Also, $T(n) = O(n)$ obviously implies that $T(n) = O(n^2)$ as well as $T(n) = O(n^{5/2})$ or $T(n) = O(2^n)$, and in general $T(n) = O(g(n))$ if $g(n) \geq n$ for all n from some point on; but the smaller the function $g(n)$, the more information it will provide about the computing time $T(n)$.

In this example, the computing time depends only on the size of the input. In other problems, however, it may depend on the arrangement of the input items as well. For example, it may take less time to sort a list of items that are nearly in order initially than to sort a list in which the items are in reverse order. We might then attempt to measure T in the **worst case** or in the **best case**, or we might attempt to compute the **average** value of T over all possible cases. The best-case performance of an algorithm is usually not very informative, and the average performance is usually more difficult to determine than the worst-case performance. Consequently, $T(n)$ is frequently taken as a measure of the algorithm's performance in the worst case.

As an illustration, consider the following sorting algorithm. (Again, we have numbered the statements for easy reference.)

SIMPLE SELECTION SORTING ALGORITHM

(* Algorithm for sorting into ascending order a list of n elements stored in an array $X[1], X[2], \ldots, X[n]$. *)

1. For $i = 1$ to $n - 1$ do the following:

   (* On the ith pass, first find the smallest element in the sublist $X[i], \ldots, X[n]$. *)

2. a. Set *SmallPos* equal to i.
3. b. Set *Smallest* equal to $X[SmallPos]$.
4. c. For $j = i + 1$ to n do the following:
5.   If $X[j] < Smallest$ then (* smaller element found *)
6.   i. Set *SmallPos* equal to j.
7.   ii. Set *Smallest* equal to $X[SmallPos]$.

   (* Now interchange this smallest element with the element at the beginning of this sublist. *)

8. d. Set $X[SmallPos]$ equal to $X[i]$.
9. e. Set $X[i]$ equal to *Smallest*.

Statement 1 is executed n times (for i ranging from 1 through the value n, which causes termination); and Statements 2, 3, 8, and 9 each are executed $n - 1$ times, once on each pass through the outer loop. On the first pass through this loop with $i = 1$, Statement 4 is executed n times; Statement 5 is executed $n - 1$ times, and assuming a worst case when the items are in descending order, so are Statements 6 and 7. On the second pass with $i = 2$, Statement 4 is executed $n - 1$ times and Statements 5, 6, and 7 $n - 2$ times, and so on. Thus Statement 4 is executed a total of $n + (n - 1) + \cdots + 2$ times, and Statements 5, 6, and 7 each are executed a total of $(n - 1) + (n - 2) + \cdots + 1$ times. These sums are equal to $n(n + 1)/2 - 1$ and $n(n - 1)/2$, respectively; thus the total computing time is given by

$$T(n) = n + 4(n - 1) + \frac{n(n + 1)}{2} - 1 + 3\left(\frac{n(n - 1)}{2}\right)$$

which simplifies to

$$T(n) = 2n^2 + 4n - 5$$

Since $n \leq n^2$ for all $n \geq 0$, we see that

$$2n^2 + 4n - 5 \leq 2n^2 + 4n^2 = 6n^2$$

and hence that

$$T(n) \leq 6n^2 \text{ for all } n \geq 0$$

Thus, taking $f(n) = n^2$ and $C = 6$ in the definition of big Oh notation, we may write

$$T(n) = O(n^2)$$

The big Oh notation gives an approximate measure of the computing time of an algorithm for a large number of inputs. If two algorithms for performing the same task have different complexities, the algorithm with the lower order of magnitude for computing time is usually to be preferred. For example, if the computing time $T_1(n)$ of Algorithm 1 is $O(n)$ and the computing time $T_2(n)$ for Algorithm 2 is $O(n^2)$, then Algorithm 1 is usually considered better than Algorithm 2, since it will perform more efficiently for large values of n. It must be noted, however, that for small values of n, Algorithm 2 might well outperform Algorithm 1. For example, suppose that $T_1(n) = 10n$ and $T_2(n) = 0.1n^2$. Since $10n > 0.1n^2$ for values of n up to 100, we see that

$$T_1(n) < T_2(n) \text{ only for } n > 100$$

Thus Algorithm 2 is more efficient than Algorithm 1 only for inputs of size greater than 100.

To illustrate, consider the problem of searching an array of n elements $A[1], \ldots, A[n]$ to determine whether a specified value *Item* appears in this list and, if so, to determine its location. A simple algorithm for performing this search is **linear search**, in which we start at the beginning of the list and examine successive elements until either *Item* is found or we reach the end of the list.

LINEAR SEARCH ALGORITHM

(∗ Algorithm to search the list $A[1], \ldots, A[n]$ for *Item*. *Found* is set to true and *Loc* to the position of *Item* if the search is successful; otherwise, *Found* is set to false. ∗)

1. Set *Loc* equal to 1.
2. While $Loc \leq n$ and $Item \neq A[Loc]$
3.   Increment *Loc* by 1.
4. If $Loc \leq n$ then
5.   Set *Found* to true.
6. Otherwise
       Set *Found* to false.

The worst case is obviously that in which *Item* is not in the list, and in this case, we find the computing time $T_L(n)$ for the linear search algorithm as follows:

Statement	# of times executed
1	1
2	$n + 1$
3	n
4	1
5	0
6	1

Thus $T_L(n) = 2n + 4$ so that

$$T_L(n) = O(n)$$

since $2n + 4 \leq 3n$ for all $n \geq 4$.

If the list being searched has previously been sorted so that the elements are in ascending order, a **binary search** can be used instead of a linear search. To locate *Item* in such a list, the element $A[Mid]$ in the middle of the list is examined. There are three possibilities:

$Item < A[Mid]$: Search the first half of the list.
$Item > A[Mid]$: Search the last half of the list.
$Item = A[Mid]$: Search is successful.

We continue this halving process until either *Item* is located or the sublist to be searched becomes empty. The following algorithm gives the details:

BINARY SEARCH ALGORITHM

(∗ Algorithm to search the ordered list $A[1], \ldots, A[n]$ for *Item* using a binary search. *Found* is set to true and *Mid* to the position of *Item* if the search is successful; otherwise, *Found* is set to false. ∗)

1. Set *Found* equal to false.
2. Set *First* equal to 1.
3. Set *Last* equal to n.
4. While *First* ≤ *Last* and not *Found* do the following:
5.   Calculate $Mid = (First + Last) / 2$.
6.   If $Item < A[Mid]$ then
7.   Set *Last* equal to $Mid - 1$.
8.   Else if $Item > A[Mid]$ then
9.   Set *First* equal to $Mid + 1$.
10.   Else
        Set *Found* equal to true.

In this algorithm, Statements 1, 2, and 3 are clearly executed exactly once, and to calculate the worst case computing time $T_B(n)$, we must determine the number of times the loop composed of Statements 4 through 10 is executed. Each pass through this loop reduces the size of the sublist still to be searched by at least one-half. The last pass occurs when the sublist reaches size one. Thus the total number of iterations of this loop is 1 plus the number k of passes required to produce a sublist of size one. Since the size of the sublist after k passes is at most $n/2^k$, we must have

$$\frac{n}{2^k} < 2$$

that is,

$$n < 2^{k+1}$$

or equivalently

$$\log_2 n < k + 1$$

The required number of passes, therefore, is the least integer that satisfies this inequality, that is, the integer part of $\log_2 n$. Thus, in the worst case, when *Item* is greater than each of $A[1], \ldots, A[n]$, Statement 4 is executed no more than

$2 + \log_2 n$ times, Statements 5, 6, and 8 no more than $1 + \log_2 n$ times, and Statements 7, 9, and 10 zero times. The total computing time, therefore, is no more than $8 + 4 \log_2 n$, so that

$$T_B(n) = O(\log_2 n)$$

Since the complexity of linear search is $O(n)$ and that of binary search is $O(\log_2 n)$, it is clear that binary search will be more efficient than linear search for large lists. For small lists, however, linear search may—and in fact, does— outperform binary search. Empirical studies indicate that linear search is more efficient than binary search for lists of up to twenty elements.

In addition to $O(\log_2 n)$, $O(n)$, and $O(n^2)$, other computing times that frequently arise in algorithm analysis are $O(1)$, $O(\log_2 \log_2 n)$, $O(n \log_2 n)$, $O(n^3)$, and $O(2^n)$. $O(1)$ denotes a **constant** computing time, that is, one that does not depend on the size of the input. A computing time of $O(n)$ is said to be **linear**; $O(n^2)$ is called **quadratic**; $O(n^3)$ is called **cubic**; and $O(2^n)$ is called **exponential**. The following table displays the values of these computing functions for several values of n:

$\log_2 \log_2 n$	$\log_2 n$	n	$n \log_2 n$	n^2	n^3	2^n
—	0	1	0	1	1	2
0	1	2	2	4	8	4
1	2	4	8	16	64	16
1.58	3	8	24	64	512	256
2	4	16	64	256	4096	65536
2.32	5	32	160	1024	32768	4294967296
2.6	6	64	384	4096	2.6×10^5	1.85×10^{19}
3	8	256	2.05×10^3	6.55×10^4	1.68×10^7	1.16×10^{77}
3.32	10	1024	1.02×10^4	1.05×10^6	1.07×10^9	1.8×10^{308}
4.32	20	1048576	2.1×10^7	1.1×10^{12}	1.15×10^{18}	6.7×10^{315652}

It should be clear from this table that algorithms with exponential complexity are practical only for solving problems in which the number of inputs is small. To emphasize this, suppose that each instruction in some algorithm can be executed in 1 microsecond. The following table shows the time required to execute $f(n)$ instructions for the common complexity functions f with $n = 256$ inputs:

Function	Time
$\log_2 \log_2 n$	3 microseconds
$\log_2 n$	8 microseconds
n	.25 milliseconds
$n \log_2 n$	2 milliseconds
n^2	65 milliseconds
n^3	17 seconds
2^n	3.7×10^{61} centuries

Exercises

1. Which of the orders of magnitude given in this section is the best O notation to describe the following computing times?

   (a) $T(n) = n^3 + 100n \cdot \log_2 n + 5000$

   (b) $T(n) = 2^n + n^{99} + 7$

   (c) $T(n) = \dfrac{n^2 - 1}{n + 1} + 8 \log_2 n$

   (d) $T(n) = 1 + 2 + 4 + \cdots + 2^{n-1}$

2. Give an example of an algorithm with complexity O(1).

3. Explain why if $T(n) = O(n)$ then it is also correct to say $T(n) = O(n^2)$.

4. For each of the following segments, determine which of the orders of magnitude given in this section is the best O notation to use to express the worst-case computing time as a function of n:

   (a) (* Calculate mean *)
   ```
   Sum := 0;
   FOR i := 1 TO n DO
       ReadReal(R);
       Sum := Sum + R
   END (* FOR *);
   Mean := Sum / FLOAT(n);
   ```

   (b) (* Matrix addition *)
   ```
   FOR i := 1 TO n DO
       FOR j := 1 TO n DO
           C[i, j] := A[i, j] + B[i, j]
       END (* FOR j *)
   END (* FOR i *);
   ```

   (c) (* Matrix multiplication *)
   ```
   FOR i := 1 TO n DO
       FOR j := 1 TO n DO
           C[i, j] := 0;
           FOR k := 1 TO n DO
               C[i, j] := C[i, j] + A[i, k] * B[k, j]
           END (* FOR k *)
       END (* FOR j *)
   END (* FOR i *);
   ```

   (d) (* Bubble sort *)
   ```
   FOR i := 1 TO n - 1 DO
       FOR j := i TO n - 1 DO
           IF X[j] > X[j + 1] THEN
               Temp := X[j];
               X[j] := X[j + 1];
               X[j + 1] := Temp
           END (* IF *)
       END (* FOR j *)
   END (* FOR i *);
   ```

(e) WHILE $n >= 1$ DO
        $n := n$ DIV 2
     END (* WHILE *);

(f) $x := 1$;
     FOR $i := 1$ TO $n - 1$ DO
        FOR $j := 1$ TO x DO
           WriteCard(i, 1);
           WriteLn
        END (* FOR j *);
        $x := 2 * x$
     END (* FOR i *);

5.2 Recursion in Modula-2

We have seen several examples of procedures that reference other procedures. In some programming languages, such as Modula-2, a procedure may also reference itself, a phenomenon known as **recursion**, and in this section we review how recursion, both **direct** and **indirect**, is supported in Modula-2.

To illustrate the basic idea of recursion, we consider the problem of calculating x^n, where x is a real value and n is a cardinal number. The first definition of x^n that one learns is usually an iterative (nonrecursive) one:

$$x^n = \underbrace{x \times x \times \cdots \times x}_{n \ x\text{'s}}$$

and later one learns that x^0 is defined to be 1. (For convenience, we assume here that x^0 is 1 also when x is 0, although in this case, it is usually left undefined.)

In calculating a sequence of consecutive powers of some number, however, it would be foolish to calculate each one using this definition, that is, to multiply the number by itself the required number of times; for example,

$$3^0 = 1$$
$$3^1 = 3$$
$$3^2 = 3 \times 3 = 9$$
$$3^3 = 3 \times 3 \times 3 = 27$$
$$3^4 = 3 \times 3 \times 3 \times 3 = 81$$
$$3^5 = 3 \times 3 \times 3 \times 3 \times 3 = 243$$
$$\vdots$$

Once some power of 3 has been calculated, it can be used to calculate the next power; for example, given the value of $3^3 = 27$, we can use this value to calculate

$$3^4 = 3 \times 3^3 = 3 \times 27 = 81$$

and this value to calculate

$$3^5 = 3 \times 3^4 = 3 \times 81 = 243$$

and so on. Indeed, to calculate any power of 3, we only need know the value of 3^0,

$$3^0 = 1$$

and the fundamental relation between one power of 3 and the next:

$$3^n = 3 \times 3^{n-1}$$

This approach to calculating powers leads to the following recursive definition of the power function:

$$x^0 = 1$$
$$\text{For } n > 0, x^n = x \times x^{n-1}$$

Another classic example of a function that can be calculated recursively is the factorial function. The first definition of the factorial $n!$ of a nonnegative integer n that one usually learns is

$$n! = 1 \times 2 \times \cdots \times n, \text{ for } n > 0$$

and that $0!$ is 1. Thus, for example,

$$0! = 1$$
$$1! = 1$$
$$2! = 1 \times 2 = 2$$
$$3! = 1 \times 2 \times 3 = 6$$
$$4! = 1 \times 2 \times 3 \times 4 = 24$$
$$5! = 1 \times 2 \times 3 \times 4 \times 5 = 120$$

Once again the value of this function at a given integer can be used to calculate the value at the next integer. For example, to calculate $5!$, we can simply multiply the value of $4!$ by 5:

$$5! = 4! \times 5 = 24 \times 5 = 120$$

Similarly, we can use $5!$ to calculate $6!$,

$$6! = 5! \times 6 = 120 \times 6 = 720$$

and so on. One need only know the value of $0!$,

$$0! = 1$$

and the fundamental relation between one factorial and the next:

$$n! = n \times (n - 1)!$$

This suggests the following recursive definition of $n!$:

$$0! = 1$$
$$\text{For } n > 0, n! = n \times (n - 1)!$$

In general, a function is said to be **defined recursively** if its definition consists of two parts:

1. An **anchor** or **base case**, in which the value of the function is specified for one or more values of the parameter(s).

2. An ***inductive*** or ***recursive step,*** in which the function's value for the current value of the parameter(s) is defined in terms of previously defined function values and/or parameter values.

We have seen two examples of such recursive definitions of functions, the power function

$$x^0 = 1 \qquad \text{(the anchor or base case)}$$
$$\text{For } n > 0, \; x^n = x \times x^{n-1} \quad \text{(the inductive or recursive step)}$$

and the factorial function

$$0! = 1 \qquad \text{(the anchor or base case)}$$
$$\text{For } n > 0, \; n! = n \times (n - 1)! \quad \text{(the inductive or recursive step)}$$

In each definition, the first statement specifies a particular value of the function, and the second statement defines its value for n in terms of its value for $n - 1$.

As we noted in these examples, such recursive definitions are useful in calculating function values $f(n)$ for a sequence of consecutive values of n. Using them to calculate any one particular value, however, requires computing earlier values. For example, consider using the recursive definition of the power function to calculate 3^5. We must first calculate 3^4, because 3^5 is defined as the product of 3 and 3^4. But to calculate 3^4 we must calculate 3^3 because 3^4 is defined as 3×3^3. And to calculate 3^3, we must apply the inductive step of the definition again, $3^3 = 3 \times 3^2$, then again to find 3^2, which is defined as $3^2 = 3 \times 3^1$, and once again to find $3^1 = 3 \times 3^0$. Now we have finally reached the anchor case:

$$3^5 = 3 \times 3^4$$
$$\downarrow$$
$$3^4 = 3 \times 3^3$$
$$\downarrow$$
$$3^3 = 3 \times 3^2$$
$$\downarrow$$
$$3^2 = 3 \times 3^1$$
$$\downarrow$$
$$3^1 = 3 \times 3^0$$
$$\downarrow$$
$$3^0 = 1$$

Since the value of 3^0 is given, we can now backtrack to find the value of 3^1,

$$3^5 = 3 \times 3^4$$
$$\downarrow$$
$$3^4 = 3 \times 3^3$$
$$\downarrow$$
$$3^3 = 3 \times 3^2$$
$$\downarrow$$
$$3^2 = 3 \times 3^1$$
$$\downarrow$$
$$3^1 = 3 \times 3^0 = 3 \times 1 = 3$$
$$\downarrow \qquad \nearrow$$
$$3^0 = 1$$

then backtrack again to find the value of 3^2,

$3^5 = 3 \times 3^4$
$\quad\quad\downarrow$
$\quad\quad 3^4 = 3 \times 3^3$
$\quad\quad\quad\quad\downarrow$
$\quad\quad\quad\quad 3^3 = 3 \times 3^2$
$\quad\quad\quad\quad\quad\quad\downarrow$
$\quad\quad\quad\quad\quad\quad 3^2 = 3 \times 3^1 = 3 \times 3 = 9$
$\quad\quad\quad\quad\quad\quad\quad\quad\downarrow$
$\quad\quad\quad\quad\quad\quad\quad\quad 3^1 = 3 \times 3^0 = 3 \times 1 = 3$
$\quad\quad\quad\quad\quad\quad\quad\quad\quad\quad\downarrow$
$\quad\quad\quad\quad\quad\quad\quad\quad\quad\quad 3^0 = 1$

and so on until we eventually obtain the value 243 for 3^5:

$3^5 = 3 \times 3^4 = 3 \times 81 = 243$
$\quad\quad\downarrow$
$\quad\quad 3^4 = 3 \times 3^3 = 3 \times 27 = 81$
$\quad\quad\quad\quad\downarrow$
$\quad\quad\quad\quad 3^3 = 3 \times 3^2 = 3 \times 9 = 27$
$\quad\quad\quad\quad\quad\quad\downarrow$
$\quad\quad\quad\quad\quad\quad 3^2 = 3 \times 3^1 = 3 \times 3 = 9$
$\quad\quad\quad\quad\quad\quad\quad\quad\downarrow$
$\quad\quad\quad\quad\quad\quad\quad\quad 3^1 = 3 \times 3^0 = 3 \times 1 = 3$
$\quad\quad\quad\quad\quad\quad\quad\quad\quad\quad\downarrow$
$\quad\quad\quad\quad\quad\quad\quad\quad\quad\quad 3^0 = 1$

As this example demonstrates, calculating function values by hand using recursive definitions may require considerable bookkeeping to record information at the various levels of the recursive evaluation so that after the anchor case is reached, this information can be used to backtrack from one level to the preceding one. Fortunately, most modern high-level languages, including Modula-2, allow recursive functions and/or procedures, and all of the necessary bookkeeping and backtracking are done automatically by the computer.

To illustrate, consider the power function again. The recursive definition of this function can be implemented as a recursive function procedure in Modula-2 in a straightforward manner:

```
PROCEDURE Power(x : REAL; n : CARDINAL) : REAL;

    (* Recursive function procedure to calculate xⁿ *)

    BEGIN
        IF n = 0 THEN                          (* anchor *)
            RETURN 1
        ELSE
            RETURN x * Power(x, n − 1)   (* inductive step *)
        END (* IF *)
    END Power;
```

When this function procedure is referenced, the inductive step is applied repeatedly until the anchor case is reached. For example, when the reference

Power(3.0, 5) is made to calculate 3.0^5, the inductive step generates another reference *Power*(3.0, 4). The inductive step in this second reference to *Power* then generates another reference *Power*(3.0, 3), which in turn generates another reference *Power*(3.0, 2), then another, *Power*(3.0, 1), and finally the reference *Power*(3.0, 0). Because the anchor condition is now satisfied, no additional references are generated.

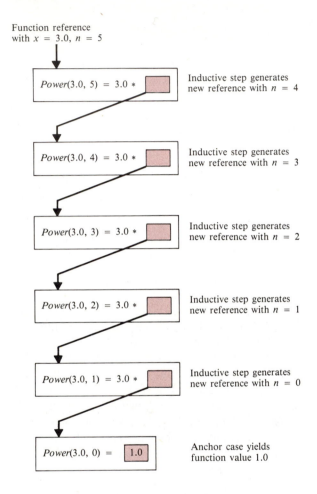

Function reference
with $x = 3.0$, $n = 5$

Power(3.0, 5) = 3.0 *   Inductive step generates
                                new reference with $n = 4$

Power(3.0, 4) = 3.0 *   Inductive step generates
                                new reference with $n = 3$

Power(3.0, 3) = 3.0 *   Inductive step generates
                                new reference with $n = 2$

Power(3.0, 2) = 3.0 *   Inductive step generates
                                new reference with $n = 1$

Power(3.0, 1) = 3.0 *   Inductive step generates
                                new reference with $n = 0$

Power(3.0, 0) =   1.0   Anchor case yields
                                function value 1.0

The value 1.0 is returned for *Power*(3.0, 0) which is then used to calculate the value of *Power*(3.0, 1), and so on until the value 243.0 is eventually returned as the value for the original function reference *Power*(3.0, 5):

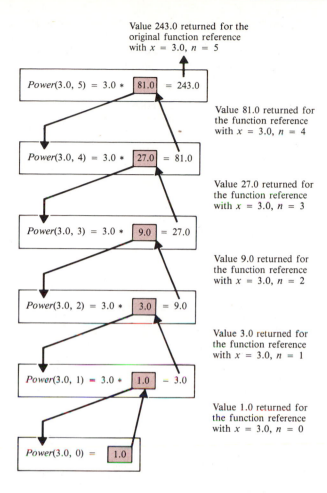

Value 243.0 returned for the original function reference with $x = 3.0$, $n = 5$

$Power(3.0, 5) = 3.0 * \boxed{81.0} = 243.0$

Value 81.0 returned for the function reference with $x = 3.0$, $n = 4$

$Power(3.0, 4) = 3.0 * \boxed{27.0} = 81.0$

Value 27.0 returned for the function reference with $x = 3.0$, $n = 3$

$Power(3.0, 3) = 3.0 * \boxed{9.0} = 27.0$

Value 9.0 returned for the function reference with $x = 3.0$, $n = 2$

$Power(3.0, 2) = 3.0 * \boxed{3.0} = 9.0$

Value 3.0 returned for the function reference with $x = 3.0$, $n = 1$

$Power(3.0, 1) = 3.0 * \boxed{1.0} = 3.0$

Value 1.0 returned for the function reference with $x = 3.0$, $n = 0$

$Power(3.0, 0) = \boxed{1.0}$

The recursive definition of the factorial function is also easily implemented as a recursive function procedure in Modula-2. Writing this function procedure and tracing its execution, as we did for the function *Power*, is left as an exercise.

Each execution of the inductive step in the definitions of the power function and the factorial function generates only one reference to the function itself, but recursive definitions of other functions may require more than one such reference. To illustrate, consider the sequence of ***Fibonacci numbers***,

$$1, 1, 2, 3, 5, 8, 13, 21, 34, 53, \ldots$$

which begins with two 1's and in which each number thereafter is the sum of the two preceding numbers. This infinite sequence is defined recursively by

$$f_1 = 1$$
$$f_2 = 1$$
$$\text{For } n > 2, f_n = f_{n-1} + f_{n-2}$$

where f_n denotes the n-th term in the sequence. This definition leads naturally to the following recursive function procedure:

PROCEDURE *Fib*(*n* : CARDINAL) : CARDINAL;

(* Recursive function procedure to calculate the
*n*th Fibonacci number *)

BEGIN
    IF *n* <= 2 THEN   (* anchor *)
        RETURN 1
    ELSE
        RETURN *Fib*(*n* − 1) + *Fib*(*n* − 2)   (* inductive step *)
    END (* IF *)
END *Fib*;

If the function reference *Fib*(5) is made to obtain the fifth Fibonacci number, the inductive step

ELSE
    RETURN *Fib*(*n* − 1) + *Fib*(*n* − 2)

immediately generates the reference *Fib*(4) with parameter $5 - 1 = 4$:

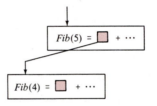

This generates another function reference *Fib*(3), which in turn generates the reference *Fib*(2):

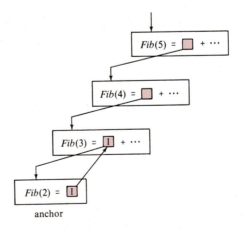

anchor

Because the anchor condition is now satisfied, the value 1 is returned for *Fib*(2), and the second reference *Fib*(1) needed to calculate *Fib*(3) is generated:

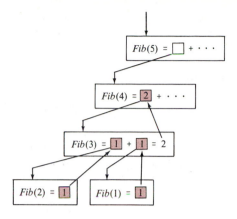

Here again, the value 1 is returned, and the function reference $Fib(3)$ is completed so that the value $1 + 1 = 2$ is returned. The first term in the sum for the reference $Fib(4)$ has thus been calculated, and the reference $Fib(2)$ is generated to determine the second term. This process continues until eventually the value 5 is returned for $Fib(5)$:

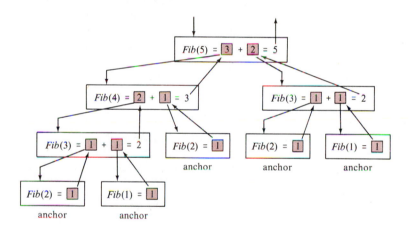

Note the function references with the same parameter in this **recursion tree**; there are three references with parameter 1, three with parameter 2, and two with parameter 3. These multiple references suggest that this is not the most efficient way to calculate Fibonacci numbers. This inefficiency is confirmed by comparing the computing time of this recursive Fibonacci function procedure with a nonrecursive version in the next section.

In Modula-2, proper procedures as well as function procedures may be recursive. To illustrate, consider the binary search algorithm, which was described in the preceding section. Although the algorithm given there is an iterative one, the approach of the binary search method is recursive. If the (sub)list we are currently examining is empty, the item for which we are searching is obviously not in the (sub)list, and so we can stop searching (anchor condition 1). If the (sub)list is not empty, we examine its middle element, and if this is the item for which we are searching, we are finished (anchor condition

2). Otherwise, either the sublist of items preceding this middle item or the sublist of items that follows it is searched *in the same manner* (inductive step). A recursive procedure for binary search is therefore quite natural:

PROCEDURE *RecBinarySearch*(VAR *A*:*ArrayType*;

First,*Last* : CARDINAL;

Item : *ElementType*;

VAR *Found* : BOOLEAN;

VAR *Mid* : CARDINAL);

(∗ Recursive procedure to search the (sub)list *A*[*First*], . . . , *A*[*Last*] for *Item* using a binary search. *Found* is returned as TRUE, and *Mid* is the position of *Item* if the search is successful; otherwise, *Found* is returned as FALSE. ∗)

```
BEGIN
    IF First > Last THEN                (* anchor 1—empty sublist *)
        Found := FALSE
    ELSE
        Mid := (First + Last) DIV 2;
        IF Item < A[Mid] THEN           (* inductive step—search first half
            RecBinarySearch(A, First, Mid − 1, Item, Found, Mid)
        ELSIF Item > A[Mid] THEN   (* inductive step—search last half
            RecBinarySearch(A, Mid + 1, Last, Item, Found, Mid)
        ELSE
            Found := TRUE               (* anchor 2—item found *)
    END(* IF *)
END RecBinarySearch;
```

To illustrate the action of this procedure, suppose that the list 11, 22, 33, 44, 55, 66, 77, 88, 99 is stored in positions 1 through 9 of array A and that we wish to search this list for the number 66. We begin with the procedure reference statement

RecBinarySearch(*A*, 1, 9, 66, *ItemFound*, *Position*)

The procedure calculates *Mid* = 5, and since 66 > *A*[5] = 55, the second part of the inductive step generates another reference,

RecBinarySearch(*A*, 6, 9, 66, *ItemFound*, *Position*):

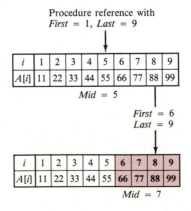

Since the sublist is nonempty, this procedure call calculates $Mid = 7$, and since $66 < A[7] = 77$, the first part of the inductive step generates another function reference with $First = 6$ and $Last = 6$:

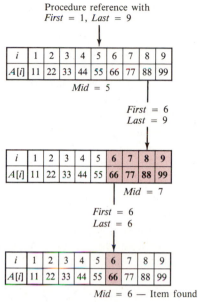

The sublist being searched still has one element, and so in this third procedure reference, the value $Mid = 6$ is calculated, and since $A[6] = 66$ is the desired item, the second anchor condition assigns the value TRUE to *Found*. This third execution of *RecBinarySearch* then terminates and returns the values $Found = $ TRUE and $Mid = 6$ to the second procedure reference. This second execution likewise terminates and returns these same values to the first execution of *RecBinarySearch*. The original reference to this procedure is thus completed, and the value TRUE is returned to the actual parameter *ItemFound* and the value 6 to the actual parameter *Position*:

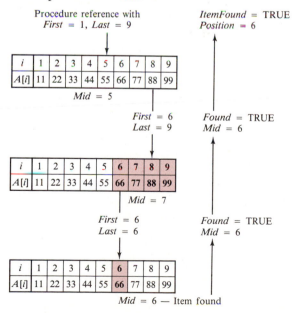

Developing recursive algorithms is difficult for many beginning programmers. Practice, practice, and more practice seems to be the only way to develop the ability to think recursively. Consequently, we present one more example of a recursive algorithm here; many more will appear in subsequent chapters.

A cardinal number is said to be a ***palindrome*** if its value does not change when its digits are reversed; that is, the number reads the same from left to right as it does from right to left. For example, 1, 33, 5665, and 123454321 are palindromes. Now, suppose we wish to develop a boolean-valued function procedure that checks if a given cardinal number is a palindrome, returning TRUE if it is and FALSE otherwise.

Thinking nonrecursively, we might begin by trying to decompose the number into its separate digits, then put them together in reverse order, and finally check if this reversed number is equal to the original number. A similar approach would be to decompose the number into its separate digits, pushing each one onto a stack. Because of a stack's LIFO property, when these digits are popped from the stack, they will appear in the opposite order from that in the original number, and so we can check if the number's reversal is the same as the number. Another nonrecursive approach might be to convert the number into a string of characters stored in an array and then to scan this array from both ends, checking to see if the digits match.

A more straightforward solution to the problem is a recursive one and is obtained simply by analyzing how one would solve this problem by hand. In checking a number like

8507058

most people first check the first and last digits, and if they agree, cross them out (perhaps only mentally) and consider the number that remains:

8̸ 50705 8̸

The resulting number 50705 is then checked *in the same way*, which is a recursive approach to the problem. After two more applications of this inductive step of checking and truncating the first and last digits,

5̸ 070 5̸
0̸ 7 0̸

a one-digit number results:

7

and this obviously is a palindrome (anchor case 1). If the original number had an even number of digits, then at this last step, no digits would remain and the number would be a palindrome. If at any point along the way, the first and last digits did not match (anchor case 2), we would stop checking, since the number obviously is not a palindrome.

This leads to the following recursive algorithm:

RECURSIVE PALINDROME CHECKER

(∗ Recursive algorithm to check if a cardinal *Number* having
   NumDigits digits is a palindrome ∗)

1. If *NumDigits* $\leq$ 1 then   (* anchor case 1 *)
   Return the value true.

   (* Otherwise check if the first and last digits match, and if not,
   return the value false *)

2. Divide Number by $10^{NumDigits-1}$ to obtain *FirstDigit*.
3. Set *LastDigit* equal to *Number* MOD 10.
4. If *FirstDigit* $\neq$ *LastDigit* then   (* anchor case 2 *)
   Return the value false.

   (* Otherwise, the first and last digits match,
   so more digits must be checked—inductive step *)

5. Apply the algorithm recursively to *Number* with *FirstDigit* and
   LastDigit removed, that is, to *Number* MOD $10^{NumDigits-1}$ MOD 10,
   and *NumDigits* $-$ 2.

Implementing this algorithm as a recursive function procedure is straightforward
and is left as an exercise.

The examples of recursion given thus far have illustrated ***direct recursion***;
that is, the procedures have referenced themselves directly. ***Indirect recursion***
occurs when a procedure references other procedures, and some chain of procedure references eventually results in a reference again to the first procedure.
For example, procedure *A* may reference procedure *B*, which references procedure *C*, which references procedure *A* again. Indirect recursion is illustrated
in Section 5.4.

5.3   Correctness and Efficiency of Recursive Algorithms

In Section 1.6 we described some techniques for proving the correctness of
algorithms, and in Section 5.1 we considered in some detail how their efficiency
can be measured. All the examples we considered, however, were nonrecursive,
and so in this section we demonstrate how these techniques can be applied to
recursive algorithms.

Recall that to prove that an algorithm is correct, one must prove that the
algorithm terminates and that when it does, it produces the correct result. In
Section 1.6 we noted that mathematical induction is a useful tool in proving
the correctness of algorithms and programs that involve repetition. Mathematical induction is also useful in proving the correctness of recursive algorithms,
since by its very nature, recursion involves induction.

As an illustration, consider the recursive power function of the preceding
section:

PROCEDURE *Power*(*x* : REAL; *n* : CARDINAL) : REAL;

    (* Recursive function procedure to calculate x^n *)

    BEGIN
        IF *n* = 0 THEN   (* anchor *)
            RETURN 1.0

ELSE
RETURN $x * Power(x, n - 1)$ (* inductive step *)
END(* IF *)
END *Power*;

Here the input and output assertions are

I : Input consists of a real number x and a cardinal number n.
O: Execution of the function procedure terminates, and when it does, the
value returned by the function is x^n.

We can use mathematical induction on n to show that the output assertion
O follows from the input assertion I. If n is 0, the anchor statement

RETURN 1.0

is executed immediately, so that execution terminates and the correct value 1.0
is returned for x^0. Now assume that for $n = k$, execution terminates and returns
the correct value for x^n. When it is referenced with $n = k + 1$, the inductive
step

RETURN $x * Power(x, n - 1)$

is executed. The value of $n - 1$ is k, and thus by the induction hypothesis,
the function reference $Power(x, n - 1)$ terminates and returns the correct value
of x^k. It follows that the function reference with $n = k + 1$ terminates and
returns the value $x * x^k = x^{k+1}$, which is the correct value of x^n. We have thus
established that in all cases, the output assertion follows from the input assertion.

The computing time $T(n)$ of a recursive algorithm is naturally given by a
recurrence relation, which expresses the computing time for inputs of size n
in terms of inputs of smaller size. For example, when the function *Power* is
referenced with $n > 0$, the boolean expression

$n = 0$

is first evaluated, and since it is false, the inductive statement

RETURN $x * Power(x, n - 1)$

is executed. The total computing time is thus 2 plus the time required to compute
$Power(x, n - 1)$. Thus $T(n)$ is given by the recurrence relation

$$T(n) = 2 + T(n - 1)$$

Similarly, if $n - 1 > 0$,

$$T(n - 1) = 2 + T(n - 2)$$

and combining these gives

$$T(n) = 2 + 2 + T(n - 2)$$

Continuing this process, we eventually obtain

$$T(n) = 2 + 2 + \cdots + 2 + T(0)$$

The time $T(0)$ to compute x^0 is clearly 2, since the boolean expression $n = 0$ is first evaluated and the anchor statement

RETURN 1.0

is executed. Thus we have

$$T(n) = 2(n + 1)$$

so that

$$T(n) = O(n)$$

As we noted in the preceding section, the power function may also be defined iteratively as

$$x^0 = 1$$
For $n > 0$, $x^n = \underbrace{x \times x \times \cdots \times x}_{n \ x\text{'s}}$

and this definition leads to the following nonrecursive function procedure:

```
PROCEDURE NRPower(x : REAL; n : CARDINAL) : REAL;

    (* Nonrecursive function procedure to calculate xⁿ *)

    VAR
        i,                      (* loop index *)
        Prod : CARDINAL;        (* the product x * x * ⋯ * x *)
    BEGIN
        Prod := 1;
        FOR i := 1 TO n DO
            Prod := Prod * x
        END (* FOR *);
        RETURN Prod
    END NRPower;
```

The computing time of this procedure is easily computed as

$$T_{NR}(n) = O(n)$$

Although the computational complexity of the recursive and nonrecursive procedures is the same, the overhead involved in implementing recursion (as described in the next section) does produce some inefficiency. Consequently, in cases such as this, in which both a recursive algorithm and a nonrecursive one can be developed with little difference in effort, the nonrecursive solution is usually preferred.

In some cases, the computing time of a recursive algorithm to solve a problem may be much greater than that of a nonrecursive algorithm for the same problem. This is especially true of those like the recursive function procedure *Fib* for calculating Fibonacci numbers in the preceding section, in which the inductive step requires more than one reference to the function itself:

> PROCEDURE *Fib*(n : CARDINAL) : CARDINAL;
>
>> (* Recursive function procedure to calculate the
>> nth Fibonacci number *)
>
>> BEGIN
>>> IF $n <= 2$ THEN   (* anchor *)
>>>> RETURN 1
>>> ELSE
>>>> RETURN *Fib*($n - 1$) + *Fib*($n - 2$)   (* inductive step *)
>>> END (* IF *)
>> END *Fib*;

We noted that multiple function references with the same parameter indicàte that this is not a particularly efficient method of calculating Fibonacci numbers. Indeed, it is horribly inefficient!

The recurrence relation that gives the computing time $T(n)$ of this function procedure *Fib* for $n > 2$ is easily seen to be

$$T(n) = 2 + T(n - 1) + T(n - 2)$$

Since this recurrence relation is not especially easy to solve to obtain an explicit formula for $T(n)$, we will use it instead to obtain a lower bound for $T(n)$, which grows exponentially with n, and thus to show that $T(n)$ grows exponentially.

This recurrence relation holds for all integers n greater than 2, and thus if $n > 3$ (so that $n - 1$ is greater than 2), we may apply it to $n - 1$ to say that

$$T(n - 1) = 2 + T(n - 2) + T(n - 3)$$

Substituting this in the original relation gives

$$T(n) = 4 + 2T(n - 2) + T(n - 3) \text{ for all } n > 3$$

and thus

$$T(n) > 2T(n - 2) \text{ for all } n > 3$$

If $n > 5$ so that $n - 2 > 3$, we may apply this inequality to $n - 2$ and obtain

$$T(n) > 2T(n - 2) > 4T(n - 4)$$

Continuing in this manner, we obtain

$$T(n) > 2T(n - 2) > 4T(n - 4) > \cdots > 2^{(n-2)/2}T(2) \text{ if } n \text{ is even}$$

or

$$T(n) > 2T(n - 2) > 4T(n - 4) > \cdots > 2^{(n-1)/2}T(1) \text{ if } n \text{ is odd}$$

and since $T(2) = T(1) = 2$, we conclude in either case that

$$T(n) > 2^{n/2} = (2^{1/2})^n = (\sqrt{2})^n > (1.4)^n \text{ for all } n > 2$$

The recursive function procedure *Fib* thus has computing time that is at least exponential. In fact, it can be shown that

$$T(n) = O\left(\left(\frac{1 + \sqrt{5}}{2}\right)^n\right)$$

where $\dfrac{1 + \sqrt{5}}{2} = 1.618034 \cdots$ is the *golden ratio* approached by ratios of consecutive Fibonacci numbers:

$$\frac{1}{1} = 1$$

$$\frac{2}{1} = 2$$

$$\frac{3}{2} = 1.5$$

$$\frac{5}{3} = 1.6666 \cdots$$

$$\frac{8}{5} = 1.6$$

$$\frac{13}{8} = 1.61825$$

$$\downarrow$$

$$\frac{1 + \sqrt{5}}{2} = 1.618034 \cdots$$

In contrast, the computing time of the following nonrecursive Fibonacci function procedure is easily seen to grow linearly with *n*; that is,

$$T_{NR}(n) = O(n)$$

PROCEDURE *NRFib* (*n* : CARDINAL) : CARDINAL;

    (∗ Nonrecursive function procedure to compute the
      *n*th Fibonacci number ∗)

    VAR
        Fib1, Fib2, Fib3,   (∗ 3 consecutive Fibonacci numbers ∗)
        i : CARDINAL;   (∗ index ∗)

    BEGIN
        Fib1 := 1;
        Fib2 := 1;
        FOR *i* := 3 TO *n* DO
            Fib3 := *Fib1* + *Fib2*;
            Fib1 := *Fib2*;
            Fib2 := *Fib3*
        END (∗ FOR ∗);
        RETURN *Fib2*
    END *NRFib*;

On one machine, the time required to compute $NRFib(n)$ for $n \le 30$ was less than 3 milliseconds, whereas the time to compute $Fib(n)$ was much greater, as shown by the following table (time is in milliseconds):

n	10	15	20	22	24	26	28	30
Time	6	69	784	2054	5465	14121	36921	96494

Quite obviously, the nonrecursive function procedure $NRFib$ is to be preferred over the recursive procedure Fib.

In summary, calculating powers and finding Fibonacci numbers are examples of problems that can be solved with nearly equal ease with the use of either a nonrecursive algorithm or a recursive one. For reasons that will become apparent in Section 5.5, nonrecursive procedures usually (but not always) execute more rapidly and use memory more efficiently than do the corresponding recursive procedures. Thus, if the problem can be solved recursively or nonrecursively with little difference in effort, it is usually appropriate to use the nonrecursive version.

There are many problems, however, in which it is more natural and straightforward to give a recursive algorithm for solving the problem. Two examples are the Towers of Hanoi and parsing problems described in the next section. Other examples will arise in later chapters when we consider data structures that are defined recursively. For such problems, it is often not obvious how the nonrecursive procedures used to implement the basic algorithms should be formulated. A good deal of effort may be required to develop them, and the results are often much less readable and understandable than the recursive versions. In such cases, the simplicity and elegance of the recursive procedures more than compensate for any inefficiency they may have. Unless these procedures are to be executed a large number of times and it can be demonstrated that the corresponding nonrecursive formulations are more efficient, the extra effort required to develop the nonrecursive versions is not warranted.

Exercises

1. Determine what is calculated by the following recursive function procedures:

   (a) PROCEDURE $F(n$: CARDINAL) : CARDINAL;

   ```
   BEGIN
       IF n = 0 THEN
           RETURN 0
       ELSE
           RETURN n * F(n - 1)
       END (* IF *)
   END F;
   ```

(b) PROCEDURE $F(x : \text{REAL}; n : \text{CARDINAL}) : \text{REAL};$

    BEGIN
       IF $n = 0$ THEN
          RETURN 0.0
       ELSE
          RETURN $x + F(x, n - 1)$
       END (* IF *)
    END F;

(c) PROCEDURE $F(n : \text{CARDINAL}) : \text{CARDINAL};$

    BEGIN
       IF $n < 2$ THEN
          RETURN 0
       ELSE
          RETURN $1 + F(n \text{ DIV } 2)$
       END (* IF *)
    END F;

2. Write nonrecursive versions of the function procedures in Exercise 1.

3. Use mathematical induction to prove the correctness of the function procedures in Exercise 1.

4. Using the basic string operations length, concatenate, substring, and index (see Section 3.1), develop a recursive algorithm for reversing a string.

5. Proceed as in Exercise 4, but develop a nonrecursive algorithm.

6. **(a)** Write a recursive function procedure that implements the algorithm in this section for determining if a number is a palindrome.
   (b) Use the function procedure of part (a) in a program that checks if several numbers are palindromes.

7. **(a)** Write a recursive function procedure that returns the number of digits in a nonnegative integer.
   (b) Write a program to test the function procedure of part (a).

8. Proceed as in Exercise 7, but write a nonrecursive function procedure.

9. The *greatest common divisor* of two integers a and b, GCD(a,b), not both of which are zero, is the largest positive integer that divides both a and b. The *Euclidean algorithm* for finding this greatest common divisor of a and b is as follows: Divide a by b to obtain the integer quotient q and remainder r, so that $a = bq + r$ (if $b = 0$, GCD(a,b) $= a$). Then GCD(a,b) $=$ GCD(b,r). Replace a and b and b with r and repeat this procedure. Because the remainders are decreasing,

eventually a remainder of 0 results. The last nonzero remainder is GCD(a,b). For example:

$$1260 = 198 \cdot 6 + 72 \qquad \text{GCD}(1260, 198) = \text{GCD}(198, 72)$$
$$198 = 72 \cdot 2 + 54 \qquad\qquad\qquad\quad\;\; = \text{GCD}(72, 54)$$
$$72 = 54 \cdot 1 + 18 \qquad\qquad\qquad\quad\;\; = \text{GCD}(54, 18)$$
$$54 = 18 \cdot 3 + 0 \qquad\qquad\qquad\qquad\;\;\; = 18$$

(*Note*: if either a or b is negative, we replace them with their absolute values in this algorithm.)

(a) Write a recursive greatest common divisor function procedure.
(b) Write a program that uses the function procedure of part (a) to find the greatest common divisor of several pairs of numbers.

10. Proceed as in Exercise 9, but write a nonrecursive function procedure.

11. *Binomial coefficients* can be defined recursively as follows:

$$\left.\begin{array}{l} \dbinom{n}{0} = 1 \\[2mm] \dbinom{n}{n} = 1 \end{array}\right\} \text{(anchor)}$$

$$\text{For } 0 < k < n, \quad \binom{n}{k} = \binom{n-1}{k-1} + \binom{n-1}{k} \quad \text{(inductive step)}$$

(a) Write a recursive procedure to calculate binomial coefficients.
(b) Draw a recursion tree like that in this section showing the procedure references and returns involved in calculating the binomial coefficient $\dbinom{4}{2}$.

(c) Use your recursive procedure in a program that reads values for n and k and displays the value of $\dbinom{n}{k}$, using the procedure to obtain this value.

12. Binomial coefficients can also be defined as follows:

$$\binom{n}{k} = \frac{n!}{k!(n-k)!}$$

(a) Write a nonrecursive procedure for calculating binomial coefficients using this definition.
(b) If possible with your version of Modula-2, write a program to compare the computing time of this nonrecursive procedure for calculating binomial coefficients with the recursive procedure developed in Exercise 9. (See Exercise 5 of Section 3.4.)

13. (a) Write a recursive procedure that prints a nonnegative integer with commas in the correct locations. For example, it should print 20131 as 20,131.

(b) Write a program to test the procedure of part (a).

14. Consider a square grid, some of whose cells are empty and others contain an asterisk. Define two asterisks to be *contiguous* if they are adjacent to each other in the same row or in the same column. Now suppose we define a *blob* as follows:

(a) A blob contains at least one asterisk.

(b) If an asterisk is in a blob, then so is any asterisk that is contiguous to it.

(c) If a blob has more than two asterisks, then each asterisk in it is contiguous to at least one other asterisk in the blob.

For example, there are four blobs in the partial grid

seven blobs in

and only one in

Write a program that uses a recursive procedure to count the number of blobs in a square grid. Input to the program should consist of the locations of the asterisks in the grid, and the program should display the grid and the blob count.

15. Consider a network of streets laid out in a rectangular grid; for example,

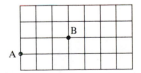

In a *northeast path* from one point in the grid to another, one may walk only to the north and to the east. For example, there are four northeast paths from A to B in the preceding grid:

Write a program that uses a recursive procedure to count the number of northeast paths from one point to another in a rectangular grid.

16. In Sections 4.1 and 4.2 we considered the problem of converting an integer from base-ten to base-two and we used a stack to store the binary digits so they could be displayed in correct order. Write a recursive procedure to accomplish this conversion without using a stack.

17. Write a recursive procedure to find the prime factorization of an integer, and display these prime factors in descending order. (See Exercise 8 of Section 4.2.)

18. Develop a recursive procedure to generate all of the $n!$ permutations of $\{1, 2, \ldots, n\}$. (*Hint*: The permutations of $\{1, 2, \ldots, k\}$ can be obtained by considering each permutation of $\{1, 2, \ldots, k - 1\}$ as an ordered list and inserting k into each of the k possible positions in this list, including at the front and at the rear. For example, the permutations of $\{1, 2\}$ are $(1,2)$ and $(2,1)$. Inserting 3 into each of the three possible positions of the first permutation yields the permutations $(3, 1, 2)$, $(1, 3, 2)$, and $(1, 2, 3)$ of $\{1, 2, 3\}$, and using the second permutation gives $(3, 2, 1)$, $(2, 3, 1)$, and $(2, 1, 3)$. Write a program to test your procedure.

5.4   Examples of Recursion: Towers of Hanoi; Parsing

Towers of Hanoi.   The Towers of Hanoi problem is a classic example of a problem for which a recursive algorithm is especially appropriate. It can be solved very easily by using recursion, but a nonrecursive solution is quite difficult. The problem is to solve the puzzle shown in Figure 5.1, in which one

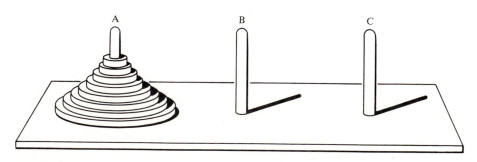

Figure 5.1

must move the disks from the left peg to the right peg according to the following rules:

1. When a disk is moved, it must be placed on one of the three pegs.
2. Only one disk may be moved at a time, and it must be the top disk on one of the pegs.
3. A larger disk may never be placed on top of a smaller one.

Legend has it that the priests in the Temple of Bramah were given a puzzle consisting of a golden platform with three golden needles on which were placed 64 golden disks. Time was to end when they had successfully finished moving the disks to another needle, following the preceding rules. (*Query*: If the priests moved one disk per second and began their work in the year 0, when would time come to an end?)

Novices usually find the puzzle easy to solve for a small number of disks, but they have considerable difficulty as the number of disks grows to seven, eight, and beyond. To a computer scientist, however, the Towers of Hanoi puzzle is easy:

If there is one disk, move it from Peg A to Peg C; thus the puzzle is solvable for $n = 1$ disk.

Assuming that a solution exists for $n - 1$ disks, a solution for n disks can easily be obtained recursively:

1. Move the topmost $n - 1$ disks from Peg A to Peg B, using C as an auxiliary peg.
2. Move the large disk remaining on Peg A to Peg C.
3. Move the $n - 1$ disks from Peg B to Peg C, using Peg A as an auxiliary peg.

This scheme is implemented by the following recursive procedure:

```
PROCEDURE Move (n : CARDINAL; StartPeg, AuxPeg, EndPeg : CHAR);

    (* Procedure to move n disks from StartPeg to EndPeg using
       AuxPeg as an auxiliary peg. *)

BEGIN
    IF n = 1 THEN
        WriteLn;
        WriteString('Move disk from ');
        Write(StartPeg);
        WriteString(' to ');
        Write(EndPeg)
    ELSE
        (* Move n - 1 disks from StartPeg to AuxPeg using EndPeg *)

        Move(n - 1, StartPeg, EndPeg, AuxPeg);

        (* Move disk from StartPeg to EndPeg * )

        Move(1, StartPeg, ' ', EndPeg);
```

(* Move $n - 1$ disks from *AuxPeg* to *EndPeg* using *StartPeg* *)

$$Move(n - 1, AuxPeg, StartPeg, EndPeg)$$
                    END (* IF *)
          END *Move*;

The program in Figure 5.2 uses this procedure to solve the problem.

```
MODULE TowersOfHanoi;

   (*************************************************************

      Program using the recursive procedure Move to solve the
      Towers Of Hanoi puzzle.

      *************************************************************)

   FROM InOut IMPORT Write, WriteString, WriteLn, ReadCard;

   CONST
       Peg1 = 'A';
       Peg2 = 'B';
       Peg3 = 'C';

   VAR
       NumDisks : CARDINAL;   (* number of disks *)

   PROCEDURE Move (n : CARDINAL; StartPeg, AuxPeg, EndPeg : CHAR);

       (*************************************************************

           Procedure to move n disks from StartPeg to EndPeg using
           AuxPeg as an auxiliary peg.

          *************************************************************)

       BEGIN
          IF n = 1 THEN
              WriteLn;
              WriteString('Move disk from ');
              Write(StartPeg);
              WriteString(' to ');
              Write(EndPeg)
          ELSE
              (* Move n-1 disks from StartPeg to AuxPeg using EndPeg *)

              Move(n - 1, StartPeg, EndPeg, AuxPeg);

              (* Move disk from StartPeg to EndPeg *)

              Move(1, StartPeg, ' ', EndPeg);

              (* Move n-1 disks from AuxPeg to EndPeg using StartPeg *)

              Move(n - 1, AuxPeg, StartPeg, EndPeg)
          END (* IF *)
       END Move;
```

Figure 5.2

Figure 5.2 (cont.)

```
BEGIN
    WriteString('Enter number of disks: ');
    ReadCard(NumDisks);
    WriteLn;
    Move (NumDisks, Peg1, Peg2, Peg3)
END TowersOfHanoi.
```

Sample run:

```
Enter number of disks: 4

Move disk from A to B
Move disk from A to C
Move disk from B to C
Move disk from A to B
Move disk from C to A
Move disk from C to B
Move disk from A to B
Move disk from A to C
Move disk from B to C
Move disk from B to A
Move disk from C to A
Move disk from B to C
Move disk from A to B
Move disk from A to C
Move disk from B to C
```

Parsing. All the examples of recursion that we have given thus far have used direct recursion. To illustrate indirect recursion, in which some chain of procedure references eventually results in a reference to the first procedure in this chain, we consider the compiler problem of processing arithmetic expressions. In particular, we consider the specific problem of parsing arithmetic expressions, that is, determining if they are well formed and, if so, what their structure is.

The *syntax rules* of a language specify how basic constructs such as assignment statements and expressions are formed. Consequently, an arithmetic expression is well formed if it is consistent with the syntax rules for generating arithmetic expressions. These syntax rules are commonly stated as *substitution rules*, or *productions*. For the simplified arithmetic expressions considered in the preceding section, the rules might be the following:

(1) *expression* → *term* + *term* | *term* − *term* | *term*
(2) *term* → *factor* * *factor* | *factor* / *factor* | *factor*
(3) *factor* → (*expression*) | *letter* | *digit*

Here the vertical bar (|) is used to separate the various alternatives. For example, the third syntax rule specifies that a factor may be a left parenthesis followed by an expression followed by a right parenthesis, or it may be a single letter or a single digit.

As an illustration of how these syntax rules are used in parsing an arith-

metic expression, consider the expression 2 * (3 + 4). According to the first
syntax rule, an expression can be a term, and by the second rule, a term may
have the form *factor * factor*. These substitutions can be displayed by the
following partially developed **parse tree** for this expression:

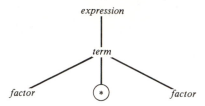

By the third syntax rule, a factor may be a digit; in particular, it may be the
digit 2;

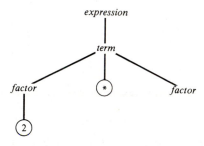

and the second alternative of the third syntax rule specifies that a factor may
be an expression enclosed in parentheses:

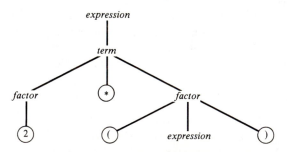

Continued application of these syntax rules produces the following complete
parse tree, which shows how 2 * (3 + 4) can be generated according to the
syntax rules and thus demonstrates that it is a legal expression:

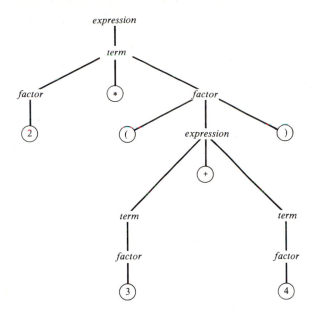

It is clear that these syntax rules for expressions involve indirect recursion. For example, an expression may be a term, which may be a factor, which may be a parenthesized expression, thus defining an expression indirectly in terms of itself.

The program in Figure 5.3 for parsing these simplified arithmetic expressions uses the three procedures *CheckForExpression*, *CheckForTerm*, and *CheckForFactor*, which are derived directly from the corresponding syntax rules. For example, consider the procedure *CheckForExpression*. According to the first syntax rule, an expression may have one of the three forms

    term + *term*
    term − *term*
    term

In each case, it must begin with a term, and so the first action in this procedure is a call to *CheckForTerm*.

If *CheckForTerm* identifies a valid term and returns the value true for *Valid*, then the procedure *CheckForExpression* must examine the next symbol to determine which of these three forms is applicable, and so it calls *GetChar*. If this symbol is + or −, *CheckForTerm* must then be called to check for one of the first two forms for an expression; *CheckForExpression* then returns the value true or false (for parameter *Valid*) to the main program according to whether *CheckForTerm* returns the value true or false. If the symbol is not + or −, then an expression of the last form has been identified, and the procedure must "back up" one symbol before resuming the parse.

The following table traces the action of these three procedures in parsing the first expression $A + B$ used in the sample run:

Active Procedure	Symbol	Pos	Valid	Action
Main program		0		Call *CheckForExpression*.
CheckForExpression		0		Call *CheckForTerm*.
CheckForTerm		0		Call *CheckForFactor*.
CheckForFactor		0		Call *GetChar* to get next symbol.
	A	1		*GetChar* returns *Symbol* = 'A' and increments *Pos*.
	A	1		ELSE clause sets *Valid* to true, and execution returns to *CheckForTerm*.
CheckForTerm	A	1	TRUE	Call *GetChar* to get next symbol.
	+	2	TRUE	"Unget" symbol because it is not * or /, and return to *CheckForExpression*.
CheckForExpression	A	1	TRUE	Call *GetChar* to get next symbol.
	+	2	TRUE	Since *Symbol* is in $\{'+', '-'\}$, call *CheckForTerm*.
CheckForTerm	+	2	TRUE	Call *CheckForFactor*.
CheckForFactor	+	2	TRUE	Call *GetChar* to get next symbol.
	B	3	TRUE	*GetChar* increments *Pos* and returns *Symbol* = 'B'.
	B	3	TRUE	ELSE clause sets *Valid* to true, and execution returns to *CheckForTerm*.
CheckForTerm	B	3	TRUE	Call *GetChar* to get next symbol.
	$	4	TRUE	"Unget" symbol because it is not * or /, and return to *CheckForExpression*.
CheckForExpression	B	3	TRUE	Return to main program.
Main Program	B	3	TRUE	Because the value TRUE is returned for *ValidExpression* and *Expr*[*Pos*] is the end-of-string mark, signaling a complete parse, print message indicating a valid expression.

For the second expression $A + B)$ in the sample run, the same trace table results, except that when execution returns to the main program, *Expr*[*Pos*] is ')' and not the end-of-string mark, and so the end of the string *Expr* has not been reached, indicating an unsuccessful parse.

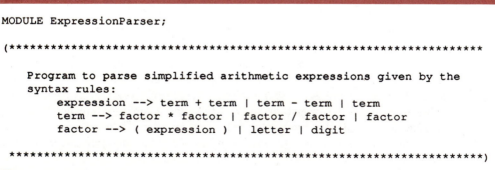

```
MODULE ExpressionParser;

(******************************************************************

    Program to parse simplified arithmetic expressions given by the
    syntax rules:
        expression --> term + term | term - term | term
        term --> factor * factor | factor / factor | factor
        factor --> ( expression ) | letter | digit

******************************************************************)
```

Figure 5.3

Figure 5.3   (cont.)

```
FROM InOut IMPORT WriteString, WriteLn, Read;
FROM SpecialInOut IMPORT ReadAString;

CONST
    MaxLength = 50;             (* maximum length of expression *)
    EOS = 0C;                   (* end-of-string mark *)

TYPE
    ArithExpression = ARRAY[0..MaxLength] OF CHAR;

VAR
    Expr : ArithExpression;     (* expression to be parsed *)
    Pos  : CARDINAL;            (* position of next character in Expr *)
    ValidExpression : BOOLEAN;  (* signals if well-formed expression found *)
    Response : CHAR;            (* user response to control repetition *)

PROCEDURE GetChar(    Expr : ArithExpression;
                  VAR Pos : CARDINAL;
                  VAR NextSymbol : CHAR);
    (***********************************************************

        Procedure to get the next nonblank symbol NextSymbol in
        expression Expr.  Pos is positioned after this symbol.

        ***********************************************************)

    BEGIN
        WHILE Expr[Pos] = ' ' DO
            INC(Pos)
        END (* WHILE *);
        NextSymbol := Expr[Pos];
        INC(Pos)
    END GetChar;

PROCEDURE CheckForExpression(    Expr : ArithExpression;
                             VAR Pos : CARDINAL;
                             VAR Valid : BOOLEAN);

    (***********************************************************

        Returns Valid = TRUE if there is a valid expression in
        Expr, beginning at the current position Pos.

        ***********************************************************)

    VAR
        Symbol : CHAR;              (* symbol in Expr *)
```

Figure 5.3   (cont.)

```
    BEGIN
        CheckForTerm (Expr, Pos, Valid);
        IF Valid THEN
            GetChar(Expr, Pos, Symbol);
            IF (Symbol = '+') OR (Symbol = '-') THEN
                CheckForTerm(Expr, Pos, Valid)
            ELSE
                (* "Unget" a character *)
                DEC(Pos)
            END (* IF *)
        END (* IF *);
    END CheckForExpression;

  PROCEDURE CheckForTerm(    Expr : ArithExpression;
                         VAR Pos : CARDINAL;
                         VAR Valid : BOOLEAN);

    (*****************************************************************

        Returns Valid = TRUE if there is a valid Term in Expr
        beginning at the current position Pos.

    *****************************************************************)

    VAR
        Symbol : CHAR;              (* symbol in Expr *)

    BEGIN
        CheckForFactor(Expr, Pos, Valid);
        IF Valid THEN
            GetChar (Expr, Pos, Symbol);
            IF (Symbol = '*') OR (Symbol = '/') THEN
                CheckForFactor(Expr, Pos, Valid)
            ELSE
                (* "Unget" a character *)
                DEC(Pos)
            END (* IF *)
        END (* IF *);
    END CheckForTerm;

  PROCEDURE CheckForFactor(    Expr : ArithExpression;
                           VAR Pos : CARDINAL;
                           VAR Valid : BOOLEAN);

    (*****************************************************************

        Returns Valid = TRUE if there is a valid factor in Expr
        beginning at the current position Pos.

    *****************************************************************)

    VAR
        Symbol : CHAR;              (* symbol in Expr *)
```

Figure 5.3   (cont.)

```
        BEGIN
            GetChar(Expr, Pos, Symbol);
            IF Symbol = '(' THEN
                CheckForExpression(Expr, Pos, Valid);
                IF Valid THEN
                    GetChar(Expr, Pos, Symbol);
                    IF Symbol # ')' THEN
                        Valid := FALSE
                    END (* IF *)
                END (* IF *)
            ELSE
                Valid := ('a' <= Symbol) AND (Symbol <= 'z') OR
                         ('A' <= Symbol) AND (Symbol <= 'Z') OR
                         ('0' <= Symbol) AND (Symbol <= '9')
            END (* IF *)
        END CheckForFactor;

BEGIN (* main program *)
    REPEAT
        WriteLn;
        WriteString('Enter arithmetic expression:  ');
        ReadAString(Expr);

        (* Parse the expression *)
        Pos := 0;
        CheckForExpression(Expr, Pos, ValidExpression);
        WriteLn;
        IF ValidExpression AND (Expr[Pos] = EOS) THEN
            WriteString('Valid Expression')
        ELSE
            WriteString('Not a Valid Expression')
        END (* IF *);
        WriteLn; WriteLn;
        WriteString('More (Y or N)?  ');
        Read(Response)
    UNTIL CAP(Response) #'Y'
END ExpressionParser.
```

Sample Run:

```
Enter arithmetic expression:  A+B
Valid Expression

More (Y or N)?  Y
Enter arithmetic expression:  A+B)
Not a Valid Expression

More (Y or N)?  Y
Enter arithmetic expression:  A*B
Valid Expression

More (Y or N)?  Y
Enter arithmetic expression:  ((((1))))
Valid Expression
```

Figure 5.3 (cont.)

```
More (Y or N)?  Y
Enter arithmetic expression:   ((A+B)  - C
Not a Valid Expression

More (Y or N)?  Y
Enter arithmetic expression:   (((A + B) * 2) - (C*D)) * 5
Valid Expression

More (Y or N)?  N
```

Exercises

1. Write a recurrence relation for the computing time of procedure *Move* in the program *TowersOfHanoi* and solve it to find this computing time.

2. Use mathematical induction to prove that the minimum number of moves required to solve the Towers of Hanoi puzzle with *n* disks is $2^n - 1$.

3. Modify the program in Figure 5.2 so that it displays a picture of each move rather than a verbal description.

4. Draw parse trees for the following expressions:

   (a) $A * B$ (b) $(A * B)$
   (c) $(((1)))$ (d) $(A * B) * C$
   (e) $A * (B * C)$ (f) $(((A + B) * 2) - (C * D)) * 5$

5. Construct trace tables like those in the text for parses of the following expressions:

   (a) $A * B$ (b) $(A * B)$
   (c) $(A - B) - C$ (d) $A - (B - C)$

6. By adding the production

   $$AssignmentStatement \rightarrow letter := expression$$

   at the beginning of the list of syntax rules for simplified expressions in this section, we obtain a list of syntax rules for simplified assignment statements. Extend the program of Figure 5.3 so it will parse such assignment statements.

7. Syntax rules for simplified boolean expressions might be the following:

   $$bexpression \rightarrow bterm \text{ OR } bterm \mid bterm$$

> *bterm* → *bfactor* AND *bfactor* | *bfactor*
> *bfactor* → NOT *bfactor* | (*bexpression*) | *letter* | TRUE | FALSE

Write a program that parses such boolean expressions. In the input string, you may simplify matters by using the symbols |, &, and ~ for OR, AND and NOT, respectively.

8. Write a program that reads lines of input, each of which is a (perhaps invalid) Modula-2 statement, and that strips each line of all valid Modula-2 comments. However, the structure of your program is restricted as follows:

(a) The only repetition structure allowed is a "while not eof" loop for reading the input; all other repetition must be carried out by using recursion.

(b) The characters must be read one at a time, and looking ahead at the next character in the input buffer is not allowed.

Execute your program with at least the following lines of input

```
Distance := Rate * Time;
Wages := ((*** regular ***) Hours * Rate (* hourly *));
WriteString('(*** DISPATCH UNIVERSITY ***)');
Temp(*erature*) := ((* Centigrade *)Deg(*rees*)*1.0);
Temp( *erature*) := (((((* zero *) 0 ))));
```

The output produced by your program for this input should be

```
Distance := Rate * Time;
Wages := ( Hours * Rate );
WriteString('(*** DISPATCH UNIVERSITY ***)');
Temp := (Deg*1.0);
Temp( *erature*) := (((( 0 ))));
```

9. Strings consisting of balanced parentheses can be generated by the productions

> *pstring* → (*pstring*) *pstring* | ( ) *pstring* | (*pstring*) | ( )

Write a program that reads a string consisting only of parentheses and that determines whether the parentheses are balanced.

10. Proceed as in Exercise 8, but design the program to read any string, ignoring all characters other than parentheses.

5.5 Implementing Recursion

Whenever execution of a program or procedure is initiated, a set of memory locations called an ***activation record*** is created for it. If execution is interrupted by a reference to another (or the same) procedure, the values of the procedure's local variables, parameters, the return address, and so on, are stored in this activation record. When execution of this program unit resumes, its activation record is used to restore these items to what they were before the interruption occurred.

Suppose, for example, that program A references procedure B, which, in turn, references procedure C. When A is initiated, its activation record is created. When A references B so that B becomes active, its activation record is also created. Similarly, when B references C, C becomes the active procedure, and its activation record is created. When execution of C terminates and control is passed back to B so that it becomes active again, the values in its activation record are the values of its parameters and local variables at the time B was interrupted; thus these values are the ones needed to resume execution of B. Likewise, when B terminates and A is reactivated, its activation record is needed to restore the values being used before its interruption. In each case, the fact that the last (sub)program interrupted is the first one to be reactivated suggests that a stack can be used to store the addresses of the activation records so they can be retrieved in a last-in–first-out order.

As an illustration, consider the recursive function procedure of Section 5.2 for calculating powers

```
      PROCEDURE Power(x : REAL; n : CARDINAL) : REAL;

           BEGIN
                IF n = 0 THEN
                     RETURN 1.0
                ELSE
(* A *)              RETURN x * Power(x, n − 1)
                END (* IF *)
           END Power;
```

and a reference to it in an assignment statement:

```
           BEGIN (* program PowerDemo *)
                .
                .
                .
(* B *)    z := Power(2.7, 3);
                .
                .
                .
           END PowerDemo;
```

Here we have indicated as A and B the return addresses, that is, the locations of the instructions where execution is to resume when the program or procedure is reactivated.

When execution of the main program is initialized, its activation record is created. This record is used to store the values of variables, actual parameters, return addresses, and so on during the time the program is active. When execution of the main program is interrupted by the function reference $Power(2.7, 3)$, this activation record, which contains the parameters 2.7 and 3 and the return address B (plus other items of information), is pushed onto a stack.

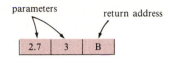

The function procedure *Power* now becomes active, and an activation record is created for it. When the statement

RETURN $x * Power(x, n - 1)$

is encountered, the execution of *Power* is interrupted. This activation record, which contains the actual parameters 2.7 and 2 for the function reference with parameters $x = 2.7$ and $n - 1 = 3 - 1 = 2$ and the return address A (and other items of information), is pushed onto the stack of activation records.

Second reference to
Power $(x=2.7, n=2)$:

2.7	2	A
2.7	3	B

Since this is a new reference to *Power*, another activation record is created, and when this reference is interrupted by the reference *Power*(2.7, 1), this activation record is pushed onto the stack:

Third reference to
Power $(x=2.7, n=1)$:

2.7	1	A
2.7	2	A
2.7	3	B

The reference *Power*(2.7, 1) results in the creation of yet another activation record, and when its execution is interrupted, this time by the reference *Power*(2.7, 0), this activation record is pushed onto the stack:

Fourth reference to
Power $(x=2.7, n=0)$:

2.7	0	A
2.7	1	A
2.7	2	A
2.7	3	B

Execution of *Power* with parameters 2.7 and 0 terminates with no interruptions and calculates the value 1.0 for *Power*(2.7, 0). The activation record for this reference is then popped from the stack, and execution resumes at the statement specified by the return address in it:

First return from *Power*:

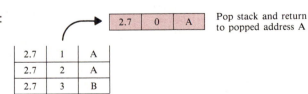

Pop stack and return
to popped address A

2.7	1	A
2.7	2	A
2.7	3	B

Execution of the preceding reference to *Power* with parameters 2.7 and 1 then resumes and terminates without interruption, so its activation record is popped from the stack and the value 2.7 returned, and the previous reference with parameters 2.7 and 2 is reactivated at statement A:

Second return from *Power*:

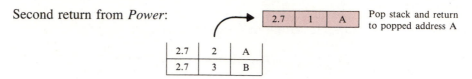

Pop stack and return to popped address A

This process continues until the value 19.683 is computed for the original reference *Power*(2.7, 3) and execution of the main program is resumed at the statement specified by the return address *B* in its activation record.

Third return from *Power*:

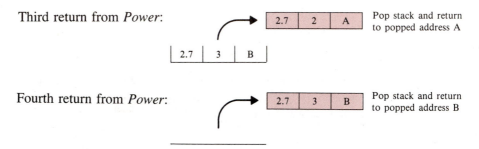

Pop stack and return to popped address A

Fourth return from *Power*:

Pop stack and return to popped address B

6

Queues

The data structure considered in the last two chapters was the stack. We defined stacks, considered array-based implementations of stacks in some detail, and looked at several of their applications, in particular, how they are used to support recursion. In this chapter we consider another data structure, the *queue*, whose definition is quite similar to that of a stack and whose applications are at least as numerous as applications of stacks. Also, like stacks, implementations of queues using arrays as the basic storage structures are common, but as we will discover, a bit more effort is required to construct an efficient array-based implementation. The chapter closes with a simulation of an information/reservations center in which an "on-hold" queue is used to store incoming telephone calls.

6.1 Introduction

According to Webster, a *queue* is a "waiting line," such as a line of persons waiting to check out at a supermarket, a line of vehicles at a toll booth, a queue of planes waiting to land at an airport, or a queue of jobs in a computer system waiting for some output device such as a printer. In each of these examples, the items are serviced in the order in which they arrive; that is, the first item in the queue is the first to be served. Thus, whereas a stack is a Last-In–First-Out (LIFO) structure, a queue is a *First-In–First-Out (FIFO)* or *First-Come–First-Served (FCFS)* structure.

As a data structure, a queue, like a stack, is a special kind of list in which the basic insert and delete operations are restricted to the ends of the list. Unlike stacks in which elements are popped and pushed at only one end of the list, items are removed from a queue at one end, called the *front* or *head* of the queue, and elements are added only at the other end, called the *rear* or *tail*.

Other basic operations are creating an empty queue and determining if a queue is empty. Thus we assume the following basic queue operations:

CreateQ: Creates an empty queue.
EmptyQ: Determines if a queue is empty.
AddQ: Adds a new element at the rear of the queue.
RemoveQ: Retrieves and removes the item at the front of the queue.

A queue is obviously an appropriate data structure for storing items that must be processed in the order in which they are generated. As a simple example, suppose that a program is to be designed to provide drill-and-practice exercises in elementary arithmetic. More precisely, suppose that these exercises are problems involving the addition of randomly generated integers having two or fewer digits. If a student answers correctly, another problem is generated; but if he or she answers incorrectly, the problem is stored so that it can be asked again at the end of the session. It seems natural to present these incorrectly answered problems in the same order in which they were presented initially, and a queue is therefore an appropriate data structure for storing these exercises.

If we assume that the data type *QueueType* can be used to declare a queue *WrongQueue* of records of the form

```
RECORD
    Addend1,
    Addend2 : integer
END;
```

and that procedures *CreateQ*, *AddQ*, and *RemoveQ* and the boolean-valued function procedure *EmptyQ* implement the basic queue operations, then statements like the following can be used to generate a problem and add it to *WrongQueue* if it is answered incorrectly:

```
CreateQ(WrongQueue);
      .
      .
      .
Problem.Addend1 := RandomCard(NumberLimit);
Problem.Addend2 := RandomCard(NumberLimit);
Ask(Problem, Correct);
IF NOT Correct THEN
    AddQ(WrongQ, Problem)
END (* IF *);
```

Here *RandomCard* is a function procedure that returns random cardinals in a specified range (see Section 0.7), and *Ask* displays an addition problem to the student, reads an answer, and returns the appropriate value TRUE or FALSE for the boolean parameter *Correct* to indicate if the answer is correct. Statements such as the following can then be used to repeat problems that were answered incorrectly:

```
WHILE NOT EmptyQ(WrongQueue) DO
    RemoveQ(WrongQueue, Problem);
    Ask(Problem, Correct);
    IF NOT Correct THEN
        INC(Wrong)
    END (* IF *)
END (* WHILE *);
```

Queues are also commonly used to model waiting lines that arise in the operation of computer systems. These queues are formed whenever more than one process requires a particular resource, such as a printer or a disk drive or the central processing unit. As processes request a particular resource, they are placed in a queue to wait for service by that resource. For example, several personal computers may be sharing the same printer, and a *spool queue* is used to schedule output requests in a first-come–first-served manner. If a request for a print job is made and the printer is free, it is immediately allocated to this job. While this output is being printed, other jobs may need the printer. They are placed in a spool queue to wait their turns. When the output from the current job terminates, the printer is released from that job and is allocated to the first job in the spool queue.

Another important use of queues in computing systems is for *input/output buffering*. The transfer of information from an input device or to an output device is a relatively slow operation, and if the processing of a program must be suspended while data is transferred, program execution is slowed dramatically. One common solution to this problem uses sections of main memory known as *buffers* and transfers data between the program and these buffers rather than between the program and the input/output device directly.

In particular, consider the problem in which data being processed by a program is to be read from a disk file. This information is transferred from the disk file to an input buffer in main memory while the central processing unit (CPU) is performing some other task. When data is required by the program, the next value(s) stored in this buffer is retrieved. While this value is being processed, additional data values can be transferred from the disk file to the buffer. Clearly, the buffer must be organized as a first-in–first-out structure, that is, as a queue. A queue-empty condition indicates that the input buffer is empty, and program execution is suspended while the operating system attempts to load more data into the buffer or signals the end of input. Of course, such a buffer has a limited size, and thus a queue-full condition must also be used to signal when the buffer is full and no more data is to be transferred from the disk file to it.

The insert and delete operations for a queue are restricted so that insertions are performed at only one end and deletions at the other. In some applications, however, insertions and deletions must be made at both ends. To model these situations, a double-ended queue, abbreviated to *deque* (pronounced ''deck'') is an appropriate data structure to use (but it could as well be called a ''dack'' for ''double-ended stack''). For example, in the case of interactive input, the user can insert data into the input buffer by entering it from the keyboard. But the user may also be able to delete information by depressing a ''delete'' or "backspace" key. A deque might therefore be a more appropriate data structure for modeling this situation; or because data values are only removed and not inserted at the other end, a better model might be a queue-stack hybrid, sometimes called a *scroll* (although more colorful names might be "queue-and-a-half," or "heque" or "quack").

Another data structure related to the queue is the so-called *priority queue*. In this structure, a certain priority is associated with each item, and these items are to be stored in such a way that those with the highest priority are near the front of the queue so they will be removed from the queue and serviced before those of lower priority are. Within this structure, items of equal priority are scheduled in the usual queuelike manner, that is, in a first-come–first-served order. Priority queues, together with deques and scrolls, are considered in more detail in the exercises at the end of the next section.

6.2   Implementation of Queues with Arrays and Records

Because a queue resembles a stack in many ways, we might imitate the array-based implementation of a stack considered in Chapter 4 to construct an array-based implementation of a queue. Thus we might use an array to store the elements of the queue and maintain two variables: *Front* to record the position in the array of the element that can be removed, that is, the first queue element; and *Rear* to record the position in the array at which an element can be added, that is, the position following the last queue element. An element is then removed from the queue by retrieving the array element at position *Front* and then incrementing *Front* by 1. An item is added to the queue by storing it at position *Rear* of the array, provided that *Rear* does not exceed some maximum size *MaxSize* allowed for the array, and then incrementing *Rear* by 1.

The difficulty with this implementation is that elements "shift to the right" in the array, so that eventually all the array elements may have to be shifted back to the beginning positions. For example, consider a queue for which *MaxSize* = 5 and whose elements are integers. The sequence of operations *AddQ* 70, *AddQ* 80, *AddQ* 50 produces the following configuration:

Now suppose that two elements are removed:

and that 90 and 60 are then added:

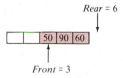

Before another item can be inserted into the queue, the elements in the array must be shifted back to the beginning of the array:

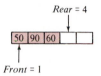

This shifting of array elements can be avoided if we think of the array as **circular**, with the first element following the last. This can be done by indexing the array beginning with 0, and incrementing *Front* and *Rear* using addition modulo *MaxSize*. For the sequence of operations just considered, this implementation yields the following configurations:

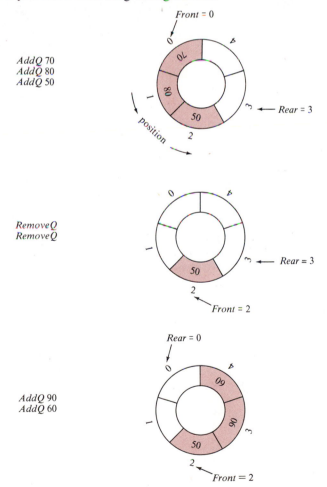

Another insertion is now possible without our having to move any array elements; we simply store the item in position *Rear* = 0.

Now consider the basic operation *EmptyQ* to determine if a queue is empty. If the queue contains a single element, it is in position *Front* of the array, and *Rear* is the vacant position following it. If this element is deleted, *Front* is incremented by 1 so that *Front* and *Rear* have the same value. Thus, to determine whether a queue is empty, we need only check the condition *Front* = *Rear*. Initially, *CreateQ* sets both *Front* and *Rear* equal to 0.

Just as the array implementation for a stack introduced the possibility of stack-full condition, the implementation of a queue raises the possibility of a queue-full condition. To see how this condition can be detected, suppose that the array is almost full, with only one empty location remaining:

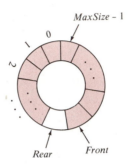

If an item is stored in this location, *Rear* would be incremented by 1 and thus would have the same value as *Front*. However, the condition *Front* = *Rear* indicates that the queue is empty. Thus, we would not be able to distinguish between an empty queue and a full queue if this location were used to store an element. We can avoid this difficulty if we maintain one empty position in the array; the condition indicating that a queue is full then becomes (*Rear* + 1) MOD *MaxSize* = *Front*.

In summary, to implement a queue, we can use for the storage structure a record consisting of a circular array to store the queue elements and fields *Front* and *Rear* to record the position of the front element and the position following the last element, respectively:

```
CONST
    MaxSize = . . .;   (* maximum number of queue elements *)

TYPE
    ElementType = . . .;   (* type of elements in the queue *)
    QueueArray = ARRAY [0 .. MaxSize − 1] OF ElementType;
    QueueType = RECORD
                    Front, Rear : [0 .. MaxSize − 1];
                    Element : QueueArray
                END;

VAR
    Queue : QueueType;
```

The operation of creating an empty queue consists of simply setting both of the fields *Front* and *Rear* of *Queue* to 0 (or to any other value in [0 .. *MaxSize* − 1]); and a queue will be empty when the boolean expression *Queue.Front* = *Queue.Rear* is true. An algorithm for the *AddQ* operation is

AddQ

(∗ Algorithm to add *Item* at the rear of *Queue*, assuming the array is not full. ∗)

1. Set *NewRear* equal to (*Queue.Rear* + 1) MOD *MaxSize*.
2. If *NewRear* = *Queue.Front*, then
   Display a queue-full message and terminate execution.
   Otherwise do the following
       a. Set *Queue.Element*[*NewRear*] equal to *Item*.
       b. Set *Queue.Rear* equal to *NewRear*.

And an algorithm for the *RemoveQ* operation is

RemoveQ

(∗ Algorithm to retrieve *Item* and delete it from the front of *Queue*, assuming the array is not empty ∗)

If the queue is empty then
    Display a queue-empty message and terminate execution.
Otherwise do the following:
    a. Set *Item* equal to the element *Queue.Element*[*Queue.Front*] at the front of the queue.
    b. Set *Queue.Front* equal to (*Queue.Front* + 1) MOD *MaxSize*.

The program in Figure 6.1 solves the drill-and-practice problem considered in the preceding section. It assumes the existence of a library module *QueuesLib1* for processing queues from which the type *QueueType* and procedures *CreateQ*, *EmptyQ*, *AddQ*, and *RemoveQ* can be imported. The development of such a module for implementing the queue data type is left as an exercise.

```
MODULE DrillAndPractice;

(*********************************************************************

   Program to randomly generate drill-and-practice addition problems.
   Problems that are answered incorrectly on the first attempt are
   queued and asked again at the end of the session.

*********************************************************************)
```

Figure 6.1

Figure 6.1 (cont.)

```
FROM InOut IMPORT WriteString, WriteCard, WriteLn, Read, ReadCard;
FROM QueuesLib1 IMPORT ElementType, QueueType, CreateQ, EmptyQ,
                       AddQ, RemoveQ, NumberLimit, ProblemRecord;
FROM Random IMPORT RandomCard;

VAR
    WrongQueue : QueueType;    (* queue of problems answered wrong *)
    Correct : BOOLEAN;         (* indicates if answer correct or not *)
    Problem : ProblemRecord;   (* an addition problem *)
    NumProblems,               (* number of problems asked *)
    Count,                     (* index *)
    Wrong : CARDINAL;          (* number gotten wrong -- on both tries *)


PROCEDURE Ask(   Problem : ProblemRecord;
               VAR Correct : BOOLEAN;
                   RoundNum : CARDINAL);

    (***************************************************************

        Procedure to display an addition Problem, read student's Answer,
        check if it agrees with Sum, and return TRUE or FALSE for
        Correct according to whether or not the answer is correct.
        If RoundNum = 2, correct answer is displayed.

    ***************************************************************)

    VAR
        Answer,                (* student's answer *)
        Sum : CARDINAL;        (* correct sum *)

    BEGIN
        WriteLn;
        WITH Problem DO
            WriteCard(Addend1, 1);
            WriteString(' + ');
            WriteCard(Addend2, 1);
            WriteString(' = ');
            Sum := Addend1 + Addend2
        END (* WITH *);
        ReadCard(Answer);
        Correct := (Answer = Sum);
        WriteLn;
        IF Correct THEN
            WriteString('Correct!')
        ELSIF RoundNum = 2 THEN
            WriteString('Wrong -- correct answer is ');
            WriteCard(Sum, 1)
        ELSE
            WriteString('Wrong.')
        END (* IF *)
    END Ask;
```

Figure 6.1 (cont.)

```
BEGIN (* main program *)
    (* Initialize queue *)
    CreateQ(WrongQueue);

    (* Carry out the practice drill *)
    WriteLn;
    WriteString('How many problems would you like? ');
    ReadCard(NumProblems);
    FOR Count := 1 TO NumProblems DO
        Problem.Addend1 := RandomCard(0, NumberLimit);
        Problem.Addend2 := RandomCard(0, NumberLimit);
        Ask(Problem, Correct, 1);
        IF NOT Correct THEN
            AddQ(WrongQueue, Problem)
        END (* IF *)
    END (* FOR *);

    (* Now reask any problems student missed *)
    WriteLn; WriteLn;
    WriteString('If you answered any problems incorrectly, you will now be');
    WriteLn;
    WriteString('given a second chance to answer them correctly.');
    WriteLn;
    Wrong := 0;
    WHILE NOT EmptyQ(WrongQueue) DO
        RemoveQ(WrongQueue, Problem);
        Ask(Problem, Correct, 2);
        IF NOT Correct THEN
            INC(Wrong)
        END (* IF *)
    END (* WHILE *);
    WriteLn;
    WriteString('You got ');
    WriteCard(Count - Wrong, 1);
    WriteString(' problems right out of ');
    WriteCard(Count, 1)
END DrillAndPractice.
```

Sample run:

```
Enter a seed for the random number generator
(preferably a prime number) 13

How many problems would you like?
4

39 + 64 = 93
Wrong.

11 + 51 = 66
Wrong.

40 + 92 = 132
Correct!
```

Figure 6.1   (cont.)

```
32 + 69 = 101
Correct!

If you answered any problems incorrectly, you will now be
given a second chance to answer them correctly.

39 + 64 = 103
Correct!

11 + 51 = 72
Wrong -- correct answer is 62
You got 3 problems right out of 4
```

Exercises

1. Write a library module *CARDINALQueues* for processing queues of cardinal numbers.

2. Write a procedure that uses the function *EmptyQ* and the procedures *CreateQ, AddQ,* and *RemoveQ* to

   (a) Retrieve the element at the rear of a queue, leaving the queue empty.
   (b) Retrieve the nth queue element, leaving the queue without its first n elements.
   (c) Retrieve the element at the front of a queue, but not deleting it from the queue.
   (d) Retrieve the element at the rear of a queue, but leaving the queue contents unchanged.
   (e) Retrieve the nth queue element, but leaving the queue contents unchanged.

3. Using the basic queue and stack operations, give an algorithm to reverse the elements in a queue.

4. In Exercise 2 of Section 4.2 we considered a railroad switching network that could be modeled with a stack. Now consider the following network:

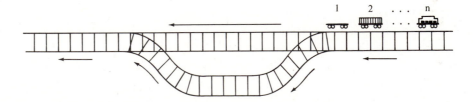

Again railroad cars numbered 1, 2, . . . , n on the right track are to be rearranged and moved along on the left track. As the diagram suggests, a car may be moved directly onto the left track, or it may be shunted onto the siding (which acts like a queue), to be removed at a later time and placed on the left track.

(a) For $n = 3$, find all possible permutations of cars that can be obtained (on the left track) by a sequence of these operations. For example, *AddQ 1, AddQ 2, Move 3, RemoveQ, RemoveQ* arranges them in the order 3, 1, 2. Are any permutations not possible?

(b) Find all possible permutations for $n = 4$. What permutations (if any) are not possible?

(c) Repeat (b) for $n = 5$.

(d) Challenge: In general, what permutations of the sequence 1, 2, . . . , n can be obtained by using a queue in this manner?

5. An alternative implementation of a queue using a circular array that does not require keeping an empty slot between the front and the rear elements to distinguish between a queue-full and a queue-empty condition is to add a field *Count* of type CARDINAL to the records of type *QueueType*, which stores the number of elements currently in the queue. Write procedures for the basic queue operations in this implementation.

6. Proceed as in Exercise 5, but use a boolean field *Full* instead of the cardinal field *Count*. It should be set to true only when the queue becomes full; it should be false otherwise.

7. In Exercise 4 of Section 4.2 we described an efficient implementation of a two-stack data structure that uses a single array for the storage structure. Describe a similar implementation of a two-queue data structure.

8. As for stacks, storing more than two queues in a single one-dimensional array in such a way that no queue-full condition occurs for any of the queues until no more array locations are available (not counting empty slots between front and rear elements) cannot be done very efficiently. Nevertheless, design such an implementation of an n-queue data structure, $n > 2$, writing the appropriate declarations and procedures for the basic queue operations.

9. Imitating the implementation of a queue using a circular array, construct an implementation of a deque. Write appropriate declarations and procedures to implement the basic operations (create an empty deque, check if the deque is empty, add at the front, add at the rear, remove at the front, remove at the rear).

10. If some location in the middle of a deque is held fixed, then the two halves of the deque behave like stacks. Devise an implementation of a deque based on this observation.

11. Construct an implementation of a scroll, giving appropriate declarations and procedures to implement the basic operations.

12. Explain why stacks and queues are special cases of a priority queue.

13. Modify the implementation of a queue given in the text for a priority queue. Items should be stored in a single array, and two "pointers" should be maintained, one for the front of the queue and another for the rear. Write appropriate declarations and procedures for the basic operations. You may assume that a function *Priority* is provided that returns the priority of a given item.

14. If the priorities of items are integers in some range $[1..p]$, then one could use p different arrays to implement a priority queue, one for each queue of items having equal priority. Construct such an implementation, giving appropriate declarations and procedures for the basic operations.

15. If the priorities of the items are not uniformly distributed, the implementation of a priority queue considered in Exercise 14 may be very inefficient. An alternative is to use a single array, as in Exercise 13, and $p + 1$ pointers, one to the front of the priority queue and one to the rear of each of the "internal" queues of items having equal priority. Construct such an implementation.

16. Write a memory-recall program that generates a random sequence of letters and/or digits, displays them one at a time for a second or so to the user, and then asks the user to reproduce the sequence. Use a queue to store the sequence of characters. (*Hint*: If your version of Modula-2 does not provide a "time" procedure or function, a **busy-wait loop** of the form

    FOR $i := 1$ TO n DO (* nothing *)
    END (* FOR *);

    might be used.)

17. Write a program that reads a string of characters, pushing each character onto a stack as it is read and simultaneously adding it to a queue. When the end of the string is encountered, use the basic stack and queue operations to determine if the string is a palindrome (see Section 5.2).

18. In text-editing and word-processing packages, one formatting convention sometimes used to indicate that a piece of text is a footnote is to mark it with some special delimiters such as { and }. When the text is formatted for output, these footnotes are not printed as normal text but are stored in a footnote queue for later output, at the end of the document (in the case of endnotes) or when an appropriate point on the current page is reached. Write a program that reads a document

containing footnotes indicated in this manner, collects them in a footnote queue, and prints them at the end of the document.

6.3   Application of Queues: Information Center Simulation

As we noted in the preceding section, queues may be used to model waiting lines. Almost all waiting lines are dynamic; that is, their lengths change over time, growing as new arrivals occur and are added to the queues and shrinking as items in the queues are removed and serviced. The term *simulation* refers to modeling such a dynamic process and using this model to study the behavior of the process. The behavior of some *deterministic* processes can be modeled with an equation or a set of equations. For queues, however, it is normally not known in advance exactly when a new arrival will occur or exactly how much time will be required to service a specified item. Thus, the behavior of a waiting line involves randomness, and a program that simulates this behavior must also incorporate randomness.

As an illustration, we consider the operation of an information/reservation center that must service calls made by customers to a toll-free number, such as one provided by an airline or a rental car company. When a call arrives at this center, it is serviced immediately if the agent is available, but if the agent is busy, the call is placed on hold in a queue to be serviced later. The program in Figure 6.2 simulates the operation of such an information center and computes several statistics to measure its performance. The program uses a random number generator of the type described in Section 0.7. It consists of three main procedures:

1. *GetSimParameters*, which obtains the simulation parameters: arrival rate, percentages for services times, and time of simulation.
2. *Simulate*, which performs the actual simulation.
3. *PrintReport*, which calculates and reports the simulation statistics.

The simulation parameters read by procedure *GetSimParameters* are stored in a record declared by

SimParameters = RECORD
          ArrivalRate : REAL;
          ServicePerc : ARRAY [1..*NumLimits*] OF CARDINAL;
          TimeLimit : CARDINAL
     END;

ArrivalRate is the probability that a call will arrive in a given minute. For example, if the average time between calls is five minutes, then the arrival rate is $1/5 = 0.2$ calls per minute. To determine whether or not a call has arrived in a particular minute, we generate a random number between 0 and 1, and if this number is less than *ArrivalRate*, we say that a call has arrived during this minute:

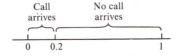

The numbers produced by a random number generator are assumed to be uniformly distributed over the interval from 0 to 1. Consequently, if many such numbers are generated, we would expect approximately 20 percent of them to be in the subinterval (0, 0.2). In terms of our simulation, this means that the probability of a call arriving in a given minute would be approximately 0.2 as desired.

The user must also enter information regarding service times; in particular, he or she must enter the percentage of calls that can be serviced in one minute or less, the percentage of calls requiring more than one minute but at most two minutes, and similar percentages for the other categories. These percentages are accumulated and stored in the array *ServicePerc*:

ServicePerc[1] = % of calls serviced in 1 minute or less;
ServicePerc[2] = % of calls serviced in 2 minutes or less;

⋮

This array is used to determine a service time for each call. For example, suppose that the user enters the percentages 0.50, 0.25, 0.15, 0.07, and 0.03, so that the elements of *ServicePerc* are 0.50, 0.75, 0.90, 0.97, and 1.00. For each call, we then generate a random number in the interval (0, 1); the subinterval (0, 0.50], (0.50, 0.75], (0.75, 0.90], (0.90, 0.97], (0.97, 1.00) in which it falls then determines the service time:

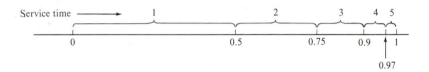

For this simulation, the basic object is a call to the information center, and such calls are characterized by the time at which they arrive and the amount of time required to service the call. These values are generated randomly by procedure *NextCall*. The number of minutes until the next call arrives is determined by generating random numbers until one is obtained that is less than *ArrivalRate*, thus indicating the arrival of a call. Adding this number of minutes to the current time (*Clock*) gives the time of arrival of the next call. The service time for this call is then determined in the manner already described.

The overall simulation for a time period of *TimeLimit* minutes proceeds as follows: The *Clock* is initialized to 0, and an empty queue *OnHold* is created. The first *Call* is generated and placed in this queue, and *Clock* is advanced to the arrival time for this call.

This call is then removed from the queue, and its (simulated) service is initiated. The next event to occur in the simulation is either the arrival of a new call or the completion of service for the current call. New calls that arrive before service for the current call is completed are placed in the queue *OnHold* for processing in a first-come–first-served manner when the agent becomes available. In any case, the *Clock* is advanced to the time of occurrence of the next event. (Simulations of this kind are thus said to be *event driven*.)

This process of moving from one event to the next continues until the specified time limit expires. After this, no new calls are accepted, but service continues until all calls in *OnHold* have been processed.

During certain peak hours, it may happen that all incoming lines are busy and an incoming call must be rejected—that is, there is no room for it on the queue *OnHold*—and it may be useful to know the number of times that this occurs. To count these rejected calls, we assume that in addition to the type *QueueType* and the procedures for the basic queue operations, the library module *QueuesLib2* exports a variable *QueueError* of type BOOLEAN that is set to TRUE each time a queue-full condition occurs. This status variable *QueueError* that is used to indicate whether or not a basic queue operation was carried out successfully is similar to the variable *StackError* described in Section 4.2.

The procedure *PrintReport* displays the number of calls processed, the average waiting time for each call, and the number of calls rejected. A number of other statistics may also be useful in measuring the performance of a given service center. Two such statistics, the average queue length and the average turnaround time, are described in the exercises.

```
MODULE InformationCenter;

(*************************************************************************

   Program that simulates the operation of an information/reservations
   center that services telephone calls.  The simulation is event-
   driven and calculates the number of calls processed, the average
   waiting time for each call, and the number of calls rejected
   because the "on-hold" queue is full.

*************************************************************************)

   FROM InOut IMPORT WriteString, WriteCard, WriteLn, ReadCard;
   FROM RealInOut IMPORT ReadReal;
   FROM SpecialInOut IMPORT FWriteReal;
   FROM QueuesLib2 IMPORT ElementType, QueueType, CreateQ, EmptyQ,
                          AddQ, RemoveQ, QueueError, CallRecord;
   FROM Random IMPORT RandomReal;

CONST
    NumLimits = 5;    (* maximum # of service time categories *)

TYPE
    SimParameters = RECORD
                       ArrivalRate : REAL;
                       ServicePerc : ARRAY [1..NumLimits] OF REAL;
                       TimeLimit : CARDINAL
                    END;
```

Figure 6.2

Figure 6.2 (cont.)

```
VAR
    SimParams : SimParameters; (* parameters needed in the simulation *)
    NumCalls,                  (* total # of calls during simulation *)
    Rejected,                  (* # of calls rejected *)
    WaitTime: CARDINAL;        (* total wait time for all calls *)

PROCEDURE GetSimParameters (VAR SimParams: SimParameters);

    (******************************************************************

         Procedure to accept from the user the parameters -- arrival
         rate, percentages for service times, and time of simulation

    ******************************************************************)

VAR
    i : CARDINAL;       (* index *)
    Perc,               (* percentage *)
    Sum : REAL;         (* sum of percentages *)

BEGIN
    WriteLn;
    WriteString('Enter arrival rate:   ');
    ReadReal(SimParams.ArrivalRate);
    WriteLn;

    WriteString('Enter percent (in decimal form) of calls serviced in ');
    Sum := 0.0;
    FOR i := 1 TO NumLimits - 1 DO
        WriteLn;
        WriteCard(i - 1, 5);
        WriteString(' - ');
        WriteCard(i, 1);
        WriteString(' minutes:  ');
        ReadReal(Perc);
        Sum := Sum + Perc;
        SimParams.ServicePerc[i] := Sum
    END (* FOR *);
    SimParams.ServicePerc[NumLimits] := 1.0;
    WriteLn;
    WriteString('Enter # of minutes to run simulation:  ');
    ReadCard(SimParams.TimeLimit)
END GetSimParameters;

PROCEDURE Simulate (    SimParams : SimParameters;
                    VAR NumCalls, Rejected, WaitTime : CARDINAL);

    (******************************************************************

         Procedure that performs the actual simulation.

    ******************************************************************)

VAR
    Clock,                                (* simulated clock (time in minutes) *)
    CallCompletionTime : CARDINAL;        (* when service is completed *)
    Call,                                 (* call being serviced *)
    NewCall : CallRecord;                 (* new incoming call *)
    OnHold : QueueType;                   (* queue of calls put on hold *)
```

Figure 6.2 (cont.)

```
PROCEDURE NextCall (    Clock : CARDINAL; SimParams : SimParameters;
                   VAR Call : CallRecord);


    (*************************************************************

        Procedure that generates a new call.  Uses system function
        Random to generate random numbers.

    *************************************************************)

    VAR
        R : REAL;              (* random number *)
        i,                     (* index *)
        Ticks : CARDINAL; (* elapsed minutes until next call *)

    BEGIN

        (* Generate time at which next call arrives *)

        Ticks := 0;
        REPEAT
            R := RandomReal();
            INC(Ticks)
        UNTIL R < SimParams.ArrivalRate;
        Call.TimeOfArrival := Clock + Ticks;

        (* Generate service time for this call *)

        R := RandomReal();
        i := 1;
        WHILE R > SimParams.ServicePerc[i] DO
            INC(i)
        END (* WHILE *);
        Call.ServiceTime := i
    END NextCall;

PROCEDURE Initialize (    SimParams : SimParameters;
                      VAR OnHold : QueueType;
                      VAR Clock, NumCalls, Rejected,
                          WaitTime : CARDINAL);


    (*************************************************************

        Procedure to initialize simulation variables, generate
        first call, and place it on the OnHold queue

    *************************************************************)

    BEGIN
        CreateQ(OnHold);
        NumCalls := 0;
        WaitTime:= 0;
        Rejected := 0;
        NextCall (0, SimParams, Call);
        Clock := Call.TimeOfArrival;
        AddQ(OnHold, Call )
    END Initialize;
```

Figure 6.2   (cont.)

```
        BEGIN (* Simulate *)
            Initialize (SimParams, OnHold, Clock, NumCalls, Rejected, WaitTime);
            WHILE Clock < SimParams.TimeLimit DO
                IF NOT EmptyQ(OnHold) THEN
                    RemoveQ (OnHold, Call);
                    INC(NumCalls);
                    WaitTime := WaitTime + Clock - Call.TimeOfArrival;
                    CallCompletionTime := Clock + Call.ServiceTime;
                    WHILE Clock < CallCompletionTime DO
                        NextCall (Clock, SimParams, NewCall);
                        IF NewCall.TimeOfArrival <= CallCompletionTime THEN
                            AddQ (OnHold, NewCall);
                            IF QueueError THEN
                                INC(Rejected)
                            END (* IF *);
                            Clock := NewCall.TimeOfArrival
                        ELSE
                            Clock := CallCompletionTime
                        END (* IF *)
                    END (* WHILE *);
                ELSE (* No calls waiting *)
                    NextCall (Clock, SimParams, NewCall);
                    IF NewCall.TimeOfArrival < SimParams.TimeLimit THEN
                        AddQ (OnHold, NewCall);
                        Clock := NewCall.TimeOfArrival
                    END (* IF *)
                END (* IF *)
            END (* WHILE *)
        END Simulate;

    PROCEDURE PrintReport (NumCalls, Rejected, WaitTime : CARDINAL);

        (*******************************************************************

            Procedure to calculate and report simulation statistics

            *******************************************************************)

        BEGIN
            WriteLn;
            WriteString('Number of calls processed:   ');
            WriteCard(NumCalls, 6);
            WriteLn;
            WriteString('Ave. waiting time per call:');
            FWriteReal(FLOAT(WaitTime) / FLOAT(NumCalls), 8, 2);
            WriteLn;
            WriteString('Number of calls rejected:    ');
            WriteCard(Rejected, 6)
        END PrintReport;

BEGIN (* main program *)
    GetSimParameters(SimParams);
    Simulate(SimParams, NumCalls, Rejected, WaitTime);
    PrintReport(NumCalls, Rejected, WaitTime)
END InformationCenter.
```

Figure 6.2   (cont.)

Sample runs:

```
Enter a seed for the random number generator
(preferably a prime number): 13

Enter arrival rate:  0.2
Enter percent (in decimal form) of calls serviced in
    0 - 1 minutes:  0.2
    1 - 2 minutes:  0.5
    2 - 3 minutes:  0.2
    3 - 4 minutes:  0:1
Enter # of minutes to run simulation:  300
Number of calls processed:     71
Ave. waiting time per call:  0.96
Number of calls rejected:      0

-----------------------------------------------------------------

Enter a seed for the random number generator
(preferably a prime number): 17

Enter arrival rate:  0.4
Enter percent (in decimal form) of calls serviced in
    0 - 1 minutes:  0.1
    1 - 2 minutes:  0.2
    2 - 3 minutes:  0.4
    3 - 4 minutes:  0.25
Enter # of minutes to run simulation:  400
Number of calls processed:    135
Ave. waiting time per call: 20.90
Number of calls rejected:     32
```

Exercises

1. Modify the program in Figure 6.2 so that it also calculates the average turnaround time, where the turnaround time for a given call is the difference between the time when service for that call is completed and the time the call arrived.

2. Modify the program in Figure 6.2 so that it also calculates the average queue length. If n minutes are simulated and $L_1, L_2, \ldots, L_n$ are the lengths of the on-hold queue at times $1, 2, \ldots, n$, respectively, then the average queue length is $(L_1 + L_2 + \cdots + L_n)/n$.

3. Modify the program in Figure 6.2 so that several agents are available to service calls. Investigate the behavior of various queue statistics as the number of agents varies.

4. Suppose that in addition to the simulation parameters given in the text, another is the percentage of calls that cannot be serviced by the agent but must be transferred to the manager. In addition to the other random information generated for each call, also generate randomly an indicator

of whether or not it can be serviced by the agent. If it cannot, it should then be added to a *ManagerQueue*, and a new service time should be generated for it. Modify the program in Figure 6.2 to simulate this information center, and calculate various statistics like those in the text and in Exercises 1 and 2 for each call, for each queue, and so on.

5. (Project) Suppose that a certain airport has one runway, that each airplane takes *LandingTime* minutes to land and *TakeOffTime* minutes to take off, and that on the average, *TakeOffRate* planes take off and *LandingRate* planes land each hour. Assume that the planes arrive at random instants of time. (Delays make the assumption of randomness quite reasonable.) There are two types of queues: a queue of airplanes waiting to land and a queue of airplanes waiting to take off. Because it is more expensive to keep a plane airborne than to have one waiting on the ground, we assume that airplanes in the landing queue have priority over those in the takeoff queue.

Write a program to simulate this airport's operation. You might assume a simulated clock that advances in one-minute intervals. For each minute, generate two random numbers; if the first is less than *LandingRate*/60, a "landing arrival" has occurred and is added to the landing queue; if the second is less than *TakeOffRate*/60, a "takeoff arrival" has occurred and is added to the takeoff queue. Next, check whether the runway is free. If it is, first check whether the landing queue is nonempty, and if so, allow the first airplane to land; otherwise, consider the takeoff queue. Have the program calculate the average queue lengths and the average time that an airplane spends in a queue. You might also investigate the effect of varying arrival and departure rates to simulate prime and slack times of day, or what happens if the amount of time it takes to land or take off is increased or decreased.

6. (Project) Suppose that in a certain computer system, jobs submitted for execution are assigned a priority from 1 through 10. Jobs with the highest priorities are executed first, and those of equal priority are executed on a first-come–first-served basis. The operating system maintains a priority queue of **job control blocks**, each of which is a record storing certain information about a particular job, such as its priority, a job identifier, its time of arrival, and the expected execution time. Using one of the implementations of a priority queue described in Exercises 12 through 14 of Section 6.2, write a program to simulate the operation of this system. It should read or generate randomly a sequence of job control blocks containing at least the four items of information given (ordered according to time of arrival), storing them in a priority queue until they can be executed. A simulated clock can be advanced by the expected execution time for a job to simulate its execution. Your program should calculate the turnaround time for each job (see Exercise 1), the average turnaround time, and any other statistics you care to use to measure the performance of the system (average wait time, amount of time the CPU is idle between jobs, and so on). You may assume *nonpreemptive* scheduling, in which the execution of a given job is not preempted by the arrival of a job of higher priority.

7

Lists

Stacks and queues, considered in the preceding chapters, are special kinds of lists. Each of these data structures is a sequence of data items, and the basic operations are insertion and deletion. For these structures, however, insertion and deletion are restricted to the ends of the list. No such limitations are imposed on a general list; items may be inserted and/or deleted at any point in the list. In this chapter we consider in more detail these general lists and several possible implementations.

7.1 An Array-Based Sequential Implementation of Lists

Lists of various kinds are common in everyday life. There are grocery lists, dean's lists, class lists, appointment lists, mailing lists, lists of seats (on TransFryslan Airlines), and even lists of lists like this one! The features that these examples have in common are abstracted to motivate the following definition of a list.

As a data structure, a *list* is a finite sequence (possibly empty) of elements. Although the basic operations performed on lists vary with each application, they commonly include the following:

1. Create an empty list.
2. Determine if a list is empty.
3. Traverse the list or a portion of it (for example, to display the elements of the list or to search the list for some item).
4. Insert a new element into the list.
5. Delete an element from the list.

Because lists, like stacks and queues, are sequences of data items, it seems natural once again to use an array as the basic storage structure. This is indeed a common method of implementing lists and is the one that we used earlier.

This **sequential implementation** is characterized by the fact that successive list elements are stored in consecutive array locations, the first list element in location 1 of the array, the second list element in location 2, and so on:

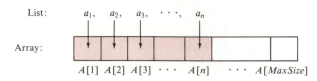

List: $a_1, \quad a_2, \quad a_3, \quad \cdots, \quad a_n$

Array:

$A[1] \quad A[2] \quad A[3] \quad \cdots \quad A[n] \quad \cdots \quad A[MaxSize]$

It is also convenient to use an auxiliary variable to maintain a count of the number of items currently in the list. Thus we might be led to make declarations such as the following:

```
CONST
    MaxSize = . . . ;      (* maximum size of the list *)

TYPE
    ElementType = . . . ; (* type of elements in the list *)
    ListArray = ARRAY [1..MaxSize] OF ElementType;
    ListType = RECORD
                    Size : [0..MaxSize];
                    Element : ListArray
               END;

VAR
    List : ListType;
```

Implementing the first three basic list operations is then easy. For example, given these declarations, the assignment statement

```
List.Size := 0
```

can be used to create an empty list, and the assignment statement

```
ListEmpty := (List.Size = 0)
```

can be used to assign the value TRUE or FALSE to the boolean variable *ListEmpty* according to whether or not *List* is empty. List traversal is easily done with a loop in which the array index varies. For example, to display all the elements in a list of cardinal numbers, we might use

```
FOR i := 1 TO List.Size DO
    WriteCard(List.Element[i], 3)
END (* FOR *)
```

Implementing the insertion operation is somewhat more complicated. For example, suppose we wish to insert the new value 56 after the element 48 in the list of ten integers

$$23, 25, 34, 48, 61, 79, 82, 89, 91, 99$$

to produce the new list

23, 25, 34, 48, 56, 61, 79, 82, 89, 91, 99

Since the definition of a list as a data structure imposes no limit on the size of the list (the length of the sequence), such an insertion is always possible theoretically. In this sequential implementation, however, the fixed size of the array used as the basic storage structure limits the size of the list. This means that before a new item can be inserted into a list, a check must be made to determine if there is room in the array for it.

Another complication arises from the fact that in this sequential implementation, list elements are stored in consecutive positions of the array. Consequently, in order to insert a new item, it usually is necessary to move array elements to make room for it. For example, for the insertion operation just described, the array elements in positions 5 through 10 must first be shifted into positions 6 through 11 before the new element can be inserted at position 5:

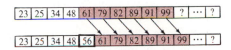

Thus a procedure for insertion must first check whether the array is full and, if it is not, carry out the necessary shifting of array elements before the new item is placed in the array. If the array is full, insertion is obviously impossible, and so some other action is required. In the following procedure, the action taken is to display a list-full message and then terminate execution by calling the procedure HALT:

```
PROCEDURE Insert(VAR List : ListType;
                     Item : ElementType;
                     Pos : CARDINAL);

    (* Procedure to insert Item after the element in position Pos in List;
       Pos = 0 indicates insertion at the beginning of the list. A list-full
       message is displayed and execution is terminated if the array
       storing the list is full. *)

VAR
    i : CARDINAL;      (* array index *)

BEGIN
    IF List.Size = MaxSize THEN
        WriteString('*** Attempt to insert into a full list ***');
        WriteLn;
        HALT
    ELSE
        (* Shift array elements right to make room for Item *)
        FOR i := List.Size TO Pos + 1 BY −1 DO
            List.Element[i + 1] := List.Element[i]
        END (* FOR *);
```

(* Insert *Item* at position *Pos* + 1 and increase list size *)
        List.Element[*Pos* + 1] := *Item*;
        INC(*List.Size*)
    END (* IF *)
END *Insert*;

The efficiency of procedure *Insert* obviously depends on the number of array elements that must be shifted to make room for the new element, that is, on the number of times that the body of the for loop is executed. In the worst case, the new item must be inserted at the beginning of the list, which requires shifting all of the array elements. In the average case, one-half of the array elements must be shifted to make room for a new item. Thus, for a list of size *n*, both the worst-case and the average-case complexities for procedure *Insert* are O(*n*). The best case occurs when the new item is inserted at the end of the list. Because no array elements need to be shifted in this case (so the body of the for loop is never executed), the computing time does not depend on the size of the list. Insertions can be carried out in constant time, and so the best-case complexity of *Insert* is O(1).

If the order in which the elements appear in a list is not important, then new items can be inserted at any convenient location in the list; in particular, they may always be inserted at the end of the list. For such lists, therefore, insertions can always be carried out in constant time. Note that for these lists, the insertion operation is nothing more than the push operation for stacks described in Chapter 4.

Implementing the deletion operation also requires shifting array elements if list elements are to be stored in consecutive array locations. For example, to delete the second item in the list

$$23, 25, 34, 48, 56, 61, 79, 82, 89, 91, 99$$

we must shift the array elements in positions 3 through 11 into locations 2 through 10 to "close the gap" in the array:

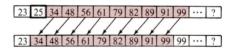

PROCEDURE *Delete*(VAR *List* : *ListType*;
                    Pos : CARDINAL);

   (* Procedure to delete item in position *Pos* from *List*. It assumes a
      boolean-valued function procedure *ListEmpty* to indicate if the
      list is empty. An attempt to delete an item from an empty list
      results in the display of a list-empty message and execution is
      terminated. *)

   VAR
       i : CARDINAL;   (* array index *)

```
BEGIN
    IF ListEmpty(List) THEN
        WriteString('*** Attempt to delete from an empty list ***');
        WriteLn;
        HALT
    ELSE
        (* Decrease list size by 1 and close the gap *)
        DEC(List.Size);
        FOR i := Pos TO List.Size DO
            List.Element[i] := List.Element[i + 1]
        END (* FOR *)
    END (* IF *)
END Delete;
```

The complexity of this procedure is easily seen to be the same as that of procedure *Insert*, $O(n)$ in the worst and average cases and $O(1)$ in the best case.

Because insertion and deletion in this sequential implementation may require shifting many array elements, they may be quite time-consuming. Thus, although the sequential implementation is adequate for **static lists**, it may not be appropriate for **dynamic lists** in which a large number of insertions and deletions are performed. In applications in which it is necessary to insert and/or delete items at any position in the list, a better implementation is to use a linked list, as described in the following sections.

Exercises

1. Explain why the best-, worst-, and average-case computing times of procedure *Delete* are $O(1)$, $O(n)$, and $O(n)$, respectively.

2. Suppose we modify the array-based implementation to allow "gaps" in the array; that is, the list elements need not be stored in consecutive array locations; they need only be stored in order. When a list element is deleted, we simply store some special value in that array location to indicate that it does not contain a list element. (For example, for a list of test scores, we might use a negative score.)

   (a) Write a procedure to traverse a list of test scores stored in an array in this manner and calculate the mean score.
   (b) Modify procedure *Delete* for this implementation, and determine its computing time.
   (c) Modify procedure *Insert* for this implementation, and determine its computing time.

3. A **polynomial of degree n** has the form

$$a_0 + a_1x + a_2x^2 + \cdots + a_nx^n$$

where $a_0, a_1, \ldots, a_n$ are numeric constants called the ***coefficients*** of the polynomial and $a_n \neq 0$. For example,

$$1 + 3x - 7x^3 + 5x^4$$

is a polynomial of degree 4 with integer coefficients. One common implementation of a polynomial stores the degree of the polynomial and the list of coefficients. Thus we might use a record consisting of a field of type CARDINAL for the degree and an array for the list of coefficients.

(a) Write appropriate declarations for this implementation of polynomials.
(b) Write a procedure to read information about a polynomial and construct such a representation.
(c) Write a procedure to implement the basic operation of polynomial addition. Determine its complexity.
(d) Write a procedure to implement the basic operation of polynomial multiplication. Determine its complexity.
(e) Use your declarations and procedures in a menu-driven program for processing polynomials. Options on the menu should include polynomial addition, polynomial multiplication, printing a polynomial using the usual mathematical format with x^n written as $x \uparrow n$, and evaluation of a polynomial for a given value of the variable.

4. The Cawker City Candy Company maintains two warehouses, one in Chicago and one in Detroit, each of which stocks at most twenty-five different items. Write a program that first reads the product numbers of items stored in the Chicago warehouse and stores them in an array *Chicago*, and then repeats this for the items stored in the Detroit warehouse, storing these product numbers in an array *Detroit*. The program should then find and display the ***intersection*** of these two lists of numbers, that is, the collection of product numbers common to both lists. Do not assume that the lists have the same number of elements.

5. Repeat Exercise 4, but find and display the ***union*** of the two lists, that is, the collection of product numbers that are elements of at least one of the lists.

7.2 Introduction to Linked Lists

A list is a sequence of data items, which means that there is an order associated with the elements in the list: It has a first element, a second element, and so on. Thus any implementation of this data structure must incorporate a method for representing this order. In the sequential implementation considered in the preceding section, this ordering of the list elements was represented *implicitly* by the natural ordering of the array elements, since the first list element was stored in the first position of the array, the second list element in the second position, and so on. It was this implicit representation of the ordering of the list elements that necessitated shifting them in the array each time an insertion or deletion was performed. In this section we begin considering an alternative implementation of lists, in which the ordering of the list elements is given *explicitly*.

In any structure used to store the elements of a list, it must be possible to perform at least the following operations if the ordering of the list elements is to be represented:

1. Locate the first list element.
2. Given the location of any element of the list, determine the location of its successor.

As we have seen, in the sequential implementation the ordering is given implicitly by the indices of the array; the first list element is stored in array location 1, and the successor of the element in location i is found in location $i + 1$ of the array.

One structure for storing the elements of a list in which the ordering is given explicitly is called a ***linked list***. It consists of a collection of elements called ***nodes***, each of which stores two items of information: (1) an element of the list and (2) a ***link*** or ***pointer*** that indicates explicitly the location of the node containing the successor of this list element. Access to the node storing the first list element must also be maintained. For example, a linked list storing the list of names

Brown, Jones, Smith

might be pictured as follows:

In this diagram, arrows represent links, and *List* points to the first node in the list. The *Data* part of each node stores one of the names in the list, and the *Next* part is a pointer to the next node; the dot in the last node having no arrow emanating from it represents a ***nil pointer*** and indicates that this list element has no successor. If p is a pointer to any of the nodes in such a linked list, we will denote the data portion of this node by *Data*(p) and the link part by *Next*(p). We will also assume that *nil* is a special value that can be assigned to p to indicate that it is a nil pointer, that is, that it points to no node.

We now consider how the five basic list operations given in the preceding section can be implemented in this setting. To create an empty list, we assign the value nil to *List* to indicate that it points to no node:

List ●

We can then perform the second list operation, determining if a list is empty, simply by checking whether *List* has the value nil.

The third basic list operation is list traversal. To traverse a linked list like the preceding list of names, we begin by initializing some auxiliary pointer *CurrPtr* to point to the first node, and we process the list element 'Brown' stored in this node:

> Initialize *CurrPtr* to *List*.
> Process *Data(CurrPtr)*.

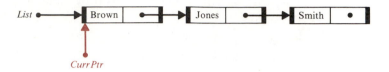

To move to the next node, we follow the link from the current node, setting *CurrPtr* equal to *Next(CurrPtr)*—analogous to incrementing an index by 1 in a sequential implementation—and process the name 'Jones' stored there:

> Set *CurrPtr* equal to *Next(CurrPtr)*.
> Process *Data(CurrPtr)*.

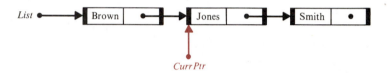

After processing the item stored in this node, we move to the next node and process the list element 'Smith' stored there:

> Set *CurrPtr* equal to *Next(CurrPtr)*.
> Process *Data(CurrPtr)*.

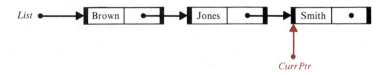

If we now attempt to move to the next node, *CurrPtr* becomes nil, signaling the end of the list:

> Set *CurrPtr* equal to *Next(CurrPtr)*.

In summary, a linked list can be traversed as follows:

ALGORITHM TO TRAVERSE A LINKED LIST

(* Traverse a linked list with first node pointed to by *List*,
processing each list element exactly once. *)

1. Initialize *CurrPtr* to *List*.
2. While *CurrPtr* ≠ nil do the following:
   a. Process *Data(CurrPtr)*.
   b. Set *CurrPtr* equal to *Next(CurrPtr)*.

Note that this algorithm is correct even for an empty list, since in this case *List* has the value nil and the while loop is bypassed.

The fourth and fifth basic list operations are insertion and deletion. In this section we illustrate these operations, leaving general algorithms and the procedures for implementing them to later sections.

To insert a new data value into a linked list, we must first obtain a new node and store the value in its data part. We assume that there is a storage pool of available nodes and some mechanism for obtaining nodes from it as needed. More precisely, we assume that some procedure *GetNode* can be called with a statement of the form *GetNode(TempPtr)* to return a pointer *TempPtr* to such a node. The second step is to connect this new node to the existing list, and for this, there are two cases to consider: (1) insertion at the beginning of the list and (2) insertion after some element in the list.

To illustrate the first case, suppose we wish to insert the name 'Adams' at the beginning of the preceding linked list. We first obtain a new node temporarily pointed to by *TempPtr* and store the name 'Adams' in its data part:

GetNode(TempPtr).
Set *Data(TempPtr)* equal to 'Adams.'

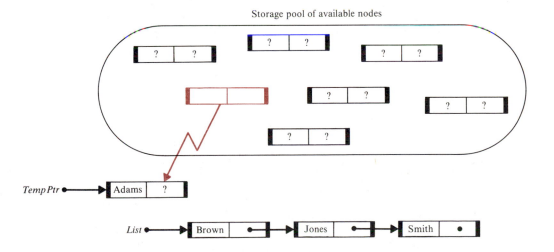

We then insert this node into the list by setting its link part to point to the first node in the list

Set *Next(TempPtr)* equal to *List*.

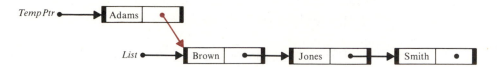

and then setting *List* to point to this new first node:

Set *List* equal to *TempPtr*.

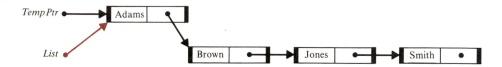

As an illustration of the second case, suppose that we wish to insert the name 'Lewis' after the node containing 'Jones' and that *PredPtr* is a pointer to this predecessor. We begin as before by obtaining a new node in which to store the name 'Lewis':

GetNode(TempPtr).
Set *Data(TempPtr)* equal to 'Lewis'.

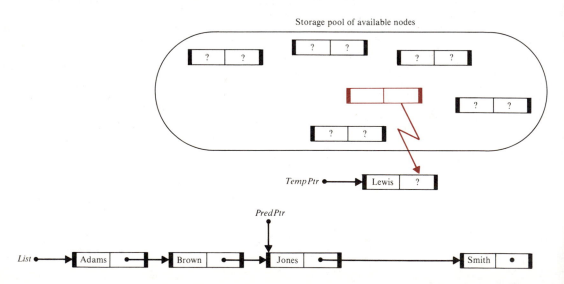

We insert it into the list by first setting its link part equal to *Next(PredPtr)* so that it points to its successor:

Set *Next(TempPtr)* equal to *Next(PredPtr)*.

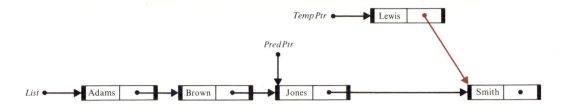

and then resetting the link part of the predecessor node to point to this new node:

Set *Next(PredPtr)* equal to *TempPtr*.

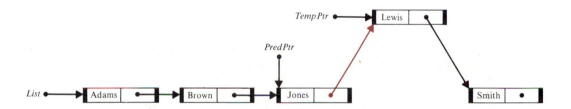

For deletion, there also are two cases to consider: (1) deleting the first element in the list and (2) deleting an element that has a predecessor. As an illustration of the first case, suppose we wish to delete the name 'Adams' from the preceding list. This case is easy and consists of simply resetting *List* to point to the second node in the list and then returning this node to the storage pool of available nodes:

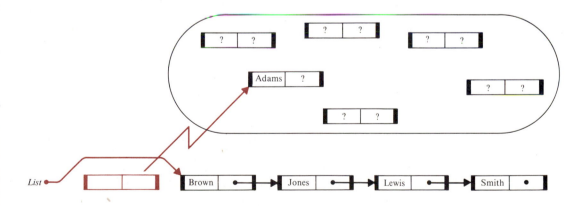

The second case is almost as easy as the first. For example, to delete the node containing 'Lewis' from the preceding list, we need only set the link of its predecessor to point to the node containing its successor (if there is one):

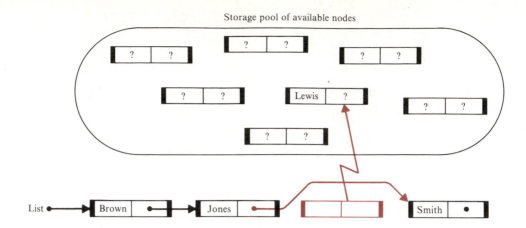

Storage pool of available nodes

As this discussion demonstrates, it is possible to carry out insertions and deletions of data items in a linked list without the shifting of array elements required by the sequential implementation. At this stage, however, we have described linked lists only abstractly, at a logical level, and have not considered an implementation for them. To implement linked lists, we need at least the following capabilities:

1. Some means of dividing memory into nodes, each having a data part and a link part, and some implementation of pointers.
2. Operations/procedures to access the values stored in each node, that is, implementations of the operations we have denoted by *Data(p)* and *Next(p)*, where *p* points to a node.
3. Some means of keeping track of the nodes in use and the available free nodes and of transferring nodes between those in use and the pool of free nodes.

Unfortunately, there are only a few programming languages (such as LISP, an acronym for LISt Processing) that provide linked lists as predefined data types. In other languages, such as Modula-2, it is necessary to implement linked lists using other predefined data types. In the next section we show how they can be implemented using arrays of records and, in Section 7.4, how they can be implemented using the pointer data type in Modula-2.

Exercises

In the following exercises you may assume that a procedure *GetNode* as described in the text may be used to obtain a new node from the storage pool of available nodes. You may also assume that a procedure reference of the form *ReleaseNode(Ptr)* returns the node pointed to by pointer *Ptr* to the storage pool.

1. Write an algorithm to count the nodes in a linked list with first node pointed to by *List*.

2. Write an algorithm to determine the average of a set of real numbers stored in a linked list with first node pointed to by *List*.

3. Write an algorithm to append a node at the end of a linked list with first node pointed to by *List*.

4. Write an algorithm to determine whether the data items in a linked list with first node pointed to by *List* are in ascending order.

5. Determine the complexity of the algorithms in Exercises 1 through 4.

6. Write an algorithm to search a linked list with first node pointed to by *List* for a given item and if found, return a pointer to the predecessor of the node containing that item.

7. Write an algorithm to insert a new node after the nth node in a linked list with first node pointed to by *List* for a given integer n.

8. Write an algorithm to delete the nth node in a linked list with first node pointed to by *List* for a given integer n.

9. The **shuffle-merge** of two lists $X_1, X_2, \ldots, X_n$ and $Y_1, Y_2, \ldots, Y_m$ is the list

$$Z = X_1, Y_1, X_2, Y_2, \ldots, X_n, Y_n, Y_{n+1}, \ldots, Y_m \text{ if } n < m$$

or

$$Z = X_1, Y_1, X_2, Y_2, \ldots, Y_m, X_m, X_{m+1}, \ldots, X_n \text{ if } n > m$$

Write an algorithm to shuffle-merge two linked lists with first nodes pointed to by *List1* and *List2*, respectively. The items in these two lists should be copied to produce the new list; the original lists should not be destroyed.

10. Proceed as in Exercise 9, but do not copy the items. Just change links in the two lists (thus destroying the original lists) to produce the merged list.

11. Suppose the items stored in two linked lists are in ascending order. Write an algorithm to merge these two lists to yield a list with the items in ascending order.

12. Write an algorithm to reverse a linked list with first node pointed to by *List*. Do not copy the list elements; rather, reset links and pointers so that *List* points to the last node and all links between nodes are reversed.

7.3 An Array-Based Implementation of Linked Lists

We have noted that a linked list is not a predefined data structure in most programming languages, and so the programmer is usually faced with the problem of implementing linked lists using other predefined structures. Because nearly every high-level language provides arrays, we first consider how arrays—and, in particular, arrays of records—can be used to implement linked lists.

Recall that the nodes in a linked list contain two parts: a data part that stores an element of the list and a link part that points to a node containing the successor of this list element or that is nil if this is the last element in the list. This suggests that each node may be represented as a record and the linked list as an array of records. Each record will contain two fields: a data field and a link field. The data field will be used to store a list element, and the link field will point to its successor by storing its index in the array. Thus, appropriate declarations for this array-based storage structure for linked lists are:

```
CONST
    NumberOfNodes = . . .;   (* number of nodes in the storage pool *)
    Nil = 0;

TYPE
    ElementType = . . .;        (* type of list elements *)
    ListPointer = [0..NumberOfNodes];
    NodeType = RECORD
                       Data : ElementType;
                       Next : ListPointer
               END;
    ArrayOfNodes = ARRAY [1..NumberOfNodes] OF NodeType;
    LinkedList = ListPointer;

VAR
    Node : ArrayOfNodes;     (* the storage pool *)
    Free : ListPointer;       (* pointer to first free node *)
    List : LinkedList;        (* pointer to first node in linked list *)
```

As an illustration, consider again a linked list containing the names Brown, Jones, and Smith in this order:

Here *List* is a variable of type *LinkedList* and points to the first node by storing its location in *Node*, the storage pool. Suppose now that *MaxSize* is 10 so that the array *Node* established by the preceding declarations consists of ten records, each of which has a *Data* field in which a name can be stored and a *Next* field for storing the location of its successor.[1] The nodes of the linked list can be stored in any three of these array locations, provided that the links are appro-

---

[1] For languages that do not provide records, *Node* can be replaced by *parallel* arrays *Data* and *Next* so that *Data*[*i*] and *Next*[*i*] correspond to the fields *Node*[*i*].*Data* and *Node*[*i*].*Next*, respectively.

priately set and *List* is maintained as a pointer to the first node. For example, the first node might be stored in location 8 in this array, the second node in location 2, and the third in location 4. Thus, *List* would have the value 8; *Node*[8].*Data* would store the string 'Brown'; and *Node*[8].*Next* would have the value 2. Similarly, we would have *Node*[2].*Data* = 'Jones' and *Node*[2].*Next* = 4. The last node would be stored in location 4 so that *Node*[4].*Data* would have the value 'Smith'. Since there is no successor for this node, the *Next* field must store a nil pointer to indicate this fact; that is, *Node*[4].*Next* must have a value that is not the index of any array location, and for this, the value 0 is a natural choice.

The following diagram displays the contents of the array *Node* and indicates how the *Next* fields connect these nodes. The question marks in some array locations indicate undetermined values because these nodes have not been used to store this linked list.

Array Index	*Data*	*Next*
1	?	?
2	Jones	4
3	?	?
4	Smith	0
5	?	?
6	?	?
7	?	?
8	Brown	2
9	?	?
10	?	?

List = 8 ⟶ 8

To traverse this list, displaying the names in order, we begin by finding the location of the first node by using the pointer *List*. Since *List* has the value 8, the first name displayed is 'Brown', stored in *Node*[8].*Data*. Following the link fields leads us to array location *Node*[8].*Next* = 2, where the name 'Jones' is stored in *Node*[2].*Data*, and then to location *Node*[2].*Next* = 4, where 'Smith' is stored. The nil value 0 for *Node*[4].*Next* signals that this is the last node in the list. The following procedure formalizes this method of traversing a linked list in this array-based implementation of linked lists; it implements the traversal algorithm given in the preceding section:

```
PROCEDURE LinkedTraverse(List : LinkedList);

    (* Procedure to traverse a linked list with first node pointed to
        by List and process each data item exactly once *)

    VAR
        CurrPtr : ListPointer; (* pointer to current node
                                    being processed *)

    BEGIN
        CurrPtr := List;
        WHILE CurrPtr # Nil (* 0 *) DO
            (* Appropriate statements to process
                Node[CurrPtr].Data are inserted here *)
            CurrPtr := Node[CurrPtr].Next
        END (* WHILE *)
    END LinkedTraverse;
```

Now suppose we wish to insert a new name into this list, for example, to insert 'Grant' after 'Brown'. We must first obtain a new node in which to store this name. Seven locations are available, namely, positions 1, 3, 5, 6, 7, 9, and 10 in the array. Let us suppose for now that this storage pool of available nodes has been organized in such a way that a call to the procedure *GetNode* returns the index 10 as the location of an available node. The new name is then inserted into the list using the method described in the preceding section: *Node*[10].*Data* is set equal to 'Grant'; *Node*[10].*Next* is set equal to 2 so that it points to the successor of 'Brown'; and the link field *Node*[8].*Next* of the predecessor is set equal to 10:

This example illustrates that the elements of the array *Node* are of two kinds. Some of the array locations—namely, 2, 4, 8, and 10—are used to store nodes of the linked list. The others represent unused "free" nodes that are available for storing new items as they are inserted into the list. We have considered in detail how the nodes used to store list elements are organized, and we must now consider how to structure the storage pool of available nodes.

One simple way to organize this pool of free nodes is as a linked list. In this case, the contents of the data parts of these nodes are irrelevant, and the link fields serve simply to link these nodes together. Initially, all nodes are available and thus must be linked together to form the storage pool. One natural way to do this is to let the first node point to the second, the second to the third, and so on. The link field of the last node will be nil, and a pointer *Free* is set equal to 1 to provide access to the first node in this storage pool. An algorithm to carry out this initialization is

InitializeStoragePool

(∗ Algorithm to initialize the storage pool consisting of *NumberOfNodes* nodes ∗)

1. For *i* ranging from 1 to *NumberOfNodes* − 1
       Set *Node*[*i*].*Next* equal to *i* + 1.
2. Set *Node*[*NumberOfNodes*].*Next* equal to 0 (∗ nil ∗).
3. Set *Free* equal to 1.

Array
Index   *Data*   *Next*

Array Index	Data	Next
Free = 1 → 1	?	2
2	?	3
3	?	4
4	?	5
5	?	6
6	?	7
7	?	8
8	?	9
9	?	10
10	?	0

A procedure call *GetNode(TempPtr)* returns the location of a free node by assigning to *TempPtr* the value *Free* and deletes that node from the free list by setting *Free* equal to *Node[Free].Next*. An algorithm for this procedure is

GetNode

(* Algorithm to return a pointer *P* to a free node; if none is available, *P* is returned as 0 (nil). *)

1. Set *P* equal to *Free*.
2. If *Free* is not zero then
   Set *Free* equal to *Node[Free].Next*.
   Otherwise
   Display message that the storage pool is empty and terminate execution.

Thus, if 'Mills' is the first name to be inserted into a linked list, it will be stored in the first position of the array *Node* because *Free* has the value 1; *List* will be set equal to 1 and *Free* equal to 2.

Array
Index   *Data*   *Next*

Array Index	Data	Next
List = 1 → 1	Mills	0
Free = 2 → 2	?	3
3	?	4
4	?	5
5	?	6
6	?	7
7	?	8
8	?	9
9	?	10
10	?	0

If 'Baker' is the next name to be inserted, it will be stored in location 2 because this is the value of *Free*, and *Free* will be set equal to 3. If the list is to be maintained in alphabetical order, *List* will be set equal to 2, *Node[2].Next* equal to 1, and *Node[1].Next* equal to 0 (nil).

Array
Index   *Data*   *Next*

Array Index	Data	Next
1	Mills	0
List = 2 → 2	Baker	1
Free = 3 --→ 3	?	4
4	?	5
5	?	6
6	?	7
7	?	8
8	?	9
9	?	10
10	?	0

If 'Wells' is the next name inserted into the list, the following configuration will result:

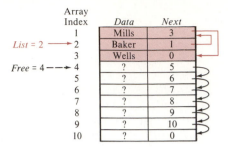

When a node is deleted from a linked list, it should be returned to the storage pool of free nodes so that it can be reused later to store some other list element. An algorithm for this procedure is

ReleaseNode

(* Algorithm to make the node pointed to by *P* a free node
    by placing it back in the storage pool. *)

1. Set *Node[P].Next* equal to *Free*.
2. Set *Free* equal to *P*.

This algorithm simply inserts the node pointed to by *P* at the beginning of the free list by first setting *Node[P].Next* equal to *Free* and then setting *Free* equal to *P*. For example, deleting the name 'Mills' from the preceding linked list produces the following configuration:

Array Index	Data	Next
Free = 1 → 1	Mills	4
List = 2 → 2	Baker	3
3	Wells	0
4	?	5
5	?	6
6	?	7
7	?	8
8	?	9
9	?	10
10	?	0

Note that it is not necessary to actually remove the string 'Mills' from the data part of this node, because changing the link of its predecessor has *logically* removed it from the linked list. This string 'Mills' will be overwritten when this node is used to store a new name.

A procedure that implements the basic list operation of creating an empty list is trivial; we need only assign the nil value to *List*:

PROCEDURE *CreateList*(VAR *List* : *LinkedList*);

   (* Procedure to create an empty linked *List* *)

BEGIN
     List := *Nil* (* 0 *)
END *CreateList*;

A function procedure that checks for an empty list likewise is simple:

PROCEDURE *EmptyList*(*List* : *LinkedList*) : BOOLEAN;

(∗ Returns TRUE if *List* is empty, otherwise FALSE ∗)

BEGIN
    RETURN *List* = *Nil* (∗ 0 ∗)
END *EmptyList*;

The procedure *LinkedTraverse* given earlier implements the basic operation of traversing a list. Procedures for the insertion and deletion operations for linked lists (in a pointer-based implementation) are given in Section 7.6.

As a simple illustration of the use of linked lists, consider the problem of reversing the characters in a string. To solve this problem, we first call procedure *CreateList* to create an empty list for storing characters. A sequence of characters is then read and stored in this linked list. As each character is read, it is added to the beginning of the list. When the end of the string is encountered, procedure *LinkedTraverse*·can be used to traverse the list and display the characters. Because the last characters read are at the beginning of the list, they are displayed in reverse order.

The program in Figure 7.1 uses this approach to solve the string-reversal problem. In addition to procedures *CreateList* and *LinkedTraverse* given in this section, it uses procedure *AddToList* to add elements at the beginning of the list in the manner described in the preceding section. It assumes that a library module *MemoryManager* has been written that initializes the storage pool of available nodes and exports the constant *Nil*, the types *ListPointer* and *ElementType* = CHAR, the array variable *Node* that represents the storage pool, and procedures *GetNode* and *ReleaseNode*. All of these items were described in this section, and the actual writing of this module is left as an exercise.

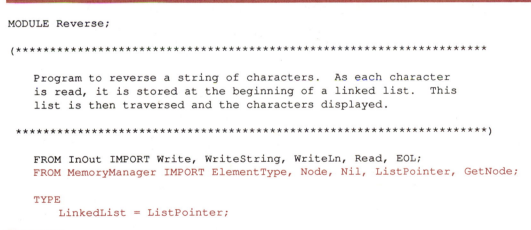

```
MODULE Reverse;

(*********************************************************************

    Program to reverse a string of characters.  As each character
    is read, it is stored at the beginning of a linked list.  This
    list is then traversed and the characters displayed.

**********************************************************************)

    FROM InOut IMPORT Write, WriteString, WriteLn, Read, EOL;
    FROM MemoryManager IMPORT ElementType, Node, Nil, ListPointer, GetNode;

    TYPE
        LinkedList = ListPointer;
```

Figure 7.1

Figure 7.1 (cont.)

```
VAR
    List : LinkedList;     (* pointer to first node in linked list *)
    Ch : CHAR;             (* current character being processed *)

PROCEDURE CreateList(VAR List : LinkedList);

    (***************************************************************


         Procedure to create an empty linked list


    **************************************************************)


    BEGIN
       List := Nil
    END CreateList;

PROCEDURE AddToList(VAR List : LinkedList; Item : ElementType);

    (***************************************************************


       Procedure to add Item at the front of a linked list with
       first node pointed to by List.


    **************************************************************)


    VAR
       TempPtr : PointerType;   (* pointer to new node *)

    BEGIN
       GetNode(TempPtr);
       Node[TempPtr].Data := Item;
       Node[TempPtr].Next := List;
       List := TempPtr
    END AddToList;

PROCEDURE LinkedTraverse(List : LinkedList);

    (***************************************************************


       Procedure to traverse a linked list with first node
       pointed to by List and display each data item


    **************************************************************)


    VAR
       CurrPtr: PointerType; (* pointer to current node being processed *)

    BEGIN
       CurrPtr:= List;
       WriteLn;
       WHILE CurrPtr # Nil DO
           Write(Node[CurrPtr].Data);
           CurrPtr:= Node[CurrPtr].Next
       END (* WHILE *);
       WriteLn
    END LinkedTraverse;
```

Figure 7.1 (cont.)

```
BEGIN (* main program *)
    CreateList(List);
    WriteString('Enter the string:');
    WriteLn;
    Read(Ch);
    WHILE Ch # EOL DO
        AddToList(List, Ch);
        Read(Ch)
    END (* WHILE *);
    WriteLn;
    WriteString('Reversed string is:');
    LinkedTraverse(List)
END Reverse.
```

Sample runs:

```
Enter the string:
SHE SELLS SEASHELLS BY THE SEASHORE$
Reversed string is:
EROHSAES EHT YB SLLEHSAES SLLES EHS


Enter the string, using $ to signal its end:
ABLE WAS I ERE I SAW ELBA$
Reversed string is:
ABLE WAS I ERE I SAW ELBA
```

Exercises

1. An ordered linked list of characters was constructed using the array-based implementation described in this section. The following diagram shows the current contents of the array that stores the elements of the linked list and the storage pool of available nodes:

Array index	Data	Next
1	J	4
2	Z	7
3	C	1
4	P	0
5	B	3
6	M	2
7	K	8
8	Q	9
9	?	10
10	?	0

List = 5
Free = 6

   (a) List the elements of this ordered list.
   (b) List the nodes in the storage pool in the order in which they are linked together.

2. Assuming the contents of the array pictured in Exercise 1, show the contents of the array after the operation Insert F.

3. Proceed as in Exercise 2, but for the operation Delete J.

4. Proceed as in Exercise 2, but for the following sequence of operations: Delete J, Delete P, Delete C, Delete B.

5. Proceed as in Exercise 2, but for the following sequence of operations: Insert A, Delete P, Insert K, Delete C.

6. Assuming an array-based implementation, write

   (a) a nonrecursive function procedure
   (b) a recursive function procedure

   to count the nodes in a linked list.

7. Assuming an array-based implementation, write

   (a) a nonrecursive boolean-valued function procedure
   (b) a recursive boolean-valued function procedure

   that determines whether the data items in a linked list are arranged in ascending order.

8. Assuming an array-based implementation, write

   (a) a nonrecursive function procedure
   (b) a recursive function procedure

   that returns a pointer to the last node in a linked list.

9. Assuming an array-based implementation, write a procedure to reverse a linked list in the manner described in Exercise 12 of Section 7.2.

10. Write the library module *MemoryManager* described in this section and used in the program of Figure 7.1. This module should initialize a storage pool of available nodes stored in the array *Node* and export the constant *Nil*, types *ListPointer* and *ElementType*, the array variable *Node*, and procedures *GetNode* and *ReleaseNode*.

11. A limited number of tickets for the Frisian Folksingers concert go on sale tomorrow, and ticket orders are to be filled in the order in which they are received. Write a program that reads the names and addresses of the persons ordering tickets together with the number of tickets requested and stores these in a linked list. The program should then produce a list of names, addresses, and number of tickets for orders that can be filled.

12. Modify the program in Exercise 11 so that multiple requests from the same person are not allowed.

7.4   Pointers and Dynamic Memory Allocation/Deallocation in Modula-2

The definition of a list as an abstract data type imposes no limit on the number of elements that a list may have. Consequently, any implementation of a list like that in the preceding section that uses an array as the basic storage structure cannot be faithful because the size of an array is fixed at compile time and cannot be changed during program execution. A faithful implementation would require the ability to allocate and deallocate memory locations for nodes dynamically during program execution without specifying some upper limit on the size of the storage pool before execution. This capability is provided in Modula-2 by the procedures ALLOCATE and DEALLOCATE which are used with pointer types. In this section we describe these procedures and Modula-2 pointers, and in the next section we show how they can be used to provide a (nearly) faithful implementation of a linked list.

The procedure ALLOCATE is exported from the library module *Storage* and is used to allocate memory locations during program execution. When it is called, it returns the address of a memory location (possibly consisting of many memory words) in which a data value can be stored. To access this memory location so that data may be stored in it or retrieved from it, a special kind of variable called a ***pointer variable***, or simply a ***pointer***, is provided, whose value is the address of a memory location.

The type of a pointer variable used to access the memory location storing some data value must be specified by

> POINTER TO *type-identifier*

where *type-identifier* specifies the type of the data value. The pointer is said to be ***bound*** to this type, as it may not be used to reference memory locations storing values of some other data type. For example, if the data values are strings, then a pointer to a memory location that may be used to store such a string can be declared by

```
CONST
    StringLimit = 7;   (* limit on number of characters in strings *)

TYPE
    String = ARRAY [0..StringLimit] OF CHAR;
    StringPointer = POINTER TO String;

VAR
    StringPtr : StringPointer;
```

The pointer variable *StringPtr* is bound to the type *String* and may be used only to reference memory locations in which values of this type can be stored.

The procedure ALLOCATE imported from the library module *Storage* may be used to acquire such memory locations.[2] This procedure is called with a

---

[2] Some Modula-2 systems provide a predefined procedure NEW for dynamic allocation. It is called with a statement of the form NEW(*pointer*).

statement of the form

ALLOCATE(*pointer*, *block-size*)

which assigns the address of a memory location to *pointer*; *block-size* is the size of this memory location (measured in words, bytes, or some other system-dependent units).

Modula-2 provides the predefined function procedure **SIZE** which can be used to determine how much memory is needed to store a value of any given type. It is referenced with an expression of the form

SIZE(*type-identifier*)

and returns the size of a memory location needed to store a value of the specified type. For example, the value of

SIZE(*String*)

is the size of a memory location needed to store a string of eight characters.[3]

It follows that a reference to procedure ALLOCATE of the form

ALLOCATE(*pointer*, SIZE(*type-identifier*))

can be used to obtain a memory location where a value of the specified type can be stored. Thus the statement

ALLOCATE(*StringPtr*, SIZE(*String*))

assigns to *StringPtr* a memory address, say 1005, of a memory location; that is, the value of *StringPtr* is this memory address:

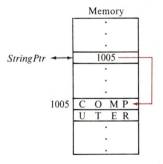

---

[3]SIZE can also be referenced in an expression of the form

SIZE(*variable*)

where *variable* is of the specified type; for example, if *Name* is of type *String*,

SIZE(*Name*)

returns the size of a memory location needed to store a value of type *String*. Some Modula-2 systems allow SIZE to be used only in this manner and require that procedure TSIZE from module SYSTEM be used for type identifiers.

This is the address of a memory location where a string such as 'COMPUTER' can be stored. (In this case, it may, in fact, be the address of the first word in a block of consecutive memory locations in which the characters of the string are stored.) We say that *StringPtr* "points" to this memory location, and we picture this, as we have done for pointers before, using a diagram such as

String Ptr ●——————▶ │ COMPUTER │

Because this area of memory can be used to store values of type *String*, it is a variable, but it has no name! Such variables are thus sometimes referred to as **anonymous variables**, and pointers can be said to point to anonymous variables. Since these variables come into existence during program execution and may later cease to exist, we shall instead refer to them as **dynamic variables**.

Each call to procedure ALLOCATE acquires a new memory location and assigns its address to the specified pointer. Thus if *TempPtr* is also a pointer of type *ListPointer*, the statement

ALLOCATE(*TempPtr*, SIZE(*String*))

acquires a new memory location pointed to by *TempPtr*:

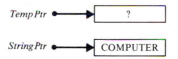

Temp Ptr ●——————▶ │ ? │

String Ptr ●——————▶ │ COMPUTER │

Modula-2 provides the special pointer constant NIL for those situations in which it is necessary to assign a value to a pointer variable that indicates that it does not point to any memory location. This value may be assigned to a pointer of any type in an assignment statement of the form

pointer := NIL

As we have done in the past, we picture a nil pointer as simply a dot with no arrow emanating from it:

pointer ●

Because the values of pointers are addresses of memory locations, the operations that may be performed on them are limited: only assignment and comparison using the relational operators =, #, and <> are allowed. If *pointer1* and *pointer2* are bound to the same type, an assignment statement of the form

pointer1 := *pointer2*

assigns the value of *pointer2* to *pointer1* so that both point to the same memory location. The previous location (if any) pointed to by *pointer1* can no longer be accessed unless pointed to by some other pointer.

As an illustration, suppose that both *StringPtr* and *TempPtr* are pointer variables of type *StringPointer* = POINTER TO *String* and point to memory locations containing the strings 'COMPUTER' and 'SOFTWARE' respectively:

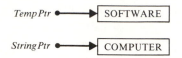

The assignment statement

　　　TempPtr := *StringPtr*

assigns the memory address that is the value of *StringPtr* to *TempPtr* so that *TempPtr* points to the same memory location as does *StringPtr*:

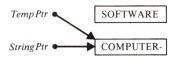

The string 'SOFTWARE' stored in the first location can no longer be accessed (unless it is pointed to by some other pointer of type *StringPointer*).

The relational operators =, #, and <> can be used to compare two pointers *bound to the same type* to determine whether they both point to the same memory locations or both are nil. Thus the boolean expression

　　　TempPtr = *StringPtr*

is valid and is true if and only if both *TempPtr* and *StringPtr* point to the same memory location or both are nil. Similarly,

　　　TempPtr # NIL

is a valid boolean expression.

Pointers may also be used as parameters in procedures. These parameters may be either value or variable parameters, but corresponding pointer parameters must be bound to the same type. The value returned by a function procedure may also be a pointer.

The value of a pointer is the *address* of the memory location to which it points, *not* the data item stored in this location. This data item can be accessed by appending the ***dereferencing operator*** ↑ (or ˆ in some systems) to the pointer:

　　　pointer ↑ (or *pointer*ˆ)

If the pointer is nil or undefined, however, then there is no memory location associated with this variable, and any attempt to use it is an error. At one point during program execution, there may be a particular memory location associated with it, and at a later time, no memory location or a different one may be associated with it. This is in contrast to ordinary variables for which memory locations are allocated at compile time and this association remains fixed throughout the execution of the program.

To illustrate, suppose that pointer variable *StringPtr* has a nonnil value. We may then append the dereferencing operator ↑ to *StringPtr* and obtain the variable *StringPtr↑* of type *String*, which is the dynamic variable (i.e., memory location) pointed to by *StringPtr*. This string variable may be used in the same manner as any other variable of this type. For example, a value can be assigned to it by an assignment statement

   StringPtr↑ := 'COMPUTER';

or by an input statement

   ReadString(StringPtr↑);

and its individual characters accessed as in

   IF *StringPtr↑[0]* = 'A'THEN
       WriteString(StringPtr↑)
   END (*IF*);

If, however, *StringPtr* is nil or undefined so that no memory location is associated with the variable *StringPtr↑*, an attempt to execute any of these statements is an error.

If both *TempPtr* and *StringPtr* have nonnil values, the statement

   TempPtr↑ := *StringPtr↑*;

is a valid assignment statement because both of the dynamic variables *TempPtr↑* and *StringPtr↑* exist and they have the same type *String* since *TempPtr* and *StringPtr* both are bound to this type. This statement copies the contents of the memory locations(s) pointed to by *StringPtr* into the location(s) pointed to by *TempPtr*:

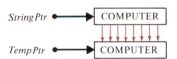

Note that this result is quite different from that produced by the assignment statement

   TempPtr := *StringPtr*;

considered earlier, which causes *TempPtr* to point to the same memory location pointed to by *StringPtr*:

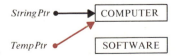

As another illustration of the difference between a pointer and a dereferenced pointer, consider the relational operators $=$, $\#$, and $<>$. As we have noted, these operators can be used to determine whether two pointers bound to the same type point to the same memory location. Thus, the boolean expression

$$TempPtr = StringPtr$$

is true only if *TempPtr* and *StringPtr* point to the same memory location. This is not equivalent to the boolean expression

$$TempPtr\uparrow := StringPtr\uparrow$$

however, since this is an attempt to compare the string pointed to by *TempPtr* with the string pointed to by *StringPtr*, and in Modula-2, strings cannot be compared with relational operators; thus this is not a valid boolean expression. (We must use a procedure like *Compare* provided in the library module *StringsLib* to compare strings.) Obviously, if *TempPtr* $=$ *StringPtr* is true, then the strings pointed to by *TempPtr* and *StringPtr*, that is, the values of *TempPtr*$\uparrow$ and *StringPtr*$\uparrow$, are identical. The converse is not true, however. These two strings may be identical, that is, *TempPtr*$\uparrow$ and *StringPtr*$\uparrow$ may have the same value, but *TempPtr* $=$ *StringPtr* may be false.

If the memory location pointed to by a pointer is no longer needed, it may be released and made available for later allocation by calling the procedure **DEALLOCATE** with a statement of the form

DEALLOCATE(*pointer, node-size*)

This procedure is provided in the module *Storage* and frees the memory location that is pointed to by *pointer* and whose size is *node-size*; it leaves *pointer* undefined.[4] For example, the statement

DEALLOCATE(*TempPtr*, SIZE(*EmployeeRecord*))

can be used to release the node pointed to by *TempPtr*.

7.5 A Pointer-Based Implementation of Linked Lists in Modula-2

Pointer variables described in the preceding section are in themselves not very useful. As we suggested, one important use of pointers is to implement a variety of linked structures. In this section we use them to implement linked lists.

Once again, as in the array-based implementation of Section 7.3, the basic structure used to store the nodes of linked lists will be records having two fields, *Data* and *Next*. The field *Data* will again be of a type that is appropriate

---

[4] Some Modula-2 systems provide a predefined procedure DISPOSE for memory deallocation. It is called with a statement of the form DISPOSE(*pointer*).

for storing a list element, and the field *Next* will store a link that points to the successor of this element. However, unlike the array-based implementation, this link will be a Modula-2 pointer rather than an array index.

The appropriate declarations for this implementation of a linked list are

```
TYPE
    ElementType = ...;                      (* type of list elements *)
    ListPointer = POINTER TO NodeType;  (* type of pointers to list nodes *)
    NodeType = RECORD
                    Data : ElementType;
                    Next : ListPointer
                END;
    LinkedList = ListPointer;

VAR
    List : LinkedList;                      (* pointer to first node in linked list *)
```

Note that the definition of the type identifier *ListPointer* precedes the definition of *NodeType*. This is the only situation in Modula-2 in which it is permissible to use an identifier (*NodeType*) in a declaration before it has been defined.

In this implementation there is no need to be concerned about initializing and maintaining a storage pool of free nodes, as required in the array-based implementation. This is done automatically by the system, with the procedures ALLOCATE and DEALLOCATE playing the roles of *GetNode* and *ReleaseNode*, respectively.

The Modula-2 procedures that carry out the basic list operations of creating an empty list, checking if a list is empty, and traversing a list are straightforward implementations of the algorithms for these operations. An empty list can be created simply by assigning the pointer value NIL to the variable *List* that maintains access to the first node of the linked list:

```
PROCEDURE CreateList(VAR List : LinkedList);

    (* Procedure to create an empty linked List *)

BEGIN
    List := NIL
END CreateList;
```

The second basic operation, checking if a list is empty, is then easily implemented by checking whether *List* has the value NIL:

```
PROCEDURE EmptyList(List : LinkedList);

    (* Returns TRUE if List is empty, otherwise FALSE *)

BEGIN
    RETURN List = NIL
END EmptyList;
```

Lists are traversed as described before, by initializing a pointer *CurrPtr* to the first node and then advancing it through the list by following the link fields,

processing the data stored in each node. The following procedure implements
this list operation:

PROCEDURE *LinkedTraverse(List : LinkedList)*;

(∗ Procedure to traverse a linked list with first node pointed to
by *List* and process each data item exactly once ∗)

VAR
  CurrPtr : *ListPointer*; (∗ pointer to current node
                                         being processed ∗)

BEGIN
  CurrPtr := *List*;
  WHILE *CurrPtr* # NIL DO
      (∗ Appropriate statements to process
          CurrPtr↑.Data are inserted here ∗)
      CurrPtr := *CurrPtr↑.Next*
  END (∗ WHILE ∗)
END *LinkedTraverse*;

It should be clear that these Modula-2 pointer-based implementations of
the basic list operations are simple restatements of the corresponding procedures
in the array-based implementation of linked lists. This is true of the other list
operations as well, and these procedures are given in the next section.

The program in Figure 7.2 is a simple illustration of this method of implementing linked lists. It is the same as the program in Figure 7.1 for reversing
a string of characters, except that the array-based implementation of the linked
list is replaced with the Modula-2 pointer-based implementation.

```
MODULE Reverse;

(*********************************************************************

    Program to reverse a string of characters.  As each character
    is read, it is stored at the beginning of a linked list.  This
    list is then traversed and the characters displayed.

*********************************************************************)

    FROM InOut IMPORT Write, WriteString, WriteLn, Read, EOL;
    FROM Storage IMPORT ALLOCATE, DEALLOCATE;

    TYPE
        ElementType = CHAR;
        PointerType = POINTER TO NodeType;
        NodeType = RECORD
                        Data : ElementType;
                        Next : PointerType
                   END;
        LinkedList = PointerType;
```

Figure 7.2

Figure 7.2 (cont.)

```
VAR
    List : LinkedList;       (* pointer to first node in linked list *)
    Ch : CHAR;               (* current character being processed *)

PROCEDURE CreateList(VAR List : LinkedList);

    (***********************************************************

            Procedure to create an empty linked list

    ***********************************************************)

    BEGIN
        List := NIL
    END CreateList;

PROCEDURE AddToList(VAR List : LinkedList; Item : ElementType);

    (***********************************************************

        Procedure to add Item at the front of a linked list with
        first node pointed to by List.

    ***********************************************************)

    VAR
        TempPtr : PointerType;    (* pointer to new node *)

    BEGIN
        ALLOCATE(TempPtr, SIZE(NodeType));
        TempPtr^.Data := Item;
        TempPtr^.Next := List;
        List := TempPtr
    END AddToList;

PROCEDURE LinkedTraverse(List : LinkedList);

    (***********************************************************

        Procedure to traverse a linked list with first node
        pointed to by List and display each data item

    ***********************************************************)

    VAR
        CurrPtr: PointerType; (* pointer to current node being processed *)

    BEGIN
        CurrPtr:= List;
        WriteLn;
        WHILE CurrPtr # NIL DO
            Write(CurrPtr^.Data);
            CurrPtr:= CurrPtr^.Next
        END (* WHILE *);
        WriteLn
    END LinkedTraverse;
```

Figure 7.2 (cont.)

```
BEGIN (* main program *)
    CreateList(List);
    WriteString('Enter the string:');
    WriteLn;
    Read(Ch);
    WHILE Ch # EOL DO
        AddToList(List, Ch);
        Read(Ch)
    END (* WHILE *);
    WriteLn;
    WriteString('Reversed string is:');
    LinkedTraverse(List)
END Reverse.
```

Sample runs:

```
Enter the string:
SHE SELLS SEASHELLS BY THE SEASHORE
Reversed string is:
EROHSAES EHT YB SLLEHSAES SLLES EHS


Enter the string:
ABLE WAS I ERE I SAW ELBA
Reversed string is:
ABLE WAS I ERE I SAW ELBA
```

Exercises

1. Assume the following declarations:

> VAR
>> X : CARDINAL;
>> $P1$, $P2$: POINTER TO INTEGER;
>> $Q1$, $Q2$: POINTER TO REAL;

What (if anything) is wrong with each of the following statements?

(a) *WriteInt(P1, 5)*;

(b) *ReadInt(P1↑)*;

(c) *P1 := Q1*;

(d) ALLOCATE(*X*, SIZE(CARDINAL));

(e) IF *P1↑* = NIL THEN
>> *Q1 := Q2*
> END (* IF *);

(f) IF *P1* # NIL THEN
      ALLOCATE(*P2↑*, SIZE(INTEGER))
END (* IF *);

2. Assume the following declarations:

TYPE
    NumberPointer = POINTER TO *NumberNode*;
    NumberNode = RECORD
                  Data : CARDINAL;
                  Next : *NumberPointer*
          END;

VAR
    P1, P2 : *NumberPointer*;
    P3 : POINTER TO CARDINAL;

and assume that the following two statements have already been executed:

ALLOCATE(*P1*, SIZE(*NumberNode*));
ALLOCATE(*P2*, SIZE(*NumberNode*));

Tell what will now be displayed by each of the following program segments, or explain why an error will occur:

(a) *P1↑.Data* := 123;
    P2↑.Data := 456;
    P1↑.Next := *P2*;
    WriteCard(P1↑.Data, 4);
    WriteCard(P1↑.Next↑.Data, 4);
    WriteLn;

(b) *P1↑.Data* := 12;
    P2↑.Data := 34;
    P1 := *P2*
    WriteCard(P1↑.Data, 3);
    WriteCard(P2↑.Data, 3);
    WriteLn;

(c) *P1↑.Data* := 123;
    P2↑.Data := 456;
    P1↑.Next := *P2*;
    WriteCard(P2↑.Data, 4);
    WriteCard(P2↑.Next↑.Data, 4);
    WriteLn;

(d) *P1↑.Data* := 12;
    P2↑.Data := 34;
    P3↑ := 34;
    P1↑.Next := *P2*;
    P2↑.Next := NIL;

> *WriteCard(P1↑.Data, 3);*
> *WriteCard(P2↑.Data, 3);*
> *WriteCard(P3↑, 3);*
> *WriteLn;*

(e) *P1↑.Data := 111;*
P2↑.Data := 222;
P1↑.Next := P2;
P2↑.Next := P1;
WriteCard(P1↑.Data, 4);
WriteCard(P2↑.Data, 4);
WriteCard(P1↑.Next↑.Data, 4);
WriteCard(P1↑.Next↑.Next↑.Data, 4);
WriteLn;

(f) *P1↑.Data := 12;*
P2↑.Data := 34;
P1 := P2;
P2↑.Next := P1;
WriteCard(P1↑.Data, 3);
WriteCard(P2↑.Data, 3);
WriteCard(P1↑.Next↑.Data, 3);
WriteCard(P2↑.Next↑.Data, 3);
WriteLn;

3. Given the following linked list and pointers, *P1*, *P2*, *P3*, and *P4* of type *NumberPointer* as defined in Exercise 2:

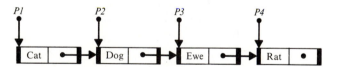

For each of the following, draw a similar diagram to show how this configuration changes when the given program segment is executed or explain why an error occurs:

(a) *P1 := P2↑.Next;*

(b) *P4 := P1;*

(c) *P4↑.Data := P1↑.Data;*

(d) *P4↑.Next↑.Data := P1↑.Data;*

(e) *P2↑.Next := P3↑.Next;*

(f) *P4↑.Next := P1;*

(g) *P1↑.Next := P3↑.Next;*
  P1 := P3;

(h) *P1 := P3;*
  P1↑.Next := P3↑.Next;

(i) $P4\uparrow.Next := P3\uparrow.Next$;
$P3\uparrow.Next := P2\uparrow.Next$;
$P2\uparrow.Next := P1\uparrow.Next$;

(j) $P4\uparrow.Next := P3$;
$P4\uparrow.Next\uparrow.Next := P2$;
$P4\uparrow.Next\uparrow.Next\uparrow.Next := P1$;
$P1 := \text{NIL}$;

4. Assuming a Modula-2 pointer-based implementation, write

   (a) a nonrecursive function procedure
   (b) a recursive function procedure

   to count the nodes in a linked list.

5. Assuming a Modula-2 pointer-based implementation, write

   (a) a nonrecursive function procedure
   (b) a resursive function procedure

   to determine whether the data items in a linked list are arranged in ascending order.

6. Assuming a Modula-2 pointer-based implementation, write

   (a) a nonrecursive function procedure
   (b) a recursive function procedure

   that returns a pointer to the last node in a linked list.

7. Assuming a Modula-2 pointer-based implementation, write a procedure to reverse a linked list in the manner described in Exercise 12 of Section 7.2.

8. In Exercise 11 of Section 7.3, a program was to be written to fill ticket orders for the Frisian Folksingers concert in the order in which these orders were received. Write this program to read the names and addresses of the persons ordering tickets together with the number of tickets requested and to store these in a linked list, but use a Modula-2 pointer-based implementation for this list. The program is to produce a list of names and addresses and the number of tickets for orders that can be filled.

9. Modify the program in Exercise 8 so that multiple requests from the same person are not allowed.

7.6 A Library Module for Processing Linked Lists

In Section 7.1 we defined the abstract data type list as a sequence of elements together with the basic operations of creating an empty list, checking if a list is empty, traversal, insertion, and deletion. And in Section 7.2 we saw that a linked implementation is better than a sequential implementation for dynamic lists. We have given algorithms for the first three operations on linked lists and have written the corresponding procedures, first in an array-based implementation and then in a pointer-based implementation. In this section we begin by developing algorithms for the basic operations of insertion and deletion for linked lists and then develop a library module for processing linked lists.

In Section 7.2 we illustrated the insertion and deletion operations for linked lists by means of diagrams and examples. In these illustrations we assumed that we knew the location at which an item was to be inserted or deleted; we did not consider how this location was determined. Here we use the same approach. We first develop algorithms and procedures for insertion and deletion, assuming that the locations at which these operations are to be performed is known. Then we will consider the problem of searching a linked list to locate a particular item or to find the location at which it should be inserted.

Recall that to insert an element into a linked list, we first obtain a new node temporarily accessed by some pointer *TempPtr* and store the item in the data part of this node. As we illustrated in Section 7.2, the second step is to connect this new node into the linked list, and there are two cases to consider here: (1) insertion at the beginning of the list and (2) insertion after some specified element in the list.

If the new node is to be inserted at the beginning of the list, we must first set its link field to point to the first node in the list:

Set *Next(TempPtr)* equal to *List*.

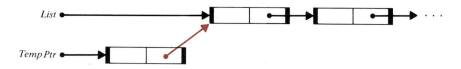

Next we reset the pointer to the former first node (if there was one) so that it points to this new first node:

Set *List* equal to *TempPtr*.

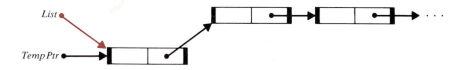

It is crucial that these operations be carried out in this order. For suppose that we first set *List* equal to *TempPtr*. Then setting *Next(TempPtr)* equal to *List* would simply cause the new node to point to itself, and access to the rest of the original list would be lost:

Set *List* equal to *TempPtr*.
Set *Next(TempPtr)* equal to *List*.

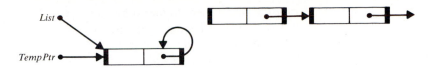

For the second case, suppose that the new node is to be inserted after the node pointed to by *PredPtr*. In this case, we first set the pointer in the link field of the new node to point to the successor of the node pointed to by *PredPtr* (if there is one):

Set *Next(TempPtr)* equal to *Next(PredPtr)*.

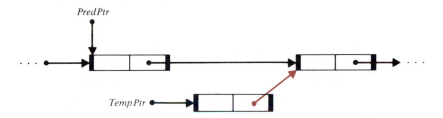

We then set the pointer in the link field of the node pointed to by *PredPtr* to point to the new node because it is the new successor for the node pointed to by *PredPtr*:

Set *Next(PredPtr)* equal to *TempPtr*.

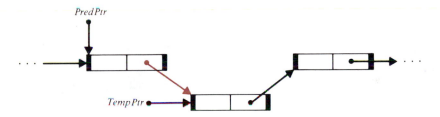

Again it is important to carry out these operations in this order so that access to part of the list is not lost.

In summary, insertion into a linked list is performed by the following algorithm:

ALGORITHM FOR INSERTION INTO A LINKED LIST

(∗ Insert *Item* into a linked list with first node pointed to by *List*. *PredPtr* points to the predecessor of the node to be inserted or is nil if *Item* is to be inserted at the beginning of the list or the list is empty. ∗)

1. Get a node pointed to by *TempPtr*.
2. Set *Data(TempPtr)* equal to *Item*.

3. If *PredPtr* = nil then do the following:
   (∗ Insert *Item* at beginning of list ∗)
   a. Set *Next(TempPtr)* equal to *List*.
   b. Set *List* equal to *TempPtr*.

Else do the following:
   (∗ There is a predecessor ∗)
   a. Set *Next(TempPtr)* equal to *Next(PredPtr)*.
   b. Set *Next(PredPtr)* equal to *TempPtr*.

When developing algorithms such as this to implement the basic operations of a data structure, it is important to verify that they work correctly in special cases. One special case for insertion that should be checked is insertion into an empty list. In this case, the new item will be the first node in the resulting one-node list, and so this case falls under the rubric "Insert *Item* at beginning of list." Since *List* has the value nil for an empty list, the first operation sets *Next(TempPtr)* equal to nil, which is correct because the new node will have no successor. The second operation then correctly sets *List* to point to the first node in this new one-node list:

Set *Next(TempPtr)* equal to *List* (= nil).

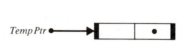

Set *List* equal to *TempPtr*.

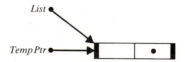

Another special case that should be checked is insertion at the end of a nonempty list. In this case, *Next(PredPtr)* is nil, so the first instruction of a "type-2" insertion correctly sets the link field *Next(TempPtr)* of the new node to nil, indicating that this is the last node in the new list. The second instruction then sets the link field in what was formerly the last node to point to this new last node.

Set *Next(TempPtr)* equal to *Next(PredPtr)* (= nil).

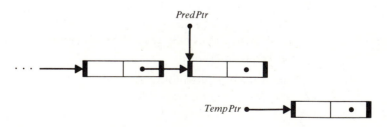

Set *Next(PredPtr)* equal to *TempPtr*.

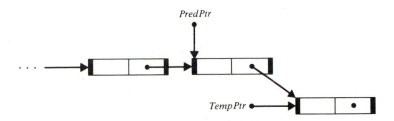

For deletion, suppose that *TempPtr* points to the node to be deleted. Once again there are two cases to consider: (1) deleting the first element in the list and (2) deleting an element that has a predecessor. We can delete the first element in a linked list by simply setting *List* to point to the second node in the list (or setting it to nil if there is none):

Set *List* equal to *Next(TempPtr)*.

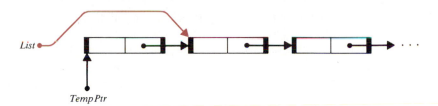

Note that in the special case of a one-node list, *Next(TempPtr)* is nil, so that *List* is correctly set to nil, as required for an empty list.

For the second kind of deletion, if *PredPtr* points to the predecessor of the node to be deleted, we need only set its link part to point to the successor of the node to be deleted (if there is one):

Set *Next(PredPtr)* equal to *Next(TempPtr)*.

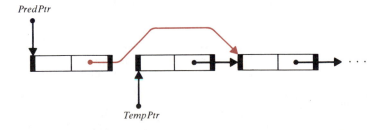

Note that in the special case where the last node is being deleted, *Next(TempPtr)* is nil so that *Next(PredPtr)* becomes nil. This is correct because the node pointed to by *PredPtr* becomes the new last node in the list.

The following algorithm implements the deletion operation for linked lists:

ALGORITHM FOR DELETION FROM A LINKED LIST

(* Delete a node from a linked list with first node pointed to by *List*. *PredPtr* points to the predecessor of the node to be deleted or is nil if the first node is being deleted. *)

If the list is empty then
Display a list-empty message and take appropriate action.

Else do the following:

1. If *PredPtr* = nil then   (* deleting the first node *)
   a. Set *TempPtr* equal to *List*.
   b. Set *List* equal to *Next(TempPtr)*.

   Else do the following: (* node has a predecessor *)
   a. Set *TempPtr* equal to *Next(PredPtr)*.
   b. Set *Next(PredPtr)* equal to *Next(TempPtr)*.
2. Return the node pointed to by *TempPtr* to the storage pool of available free nodes.

The algorithms for insertion and deletion use a pointer to the predecessor of the item to be inserted or deleted (nil if there is no predecessor). If the elements need not be arranged in any particular order, so that it makes no difference where new items are inserted in the list, then we may as well insert them at the beginning of the list. For such unordered lists, the third step of the insertion algorithm simplifies to

3. Set *Next(TempPtr)* equal to *List*.
4. Set *List* equal to *TempPtr*.

Procedure *AddToList* in the programs of Figure 7.1 and 7.2 implements this simplified insertion algorithm. (Note that the insertion operation for such lists is precisely the push operation for stacks.)

To delete an item from a linked list, however, a method is needed to position the pointer *PredPtr*, given only the value of the item to be deleted. The following algorithm, which performs a linear search of a linked list, can be used:

ALGORITHM TO SEARCH A LINKED LIST

(* Search a linked list with first node pointed to by *List* for a node containing a specified *Item*. If such a node is found, the boolean value *Found* is set to true, *CurrPtr* points to the node, and *PredPtr* points to its predecessor or is nil if there is none. *Found* is set to false if *Item* is not found. *)

1. Initialize *CurrPtr* to *List* and *PredPtr* to nil.
2. While *CurrPtr* $\neq$ nil and *Data(CurrPtr)* $\neq$ *Item* do the following:
   a. Set *PredPtr* equal to *CurrPtr*.
   b. Set *CurrPtr* equal to *Next(CurrPtr)*.
3. Set *Found* equal to true if *CurrPtr* $\neq$ nil; otherwise set *Found* to false.

In an ***ordered*** or ***sorted list***, the nodes are linked together in such a way that the items stored in the nodes are visited in ascending (or descending) order as the list is traversed. If the data part of a node is a record, then one of the fields in this record is designated as the **key field**, and the ordering is based on the values that appear in this field. When a new item is inserted, it must be inserted in such a way that this ordering is maintained. Thus both the insertion algorithm and the deletion algorithm require a pointer *PredPtr* to the predecessor of the item being inserted or deleted (if there is one), and the following modified search algorithm can be used to position this pointer:

ALGORITHM TO SEARCH AN ORDERED LINKED LIST

(* Search an ordered linked list with first node pointed to by *List* for a node containing a specified *Item*, in which case *Found* is set to true and *CurrPtr* points to the node, or for a position to insert a new node containing *Item*. *PredPtr* points to the predecessor of such a node or is nil if *Item* precedes all elements in the list. This algorithm assumes that the data items are in ascending order; for descending order, change $<$ to $>$ in Step 2. *)

1. Initialize *CurrPtr* to *List* and *PredPtr* to nil.
2. While *CurrPtr* $\neq$ nil and *Data(CurrPtr)* $<$ *Item* do the following:
    a. Set *PredPtr* equal to *CurrPtr*.
    b. Set *CurrPtr* equal to *Next(CurrPtr)*.
3. Set *Found* equal to true if *CurrPtr* $\neq$ nil and *Data(CurrPtr)* $=$ *Item*; otherwise set *Found* to false.

Procedures to implement these algorithms for insertion, deletion, and searching are straightforward in both the array-based and pointer-based implementations. To illustrate, we now construct a library module *LinkedListLib* for processing linked lists, using the pointer-based implementation. (The array-based version is left as an exercise.)

The definition part of this module might be

```
DEFINITION MODULE LinkedListLib;

(*********************************************************************

   This module exports the type ElementType of the list elements and
   the data type ListPointer together with procedures CreateList,
   Insert, Delete, and LinkedOrderdSearch and function procedure
   EmptyList for processing linked lists.

   *******************************************************************)


   TYPE
       ElementType = ...;   (* type of list elements *)
       ListPointer;
       LinkedList;
```

(cont.)

```
PROCEDURE CreateList(VAR List : LinkedList);

   (*************************************************************

         Procedure to create an empty linked List

    *************************************************************)

PROCEDURE EmptyList(List : LinkedList) : BOOLEAN;

   (*************************************************************

         Returns TRUE if List is empty, FALSE otherwise

    *************************************************************)

PROCEDURE LinkedTraverse(VAR List : LinkedList);

   (*************************************************************

        Procedure to traverse a linked list with first node pointed
        to by List and process each data item exactly once

    *************************************************************)

PROCEDURE LinkedInsert(VAR List : LinkedList;
                           Item : ElementType;
                           PredPtr : ListPointer);

   (*************************************************************

        Procedure to insert Item into a linked list with first node
        pointed to by List.  PredPtr points to the predecessor of the
        new node to be inserted or is nil if it is to be inserted
        at the beginning of the list or the list is empty.

    *************************************************************)

PROCEDURE LinkedDelete(VAR List : LinkedList;
                           PredPtr : ListPointer);

   (*************************************************************

        Procedure to delete a node from a linked list with first node
        pointed to by List.  PredPtr points to the predecessor of the
        node to be deleted or is nil if the first node is being
        deleted.  A list-empty message is displayed and execution
        terminated if an attempt is made to delete from an empty list.

    *************************************************************)
```

(cont.)

```
    PROCEDURE LinkedSearch(    List : LinkedList; Item : ElementType;
                           VAR PredPtr, CurrPtr : ListPointer;
                           VAR Found : BOOLEAN);

        (*****************************************************************

            Procedure to search a linked list with first node pointed to
            by List for a node containing a specified Item.  If such a
            node is found, Found is returned as TRUE, CurrPtr points to
            the first node containing Item and PredPtr points to its
            predecessor or is nil if there is none.  Found is returned
            as FALSE if Item is not found.

        *****************************************************************)

    PROCEDURE LinkedOrderedSearch(    List : LinkedList;
                                      Item : ElementType;
                                  VAR PredPtr, CurrPtr : ListPointer;
                                  VAR Found : BOOLEAN);

        (*****************************************************************

            Procedure to search an ordered linked list having first node
            pointed to by List for a node containing a specified Item, in
            which case Found is returned as TRUE and CurrPtr points to the
            node, or for a position to insert a new node containing PredPtr
            points to the  predecessor of such a node or is nil if Item
            precedes all elements in the list.  This procedure assumes
            the data items are in ascending order.

        *****************************************************************)

END LinkedListLib.
```

In this definition module the type *ListPointer* and *LinkedList* are called **opaque types** because the actual definitions of these types are not *visible* in the definition module. The details of their definitions are hidden in the corresponding implementation module:

```
IMPLEMENTATION MODULE LinkedListLib;

(*********************************************************************************

    This module defines the opaque data type ListPointer to be a pointer
    type for processing nodes which are records containing Data and Next
    fields and LinkedList to be a synomym for ListPointer.  It also
    contains the actual procedures CreateList, Insert, Delete,
    LinkedSearch, LinkedOrderdSearch and function procedure EmptyList
    for processing linked lists in this pointer-based implementation.

*********************************************************************************)
```

(cont.)

```
FROM Storage IMPORT ALLOCATE, DEALLOCATE;
FROM InOut IMPORT WriteString, WriteLn;

TYPE
    ListPointer = POINTER TO NodeType;
    NodeType = RECORD
                    Data : ElementType;
                    Next : ListPointer
               END;
    LinkedList = ListPointer;

PROCEDURE CreateList(VAR List : LinkedList);

    (****************************************************************


            Procedure to create an empty linked List


    ****************************************************************)


    BEGIN
        List := NIL
    END CreateList;

PROCEDURE EmptyList(List : LinkedList) : BOOLEAN;

    (****************************************************************


        Returns TRUE if List is empty, FALSE otherwise


    ****************************************************************)


    BEGIN
        RETURN List = NIL
    END EmptyList;

PROCEDURE LinkedTraverse(VAR List : LinkedList);

    (****************************************************************


        Procedure to traverse a linked list with first node pointed
        to by List and process each data item exactly once


    ****************************************************************)


    VAR
        CurrPtr : ListPointer; (* pointer to current node *)

    BEGIN
        CurrPtr := List;
        WHILE CurrPtr # NIL DO
            (* Appropriate statements to process CurrPtr^.Data
               are inserted here *)
        END (* WHILE *)
    END LinkedTraverse;
```

```
PROCEDURE LinkedInsert(VAR List : LinkedList;
                           Item : ElementType;
                           PredPtr : ListPointer);

    (*****************************************************************

        Procedure to insert Item into a linked list with first node
        pointed to by List.  PredPtr points to the predecessor of the
        new node to be inserted or is nil if it is to be inserted
        at the beginning of the list or the list is empty.

    *****************************************************************)

    VAR
        TempPtr : ListPointer;   (* points to new node to be inserted *)

    BEGIN
        ALLOCATE(TempPtr, SIZE(NodeType));
        TempPtr^.Data := Item;
        IF PredPtr = NIL THEN   (* insert at beginning of list *)
            TempPtr^.Next := List;
            List := TempPtr
        ELSE                        (* node has a precedecessor *)
            TempPtr^.Next := PredPtr^.Next;
            PredPtr^.Next := TempPtr
        END (* IF *)
    END LinkedInsert;

PROCEDURE LinkedDelete(VAR List : LinkedList;
                           PredPtr : ListPointer);

    (*****************************************************************

        Procedure to delete a node from a linked list with first node
        pointed to by List.  PredPtr points to the predecessor of the
        node to be deleted or is nil if the first node is being
        deleted.  A list-empty message is displayed and execution
        terminated if an attempt is made to delete from an empty list.

    *****************************************************************)

    VAR
        TempPtr : ListPointer; (* points to node to be deleted *)

    BEGIN
        IF EmptyList(List) THEN
            WriteString('*** Attempt to delete from an empty list ***');
            HALT
        ELSE
            IF PredPtr = NIL THEN (* first node being deleted *)
                TempPtr := List;
                List := TempPtr^.Next
            ELSE                    (* node has a precedecessor *)
                TempPtr := PredPtr^.Next;
                PredPtr^.Next := TempPtr^.Next
            END (* IF *)
        END (* IF *);
        DEALLOCATE(TempPtr, SIZE(NodeType))
    END LinkedDelete;
```

341

(cont.)

```
    PROCEDURE LinkedSearch(     List : ListPointer; Item : ElementType;
                           VAR PredPtr, CurrPtr : ListPointer;
                           VAR Found : BOOLEAN);

        (*************************************************************

            Procedure to search a linked list with first node pointed to
            by List for a node containing a specified Item.  If such a
            node is found, Found is returned as TRUE, CurrPtr points to
            the first node containing Item and PredPtr points to its
            predecessor or is nil if there is none.  Found is returned
            as FALSE if Item is not found.

        *************************************************************)

    BEGIN
        CurrPtr := List;
        PredPtr := NIL;
        WHILE (CurrPtr # NIL) AND (CurrPtr^.Data # Item) DO
            PredPtr := CurrPtr;
            CurrPtr := CurrPtr^.Next
        END (* WHILE *);
        Found := CurrPtr # NIL
    END LinkedSearch;

    PROCEDURE LinkedOrderedSearch(     List : ListPointer;
                                   Item : ElementType;
                               VAR PredPtr, CurrPtr : ListPointer;
                               VAR Found : BOOLEAN);

        (*************************************************************

            Procedure to search an ordered linked list having first node
            pointed to by List for a node containing a specified Item, in
            which case Found is returned as TRUE and CurrPtr points to the
            node, or for a position to insert a new node containing PredPtr
            points to the  predecessor of such a node or is nil if Item
            precedes all elements in the list.  This procedure assumes
            the data items are in ascending order; for descending order,
            change > to < in the WHILE clause.

        *************************************************************)

    BEGIN
        CurrPtr := List;
        PredPtr := NIL;
        WHILE (CurrPtr # NIL) AND (CurrPtr^.Data > Item) DO
            PredPtr := CurrPtr;
            CurrPtr := CurrPtr^.Next
        END (* WHILE *);
        Found := (CurrPtr # NIL) AND (CurrPtr^.Data = Item)
    END LinkedOrderedSearch;

END LinkedListLib.
```

Using an opaque type such as *LinkedList* (and *ListPointer*) in a library module makes possible a clearer separation between the definition of an abstract data type and its implementation. The definition module contains only the name of the data type and descriptions of the basic operations and relations; all of the implementation details, including the actual declaration of the data type, are contained in the corresponding implementation module. However, in Modula-2, *only pointer types may be opaque*, and opaque types are thus used with pointer-based implementations of data types. Therefore, although it may be assumed that an opaque type is a pointer type, no assumptions may be made about the structure of the type to which it points. The library module must export procedures for all operations that may be performed on this type.

7.7 Application of Linked Lists: Text Concordance

A *text concordance* is an alphabetical listing of all the distinct words in a piece of text, and in this section we consider the problem of constructing such a concordance for a document stored in a file. Because the words in a concordance are arranged in alphabetical order, a concordance is an ordered list. To construct such a concordance, we begin with an empty list, and as each word is read, it is inserted into this list in the appropriate place, provided that it does not appear in the list already. Obviously, insertions may be performed at any point in this list, and thus a linked implementation is more appropriate than a sequential one.

Each time a word is read from the document, this linked list must be searched sequentially, always beginning with the first node. For a large document, however, the concordance may grow so large that searching this single list is not efficient. In order to reduce search time, we will use several smaller linked lists. In this problem, it seems natural to construct one list of words beginning with the letter 'A', another consisting of words beginning with 'B', and so on. Consequently, we will need a total of twenty-six pointers, one for each of these linked lists, and so we will use an array of pointers indexed by 'A'..'Z'. Thus, for the document

```
Dear Marlin:

The aardvarks and the camels were
mistakenly shipped to the Azores.
Sorry about that!

Sincerely,

Jim
```

the concordance will be stored in the following array of linked lists:

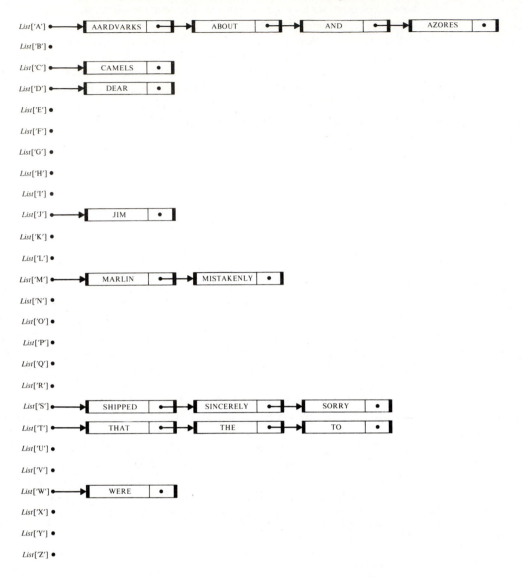

It can be displayed by simply traversing these twenty-six lists.

In summary, an algorithm for solving this text concordance problem is

ALGORITHM FOR CONSTRUCTING A TEXT CONCORDANCE

(* Algorithm to construct a text concordance from a document stored in a file. The concordance is stored in a data structure composed of an array *List* of linked lists, where *List*[*Ch*] is an ordered linked list of words beginning with the letter *Ch*. *)

1. For *Ch* ranging from 'A' to 'Z'
   Create an empty list *List*[*Ch*].

2. Open the file and get the first *Word*.
3. While there are more words to process, do the following:
   a. Search the list of words having the same first letter as *Word* to see if it already contains *Word*.
   b. Insert *Word* into this list if it is not already there.
   c. Get the next *Word*.
4. For *Ch* ranging from 'A' to 'Z' do the following:
   If *List*[*Ch*] is not empty then
      Traverse this list, displaying each word in it.

The program in Figure 7.3 implements this algorithm. It imports the type *LinkedList* and procedures *CreateList*, *EmptyList*, *LinkedOrderedSearch*, *LinkedInsert*, and *LinkedTraverse* from the library module *StringLinkedLists*. This module is obtained from *LinkedListLib* given in Section 7.6 by defining *ElementType* to be a string type in the definition part of this module and placing the statement *WriteString*(*CurrPtr*↑.*Data*) in the statement part of procedure *LinkedTraverse* in the implementation part.

```
MODULE TextConcordance;

(**********************************************************************

    Program that constructs a text concordance from a document stored
    in a file.  This concordance is stored in a data structure
    composed of an array List['A'], ..., List['Z'] of linked lists;
    List[Ch] points to an alphabetically-ordered linked list of words
    in the document that begin with the letter Ch.

**********************************************************************)

    FROM StringLinkedLists IMPORT String, LinkedList, ListPointer,
                                CreateList, EmptyList, LinkedTraverse,
                                LinkedOrderedSearch, LinkedInsert;
    FROM InOut IMPORT Write, WriteString, WriteLn, Read,
                    OpenInput, CloseInput, Done;

    TYPE
        ArrayOfLinkedLists = ARRAY ['A'..'Z'] OF LinkedList;

    VAR
        CurrPtr,                   (* pointer to a node *)
        PredPtr : ListPointer;     (* pointer to predecessor of that node *)
        Word : String;            (* current word *)
        List : ArrayOfLinkedLists; (* array of lists of words *)
        Ch : CHAR;                (* index for the array List *)
        Found,                    (* indicates if search for a word is
                                       successful *)
        MoreWords : BOOLEAN;      (* indicates if more words in file *)
```

Figure 7.3

Figure 7.3 (cont.)

```
    PROCEDURE GetAWord (VAR Word : String; VAR MoreWords : BOOLEAN);

        (***********************************************************

            Procedure that gets the next word in the file or returns
            FALSE for MoreWords if there are none (else MoreWords
            is TRUE).

            ********************************************************)

            CONST
                EOS = 0C;              (* end-of-string mark *)

            VAR
                Ch : CHAR;            (* next character read from the file *)
                i : CARDINAL;         (* index *)

            BEGIN
                (* Find first letter of next word *)
                REPEAT
                    Read(Ch)
                UNTIL NOT Done
                        OR ('a' <= Ch) AND (Ch <= 'z')
                        OR ('A' <= Ch) AND (Ch <= 'Z');

                (* Find next word, if there is one *)
                MoreWords := Done;
                IF MoreWords THEN
                    Word[0] := CAP(Ch);
                    i := 1;
                    Read(Ch);
                    WHILE Done AND (('a' <= Ch) AND (Ch <= 'z')
                                OR ('A' <= Ch) AND (Ch <= 'Z') ) DO
                        Word[i] := CAP(Ch);
                        INC(i);
                        Read(Ch)
                    END (* WHILE *);
                    Word[i] := EOS
                END (* IF *)
            END GetAWord;

BEGIN (* main program *)
    (* Initialization *)
    FOR Ch := 'A' TO 'Z' DO
        CreateList(List[Ch])
    END (* FOR *);
    WriteString('Enter name of input file: '); WriteLn;
    OpenInput('');
    GetAWord(Word, MoreWords);
```

Figure 7.3 (cont.)

```
    (* Construct the concordance *)
    WHILE MoreWords DO
        LinkedOrderedSearch(List[Word[0]], Word, PredPtr, CurrPtr, Found);
        IF NOT Found THEN
            LinkedInsert(List[Word[0]], Word, PredPtr)
        END (* IF *);
        GetAWord(Word, MoreWords)
    END (* WHILE *);
    CloseInput;

    (* Display the concordance *)
    FOR Ch := 'A' TO 'Z' DO
        IF NOT EmptyList(List[Ch]) THEN
            WriteLn;
            WriteString('Words beginning with ');
            Write(Ch);
            Write(':');
            LinkedTraverse (List[Ch]);
            WriteLn
        END (* IF *)
    END (* FOR *)
END TextConcordance.
```

Listing of file ANIMAL used in sample run:

```
Dear Marlin:

The aardvarks and the camels were
mistakenly shipped to the Azores.
Sorry about that!

Sincerely,

Jim
```

Sample run:

```
Enter name of input file:
in> ANIMAL

Words beginning with A:
AARDVARKS
ABOUT
AND
AZORES

Words beginning with C:
CAMELS

Words beginning with D:
DEAR

Words beginning with J:
JIM
```

Figure 7.3 (cont.)

```
Words beginning with M:
MARLIN
MISTAKENLY

Words beginning with S:
SHIPPED
SINCERELY
SORRY

Words beginning with T:
THAT
THE
TO

Words beginning with W:
WERE
```

Exercises

1. Implement the algorithms for
   (a) Insertion into a linked list.
   (b) Deletion from a linked list.
   (c) Searching a linked list.
   (d) Searching an ordered linked list.
   given in this section as procedures, using the array-based implementation of linked lists described in Section 7.3.

2. (a) Write the complete array-based version of the library module *LinkedListLib*. It should import necessary items from the library module *MemoryManager* described in Section 7.3.
   (b) Modify this module as described in this section to obtain *StringLinkedLists*. Then execute the program of Figure 7.3, importing the necessary items from this module.

3. Write a program to read the records from *StudentFile* (see Appendix E), and construct five linked lists of records, each of which contains a student's name, number, and cumulative grade-point average (GPA), one list for each class. Each list is to be an ordered linked list in which the names are in alphabetical order. After the lists have been constructed, print each of them with appropriate headings.

4. Write a menu-driven program that allows at least the following options:

   GET: Read the records from *StudentFile* (see Appendix E) and store them in five linked lists, one for each class, with each list ordered so that student numbers are in ascending order.
   INS: Insert the record for a new student, keeping the list sorted.
   RET: Retrieve and display the record for a specified student.

UPD: Update the information in the record for a specified student.
DEL: Delete the record for some student.
LIS: List the records (or perhaps selected items in the records) in order. This option should allow suboptions:

A: List for all students.
C: List for only a specified class.
G: List for students with GPAs above/below a specified value.
M: List for a given major.
S: List for a given sex.

SAV: Save the updated list of records by writing them to *New-StudentFile*.

5. In addition to the words in a section of text, a concordance usually stores the numbers of selected pages on which there is a significant use of the word. Modify the program in Figure 7.3 so that the line numbers of the first ten or fewer references to a word are stored along with the word itself. The program should display each word together with its references in ascending order.

6. Proceed as in Exercise 5, but modify the data structure used for the text concordance so that the numbers of *all* lines in which a word appears are stored.

7.8 Summary

In this chapter we considered the list data type and two important implementations: sequential and linked. The sequential implementation is useful in a wide variety of list-processing problems, and in many applications it is preferred over the linked implementation. For example, many sorting and searching schemes require direct access to each list element, and this access is provided only in the sequential implementation. The sequential implementation is also appropriate for lists whose maximum sizes can be estimated and whose actual sizes do not vary greatly during processing, especially those for which insertions and deletions are infrequent or are restricted to the ends of the lists.

As we noted, however, the sequential implementation does have its weaknesses. It is possible to declare the array that stores the list elements to have exactly the right size only if the list is static, that is, if its size does not change. Otherwise we estimate the maximum size of the list and use this to declare the array size. However, if this estimate is too small, we run the risk of an error resulting from indices that are out of range, or we may lose some list elements because there is no room for them in the array. If we make the array too large, then we may be wasting a considerable part of the memory allocated to the array. The other major weakness we observed in Section 7.1 is the shifting of array elements required when items are inserted or deleted at points other than the ends of the list.

Dynamic lists whose sizes may vary greatly during processing and those for which items are frequently inserted and/or deleted anywhere in the list are generally best processed as linked lists. There are, however, certain drawbacks to this implementation as well. One is that only the first element in the list is directly accessible; the other elements are accessible only if those that precede it are first traversed. A second weakness is the additional memory required in this implementation. Memory must be allocated not only for the list elements but also for the links used to connect nodes to their successors.

The array-based implementation of a linked list does not have one of the important characteristics of a linked list—unlimited size—because the fixed size of the array limits the size of the storage pool. In the second implementation using Modula-2 pointers, the size of a list is limited only by the total memory available. This is therefore a more faithful implementation of linked lists and is the implementation we will use for them and for other linked structures to be considered later.

Some words of warning are in order, however. Remember that the values of pointer variables are memory addresses, and, therefore, the way in which pointers are used is quite different from the way in which other kinds of variables are manipulated. Using pointers correctly can be challenging not only to beginners but to experienced programmers as well. Pointers are used to create dynamic data structures such as linked lists, and algorithms for processing such structures are quite different from those for static data structures such as arrays. The following are some important things to remember when using pointer variables to implement linked structures in Modula-2 programs:

1. *Each pointer is bound to a fixed type.* It is the address of a memory location in which only a value of that type can be stored. This means that you cannot use pointer P at one place in the program to point to a memory location that stores an integer and, sometime later, to point to a memory location that stores a string.

2. *Only limited operations can be performed on pointers, because they are memory addresses.* In particular:

   - A pointer P can be assigned a value in only the following ways:
     - i. ALLOCATE(P, SIZE(*type-to-which-P-is-bound*))
     - ii. $P := $ NIL
     - iii. $P := Q$ (∗ where Q is bound to the same type as P ∗)
   - No arithmetic operations can be performed on pointers.
   - Only $=$, $\#$, and $<>$ can be used to compare pointers.
   - Pointers cannot be read or displayed.

3. *Don't confuse memory locations with the contents of memory locations.* If P is a pointer, its value is the address of a memory location; $P\uparrow$ refers to the contents of that location. $P := P + 1$ is not valid, but $P\uparrow :=$ $P\uparrow + 1$ may be (if P is bound to a numeric type); similarly, you cannot display the value of P, but you can perhaps display the value of $P\uparrow$.

4. *You cannot access something that isn't there.* If pointer P is nil or undefined, then an attempt to use $P\uparrow$ is an error.

5. *Nil $\neq$ undefined.* A pointer becomes defined when it is assigned a memory address or the value NIL. Assigning P the value NIL is analogous to "blanking out" a character or string variable or "zeroing out" a numeric variable. (You might think of it as assigning a nonexistent address such as 0 to P.)

6. *Pay attention to special cases in processing linked structures, and be careful not to lose access to nodes.* In particular, remember the following ''programming proverbs'':

- *Don't take a long walk off a short linked list.* It is an error if you attempt to process elements beyond the end of the list. As an illustration, consider the following incorrect attempts to search the linked list with first node pointed to by *List* for some *Item*:

  Attempt 1:

  ```
  CurrPtr := List;
  WHILE CurrPtr↑.Data # Item DO
      CurrPtr := CurrPtr↑.Next
  END (* WHILE *);
  ```

  (* What happens if *Item* isn't in the list? *)

  Attempt 2:

  (* This time I'll make sure I don't fall off the end of the list
     by stopping if I find *Item* or reach a node whose link field is
     nil. *)

  ```
  Found := FALSE;
  CurrPtr := List;
  WHILE NOT Found AND (CurrPtr↑.Next # NIL) DO
      IF CurrPtr↑.Data = Item THEN
          Found := TRUE
      ELSE
          CurrPtr := CurrPtr↑.Next;
      END (* IF *)
  END (* WHILE *);
  ```

  (* Almost, but there are still a few cases in which it fails. *)

  Attempt 3:

  (* Now I see how to fix the last try! *)

  ```
  Found := FALSE;
  CurrPtr := List;
  REPEAT
      IF CurrPtr↑.Data = Item THEN
          Found := TRUE
      ELSE
          CurrPtr := CurrPtr↑.Next
      END (* IF *)
  UNTIL Found OR (CurrPtr = NIL);
  ```

  (* This is close, but there is still one case in which it fails. *)

- *You can't get water from an empty well.* Don't try to access elements in an empty list; this case usually requires special consideration. For example, if *List* is nil, then initializing *CurrPtr* to *List* and attempting to access *CurrPtr↑.Data* or *CurrPtr↑.Next* is an error. (Go back now and reconsider Attempts 2 and 3 if you didn't see when they might fail.)

● *Don't burn bridges before you cross them.* Be careful that you change links in the correct order, or you may lose access to a node or to many nodes! For example, in the following attempt to insert a new node at the beginning of a linked list,

List := *NewNodePtr*;
NewNodePtr↑.Next := *List*;

the statements are not in the correct order. As soon as the first statement is executed, *List* points to the new node, and access to the remaining nodes in the list (those formerly pointed to by *List*) is lost. The second statement then simply sets the link field of the new node to point to itself:

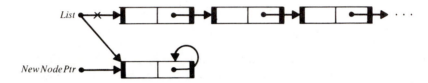

The correct sequence is first to connect the new node to the list and then reset *List*:

NewNodePtr↑.Next := *List*;
List := *NewNodePtr*;

8

More Lists

The "standard" linked lists considered in the preceding chapter are characterized by the following properties: (1) Only the first node is directly accessible,
and (2) each node consists of a data part and a single link that connects this
node to its successor (if there is one). They are, therefore, *linear structures*
that must be processed sequentially in the order in which the nodes are linked
together, from first to last.

In some applications, other kinds of list processing are required, and in
these situations it may be convenient to allow other kinds of access and/or
linkages. In this chapter we consider some of these variants of linked lists, such
as linked stacks and queues, circular linked lists, symmetrically linked lists,
and other multiply linked lists.

8.1 Linked Stacks and Queues

We have seen that implementations of lists that use arrays as the basic storage
structures are not completely faithful because the fixed size of the array limits
the size of the list. In particular, array-based implementations of stacks and
queues, like those considered in Chapter 4 and 6, are not perfect representations
of these structures. In this section we show how these data structures can be
implemented more faithfully as linked structures.

Recall that a stack is a list in which items can be accessed only at one
end, called the *top*. Thus it seems natural to implement a stack using a linked
list because, as we noted in the introduction, only the first node of a linked list
is directly accessible. Using the Modula-2 pointer-based implementation of

linked lists, we make the following declarations for a linked stack:

```
TYPE
    ElementType = . . .;   (* type of elements in the stack *)
    StackPointer = POINTER TO StackNode;
    StackNode = RECORD
                        Data : ElementType;
                        Next : StackPointer
                    END;
    StackType = StackPointer;

VAR
    Stack : StackType;
```

A procedure to create an empty stack and a function procedure to check for a stack-empty condition are basically the same as those for the corresponding operations for general linked lists considered in the preceding chapter. And since the pop operation for stacks is simply the deletion operation restricted to the beginning of the linked list, a procedure for it is a simplification of the procedure *LinkedDelete* for a linked list. Similarly, a procedure that implements the push operation is a simple modification of the procedure *LinkedInsert*. It is basically the same as the procedure *AddToList* in the program of Figure 7.2.

As we have done with several other abstract data types, these declarations and procedures can be packaged into a library module for processing linked stacks. For example, we might develop an alternative version of the library module *StacksLib* for processing stacks as described in Section 4.2. The definition part of this revised module could be

```
DEFINITION MODULE LinkedStacksLib;

(*******************************************************************

    This module exports the data types ElementType and StackType for
    processing stacks whose elements are of type ElementType together
    with procedures Create, Empty, Pop, and Push, which implement the
    basic stack operations.

********************************************************************)

    TYPE
        ElementType = . . .;   (* type of stack elements *)
        StackType;

    PROCEDURE CreateStack(VAR Stack : StackType );

        (********************************************************

                Procedure to create an empty stack

         ********************************************************)
```

(cont.)

```
    PROCEDURE EmptyStack(Stack : StackType) : BOOLEAN;

        (*************************************************************

                Returns TRUE if Stack is empty, FALSE otherwise

         ************************************************************)

    PROCEDURE Pop(VAR Stack : StackType; VAR Item : ElementType);

        (*************************************************************

            Procedure to pop Item from the top of Stack.  Execution
            is terminated if an attempt is made to pop from an
            empty stack.

         ************************************************************)

    PROCEDURE Push(VAR Stack : StackType; Item : ElementType);

        (*************************************************************

                Procedure to push Item onto Stack

         ************************************************************)

END LinkedStacksLib.
```

The corresponding implementation module that defines the opaque type *StackType* and contains the actual procedures *CreateStack*, *EmptyStack*, *Pop*, and *Push* is

```
IMPLEMENTATION MODULE LinkedStacksLib;

(*********************************************************************

    This module defines the opaque types StackPointer and StackType
    and contains the actual procedures Crete, EmptyStack, Pop, and
    Push for the basic stack operations.

 ********************************************************************)

    FROM InOut IMPORT WriteString, WriteLn;
    FROM Storage IMPORT ALLOCATE, DEALLOCATE;
```

(cont.)

```
TYPE
    StackPointer  = POINTER TO StackNode;
    StackNode = RECORD
                    Data : ElementType;
                    Next : StackPointer
                END;
    StackType = StackPointer;

PROCEDURE CreateStack(VAR Stack : StackType );

    (****************************************************************

            Procedure to create an empty stack

    ****************************************************************)

    BEGIN
        Stack := NIL
    END CreateStack;

PROCEDURE EmptyStack(Stack : StackType) : BOOLEAN;

    (****************************************************************

            Returns TRUE if Stack is empty, FALSE otherwise

    ****************************************************************)

    BEGIN
        RETURN Stack = NIL
    END EmptyStack;

PROCEDURE Pop(VAR Stack : StackType; VAR Item : ElementType);

    (****************************************************************

        Procedure to pop Item from the top of Stack.  Execution
        is terminated if an attempt is made to pop from an
        empty stack.

    ****************************************************************)

    VAR
        TempPtr : StackPointer;

    BEGIN
        IF EmptyStack(Stack) THEN
            WriteString('*** Attempt to pop from an empty stack ***');
            WriteLn;
            RETURN
        ELSE
            Item := Stack^.Data;
            TempPtr := Stack;
            Stack := Stack^.Next;
            DEALLOCATE(TempPtr, SIZE(StackNode))
        END (* IF *)
    END Pop;
```

(cont.)

```
    PROCEDURE Push(VAR Stack : StackType; Item : ElementType);

        (************************************************************

                Procedure to push Item onto Stack

        ***********************************************************)

        VAR
            TempPtr : StackPointer;    (* temporary pointer to a new node *)

        BEGIN
            ALLOCATE(TempPtr, SIZE(StackNode));
            TempPtr^.Data := Item;
            TempPtr^.Next := Stack;
            Stack := TempPtr
        END Push;

END LinkedStacksLib.
```

A linked implementation of a queue is a simple extension of that for stacks. Recall that a queue is a list in which items may be removed only at one end, called the *front* or *head*, and items may be inserted only at the other end, called the *rear* or *tail* of the queue. In a linked-list implementation of a queue, it seems natural to identify the first element in the list as the front of the queue. The deletion operation is then implemented in the same way as the pop operation is for a stack, but the insertion operation requires traversing the entire list to find the rear of the queue. This list traversal can be avoided if we adopt the approach of the array-based implementation in Chapter 6 and maintain two pointers, one to the first node (the front of the queue) and another to the last node (the rear of the queue).

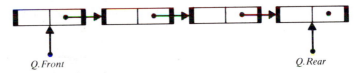

Q.Front   *Q.Rear*

We are thus led to declarations of the form

TYPE
    ElementType = . . . ;   (∗ type of elements in the queue ∗)
    QueuePointer = POINTER TO *QueueNode*;
    QueueNode = RECORD
                Data : *ElementType*;
                Next : *QueuePointer*
        END;
    QueueType = RECORD
                Front,
                Rear : *QueuePointer*;
        END;

VAR
    Q : *QueueType*;

Procedures that implement the basic queue operations are much like those for linked stacks and are left as exercises.

8.2 Other Variants of Singly Linked Lists

In the linked implementation of a queue described in the preceding section, two pointers are maintained, one to the front of the queue and another to the rear. This modification of the standard linked list is convenient because the basic queue operations are performed at the ends of the list. In this section we consider other variants of linked lists that are appropriate for certain list applications and that make algorithms for some of the basic list operations simpler and more efficient.

Lists with Head Nodes.   The first node in a standard linked list differs from the other nodes in that it does not have a predecessor. As we saw in Chapter 7, this means that two cases must be considered for some basic list operations such as insertion and deletion. This would not be necessary if we could ensure that every node that stores a list element has a predecessor. And we can do this by simply introducing a dummy first node, called a ***head node***, at the beginning of a linked list. No actual list element is stored in the data part of this head node; instead, it serves as a predecessor of the node that stores the actual first element because its link field points to this "real" first node. For example, the list of names Brown, Jones, Smith can be stored in a linked list with a head node as follows:

In this implementation, every linked list is required to have a head node. In particular, an empty list has a head node:

To create an empty list, therefore, instead of simply initializing a pointer *List* to have the value nil, we must obtain a head node pointed to by *List* and set its link field to nil. In the Modula-2 pointer-based implementation of linked lists, the following two statements could be used:

    ALLOCATE (*List*, SIZE(*ListNode*));
    List↑.Next := NIL;

Similarly, a function procedure to check for a list-empty condition would require checking *List↑.Next* = NIL rather than *List* = NIL.

    In the creation of an empty list, a value (nil) has been assigned only to the link part of the head node; the data part has been left undefined (as denoted by the question mark in the preceding diagrams). In some situations the data part of the head node might be used to store some information about the list. For example, if Brown, Jones, and Smith all are members of some organization, we might store the name of this organization in the head node:

The fact that every node in a linked list now has a predecessor simplifies the algorithms for the insertion and deletion operations because no special consideration of nodes without predecessors is required. For example, the insertion algorithm given in Section 7.4 for standard linked lists (without head nodes) simplifies in this implementation to

ALGORITHM FOR INSERTION INTO A LINKED LIST WITH HEAD NODE

(* Insert *Item* into a linked list with the head node pointed to by *List*. *PredPtr* points to the predecessor of the node to be inserted. *)

1. Get a node pointed to by *TempPtr*.
2. Set *Data(TempPtr)* equal to *Item*.
3. Set *Next(TempPtr)* equal to *Next(PredPtr)*.
4. Set *Next(PredPtr)* equal to *TempPtr*.

The deletion algorithm simplifies in a similar manner.

Algorithms for traversing a standard linked list or a part of it can easily be modified for use with linked lists that have head nodes. Usually only instructions that initialize some auxiliary pointer to the first node in the list need to be altered. For example, in the traversal algorithm of Section 7.2, only the first instruction requires modification:

ALGORITHM TO TRAVERSE A LINKED LIST WITH HEAD NODE

(* Traverse a linked list with head node pointed to by *List*, processing each element exactly once. *)

1. Initialize *CurrPtr* to *Next(List)*.
2. While *CurrPtr* ≠ nil do the following:
   a. Process *Data(CurrPtr)*.
   b. Set *CurrPtr* equal to *Next(CurrPtr)*.

Circular Linked Lists. We saw in Chapter 6 that a feasible implementation of a queue using an array was obtained if we thought of the array as being circular, with the first element following the last. This suggests that an analogous *circular linked list* obtained by setting the link of the last node in a standard linear linked list to point to the first node might also be a useful data structure:

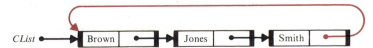

As this diagram illustrates, each node in a circular linked list has a predecessor (and a successor), provided the list is nonempty. Consequently, as in the case of linked lists with head nodes, the algorithms for insertion and deletion do not require special consideration of nodes without predecessors. For example, an algorithm for inserting an item into a circular linked list is as follows:

ALGORITHM FOR INSERTION INTO A CIRCULAR LINKED LIST

(* Insert *Item* into a circular linked list with first node pointed to by *CList*. *PredPtr* points to the predecessor of the node to be inserted (if there is one). *)

1. *GetNode(TempPtr)*.
2. Set *Data(TempPtr)* equal to *Item*.
3. If the list is empty then do the following:
       a. Set *Next(TempPtr)* equal to *TempPtr*.
       b. Set *CList* equal to *TempPtr*.

   Else do the following:

       a. Set *Next(TempPtr)* equal to *Next(PredPtr)*.
       b. Set *Next(PredPtr)* equal to *TempPtr*.

Note, however, that insertion into an empty list requires special consideration because, in this case, the link in the one-node list that results must point to the node itself:

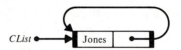

The deletion operation for a circular list is implemented by the following algorithm:

ALGORITHM FOR DELETION FROM A CIRCULAR LINKED LIST

(* Delete a node from a circular linked list with first node pointed to by *CList*. *PredPtr* points to the predecessor of the node to be deleted (if there is one). *)

If the list is empty then
    Display a list-empty message and take appropriate action.

Else do the following:

1. Set *TempPtr* equal to *Next(PredPtr)*.

2. If *TempPtr* = *PredPtr* then   (* one-node list *)
         Set *CList* equal to nil.
     Else   (* list with more than one node *)
         Set *Next(PredPtr)* equal to *Next(TempPtr)*.

3. Return the node pointed to by *TempPtr* to the storage pool of available free nodes.

Notice here that in addition to an empty list, a one-element list also requires special treatment because, in this case, the list becomes empty after this node is deleted. This case is detected in the algorithm by finding that the node is its own predecessor, that is, that its link field points to itself.

Most other algorithms for standard linear linked lists also require modification when applied to circular lists. To illustrate, consider again the general traversal algorithm given in Section 7.2:

ALGORITHM TO TRAVERSE A STANDARD LINKED LIST

(* Traverse a standard linked list with first node pointed to by *List*, processing each list element exactly once. *)

1. Initialize *CurrPtr* to *List*.
2. While *CurrPtr* ≠ nil do the following:
   a. Process *Data(CurrPtr)*.
   b. Set *CurrPtr* equal to *Next(CurrPtr)*.

In this algorithm, the list traversal terminates when *CurrPtr* attains the value nil, signaling that the last node has been processed.

For a circular linked list, the link in the last node points to the first node. Thus a naive attempt to modify this traversal algorithm for a circular list might produce the following:

(* INCORRECT attempt to traverse a circular linked list with first node pointed to by *CList*, processing each list element exactly once. *)

1. Initialize *CurrPtr* to *CList*.
2. While *CurrPtr* ≠ *CList* do the following:
   a. Process *Data(CurrPtr)*.
   b. Set *CurrPtr* equal to *Next(CurrPtr)*.

Here the expression *CurrPtr* ≠ *CList* is false immediately, and thus this algorithm correctly traverses only an empty list!

To obtain an algorithm that correctly traverses all circular linked lists, we can replace the while loop with a repeat-until loop, provided we have made sure that the list is not empty:

ALGORITHM TO TRAVERSE A CIRCULAR LINKED LIST

(* Traverse a circular linked list with first node pointed to by *CList*, processing each list element exactly once. *)

If the list is not empty then do the following:

1. Initialize *CurrPtr* to *CList*.
2. Repeat the following steps:
   a. Process *Data(CurrPtr)*.
   b. Set *CurrPtr* equal to *Next(CurrPtr)*.
   Until *CurrPtr* = *CList*.

Another option is to use a circular linked list with a head node, for example,

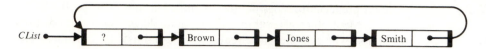

Version 1 of the traversal algorithm then correctly traverses such lists if the initialization instruction is changed to

    1. Initialize *CurrPtr* to *Next(CList)*.

You should check this revised algorithm for circular lists like the preceding one and for one-element lists such as

as well as empty lists that consist only of a head node that points to itself:

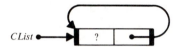

For some applications of circular linked lists, it is advantageous to maintain a pointer *CList* to the last node rather than the first; for example,

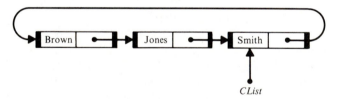

In this case we have direct access to the last node and almost direct access to the first node since *Next(CList)* points to the first node in the list. This variation is thus especially appropriate when it is necessary to repeatedly access the elements at the ends of the list. In particular, it is well suited for linked queues and deques.

Exercises

1. Beginning with an empty stack, draw a diagram of the linked stack that results when the following sequence of operations is performed: *Push 'X', Push 'L', Push 'R', Pop, Push 'A', Pop, Pop, Push 'Q'.*

2. Beginning with an empty queue, draw a diagram of the linked queue that results when the following sequence of operations is performed:

AddQ 'X', *AddQ* 'L', *AddQ* 'R', *RemoveQ*, *AddQ* 'A', *RemoveQ*, *RemoveQ*, *AddQ* 'Q'.

3. **(a)** Assuming a Modula-2 pointer-based implementation, write procedures to implement the basic operations *CreateQ*, *EmptyQ*, *AddQ*, and *RemoveQ* for a linked queue.
   (b) Develop a linked-list version of the library module for the ADT queue.

4. In Section 6.1 a *priority queue* was described as a queuelike structure in which each item has a certain priority and is inserted ahead of all items that have a lower priority but behind all those with an equal or higher priority. Assuming that such a priority queue is implemented as a linked list, write a procedure for the insertion operation.

5. **(a)** Extend Exercise 4 by developing a library module for the ADT *PriorityQueueType*.
   (b) Importing the necessary types and procedures from this module, write a program that simulates the operation of a computer system as described in Exercise 6 of Section 6.3.

6. **(a)** Write a procedure for deleting an item from a linked list with a head node.
   (b) Develop a complete library module for the ADT *LinkedListWithHeadNode*.

7. Write a procedure for searching a circular linked list for a given item.

8. **(a)** Write a procedure for searching an ordered circular linked list for a given item.
   (b) Develop a complete library module for the ADT *CircularLinkedList*. Include both of the search procedures from part (a) and from Exercise 7.

9. Write an algorithm for locating the nth successor of an item in a circular linked list. (If the list has fewer than $n + 1$ items, there is no nth successor; otherwise, it is the nth item that follows the given item in the list.)

10. **(a)** Write procedures *Create*, *Insert*, *Delete*, and *Empty* for a circular linked list with a head node.
   (b) Develop a complete library module for the ADT *CircularLinkedListWithHeadNode*.

11. Redo Exercise 2 for a queue implemented as a circular linked list with a single pointer to the last node.

12. Write procedures for the basic operations *CreateQ*, *EmptyQ*, *AddQ*, and *RemoveQ* for a queue implemented as a circular linked list with a single pointer to the last node.

13. Repeat Exercise 12 for a deque.

14. The *shuffle-merge* operation on two lists was defined in Exercise 9 of Section 7.2. Write an algorithm to shuffle-merge two circularly linked lists. The items in the lists are to be copied to produce the new circularly linked list; the original lists are not to be destroyed.

15. Proceed as in Exercise 14, but do not copy the items. Just change links in the two lists (thus destroying the original lists) to produce the merged list.

16. In the *Josephus problem*, a group of soldiers is surrounded by the enemy, and one soldier is to be selected to ride for help. The selection is made in the following manner: An integer *n* and a soldier are selected randomly. The soldiers are arranged in a circle, and they count off, beginning with the randomly selected soldier. When the count reaches *n*, that soldier is removed from the circle, and the counting begins again with the next soldier. This process continues until only one soldier remains, who is then the (un)fortunate one selected to ride for help. Write an algorithm that implements this selection strategy, assuming that a circular linked list is used to store the names (or numbers) of the soldiers.

17. Write a program that solves the Josephus problem described in Exercise 16. Use output statements to trace the selection process, showing the contents of the list at each stage.

18. Write a program that reads a string of characters, inserting each character as it is read into both a linked stack and a linked queue. When the end of the string is encountered, use basic stack and queue operations to determine whether the string is a palindrome (see Exercise 7 of Section 3.2).

8.3 Linked Implementations of Sets

Implementations of sets as bit strings, as described in Section 2.5, usually impose two limitations on the kinds of sets that can be processed. One limitation is that a fixed number of memory words and thus a fixed number of bits are allocated by the system for any set, which limits the size of the set. A second common restriction is that the elements in the universal set must be ordered so that the first element can be associated with the first bit in a bit string, the second element with the second bit, and so on. This is why the type of the elements of a set in Modula-2 must be an ordinal type; sets of real numbers, sets of strings, and sets of records are not allowed.

There are various alternatives to the bit-string implementation of sets, such as the array-based implementation described in Section 2.6. This implementation uses a boolean array *S* as the basic storage structure. The size of the array is the number of elements in the universal set, and each array component is associated with a unique element of the universal set. A particular subset S of the universal set is represented by setting $S[i]$ to TRUE or FALSE according to whether or not the ith element of the universal set belongs to S.

One obvious weakness of this implementation is that all sets, even those with only a few elements, are represented using arrays whose size is equal to the size of the universal set, and this may be very large. It seems very inefficient to store all of the false entries in these arrays when a set is completely specified by the true entries. A second weakness is that just as in the bit-string implementation, the elements of the universal set must be ordered because they must correspond to array indices.

An alternative approach that removes these deficiencies is to use a linked list to represent a set. For example, the set of even digits can be represented by the following linked list with a head node

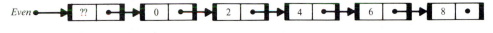

or

Even●———▶[?? |]→[6 |]→[2 |]→[4 |]→[8 |]→[0 | ●]

or by any other linked list that contains nodes storing the digits 0, 2, 4, 6, and 8 in some order. The empty set is represented by

Empty ●———▶[?? | ●]

Of course, circular linked lists can also be used.

These linked lists can represent the set of even digits and the empty set for any universal set containing the even digits. In the array-based implementation, however, the array must change when the universal set changes. Note also that whereas the array-based implementation requires an ordered universal set, the linked implementation does not.

Because the order of the elements in these linked lists is not important, it is very easy to construct this linked representation for a set. We can simply insert each element at the front of the list; that is, we can use the push operation for a linked stack. Beginning with an empty list that consists only of a head node, we repeatedly call the following procedure for each new set element:

PROCEDURE *Include* (VAR S : *SetType*; X : *ElementType*);

    (∗ Procedure to add element X to set S implemented as
      a linked list with a head node. ∗)

VAR
    TempPtr : *SetPointer*;   (∗ pointer to new node for X ∗)

BEGIN
    ALLOCATE(*TempPtr*, SIZE(*SetNode*));
    TempPtr↑.Element := X;
    TempPtr↑.Next := $S↑.Next$;
    $S↑.Next$:= *TempPtr*
END *Include*;

Here *SetType* and *SetPointer* are type identifiers defined by declarations of the form:

```
TYPE
    ElementType = . . .;   (* type of elements for set *)
    SetPointer = POINTER TO SetNode;
    SetNode = RECORD
                    Element : ElementType;
                    Next : SetPointer
              END;
    SetType = SetPointer;
```

The other basic set operations and relations can also be implemented quite easily in this linked implementation. For example, the membership relation can be implemented by the following function procedure *IsAMember*, which simply performs a linear search of the linked list representing the set. Note, however, that this procedure is slower than the corresponding procedure in the array-based implementation of sets.

```
PROCEDURE IsAMember(S : SetType; X : ElementType) : BOOLEAN;

    (* Function procedure returns TRUE or FALSE according to
        whether X is or is not an element of S. S is implemented as a
        linked list with head node pointed to by S. *)

    VAR
        p : SetPointer;     (* auxiliary pointer to run through S *)

    BEGIN
        p := S↑.Next;
        WHILE (p # NIL) AND (p↑.Element # X) DO
            p := p↑.Next
        END (* WHILE *);
        RETURN p # NIL
    END IsAMember;
```

The program in Figure 8.1 illustrates the use of this linked implementation of sets. It determines the number of distinct users logged in to a particular computer system for some given period of time. User identifications (user-ids) are automatically entered into a log file each time they log in to the system. Because the same user may log in many times, this file will contain many duplicate user-ids. As the program reads each user-id from the file, it uses the function procedure *IsAMember* to check whether it is an element of the set *Users* that contains the user-ids read thus far. If it is not, the user-id is added to the set using procedure *Include*, and a counter is incremented by 1. Note that the elements in the set *Users* are strings. Such a set cannot be constructed with the Modula-2 set data type, which requires an ordinal base type for all sets. Also, in procedure *IsAMember*, strings must be compared to determine whether they are equal. Thus the program imports a procedure *Compare* from a module *StringsLib* that was described in Section 3.2.

```
MODULE CountUsers1;

(**********************************************************************

    Program to determine the number of distinct users logged into a
    computer system for a given period of time.  User-ids are read
    from the file UserIdFile and each new one is counted and added to
    the set Users of user-ids already found in the file.  The program
    uses a linked implementation of sets.

**********************************************************************)

    FROM InOut IMPORT Write, WriteString, WriteCard, WriteLn,
                    ReadString, Done, OpenInput, CloseInput;
    FROM StringsLib IMPORT Compare;
    FROM Storage IMPORT ALLOCATE, DEALLOCATE;

    CONST
        MaxString = 8;   (* maximum number of characters in strings *)

    TYPE
        String = ARRAY [0..MaxString] OF CHAR;
        ElementType = String;
        SetPointer = POINTER TO SetNode;
        SetNode = RECORD
                    Element : ElementType;
                    Next : SetPointer
                END;
        SetType = SetPointer;

    VAR
        UserId : String;        (* current user-id being processed *)
        Users : SetType;        (* set of user-ids already found in file *)
        NumUsers : CARDINAL;    (* count of distinct user-ids *)

    PROCEDURE EmptySet() : SetPointer;

        (**********************************************************************

            Function returns a pointer to an empty list consisting of
            only a head hode.  This is the linked implementation of an
            empty set.

        **********************************************************************)

        VAR
            TempPtr : SetType;    (* temporary pointer *)

        BEGIN
            ALLOCATE(TempPtr, SIZE(SetNode));
            TempPtr^.Next := NIL;
            RETURN TempPtr
        END EmptySet;
```

Figure 8.1

Figure 8.1 (cont.)

```
    PROCEDURE IsAMember(S : SetType; X : ElementType): BOOLEAN;

      (***************************************************************

          Function procedure returns TRUE or FALSE according to whether
          X is or is not an element of S.  S is implemented as a
          linked list with head node pointed to by S.

       ***************************************************************)

      VAR
          p : SetType;    (* auxiliary pointer to run through S *)

      BEGIN
          p := S^.Next;
          WHILE (p # NIL) AND (Compare(p^.Element, X) # 0) DO
              p := p^.Next
          END (* WHILE *);
          RETURN p # NIL
      END IsAMember;

    PROCEDURE Include(VAR S : SetType; X : ElementType);

      (***************************************************************

          Procedure to add element X to set S implemented as
          a linked list with a head node.

       ***************************************************************)

      VAR
          TempPtr : SetType;   (* pointer to new node for X *)

      BEGIN
          ALLOCATE(TempPtr, SIZE(SetNode));
          TempPtr^.Element := X;
          TempPtr^.Next := S^.Next;
          S^.Next := TempPtr
      END Include;

BEGIN (* main program *)
    WriteString('Enter name of input file.'); WriteLn;
    OpenInput('');
    Users := EmptySet();
    NumUsers := 0;
    ReadString(UserId);
    WHILE UserId[0] # '*' DO
        IF NOT IsAMember(Users, UserId) THEN
            INC(NumUsers);
            Include(Users, UserId)
        END (* IF *);
        ReadString(UserId)
    END (* WHILE *);
    WriteLn;
    WriteString('Number of users who logged in:  ');
    WriteCard(NumUsers, 1);
    CloseInput
END CountUsers1.
```

Figure 8.1 (cont.)

Listing of file USERIDS used in sample run:

```
S31416PI
S12345SL
S31416PI
S31313LN
S12345SL
S31416PI
S21718EX
S13331RC
S77777UP
S12345SL
S31416PI
S21718EX
S99099RR
S12345SL
S77777UP
S31313LN
S31416PI
*
```

Sample run:

```
Enter name of input file.
in> USERIDS

Number of users who logged in:   7
```

The procedures *EmptySet*, which creates an empty set, *IsAMember*, and *Include* implement three of the basic set operations and relations. Procedures for the others are similar. For example, to form the union *AUB* of two sets *A* and *B* in this linked implementation, we first get a head node pointed to by *AUB* and then traverse *A*, copying each of its elements to *AUB* using procedure *Include*. Next we traverse *B* and use the function procedure *IsAMember* to determine which elements of *B* do not belong to *A* and add them to *AUB* using *Include*. The following function procedure implements set union in precisely this manner:

PROCEDURE *Union*(*A*, *B* : *SetType*) : *SetType*;

    (* Function procedure to compute the union of two sets *A* and *B*
      implemented as linked lists with head nodes *)

VAR
    ptr,   (* pointer to run through *A* and *B* *)
    AUB : *SetPointer*;   (* pointer to list for union of *A* and *B* *)

BEGIN
    (* get head node for union *)
    ALLOCATE(*AUB*, SIZE(*SetNode*));
    AUB↑.*Next* := NIL;

```
(* copy A to AUB *)
ptr := A↑.Next;
WHILE ptr # NIL DO
    Include(AUB, ptr↑.Element);
    ptr := ptr↑.Next
END (* WHILE *);

(* copy elements of B not in A to AUB *)
ptr := B↑.Next;
WHILE ptr # NIL DO
    IF NOT IsAMember(A, ptr↑.Element) THEN;
        Include(AUB, ptr↑.Element)
    END (* IF *);
    ptr := ptr↑.Next
END (* WHILE *);

    RETURN AUB
END Union;
```

Procedures for the other set operations and relations are similar to those given in this section and are left as exercises. These procedures can be collected in a library module for processing more general sets than those allowed in Modula-2 or those processed by the module *ExtendedSets* described in Section 2.6.

Exercises

1. Determine the complexity of the function procedure *Union* for sets A and B having m and n elements, respectively.

2. Assuming the linked implementation of sets of this section, write a function procedure for set intersection. Determine its complexity for sets A and B having m and n elements, respectively.

3. Proceed as in Exercise 2, but write a function procedure to implement the operation of set difference.

4. Assuming the linked implementation of sets in this section, write a

   (a) nonrecursive boolean-valued function procedure
   (b) recursive boolean-valued function procedure

   Subset so that the function reference *Subset(A, B)* returns the value TRUE if A is a subset of B and FALSE otherwise.

5. Write a function procedure *CardinalNumber* that returns the cardinal number (number of elements) of a set implemented as a linked list with a head node.

6. Suppose sets are maintained as ordered linked lists. Write an algorithm for set intersection that is more efficient than that in Exercise 2. (It should have complexity $O(m + n)$ where the two sets have m elements and n elements, respectively.)

7. Repeat Exercise 6 for set union.

8. The **Cartesian product** $A \times B$ of two sets A and B is the set of all ordered pairs (x, y) where $x \in A$ and $y \in B$. For example, if $A = \{1, 2\}$ and $B = \{a, b, c\}$, then

$$A \times B = \{(1,a), (1,b), (1,c), (2,a), (2,b), (2,c)\}$$

Write a procedure that accepts linked lists (with head nodes) representing sets A and B and returns a pointer to a linked list representing $A \times B$. Give appropriate type definitions for the case when A is some set of integers and B is some set of characters.

9. Write a procedure for the inverse of the operation in Exercise 8. It should accept a pointer to a linked list representing the Cartesian product $A \times B$ of two sets and should return pointers to the linked lists for A and B. (This operation is commonly referred to as projecting onto the first/second component.)

10. Write a linked-list version of the module *ExtendedSets* in Section 2.6, using the linked implementation of sets described in this section. It should export the types *ElementType* and *SetType*, the variable *EmptySet* initialized to the empty set by the module, and procedures for the basic set operations: *Union, Intersection, Difference, SymmetricDifference, IsAMember, Equal, Subset, Include,* and *Exclude*, and a procedure *Assign* that assigns a copy of a set to a set variable.

11. Using the linked implementation of sets described in this section, write a program for finding prime numbers using the Sieve Method of Eratosthenes (see Exercise 10 of Section 2.5).

12. Using the linked implementation of sets described in this section, write a program that reads records from *StudentFile* (see Appendix E), constructs the set of all distinct majors, and displays this set.

13. Using the linked implementation of sets described in this section, write a program to simulate dealing hands of cards from a deck of cards. Use an array of sets to represent the various hands. (See Section 0.7 for the description of a library module for generating random numbers if your system does not provide one.)

8.4 Linked Implementations of Strings

The implementation of strings in Chapter 3 uses arrays of characters as the basic storage structure. For example, the usual implementation in Modula-2 uses declarations of the form

        CONST
            StringLimit = . . .;   (* limit on number of characters in strings *)

        TYPE
            String = ARRAY [0..*StringLimit*] OF CHAR;

This implementation has the usual weaknesses of array-based implementations. In particular, it imposes a limit on the lengths of strings and does not allow efficient insertion and/or deletion of characters. Since strings are lists of characters, we might attempt to remedy these deficiencies by using a linked implementation.

An obvious way to change to a linked representation of strings is to replace the array of characters by a linked list in which each node stores a single character. For example, the string 'COMPUTE' can be stored in a linked list as

If we use a linked list like this as the storage structure for strings, determining the length of a string will require traversing the list to count the nodes. An alternative is to use a head node to store CHR(*count*), where *count* is the number of characters in the string. However, this has the undesirable feature that it imposes an upper limit on the length of a string, since the CHR function is defined over only a small subrange of integers, such as [0..255].

A better alternative is to use a record containing two fields, one to store the length of a string and another to store a pointer to a linked list containing the characters that make up the string. Appropriate declarations for this implementation have the form

        TYPE
            StringPointer = POINTER TO *StringNode*;
            StringNode = RECORD
                                Ch : CHAR;
                                Next : *StringPointer*
                            END;

            String = RECORD
                                Length : CARDINAL;
                                List : *StringPointer*
                            END;

        VAR
            Str : *String*;

Algorithms for basic string operations in this linked implementation are not difficult. For example, two strings can be concatenated to form a third string using the following algorithm:

ALGORITHM FOR CONCATENATION

(∗ Algorithm to concatenate string *Str1* with string *Str2* to form the string *Str*, where all strings are implemented as linked lists with head nodes, with one character per node. ∗)

1. Set the length of *Str* equal to the sum of the lengths of *Str1* and *Str2*.
2. Get a head node for *Str*.
3. Traverse *Str1*, copying its nodes and attaching them to the end of the linked list for *Str*.
4. Traverse *Str2*, copying its nodes and attaching them to the end of the linked list for *Str*.
5. Set the link in the last node of *Str* to nil.

The following procedure implements this algorithm:

PROCEDURE *Concat*(*Str1*, *Str2*: *String*; VAR *Str* : *String*);

(∗ Procedure returns the string *Str* obtained by concatenating *Str2* onto the end of *Str1*. Strings are implemented as linked lists with head nodes, with one character per node. ∗)

```
VAR
    P, Q : StringPointer;          (* auxiliary pointers *)
BEGIN
    Str.Length := Str1.Length + Str2.Length;
    ALLOCATE(Str.List, SIZE(StringNode));

    Q := Str.List;
    P := Str1.List;                (* First copy Str1 into Str *)
    WHILE P # NIL DO
        Attach(P↑.Ch, Q);
        P := P↑.Next
    END (* WHILE *);

    P := Str2.List;                (* Now copy Str2 into Str *)
    WHILE P # NIL DO
        Attach(P↑.Ch, Q);
        P := P↑.Next
    END (* WHILE *);

    Q↑.Next = NIL
END Concat;
```

Here *Attach* is a procedure like the following that is used to attach nodes at the end of a linked list:

PROCEDURE *Attach*(*Character* : CHAR; VAR *Last* : *StringPointer*);

(∗ Procedure to create a node containing *Character*, attach it to a linked list with last node pointed to by *Last*, and advance *Last* to point to this node. ∗)

VAR
    TempPtr : *StringPointer*; (∗ pointer to new node ∗)

BEGIN
    ALLOCATE (*TempPtr*, SIZE (*StringNode*));
    TempPtr↑.*Ch* := *Character*;
    TempPtr↑.*Next* := NIL;
    Last↑.*Next* := *TempPtr*;
    Last := *TempPtr*
END *Attach*;

This procedure *Attach* can also be used to develop a procedure *ReadLinkedString* for reading a string and constructing its linked representation. This procedure is used in the program of Figure 8.2, which is a revision of that in Figure 8.1 for counting users logged into a computer system for some given period of time. This revised program uses the linked implementation of strings in place of the usual array implementation. Note the function procedure *EqualStrings* used to compare two linked strings. It first checks that the strings have the same length, and if so, it traverses each of the strings, comparing them character by character, returning FALSE if a mismatch occurs and TRUE otherwise.

```
MODULE CountUsers2;

(*************************************************************************

   Program to determine the number of distinct users logged into a
   computer system for a given period of time.  User-ids are read
   from the file UserIdFile, and each new one is counted and added to
   the set Users of user-ids already found in the file.  The program
   uses a linked implementation of sets and a linked implementation
   of strings.

   *************************************************************************)

   FROM InOut IMPORT Write, WriteString, WriteCard, WriteLn, Read,
                     Done, EOL, OpenInput, CloseInput;
   FROM Storage IMPORT ALLOCATE, DEALLOCATE;
```

Figure 8.2

Figure 8.2 (cont.)

```
TYPE
    StringPointer = POINTER TO StringNode;
    StringNode = RECORD
                    Ch : CHAR;
                    Next : StringPointer
                 END;
    String = RECORD
                Length : CARDINAL;
                List : StringPointer
             END;
    ElementType = String;
    SetPointer = POINTER TO SetNode;
    SetNode = RECORD
                Element : ElementType;
                Next : SetPointer
              END;

    SetType = SetPointer;

VAR
    UserId : String;        (* current user-id being processed *)
    Users : SetPointer;     (* set of user-ids already found in file *)
    NumUsers : CARDINAL;    (* count of distinct user-ids *)
    MoreData : BOOLEAN;     (* indicates if more data in file *)

PROCEDURE ReadLinkedString(VAR Str : String; VAR MoreData : BOOLEAN);

    (****************************************************************

        Procedure to read characters from a file until an end-of-line
        mark is reached, storing these in a linked list with head node
        pointed to by Str.  Procedure Attach is used to attach nodes
        containing these characters to the end of this linked list.
        MoreData is returned as TRUE or FALSE according to whether or
        not a string is read.

    ****************************************************************)

    VAR
        Character : CHAR;       (* next character read from file *)
        Last : StringPointer;   (* pointer to last node in linked list *)

    PROCEDURE Attach(Character : CHAR; VAR Last : StringPointer);

        (************************************************************

            Procedure to create a node containing Character, attach
            it to a linked list with last node pointed to by Last,
            and advance Last to point to this node.

        ************************************************************)

        VAR
            TempPtr : StringPointer;    (* pointer to new node *)
```

Figure 8.2 (cont.)

```
        BEGIN (* Attach *)
            ALLOCATE(TempPtr, SIZE(StringNode));
            TempPtr^.Ch := Character;
            TempPtr^.Next := NIL;
            Last^.Next := TempPtr;
            Last := TempPtr
        END Attach;

    BEGIN (* ReadAString *)
        Str.Length := 0;
        ALLOCATE(Str.List, SIZE(StringNode));
        Str.List^.Next := NIL;
        Last := Str.List;
        Read(Character);
        MoreData := Done;
        WHILE MoreData AND (Character # EOL) DO
            INC(Str.Length);
            Attach(Character, Last);
            Read(Character)
        END (* WHILE *)
    END ReadLinkedString;

PROCEDURE EqualStrings (A, B : String) : BOOLEAN;

    (*****************************************************************

        Function returns TRUE or FALSE according to whether or not
        strings A and B are the same.   A linked list implementation
        of strings is assumed.

        ****************************************************************)

    VAR
        ptrA, ptrB : StringPointer;  (* pointers to run through A and B *)
        Same : BOOLEAN;               (* signals if strings are same *)

    BEGIN
        IF A.Length # B.Length THEN
            RETURN FALSE            .(* different lengths, so A # B *)
        ELSE
            ptrA := A.List^.Next;
            ptrB := B.List^.Next;
            WHILE (ptrA # NIL) AND (ptrA^.Ch = ptrB^.Ch) DO
                ptrA := ptrA^.Next;
                ptrB := ptrB^.Next
            END (* WHILE *);
            RETURN ptrA = NIL (* A = B if both completely traversed *)
        END (* IF *)
    END EqualStrings;
```

Figure 8.2 (cont.)

```
PROCEDURE EmptySet() : SetType;

    (********************************************************************

        Function returns a pointer to an empty list consisting of only
        a head hode.  This is the linked implementation of an empty set.

    *******************************************************************)

    VAR
        TempPtr : SetType;    (* temporary pointer *)

    BEGIN
        ALLOCATE(TempPtr, SIZE(SetNode));
        TempPtr^.Next := NIL;
        RETURN TempPtr
    END EmptySet;

PROCEDURE IsAMember(S : SetType; X : ElementType): BOOLEAN;

    (********************************************************************

        Function procedure returns TRUE or FALSE according as X is
        or is not an element of S.  S is implemented as a linked
        list with head node pointed to by S.

    *******************************************************************)

    VAR
        p : SetType;    (* auxiliary pointer to run through S *)

    BEGIN
        p := S^.Next;
        WHILE (p # NIL) AND NOT EqualStrings(p^.Element, X) DO
            p := p^.Next
        END (* WHILE *);
        RETURN p # NIL
    END IsAMember;

PROCEDURE Include( X : ElementType; VAR S : SetType);

    (********************************************************************

        Procedure to add element X to set S implemented as
        a linked list with head node.

    *******************************************************************)

    VAR
        TempPtr : SetType;    (* pointer to new node for X *)

    BEGIN
        ALLOCATE(TempPtr, SIZE(SetNode));
        TempPtr^.Element := X;
        TempPtr^.Next := S^.Next;
        S^.Next := TempPtr
    END Include;
```

Figure 8.2 (cont.)

```
BEGIN   (* main program *)
    WriteString('Enter name of input file.'); WriteLn;
    OpenInput('');
    Users := EmptySet();
    NumUsers := 0;
    ReadLinkedString(UserId, MoreData);
    WHILE MoreData DO
        IF NOT IsAMember(Users, UserId) THEN
            INC(NumUsers);
            Include(UserId, Users)
        END (* IF *);
        ReadLinkedString(UserId, MoreData)
    END (* WHILE *);
    WriteLn;
    WriteString('Number of users who logged in:  ');
    WriteCard(NumUsers, 1);
    CloseInput
END CountUsers2.
```

Listing of file USERIDS used in sample run:

```
S31416PI
S12345SL
S31416PI
S31313LN
S12345SL
S31416PI
S21718EX
S13331RC
S77777UP
S12345SL
S31416PI
S21718EX
S99099RR
S12345SL
S77777UP
S31313LN
S31416PI
```

Sample run:

```
Enter name of input file.
in> USERIDS

Number of users who logged in:  7
```

In a linear linked list, direct access is possible only to the first node, but some string operations may require fast access to characters other than the first one. For example, to implement an append operation efficiently, we must be able to access the last character rapidly. This is not possible if direct access to only the first node is maintained, since the entire list of characters must then be traversed each time to find the last node. One alternative is to maintain an auxiliary pointer to the last node as in procedure *Concat*. Another alternative is to use a circular linked list with a pointer to the last node, as described in Section 8.2. The following procedure *Append* uses this approach:

PROCEDURE *Append*(*Character* : CHAR; VAR *Str* : *String*);

   (* Procedure to modify string *Str* by appending *Character* to it.
      Strings are implemented as circular linked lists with a pointer to
      the last node. *)

   VAR
      First : *StringPointer*;   (* pointer to first node *)

   BEGIN
      First := *Str.List↑.Next*;
      Attach (*Character*, *Str.List*);
      Str.List↑.Next := *First*
   END *Append*;

The following diagrams summarize the action of this procedure and *Attach* in appending R to the string 'COMPUTE':

First := Str.List↑.Next;

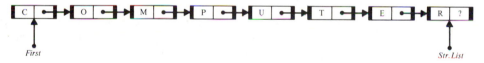

Attach('R', Str.List);

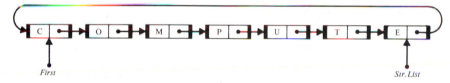

Str.List↑.Next := First

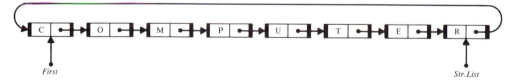

Exercises

1. Using the linked list implementation of strings described in this section, write a function procedure for the *Compare* operation (see Section 3.2). A reference of the form *Compare(Str1, Str2)* should return −1, 0, or 1, according to whether *Str1* is less than *Str2*, *Str1* is equal to *Str2*, or *Str1* is greater than *Str2*.

2. Assuming the linked list implementation of strings described in this section, write procedures for the basic string operations:

   (a) length   **(b)** position   **(c)** copy

3. Assuming the linked list implementation of strings described in this section, write a **(a)** nonrecursive procedure, **(b)** recursive procedure *WriteLinkedString* to print a string.

4. Write a complete linked-list version of the library module *StringsLib* described in Section 3.2, using the linked-list implementation of strings described in this section. In addition to procedures for the basic string operations, it should also export special input/output procedures *ReadLinkedString* and *WriteLinkedString* (see Exercise 3).

5. Assuming a circular linked list representation for strings, write procedures for the basic string operations:

   (a) length   **(b)** position   **(c)** copy   **(d)** concatenate

6. Assuming a linked list implementation of strings, write a boolean-valued function procedure that determines whether a string is a palindrome:

   (a) Using an auxiliary linked stack.
   (b) Constructing another string that is the reversal of the original string.
   (c) Using recursion.

7. Write a recursive version of the function procedure in Exercise 6 assuming a circular linked-list implementation of strings.

8. Write a program that reads a string, stores it in a linked list, prints it, and checks whether the string is a palindrome, using one of the functions in Exercises 6 or 7.

9. Write a program that reads names of the form First Middle Last and prints them in the format Last, F. M. Use a linked-list implementation for all strings.

10. Extend the program in Exercise 9 to store these rearranged names in an array and sort them. Use the function procedure in Exercise 1 to compare strings.

*8.5 Linked Implementation of Sparse Polynomials

A *polynomial in one variable x*, $P(x)$, has the form

$$P(x) = a_0 + a_1 x + a_2 x^2 + \cdots + a_n x^n$$

where $a_0, a_1, a_2 \ldots, a_n$ are called the **coefficients** of the polynomial. The **degree** of $P(x)$ is the largest power of x that appears in the polynomial with a nonzero coefficient; for example, the polynomial

$$P(x) = 5 + 7x - 8x^3 + 4x^5$$

has degree 5. Constant polynomials such as $Q(x) = 3.78$ have degree 0, and the zero polynomial is also said to have degree 0.

A polynomial can be viewed abstractly as a list of coefficients

$$(a_0, a_1, a_2, \ldots, a_n)$$

and can be represented using any of the list implementations we have considered. For example, the polynomial $P(x) = 5 + 7x - 8x^3 + 4x^5$, which can also be written as

$$P(x) = 5 + 7x + 0x^2 - 8x^3 + 0x^4 + 4x^5 \\ + 0x^6 + 0x^7 + 0x^8 + 0x^9 + 0x^{10}$$

can be identified with the list of coefficients

$$(5, 7, 0, -8, 0, 4, 0, 0, 0, 0, 0)$$

and this can be stored in an array P indexed $[0..10]$:

i	0	1	2	3	4	5	6	7	8	9	10
$P[i]$	5	7	0	-8	0	4	0	0	0	0	0

If the degrees of the polynomials being processed do not vary too much from the upper limit imposed by the array size and do not have a large number of zero coefficients, this representation may be satisfactory. However, for *sparse* polynomials—that is, those that have only a few nonzero terms—this array implementation is not very efficient. For example, storing the polynomial

$$Q(x) = 5 + x^{99}$$

or equivalently,

$$Q(x) = 5 + 0x + 0x^2 + 0x^3 + \cdots + 0x^{98} + 1x^{99}$$

would require an array having 2 nonzero elements and at least 98 zero elements.

The obvious waste of memory caused by storing all of the zero coefficients can be eliminated if only the nonzero coefficients are stored. In such an implementation, however, it is clear that it would also be necessary to store the power of x that corresponds to each coefficient. Thus, rather than identifying a polynomial with its list of coefficients, we might represent it as a list of coefficient-exponent pairs; for example,

$$P(x) = 5 + 7x - 8x^3 + 4x^5 \longleftrightarrow ((5,0), (7,1), (-8,3), (4,5)) \\ Q(x) = 5 + x^{99} \longleftrightarrow ((5,0), (1,99))$$

Note that the pairs are ordered in such a way that the exponents are in increasing order.

Such lists could be implemented sequentially by arrays of records, each of which contains a coefficient field and an exponent field. However, the fixed array size again imposes a limit on the size of the list and results in considerable waste of memory in applications in which the sizes of the lists—that is, the number of nonzero coefficients in the polynomials—varies considerably from this upper limit.

For this application, a linked list implementation is appropriate. Each node will have the form

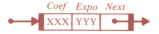

in which the three parts *Coef*, *Expo*, and *Next* store a nonzero coefficient, the corresponding exponent, and a pointer to the node representing the next term, respectively. For example, the preceding polynomials $P(x)$ and $Q(x)$ can be represented by the following linked lists with head nodes that store the polynomials' degrees in their *Expo* fields:

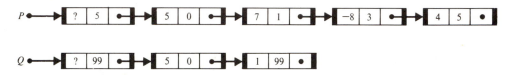

and the zero polynomial by simply a head node:

$$Z \quad \rightarrow \boxed{? \mid 0 \mid \bullet}$$

For such linked polynomials we can use declarations of the following form:

```
TYPE
    CoefType = REAL;    (* type of coefficients *)
    PolyPointer = POINTER TO PolyNode;
    PolyNode = RECORD
                    Coef : CoefType;
                    Expo : CARDINAL;
                    Next : PolyPointer
               END;
    Polynomial = PolyPointer;

VAR
    P, Q, . . . : Polynomial;
```

Of course, we could have used the "standard" node format of a *Data* field and a *Next* field by making the type of the *Data* field a record with a *Coef* field and an *Expo* field. This does not produce any real benefits, however, and would require double field designation to access these items, for example, $P\uparrow.Data.Coef$ rather than simply $P\uparrow.Coef$.

As an illustration of how such linked polynomials are processed, we consider the operation of polynomial addition. For example, suppose we wish to add the following polynomials $A(x)$ and $B(x)$;

$$A(x) = 5 + 6x^3 + 2x^5 + x^7$$
$$B(x) = x^3 - 2x^5 + 13x^7 - 2x^8 + 26x^9$$

Recall that this sum is calculated by adding coefficients of terms that have matching powers of x. Thus, the sum of polynomials $A(x)$ and $B(x)$ is

$$C(x) = A(x) + B(x) = 5 + 7x^3 + 14x^7 - 2x^8 + 26x^9$$

Now consider the linked representations of these polynomials:

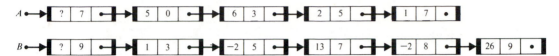

Since we have decided to use linked lists with head nodes, we begin by initializing C to point to a head node:

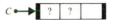

Three auxiliary pointers, *ptrA*, *ptrB*, and *ptrC*, will run through the lists A, B, and C, respectively; *ptrA* and *ptrB* will point to the current nodes being processed; and *ptrC* will point to the last node attached to C. Thus, *ptrA*, *ptrB*, and *ptrC* are initialized to $A\uparrow.Next$, $B\uparrow.Next$, and C, respectively:

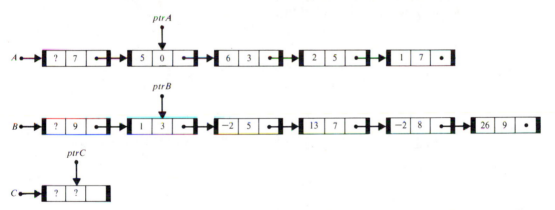

At each step of the computation, we compare the exponents in the nodes pointed to by *ptrA* and *ptrB*. If they are different, a node containing the smaller exponent and the corresponding coefficient is attached to C, and the pointer for this list and *ptrC* are advanced:

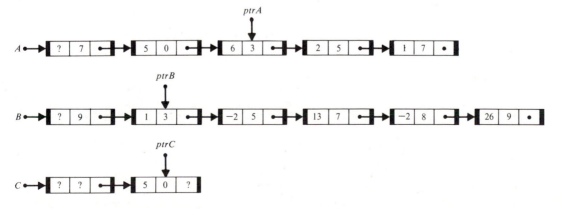

If the exponents in the nodes pointed to by *ptrA* and *ptrB* match, then the coefficients in these nodes are added. If this sum is not zero, a new node is created with coefficient field equal to this sum and exponent field equal to the common exponent, and this node is attached to *C*. Pointers for all three lists are then advanced:

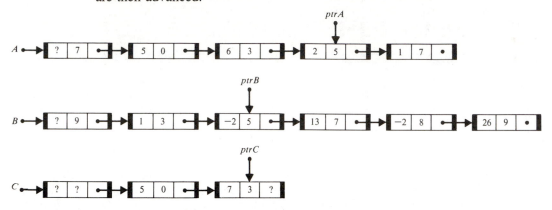

If the sum of the coefficients is zero, then *ptrA* and *ptrB* are simply advanced, and no new node is attached to *C*:

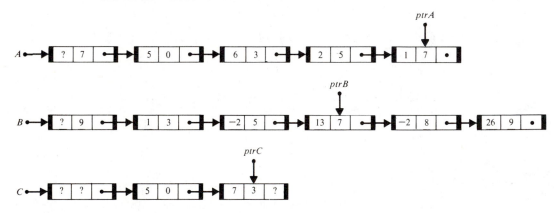

We continue in this manner until the end of *A* or *B* is reached, that is, until one of *ptrA* or *ptrB* becomes nil:

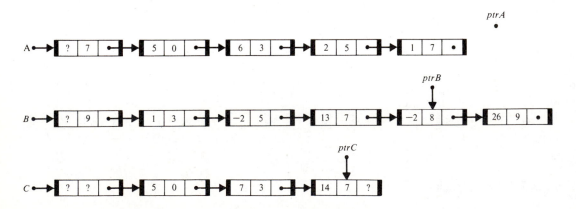

If the end of the other list has not been reached, we simply copy the remaining nodes in it, attaching each to C, and then set the link field in the last node of C to nil and store the degree of C in its head node to complete the construction of the linked list C representing the sum $A(x) + B(x)$:

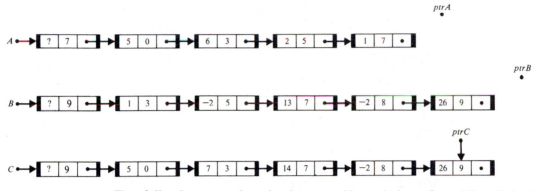

The following procedure implements this technique for adding linked polynomials:

PROCEDURE *LinkedPolyAdd*(*A*, *B* : *Polynomial*; VAR *C* : *Polynomial*);

    (∗ Procedure to add two linked polynomials *A* and *B* and return a pointer *C* to their sum. Linked lists representing polynomials are assumed to have head nodes that store their degrees. ∗)

VAR
    ptrA, *ptrB*, *ptrC*, *TempPtr* : *PolyPointer*;
    Sum : *CoefType*;
    Degree : CARDINAL;

BEGIN
    ptrA := *A*↑.*Next*;
    ptrB := *B*↑.*Next*;
    ALLOCATE(*C*, SIZE(*PolyNode*));
    ptrC := *C*;
    Degree := 0;
    WHILE (*ptrA* # NIL) AND (*ptrB* # NIL) DO
        IF *ptrA*↑.*Expo* < *ptrB*↑.*Expo* THEN   (∗ copy term from *A* ∗)
            Attach(*ptrA*↑.*Coef*, *ptrA*↑.*Expo*, *ptrC*);
            ptrA := *ptrA*↑.*Next*
        ELSIF *ptrA*↑.*Expo* > *ptrB*↑.*Expo* THEN (∗ copy term from *B* ∗)
            Attach(*ptrB*↑.*Coef*, *ptrB*↑.*Expo*, *ptrC*);
            ptrB := *ptrB*↑.*Next*
        ELSE   (∗ exponents match ∗)

```
                    Sum := ptrA↑.Coef + ptrB↑.Coef;
                    IF Sum # 0.0 THEN                    (* nonzero sum — put in C *)
                        Attach(Sum, ptrA↑.Expo, ptrC);
                        Degree := ptrA↑.Expo;
                        ptrA := ptrA↑.Next;
                        ptrB := ptrB↑.Next
                    END (* IF *)
                END (* IF *)
            END (* WHILE *);

            (* Copy any remaining terms in A or B to C *)

            IF ptrA # NIL THEN
                TempPtr := ptrA
            ELSE
                TempPtr := ptrB
            END (* IF *);
            WHILE TempPtr # NIL DO
                Attach(TempPtr↑.Coef, TempPtr↑.Expo, ptrC);
                Degree := TempPtr↑.Expo;
                TempPtr := TempPtr↑.Next
            END (* WHILE *);

            ptrC↑.Next := NIL;
            C↑.Expo := Degree
        END LinkedPolyAdd;
```

This procedure uses a procedure *Attach* similar to that used in the preceding section to create and attach new nodes to *C* as needed:

```
    PROCEDURE Attach(       Co : CoefType; Ex : CARDINAL;
                        VAR Last : PolyPointer);

        (* Procedure to create a node containing Co and Ex, attach it to a
           linked list with last node pointed to by Last, and advance Last to
           point to this node. *)

    VAR
        TempPtr : PolyPointer;    (* pointer to new node *)

    BEGIN
        ALLOCATE (TempPtr, SIZE(PolyNode));
        TempPtr↑.Coef := Co;
        TempPtr↑.Expo := Ex;
        TempPtr↑.Next := NIL;
        Last↑.Next := TempPtr;
        Last := TempPtr
    END Attach;
```

The procedure for adding linked polynomials is more complex and less understandable than the corresponding procedure for the array-based implementation described at the beginning of this section, in which the *i*th coefficient is stored in the *i*th location of an array. In this case, two polynomials *A* and *B* can be added to produce *C* very simply:

```
FOR i := 0 TO MaxDegree DO
    C[i] := A[i] + B[i]
END (* FOR *);
```

Here *MaxDegree* denotes the maximum degree of A and B.

Procedures for other basic polynomial operations, such as evaluation for a given value of x and multiplication, are likewise more complex in the linked implementation than in the array-based implementation. However, in applications in which the polynomials are sparse and of large degree, the memory saved compensates for the increased complexity of the algorithms.

Exercises

1. Write a procedure that reads the nonzero coefficients and exponents of a polynomial, constructs the linked list implementation of it, and returns a pointer to this linked list.

2. Write a procedure that prints a polynomial implemented as a linked list in the usual mathematical format, with x^n written as $x \uparrow n$ or $x \char94 n$.

3. Write a function procedure that accepts a pointer to a linked list representing a polynomial $P(x)$ and a value a of x and returns $P(a)$, the value of $P(x)$ at $x = a$.

4. The ***derivative*** of a polynomial $P(x) = a_0 + a_1 x + a_2 x^2 + a_3 x^3 + \cdots + a_n x^n$ of degree n is the polynomial $P'(x)$ of degree $n - 1$ defined by $P'(x) = a_1 + 2a_2 x + 3a_3 x^2 + \cdots + na_n x^{n-1}$. Write a function procedure that accepts a pointer to a linked list representing a polynomial and returns a pointer to a linked list that represents its derivative.

5. A ***root*** of a polynomial $P(x)$ is a number c for which $P(c) = 0$. The ***bisection method*** is one scheme that can be used to find an approximate root of $P(x)$ in some given interval $[a, b]$ where $P(a)$ and $P(b)$ have opposite signs (thus guaranteeing that $P(x)$ has a root in $[a, b]$). In this method, we begin by bisecting the interval $[a, b]$ and determining in which half $P(x)$ changes sign, because P must have a root in that half of the interval. Now bisect this subinterval and determine in which half of this subinterval $P(x)$ changes sign. Repeating this process gives a sequence of smaller and smaller subintervals, each of which contains a root of $P(x)$, as pictured in the following diagram. The process can be terminated when a small subinterval—say, of length less than 0.0001—is obtained or $P(x)$ has the value 0 at one of the endpoints. Assuming a linked implementation of polynomials and using the procedures in Exercises 1 and 3, write a program that uses the bisection method to find a root of a given polynomial.

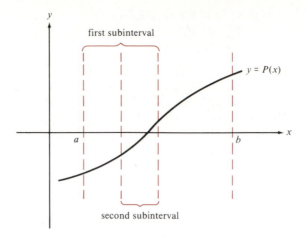

6. Another method for finding a root of a polynomial $P(x)$ is **Newton's method**. This method consists of taking an initial approximation x_1 and constructing a tangent line to the graph of $P(x)$ at that point. The point x_2 where this tangent line crosses the x axis is taken as the second approximation to the root. Then another tangent line is constructed at x_2, and the point x_3 where this tangent line crosses the x axis is the next approximation. The following diagram shows this process:

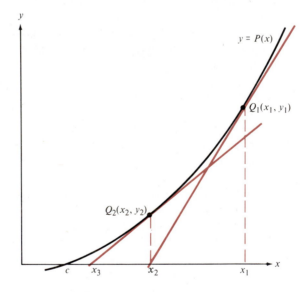

If c is an approximation to the root of $P(x)$, then the formula for obtaining the new approximation is

$$\text{new approximation} = c - \frac{P(c)}{P'(c)}$$

where $P'(x)$ is the derivative of $P(x)$. Assuming a linked implementation of polynomials and using the procedures in Exercises 1, 3, and 4, write a program to locate a root of a polynomial using Newton's method.

The process should terminate when a value of $P(x)$ is sufficiently small in absolute value or when the number of iterations exceeds some upper limit. Display the sequence of successive approximations.

7. Use the procedures in Exercises 1 through 3 and those given in the text in a library module for processing polynomials. The module should export (at least) procedures for reading a polynomial, printing a polynomial using the usual mathematical format described in Exercise 2, evaluating the polynomial for a given value of x, and polynomial addition.

8. Write a procedure to do polynomial multiplication, and determine its complexity.

9. Extend the library module in Exercise 7 to include procedures for

   (a) Calculating the derivative of a polynomial (see Exercise 4).
   (b) Finding a root of a polynomial.
   (c) Polynomial multiplication.

8.6 Symmetrically Linked Lists; Large-Number Arithmetic

One characteristic of singly linked lists is that they are unidirectional. This means that it is possible to move easily from a node to its successor. To find its predecessor, however, requires searching from the beginning of the list. In many applications, the need to locate the predecessor of an element arises just as often as does the need to locate its successor. In this section we consider how bidirectional lists can be constructed and processed, and we apply them to the problem of doing arithmetic with large integers.

Bidirectional lists can be easily constructed by using nodes that contain, in addition to a data part, two links: a forward link (*FLink*) pointing to the successor of the node and a backward link (*BLink*) pointing to its predecessor:

A linked list constructed from such nodes is usually called a ***symmetrically linked*** (or ***doubly linked***) *list*. As in the singly linked case, using head nodes for symmetrically linked lists eliminates some special cases (e.g., empty list and first node), and making the lists circular provides easy access to either end of the list. Thus we use head nodes for the symmetrically linked lists that we consider and assume that they are circular, and so they have a structure like the following:

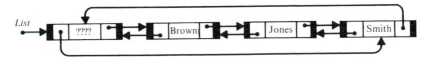

Symmetrically linked lists can be implemented using arrays of records (or parallel arrays), by a simple extension of the implementation described for singly linked lists in Section 7.3, or they can be implemented using Modula-2 pointers. In this latter implementation, the following declarations might be used:

```
TYPE
    ElementType = . . . ;   (* type of list elements *)
    SymmListPointer = POINTER TO NodeType;
    NodeType = RECORD
                    Data : ElementType;
                    FLink, BLink : SymmListPointer
               END;
    SymmLinkedList = SymmListPointer;

VAR
    List : SymmLinkedList;
```

Algorithms for the basic list operations are similar to those for the singly linked case, the main difference being the need to set some additional links. An empty symmetrically linked list is created by the following statements:

$List\uparrow.FLink := List;$
$List\uparrow.BLink := List;$

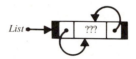

An empty-list condition can then be detected by using either of the boolean expressions $List\uparrow.BLink = List$ or $List\uparrow.FLink = List$.

Inserting a new node into a symmetrically linked list involves first setting its backward and forward links to point to its predecessor and successor, respectively, and then resetting the forward link of its predecessor and the back link of its successor to point to this new node:

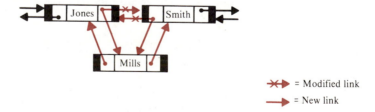

The following procedure implements this insertion operation:

```
PROCEDURE SymmLinkedInsert (VAR List : SymmLinkedList;
                                 Item : ElementType;
                                 PredPtr : SymmListPointer);
```

(* Procedure to insert *Item* into a circular symmetrically linked list with head node pointed to by *List*. *PredPtr* points to the predecessor of the node to be inserted. *)

```
         VAR
             TempPtr : SymmListPointer;      (* pointer to new node to be inserted *)

         BEGIN
             ALLOCATE (TempPtr, SIZE (NodeType));
             TempPtr↑.Data := Item;
             TempPtr↑.BLink := PredPtr;
             TempPtr↑.FLink := PredPtr↑.FLink;
             PredPtr↑.FLink := TempPtr;
             TempPtr↑.FLink↑.BLink := TempPtr
         END SymmLinkedInsert;
```

Note the last four statements, which set/reset the links as needed to connect the new node to the list. It is important that these be done in the correct order: You should study examples to see what happens if this order is changed.

A node can be deleted simply by resetting the forward link of its predecessor and the backward link of its successor to bypass the node:

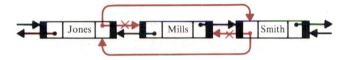

A procedure that implements deletion is

```
    PROCEDURE SymmLinkedDelete (VAR List : SymmLinkedList;
                                    CurrPtr : SymmListPointer);
```

(* Procedure to delete a node pointed to by *CurrPtr* from a circular symmetrically linked list with head node pointed to by *List*. *)

```
    BEGIN
        CurrPtr↑.BLink↑.FLink := CurrPtr↑.FLink;
        CurrPtr↑.FLink↑.BLink := CurrPtr↑.BLink;
        DEALLOCATE(CurrPtr, SIZE (NodeType))
    END SymmLinkedDelete;
```

As an application of symmetrically linked lists, we consider large-integer arithmetic. Recall that the size of a number that can be stored in computer memory is limited by the word size of the particular system being used. For example, the largest cardinal number that can be stored in a 16-bit word with the usual binary representation described in Section 2.2 is $2^{16} - 1 = 65535$. In some applications (e.g., storing zip codes or keeping track of the national debt), it obviously is necessary to process numbers that are larger than this value.

The first step in solving the problem of how to compute with large integers is to select a data structure for representing these numbers. Because the number of digits in these integers may vary considerably, a linked list seems appropriate. And because it is necessary to traverse this list in both directions, we use a symmetrically linked list. Each integer to be processed will be stored in a separate linked list, with each node storing a three-digit integer corresponding to a block of three consecutive digits in the number. And for simplicity, we consider only nonnegative integers. For example, the integer 9,145,632,884 is represented by the symmetrically linked list

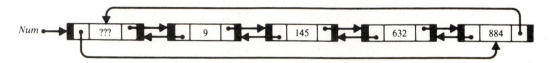

This linked representation of large integers is used in the program of Figure 8.3, which performs large-integer addition. The procedure *ReadLargeInt* reads a long integer in three-digit blocks, separated by blanks, and attaches a node containing the value of each of these three-digit blocks to the symmetrically linked list pointed to by *Num*. For example, suppose that the input data is

9 145 632 884

and that the first three blocks have already been read so that *Num* is the list

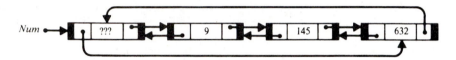

When the block 884 is read, a new node pointed to by *TempPtr* is created for it and is attached to the end of this list by setting the backward link in this new node to point to the last node in the list,

$TempPtr{\uparrow}.BLink := Num{\uparrow}.BLink;$

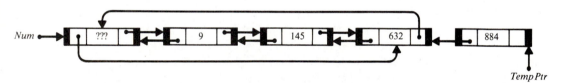

its forward link to point to the head node,

$TempPtr{\uparrow}.FLink := Num;$

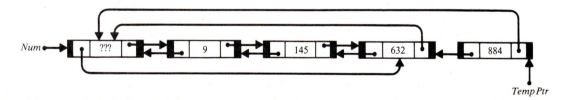

and then setting the forward link in the last node and the backward link in the head node to point to this new node.

$Num{\uparrow}.BLink{\uparrow}.FLink := TempPtr;$
$Num{\uparrow}.BLink := TempPtr;$

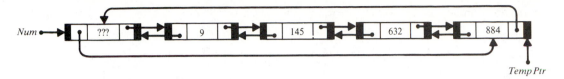

The procedure *AddLargeInt* carries out the addition of two long integers, *Num1* and *Num2*. It traverses the symmetrically linked lists representing these two numbers, from right to left, adding the two three-digit integers in corresponding nodes and the carry digit from the preceding nodes to obtain a three-digit sum and a carry digit. A node is created to store this three-digit sum and is attached at the front of the list representing the sum of *Num1* and *Num2*. The following diagram shows the linked lists corresponding to the computation:

$$
\begin{array}{r@{\quad}rrrr}
\text{carry digits} \quad \rightarrow 1 & 1 & & 1 & \\
& & 65 & 313 & 750 \\
+ & 999 & 981 & 404 & 873 \\
\hline
1 & 000 & 046 & 718 & 623 \\
\end{array}
$$

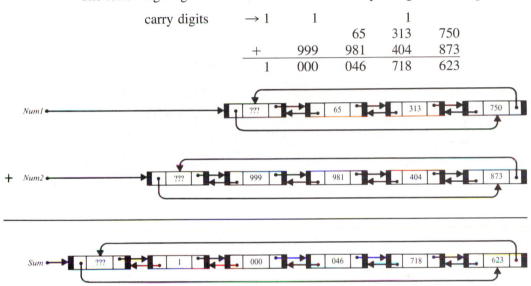

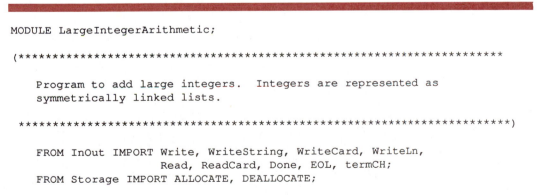

After the sum has been calculated, the procedure *WriteLargeInt* is called to display the sum. It traverses a symmetrically linked list pointed to by *Num* from left to right, displaying the three digits corresponding to the value stored in each node.

```
MODULE LargeIntegerArithmetic;

(*******************************************************************

    Program to add large integers.  Integers are represented as
    symmetrically linked lists.

 *******************************************************************)

    FROM InOut IMPORT Write, WriteString, WriteCard, WriteLn,
                Read, ReadCard, Done, EOL, termCH;
    FROM Storage IMPORT ALLOCATE, DEALLOCATE;
```

Figure 8.3

Figure 8.3 (cont.)

```
CONST
    BlockLength = 3;  (* number of digits in blocks *)
    Limit = 1000;     (* 1 + largest integer having BlockLength digits *)

TYPE
    ElementType = [0..Limit];
    SymmListPointer = POINTER TO ListNode;
    ListNode = RECORD
                    Data : ElementType;
                    BLink, FLink : SymmListPointer;
               END;
    SymmLinkedList = SymmListPointer;

VAR
    Num1, Num2,                   (* symmetric linked list storing the
                                     numbers being added *)
    Sum : SymmLinkedList;         (* pointer to sum *)
    Response : CHAR;              (* user respone *)

PROCEDURE InsertFront (Item : ElementType; VAR List : SymmLinkedList);

    (*****************************************************************

        Procedure to create a node containing Item and insert it at
        the front of the circular symmetrically linked list having
        head node pointed to by List.

        ****************************************************************)

    VAR
        TempPtr : SymmListPointer;  (* pointer to new node *)

    BEGIN (* InsertFront *)
        ALLOCATE(TempPtr, SIZE(ListNode));
        TempPtr^.Data := Item;
        TempPtr^.FLink := List^.FLink;
        TempPtr^.BLink := List;
        List^.FLink^.BLink := TempPtr;
        List^.FLink := TempPtr
    END InsertFront;

PROCEDURE ReadLargeInt (VAR Num : SymmLinkedList);

    (*****************************************************************

        Procedure to read a large integer in blocks of size BlockLength
        and store these blocks in nodes of a circular symmetrically
        linked list with head node pointed to by Num.

        ****************************************************************)

    VAR
        TempPtr : SymmListPointer;   (* pointer to new node *)
        Block : CARDINAL;            (* next block of digits *)
```

Figure 8.3 (cont.)

```
    BEGIN
        (* Set up head node *)
        ALLOCATE(Num, SIZE(ListNode));
        Num^.FLink := Num;
        Num^.BLink := Num;

        (* Read and store blocks of digits *)
        REPEAT
            ReadCard(Block);
            ALLOCATE(TempPtr, SIZE(ListNode));
            TempPtr^.Data := Block;
            TempPtr^.BLink := Num^.BLink;
            TempPtr^.FLink := Num;
            Num^.BLink^.FLink := TempPtr;
            Num^.BLink := TempPtr
        UNTIL termCH = EOL
    END ReadLargeInt;

PROCEDURE AddLargeInt (    Num1, Num2 : SymmLinkedList;
                       VAR Sum : SymmLinkedList);

    (*********************************************************************

        Procedure to add two large integers represented as circular
        symmetrically linked lists with head nodes pointed to by
        Num1 and Num2 and return the large integer pointed to by Sum.

        *********************************************************************)

    VAR
        p1, p2, p, Head : SymmListPointer;  (* auxiliary pointers *)
        Carry,                              (* carry digit *)
        NodeSum : CARDINAL;                 (* sum of numbers in list nodes *)

    BEGIN
        p1 := Num1^.BLink;
        p2 := Num2^.BLink;
        Carry := 0;

        (* Set up head node *)
        ALLOCATE(Sum, SIZE(ListNode));
        Sum^.FLink := Sum;
        Sum^.BLink := Sum;

        (* Add blocks in corresponding nodes of Num1 and Num2 *)
        WHILE (p1 # Num1) AND (p2 # Num2) DO
            NodeSum := p1^.Data + p2^.Data + Carry;
            Carry := NodeSum DIV Limit;
            InsertFront (NodeSum MOD Limit, Sum);
            p1 := p1^.BLink;
            p2 := p2^.BLink
        END (* WHILE *);

        IF p1 = Num1 THEN  (* continue with Num2 *)
            p := p2;
            Head := Num2
        ELSE               (* continue with Num1 *)
            p := p1;
            Head := Num1
        END (* IF *);
```

Figure 8.3 (cont.)

```
        WHILE p # Head DO
            NodeSum := p^.Data + Carry;
            Carry := NodeSum DIV Limit;
            InsertFront (NodeSum MOD Limit, Sum);
            p := p^.BLink
        END (* WHILE *);
        IF Carry > 0 THEN
            InsertFront (Carry, Sum)
        END (* IF *)
    END AddLargeInt;

PROCEDURE WriteLargeInt (Num : SymmLinkedList);

    (****************************************************************

        Procedure to traverse circular symmetrically linked list,
        displaying the digits of the integers stored in each node.

    ****************************************************************)

    VAR
        p : SymmListPointer;        (* auxiliary pointer *)
        Block,                      (* a block of digits to be displayed *)
        PowerOfTen : ElementType; (* power of 10 -- to split off digits *)

    BEGIN
        p := Num^.FLink;

        (* Print first block of digits *)

        IF p # Num THEN
            WriteCard(p^.Data, 1);
            Write(' ');
            p := p^.FLink
        END (* IF *);

        (* Print remaining blocks, digit by digit *)
        WHILE p # Num DO
            Block := p^.Data;
            PowerOfTen := Limit DIV 10;
            WHILE PowerOfTen > 0 DO
                WriteCard(Block DIV PowerOfTen, 1);
                Block := Block MOD PowerOfTen;
                PowerOfTen := PowerOfTen DIV 10
            END (* WHILE *);
            Write(' ');
            p := p^.FLink
        END (* WHILE *);
        WriteLn
    END WriteLargeInt;
```

Figure 8.3 (cont.)

```
BEGIN (* main program *)
    WriteString('Enter two integers in blocks of size ');
    WriteCard(BlockLength, 1);
    WriteLn;
    WriteString ('separating these blocks by at least one space.');
    WriteLn;
    WriteString('Depress the RETURN key immediately after the last block.');
    WriteLn;
    REPEAT
        WriteLn;
        WriteString(' First #:  ');
        ReadLargeInt(Num1);
        WriteLn;
        WriteString('Second #:  ');
        ReadLargeInt(Num2);
        AddLargeInt(Num1, Num2, Sum);
        WriteLn; WriteLn;
        WriteString('  Sum is:  ');
        WriteLargeInt(Sum);
        WriteLn;
        WriteString('More (Y or N)?  ');
        Read(Response)
    UNTIL CAP(Response) # 'Y'
END LargeIntegerArithmetic.
```

Sample run:

```
Enter two integers in blocks of size 3
separating these blocks by at least one space:

 First #:  1
Second #:  1

  Sum is:  2

More (Y or N)?  Y

 First #:    999 999 999 999 999 999 999 999
Second #:                                  1

  Sum is:  1 000 000 000 000 000 000 000 000

More (Y or N)?  Y

 First #:           65 313 750
Second #:     999 981 404 873

  Sum is:  1 000 046 718 623

More (Y or N)?  N
```

Exercises

1. Given the following symmetrically linked list with the two pointers *P1* and *P2*:

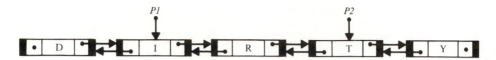

Find the value of each of the following:

(a) *P1↑.Data*
(b) *P1↑.FLink↑.Data*
(c) *P1↑.BLink↑.BLink*
(d) *P1↑.FLink↑.FLink*
(e) *P1↑.BLink↑.FLink*
(f) *P2↑.BLink↑.BLink↑.Data*
(g) *P2↑.BLink↑.BLink↑.BLink↑.BLink*
(h) *P2↑.BLink↑.BLink↑.FLink↑.Data*

2. Using only pointer *P1* to access the symmetrically linked list in Exercise 1, write statements to

(a) Display the contents of the nodes, in alphabetical order.
(b) Replace 'D' by 'M' and 'R' by 'S'.
(c) Delete the node containing 'T'.

3. Repeat Exercise 2, but using only pointer *P2* to access the list.

4. Repeat Exercise 1, but for the following circular symmetrically linked list:

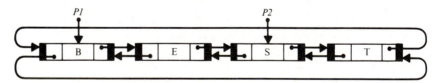

5. Using only pointer *P1* to access the symmetrically linked list in Exercise 4, write statements to

(a) Display the contents of the nodes, in alphabetical order.
(b) Insert a node containing 'L' after the node containing 'B' and replace 'E' with 'A'.
(c) Delete the node containing 'T'.

6. Repeat Exercise 5, but using only pointer *P2* to access the list.

7. Assuming the linked implementation of large integers described in this section, write a boolean-valued function procedure *LEQ* that determines if one large integer is less than or equal to another large integer.

8. What information might be stored in the head node of a linked list for a large integer so that a more efficient version of the less-than-or-equal-to procedure in Exercise 7 is possible?

9. Write a function procedure *Difference* that implements subtraction for nonnegative large integers; a reference of the form *Difference*(*A*, *B*) where $A \geq B$ should return the value of $A - B$. (If $A < B$, no value need be returned.)

10. Using the procedures in Exercises 7 and 9, modify the program in Figure 8.3 to process both positive and negative large integers. Use the head node in the linked list for a large integer to indicate the sign of the number.

11. The sequence of *Fibonacci numbers* begins with the integers

$$1, 1, 2, 3, 5, 8, 13, 21, 34, 55, 89, \ldots$$

where each number after the first two is the sum of the two preceding numbers. Write a program to calculate and display large Fibonacci numbers.

12. Write a function procedure for multiplying large integers implemented as linked lists as described in the text.

13. Use the procedure in Exercise 12 in a program that calculates large factorials.

14. Write a library module for the ADT *LargeInteger*, using the linked representation of large integers described in this section. It should export (at least) procedures for the basic operations of addition, subtraction (Exercise 9), multiplication (Exercise 12), comparison (Exercise 7), and procedures for reading, writing, and assigning large integer values.

15. Write a procedure for reversing a symmetrically linked list.

16. In a multiuser environment, jobs with various memory requirements are submitted to the computer system, and the operating system allocates a portion of memory to each job using some memory-management scheme. One popular scheme maintains a symmetrically linked list of records describing free memory blocks. When a memory request is received, this list is searched to locate the first available block that is large enough to satisfy the request. An appropriate portion of this block is allocated to the job, and any remaining portion remains on the free list.

   Write a procedure to implement this *first-fit* memory-management scheme. Assume that records in the free list contain the beginning address of an available block and its size, together with the links necessary to maintain a circular symmetrically linked list. Parameters for this procedure are a pointer to the first node in the free list and the size of the request. The procedure should return the address of the allocated block or an indication that the request cannot be satisfied.

17. Another common memory-allocation strategy is the ***best-fit*** scheme, in which the free list is scanned and the memory block that best fits the request is allocated. This block is either the first block whose size is equal to the request or the block whose size least exceeds the request. Rewrite the procedure in Exercise 16, using this best-fit scheme.

8.7 Other Multiply Linked Lists

We have seen that symmetrically linked lists are useful data structures in those applications in which it is necessary to move in either direction in a list. In this section we consider an assortment of other kinds of list processing in which linked lists whose nodes contain more than one link are useful. Such structures are usually considered in detail in advanced data structures courses and are only previewed here.

Multiply Ordered Lists.   In Chapter 7 we considered ordered linked lists in which the nodes were ordered so that the values in some key field of the data items stored in these nodes were in ascending order. In some applications, however, it is necessary to maintain a collection of records ordered in two or more different ways. For example, we might wish to have a collection of student records ordered both by name and by id number.

One way to accomplish such multiple orderings is to maintain separate ordered linked lists, one for each of the desired orders. But this is obviously inefficient, especially for large records, because multiple copies of each record are required. A better approach is to use a single list in which multiple links are used to link the nodes together in the different orders. For example, to store a collection of records containing student names and id numbers with names in alphabetical order and id numbers in ascending order, we might use the following multiply linked list having two links per node:

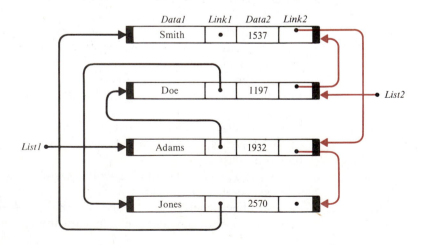

If this list is traversed and the data fields are displayed by using *List1* to point to the first node and following the pointers in the field *Link1*, the names will be in alphabetical order:

Adams   1932
Doe   1197
Jones   2570
Smith   1537

A traversal using *List2* to point to the first node and following pointers in the field *Link2* gives the id numbers in ascending order:

Doe   1197
Smith   1537
Adams   1932
Jones   2570

This list is logically ordered, therefore, in two different ways.

Sparse Matrices.   An **m** × **n matrix** is a rectangular array containing *m* rows and *n* columns. The usual storage structure for matrices is thus quite naturally a two-dimensional array, especially since arrays are provided in nearly every programming language.

In some applications, however (for example, solving differential equations), it is necessary to process very large matrices having few nonzero entries. Using a two-dimensional array to store all the entries (including 0s) of such *sparse matrices* is not very efficient. They can be stored more efficiently using a linked structure analogous to that for sparse polynomials described in Section 8.5.

One common linked implementation is to represent each row of the matrix as a linked list, storing only the nonzero entries in each row. In this scheme, the matrix is represented as an array of pointers $A[1], A[2], \ldots, A[m]$, one for each row of the matrix. Each array element $A[i]$ points to a linked list of nodes, each of which stores a nonzero entry in that row and the number of the column in which it appears, together with a link to the node for the next nonzero entry in that row:

For example, the 4 × 5 matrix

$$A = \begin{bmatrix} 9 & 0 & 0 & 8 & 0 \\ 7 & 0 & 0 & 0 & 0 \\ 0 & 0 & 0 & 0 & 0 \\ -1 & 6 & 0 & -8 & 0 \end{bmatrix}$$

can be represented by

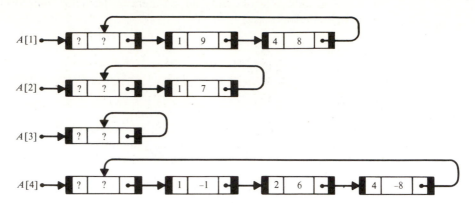

Although this is a very useful linked storage structure for matrices, the size of the array imposes a limit on the number of rows that such matrices may have. Moreover, for smaller matrices and/or those having a large number of rows with all zero entries, many of the elements in this array will be wasted.

An alternative implementation is to create a single linked list. Each node contains a row number, a column number, the nonzero entry in that row and column, and a link to the next node:

These nodes are usually arranged in the list so that traversing the list visits the entries of the matrix in rowwise order. For example, the preceding 4×5 matrix can be represented by the following circular linked list, which uses a head node to store the dimensions of the matrix:

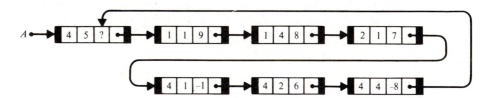

In this implementation, however, we lose direct access to each of the rows of the matrix. If rowwise processing is important in a particular application, such as the addition of matrices, it might be better to replace the array of pointers with a linked list of row head nodes, each of which contains a pointer to a nonempty row list. Each row head node will also contain the number of that row and a pointer to the next row head node, and these row head nodes will be ordered so that the row numbers are in ascending order. In this implementation, the preceding 4×5 matrix might be represented by the following linked structure:

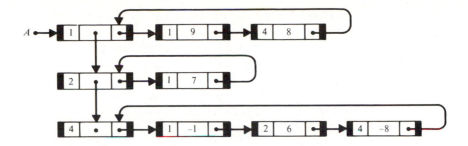

One drawback of all of these linked implementations is that it is difficult to process a matrix columnwise as required, for example, when multiplying two matrices. One linked structure that provides easy access to both the rows and the columns of a matrix is known as an **orthogonal list**. Each node stores a row number, a column number, and the nonzero entry in that row and column, and it appears in both a row list and a column list. This is accomplished by using two links in each node, one pointing to its successor in the row list and another pointing to its successor in the column list:

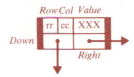

Usually each of the row lists and column lists is a circular list with a head node, and these head nodes are linked together to form circular lists with a master head node. For example, the orthogonal list representation of the preceding 4 × 5 matrix might be as shown in Figure 8.4.

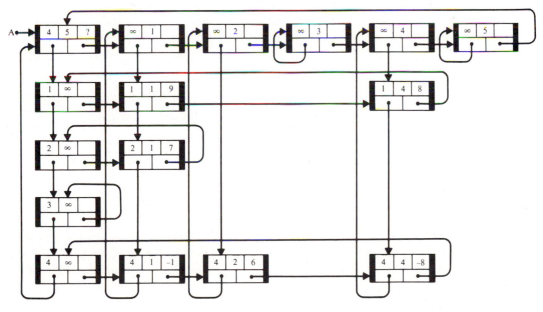

Figure 8.4

Generalized Lists.   In nearly all of our examples of list thus far, the list elements have been *atomic*, which means that they themselves are not lists. We considered, for example, lists of integers and lists of records. However, we just described a representation of sparse matrices that is a list of row lists. We also considered lists of strings on several occasions, and a string is itself a list. In particular, the program in Figure 8.2 represents a set of strings as a linked list of strings and each string as a linked list of characters. In this "linked list of linked lists" implementation, the set $S = \{AL, FRED, JOE\}$ would be represented as

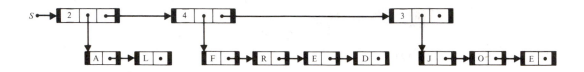

Lists in which the elements are allowed to be lists are called *generalized lists*. As illustrations, consider the following examples of lists:

$$A = (4, 6)$$
$$B = ((4, 6), 8)$$
$$C = (((4)), 6)$$
$$D = (2, A, A)$$
$$E = (2, 4, E)$$

A is an ordinary list containing two atomic elements, the integers 4 and 6. B is also a list of two elements, but the first element $(4, 6)$ is itself a list with two elements. C is also a list with two elements; its first element is $((4))$, which is a list of one element (4), and this element is itself a list of one element, namely, the integer 4. D is a list with three elements in which the second and third are themselves lists. The list E also has three elements, but it differs dramatically from D in that it has itself as a member. Such lists are said to be *recursive lists*.

Generalized lists are commonly represented as linked lists in which the nodes have a tag field in addition to a data part and a link part:

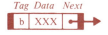

This tag is used to indicate whether the data field stores an atom or a pointer to a list. It can be implemented as a single bit with 0 indicating an atom and 1 indicating a pointer, or as a boolean variable with false and true playing the roles of 0 and 1. Thus lists A, B, and C can be represented by the following linked lists:

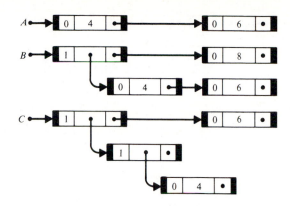

Of course, linked lists with head nodes, circular lists, and other variations might also be used.

Two implementations of D are possible. Because A is the list $(4, 6)$, we can think of D as the list

$$(2, (4, 6), (4,6))$$

and represent it as

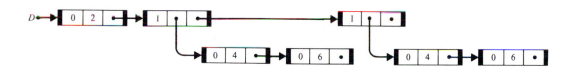

The second possibility is to allow **shared lists** and represent D and A as follows:

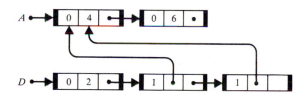

Note that in this case, modifying A also changes D.

The recursive list E can be represented as a circular linked structure:

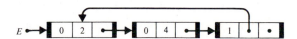

This is equivalent to the following infinite linked structure:

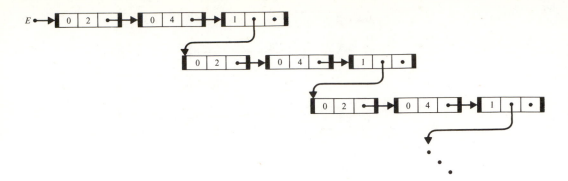

In Section 8.5 we described a linked implementation of polynomials in a single variable. Polynomials in more than one variable can be represented as generalized lists and can thus be implemented using linked structures similar to these. For example consider the polynomial $P(x,y)$ in two variables

$$P(x,y) = 3 + 7x + 14y^2 + 25y^7 - 9x^2y^7 + 18x^6y^7$$

This can be written as a polynomial in y whose coefficients are polynomials in x:

$$P(x,y) = (3 + 7x) + 14y^2 + (25 - 9x^2 + 18x^6)y^7$$

If we use nodes of the form

in which $Tag = 0$ indicates that the field *Coef* stores a number and $Tag = 1$ that it stores a pointer to a linked list representing a polynomial in x, we can represent the preceding polynomial $P(x,y)$ as

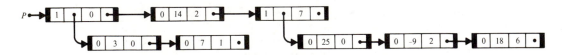

Linked representations of generalized lists are used extensively in implementing the programming language LISP (LISt Processing). As an illustration, the assignment statement that would be written in Modula-2 as

$$Z := X + 3 * (Y - 1)$$

is written in LISP as

(setq Z (plus X (times 3 (sub1 Y))))

This is, in fact, a list of three elements (without the separating commas we are accustomed to using). The first element is the key word *setq*, which denotes an assignment operator in LISP. The second element is a variable Z, to which a value is to be assigned. The third element is the list

(plus X (times 3 (sub1 Y)))

which corresponds to the Modula-2 expression $X + 3 * (Y - 1)$. This three-element list consists of the keyword *plus* denoting an addition operation, the variable X, and a list corresponding to the subexpression $3 * (Y - 1)$:

$$(times\ 3\ (sub1\ Y))$$

Similarly, this list contains the keyword *times* denoting multiplication, the integer constant 3, and a two-element list corresponding to the subexpression $Y - 1$:

$$(sub1\ Y)$$

The keyword *sub1* in this list specifies that 1 is to be subtracted from the variable Y that follows it to obtain the value of this expression.

If we use nodes in which a tag value of 0 denotes atomic list elements, such as keywords, variable names, and constants, and the tag value 1 denotes lists, this assignment statement can be represented by the following linked structure:

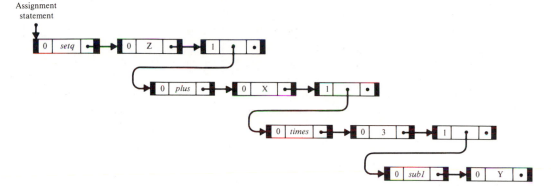

Looking Ahead. In this section we introduced several kinds of multiply linked structures and noted some of their applications. These are many other problems in which multiply linked structures can be used effectively. Several of these applications, including the study of trees and graphs, are considered in detail in later chapters.

Exercises

1. Write appropriate declarations for a multiply ordered linked list of names and id numbers like that described in the text.

2. Beginning with the multiply ordered linked list of names and id numbers pictured in the text, show the linked list that results from each of the following operations or sequence of operations:

   (a) Insert Brown with id number 2250.
   (b) Delete Smith with id number 1537.
   (c) Insert Zzyzk with id number 1025.
   (d) Insert Evans with id number 1620; insert Harris with id number 1750; delete Adams with id number 1932.

3. Write a program to read the records from *StudentFile* (see Appendix E) and store them in a multiply ordered linked list with two link fields, in which one link is used to order the nodes so that the id numbers are in ascending order and another link orders the nodes so that the names are in alphabetical order. (Note that the records in *StudentFile* are already arranged in order of ascending id numbers.) Then search this list for a given student id or a given student name, and display the other information in the record.

4. Extend the program in Exercise 3 so that new records can be inserted or existing records deleted.

5. Suppose that the following sparse matrix is implemented by an array of pointers to row lists. Give a diagram of the resulting linked lists similar to that in the text.

$$A = \begin{bmatrix} 1 & 0 & 0 & 0 & 8 & 0 & 0 \\ -5 & -6 & 0 & 0 & 0 & 0 & 0 \\ 0 & 0 & 0 & 0 & 0 & 0 & 10 \\ 0 & 0 & 0 & 0 & 0 & 0 & 0 \\ 9 & 8 & 7 & 0 & 0 & 0 & 0 \end{bmatrix}$$

6. Repeat Exercise 5, but implement the matrix as a circular linked list having a head node that stores its dimensions as described in the text.

7. Repeat Exercise 5, but implement the matrix as a linked list of head nodes containing pointers to linked row lists as described in the text.

8. Repeat Exercise 5, but give an orthogonal list representation like that described in this section.

9. Write the declarations needed to store a sparse matrix of integers using the implementation in

   (a) Exercise 5.   (b) Exercise 6.   (c) Exercise 7.
   (d) Exercise 8.

10. Write a procedure to add two sparse matrices, assuming the array of linked row lists implementation described in this section.

11. Repeat Exercise 10, but assume that each matrix is implemented as a circular linked list having a head node that stores its dimensions as described in the text.

12. Repeat Exercise 10, but assume that each matrix is implemented as a linked list of head nodes containing pointers to linked row lists as described in the text.

13. Repeat Exercise 10, but assume that each matrix is implemented using an orthogonal list representation like that described in this section.

14. Write a program that reads the dimensions of a sparse matrix and its entries, that constructs one of the linked list implementations described in this section, and that then prints the matrix in its usual tabular format.

15. Extend the program in Exercise 14 to read and calculate the sum of two matrices.

16. Give a diagram of the linked list implementation of each of the following generalized lists:

    (a) (1, (2, 3))
    (b) ((1, 2), (3, 4), 5)
    (c) (1, (2, 3), ( ), 4)   [( ) denotes an empty list.]
    (d) ((1, (2, 3)), ((4)))

17. Give a diagram of the linked list implementation of the following polynomials in two variables:

    (a) $P(x,y) = 7 + 3xy + 5x^3y - 17y^2$
    (b) $P(x,y) = 6 - 5x + 4x^2 - 2x^3y^4 + 6x^5y^4 - x^9y^4 + y^8$

18. Describe how a polynomial $P(x,y,z)$ in three variables can be implemented as a linked list, and illustrate your implementation for the polynomial

$$P(x,y) = 6 - 5x + 4x^2 - 2x^3y^4 + 6x^5y^4z^3 - x^9y^4z^3 + y^8z^3 + z^7$$

9

Searching

The problem of searching a collection of data items to determine whether or not a particular item appears in the collection is one of the most important data-processing problems and has arisen in many places in previous chapters. It is thus worthy of study in its own right, and so this chapter is devoted to this problem. We first review linear and binary search for lists and then introduce other searching schemes and describe the data structures required to support them. In particular, we consider binary search trees and hash tables.

9.1 Review of Linear Search and Binary Search

In many applications, the collection of data items to be searched is organized as a list,

$$X_1, X_2, \ldots, X_n$$

This list is to be searched to determine if one of the X_i's has some specified value.

In practice, the list elements are records, and the search is based on some key field in these records; that is, we search the list for a record X_i containing some specified value in its key field. In our discussion of the searching problem in this section, however, we assume for simplicity that the X_i's are simple items. The algorithms we describe can be easily modified to handle the case of records.

The most straightforward searching scheme is **_linear search_**, in which we begin with the first list element and then search the list sequentially until either we find the specified item or we reach the end of the list. An algorithm for linear search was given in Section 5.1, and for the array-based sequential implementation of lists, this algorithm is implemented by the following procedure:

```
PROCEDURE LinearSearch (VAR X : ListType; n : CARDINAL;
                              Item : ElementType;
                        VAR Found : BOOLEAN;
                        VAR Loc : CARDINAL);
```

(* Procedure to search the list of array elements $X[1], \ldots, X[n]$ for *Item*. *Found* is returned as TRUE and *Loc* as the position of *Item* if the search is successful; otherwise, *Found* is set to FALSE. *)

```
BEGIN
    Loc := 1;
    WHILE (Loc <= n) AND (X[Loc] # Item) DO
        INC (Loc)
    END (* WHILE *);
    Found := (Loc <= n)   .
END LinearSearch;
```

Here we assume that the type identifier *ListType* has been defined as an array of elements of some type *ElementType* and with index type [1..*MaxSize*] for some constant *MaxSize*.

To linearly search a linked list, we initialize some auxiliary pointer *LocPtr* to the first node and advance it from one node to the next following the links:

```
PROCEDURE LinkedLinearSearch (       L : ListPointer;
                                  Item : ElementType;
                            VAR Found : BOOLEAN;
                            VAR LocPtr : ListPointer);
```

(* Procedure to search the linked list with first node pointed to by *L* for *Item*. *Found* is returned as TRUE and *LocPtr* points to the node containing *Item* if the search is successful; otherwise, *Found* is set to FALSE. *)

```
BEGIN
    LocPtr := L;
    WHILE (LocPtr # NIL) AND (LocPtr↑.Data # Item) DO
        LocPtr := LocPtr↑.Next
    END (* WHILE *);
    Found := (LocPtr # NIL)
END LinkedLinearSearch;
```

Here we assume that the types *LinkedList, ListPointer,* and *ElementType* have been defined as indicated in Chapter 7 for linked lists.

The worst case for linear search is obviously that in which the item for which we are searching is not in the list, because in this case, each of the n items in the list must be examined. The worst-case computing time for linear search is thus O(n).

If the list being searched is an ordered list, that is, if the elements are arranged in ascending (or descending) order, then it is usually possible to determine that a specified item is not in the list without examining every element of the list. As soon as a list element is encountered that is greater than (less than) the item, the search can be terminated. For example, in searching the list

$$10, 20, 30, 40, 50, 60, 70, 80, 90, 100$$

for the value 35, there is no need to search beyond the list element 40, because it—and therefore all the list elements that follow it—are greater than 35. This improved linear search algorithm for ordered lists is

LINEAR SEARCH FOR ORDERED LISTS

(∗ Algorithm to linearly search an ordered list $X_1, \ldots, X_n$ for some specified *Item*. *Found* is set to true and *Loc* to the location of *Item* if the search is successful; otherwise, *Found* is set to false. The list elements are assumed to be in ascending order; for descending order, change $>$ to $<$ in the while loop. ∗)

1. Initialize *Loc* to 1.
2. While $Loc \leq n$ and $Item > X_{Loc}$
        Increment *Loc* by 1.
3. If $Loc \leq n$ and $Item = X_{Loc}$ then
        Set *Found* to true.
    Otherwise
        Set *Found* to false.

If *Item* is less than every X_i, the comparison of *Item* with X_{Loc} causes the while loop in Step 2 to terminate immediately. If *Item* is in the range X_1 through X_n (and the possible values for it are uniformly distributed over this range), then, on the average, $n/2$ comparisons of *Item* with the X_i are made before repetition terminates. Thus, in many cases, linear search for ordered lists will require fewer comparisons than are needed for unordered lists. The worst-case complexity is still $O(n)$, however, since n comparisons are required if $Item > X_n$.

An alternative scheme for searching an ordered list is **binary search**, also described in Chapter 5:

BINARY SEARCH

(∗ Algorithm to search the ordered list $X_1, \ldots, X_n$, assumed to be in ascending order, for some specified *Item* using a binary search. *Found* is set to true and *Mid* to the position of *Item* if the search is successful; otherwise, *Found* is set to false. ∗)

1. Initialize *Found* to false, *First* to 1, and *Last* to n.
2. While not *Found* and $First \leq Last$ do the following:
        a. Calculate $Mid = (First + Last) / 2$.
        b. If $Item < X_{Mid}$ then
            Set *Last* equal to $Mid - 1$.
        Else if $Item > X_{Mid}$ then
            Set *First* equal to $Mid + 1$.
        Else
            Set *Found* to true.

Here the middle list element is examined first, and if it is not the desired item, the search continues with either the first half or the last half of the list. Thus, on each pass through the while loop, the size of the sublist being searched is reduced by one-half. We showed in some detail in Section 5.1 that it follows from this observation that the worst-case computing time for binary search is $O(\log_2 n)$. It is therefore more efficient than linear search for large n ($n \geq 20$, as indicated by empirical studies).

We noted in Chapter 5 that although the preceding binary search algorithm is iterative, it can also naturally be described recursively. The basic idea at each stage is to examine the middle element of the (sub)list and, if it is not the desired item, then to search one of the two halves of the (sub)list *in exactly the same manner*.

RECURSIVE BINARY SEARCH

(* Algorithm to recursively search the ordered list $X_1, \ldots, X_n$, assumed
to be in ascending order, for some specified *Item* using a binary
search. *Found* is set to true and *Mid* to the postion of *Item* if the
search is successful; otherwise, *Found* is set to false. *)

1. Initialize *First* to 1 and *Last* to n.
2. If *First* > *Last* than   (* empty (sub)list *)
    Set *Found* to false.
   Else do the following:
    a. Calculate *Mid* = (*First* + *Last*) / 2.
    b. If *Item* < X_{Mid} then
        Apply the binary search algorithm with *Last* = *Mid* − 1.
       Else if *Item* > X_{Mid} then
        Apply the binary search algorithm with *First* = *Mid* + 1.
       Else
        Set *Found* to true.

Because the complexity of this recursive algorithm is $O(\log_2 n)$ and because it is no simpler than the iterative version, the guidelines given in Chapter 5 for choosing between recursive and iterative formulations of an algorithm suggest that we opt for the nonrecursive version.

Although binary search usually outperforms linear search, it does require an array-based sequential implementation so that list elements can be accessed directly. It is not appropriate for linked lists, because locating the middle element would require traversing the sublist of elements that precede it to reach the middle of the list. As the exercises ask you to show, this causes the worst-case computing time to become $O(n)$ for a list of size n.

It is possible, however, to store the elements of an ordered list in a linked structure that can be searched in a binary fashion. To illustrate, consider the following ordered list of integers:

$$13, 28, 35, 49, 62, 66, 80$$

The first step in binary search requires examining the middle element in the list. Direct access to this element is possible if we maintain a pointer to the node storing it:

At the next stage, one of the two sublists, the left half or the right half, must be searched and must therefore be accessible from this node. This is possible if we maintain two pointers, one to each of these sublists. Since these sublists are searched in the same manner, these pointers should point to nodes containing the middle elements in these sublists:

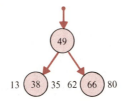

By the same reasoning, pointers from each of these "second-level" nodes are needed to access the middle elements in the sublists at the next stage:

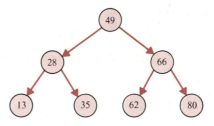

The resulting treelike structure is called a **binary search tree** and is the data structure studied in the next section.

Exercises

1. The performance of procedure *LinearSearch* can be improved slightly if the item being searched for is put at the end of the list (in position $n + 1$). This makes it possible to replace the compound boolean expression in the WHILE statement by a simple one. Write this improved version of *LinearSearch*.

2. Write a recursive version of procedure

   (a) *LinearSearch*.
   (b) *LinkedLinearSearch*.

3. In many cases of list searching, certain items in the list are retrieved more frequently than others are. The average performance of linear

search in such cases improves if these frequently sought items are placed at or near the beginning of the list. One data structure that allows this is a *self-organizing list*, in which list elements are rearranged so that frequently accessed items move to or toward the front of the list. Write a linear search procedure for such a self-organizing list using a *move-to-the-front strategy* in which the item being retrieved is moved to the front of the list. Assume that the list is implemented as

(a) an array.
(b) a linked list.

4. Proceed as in Exercise 3, but use a *move-ahead-one strategy* in which the item begin retrieved is interchanged with its predecessor.

5. Linear search is not practical for large lists because the search time becomes unacceptably large. In a dictionary this problem is alleviated by providing thumb cutouts that allow direct access to the beginnings of sublists, which can then be searched. Imitating this approach, we might break a long list into a number of sublists and construct an *index array* of pointers to the beginnings of these sublists. Write a program to read records from *StudentFile*, storing them in a linked list, and construct an array of pointers to the sublists of words beginning with 'A', 'B', 'C', ... The program should then accept a name and retrieve the record for this student.

6. Linear search outperforms binary search for small lists. If possible with your version of Modula-2, write a program to compare the computing times of linear search and binary search (see Exercise 5 of Section 3.4).

7. As noted in the text, binary search is not practical for linked lists because the worst-case complexity would be $O(n)$. Show that this is true by designing an algorithm to carry out a binary search of a linked list and analyzing its complexity.

8. In binary search, *probes* are always made at the middle of the (sub)list. In many situations, however, we have some idea of approximately where the item is located; for example, in searching a telephone directory for ''Doe, John,'' we might estimate that this name is approximately ⅙ of the way through the list. This idea is the basis for *interpolation search*, in which probes of a sublist of size L are made at position $First + F*L$ for some fraction F (not necessarily ½). Write a procedure to implement interpolation search for an ordered list of integers using the fraction F given by

$$F = (Item - X_{First}) \text{ DIV } (X_{Last} - X_{First})$$

9. If possible with your version of Modula-2, write a program to compare the computing times of

(a) linear search,

(b) binary search, and

(c) interpolation search (see Exercise 8).

(See Exercise 5 of Section 3.4)

9.2 Binary Search Trees

We have seen that a linked list is a very useful structure for processing dynamic lists whose maximum sizes are not known in advance and whose sizes change significantly because of repeated insertions and deletions. It is unfortunate that the binary search algorithm cannot be used for linked lists, because it is more efficient than linear search. In this section we describe another data structure, a *binary search tree*, which makes a binary search possible while still maintaining the flexibility of a linked structure. These are special instances of a general structure, called a *tree*, that has a variety of applications. Here we confine our attention to the searching problem and consider some of the other applications in Chapter 12.

A *tree* consists of a finite set of elements called *nodes*, or *vertices*, and a finite set of *directed arcs* that connect pairs of nodes. If the tree is nonempty, then one of the nodes, called the *root*, has no incoming arcs, but every other node in the tree can be reached from it by following a unique sequence of consecutive arcs.

Trees derive their names from the treelike diagrams that are used to picture them. For example,

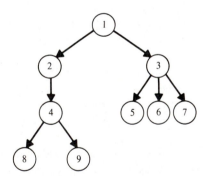

shows a tree having nine vertices in which vertex 1 is the root. As this diagram indicates, trees are usually drawn upside down, with the root at the top and the *leaves*—that is, vertices with no outgoing arcs—at the bottom. Nodes that are directly accessible from a given node (by using only one directed arc) are called the *children* of that node, and a node is said to be the *parent* of its children. For example, in the preceding tree, vertex 3 is the parent of vertices 5, 6, 7, and these vertices are the children of vertex 3 and are called *siblings*.

Trees in which each node has at most two children are called *binary trees*. They can be implemented as linked structures in which each node has two links, one pointing to the left child of that node (this link is nil if there is no left child), and another pointing to the right child (if there is one). Access to any node in the tree is possible if we maintain a pointer to the root of the tree. Using records to represent the nodes and Modula-2 pointers, we make the following declarations for a binary tree:

```
TYPE
    ElementType = . . .;   (* type of data items stored in nodes *)
    TreePointer = POINTER TO TreeNode;
    TreeNode = RECORD
                    Data : ElementType;
                    LChild, RChild : TreePointer
            END;
    BinaryTree = TreePointer;

VAR
    Root: BinaryTree;
```

The two link fields *LChild* and *RChild* in a node are pointers to nodes representing its left and right children, respectively.

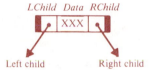

or are nil if the node does not have a left or right child. A leaf node is thus characterized by having nil values for both *LChild* and *RChild*:

The binary tree

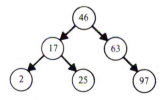

can thus be represented as the following linked tree of records:

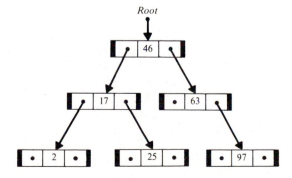

Note that in this binary tree, the value in each node is greater than the value in its left child (if there is one) and less than the value in its right child (if there is one). A binary tree having this property is called a **binary search tree (BST)** because it can be searched using an algorithm much like the binary search algorithm for lists. To illustrate, suppose we wish to search this BST for 25. We begin at the root, and since 25 is less than the value 46 in the root, we know that the desired value is located to the left of the root; that is, it must be in the left *subtree*, whose root is 17:

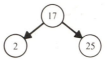

Now we continue the search by comparing 25 with the value in the root of this subtree. Since $25 > 17$, we know that the right subtree should be searched:

Examining the value in the root of this one-node subtree locates the value 25.

Similarly, to search for the value 55, after comparing 55 with the value in the root, we are led to search its right subtree:

Now, because $55 < 63$, if the desired value is in the tree, it must be in the left subtree. However, since this left subtree is empty, we conclude that the value 55 is not in the tree.

The following procedure *BSTSearch* incorporates these techniques for searching a binary search tree. The pointer *LocPtr* begins at the root of the BST and then is repeatedly replaced with the left or right link of the current node, according to whether the item for which we are searching is less than or greater than the value stored in this node. This process continues until either the desired item is found or *LocPtr* becomes nil, indicating an empty subtree, in which case the item is not in the tree. The procedure is designed to handle trees in which the data parts of the nodes are records containing more than one field; *Item* is compared with some key field in these nodes, and the outcome of this comparison is used to determine whether to descend to the left subtree or to the right subtree or to terminate the search because the item has been found.

PROCEDURE *BSTSearch*(*Root* : *BinaryTree*; *Item* : *KeyType*;
                    VAR *Found* : BOOLEAN;
                    VAR *LocPtr* : *TreePointer*);

(∗ Procedure to search the BST with the specified *Root* for *Item*. *Found* is returned as TRUE and *LocPtr* points to a node containing *Item* if the search is successful; otherwise, *Found* is returned as FALSE. ∗)

```
BEGIN
     LocPtr := Root;                              (* begin at the root *)
     Found := FALSE;
     WHILE NOT Found and (LocPtr # NIL) DO
          IF Item < LocPtr↑.Data.Key THEN        (* search left subtree *)
               LocPtr := LocPtr↑.LChild
          ELSIF Item > LocPtr↑.Data.Key THEN      (* search right subtree *)
               LocPtr := LocPtr↑.RChild
          ELSE                                     (* Item found *)
               Found := TRUE
          END (* IF *)
     END (* WHILE *)
END BSTSearch;
```

As was the case for the binary search algorithm in the preceding section, *BSTSearch* can be written either iteratively (as was done here) or recursively, with little difference of effort. The recursive version is left as an exercise.

A binary search tree can be constructed by repeatedly calling a procedure to insert elements into a BST that is initially empty (*Root* = NIL). The method used to determine where an element is to be inserted is similar to that used to search the tree. In fact, we need only modify *BSTSearch* to maintain a pointer to the parent of the node currently being examined as we descend the tree, looking for a place to insert the item.

To illustrate, suppose that the following BST has already been constructed

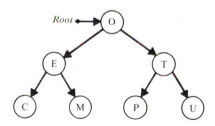

and we wish to insert the letter *R*. We begin at the root and compare 'R' with the letter there:

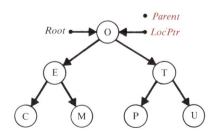

Since 'R' > 'O', we descend to the right subtree:

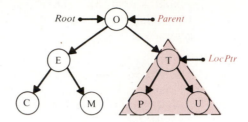

After comparing 'R' with the letter 'T' stored in the root of this subtree pointed to by *LocPtr*, we descend to the left subtree since 'R' < 'T';

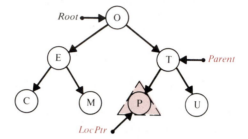

Since 'R' > 'P', we descend to the right subtree of this one-node subtree containing 'P':

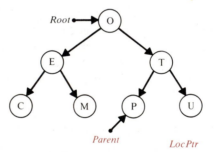

The fact that this right subtree is empty (*LocPtr* = NIL) indicates that 'R' is not in the BST and should be inserted as a right child of its parent node:

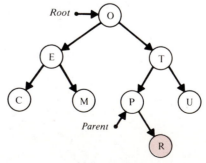

The following procedure uses this modified version of *BSTSearch* to locate the position where a given item is to be inserted (or is found). The pointer *Parent* that trails the search pointer *LocPtr* down the tree keeps track of the parent node so that the new node can be attached to the BST in the proper place.

```
PROCEDURE BSTInsert(VAR Root : BinaryTree; Element : ElementType);

(* Procedure to insert Element into the BST with the specified Root. *)

VAR
    LocPtr,                    (* search pointer *)
    Parent : TreePointer;      (* pointer to parent of current node *)
    Found : BOOLEAN;           (* indicates if Element is already in BST *)

BEGIN
    LocPtr := Root;
    Parent := NIL;
    Found := FALSE;
    WHILE NOT Found and (LocPtr # NIL) DO
        Parent := LocPtr;
        IF Element.Data.Key < LocPtr↑.Data.Key THEN
            LocPtr := LocPtr↑.LChild         (* descend left *)
        ELSIF Element.Data.Key > LocPtr↑.Data.Key THEN
            LocPtr := LocPtr↑.RChild         (* descend right *)
        ELSE
            Found := TRUE                    (* Element found *)
        END (* IF *)
    END (* WHILE *);
    IF Found THEN
        WriteString('Element already in the tree');
        WriteLn;
        RETURN
    END (* IF *);

    (* Else, insert a new node in the BST for Element *)

    ALLOCATE(LocPtr, SIZE(TreeNode));
    WITH LocPtr↑ DO
        Data := Element;
        LChild := NIL;
        RChild := NIL
    END (* WITH *);
    IF Parent = NIL THEN        (* empty tree *)
        Root := LocPtr
    ELSE
        WITH Parent↑ DO
            IF Element.Data.Key < Data.Key THEN
                LChild := LocPtr   (* insert to left of parent *)
            ELSE
                RChild := LocPtr   (* insert to right of parent *)
            END (* IF *)
        END (* WITH *)
    END (* IF *)
END BSTInsert;
```

To illustrate the use of BSTs, consider the problem of organizing a collection of computer user-ids and passwords. Each time a user logs in to the system by entering his or her user-id and a secret password, the system must check this user-id and password to verify that this is a legitimate user. Because this user validation must be done many times every day, it is necessary to structure this information in such a way that it can be searched rapidly. Moreover, this must be a dynamic structure because new users are regularly added to the system. One possible candidate is a BST in which the data part of each node is a record with two fields, *UserId* and *Password*, the first of which is the key field on which searches are based.

The program in Figure 9.1 solves this user-validation problem. It assumes that a library module *BSTLib* for processing such BSTs of user records has been written. Among other items this module exports the types *BinaryTree* and *TreePointer*; the procedure *CreateBST*, which creates an empty BST; procedures *BSTInsert* and *BSTSearch* like those described in this section; and procedures for other basic tree operations as described in Chapter 12. Note that in this example, procedure *BSTSearch* and *BSTInsert* must compare strings. Thus the module *BSTLib* must import a procedure like *Compare* from the module *StringsLib* described in Section 3.2.

```
MODULE ValidateUsers1;

(**********************************************************************

   Program to validate computer user-ids and passwords.  A list of
   valid ids and passwords is read from UsersFile and stored in a
   BST.  When user-ids and passwords are entered during execution
   this BST is searched to determine if they are legal.

   **********************************************************************)

   FROM InOut IMPORT WriteString, WriteLn, ReadString,
                   OpenInput, CloseInput, Done;
   FROM StringsLib IMPORT Compare;
   FROM BSTLib IMPORT UserRecord, ElementType, BinaryTree, TreePointer,
                   CreateBST, BSTInsert, BSTSearch, Retrieve;

   VAR
      DataPart,                    (* data part of a tree node *)
      UserRec : UserRecord;        (* current user record being validated *)
      UserTree : BinaryTree;       (* hash table of user records *)
      LocPtr : TreePointer;        (* pointer to a node in the BST *)
      Found,                       (* signals if search of BST was successful *)
      MoreUsers : BOOLEAN;         (* signals end of processing *)
```

Figure 9.1

Figure 9.1   (cont.)

```
PROCEDURE BuildTree(VAR UserTree : BinaryTree);

    (***********************************************************

        Procedure to construct the BST of legal user records

     **********************************************************)

    CONST
        EOF = '*';       (* end-of-file mark *)

    BEGIN
        WriteString('Enter name of input file.'); WriteLn;
        OpenInput('');
        CreateBST(UserTree);
        ReadString(UserRec.Id);
        WHILE UserRec.Id[0] # EOF DO
            ReadString(UserRec.Password);
            BSTInsert(UserTree, UserRec);
            ReadString(UserRec.Id)
        END (* WHILE *);
        CloseInput
    END BuildTree;

PROCEDURE Login (VAR UserRec : UserRecord;
                 VAR MoreUsers : BOOLEAN);

    (***********************************************************

        Procedure to read a user-id and password.  A special QuitSignal
        for the id sets MoreUsers to FALSE to signal end of processing.

     **********************************************************)

    CONST
        QuitSignal = 'QUIT';

    BEGIN
        WriteLn;
        WriteString('User-id (');
        WriteString(QuitSignal);
        WriteString(' to stop)?  ');
        ReadString (UserRec.Id);
        IF Compare(UserRec.Id, QuitSignal) = 0 THEN
            MoreUsers := FALSE;
            RETURN
        ELSE
            MoreUsers := TRUE;
            WriteLn;
            WriteString('Password?  ');
            ReadString (UserRec.Password)
        END (* IF *)
    END Login;
```

Figure 9.1   (cont.)

```
BEGIN (* main program *)
    BuildTree(UserTree);

    (* Validate users *)
    Login (UserRec, MoreUsers);
    WHILE MoreUsers DO
        BSTSearch(UserTree, UserRec.Id, Found, LocPtr);
        WriteLn;
        IF Found THEN
            Retrieve(LocPtr, DataPart);
            IF Compare(UserRec.Password, DataPart.Password) = 0 THEN
                WriteString('Valid user')
            ELSE
                WriteString('*** Invalid Password ***')
            END (* IF *)
        ELSE
            WriteString('*** Invalid User-Id ***')
        END (* IF *);
        WriteLn;
        Login (UserRec, MoreUsers)
    END (* WHILE *)
END ValidateUsers1.
```

Listing of UsersFile used in sample run:

```
S31416PI CHERRY
S12345SL CLAY
S31313LN KANSAS
S21718EX LOG
S13331RC COLA
S77777UP UNCOLA
S99099RR RAILROAD
*
```

Sample run:

```
Enter name of input file.
in> UsersFile
User-id?    S31416PI
Password?   CHERRY
Valid user

User-id?    S12345SL
Password?   SAND
*** Invalid Password ***

User-id?    S11111AB
Password?   ALPHA
*** Invalid User-Id ***
```

The order in which items are inserted into a BST determines the shape of the tree. For example, inserting the letters O, E, T, C, U, M, P into a BST of characters in this order gives the nicely *balanced* tree

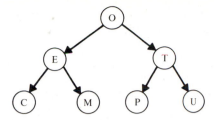

but inserting then in the order C, O, M, P, U, T, E yields the unbalanced tree

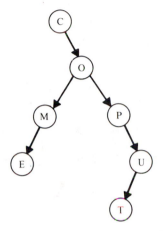

and inserting them in alphabetical order, C, E, M, O, P, T, U, causes the tree to degenerate into a linked list:

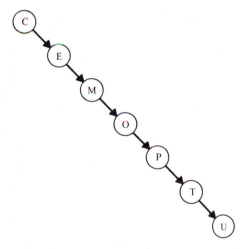

The time required to carry out most of the basic operations on a BST clearly depends on its "shape." If it is balanced so that the left and right subtrees of each node contain approximately the same number of nodes, then as a search pointer moves down the tree from one level to the next, the size of the subtree to be examined is reduced by one-half. By an analysis like that for binary search in Section 5.1, it is easy to show that the computing time for

BSTSearch and *BSTInsert* is $O(\log_2 n)$ in this case. As the BST becomes increasingly unbalanced, however, the performance of these procedures deteriorates. For trees that degenerate into linked lists as in the last example, *BSTSearch* degenerates into linear search, so that the computing time is $O(n)$ for such BSTs.

It is usually not possible to determine a priori the optimal order in which to insert items into a BST, that is, to preorder the items so that inserting them into a BST will result in a balanced tree. The usual solution is to rebalance the tree after each new element is inserted using rebalancing algorithms. One common rebalancing scheme is described in Chapter 12.

Exercises

1. For each of the following lists of letters, draw the BST that results when the letters are inserted in the order given:

   (a) A, C, R, E, S   (b) R, A, C, E, S
   (c) C, A, R, E, S   (d) S, C, A, R, E
   (e) C, O, R, N, F, L, A, K, E, S

2. Write a recursive version of procedure *BSTSearch*.

3. Write a

   (a) nonrecursive function procedure
   (b) recursive function procedure

   that determines the *level* in a BST at which a specified item in the tree is located. The root of the BST is at level 0; its children are at level 1; and so on.

4. The worst-case number of comparisons in searching a BST is equal to its *height*, that is, the number of levels in the tree. Write a recursive function procedure to determine the height of a BST.

5. In Section 7.7 we designed a program for constructing a text concordance. The basic storage structure was an array of pointers to ordered linked lists of words. This concordance can be searched more quickly if binary search trees are used in place of ordered linked lists. Write a program that reads a piece of text, constructs a concordance that contains the distinct words that appear in the text together with the line (or page) numbers of their first occurrences, and then allows the user to search this concordance. Use an array of pointers to BSTs as a storage structure for the concordance.

6. Extend the program in Exercise 5 so that an ordered linked list of *all* occurrences of each word is stored. When the concordance is searched for a particular word, the program should display the line (or page) numbers of all occurrences of this word.

7. In this section, binary search trees were implemented using Modula-2 pointers, but it is also possible to use an array-based implementation similar to that for linked lists described in Section 7.3. In this implementation, each node is represented as a record and the BST as an array of records. Each record contains three fields: a data field and two link fields that point to the left and right child, respectively, by storing their indices in the array. Imitating the array-based implementation of linked lists in Section 7.3,

   (a) Write appropriate declarations for this array-based implementation of binary search trees.
   (b) Devise a scheme for maintaining a storage pool of available nodes, and write procedures *InitializeStoragePool*, *GetNode*, and *ReleaseNode* for maintaining this storage pool.

8. Assuming that an array of ten records constitutes the storage pool for an array-based implementation of a BST as described in Exercise 7, draw diagrams similar to those in Section 7.3 for the BSTs of Exercise 1.

9. Assuming the array-based implementation of BSTs in Exercise 7, write a procedure

   (a) *BSTSearch* for searching a BST.
   (b) *BSTInsert* for inserting an item into a BST.

9.3 Hash Tables

In all of the search algorithms considered thus far, the location of an item is determined by a sequence of comparisons. In each case, the item being sought is repeatedly compared with items in certain locations of the structure. For a collection of n items, linear search requires $O(n)$ comparisons, whereas for binary search, $O(\log_2 n)$ comparisons are required. In some situations, these algorithms perform too slowly. For example, a **symbol table** constructed by a compiler stores identifiers and information about them. The speed with which this table can be constructed and searched is critical to the speed of compilation. A data structure known as a **hash table**, in which the location of an item is determined directly as a function of the item itself rather than by a sequence of trial-and-error comparisons, is commonly used to provide faster searching. Under ideal circumstances, the time required to locate an item in a hash table is $O(1)$; that is, it is constant and does not depend on the number of items stored.

As an illustration, suppose that up to 25 integers in the range 0 through 999 are to be stored in a hash table. This hash table could be implemented as an array *Table* of type CARDINAL with index type [0..999], in which each array element is initialized with some dummy value, such as 9999. If we use each number i in the set as an index, that is, if we store i in *Table*[i], then to determine whether a particular integer *Number* has been stored, we need only check whether *Table*[*Number*] = *Number*. The function *h* defined by $h(i) = i$ determines the location of an item *i* in the hash table is called a ***hash function***.

The hash function in this example works perfectly, since the time required to search the table for a given value is constant; only one location needs to be examined. This scheme is thus very time efficient, but it is surely not space efficient. Only 25 of the 1000 available locations are used to store items, leaving 975 unused locations; only 2.5 percent of the available space is used, and 97.5 percent is wasted!

Because it is possible to store 25 values in 25 locations, we might try improving space utilization by using an array *Table* indexed [0..24]. Obviously, the original hash function $h(i) = i$ can no longer be used. Instead we might use

$$h(i) = i \text{ MOD } 25$$

since this function always produces a cardinal number in the range 0 through 24. The integer 52 would thus be stored in *Table*[2], since $h(52)$ = 52 MOD 25 = 2. Similarly, 129, 500, 273, and 49 would be stored in locations 4, 0, 23, and 24, respectively.

	Hash table
Table[0]	500
Table[1]	9999
Table[2]	52
Table[3]	9999
Table[4]	129
Table[5]	9999
⋮	⋮
Table[23]	273
Table[24]	49

A difficulty arises, however, in that ***collisions*** may occur. For example, if 77 is also to be stored, it should be placed at location $h(77)$ = 77 MOD 25 = 2, but this location is already occupied by 52. In the same way, many other values may collide at a given position, for example, 2, 27, 102, and, in fact, all integers of the form $25k + 2$ "hash" to location 2. Obviously, some strategy is needed to resolve such collisions.

One simple strategy for handling collisions is known as ***linear probing***. In this scheme, a linear search of the table begins at the location where a collision occurs and continues until an empty slot is found in which the item can be stored. Thus, in the preceding example, when 77 collides with the value 52 at location 2, we simply put 77 in position 3; to insert 102, we follow the ***probe sequence*** consisting of locations 2, 3, 4, and 5 to locate the first available location and thus store 102 in *Table*[5]. If the search reaches the bottom of the table, we continue at the first location. For example, 123 is stored in Location 1, since it collides with 273 at location 23, and the probe sequence 23, 24, 0, 1 locates the first empty slot at position 1.

Table[0]	500
Table[1]	123
Table[2]	52
Table[3]	77
Table[4]	129
Table[5]	102
⋮	⋮
Table[23]	273
Table[24]	49

To determine if a specified value is in this hash table, we first apply the hash function to compute the position at which this value should be found. There are three cases to consider. First, if this location is empty (contains 9999), we can conclude immediately that the value is not in the table. Second, if this location contains the specified value, the search is immediately successful. In the third case, this location contains a value other than the one for which we are searching, because of the way that collisions were resolved in constructing the table. In this case, we begin a "circular" linear search at this location and continue until either the item is found or we reach an empty location or the starting location, indicating that the item is not in the table. Thus, the search time in the first two cases is constant, but in this last case, it is not. If the table is nearly full, we may, in fact, have to examine almost every location before we find the item or conclude that it is not in the table.

There seem to be three things we might do to improve performance:

1. Increase the table size.
2. Use a different strategy for resolving collisions.
3. Use a different hash function.

Making the table size equal to the number of items to be stored is usually not practical, but using any smaller table leaves open the possibility of collisions. In fact, even though the table is capable of storing considerably more items than necessary, collisions may be quite likely. For example, for a hash table with 365 locations in which 23 randomly selected items are to be stored, the probability that a collision will occur is greater than 0.5! (This is related to the birthday problem, whose solution states that in a room containing twenty-three people, there is a greater than 50 percent chance that two or more of them will have the same birthday.) Thus it is clearly unreasonable to expect a hashing scheme to prevent collisions completely. Instead, we must be satisfied with hash tables in which reasonably few collisions occur. Empirical studies suggest using tables whose sizes are aproximately 1½ to 2 times the number of items that must be stored.

A second way to improve performance is to design a better method for handling collisions. In the linear probe scheme, whenever collisions occur, the colliding values are stored in locations that should be reserved for items that hash directly to these locations. This approach of "robbing Peter to pay Paul" makes subsequent collisions more likely, thus compounding the problem.

A better approach, known as ***chaining***, uses linked lists to store the values. In this scheme, the hash table is an array of pointers to these linked lists. To illustrate, suppose we wish to store a collection of names. We might use an array *Table* indexed 'A'..'Z' of pointers, initially nil, and the simple hash function *h(Name)* = *Name*[1]. Thus, for example, 'Adams, John' and 'Doe, Mary' are stored in nodes pointed to by *Table*['A'] and *Table*['D'], respectively.

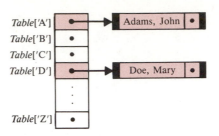

When a collision occurs, we simply insert the new item into the appropriate linked list using the techniques developed in Chapter 7. For example, since *h*('Davis, Joe') = *h*('Doe, Mary') = 'D', a collision occurs when we attempt to store the name 'Davis, Joe', and thus we add a new node containing this name to the linked list pointed to by *Table*['D']:

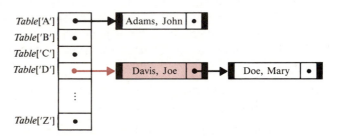

Searching such a hash table is also straightforward. We simply apply the hash function to the item being sought and then use one of the search procedures for linked lists described in Chapter 7,

LinkedSearch(Table[h(Item)], Item, Found)

if the lists are unordered, or

LinkedOrderedSearch(Table[h(Item)], Item, Found)

if they are ordered.

Several other strategies may be used to resolve collisions. For example, one might use an array of pointers to roots of binary search trees and use the insert and search procedures of the preceding section. Another common scheme, called ***double hashing***, is described in the exercises.

A third factor in the design of a hash table is the selection of the hash function. The behavior of this function obviously affects the frequency of collisions. For example, the hash function $h(Name) = Name[1]$ in the preceding example is not a good choice because some letters occur much more frequently than others do as the first letters of names. Thus the linked list of names beginning with $'S'$ tends to be much longer than that containing names that begin with $'Z'$. This clustering effect results in longer search times for S-names than for Z-names. A better hash function that distributes the names more uniformly throughout the hash table might be the "average" of the first and last letters in the name.

$$h(Name) = \text{CHR}((\text{ORD}(FirstLetter) + \text{ORD}(LastLetter)) \text{ DIV } 2)$$

or one might use the "average" of all the letters. The hash function must not, however, be so complex that the time required to evaluate it makes the search time unacceptable.

An ideal hash function is one that is simple to evaluate and that scatters the items throughout the hash table, thus minimizing the probability of collisions. Although no single hashing method performs perfectly in all situations, a currently popular method known as **random hashing** uses a simple random number generation technique to scatter the items "randomly" throughout the hash table. The item is first transformed into a large random cardinal number using a statement of the form

$$RandCardNum := (Multiplier * Item + Addend) \text{ MOD } Modulus$$

and this value is then reduced modulo the table size to determine the location of the item:

$$Location := RandCardNum \text{ MOD } TableSize;$$

(See the description of the library module *Random* in Section 0.7 for a discussion of appropriate values of *Multiplier*, *Addend*, and *Modulus*.) This hash function can be used with nonnumeric items if we first encode such items as integers; for example, a name might be encoded as the sum of the ASCII codes of some or all of its letters.

The program in Figure 9.2 is a modification of that in Figure 9.1 for processing user-ids and passwords that stores these items of information in a hash table rather than in a BST. It assumes that the module *UserIdHashTable* has been designed to manage hash tables in which the elements are records in which the key field is the user-id. The definition part of this module might be

```
DEFINITION MODULE UserIdHashTable;

(********************************************************************

    Module to manage hash tables in which the elements are records.
    Searching is based on some key field in these records.  Collisions
    are resolved by chaining.  It exports the types ElementType,
    UserRecord, IndexRange, Chain, and HashTable and procedures
    CreateHashTable, Hash, Search, and Insert.

    *******************************************************************)

    (* In this instance of the module, ElementType = UserRecord and the
       key field is the field Id in these records. *)

    CONST
        MaxString = 9;
        TableSize = 13;
        MaxIndex = TableSize - 1;

    TYPE
        String = ARRAY [0..MaxString] OF CHAR;
        UserRecord = RECORD
                         Id,
                         Password : String
                     END;
        ElementType = UserRecord;
        KeyType = String;
        Chain = POINTER TO HashTableNode;
        HashTableNode = RECORD
                            Data : ElementType;
                            Next : Chain
                        END;
        IndexRange = [0..MaxIndex];
        HashTable = ARRAY IndexRange OF Chain;

    PROCEDURE CreateHashTable(VAR Table : HashTable);

        (*************************************************************

            Create a hash Table, setting all entries equal to NIL.

            ************************************************************)

    PROCEDURE Hash(Str : String; TableSize : CARDINAL) : IndexRange;

        (*************************************************************

            Hash function -- string Str is encoded as integer by summing
            the ASCII codes of its characters.

            ************************************************************)
```

(cont.)

```
      PROCEDURE HashSearch(    Table : HashTable; Item : KeyType;
                           VAR Loc : IndexRange;
                           VAR Found : BOOLEAN; VAR LocPtr : Chain);

          (*********************************************************

             Procedure to search hash Table for Item in the key field of
             a record.  Loc is the location in the table to which Item
             hashes.  Found is returned as TRUE and LocPtr points to a
             node in a chain whose Data part contains Item in its key
             field, if such a node is found; otherwise, Found is
             returned as FALSE.

             *********************************************************)

      PROCEDURE HashInsert (VAR Table : HashTable; Element : ElementType);

          (*********************************************************

             Procedure to insert Element (user record) into the hash Table.
             Collisions are resolved by chaining.

             *********************************************************)

END UserIdHashTable.
```

The corresponding implementation module might be

```
IMPLEMENTATION MODULE UserIdHashTable;

(*************************************************************************

   Module to manage hash tables in which the elements are commputer
   user records. Searching is based on the field Id in these records.
   Collisions are resolved by chaining.

   *************************************************************************)

   FROM InOut IMPORT WriteString, WriteLn;
   FROM StringsLib IMPORT Compare;
   FROM Storage IMPORT ALLOCATE, DEALLOCATE;

   PROCEDURE CreateHashTable(VAR Table : HashTable);

      (*********************************************************

         Create a hash Table, setting all entries equal to NIL.

         *********************************************************)

      VAR
         i : IndexRange;    (* index *)
```

(cont.)

```
        BEGIN
            FOR i := 0 TO MaxIndex DO
                Table[i] := NIL
            END (* FOR *)
        END CreateHashTable;

    PROCEDURE Hash(Str : String; TableSize : CARDINAL) : IndexRange;

        (***********************************************************

            Hash function -- string Str is encoded as integer by summing
            the ASCII codes of its characters.

        ***********************************************************)

        CONST
            EOS = 0C;                  (* end-of-string mark *)
        VAR
            Sum : CARDINAL;            (* sum of ASCII codes of characters in Str *)
            i : [0..MaxString];   (* index *)

        BEGIN
            i := 0;
            Sum := 0;
            WHILE (i <= MaxString) AND (Str[i] # EOS) DO
                Sum := Sum + ORD(Str[i]);
                INC(i)
            END (* WHILE *);
            RETURN Sum MOD TableSize
        END  Hash ;

    PROCEDURE HashSearch(    Table : HashTable; Item : KeyType;
                         VAR Loc : IndexRange;
                         VAR Found : BOOLEAN; VAR LocPtr : Chain);

        (***********************************************************

            Procedure to search hash Table for Item in the Id field of
            a user record.  Loc is the location in the table to which Item
            hashes.  Found is returned as TRUE,  and LocPtr points to a
            node in a chain whose Data part contains Item in its Id
            field, if such a node is found; otherwise, Found is
            returned as FALSE.

        ***********************************************************)

        BEGIN
            Loc := Hash(Item, TableSize);
            LocPtr := Table[Loc];
            WHILE (LocPtr <> NIL) AND (Compare(LocPtr^.Data.Id, Item) # 0) DO
                LocPtr := LocPtr^.Next
            END (* WHILE *);
            Found := (LocPtr # NIL)
        END HashSearch;
```

(cont.)

```
    PROCEDURE HashInsert (VAR Table : HashTable; Element : ElementType);

        (************************************************************

            Procedure to insert the user record Element into the hash
            Table.  Collisions are resolved by chaining.

            ************************************************************)

        VAR
            Loc : IndexRange;        (* location in Table *)
            LocPtr : Chain;          (* pointer to node in chain *)
            Found : BOOLEAN;         (* indicates if Item already in Table *)

        BEGIN
            HashSearch(Table, Element.Id, Loc, Found, LocPtr);
            IF Found THEN
                WriteString('Item is already in the hash table');
                WriteLn
            ELSE
                ALLOCATE(LocPtr, SIZE(HashTableNode));
                LocPtr^.Data := Element;
                LocPtr^.Next := Table[Loc];
                Table[Loc] := LocPtr
            END (* IF *)
        END HashInsert;

END UserIdHashTable.
```

```
MODULE ValidateUsers2;

(****************************************************************************

    Program to validate computer user-ids and passwords.  A list of
    valid ids and passwords is read from UsersFile and stored in a hash
    table.  When user-ids and passwords are entered during execution
    this hash table is searched to determine if they are legal.

    ****************************************************************)

    FROM InOut IMPORT WriteString, WriteLn, ReadString,
                      OpenInput, CloseInput, Done;
    FROM StringsLib IMPORT Compare;
    FROM UserIdHashTable IMPORT UserRecord, HashTable, IndexRange, Chain,
                      CreateHashTable, HashSearch, HashInsert;
```

Figure 9.2

Figure 9.2   (cont.)

```
VAR
    UserRec : UserRecord;        (* user record being validated *)
    UserTable  : HashTable;      (* hash table of user records *)
    Found,                       (* signals if search of UserTable was
                                    successful *)
    MoreUsers : BOOLEAN;         (* signals end of processing *)
    Loc : IndexRange;            (* location in hash table *)
    LocPtr : Chain;              (* points to a node in chain from Table[Loc] *)

PROCEDURE BuildHashTable(VAR UserTable : HashTable);

    (****************************************************************

        Procedure to construct the hash table of legal user records

     ***************************************************************)

    CONST
        EOF = '*';        (* end-of-file mark *)

    BEGIN
        WriteString('Enter name of input file.'); WriteLn;
        OpenInput('');
        CreateHashTable(UserTable);
        ReadString(UserRec.Id);
        WHILE UserRec.Id[0] # EOF DO
            ReadString(UserRec.Password);
            HashInsert(UserTable, UserRec);
            ReadString(UserRec.Id)
        END (* WHILE *);
        CloseInput
    END BuildHashTable;

PROCEDURE Login (VAR UserRec : UserRecord;
                 VAR MoreUsers : BOOLEAN);

    (****************************************************************

        Procedure to read a user-id and password.  A special QuitSignal
        for the id sets MoreUsers to true to signal end of processing.

     ***************************************************************)

    CONST
        QuitSignal = 'QUIT';
```

Figure 9.2 (cont.)

```
        BEGIN
            WriteLn;
            WriteString('User-id (');
            WriteString(QuitSignal);
            WriteString(' to stop)?  ');
            ReadString (UserRec.Id);
            IF Compare(UserRec.Id, QuitSignal) = 0 THEN
                MoreUsers := FALSE;
                RETURN
            ELSE
                MoreUsers := TRUE;
                WriteLn;
                WriteString('Password?  ');
                ReadString (UserRec.Password)
            END (* IF *)
        END Login;

BEGIN (* main program *)
    BuildHashTable(UserTable);

    (* Validate users *)
    Login (UserRec, MoreUsers);
    WHILE MoreUsers DO
        HashSearch(UserTable, UserRec.Id, Loc, Found, LocPtr);
        WriteLn;
        IF Found THEN
            IF Compare(LocPtr^.Data.Password, UserRec.Password) = 0 THEN
                WriteString('Valid user')
            ELSE
                WriteString('*** Invalid Password ***')
            END (* IF *)
        ELSE
            WriteString('*** Invalid User-Id ***')
        END (* IF *);
        WriteLn;
        Login (UserRec, MoreUsers)
    END (* WHILE *)
END ValidateUsers2.
```

Listing of UsersFile used in sample run:

```
S31416PI CHERRY
S12345SL CLAY
S31313LN KANSAS
S21718EX LOG
S13331RC COLA
S77777UP UNCOLA
S99099RR RAILROAD
*
```

Figure 9.2 (cont.)

```
Sample run:

Enter name of input file.
in> UsersFile
User-id?    S31416PI
Password?   CHERRY
Valid user

User-id?    S12345SL
Password?   SAND
*** Invalid Password ***

User-id?    S11111AB
Password?   ALPHA
*** Invalid User-Id ***

User-id?    QUIT
```

Exercises

1. Using a hash table with eleven locations and the hashing function $h(i) = i$ MOD 11, show the hash table that results when the following integers are inserted in the order given: 26, 42, 5, 44, 92, 59, 40, 36, 12, 60, 80. Assume that collisions are resolved using (a) linear probing and (b) chaining.

2. Suppose that the following character codes are used: $'A' = 1$, $'B' = 2, \ldots, 'Y' = 25$, $'Z' = 26$. Using a hash table with eleven locations and the hashing function $h(identifier) = average$ MOD 11, where *average* is the average of the codes of the first and last letters in *identifier*, show the hash table that results when the following identifiers are inserted in the order given, assuming (a) linear probing (b) chaining:

   BETA, RATE, FREQ, ALPHA, MEAN, SUM, NUM, BAR, WAGE, PAY, KAPPA

3. The method of *double hashing* for handling collisions is as follows: If item i collides with another table entry at location a, then apply a second hash function h_2 to the item to determine $k = h_2(i)$. Now proceed as in linear probing, but instead of examining consecutive locations, examine the elements of the table in the order a, $a + k$, $a + 2k$, ..., reducing all these values MOD n (n is the table size). Give the hash table that results using the numbers in Exercise 1, but using double hashing to resolve collisions with secondary hash function

$$h_2(i) = \begin{cases} 2i \text{ MOD } 11 \text{ if this is nonzero} \\ 1 \text{ otherwise} \end{cases}$$

4. Modify the program in Figure 9.2 so that linear probing rather than chaining is used to resolve collisions.

5. Modify the program in Figure 9.2 so that passwords, rather than identification numbers, are hashed; that is, the user can enter a password, and the corresponding identification number is then retrieved from the hash table and is displayed.

6. Suppose that integers in the range 1 through 100 are to be stored in a hash table using the hashing function $h(i) = i$ MOD *TableSize*. Write a program that generates random integers in this range and inserts them into the hash table until a collision occurs. The program should carry out this experiment 100 times and calculate the average number of integers that can be inserted into the hash table before a collision occurs. Run the program with various values for *TableSize*.

10

Sorting

Like the searching problem considered in the preceding chapter, the problem of sorting a collection of data is important in data processing. Indeed, the two problems go hand in hand because, as we have seen, some of the more efficient search algorithms can be used only if the data items are first organized in an ordered list. In this chapter we turn to the problem of sorting a list,

$$X_1, X_2, \ldots, X_n$$

that is, arranging the list elements so that they (or some key fields in them) are in ascending order,

$$X_1 \leq X_2 \leq \cdots \leq X_n$$

or in descending order

$$X_1 \geq X_2 \geq \cdots \geq X_n$$

10.1 Some $O(n^2)$ Sorting Schemes

We begin our discussion of sorting algorithms by considering two simple sorting schemes that are typically studied in introductory programming courses: *simple selection sort* and *bubble sort*. Neither of these schemes is very efficient; their principal virtue is their simplicity. Another sorting technique that we consider in this section is *insertion sort*. It is as straightforward as the other two and is preferable to them, especially for small lists.

Simple Selection Sort.   The basic idea of a selection sort of a list is to make a number of passes through the list or a part of the list, and on each pass to select one element to be correctly positioned. For example, on each pass through a sublist, the smallest element in this sublist might be found and then moved to its proper location.

As an illustration, suppose that the following list is to be sorted into ascending order:

$$67 \;,\; 33 \;,\; 21 \;,\; 84 \;,\; 49 \;,\; 50 \;,\; 75$$

We scan the list to locate the smallest element and find it in position 3:

$$67 \;,\; 33 \;,\; \boxed{21} \;,\; 84 \;,\; 49 \;,\; 50 \;,\; 75$$

We interchange this element with the first element and thus properly position the smallest element at the beginning of the list:

$$\boxed{21} \;,\; 33 \;,\; 67 \;,\; 84 \;,\; 49 \;,\; 50 \;,\; 75$$

We now scan the sublist consisting of the elements from position 2 on to find the smallest element

$$21 \;,\; \boxed{33} \;,\; 67 \;,\; 84 \;,\; 49 \;,\; 50 \;,\; 75$$

and exchange it with the second element (itself in this case) and thus properly position the next-to-smallest element in position 2:

$$21 \;,\; \boxed{33} \;,\; 67 \;,\; 84 \;,\; 49 \;,\; 50 \;,\; 75$$

We continue in this manner, locating the smallest element in the sublist of elements from position 3 on and interchanging it with the third element, then properly positioning the smallest element in the sublist of elements from position 4 on, and so on until we eventually do this for the sublist consisting of the last two elements:

$$21 \;,\; 33 \;,\; \boxed{49} \;,\; 84 \;,\; 67 \;,\; 50 \;,\; 75$$

$$21 \;,\; 33 \;,\; 49 \;,\; \boxed{50} \;,\; 67 \;,\; 84 \;,\; 75$$

$$21 \;,\; 33 \;,\; 49 \;,\; 50 \;,\; \boxed{67} \;,\; 84 \;,\; 75$$

$$21 \;,\; 33 \;,\; 49 \;,\; 50 \;,\; 67 \;,\; \boxed{75} \;,\; \boxed{84}$$

Positioning the smallest element in this last sublist obviously also positions the last element correctly and thus completes the sort.

An algorithm for this simple selection sort was given in Section 5.1 for lists implemented as arrays:

SIMPLE SELECTION SORT FOR ARRAY-BASED LISTS

(* Algorithm to sort a list of n elements stored in an array $X[1]$, $X[2]$, . . . , $X[n]$ into ascending order. *)

For $i = 1$ to $n - 1$ do the following:

(* On the ith pass, first find the smallest element in the sublist $X[i]$, . . . , $X[n]$. *)

a. Set *SmallPos* equal to i.
b. Set *Smallest* equal to $X[SmallPos]$.
c. For $j = i + 1$ to n do the following:
   If $X[j] <$ *Smallest* then (* smaller element found *)
      i. Set *SmallPos* equal to j.
      ii. Set *Smallest* equal to $X[SmallPos]$.

(* Now interchange this smallest element with the element at the beginning of this sublist. *)

d. Set $X[SmallPos]$ equal to $X[i]$.
e. Set $X[i]$ equal to *Smallest*.

A version that can be used for linked lists is just as easy. We need only replace the indices i and j with pointers that move through the list and sublists. Using the notation introduced in Section 7.2 for abstract linked lists, we can express this algorithm as

SIMPLE SELECTION SORT FOR LINKED LISTS

(* Algorithm to sort a list of elements stored in a linked list into ascending order. *)

1. Initialize pointer p to the first node.
2. While $p \neq$ nil do the following:

(* First find the smallest element in the sublist pointed to by p. *)

a. Set pointer *SmallPtr* equal to p.
b. Set *Smallest* equal to *Data(SmallPtr)*.
c. Set pointer q equal to *Next(p)*.
d. While $q \neq$ nil do the following:
      i. If *Data(q)* < *Smallest* then   (* smaller element found *)
         Set *SmallPtr* equal to q and *Smallest* equal to *Data(q)*.
      ii. Set q equal to *Next(q)*.

(* Now interchange this smallest element with the element in the node at the beginning of this sublist *)

e. Set *Data(SmallPtr)* equal to *Data(p)*.
f. Set *Data(p)* equal to *Smallest*.
g. Set p equal to *Next(p)*.

In Section 5.1 we derived a worst-case computing time of O(n^2) for this sorting method. This is, in fact, the computing time for all cases. On the first pass through the list, the first item is compared with each of the $n - 1$ elements that follow it; on the second pass, the second element is compared with the $n - 2$ elements following it; and so on. A total of

$$(n - 1) + (n - 2) + \cdots + 2 + 1 = \frac{n(n - 1)}{2}$$

comparisons is thus required for any list, and it follows that the complexity is O(n^2) in all cases.

Bubble Sort. A second simple sorting scheme, bubble sort, also makes repeated passes through the list and sublists, comparing and interchanging various pairs of list elements. However, instead of only one interchange being performed on each pass, each pair of consecutive elements that are out of order are interchanged.

As an illustration, consider again the list

67 , 33 , 21 , 84 , 49 , 50 , 75

On the first pass, we compare the first two elements, 67 and 33, and interchange them because they are in the wrong order:

67 , 33 , 21 , 84 , 49 , 50 , 75
33 , 67 , 21 , 84 , 49 , 50 , 75

Now we compare the second and third elements, 67 and 21, and interchange them:

33 , 67 , 21 , 84 , 49 , 50 , 75
33 , 21 , 67 , 84 , 49 , 50 , 75

Next we compare 67 and 84 but do not interchange them because they are already in the correct order:

33 , 21 , 67 , 84 , 49 , 50 , 75
33 , 21 , 67 , 84 , 49 , 50 , 75

Next, 84 and 49 are compared and interchanged:

33 , 21 , 67 , 84 , 49 , 50 , 75
33 , 21 , 67 , 49 , 84 , 50 , 75

Then 84 and 50 are compared and interchanged:

33 , 21 , 67 , 49 , 84 , 50 , 75
33 , 21 , 67 , 49 , 50 , 84 , 75

Then 84 and 75 are compared and interchanged:

$$33\ ,\ \ 21\ ,\ \ 67\ ,\ \ 49\ ,\ \ 50\ ,\ \ 84\ ,\ \ 75$$

$$33\ ,\ \ 21\ ,\ \ 67\ ,\ \ 49\ ,\ \ 50\ ,\ \ 75\ ,\ \ 84$$

The first pass through the list is now complete.

We are guaranteed that on this pass, the largest element in the list will "sink" to the end of the list, since it will obviously be moved past all smaller elements. But notice also that some of the smaller items have "bubbled up" toward their proper positions nearer the front of the list.

We now scan the list again, but this time we leave out the last item because it is already in its proper position.

$$33\ ,\ \ 21\ ,\ \ 67\ ,\ \ 49\ ,\ \ 50\ ,\ \ 75\ ,\ \ \boxed{84}$$

The comparisons and interchanges that take place on this pass are summarized in the following diagram:

$$33\ ,\ \ 21\ ,\ \ 67\ ,\ \ 49\ ,\ \ 50\ ,\ \ 75\ ,\ \ \boxed{84}$$
$$21\ ,\ \ 33\ ,\ \ 67\ ,\ \ 49\ ,\ \ 50\ ,\ \ 75\ ,\ \ \boxed{84}$$
$$21\ ,\ \ 33\ ,\ \ 67\ ,\ \ 49\ ,\ \ 50\ ,\ \ 75\ ,\ \ \boxed{84}$$
$$21\ ,\ \ 33\ ,\ \ 49\ ,\ \ 67\ ,\ \ 50\ ,\ \ 75\ ,\ \ \boxed{84}$$
$$21\ ,\ \ 33\ ,\ \ 49\ ,\ \ 50\ ,\ \ 67\ ,\ \ 75\ ,\ \ \boxed{84}$$
$$21\ ,\ \ 33\ ,\ \ 49\ ,\ \ 50\ ,\ \ 67\ ,\ \ 75\ ,\ \ \boxed{84}$$

On this pass, the last element involved in an interchange was in position 5, which means that this element and all those that follow it have been properly positioned and can thus be omitted on the next pass.

On the next pass, therefore, we consider only the sublist consisting of the elements in positions 1 through 4:

$$21,\ 33,\ 49,\ 50,\ \boxed{67},\ \boxed{75},\ \boxed{84}$$

In scanning this sublist, we find that no interchanges are necessary, and so we conclude that the sorting is complete. The details of this sorting scheme are given in the following algorithm:

BUBBLE SORT

(* Algorithm to bubble sort a list of items $X_1, X_2, \ldots, X_n$ into ascending order. *)

1. Initialize *NumPairs* to $n - 1$ and *Last* to 1.
   (* *NumPairs* is the number of pairs to be compared on the current pass, and *Last* marks the location of the last element involved in an interchange. *)

2. Repeat the following steps:

    a. For $i = 1$ to *NumPairs* do:

      If $X_i > X_{i+1}$ then:
        i. Interchange X_i and X_{i+1}.
        ii. Set *Last* equal to i.
    b. Set *NumPairs* equal to *Last* $-$ 1.

    Until *NumPairs* $= 0$.

The worst case for bubble sort occurs when the list elements are in reverse order because, in this case, only one item (the largest) is positioned correctly on each pass through the repeat loop. On the first pass through the list, $n - 1$ comparisons and interchanges are made, and only the largest element is correctly positioned. On the next pass, the sublist consisting of the first $n - 1$ elements is scanned; $n - 2$ comparisons and interchanges occur; and the next largest element sinks to position $n - 1$. This continues until the sublist consisting of the first two elements is scanned, and on this pass, one comparison and interchange occurs. Thus, a total of $(n - 1) + (n - 2) + \cdots + 1 = n(n - 1)/2$ comparisons and interchanges is required. Since the instructions that carry out these comparisons and interchanges are the instructions in the algorithm executed most often, they determine its complexity. It follows that the worst-case computing time for bubble sort is O(n^2). The average complexity is also O(n^2), but this is considerably more difficult to show.

Insertion Sort. Insertion sort is based on the same idea as the algorithms for inserting into ordered linked lists described in the preceding chapter: Repeatedly insert a new element into a list of already sorted elements so that the resulting list is still sorted.

The method used is similar to that used by a card player in ordering the cards in his or her hand as they are dealt. To illustrate, suppose that the first card dealt is a 7. (We will ignore all other attributes, such as suit or color.) This card is trivially in its proper place in the hand:

When the second card is dealt, it is inserted into its proper place, either before or after the first card. For example, if the second card is a 2, it is placed ahead of the 7:

When the third card is dealt, it is inserted into its proper place among the first two cards so that the resulting three-card hand is properly ordered. For example, if it is a 4, the 7 is moved over a bit to make room for the 4, which must be inserted between the 2 and the 7:

This process continues. At each stage the newly dealt card is inserted into the proper place among the cards already in the hand so that the newly formed hand is correctly ordered:

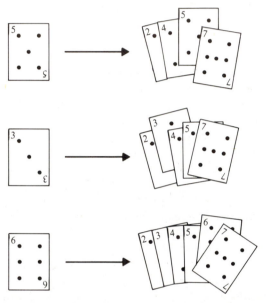

The following algorithm describes this procedure for lists stored in arrays. At the ith stage, X_i is inserted into its proper place among the already sorted $X_1, X_2, \ldots, X_{i-1}$. We do this by comparing X_i with each of these elements, starting from the right end, and shifting them to the right as necessary. Array position 0 is assumed to be occupied by some dummy value (denoted in the algorithm by $-\infty$) that is smaller than any possible list element to prevent ''falling off the left end'' in these right-to-left scans.

INSERTION SORT FOR ARRAY-BASED LISTS

($*$ Algorithm to sort a list of elements stored in an array $X[1]$, $X[2]$,
  $\ldots$, $X[n]$ into ascending order using insertion sort; $-\infty$ denotes
  some value smaller than any possible list element. $*$)

1. Initialize $X[0]$ to $-\infty$.
2. For $i = 2$ to n do the following:
      ($*$ Insert $X[i]$ into its proper position among $X[1], \ldots,$
      $X[i-1]$ $*$)

    a. Set *NextElement* equal to $X[i]$.
    b. Set j equal to $i - 1$.
    c. While *NextElement* < $X[j]$ do the following:

        (* Shift element to right to open up a spot *)
        i. Set $X[j + 1]$ equal to $X[j]$.
        ii. Decrement j by 1.

    (* Now drop *NextElement* into the open spot. *)
    d. Set $X[j + 1]$ equal to *NextElement*.

The following sequence of diagrams demonstrates this algorithm for the list 67, 33, 21, 84, 49, 50, 75. The sorted sublist produced at each stage is highlighted; the other list elements are waiting for their turn to be inserted:

67 ,	33 ,	21 ,	84 ,	49 ,	50 ,	75	Initial sorted sublist of 1 element
33 ,	67 ,	21 ,	84 ,	49 ,	50 ,	75	Insert 33 to get 2-element sorted sublist
21 ,	33 ,	67 ,	84 ,	49 ,	50 ,	75	Insert 21 to get 3-element sorted sublist
21 ,	33 ,	67 ,	84 ,	49 ,	50 ,	75	Insert 84 to get 4-element sorted sublist
21 ,	33 ,	49 ,	67 ,	84 ,	50 ,	75	Insert 49 to get 5-element sorted sublist
21 ,	33 ,	49 ,	50 ,	67 ,	84 ,	75	Insert 50 to get 6-element sorted sublist
21 ,	33 ,	49 ,	50 ,	67 ,	75 ,	84	Insert 75 to get 7-element sorted sublist

The worst case for insertion sort is once again the case in which the list elements are in reverse order. Inserting $X[2]$ requires two comparisons (with $X[1]$ and then with $X[0]$); inserting $X[3]$ requires three; and so on. The total number of comparisons is thus

$$2 + 3 + \cdots + n = \frac{n(n + 1)}{2} - 1$$

so the computing time is again O(n^2). This is also the average-case complexity, since one would expect that on the average, the item being inserted must be compared with one-half the items in the already-sorted sublist.

    Insertion sort can also be used with linked lists. For singly linked lists, however, the algorithm will obviously be quite different from the preceding one because we have direct access to only the first element. Combining the basic techniques of *LinkedInsert* and *LinkedOrderedSearch* from Chapter 7 to obtain an insertion sort algorithm for linked lists is not difficult and is left as an exercise.

Comparison of These Sorting Schemes.   All of the sorting algorithms that we have considered have the same complexity, O(n^2), in the worst and average cases, and so this measure of efficiency provides no clue to which is preferable. More careful analysis, together with empirical results, however, shows that both selection sort and bubble sort are very inefficient and have little to recommend them other than their simplicity. They are inferior in almost every regard to the other sorting schemes described in the following sections. A variation of bubble sort known as *Shell sort*, which does perform considerably better, is described in the exercises, and an efficient variation of simple selection sort known as *heapsort* is described in the next section.

Insertion sort is too inefficient to be used as a general-purpose sorting scheme (indeed there is no such thing as one universally good sorting scheme). However, the low overhead that it requires makes it better than simple selection sort and bubble sort. In fact, it is the best choice of all the sorting schemes that we will consider for small lists (with a maximum of fifteen to twenty elements) and for lists that are already partially sorted.

Exercises

1. The basic operation in the simple selection sort algorithm is to scan a list $X_1, \ldots, X_n$ to locate the smallest element and to position it at the beginning of the list. A variation of this approach is to locate both the smallest and the largest elements while scanning the list and to position them at the beginning and the end of the list, respectively. On the next scan this process is repeated for the sublist $X_2, \ldots, X_{n-1}$, and so on. Write an algorithm to implement this double-ended simple selection sort, and determine its complexity.

2. The double-ended selection sort algorithm described in Exercise 1 can be improved by using a more efficient method for determining the smallest and largest elements in a (sub)list. One such algorithm is known as **Min-Max Sort**[1]:

   Consider a list $X_1, \ldots, X_n$, where n is even.

   1. For i ranging from 1 to n DIV 2, compare X_i with X_{n+1-i} and interchange them if $X_i > X_{n+1-i}$. This establishes a "rainbow pattern" in which $X_1 \le X_n$, $X_2 \le X_{n-1}$, $X_3 \le X_{n-2}$, and so on, and guarantees that the smallest element of the list is in the first half of the list and that the largest element is in the second half.
   2. Repeat the following for the list $X_1, \ldots, X_n$, then for the sublist $X_2, \ldots, X_{n-1}$, and so on:
      a. Find the smallest element X_S in the first half and the largest element x_L in the second half, and swap them with the elements in the first and last positions of these sublists, respectively.
      b. Restore the rainbow pattern by comparing X_S with X_{n+1-S} and X_L with X_{n+1-L}, interchanging as necessary.

   Write a program to implement this sorting algorithm.

3. One problem with bubble sort is that although larger values move rapidly toward their proper positions, smaller values move slowly in the other direction. **Shell sort** (named after Donald Shell) attempts to im-

---

[1] Narayan Murthy, "Min-Max Sort: A Simple Sorting Method," *CSC'87 Proceedings* (Association of Computing Machinery, 1987).

prove this. A series of compare–interchange scans are made, but consecutive items are not compared on each scan. Instead, there is a fixed distance between the items that are compared. When no more interchanges can be made for a given distance, the distance is cut in half, and the compare–interchange scans continue. The initial distance is commonly taken to be $n/2$ for a list of n items. For example, for the list

$$6,1,5,2,3,4,0$$

the following sequence of distances and scans would be used:

Scan #	Distance	Rearranged List	Interchanges
1	3	2,1,4,0,3,5,6	(6,2), (5,4), (6,0)
2	3	0,1,4,2,3,5,6	(2,0)
3	3	0,1,4,2,3,5,6	none
4	1	0,1,2,3,4,5,6	(4,2), (4,3)
5	1	0,1,2,3,4,5,6	none

Write a program to sort a list of items, using the Shell sort method.

4. Write a bubble sort algorithm that is appropriate for a linked list.

5. Write an insertion sort algorithm that is appropriate for a linked list.

6. Write a recursive procedure to implement simple selection sort.

7. Write a recursive procedure to implement bubble sort.

8. Each of the sorting schemes described in this section requires moving list elements from one array position to another. If these list elements are records containing many fields, then the time required for such data transfers may be unacceptable. For such arrays of large records, an alternative is to use an ***index table*** that stores the positions of the records in the array, and to move entries in this index rather than the records themselves. For example, for an array $X[1], \ldots , X[5]$ of records, we initialize an array $Index$ with $Index[1] = 1, Index[2] = 2, \ldots , Index[5] = 5$. If it is necessary while sorting these records to interchange the first and third records as well as the second and fifth, we interchange these items in the index table to obtain $Index[1] = 3, Index[2] = 5, Index[3] = 1, Index[4] = 4, Index[5] = 2$. At this stage the records are arranged in the *logical* order $X[Index[1]], X[Index[2]], \ldots , X[Index[5]]$, that is, $X[3], X[5], X[1], X[4], X[2]$. Write a program that reads the records in *UsersFile* (see Appendix E) and stores them in an array. Then sort the records so that the resources used to date are in descending order, using one of the sorting schemes in this section together with an index table.

9. If possible with your version of Modula-2, write a program that compares the execution times of the various $O(n^2)$ sorting algorithms described in this section for randomly generated lists of integers. (See Exercise 5 of Section 3.4 regarding how to measure execution time and Section 0.7 concerning random number generation.)

10.2 Heaps and Heapsort

In the preceding section we looked at three sorting algorithms, simple selection sort, bubble sort, and insertion sort, all of which have worst-case and average-case complexity $O(n^2)$, where n is the size of the list being sorted. There are other schemes that have complexity $O(n \log_2 n)$ and thus in most cases are more efficient than these three. In fact, it can be shown that any sorting scheme based on comparisons and interchanges like those we are considering must have worst-case complexity of at least $O(n \log_2 n)$. In this section we describe one of these, known as **heapsort**, which, as we mentioned, is a variation of the simple selection sort. It was discovered by John Williams in 1964 and uses a new data structure called a *heap* to organize the list elements in such a way that the selection can be carried out more efficiently.[2]

Like the binary search trees considered in the previous chapter, a **heap** is a special kind of binary tree. It differs from BSTs, however, in two respects:

1. It is *complete*; that is, each level of the tree is completely filled, except possibly the bottom level, and in this level, the nodes are in the leftmost positions.
2. The data item stored in each node is greater than the data items stored in each of its children. (Of course, if the data items are records, then some key field in these records must satisfy this condition.)

For example, the first binary tree pictured here is a heap; the second tree is not, because it is not complete; the third binary tree is complete, but it is not a heap because the second condition is not satisfied.

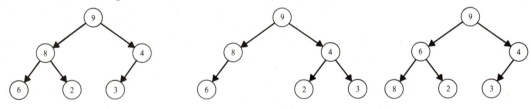

To implement a heap, we could use a linked structure like that for binary search trees, but an array can be used more effectively. We simply number the nodes in the heap from top to bottom, numbering the nodes on each level from left to right:

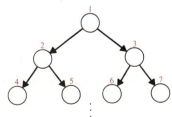

    [2] J. W. J. Williams, "Algorithm 232: Heapsort," *Communication of the Association of Computing Machinery* 7(1964): 347–348.

and store the data in the *i*th node in the *i*th location of the array. The completeness property of a heap guarantees that these data items will be stored in consecutive locations at the beginning of the array. Such an array *Heap* might be declared by

    CONST
        HeapLimit = …;   (* limit on number of nodes in the heap *)

    TYPE
        ElementType = …;   (* type of data items in the heap *)
        HeapType = ARRAY [1..*HeapLimit*] OF *ElementType*;

    VAR
        Heap : *HeapType*;

The items in the preceding heap are then stored as follows: $Heap[1] = 9$, $Heap[2] = 8$, $Heap[3] = 4$, $Heap[4] = 6$, $Heap[5] = 2$, $Heap[6] = 3$.

Note that in such an array implementation, finding the children of a given node is easy; the children of the *i*th node are at locations $2*i$ and $2*i + 1$. Similarly, the parent of the *i*th node is easily seen to be in location *i* DIV 2.

An algorithm for converting a complete binary tree into a heap is basic to most other heap operations. The simplest instance of this problem is a tree that is almost a heap, in that both subtrees of the root are heaps, but the tree itself is not, for example,

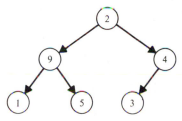

As this tree is complete and both subtrees are heaps, the only reason it is not a heap is that the root item is smaller than one of its children. The first step, therefore, is to interchange this root with the larger of its two children, in this case, the left child:

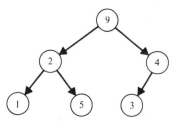

This guarantees that the new root will be greater than both of its children and that one of its subtrees, the right one in this case, will still be a heap. The other subtree may or may not be a heap. If it is, the entire tree is a heap, and we are finished. If it is not, as in this example, we simply repeat this "swapdown" procedure on this subtree. This process is repeated until at some stage, both subtrees of the node being examined are heaps; the process will be repeated only a finite number of times because eventually we reach the bottom of the tree.

For the general problem of converting a complete binary tree into a heap, we begin at the last node that is not a leaf, apply the swap-down procedure to convert the subtree rooted at this node into a heap, move to the preceding node and swap down in that subtree, and so on, working our way up the tree until the root of the given tree is reached. The following sequence of diagrams illustrates this "heapify" process; the subtree being heapified at each stage is highlighted.

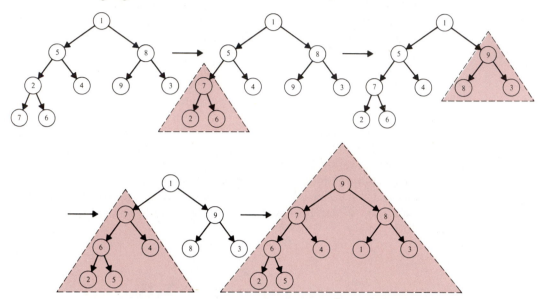

An algorithm to implement the swapdown process is as follows:

SWAPDOWN

(* Given a complete binary tree stored in locations r through n of the array *Heap* and left and right subtrees that are heaps, this algorithm converts the tree into a heap. *)

1. Initialize a boolean variable *Finished* to false and an index c (* child *) to $2 * r$.

2. While not *Finished* and $c \leq n$ do the following:

    (* Find the largest child *)
    a. If $c < n$ and $Heap[c] < Heap[c + 1]$ then
       set c equal to $c + 1$.

    (* Interchange node and largest child if necessary, and move down to the next subtree *)
    b. If $Heap[r] < Heap[c]$ then
         i. Interchange $Heap[r]$ and $Heap[c]$.
        ii. Set r equal to c.
       iii. Set c equal to $2 * c$.
       Else
          Set *Finished* to true.

An algorithm for converting any complete binary tree into a heap is then easy to write:

HEAPIFY

(* Algorithm to convert a complete binary tree stored in positions 1 through *n* of array *Heap* into a heap. *)

For *r* = *n* DIV 2 down to 1 do: (* start at last nonleaf *)

Apply *SwapDown* to the tree stored in locations *r* through *n* of *Heap*.

To see how these algorithms can now be used to sort a list stored in an array, consider the following list:

35, 15, 77, 60, 22, 41

We think of the array storing these items as a complete binary tree

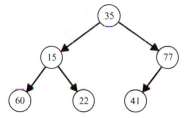

and we use the *Heapify* algorithm to convert it into a heap:

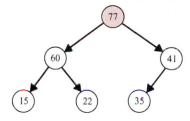

This puts the largest element in the list at the root of the tree, that is, at position 1 of the array. We now use the strategy of a selection sort and correctly position this largest element by placing it at the end of the list and turn our attention to sorting the sublist consisting of the first five elements. In terms of the tree, we are exchanging the root element and the rightmost leaf element, and then "pruning" this leaf from the tree, as indicated by the dotted arrow in the following diagram:

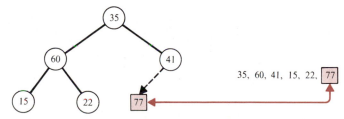

Quite obviously, the tree that results when we perform this root–leaf exchange, followed by pruning the leaf, is not usually a heap. In particular, the five-node tree that corresponds to the sublist 35, 60, 41, 15, 22 is not a heap. However, since we have changed only the root, the tree is almost a heap in the sense described earlier; namely, each of its subtrees is a heap. Thus we can use the *SwapDown* algorithm rather than the more time-consuming *Heapify* algorithm to convert this tree to a heap:

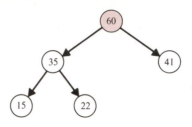

Now we use the same technique of exchanging the root with the rightmost leaf to correctly position the second largest element in the list, and then we prune this leaf from the tree to prepare for the next stage:

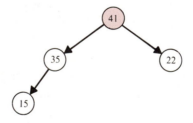

Now we use *SwapDown* to convert to a heap the tree corresponding to the sublist consisting of the first four elements

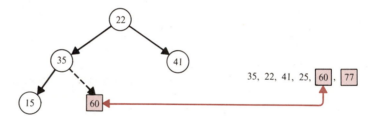

and do the root–leaf exchange and the leaf pruning to correctly position the third largest element in the list:

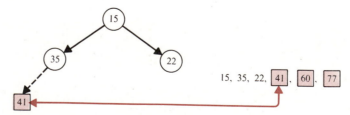

Next the three-node tree corresponding to the sublist 15, 35, 22 is converted to a heap using *SwapDown*

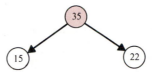

and the root–leaf exchange and pruning operation are used to correctly position the next largest element in the list:

Finally, the two-node tree corresponding to the two-element sublist 22, 15 is converted to a heap

and one last root–leaf swap and leaf pruning is performed to correctly position the element 22, which obviously also correctly positions the smallest element 15 at the beginning of the list:

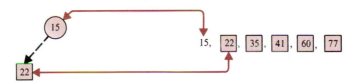

The following algorithm summarizes this simple but efficient sorting scheme, known as *heapsort*:

HEAPSORT

(∗ Algorithm to heapsort a list of n elements stored in an array $X[1]$, $X[2], \ldots, X[n]$, so they are in ascending order. ∗)

1. Consider X as a complete binary tree and use the *Heapify* algorithm to convert this tree into a heap.
2. For $i = n$ down to 2, do the following:
   a. Interchange $X[1]$ and $X[i]$, thus putting the largest element in the sublist $X[1], \ldots, X[i]$ at the end of the sublist.
   b. Apply the *SwapDown* algorithm to convert the binary tree corresponding to the sublist stored in positions 1 through $i - 1$ of X to a heap.

The following program implements this algorithm and the *Heapify* and *SwapDown* algorithms that it uses.

```
MODULE SortWithHeapsort;

(************************************************************************

    Program to read and count a list of items, sort them using the
    heapsort algorithm, and then display the sorted list.

 ***********************************************************************)

    FROM InOut IMPORT ReadInt, WriteString, WriteLn,
                      WriteCard, WriteInt, Done;

    CONST
        HeapLimit = 100;

    TYPE
        ElementType = INTEGER;
        HeapType = ARRAY[1..HeapLimit] OF ElementType;

    VAR
        Item : HeapType;      (* list of items to be sorted *)
        Temp : ElementType;   (* temporary item read *)
        NumItems,             (* number of items *)
        i : CARDINAL;         (* index *)

    PROCEDURE Interchange(VAR A, B : ElementType);

        (*****************************************************************

                Procedure to interchange two items A and B

         ****************************************************************)

        VAR
            Temp : ElementType;   (* temporary location used to swap A and B *)

        BEGIN
            Temp := A;
            A := B;
            B := Temp
        END Interchange;

    PROCEDURE Heapsort (VAR X : HeapType; n : CARDINAL);

        (**************************************************************

            Procedure to heapsort an array X of n items so they
            are in ascending order.

         *************************************************************)
```

Figure 10.1

Figure 10.1   (cont.)

```
VAR
    i : CARDINAL;              (* index *)

PROCEDURE SwapDown (VAR Heap : HeapType; r, n : CARDINAL);

    (**************************************************************

        Given a complete binary tree stored in locations r
        through n of array Heap with left and right subtrees
        that are heaps.  This procedure converts this tree
        into a heap.

    **************************************************************)

    VAR
        Child : CARDINAL;     (* largest child *)
        Finished : BOOLEAN; (* signals when swapping down is complete *)

    BEGIN
        Finished := FALSE;
        Child := 2 * r;
        WHILE (NOT Finished) AND (Child <= n) DO

            (* Find the largest child *)

            IF (Child < n) AND (Heap[Child] < Heap[Child + 1]) THEN
                INC(Child)
            END (* IF *);

            (* Interchange node and largest child if necessary,
               and move down to the next subtree *)

            IF Heap[r] < Heap[Child] THEN
                Interchange (Heap[r], Heap[Child]);
                r := Child;
                Child := 2 * Child
            ELSE
                Finished := TRUE
            END (* IF *)
        END (* WHILE *)
    END SwapDown;

PROCEDURE Heapify (VAR Heap : HeapType; n : CARDINAL);

    (**************************************************************

        Procedure to convert a complete binary tree stored in
        positions 1 through n of array Heap into a heap.

    **************************************************************)

    VAR
        r : CARDINAL;          (* index *)
```

Figure 10.1   (cont.)

```
        BEGIN
            FOR r := n DIV 2 TO 1 BY -1 DO
                SwapDown(Heap, r, n)
            END (* FOR *)
        END Heapify;

    BEGIN (* Heapsort *)
        (* Convert tree represented by X[1], ..., X[n] into a heap *)

        Heapify(X, n);

        (* Repeatedly put largest item in root at end of list, prune
            it from the tree and apply SwapDown to rest of tree *)

        FOR i := n TO 2 BY -1 DO
            Interchange(X[1], X[i]);
            SwapDown(X, 1, i - 1)
        END (* FOR *)
    END Heapsort;

BEGIN (* main program *)
    NumItems := 0;
    WriteString('Enter the list of items.  Maximum of ');
    WriteCard(HeapLimit, 1);
    WriteString(' items allowed.');
    WriteLn;
    WriteString('Enter any nondigit to signal the end of the list.');
    WriteLn; WriteLn;
    ReadInt(Temp);
    WHILE Done AND (NumItems < HeapLimit) DO
        INC(NumItems);
        Item[NumItems] := Temp;
        ReadInt(Temp)
    END (* WHILE *);
    Heapsort (Item, NumItems);
    WriteLn; WriteLn;
    WriteString('Sorted list:');
    WriteLn;
    FOR i := 1 TO NumItems DO
        WriteInt(Item[i], 8);
        WriteLn
    END (* FOR *)
END SortWithHeapsort.
```

Sample run:

```
Enter the list of items.  Maximum of 100 items allowed.
Enter any nondigit to signal the end of the list.

35 15 77 60 22 41
*

Sorted list:
        15
        22
        35
        41
        60
        77
```

In the introduction to this section we claimed that the complexity of heap-sort is O($n \log_2 n$). To see this, we must first analyze the *SwapDown* and *Heapify* algorithms.

In *SwapDown*, the number of items in the subtree considered at each stage is one-half the number of items in the subtree at the preceding stage. Thus, by an analysis similar to that for binary search trees, the worst-case computing time for this algorithm is easily seen to be O($\log_2 n$). Since the *Heapify* algorithm executes *SwapDown* $n/2$ times, its worst-case computing time is O($n \log_2 n$). *Heapsort* executes *Heapify* one time and *SwapDown* $n - 1$ times; consequently, its worst-case complexity is O($n \log_2 n$).

Exercises

1. Convert each of the following binary trees into a heap using the *Heapify* algorithm if possible, or explain why it is not possible:

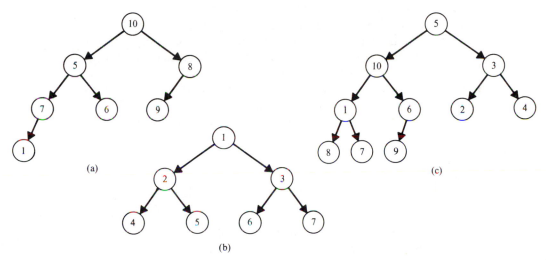

(a)

(b)

(c)

2. Using diagrams like those in this section, trace the action of heapsort on the following lists:

(a) 7, 1, 6, 5, 4, 2, 3   (b) 1, 7, 2, 6, 3, 5, 4
(c) 7, 6, 5, 4, 3, 2, 1   (d) 1, 2, 3, 4, 5, 6, 7

3. (a) Design an efficient algorithm for inserting an item into a heap having n elements to produce a heap with $n + 1$ elements. (*Hint:* Put the item in location $n + 1$ and then . . . .)
   (b) Design an efficient algorithm for deleting an item at location *Loc* from a heap having n nodes to produce a heap with $n - 1$ nodes.
   (c) Determine the computing times for the algorithms in parts (a) and (b).

4. Write procedures implementing the insert and delete algorithms of Exercise 3. Use these procedures in a program that reads records containing an employee number and an hourly rate for several employees and that stores these in a heap, using the employee number as the key field. The program should then allow the user to insert or delete records and, finally, use heapsort to sort the updated list so that employee numbers are in ascending order and display this sorted list.

10.3   Quicksort

In several of the preceding internal sorts, the basic idea was to select the smallest or largest element in some sublist of the list and place it in its proper position in that sublist. In this section we consider a sorting scheme developed by C. A. R. Hoare known as *quicksort*, which also selects an item in the list and properly positions it.[3] In this scheme, however, the item is not necessarily the smallest or largest element; in fact, quicksort works the best if the element is not one of these extreme values but is instead some element that properly belongs somewhere in the middle of the sublist.

The element selected is correctly positioned by rearranging the list or sublist so that all list elements to the left of the selected element are less than or equal to it, and all those to the right are greater than this element. This divides the (sub)list into two smaller sublists, each of which may then be sorted independently in the *same* way. This *divide-and-conquer strategy* leads naturally to a recursive sorting algorithm.

As an illustration, consider the following list of test scores:

$$75, 70, 65, 84, 98, 78, 100, 93, 55, 61, 81, 68$$

Suppose, for simplicity, that we select the first number 75 to be correctly positioned. We must rearrange the list so that 70, 65, 55, 61, and 68 are to the left of 75 (but not necessarily in the order listed here), and the numbers 84, 98, 78, 100, 93, and 81 are to the right of 75.

The only thing we require of this rearrangement is that all numbers in the sublist to the left of 75 be less than or equal to 75 and that those in the right sublist be greater than 75. We do not care how the elements in each of these sublists are themselves ordered. And it is precisely this flexibility that makes it possible to rearrange them very efficiently.

We carry out two searches, one from the right end of the list for elements less than or equal to the selected element 75, and another from the left end for elements greater than 75. In our example, the first element located on the search from the right is 68, and that on the search from the left is 84:

---

[3] C. A. R. Hoare, "Quicksort," *Computer Journal* 5(1962): 10–15.

These elements are then interchanged:

75 , 70 , 65 , 68 , 98 , 78 , 100 , 93 , 55 , 61 , 81 , 84

The searches are then resumed, from the right to locate another element less than or equal to 75, and from the left to find another element greater than 75,

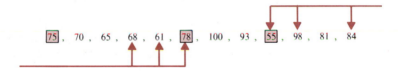

and these elements, 61 and 98, are interchanged:

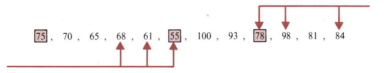

A continuation of the searches next locates 78 and 55:

75 , 70 , 65 , 68 , 61 , 78 , 100 , 93 , 55 , 98 , 81 , 84

and interchanging them yields:

75 , 70 , 65 , 68 , 61 , 55 , 100 , 93 , 78 , 98 , 81 , 84

Now, when we resume our search from the right, we locate the element 55 that was found on the previous search from the left:

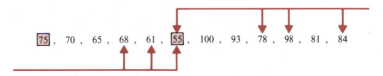

The ''pointers'' for the left and right searches have thus met, and this signals the end of the two searches. We now interchange 55 and 75:

55 , 70 , 65 , 68 , 61 , 75 , 100 , 93 , 78 , 98 , 81 , 84

Note that all elements to the left of 75 are now less than 75 and that all those to its right are greater than 75, and thus 75 has been properly positioned.
The left sublist

55 , 70 , 65 , 68 , 61

and the right sublist

100 , 93 , 78 , 98 , 81 , 84

can now be sorted *independently, using any sorting scheme desired.* Quicksort uses the same scheme we have just illustrated for the entire list; that is, these sublists must themselves be split by selecting and correctly positioning one element (the first) in each of them. The following procedure *Split* can be used for this; it assumes that the list is stored in an array.

```
PROCEDURE Split(VAR X : List; First, Last : INTEGER;
                VAR Pos : CARDINAL);

    (* Procedure to rearrange X[First], . . . , X[Last] so that the first
       element X[First] is properly positioned; it returns the rearranged
       list and the final position Pos of that element. *)

VAR
    Left,                           (* index for searching from the left *)
    Right : CARDINAL;               (* index for searching from the right *)
    TempItem : ElementType;         (* temporary element used for interchangin

BEGIN
    (* Initialize indices for left and right searches *)
    Left := First;
    Right := Last;

    WHILE Left < Right DO (* While searches haven't met *)

        (* Search from the right for element <= X[First] *)
        WHILE X[Right] > X[First] DO
            DEC (Right)
        END (* WHILE *);

        (* Search from the left for element > X[First] *)
        WHILE (Left < Right) AND (X[Left] <= X[First]) DO
            INC (Left)
        END (* WHILE *);
```

(* Interchange elements if searches haven't met *)
IF *Left* < *Right* THEN
    TempItem := *X[Left]*;
    X[Left] := *X[Right]*;
    X[Right] := *TempItem*
END (* IF *)
END (* WHILE *);

(* End of searches; place selected element in proper position *)

Pos := *Right*;
TempItem := *X[Pos]*;
X[Pos] := *X[First]*;
X[First] := *TempItem*
END *Split*;

A recursive procedure to sort a list is now easy to write:

PROCEDURE *QuickSort*(VAR *X* : *List*; *First*, *Last* : CARDINAL);

(* Procedure to quicksort array elements *X[First]*, . . . , *X[Last]* *)

VAR
    Mid : CARDINAL;   (* final position of selected element *)

BEGIN
(* 1 *)   If *First* < *Last* THEN (* list has more than one element *)
(* 2 *)   *Split*(*X*, *First*, *Last*, *Mid*);   (* split into two sublists *)
(* 3 *)   *QuickSort*(*X*, *First*, *Mid* − 1);   (* sort first sublist *)
(* 4 *)   *QuickSort*(*X*, *Mid* + 1, *Last*)   (* sort second sublist *)
      (* else
      list has 0 or 1 element and requires no sorting *)
      END (* IF *)
(* 5 *) END *QuickSort*;

This procedure is called with a statement of the form

Quicksort (*X*, 1, *n*)

where $X[1]$, $X[2]$, . . . , $X[n]$ is the list of elements to be sorted.

The following sequence of treelike diagrams traces the action of *Quicksort* as it sorts the list of integers

$$8, 2, 13, 5, 14, 3, 7$$

In each tree, a circle indicates an item that has been correctly positioned, a shaded circle indicating the item currently being positioned. Rectangles represent sublists to be sorted, and a highlighted rectangle indicates the next sublist to be sorted.

8,2,13,5,14,3,7

First call to *Quicksort*(*Low* = 1, *High* = 7)

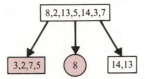

$1 < 7$ so *Split* is called to correctly position 8. Now call *Quicksort* for the left sublist 3, 2, 7, 5 (*Low* = 1, *High* = 4)

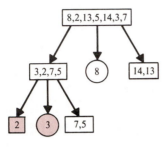

$1 < 4$ so call *Split* which correctly positions 3. Now call *Quicksort* for the left sublist which consists of the single element 2 (*Low* = 1, *High* = 1)

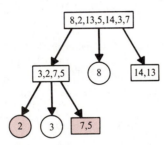

$1 \not< 1$ (one-element sublist) so nothing happens on this call to *Quicksort*. We return to the previous level and call *Quicksort* for the right sublist 7, 5 (*Low* = 3, *High* = 4)

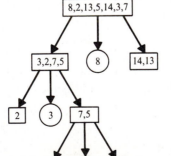

Since $3 < 4$, *Split* is called which correctly positions 7. Now call *Quicksort* for the left sublist consisting of the single element 5 (*Low* = 3, *High* = 3)

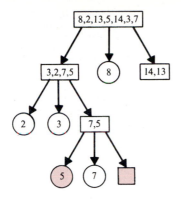

3 ⊀ 3 (one-element sublist) so nothing happens on this call to *Quicksort*. We return to the previous level and call *Quicksort* for the right sublist which is empty (*Low* = 5, *High* = 4).

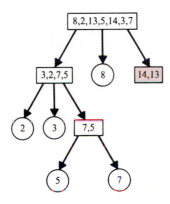

5 ⊀ 4 (empty sublist) so again nothing happens on this call to *Quicksort*. We return to the previous level and find the call to *Quicksort* for sublist 7,5 is complete. So we back up to the previous level and call *Quicksort* for the right sublist 14,13 at this level (*Low* = 6, *High* = 7).

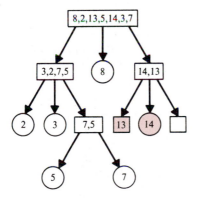

Since 6 < 7, *Split* is called to correctly position 14. Now *Quicksort* is called for the resulting left sublist which consists of the single element 13 (*Low* = 6, *High* = 6)

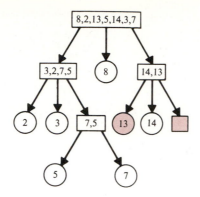

6 ⊄ 6 (one-element sublist) so nothing is done on this call to *Quicksort*. We return to the previous level and call *Quicksort* for the right sublist, which is empty (*Low* = 8, *High* = 7).

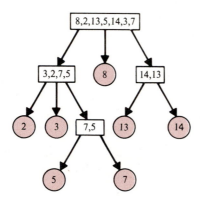

8 ⊄ 7 (empty sublist), so do nothing on this call to *Quicksort*; simply return to the previous level. But this completes the call to *Quicksort* for the sublist 14,13, and we return to the previous level. Now we find that the original call to *Quicksort* is complete.

The worst case for quicksort occurs when the list is already ordered or the elements are in reverse order. The worst-case complexity is $O(n^2)$, and the average-case complexity is $O(n \log_2 n)$. Although a rigorous derivation of these computing times is rather difficult, we can see intuitively why they are correct, by considering the treelike diagrams used to describe the action of *Quicksort*. At each level of the tree, the procedure *Split* is applied to several sublists, whose total size is, of course, at most *n*; hence, each of the statements in the while loop of *Split* is executed at most *n* times on each level. The computing time for quicksort is thus $O(n \cdot L)$, where *L* is the number of levels in the tree. In the worst case, one of the sublists produced by *Split* is always empty, so that the tree has *n* levels. It follows that the worst-case computing time is $O(n^2)$. If, however, the two sublists produced by *Split* are approximately the same size, the number of levels will be approximately $\log_2 n$, thus giving $O(n \log_2 n)$ as the computing time in the average case.

A number of changes can be made in quicksort to improve its performance. The first of these is to select more carefully the item to be properly positioned at each stage in an attempt to produce more uniform splitting. One common method is the **median-of-three rule**, which selects the median of the first, middle, and last elements in each sublist as the item to be positioned correctly. In practice, it is often the case that the list to be sorted is already partially ordered, and then it is likely that the median-of-three rule will select an item closer to the middle of the sublist than will the "first-element" rule.

A second improvement is to switch to a faster sorting method when the sublist is small. We noted in Section 10.1, for example, that insertion sort is one of the best sorting schemes for small lists, say of size up to fifteen or twenty. Thus we might modify quicksort so that insertion sort is used when *High* − *Low* is less than 20.

Quicksort is a recursive procedure, and as we have seen (see Section 5.5), a stack of activation records must be maintained by the system to manage recursion. The deeper the recursion is, the larger this stack will become. The depth of the recursion can be reduced if we first sort the smaller sublist at each stage, rather than always selecting the left sublist. If quicksort is to be used extensively, it may even be worthwhile to remove recursion by writing it iteratively, as described in the exercises.

Exercises

1. Draw a sequence of trees like those in the text to illustrate the actions of *Split* and *Quicksort* while sorting the following lists:

   (a) E, A, F, D, C, B   **(b)** A, B, C, F, E, D
   (c) F, E, D, C, B, A   **(d)** A, B, C, D, E, F

2. One of the lists in Exercise 1 shows why the compound boolean condition is needed to control the search from the left in procedure *Split*. Which list is it? What would happen if we were to omit the boolean expression *Left* < *Right*?

3. The procedure *Quicksort* always sorts the left sublist before the right. The size of the stack used to implement the recursion required by *Quicksort* is reduced if the shorter sublist is sorted first. Modify *Quicksort* to do this.

4. Another way to improve quicksort is to use some other sorting algorithm to sort small sublists. For example, insertion sort is one of the fastest sorting schemes for lists having up to twenty elements. Modify *Quicksort* to use insertion sort if the sublist has fewer than *LBound* elements for some constant *LBound* and otherwise uses quicksort.

5. An alternative to the approach in Exercise 4 is simply to ignore all sublists with fewer than *LBound* elements, not splitting them further. When execution of the quicksort algorithm terminates, the file will not be sorted. It will be nearly sorted, however, in that it will contain small unordered groups of elements, but all of the elements in each such group will be smaller than those in the next group. One then simply sorts the list using insertion sort. Modify *Quicksort* to incorporate this modification.

6. The procedure *Split* always selects the first element of the sublist to position. If the list is already sorted or nearly sorted, this is a poor choice for a *pivot* element to be correctly positioned. An alternative method for choosing the pivot and one that works better for partially sorted lists is the *median-of-three rule*, in which the median of the first, middle, and last elements in the list is selected. (The median of three numbers a, b, and c, arranged so that $a \leq b \leq c$ is the middle number b.) Modify *Split* to use this median-of-three rule.

7. As we saw in Section 5.5, recursion is usually implemented using a stack; parameters, local variables, and return addresses are pushed onto the stack when a recursive subprogram is called, and values are popped from the stack upon return from the subprogram. Generally, we can transform a recursive subprogram into a nonrecursive one by maintaining such a stack within the subprogram itself. Use this approach to design a nonrecursive version of procedure *Quicksort*; use a stack to store the first and last positions of the sublists that arise in quicksort.

8. The *median* of a set with an odd number of elements is the middle value if the data items are arranged in order. An efficient algorithm to find the median that does not require first ordering the entire set can be obtained by modifying the quicksort algorithm. We use procedure *Split* to position one element in the list so that the items preceding it are less than or equal to that element, and those following it are greater than that element. If this element is positioned at location $(n + 1)/2$, it is the median; otherwise, one of the two sublists produced by *Split* contains the median, and that sublist can be processed recursively. Write a procedure to find the median of a list using this method.

9. The technique described in Exercise 8 for finding the median of a set of data items can be modified easily to find the *k*th smallest element in the set. Write such a procedure.

11

Sorting and Searching Files

In the sorting and searching schemes considered up to now, we have assumed that the collection of items to be processed is stored in internal memory and can thus be accessed very quickly. The storage capacity of main memory may be too small, however, for large collections of student records, motor vehicle registrations, telephone listings, and so on. Such collections must be stored in external memory, such as magnetic tapes or disks, which provide less expensive mass storage but for which the access time is considerably greater. These collections of data items are called *files*, and the individual items are called *components* or *records*.

There are two basic types of files: *sequential* and *direct* (or *random*) *access*. In a sequential file the data items must be accessed in the order in which they are stored; that is, to access any particular component, we must start at the beginning of the file and pass through all the components that precede it. In contrast, each record in a direct access file can be accessed directly by specifying its location in the file.

Another distinction between files is based on the way in which information is represented in them. Files in which information is stored in external character form are called *text files*, and those in which the information is stored in internal form are called *binary files*.

In this chapter we describe the file capabilities provided in Modula-2 systems and consider several important file-processing problems, including sorting and updating. We also describe how binary files and direct access files are supported in Modula-2 systems.

11.1 The Library Module *FileSystem*

A *file* is a collection of related data items, usually stored in external memory, for which the basic operations are input and output; that is, information can be read from the file and/or written to the file. Usually the programmer is not concerned with the details of the actual external medium on which the data is stored because these details are handled by the operating system. Instead, the programmer deals with the *logical* structure of the file, that is, with the relationship between the items stored in the file and with the algorithms needed to process them.

Programs that read and write only character and/or numeric data and use only one input stream and one output stream can usually be written using the input and output redirection services provided by the module *InOut* (and *RealInOut*), as described in Section 0.5. Although *InOut* is easy to use, its services are somewhat limited; in particular:

1. It allows only one input stream and one output stream to be in use at any one time.
2. It supports only input and output of character and numeric data; it does not allow input/output of other data types.
3. It supports only sequential files; no provision is made for direct access files.

To overcome some of these limitations, most Modula-2 systems provide additional library modules for processing files. However, because there is (as yet) no standard set of Modula-2 library modules, it is somewhat difficult to describe the details of file processing in Modula-2. In our discussion here we use the library module *FileSystem* described by Wirth in *Programming in Modula-2*. The collection of library modules provided in most implementations of Modula-2 include such a module, although in many cases its contents are modified and/or extended and it may have a different name.

File Declarations.   In Modula-2 programs, files are processed using *file variables* of type *File*, where *File* must be imported from the module *FileSystem* (or some similar file-handling module). In Wirth's version of *FileSystem*, *File* is defined to be a record; in some other systems, *File* (or some other type identifier such as *FileDescr*) is a synonym for INTEGER; in still other systems, files may be implemented as pointers (and a type identifier such as *FilePtr* may be used to indicate this fact). The exact structure of this record varies from one implementation to another; two of its fields as specified in Wirth's *FileSystem* are named *res* and *eof*. The type of the field *res* is an enumeration type whose values represent possible errors that can occur in the various file operations. One value of this enumeration type is *done*, and this value is assigned to *res* when a file operation is performed successfully. For example, if the file variable *InFile* has been declared by

FROM *FileSystem* IMPORT *File*, . . . ;
.
.
.
VAR
    InFile : *File*;

and some operation has been attempted on it, an IF statement of the form

```
IF InFile.res # done THEN
        ⋮
        ⋮
END (* IF *)
```

might be used to specify some error-handling action to be taken if the operation could not be carried out.

The field *eof* in *File* is of type BOOLEAN. Its value is TRUE when the end of the file is reached. More precisely, it is FALSE until an attempt is made to read beyond the end of the file. Thus a loop of the form

```
Read an item from InFile
WHILE NOT InFile.eof DO
    Process the item
    Read next item from InFile
END (* LOOP *)
```

or

```
LOOP
    Read an item from InFile
    IF InFile.eof THEN EXIT END;
    Process the item
END (* LOOP *)
```

can be used to read and process the items in the file *InFile*. In some Modula-2 systems the end-of-file checking is done by using a function procedure *Eof*. In such systems the preceding loops would have the forms

```
Read an item from InFile
WHILE NOT Eof(InFile) DO
    Process the item
    Read next item from InFile
END (* LOOP *)
```

and

```
LOOP
    Read an item from InFile
    If Eof(InFile) THEN EXIT END;
    Process the item
END (* LOOP *)
```

Connecting, Creating, Renaming, and Closing Files.　Files that exist before and/or after execution of a program are called *permanent* files, and those that exist only during execution are called *temporary* files. Before a permanent file can be processed, it must be connected to a file variable. In Wirth's

FileSystem, this is done using the procedure *Lookup*. This procedure is called with a statement of the form

> *Lookup(file-variable, file-name, new)*

where *file-variable* is of type *File*, *file-name* is the actual name of the permanent file and is of string type, and *new* is a boolean expression. In some Modula-2 systems, the procedure is named *Open* and may be called with a different set of parameters.

When called, this procedure searches for a file with the specified name. If it is found, it connects this file to the specified file variable so that all subsequent operations specified for this file variable will actually be performed on the associated permanent file. If a file with the specified name is not found and the value of the boolean expression *new* is TRUE, then a new (empty) file having this name will be created. Thus, for example, if a file with the name 'TestData1' exists, the statement

> *Lookup(InFile,* 'TestData1', TRUE)

will locate this file and connect it to the file variable *InFile*. If it does not exist, an empty file with the name 'TestData1' will be created and associated with *InFile*.

In Modula-2 systems in which the file-handling module is or closely resembles the module *FileSystem*, temporary files can be created by using the procedure *Create* in a reference of the form

> *Create (file-variable, medium-name)*

where *file-variable* is of type *File* and *medium-name* is a string specifying the device on which the temporary (nameless) file is to be created. For example, the statement

> *Create(TempFile,* 'A:')

might be used to create a temporary file on disk drive A and connect it to the file variable *TempFile*. Some Modula-2 systems make no such provision for temporary files. They may include a procedure *Delete*, however, that can be used to remove unneeded files.

The module *FileSystem* also provides the procedure *Rename*, which may be used to change the name of the file connected to a file variable. It is called with a statement of the form

> *Rename(file-variable, new-file-name)*

For example, the statement

> *Rename(InFile,* 'TestData2')

changes the name of the file associated with *InFile* from 'TestData1' to

'TestData2'. If the file whose name is being changed is a (nameless) temporary file, it is given the specified name and becomes a permanent file. Conversely, if *new-file-name* is an empty string, the file loses its name and becomes a temporary file.

Operations on a file are terminated by calling the procedure *Close*, also provided in module *FileSystem*, with a statement of the form

    Close(file-variable)

This procedure terminates the connection between the file variable and the permanent or temporary file associated with it.

Closing a temporary file deletes it from the system. In Modula-2 systems that provide no *Delete* procedure, it may be possible to delete a permanent file by first using the procedure *Rename* to change the file to a temporary file and then using the procedure *Close* to delete this temporary file.

File Modes. The input/output operations that may be performed on a file are controlled by the **mode** of the file. The four possible modes specified in *FileSystem* are

> ***read***:   Data can be read from the file but cannot be written to it.
> ***write***:   Data can be written at the end of the file but cannot be read from it.
> ***modify***:   Data can be both read and written at the current location in the file.
> ***open***:   This is the initial mode of a file.

Some Modula-2 systems use other names for these modes such as *readOnly*, *writeOnly* and *readWrite* and may allow other modes as well.

When a file is connected to a file variable by using the procedures *Lookup* or *Create*, it is initially in open mode. These operations are thus usually referred to as **opening the file**. If the first operation performed on a file is a read operation, the file mode will be changed from open to read. If a write operation is performed first, its mode will be changed from open to write.

To place the file in modify mode, the procedure *SetModify* can be used. It is called with a statement of the form

    SetModify(file-variable)

Procedures *SetRead*, *SetWrite*, and *SetOpen* can be called with similar statements to place the file in a read, write, and open mode, respectively. In some Modula-2 systems, the file mode is specified by a parameter of the *Open* procedure.

The module *FileSystem* also provides the procedure *Reset* which can be called with a statement of the form

    Reset(file-variable)

This procedure returns the specified file to its initial mode.

File Input/Output.   File input/output procedures vary from one Modula-2 system to another. Wirth's version of *FileSystem* provides five procedures: *ReadChar*, *WriteChar*, *Again, ReadWord*, and *WriteWord*. *ReadChar* and *WriteChar* are used for text files and are called with statements of the form

> *ReadChar(file-variable, ch)*

and

> *WriteChar(file-variable, ch)*

ReadChar reads the next character from the specified file and assigns it to the variable *ch* of type CHAR. *WriteChar* appends the value of the expression *ch* of type *CHAR* to the specified text file.

The procedure *Again* can be used to reread the previous data value. It is called with a statement of the form

> *Again(file-variable)*

Procedures *ReadWord* and *WriteWord* are used for input from and output to binary files and are described later in this section. Other file-processing facilities provided in the module *FileSystem* are described in Appendix F.

To illustrate how text files are processed using the file-processing facilities provided in a module like *FileSystem*, we reconsider the text-editing problem in Section 3.1. In the solution given there, lines of text are read from a file (using input redirection) into an array of strings, and these lines are then edited one by one using editing commands of the form

> *old-string/new-string/*

where *old-string* is a part of the current text line that is to be replaced with *new-string*. The program in Figure 11.1 solves this same problem, implementing the algorithms given in Section 3.1, but does not store the entire document in an array before the editing is begun. Rather, a line of text is read from the file into a string variable and is edited, and the resulting line is then written to another file. The basic algorithm thus is

TEXT-EDITING ALGORITHM

1. Open the input file *TextFile* and a new file *NewTextFile* for the edited output.
2. Read the first line from *TextFile*.
3. While the end of *TextFile* has not been reached, do the following:
   a. Edit the line of text and write it to *NewTextFile*.
   b. Read the next line from *TextFile*.
4. Close the files *TextFile* and *NewTextFile*.

The procedures *LookUp* and *Close* from the library module *FileSystem* can be used to open and close the files, as required in Steps 1 and 4. And the procedure

ReadAString in the module *SpecialInOut* can easily be modified to read a line from a file, as required in Steps 2 and 3, by simply using procedure *ReadChar* from *FileSystem* in place of *Read* from *InOut*; procedure *ReadTextLine* in the program in Figure 11.1 is the result. The editing required in Step 3-a is done in the same manner as described in Section 3.1, with the exception that edited lines are written to a file, rather than stored in the array of lines. In the program, procedures *Edit* and *Replace* carry out the editing operations and are the same as in the program of Figure 3.1; procedure *WriteTextLine* performs the file output.

```
MODULE TextEditor2;

(**********************************************************************

   Program to perform some basic text-editing functions on lines of
   text.  The basic operation is that of replacing a substring of
   the text by another string.  This replacement is accomplished
   by a command of the form
                        OldString/NewString/
   where OldString specifies the substring in the text to be replaced
   by the specified string NewString; NewString may be an empty
   string which then causes the substring OldString (if found) to be
   deleted.  The text lines are read from TextFile, and after editing
   has been completed, the edited lines are written to NewTextFile.

 ********************************************************************* *)

   FROM FileSystem IMPORT File, Lookup, Close, ReadChar, WriteChar;
   FROM InOut IMPORT Write, WriteString, WriteLn, Read, EOL, Done;
   FROM StringsLib IMPORT Length, Concat, Copy, Position, Insert, Delete;
   FROM SpecialInOut IMPORT ReadAString;

   CONST
       StringLimit = 80;

   TYPE
       String = ARRAY [0..StringLimit] OF CHAR;

   VAR
       TextFile,                   (* file of original text *)
       NewTextFile : File;         (* file of edited text *)
       OldFileName,                (* actual name of text file to be edited *)
       NewFileName,                (* actual name for new file to be produced *)
       TextLine : String;          (* line of text to be edited *)
       EOF : BOOLEAN;              (* signals end of file *)

   PROCEDURE ReadTextLine(    TextFile : File;
                          VAR TextLine : String; VAR EOF : BOOLEAN);

       (***********************************************************
```

Figure 11.1

Figure 11.1   (cont.)

```
        Procedure to read and echo a line of text from TextFile or
        signal end of file (EOF).

    ****************************************************************)

    VAR
        i : CARDINAL;    (* index *)
        Ch : CHAR;       (* character read from file *)

    BEGIN
        i := 0;
        TextLine := '  ';
        ReadChar(TextFile, Ch);
        WHILE NOT TextFile.eof AND (Ch # EOL) DO
            IF (i <= StringLimit) THEN
                Write(Ch);
                TextLine[i] := Ch;
                INC(i);
                ReadChar(TextFile, Ch)
            END (* IF *)
        END (* WHILE *);
        TextLine[i] := 0C;
        WriteLn;

        EOF :=  TextFile.eof

    END ReadTextLine;

PROCEDURE WriteTextLine (TextFile : File; Line : String);

    (***************************************************************

        Procedure to write a Line of text to TextFile.

    ****************************************************************)

    VAR
        i : CARDINAL;      (* index *)

    BEGIN
        WriteLn;
        FOR i := 0 TO Length(TextLine) DO
            WriteChar(NewTextFile, TextLine[i])
        END (* FOR *);
        WriteChar(TextFile, EOL)
    END WriteTextLine;

PROCEDURE Edit (TextLine : String);

    (***************************************************************

        Procedure to carry out the editing operations on TextLine.
        After editing is completed, the edited line is written to
        NewTextFile.

    ****************************************************************)
```

Figure 11.1 (cont.)

```
VAR
    OldString,              (* old string in edit change *)
    NewString : String;     (* new string in edit change *)
    i,                      (* index *)
    Location : CARDINAL;    (* location of OldString in TextLine *)
    Response : String;      (* user response *)

PROCEDURE GetEditCommand (VAR OldString, NewString : String);

    (**************************************************************

        Procedure to read the edit change of the form
                    OldString/NewString/
        It returns OldString and NewString.

    **************************************************************)

    VAR
        EditChange : String;     (* editing change *)
        i,                       (* index *)
        OldLength,               (* length of OldString *)
        NewLength : CARDINAL;    (* length of NewString *)

BEGIN
    WriteLn;
    WriteString('Edit change:  ');
    WriteLn;
    ReadAString(EditChange);
    OldLength := Position('/', EditChange);
    Copy(EditChange, 0, OldLength, OldString);
    Delete(EditChange, 0, OldLength + 1);
    NewLength := Length(EditChange) - 1;
    Copy(EditChange, 0, NewLength, NewString)
END GetEditCommand;

PROCEDURE Replace (VAR TextLine: String;
                       OldString, NewString : String;
                       Start : CARDINAL);

(**************************************************************

    Procedure to replace a substring OldString beginning at
    position Start of TextLine with NewString.

**************************************************************)

BEGIN
    Delete(TextLine, Start, Length(OldString));
    IF Start < Length(TextLine) THEN
        Insert(NewString, Start, TextLine)
    ELSE
        Concat(TextLine, NewString, TextLine)
    END (* IF *);
    WriteLn;
    WriteString(TextLine)
END Replace;
```

Figure 11.1   (cont.)

```
        BEGIN (* Edit *)
            WriteString('Edit this line? ');
            ReadAString(Response);
            WHILE CAP(Response[0]) = 'Y' DO
                GetEditCommand(OldString, NewString);
                Location := Position(OldString, TextLine);
                IF Location >= Length(TextLine) THEN
                    WriteString(OldString);
                    WriteString(' not found');
                    WriteLn
                ELSE
                    Replace (TextLine, OldString, NewString, Location)
                END (* IF *);
                WriteLn;
                WriteString('More editing (Y or N)? ');
                ReadAString(Response)
            END (* WHILE *);
            WriteTextLine(TextFile, TextLine)
        END Edit;


BEGIN (* main program *)
    (* Open the file to be edited and a new file for the edited output *)

    WriteString('Name of file to be edited?  ');
    ReadAString(OldFileName);
    Lookup(TextFile, OldFileName, FALSE);
    WriteLn;
    WriteString('Name of new file to be produced?  ');
    ReadAString(NewFileName);
    Lookup(NewTextFile, NewFileName, TRUE);

    (* Read and edit the lines of text *)

    WriteLn; WriteLn;
    EOF := FALSE;
    ReadTextLine(TextFile, TextLine, EOF);
    WHILE NOT EOF DO
        Edit(TextLine);
        ReadTextLine(TextFile, TextLine, EOF)
    END (* WHILE *);

    (* Close the files *)

    Close(TextFile);
    Close(NewTextFile)
END TextEditor2.
```

Listing of file LINCOLN:

```
FOURSCORE AND FIVE YEARS AGO, OUR MOTHERS
BROUGHT FORTH ON CONTINENT
A NATION CONCEIVED IN LIBERTY AND AND DEDICATED
TO THE PREPOSITION THAT ALL MEN
ARE CREATED EQUAL.
```

Figure 11.1 (cont.)

```
Sample run:

Name of file to be edited?  LINCOLN
Name of new file to be produced?  EDITED

FOURSCORE AND FIVE YEARS AGO, OUR MOTHERS
Edit this line? Y
Edit change:
FIVE/SEVEN/
FOURSCORE AND SEVEN YEARS AGO, OUR MOTHERS
More editing (Y or N)? Y
Edit change:
MOTH/FATH/
FOURSCORE AND SEVEN YEARS AGO, OUR FATHERS
More editing (Y or N)? N

BROUGHT FORTH ON CONTINENT
Edit this line? Y
Edit change:
ONC/ON THIS C/
ONC not found
More editing (Y or N)? Y
Edit change:
ON/ON THIS/
BROUGHT FORTH ON THIS CONTINENT
More editing (Y or N)? N

A NATION CONCEIVED IN LIBERTY AND AND DEDICATED
Edit this line? Y
Edit change:
A/A NEW/
A NEW NATION CONCEIVED IN LIBERTY AND AND DEDICATED
More editing (Y or N)? Y
Edit change:
AND //
A NEW NATION CONCEIVED IN LIBERTY AND DEDICATED
More editing (Y or N)? N

TO THE PREPOSITION THAT ALL MEN
Edit this line? Y
Edit change:
RE/RO/
TO THE PROPOSITION THAT ALL MEN
More editing (Y or N)? N

ARE CREATED EQUAL.
Edit this line? N

Enter name of output file.
out> EDITED
```

Figure 11.1 (cont.)

<u>Listing of file EDITED:</u>

```
FOURSCORE AND SEVEN YEARS AGO, OUR FATHERS
BROUGHT FORTH ON THIS CONTINENT
A NEW NATION CONCEIVED IN LIBERTY AND DEDICATED
TO THE PROPOSITION THAT ALL MEN
ARE CREATED EQUAL.
```

The characters that comprise a text file like that used in Figure 11.1 are stored using a standard coding scheme such as ASCII and EBCDIC, and when a text file is listed, these codes are automatically converted to the corresponding characters by the terminal, printer, or other output device and become *legible* to the user. On the other hand, the information in a binary file is *illegible* because it is stored using the internal representation scheme for the particular computer being used, and this representation usually cannot be displayed correctly in character form by the output device. The diagram in Figure 11.2 illustrates this difference for the number 32767.

Binary files usually can be created only with a program, and their contents can be accessed only within a program. Attempting to list the contents of such a file by using the system text editor or some other system command usually causes "garbage" or some error message to be displayed. For example, listing the contents of the binary file *GPAFile* produced by the program in Figure 11.3 produced the following on one system:

@Ä @|ÃÃ@h₁¬ @Iôô@8₁¬ @@£◇ @KÖæ@6ff@
p£@ææΠ?Δff?Bè[?¯QÎ@æè\@Ä @Ä @æ @æ @@£◇ @?\)

There are, however, some advantages in using binary files. The primary advantage is that the information in such files can be transferred between main memory and secondary memory more rapidly, since it is already in a form that requires no decoding or encoding. Another advantage is that the data is usually

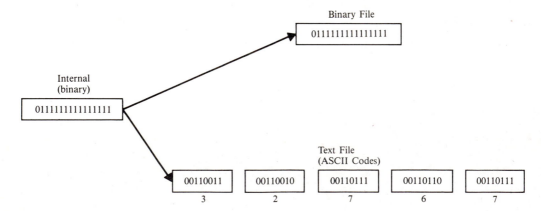

Figure 11.2

stored more compactly if it is stored using its internal rather than its external representation in one of the standard coding schemes; Figure 11.2 illustrates this.

The library module *FileSystem* supports both text files and binary files. The file-processing facilities described in the preceding section, with the exception of procedures *ReadChar* and *WriteChar*, may be used with both kinds of files. Whereas text files are viewed as sequences of characters or bytes, binary files are viewed as sequences of words. Thus, although *ReadChar* and *WriteChar* are appropriate for text files, they are not appropriate for binary files. In their place, a file-processing module like *FileSystem* provides procedures *ReadWord* and *WriteWord* for processing binary files.

The procedure *ReadWord* in *Filesystem* is called with a statement of the form

> *ReadWord(file-variable, w)*

where *file-variable* is of type *File* and *w* is a variable of type WORD. The type **WORD** must be imported from the library module SYSTEM. Values of type WORD are simply bit strings that can be stored in one word of memory. Since these bit strings are not interpreted as any particular type, no operations can be performed on them other than assignment to variables of type WORD.

The procedure *WriteWord* in *FileSystem* is used to write the value of a variable of type WORD at the end of a binary file. It is called with a statement of the form

> *WriteWord(file-variable, w)*

where *file-variable* is of type *File* and *w* is of type WORD. This procedure simply appends the bit string stored in the memory word associated with *w* to the specified file.

Wirth's version of *FileSystem* does not include procedures for reading and writing blocks of words. However, the procedures *ReadWord* and *WriteWord* can be used in the design of such procedures:

```
PROCEDURE ReadBlock(InFile : FILE; Block : ARRAY OF WORD);

    (* Procedure to read a Block of words from binary file InFile *)

    VAR
        i : CARDINAL;     (* index *)
    BEGIN
        FOR i := 0 TO HIGH(Block) DO
            ReadWord(InFile, Block[i])
        END (* FOR *)
    END ReadBlock;

PROCEDURE WriteBlock(InFile : FILE; Block : ARRAY OF WORD);

    (* Procedure to write a Block of words at the end of binary file
        InFile *)
```

```
VAR
    i : CARDINAL;      (* index *)
BEGIN
    FOR i := 0 TO HIGH(Block) DO
        WriteWord(InFile, Block[i])
    END (* FOR *)
END WriteBlock;
```

It is important to note that in procedure references, *an actual parameter corresponding to a formal open array parameter of type* WORD *may be of any type*. Thus an actual parameter corresponding to the formal parameter *Block* in procedures *ReadBlock* and *WriteBlock* may be of any type—an integer, an array of real numbers, a string, a record, an array of records, and so on. Because of this generality, we assume that these procedures are included in the special library module *SpecialInOut* (see Appendix F).

As a simple illustration, suppose that high school and college grade-point averages (GPAs) are to be compared and that we wish to read pairs of such GPAs, one pair for each student, and store these in a binary file *GPAFile*. This file can be created by a program in which pairs of real values representing GPAs are entered by the user and stored in a record of type

```
GPARecord = RECORD
                HighSchool, College : REAL
            END;
```

Each record is written to *GPAFile* using the procedure *WriteBlock*.

The program in Figure 11.3 creates the desired file. It first opens the file *GPAFile* and then has the user enter pairs of real numbers representing pairs of GPAs, using the procedure *WriteBlock* to write each pair to *GPAFile*.

```
MODULE CreateGPAFile;

(**********************************************************************

   Program to create the binary file GPAFile storing pairs of grade
   point averages which are input by the user during execution.

 **********************************************************************)

   FROM FileSystem IMPORT File, Lookup, Close, WriteWord;
   FROM InOut IMPORT Write, WriteString, WriteLn, ReadString;
   FROM RealInOut IMPORT ReadReal;
   FROM SpecialInOut IMPORT WriteBlock;

   CONST
       StringLimit = 32;
```

Figure 11.3

Figure 11.3 (cont.)

```
TYPE
    GPARecord = RECORD
                    HighSchool, College: REAL
                END;
    String = ARRAY [0..StringLimit] OF CHAR;

VAR
    GPAPair : GPARecord;        (* pair of grade point averages *)
    GPAFile : File;             (* file of GPA records created *)
    FileName : String;          (* name of file to be created *)

BEGIN
    WriteString('Name of file to be created?  ');
    ReadString(FileName);
    Lookup(TextFile, OldFileName, TRUE);
    WriteLn;
    WriteString(Enter negative GPA's to stop.');
    LOOP
        WriteLn;
        WriteString('GPA pair?  ');
        ReadReal(GPAPair.HighSchool);
        ReadReal(GPAPair.College);
        IF (GPAPair.HighSchool < 0.0) THEN EXIT END;
        WriteBlock(GPAFile, GPAPair)
    END (* LOOP *);
    WriteLn;
    WriteString('Creation of GPAFile completed');
    WriteLn;
    Close(GPAFile)
END CreateGPAFile.
```

Sample run:

```
Enter negative GPA's to stop.
GPA pair?  4.00 3.95
GPA pair?  3.64 3.15
GPA pair?  2.89 3.01
GPA pair?  3.18 2.85
GPA pair?  2.21 2.33
GPA pair?  1.55 0.76
GPA pair?  1.94 2.04
GPA pair?  4.00 4.00
GPA pair?  2.25 2.25
GPA pair?  3.01 2.99
GPA pair?  -1-1
Creation of GPAFile completed
```

As an illustration of input from binary files, suppose that we wish to examine the contents of the file *GPAFile* created by the program in Figure 11.3. Blocks of words can be read from the file and assigned to the variable *GPAPair* of type *GPARecord* with the statement

ReadBlock(GPAFile, GPAPair)

and the values of the two fields of *GPAPair* can then be displayed:

FWriteReal(GPAPair.HighSchool, 4, 2);
FWriteReal(GPAPair.College, 7, 2);

In the program in Figure 11.4, these two statements are repeated until the end of *GPAFile* is encountered.

```
MODULE ReadGPAFile;

(*********************************************************************

   Program to read and display the contents of the permanent file
   GPAFile created by the program of Figure 11.2 or 11.3.

   *********************************************************************)

   FROM FileSystem IMPORT File, Lookup, Close, ReadWord;
   FROM InOut IMPORT WriteString, WriteLn, ReadString;
   FROM SpecialInOut IMPORT FWriteReal, ReadBlock;

   CONST
       StringLimit = 32;

   TYPE
       GPARecord = RECORD
                       HighSchool, College: REAL
                   END;
       String = ARRAY [0..StringLimit] OF CHAR;

   VAR
       GPAPair : GPARecord;       (* pair of grade point averages *)
       GPAFile : File;            (* file of GPA records to read *)
       FileName : String;         (* name of file to be read *)

BEGIN
    WriteString('Name of file to be read?  ');
    ReadString(FileName);
    Lookup(TextFile, OldFileName, FALSE);
    WriteLn;
    WriteString('Contents of GPAFile:');
    WriteLn;
    ReadBlock(GPAFile, GPAPair);
    WHILE NOT GPAFile.EOF DO
        FWriteReal(GPAPair.HighSchool, 5, 2);
        FWriteReal(GPAPair.College, 7, 2);
        WriteLn;
        ReadBlock(GPAFile, GPAPair);
    END (* WHILE *)
    Close(GPAFile)
END ReadGPAFile.
```

Figure 11.4

Figure 11.4 (cont.)

Sample run:

Contents of GPAFile:
```
 4.00   3.95
 3.64   3.15
 2.89   3.01
 3.18   2.85
 2.21   2.33
 1.55   0.76
 1.94   2.04
 4.00   4.00
 2.25   2.25
 3.01   2.99
```

11.2 File Updating

One important file-processing problem is file updating, that is, changing the contents of a file by inserting new records into the file, by deleting some records from the file, or by modifying existing records in the file. We have already considered several instances of this problem. For example, the program developed in Section 1.6 copied financial aid information from a text file into an array of records. The user could then modify any number of these records, and these records were written back into a file after the updating was completed. In other applications in which items of information in a file were processed, we copied these items into linked lists (see Section 7.7), a binary search tree (see Section 9.2), or a hash table (see Section 9.3). In all of these examples we assumed that the file was small enough that its contents could be copied and stored in their entirety in main memory. In this section we consider a file-updating problem in which no such assumption is made. In particular, we consider the problem of modifying the records in a master file using the information in a transaction file, where both files are to be processed sequentially. For example, the master file may be an inventory file that is to be updated with a transactions file containing the day's sales and returns; or the master file may be a file of student records that is to be updated with a transaction file containing student grades for a given semester.

Here we consider the problem of updating a master file containing information regarding the users of a university's computing system. The components of the master file *UsersFile* are records, each of which consists of the identification number, name, password, limit on resources, and resources used to date for one user. A daily log of the system's activity is also maintained. Among other items of information, this log contains a list of user identification numbers and resources used for each job entered into the system. This list is maintained in the transaction file *UpdateFile*. At the end of each day, the master file *UsersFile* must be updated with the contents of *UpdateFile* to incorporate the activities of that day.

This type of updating of sequential files can be done most easily and efficiently if both files have been previously sorted (using some sorting scheme like that in the next section) so that the values in some common key field appear

in ascending (or descending) order. An algorithm for performing such file updating is as follows:

ALGORITHM FOR UPDATING A MASTER FILE
USING A TRANSACTIONS FILE

(* Algorithm to update records in a file *MasterFile* with information
from a transactions file *TransFile* to produce *NewMasterFile*. It is
assumed that the records in these files are ordered so that values in
some common key field are in ascending order and that all values in
both files are valid. *)

1. Read the first record from *MasterFile* and assign it to *MasterRec*.
2. Read the first record from *TransFile* and assign it to *TransRec*.
3. Initialize a boolean variable *EndOfUpdate* to false.
4. While not *EndOfUpdate* do the following updating:

   Compare the key fields of *MasterRec* and *TransRec*. If they
   match, do the following:
   a. Update *MasterRec* using the information in *TransRec*.
   b. If the end of *TransFile* has been reached, set *EndOfUpdate*
      to true; otherwise read the next value for *TransRec* from
      TransFile.

   If the key fields do not match, do the following:
   a. Write *MasterRec* to *NewMasterFile*.
   b. Read a new value for *MasterRec* from *MasterFile*.

5. Because the last updated master record has not been written, write
   MasterRec to *NewMasterFile*.
6. Copy any remaining records in *MasterFile* into *NewMasterFile*.

The program in Figure 11.5 uses this algorithm to update the contents of
UsersFile with the entries in *UpdateFile* and produces *NewUsersFile*. Also
shown are the contents of two small files used in a sample run and the updated
file produced. The listings of these nontext files were obtained using programs
like those in Figure 11.4.

```
MODULE UserFileUpdate;

(***********************************************************************

    Program to update the entries in the master file UsersFile with
    the entries in the transactions file UpdateFile.  The records
    in UsersFile contain the id-number, name, password, resource
    limit, and resources used to date for each system user.
    UpdateFile represents the log of a day's activities; each
    record contains a user's id-number and resources used for a
```

Figure 11.5

Figure 11.5 (cont.)

```
        job entered into the system.  Both files are sorted so that
        id-numbers are in ascending order, and all id-numbers in
        UsersFile are assumed to be valid.  The updated records are
        written to the output file NewUsersFile.


*********************************************************************)

        FROM FileSystem IMPORT File, Lookup, Close, ReadWord, WriteWord;
        FROM InOut IMPORT Write, WriteString, WriteLn, ReadString;
        FROM RealInOut IMPORT ReadReal;
        FROM SpecialInOut IMPORT ReadBlock, WriteBlock;

        CONST
            NameLength = 20;              (* lengths of names *)
            PasswordLength = 4;           (* lengths of passwords *)

        TYPE
            NameString = ARRAY[0..NameLength] OF CHAR;
            PasswordString = ARRAY[0..PasswordLength] OF CHAR;
            UserRecord = RECORD
                            IdNumber : CARDINAL;
                            Name : NameString;
                            Password : PasswordString;
                            ResourceLimit,
                            UsedToDate : CARDINAL
                         END;
            UserUpdateRecord = RECORD
                                  IdNumber,
                                  ResourcesUsed : CARDINAL
                               END;

    VAR
        UserRec : UserRecord;             (* record from UsersFile *)
        UpdateRec : UserUpdateRecord;     (* record from UpdateFile *)
        UsersFile,                        (* file containing user information *)
        UpdateFile,                       (* file to update UsersFile *)
        NewUsersFile : File;              (* updated user file *)
        UsersFileName,                    (* actual name of UsersFile *)
        UpdateFileName,                   (* actual name of UpdateFile *)
        NewFileName : NameString;         (* actual name of new updated file *)
        EndOfUpdate : BOOLEAN;            (* signals end of UpdateFile *)

BEGIN
    (* Open the files *)
    WriteString('Name of master users file? ');
    ReadString(UsersFileName);
    WriteString('Name of update file? ');
    ReadString(UpdateFileName);
    WriteString('Name of new file to be created? ');
    ReadString(NewFileName);

    Lookup(UsersFile, UsersFileName, FALSE);
    Lookup(UpdateFile, UpdateFileName, FALSE);
    Lookup(NewUsersFile, NewFileName, TRUE);
```

Figure 11.5   (cont.)

```
(* Read first record from each file *)

ReadBlock(UsersFile, UserRec);
ReadBlock(UpdateFile, UpdateRec);

(* Update records of UsersFile with records of UpdateFile *)

EndOfUpdate := FALSE;
WHILE NOT EndOfUpdate DO
    IF UserRec.IdNumber = UpdateRec.IdNumber THEN   (* id-numbers match *)
        WITH UserRec DO
            UsedToDate := UsedToDate + UpdateRec.ResourcesUsed
        END (* WITH *);
        IF  UpdateFile.eof THEN
            EndOfUpdate := TRUE
        ELSE
            ReadBlock(UpdateFile, UpdateRec)
        END (* IF *)
    ELSE                                            (* no match *)
        WriteBlock(NewUsersFile, UserRec);
        ReadBlock(UsersFile, UserRec)
    END (* IF *)
END (* WHILE *);

(* Write UserRec to NewUsersFile; then copy any
    remaining records from UsersFile *)

WriteBlock(NewUsersFile, UserRec);
ReadBlock(UsersFile, UserRec);
WHILE NOT  UsersFile.eof DO
    WriteBlock(NewUsersFile, UserRec);
    ReadBlock(UsersFile, UserRec);
END (* WHILE *);

Close(UsersFile);
Close(UpdateFile);
Close(NewUsersFile);

END UserFileUpdate.
```

Sample run:

```
Name of master users file? USERS
Name of update file? USERUPDATE
Name of new file to be created? NEWUSERS
```

Contents of USERS: Contents of USERUPDATE:

```
12300 JOHN DOE                                        12300 10
GERM 200 125                                          12300 24
12310 MARY SMITH                                      12310 17
SNOW 200  75                                          12310 3
13320 PETE VANDERVAN                                  12310 5
RAIN 300 228                                          12310 10
13400 FRED JONES                                      13400 28
```

Figure 11.5   (cont.)

```
FROM 100    0                          13450 25
13450 JANE TARZAN                      13450 3
JUST 200   63                          13450 1
13490 JACK JACKSON                     13450 13
DATE 300 128                           14010 22
14000 ALBERT ALBERTS                   14010 5
LIST 400 255                           14010 12
14010 JESSE JAMES                      14010 7
GUNS 100   38
14040 DIRTY GERTIE
MESS 100   17
14100 PRINCE ALBERT
CANS 300 185
```

Contents of NEWUSERS:

```
12300 JOHN DOE
GERM 200 159
12310 MARY SMITH
SNOW 200 110
13320 PETE VANDERVAN
RAIN 300 228
13400 FRED JONES
FROM 100   28
13450 JANE TARZAN
JUST 200 105
13490 JACK JACKSON
DATE 300 128
14000 ALBERT ALBERTS
LIST 400 255
14010 JESSE JAMES
GUNS 100   84
14040 DIRTY GERTIE
MESS 100   17
14100 PRINCE ALBERT
CANS 300 185
```

Exercises

1. Write a procedure to concatenate two text files.

2. Write a text-file version of procedure *WriteLn*; that is, write a procedure that writes an end-of-line character to a specified text file.

3. Write a text-file version of procedure *WriteCard*; that is, write a procedure for output of a CARDINAL value to a specified text file.

4. Using the procedure in Exercise 3, write a text-file version of procedure *WriteInt*; that is, write a procedure for output of an INTEGER value to a specified text file.

In each of the following exercises, the files *InventoryFile*, *Inventory-Update*, *UsersFile*, *StudentFile*, and *StudentUpdate* should be processed as binary files, and the contents read and interpreted as records. See Appendix E for descriptions of these records.

5. Write a program to search *InventoryFile* to find an item with a specified stock number. If a match is found, display the item name and the number currently in stock; otherwise, display a message indicating that it was not found.

6. At the end of each month, a report is produced that shows the status of the account of each user in *UsersFile*. Write a program to read the current date and produce a report of the following form:

USER ACCOUNTS—09/30/89

USER NAME	USER-ID	RESOURCE LIMIT	RESOURCES USED
Joseph Miltgen	10101	$750	$381
Isaac Small	10102	$650	$599***
.	.	.	.
.	.	.	.
.	.	.	.

where the three asterisks (***) indicate that the user has already used 90 percent or more of the resources available to him or her.

7. Write a program to update *InventoryFile* with *InventoryUpdate* to produce a new inventory file. Each record in *InventoryFile* for which there is no record in *InventoryUpdate* with a matching item number should remain unchanged. Each record with one or more corresponding records in *InventoryUpdate* should be updated with the entries in the update file. For transaction code R, the number of items returned should be added to the number in stock. For transaction code S, the number of items sold should be subtracted from the number currently in stock; if more items are sold than are in stock, display a message showing the order number, stock number, item name, and how many should be backordered (that is, the difference between the number ordered and the number in stock), and set the number currently in stock to zero.

8. (Project) Write a program to read the files *StudentFile* and *StudentUpdate* and produce an updated grade report. This grade report should show

(a) The current date.
(b) The student's name and student number.
(c) A list of the names, grades, and credits for each of the current courses under the headings COURSE, GRADE, and CREDITS.
(d) Current GPA (multiply credits by numeric grade—A = 4.0, A− = 3.7, B+ = 3.3, B = 3.0, . . . , D− = 0.7, F = 0.0—

for each course to find honor points earned for that course; sum these to find total new honor points; and then divide total new honor points by total new credits to give the current GPA, rounded to two decimal places).

(e) Total credits taken (old credits from *StudentFile* plus total new credits).

(f) New cumulative GPA (first calculate old honor points = old credits times old cumulative GPA and then new cumulative GPA = sum of old honor points and new honor points divided by updated total credits.)

9. (Project) Write a *text editor* that performs editing operations on the lines of a text file. Include commands of the following forms in the menu of options:

F *n*	Find and display the *n*th line of the file.
P *n*	Print *n* consecutive lines beginning with the current line.
M *n*	Move ahead *n* lines from the current line.
T	Move to the top line of the file.
C/*string1*/*string2*/	Change the current line by replacing *string1* with *string2*.
L *string*	Search the file starting from the current line to find a line containing *string*.
D *n*	Delete *n* consecutive lines beginning with the current line.
I *line*	Insert the given *line* after the current line.

10. (Project) Write a program to implement a computer dating service. It should accept a person's name, sex, and interests (sports, music preference, religion, and the like) and then search a file containing records having these items of information to find the person(s) of the opposite sex who has the most interests in common with the given individual.

11. (Project) Write a menu-driven program that uses *Studentfile* and *StudentUpdate* and allows (some of) the following options. For each option, write a separate procedure so that options and corresponding procedures can be easily added or removed.

1. Locate a student's permanent record when given his or her student number and print it in a nice format.
2. Same as Option 1, but locate the record when given his or her name.
3. Print a list of all student names and numbers in a given class (1, 2, 3, 4, 5).
4. Same as Option 3, but for a given major.
5. Same as Option 3, but for a given range of cumulative GPAs.
6. Find the average cumulative GPAs for all
   (a) females   (b) males   (c) students with a specified major
   (d) all students. (These are suboptions of Menu Option 6.)

11.3 Mergesort

Sorting schemes can be classified as *internal* or *external* according to whether the collection of data items to be sorted is stored in main memory or in secondary memory. The sorting schemes described in the preceding chapter were internal sorts. In this section we describe two versions of a popular external sorting scheme known as *mergesort*.

As the name suggests, the basic operation in mergesort is *file merging*, that is, combining two files that have previously been sorted so that the resulting file is also sorted. As a simple illustration, suppose that *File1* contains eight integers in increasing order,

File1: 15 20 25 35 45 60 65 70

and *File2* contains five integers in increasing order:

File2: 10 30 40 50 55

In practice, of course, files contain many more items, and each item is usually a record containing several different types of information, and as we have commented before, sorting is then based on some key field within these records.

To merge files *File1* and *File2* to produce sorted *File3*, we read one element from each file, say *X* from *File1* and *Y* from *File2*:

File1: 15 20 25 35 45 60 65 70
X

File2: 10 30 40 50 55
Y

We compare these items and write the smaller, in this case *Y*, to *File3*:

File3: 10

and then read another value for *Y* from *File2*:

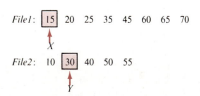

Now *X* is smaller than *Y*, and so it is written to *File3*, and a new value for *X* is read from *File1*:

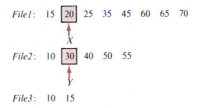

Again, *X* is less than *Y*, and so it is written to *File3* and a new *X* value is read from *File1*:

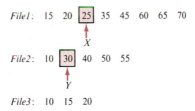

Continuing in this manner, we eventually reach the value 60 for *X* and the last value in *File2*, 55, for *Y*:

```
File1:  15  20  25  35  45  60  65  70
                            X
File2:  10  30  40  50  55
                        Y
File3:  15  20  25  30  35  40  45  50
```

Because *Y* < *X*, we write *Y* to *File3*:

```
File3:  15  20  25  30  35  40  45  50  55
```

Because the end of *File2* has been reached, we simply copy the remaining items in *File1* to *File3* to complete the merging:

```
File3:  15  20  25  30  35  40  45  50  55  60  65  70
```

The general algorithm for merging two sorted files is

MERGE

(∗ Algorithm to merge sorted files *File1* and *File2* giving *File3* ∗)

1. Open *File1* and *File2* for input, *File3* for output.
2. Read the first element *X* from *File1* and the first element *Y* from *File2*.
3. Repeat the following until the end of either *File1* or *File2* is reached:

If $X < Y$, then
    (i) Write X to *File3*.
    (ii) Read a new X value from *File1*.
Otherwise
    (i) Write Y to *File3*.
    (ii) Read a new Y value from *File2*.
4. If the end of *File1* was encountered, copy any remaining elements from *File2* into *File3*. If the end of *File2* was encountered, copy the rest of *File1* into *File3*.

To see how the merge operation can be used in sorting a file, consider the following file F containing sixteen integers:

$$F: \quad 75 \quad 55 \quad 15 \quad 20 \quad 85 \quad 30 \quad 35 \quad 10 \quad 60 \quad 40 \quad 50 \quad 25 \quad 45 \quad 80 \quad 70 \quad 65$$

We begin by copying the elements of F alternately into two other files $F1$ and $F2$:

$$F1: \quad 75 \quad 15 \quad 85 \quad 35 \quad 60 \quad 50 \quad 45 \quad 70$$

$$F2: \quad 55 \quad 20 \quad 30 \quad 10 \quad 40 \quad 25 \quad 80 \quad 65$$

We now merge the first one-element subfile of $F1$ with the first one-element subfile of $F2$ to give a sorted two-element subfile of F:

$$F1: \quad \boxed{75} \quad 15 \quad 85 \quad 35 \quad 60 \quad 50 \quad 45 \quad 70$$

$$F2: \quad \boxed{55} \quad 20 \quad 30 \quad 10 \quad 40 \quad 25 \quad 80 \quad 65$$

$$F: \quad \boxed{55 \quad 75}$$

Next the second one-element subfile of $F1$ is merged with the second one-element subfile of $F2$ and written to F:

$$F1: \quad 75 \quad \boxed{15} \quad 85 \quad 35 \quad 60 \quad 50 \quad 45 \quad 70$$

$$F2: \quad 55 \quad \boxed{20} \quad 30 \quad 10 \quad 40 \quad 25 \quad 80 \quad 65$$

$$F: \quad 55 \quad 75 \quad \boxed{15 \quad 20}$$

This merging of corresponding one-element subfiles continues until the end of either or both of the files $F1$ and $F2$ is reached. If either file still contains a subfile, it is simply copied into F:

$$F: \quad \boxed{55 \quad 75} \quad \boxed{15 \quad 20} \quad \boxed{30 \quad 85} \quad \boxed{10 \quad 35} \quad \boxed{40 \quad 60} \quad \boxed{25 \quad 50} \quad \boxed{45 \quad 80} \quad \boxed{65 \quad 70}$$

As the highlighted blocks indicate, the file F now consists of a sequence of two-element subfiles. We again split it into files $F1$ and $F2$, copying these two-element subfiles alternately to $F1$ and $F2$:

Now we merge corresponding subfiles in *F1* and *F2* to produce four-element sorted subfiles in *F*:

Now, using four-element subfiles, we again split *F* by copying subfiles alternately to *F1* and *F2*:

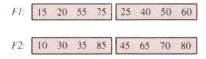

and then merge corresponding four-element subfiles to produce eight-element sorted subfiles in *F*:

F: | 10 15 20 30 35 55 75 85 | 25 40 45 50 60 65 70 80 |

The next splitting into files *F1* and *F2* produces

F1: | 10 15 20 30 35 55 75 85 |

F2: | 25 40 45 50 60 65 70 80 |

and merging corresponding eight-element subfiles in *F1* and *F2* produces one sorted sixteen-element sorted subfile in *F*:

F: | 10 15 20 25 30 35 40 45 50 55 60 65 70 75 80 85 |

Because there are only sixteen elements in *F*, they are now in order; that is, *F* has been sorted.

In this example, the size of *F* is a power of 2, so that all the subfiles produced by the split and merge operations are of the same size, and this size is also a power of 2. In general, this is true for all of the subfiles except possibly for the last one, which may have fewer elements. Although this means that some care must be exercised in checking for the ends of files and subfiles in this version of mergesort, known as **binary mergesort**, it does not present any serious difficulties in designing the required split and merge algorithms.

A more serious criticism of binary mergesort is that it restricts itself to subfiles of sizes 1, 2, 4, 8, . . . , 2^k, where $2^k \geq$ size of *F* and must therefore always go through a series of *k* split–merge phases. If sorted subfiles of other sizes are allowed, the number of phases can be reduced in those situations in which the file contains longer "runs" of elements that are already in order. A version of mergesort that takes advantage of these "natural" sorted subfiles (in contrast with the "artificial" sizes and subfiles created by binary mergesort) is called *natural mergesort*, naturally.

As an illustration of natural mergesort, consider again the file F used to demonstrate binary mergesort:

F: 75   55   15   20   85   30   35   10   60   40   50   25   45   80   70   65

Notice that several segments of F consist of elements that are already in order

F: 75 | 55 | 15   20   85 | 30   35 | 10   60 | 40   50 | 25   45   80 | 70 | 65

and that these sorted subfiles subdivide F in a natural way.

We begin as before by copying subfiles of F alternately to two other files, $F1$ and $F2$, but using these natural subfiles rather than requiring that, at each stage, their sizes be a power of 2:

$F1$:   75 | 15   20   85 | 10   60 | 25   45   80 | 65

$F2$:   55 | 30   35 | 40   50 | 70

We now identify the natural sorted subfiles in each of $F1$ and $F2$:

$F1$:   75 | 15   20   85 | 10   60 | 25   45   80 | 65

$F2$:   55 | 30   35   40   50   70

Notice that although the subfiles of $F1$ are the same as those copied from F, the last three subfiles written to $F2$ have combined to form a larger subfile.

Now, proceeding as in binary mergesort, we merge the first subfile of $F1$ with the first one in $F2$ to produce a sorted subfile in F.

F: 55   75

and then merge the second subfiles:

F: 55   75 | 15   20   30   35   40   50   70   85

Since we have now reached the end of $F2$, we simply copy the remaining subfiles of $F1$ back to F:

F: 55   75 | 15   20   30   35   40   50   70   85 | 10   60 | 25   45   80 | 65

Now we again split F, alternately copying sorted subfiles to $F1$ and $F2$:

$F1$: | 55 75 | 10 60 | 65 |

$F2$: | 15 20 30 35 40 50 70 85 | 25 45 80 |

This time we see that two subfiles of $F1$ combine to form a larger subfile:

$F1$: | 55 75 | 10 60 65 |

$F2$: | 15 20 30 35 40 50 70 85 | 25 45 80 |

As before, we merge corresponding subfiles of $F1$ and $F2$, writing the results back to F:

F: | 15 20 30 35 40 50 55 70 75 85 | 10 25 45 60 65 80 |

In the next phase, splitting F produces files $F1$ and $F2$, each of which contains only one sorted subfile, and thus they are themselves completely sorted files:

$F1$: | 15 20 30 35 40 50 55 70 75 85 |

$F2$: | 10 25 45 60 65 80 |

Consequently, when we perform the merge operation in this phase, F will be a sorted file:

F: | 10 15 20 25 30 35 40 45 50 55 60 65 70 75 80 85 |

Notice that one less split–merge phase was required here than in binary mergesort.

The splitting operation in natural mergesort is carried out by the following algorithm:

SPLIT ALGORITHM FOR NATURAL MERGESORT

($*$ Algorithm to split file F into files $F1$ and $F2$ by copying natural sorted subfiles of F alternately to $F1$ and $F2$. $*$)

1. Open the file F for input and the files $F1$ and $F2$ for output.
2. While the end of F has not been reached, do the following:
   a. Copy a sorted subfile of F into $F1$ as follows: Repeatedly read an element of F and write it into $F1$ until the next element in F is smaller than this copied item or the end of F is reached.
   b. If the end of F has not been reached, copy the next sorted subfile of F into $F2$ in a similar manner.

And the following algorithm implements the merge operation illustrated in the example:

MERGE ALGORITHM FOR NATURAL MERGESORT

(* Algorithm to merge corresponding sorted subfiles in *F1* and *F2* back into file *F*. *NumSubFiles* is the number of sorted subfiles produced in F. *)

1. Open files *F1* and *F2* for input, *F* for output.
2. Initialize *NumSubFiles* to 0.
3. While neither the end of *F1* nor the end of *F2* has been reached, do the following:
    a. While the end of no subfile in *F1* or in *F2* has been reached, do the following:

    If the next element in *F1* is less than the next element in *F2*, then copy the next element from *F1* into *F*; otherwise, copy the next element from *F2* into *F*.

    b. If the end of a subfile in *F1* has been reached, then copy the rest of the corresponding subfile in *F2* to *F*; otherwise, copy the rest of the corresponding subfile in *F1* to *F*.
    c. Increment *NumSubFiles* by 1.
4. Copy any remaining subfiles remaining in *F1* or *F2* to *F*, incrementing *NumSubFiles* by 1 for each.

An algorithm for natural mergesort consists of simply calling these two algorithms repeatedly until the file is sorted:

NATURAL MERGESORT

(* Algorithm to sort a file *F* using the two auxiliary files *F1* and *F2*. *)

Repeat the following steps

1. Call the *Split* algorithm to split *F* into files *F1* and *F2*.
2. Call the *Merge* algorithm to merge corresponding subfiles in *F1* and *F2* back into *F*.

Until *NumSubFiles* = 1.

Mergesort can also be used as an internal sorting method for lists. The split and merge algorithms can easily be modified to use arrays or linked lists in place of the files *F*, *F1*, and *F2*.

The worst case for natural mergesort occurs when the items are in reverse order. In this case, natural mergesort functions in exactly the same way as binary mergesort does, using subfiles of sizes 1, 2, 4, 8, and so on. It follows that to sort a file or list of *n* items, $\log_2 n$ split and merge operations are required, and each of the *n* items must be examined in each of them. Hence, in the worst case, and as can be shown for the average case also, the complexity of natural mergesort is $O(n \log_2 n)$.

Exercises

1. Using diagrams like those in the text, show the various splitting–merging stages of binary mergesort for the following lists of numbers:

   (a) 13, 57, 39, 85, 70, 22, 64, 48
   (b) 13, 57, 39, 85, 99, 70, 22, 48, 64
   (c) 13, 22, 57, 99, 39, 64, 57, 48, 70
   (d) 13, 22, 39, 48, 57, 64, 70, 85
   (e) 85, 70, 64, 57, 48, 39, 22, 13

2. Repeat Exercise 1 but use natural mergesort.

3. Write a program that sorts a file of names using

   (a) binary mergesort
   (b) natural mergesort

4. Write a program to read records from *UsersFile* (see Appendix E) and then sort them using

   (a) binary mergesort
   (b) natural mergesort

   so that the resources used to date are in increasing order.

5. Write a program that uses

   (a) binary mergesort
   (b) natural mergesort

   appropriately modified, to sort a list stored in an array.

6. Proceed as in Exercise 4, but for a linked list. For the merge operation, merge the two linked lists by simply changing links rather than actually copying the list elements into a third list.

7. Suppose that we sort a list of records in which some of the values in the key field may be the same. A sorting scheme is said to be **stable** if it does not change the order of such records. For example, consider a list of records containing a person's name and age that is to be sorted so that the ages are in ascending order. Suppose that

   comes before

   in the original list (with possibly several records between them). For a stable sorting scheme, Doe's record still comes before Smith's after the sorting is carried out. Determine whether each of the following is a stable sorting method:

(a) Selection sort
(b) Bubble sort
(c) Insertion sort
(d) Heapsort
(e) Quicksort
(f) Binary mergesort
(g) Natural mergesort

8. One variation of the mergesort method is obtained by modifying the splitting operation as follows: Copy some fixed number of elements into main memory, sort them using an internal sorting method such as quicksort, and write this sorted list to *F1*; then read the same number of elements from *F* into main memory, sort them internally, and write this sorted list to *F2*, and so on, alternating between *F1* and *F2*. Write procedures for this modified mergesort scheme, using quicksort to sort internally the sublists containing *Size* elements for some constant *Size*.

9. Write a procedure to carry out a ***three-way merge***, that is, a procedure that merges three sorted files to form another sorted file.

10. Use the procedure in Exercise 9 to merge three files of records containing names and phone numbers, sorted so that the names are in alphabetical order. For duplicate entries in the files, put only one entry in the final file.

11. Use the procedure in Exercise 9 in a program that performs a ***ternary mergesort***, which differs from binary mergesort in that three files rather than two are used to split a given file.

12. (Project) Write a program to read titles of books or magazine articles and prepare a KWIC (Key Word In Context) index. Each word in a title except for such simple words as AND, OF, THE, A, and the like is considered to be a keyword. The program should read the titles and construct a file containing the keywords together with the corresponding title, sort the file using the mergesort method, and then display the KWIC index. For example, the titles

FUNDAMENTALS OF PROGRAMMING

PROGRAMMING FUNDAMENTALS FOR DATA STRUCTURES

should produce the following KWIC index:

DATA STRUCTURES // PROGRAMMING FUNDAMENTALS FOR

FUNDAMENTALS FOR DATA STRUCTURES // PROGRAMMING
OF PROGRAMMING

PROGRAMMING FUNDAMENTALS FOR DATA STRUCTURES
// FUNDAMENTALS OF

STRUCTURES // PROGRAMMING FUNDAMENTALS FOR DATA

13. If possible with your version of Modula-2, write a program to compare the computing times of binary mergesort and natural mergesort for files of randomly generated integers. (See Exercise 5 of Section 3.4 regarding how to measure execution time and Section 0.7 concerning random number generation.)

14. **Polyphase sort** is another external sorting scheme of the mergesort variety. A simple version of it begins by merging one-element subfiles in two files, *F1* and *F2*, forming sorted subfiles of size 2 in a third file, *F3*. However, only enough subfiles are merged to empty one of *F1* and *F2*—say, *F1*. The remaining one-element subfiles in *F2* are then merged with the two-element subfiles in *F3* to produce subfiles of length 3 and written to *F1* until *F2* becomes empty. The remaining two-element subfiles of *F3* are then merged with three-element subfiles of *F2* to form subfiles of length 5 in *F1* until the end of *F1* becomes empty. This process continues until sorting is complete.

Note that the sequence of subfile lengths in polyphase sort is 1, 1, 2, 3, 5, 8, 13, 21, 34, . . . , the sequence of **Fibonacci numbers** (see Section 5.2). The final subfile length (which is also the size of the original file *F3* to be sorted) must therefore be some Fibonacci number f_n. It also follows that the sizes of the initial subfiles *F1* and *F2* must be the two Fibonacci numbers f_{n-1} and f_{n-2}, which precede f_n. Write a program to sort a file using polyphase sort, adding "dummy" subfiles to one of *F1* to *F2* if necessary to make their sizes two consecutive Fibonacci numbers, and removing them when sorting is completed.

11.4 Direct Access Files

Direct access or **random access files** are files in which each component can be accessed directly by specifying its location in the file, thus making it possible to read or write components anywhere in the file. A direct access file can be thought of, therefore, as a very large array that is stored in secondary memory instead of in main memory (and so access to its components is slower than for arrays). In this section we illustrate some of the techniques used in processing direct access files.

Direct access files are opened in the same manner as are sequential files. As described in Section 11.1, the library module *FileSystem* provides procedures *LookUp* and *Create* for this purpose. The file should then be put in modify (read-write) mode using procedure *SetModify* if the file is to be updated by reading records from the file, modifying them, and writing them back to the file.

Before any component in a direct access file can be accessed, its location in the file must be determined. The procedure *SetPos* provided in Wirth's module *FileSystem* can then be used to position the file at that location. (*Seek* is the name of the corresponding procedure in some Modula-2 systems.) *SetPos* is called with a statement of the form

    SetPos(FileVar, HighPos, LowPos)

This statement sets the current position of the file associated with the specified file variable *FileVar* to byte

    $CurrPos = MaxCard * HighPos + LowPos$

Here *MaxCard* is the largest cardinal number allowed in a given system; a common value is 2^{16} for smaller machines and 2^{32} for larger ones.

To position the file at a particular component thus requires determining the component size in bytes (or words), and the predefined function procedure SIZE described in Section 7.4 can be used for this. Thus, for example, if *EmpFile* is a small file of employee records of type *EmployeeRecord* and we wish to position the file at the *RecNum*th record, we might use statements like the following:

    RecSize := SIZE(*EmployeeRecord*);
    RecPos := *RecNum* * *RecSize*;
    SetPos(EmpFile, 0, *RecPos*);

Here we have assumed that the file size and record size are sufficiently small that the value of *RecPos* does not exceed *MaxCard*. For larger files and/or larger records in which this might not be the case, we must assign *HighPos* and *LowPos* the values *RecPos* DIV (*MaxCard* + 1) and *RecPos* MOD (*MaxCard* + 1), respectively. However, these expressions cannot be calculated as written, since the value of *MaxCard* + 1 exceeds the maximum cardinal value allowed. Calculating these values without using the DIV and MOD operations is left as an exercise.

Once the file is positioned at the desired component, the procedures *ReadWord* and *WriteWord* (or *ReadByte* and *WriteByte* in some systems) can be used to read or write this file component. Since these procedures read from and write to a single memory word (byte), it is again convenient to use the procedures *ReadBlock* and *WriteBlock* described in Section 11.2 to read and write blocks of words. We have assumed that these procedures are available in the library module *SpecialInOut*.

In summary, the usual method for processing a given record is to position the file at that record and then use procedures such as *ReadBlock* to read this record and/or *WriteBlock* to write a new value at this position. For example, to display the social security number and name of the employee whose record is the *RecNum*th record in *EmpFile* and then modify some of the other fields in this record such as the pay rate, we could use

    RecSize := *BytesPerWord* * SIZE(*EmployeeRecord*);

```
RecPos := RecNum * RecSize;
SetPos(EmpFile, 0, RecPos);   (* assuming HighPos = 0 *)
ReadBlock(EmpFile, EmpRec);
WITH EmpRec DO
    WriteLn;
    WriteString('Employee: ');
    WriteString(SocSecNumber);
    Write(' ');
    WriteString(FirstName);
    Write(' ');
    WriteString(LastName);
    WriteLn;
    WriteString('Hourly rate: $');
    FWriteReal(HourlyRate, 8, 2);
    WriteLn;
    WriteString(' Enter new hourly pay rate: ');
    ReadReal(HourlyRate)
END (* WITH *);
SetPos(EmpFile, 0, RecPos);
WriteBlock(EmpFile, EmpRec);
```

Here *BytesPerWord* is a system-dependent constant that specifies the number of bytes in a memory word.

Of course, to access a particular component in a direct access file, it is necessary to know its component number. For example, suppose we wish to locate the record for an employee whose number *NumDesired* has been entered by the user during program execution. If the file were constructed so that the *n*th record in the file corresponds to the employee whose number is *n*, then the task would be trivial. However, this is not likely because, for example, if social security numbers are used for employee numbers, the record for employee 567-34-9999 would be stored in the 567,349,999th record in the file, but most of the file components numbered 0 through 567349998 would probably not be used.

Of course, we could simply perform a linear search of the file, but this does not take advantage of the fact that we have direct access to each component. An alternative strategy might be to use a hash function *h* so that *h(NumDesired)* is the number of the file component where this employee's record should be found and, if it is not, to search for it using the probe sequence or other search strategy consistent with the way the hash table was created. If the file has been sorted so that the employee numbers are in ascending order, for example, by using mergesort, then a binary search could be used since we have direct access to each file component.

One difficulty with most of these search techniques is the large number of file components that must be transferred from secondary memory to main memory, where they can be examined by the search procedure. Such transfers may be prohibitively time-consuming, especially if the records are large.

An alternative is to use an *index* to establish a correspondence between key values and component numbers. This index is a list of key values stored in main memory—in an array, for example—arranged in the same order as they appear in the file. Thus the location of a given key value in this list is the same as the number of the corresponding record in the file. We search this index for some particular key value using some internal search method such as binary search, and its position in this index is the number of the desired record in the file:

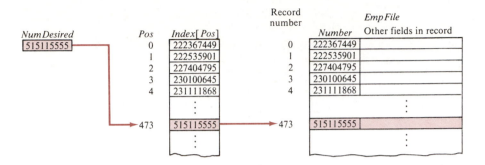

This record can then be fetched using only one transfer from secondary memory to main memory.

The file update program in Figure 11.6 illustrates the use of an index to locate an employee record in a direct access file *EmpFile*. This index is stored in the array *Index*, which is constructed by reading the employee numbers from a file. This program assumes that both files are sorted with employee numbers in ascending order, so that binary search can be used to locate an employee number entered by the user in this index. Once the record for that employee is retrieved from *EmpFile*, the user can then modify it. For simplicity, this program allows a change only in the hourly rate, but it can easily be modified to allow changes in the other fields of the employee records.

```
MODULE EmployeeFileUpdate;

(****************************************************************************

    Program to update a direct access file of employee records.
    An employee number is entered by the user, the number of the
    record in the file for this employee is looked up in Index, the
    record is retrieved and displayed, modifications are made, and
    the updated record is then rewritten to the file.

 *************************************************************************)

    FROM FileSystem IMPORT File, Lookup, Close, ReadWord, WriteWord,
                        SetModify, SetPos;
    FROM InOut IMPORT Write, WriteString, WriteLn, ReadString, ReadCard,
                        OpenInput, CloseInput;
    FROM RealInOut IMPORT ReadReal;
    FROM StringsLib IMPORT Compare;
    FROM SpecialInOut IMPORT FWriteReal, ReadBlock, WriteBlock;
```

Figure 11.6

Figure 11.6 (cont.)

```
CONST
    MaxRecNum = 100;    (* maximum number of records in the file *)
    StringLimit = 19;   (* limit on number of characters in strings *)
    BytesPerWord = 2;   (* number of bytes per memory word *)

TYPE
    String = ARRAY [0..StringLimit] OF CHAR;
    DeptType = (Factory, Office, Sales);
    EmployeeRecord =  RECORD
                        SocSecNumber,
                        LastName,
                        FirstName : String;
                        MidInitial : CHAR;
                        StreetAddress,
                        CityState,
                        PhoneNumber : String;
                        Sex : CHAR;
                        Age,
                        Dependents : CARDINAL;
                        Dept : DeptType;
                        Union : BOOLEAN;
                        HourlyRate : REAL
                      END;
    IndexArray = ARRAY[0..MaxRecNum] OF String;

VAR
    EmpFile : File;            (* direct access employee file *)
    RecNum,                    (* number of a record in EmpFile *)
    LastRecNum : CARDINAL;     (* number of last record in EmpFile *)
    EmpNumber,                 (* employee's social security number *)
    FileName : String;         (* actual name of  file *)
    Index : IndexArray;        (* index for EmpFile *)
    Found  : BOOLEAN;          (* signals if entry found in Index *)

PROCEDURE ConstructIndex(VAR Index : ARRAY OF String;
                         VAR Last : CARDINAL);

    (*****************************************************************

        Procedure to construct an Index of employee numbers by reading
        them in order from a file.   Returns this Index and Last
        location used in Index.

     *****************************************************************)

    VAR
        MaxIndex : CARDINAL;      (* maximum index in the array Index *)
        FileName,                 (* name of file to be read *)
        EmpNumber : String;       (* an employee's social security number *)
```

Figure 11.6   (cont.)

```
    BEGIN (* ConstructIndex *)
        WriteString('Enter name of file of employee numbers');
        WriteLn;
        OpenInput('');
        MaxIndex := HIGH(Index);
        Last := 0;
        ReadString(EmpNumber);
        WHILE EmpNumber[0] # '*' DO
            Index[Last] := EmpNumber;
            INC(Last);
            IF (Last > MaxIndex) THEN
                WriteString('Index array is full');
                WriteLn;
                RETURN
            ELSE
                ReadString(EmpNumber)
            END (* IF *);
        END (* WHILE *);
        DEC(Last);
        CloseInput
    END ConstructIndex;

PROCEDURE Search(VAR Index : IndexArray; Last : INTEGER;
                     EmpNumber : String;
                 VAR Found : BOOLEAN; VAR Location : CARDINAL);

    (******************************************************************

        Procedure uses a binary search to look EmpNum up in Index
        which has first entry in location 0, last in location Last.
        It returns its Location and Found = TRUE if found;
        otherwise Found is set to FALSE

    ******************************************************************)

    VAR
        First,                 (* first item in sublist being searched *)
        Middle : INTEGER;  (* middle item in sublist *)

    BEGIN
        First := 0;
        Found := FALSE;
        WHILE (First <= Last) AND (NOT Found) DO
            Middle := (First + Last) DIV 2;
            IF Compare(EmpNumber, Index[Middle]) < 0 THEN
                Last := Middle - 1     (* EmpNum in first half of sublist *)
            ELSIF Compare(EmpNumber, Index[Middle]) > 0 THEN
                First := Middle + 1   (* EmpNum in last half of sublist *)
            ELSE
                Found := TRUE;          (* EmpNum found *)
                Location := Middle
            END (* IF *)
        END (* WHILE *)
    END Search;
```

Figure 11.6 (cont.)

```
PROCEDURE Update(VAR EmpFile: File; Index : IndexArray);

    (****************************************************************

        Procedure to update hourly rates for employees in EmpFile.
        The user enters an employee number which is then looked up in
        Index.  Its location in Index is then used as the number of
        the employee's record in the direct access file EmpFile.

     ***************************************************************)

    VAR
        FileName,               (* name of file to be updated *)
        EmpNumber: String;      (* an employee's social security number *)
        RecSize,                (* size of a record *)
        RecPos : CARDINAL;      (* current position in the file *)
        EmpRec : EmployeeRecord; (* an employee record *)

    BEGIN
        (* open EmpFile *)
        WriteLn;
        WriteString('Name of file to be updated? ');
        ReadString(FileName);
        WriteLn;
        Lookup(EmpFile, FileName, FALSE);
        SetModify(EmpFile);

        (* update the file *)
        WriteLn;
        WriteString('Enter employee number beginning with * to stop.');
        WriteLn; WriteLn;
        RecSize := BytesPerWord * SIZE(EmployeeRecord);
        WriteString('Employee #?  ');
        ReadString(EmpNumber);
        WHILE EmpNumber[0] # '*' DO
            Search (Index, LastRecNum, EmpNumber, Found, RecNum);
            IF NOT Found THEN
                WriteLn;
                WriteString('No such employee number')
            ELSE
                RecPos := RecNum * RecSize;
                SetPos(EmpFile, 0, RecPos);    (* assuming HighPos = 0 *)
                ReadBlock(EmpFile, EmpRec);
                WITH EmpRec DO
                    WriteLn;
                    WriteString('Employee:  ');
                    WriteString(SocSecNumber);
                    Write(' ');
                    WriteString(FirstName);
                    Write(' ');
                    WriteString(LastName);
                    WriteLn;
                    WriteString('Hourly rate:  $');
                    FWriteReal(HourlyRate, 8, 2);
                    WriteLn;
```

Figure 11.6   (cont.)

```
                      WriteString('Enter new hourly pay rate:  ');
                      ReadReal(HourlyRate)
                  END (* WITH *);
                  SetPos(EmpFile, 0, RecPos);
                  WriteBlock(EmpFile, EmpRec);
              END (* IF *);
              WriteLn; WriteLn;
              WriteString('Employee #?  ');
              ReadString(EmpNumber)
          END (* WHILE *);
          WriteLn; WriteLn;;
          WriteString('File updating completed');

          Close(EmpFile);
      END Update;

      BEGIN (* main program *)
         ConstructIndex(Index, LastRecNum);
         Update(EmpFile, Index)
      END EmployeeFileUpdate.


      Sample run:

      Name of file of employee numbers?  EMPNUMBERS
      Name of file to be updated?  DAEMPFILE
      Enter employee number beginning with * to stop.

      Employee #?  222535901
      222535901 Mary A. Smith
      Hourly rate:  $9.76
      New hourly rate?  $9.95

      Employee #?  222535901
      222535901 Mary A. Smith
      Hourly rate:  $9.95
      New hourly rate?  $9.95

      Employee #?  233100645
      No such employee number

      Employee #?  231111868
      231111868 Alfred E. Newman
      Hourly rate:  $4.00
      New hourly rate?  $4.10

      Employee #?  *

      File updating completed
```

In file update programs like that in Figure 11.6, it may well be the case that the number of records is so large that even the index is too large to store in main memory and/or that searching it is not practical. One common alternative, known as *indexed sequential search*, uses a smaller index by having each entry refer to a block of consecutive file components rather than to an individual component. More precisely, the *i*th entry in the index is the largest key value in the *i*th block of components, where we assume the file has been previously sorted so that the key values are in ascending order. To locate the record containing a particular key value, we search the index for the first entry that is greater than or equal to the desired key. Its position in the index determines the block in the file where the desired record should be found, and we can search this block sequentially to locate it or to determine that it is not in the file. This is illustrated in Figure 11.7 for *EmpFile*, where a block size of 5 is used.

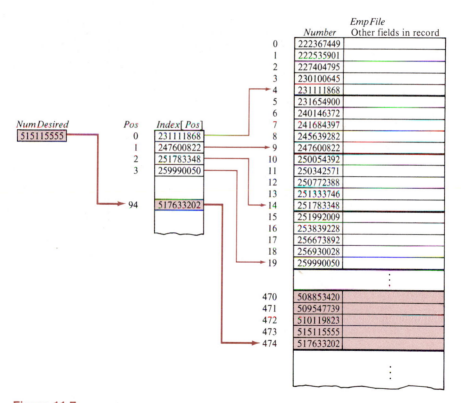

Figure 11.7

The file may be so large that even this index is too large. For the index to be sufficiently small, it may be necessary to use a large block size to keep the number of index entries manageable. But now, large parts of the file must be searched sequentially, and we are back again to the problem of slow transfer of information from secondary memory to main memory. However, what has been done once can be done again! We simply construct a secondary index that

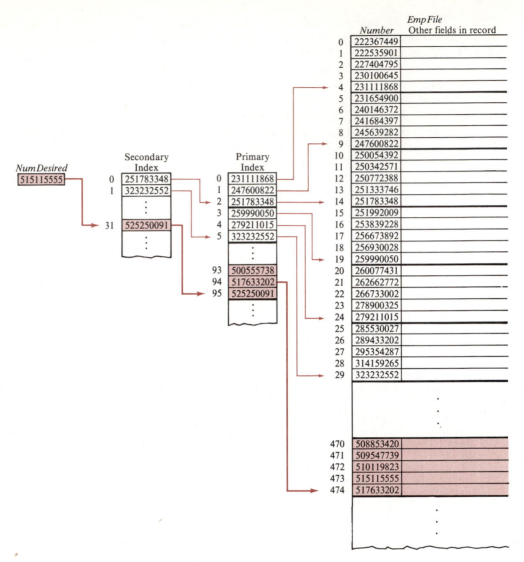

Figure 11.8

acts as an index to the primary index for the file. This is illustrated in Figure 11.8, where blocks of size 5 are used for the file and blocks of size 3 in the primary index.

Exercises

1. Write procedures *ReadDirect* and *WriteDirect* that simulate direct access file input/output using only sequential access. *ReadDirect* should accept a file variable and a record number n and should return the nth record in the file or signal a read error if there is no such record. *WriteDirect* should accept a file variable, a record number n, and a record and should modify the file by replacing the *n*th record in the file with this record.

2. Information about computer terminals in a computer network is maintained in a direct access file. The terminals are numbered 1 through 100, and information about the the *n*th terminal is stored in the *n*th record of the file. This information consists of a terminal type (string), the building in which it is located (string), its transmission rate (integer), an access code (character), and the date of last service (month, day, year). Write a program to read a terminal number, retrieve and display the information about that terminal, and modify the date of last service for that terminal.

3. Write a program similar to that in Figure 11.6 to process *InventoryFile*, considered as a direct access file of records described in Appendix E. The program should first construct an index that contains item numbers as key values. (For this, you might first write a "preprocessor" program that reads through *InventoryFile*, regarded as a sequential file, and constructs a file containing the item numbers. Note that the records in *InventoryFile* are arranged so that the item numbers are in ascending order.) The program should then allow the user to enter item numbers, and it should retrieve the information in the file for that item. This search should be carried out using a binary search of the index.

4. Write a program like that in Exercise 3 for retrieving information from *InventoryFile*, but use a hash table for the index. For the rather small sample *InventoryFile* in Appendix E, you might use a hash table of size 11 and hashing function $h(item\text{-}number) = $ (last three digits of *item-number*) MOD 11, and use chaining to resolve collisions.

5. Write a program like that in Exercise 3 for retrieving information from *InventoryFile*, but use an indexed sequential search like that described in this section.

6. Write a program like that in Exercise 3 for retrieving information from *InventoryFile*, but use two indices, a primary index and a secondary index, as described in this section.

7. (Project) In each of the examples and exercises considered thus far, it has been assumed that the file has been sorted so that the key values in the records are in ascending order. This makes it possible to use the position of a key value in the index as the number of the corresponding record in the file. If new records are added to the file or removed from the file, however, both the file and the index have to be sorted with each insertion or deletion if this approach is to be used. An alternative approach, requiring that only the index be kept sorted, is to include with each key value in the index the number of the corresponding record. A new record can then be inserted at any "free" location in the file; the key value of this record, together with this location, is then inserted into the index using, for example, insertion sort. The free locations in the file can be managed as a linked stack. (The nodes of this linked stack might be the records in the file and the record numbers used to link them together.) When a record is deleted from the file, it is pushed onto the free stack, and its entry is removed from the index.

Use this indexing scheme in a menu-driven program that manages a database of records in *InventoryFile*. The program should support at least the following operations:

(0) Display the menu.

(1) Insert a new record into the (possibly empty) database.

(2) Search the database for an item with a given number, and retrieve information about that item.

(3) Search the database for an item with a given number, and change the information (not the item number) in the record for that item.

(4) Search the database to delete the record for an item with a given number.

(5) Print a list of records for all items for which the number in stock has fallen below the minimum inventory level.

(6) Update all records in *InventoryFile* with the information in the file *InventoryUpdate*.

(7) Quit.

12

Trees

In Chapter 9 we introduced binary trees and showed how a special kind of binary tree, a binary search tree (BST), can be used to carry out a binary search in a linked structure. Then in Chapter 10 we described the heap data structure, another special kind of binary tree, and used it to transform an inefficient selection sort algorithm into one of the more efficient internal sorting schemes. In this chapter we begin by considering several operations on binary trees, including traversal, deletion, balancing, and threading, and also how they can be used to construct an efficient code known as a *Huffman code*. General trees in which each node may have any number of children are a natural extension of binary trees and are also considered in this chapter.

12.1 Binary Trees

As noted in the introduction, binary trees can be used to solve a variety of problems in addition to the searching and sorting problems considered in the preceding chapters. They are especially useful in modeling processes in which some experiment or test with two possible outcomes (e.g., off or on, 0 or 1, false or true, down or up) is performed repeatedly. For example, the following tree might be used to represent the possible outcomes in flipping a coin three times:

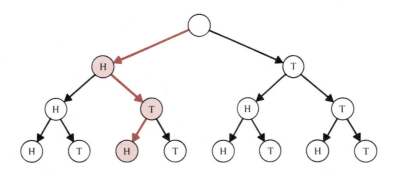

Each path from the root to one of the leaf nodes corresponds to a particular outcome, such as HTH, a head followed by a tail followed by another head, as highlighted in the diagram.

Similarly, a binary tree can be used in coding problems such as in encoding and decoding messages transmitted in Morse code, a scheme in which characters are represented as sequences of dots and dashes, as shown in the following table:

A	· —	M	— —	Y	— · — —
B	— · · ·	N	— ·	Z	— — · ·
C	— · — ·	O	— — —	1	· — — — —
D	— · ·	P	· — — ·	2	· · — — —
E	·	Q	— — · —	3	· · · — —
F	· · — ·	R	· — ·	4	· · · · —
G	— — ·	S	· · ·	5	· · · · ·
H	· · · ·	T	—	6	— · · · ·
I	· ·	U	· · —	7	— — · · ·
J	· — — —	V	· · · —	8	— — — · ·
K	— · —	W	· — —	9	— — — — ·
L	· — · ·	X	— · · —	0	— — — — —

In this case, the nodes in a binary tree are used to represent the characters, and each arc from a node to its children is labeled with a dot or a dash, according to whether it leads to a left child or a right child, respectively. Thus, part of the tree for Morse code is

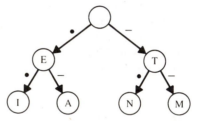

The sequence of dots and dashes labeling a path from the root to a particular node corresponds to the Morse code for that character; for example, ·· is the code for I and —· is the code for N. In Section 12.4 we use a similar tree to construct another kind of code known as *Huffman code*.

In our study of heaps in Chapter 10, we used an array to store the heap elements, an implementation that can also be used for binary trees in general. We simply number the nodes in the tree from the root down, numbering the nodes on each level from left to right,

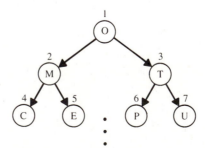

and store the contents of the *i*th node in the *i*th location of the array:

i	1	2	3	4	5	6	7	· · ·
T[*i*]	O	M	T	C	E	P	U	· · ·

This array-based implementation works very well for heaps because they are complete trees; that is, each level of the tree is completely filled, except possibly the bottom level, and in this level, the nodes are in the leftmost positions. This completeness property guarantees that the data items will be stored in consecutive locations at the beginning of the array. It should be obvious, however, that this implementation may not be space efficient for other kinds of binary trees. For example, the tree

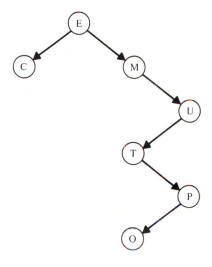

contains the same characters as the one before but requires fifty-eight positions in an array for storage:

i	1	2	3	4	5	6	7	8	9	10	11	12	13	14	15	16	17	18	19	20
T[*i*]	E	C	M				U							T						

21	22	23	24	25	26	27	28	29	30	31	32	33	34	35	36	37	38	39	40
								P											

41	42	43	44	45	46	47	48	49	50	51	52	53	54	55	56	57	58	· · ·
																	O	· · ·

To use space more efficiently and to provide additional flexibility, we instead implement binary trees using the multiply linked structure described in Chapter 9 for binary search trees. Recall that nodes in this structure have two link fields, one pointing to the left child of the node and the other to the right child:

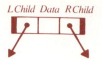

and that appropriate Modula-2 declarations for this structure have the form

```
TYPE
    ElementType = . . . ; (* type of data items in the nodes *)
    TreePointer = POINTER TO TreeNode;
    TreeNode = RECORD
                    Data : ElementType;
                    LChild, RChild : TreePointer
               END;
    BinaryTree = TreePointer;
```

All the algorithms we developed in Chapter 9 for processing binary search trees are iterative, but they can also be written recursively. The reason is that a binary tree can be defined as a *recursive data structure* in a very natural way. As an illustration, consider the following binary tree:

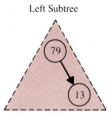

Its root node contains the integer 32 and has pointers to the nodes containing 79 and 42, each of which is itself the root of a binary *subtree*:

Left Subtree   Right Subtree

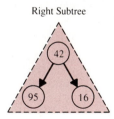

Now consider the left subtree. Its root node contains the integer 79 and has a right child but no left child. Nevertheless, we can still regard this node as having pointers to two binary subtrees, a left subtree and a right subtree, provided we allow empty binary trees:

Left Subtree   Right Subtree

Both the left and right subtrees of the one-node tree containing 13 are thus empty binary trees.

This leads to the following recursive definition of a binary tree:

Recursive Definition of a Binary Tree:

A binary tree either

a. is empty ⟵——————————————— Anchor

or

b. consists of a node called the ***root***, which has pointers to two disjoint binary subtrees called the ***left subtree*** and the ***right subtree***. ⟵——————— Inductive step

Because of the recursive nature of binary trees, many of the basic operations on them can be carried out most simply and elegantly using recursive algorithms. These algorithms are typically anchored by the special case of an empty binary tree, and the inductive step specifies how a binary tree is to be processed in terms of its root and either or both of its subtrees.

As an illustration, we first consider the operation of traversal, that is, moving through a binary tree like the preceding one, "visiting" each node exactly once. And suppose for now that the order in which the nodes are visited is not relevant. What is important is that we visit each node, not missing any, and that the information in each node is processed exactly once.

One simple recursive scheme is to traverse the binary tree as follows:

1. Visit the root and process its contents.
2. Now traverse the left subtree.
3. Then traverse the right subtree.

Thus, in our example, if we simply display a node's contents when we visit it, we begin by displaying the value 32 in the root of the binary tree. Next we must traverse the left subtree; after this traversal is finished, we then must traverse the right subtree; and when this traversal is completed, we will have traversed the entire binary tree.

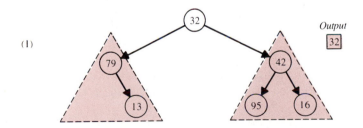

Thus the problem has been reduced to the traversal of two smaller binary trees. We consider the left subtree and visit its root. Next we must traverse its left subtree and then its right subtree.

(II)

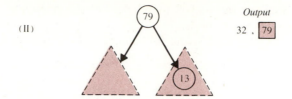

Output

32 , 79

The left subtree is empty, and so we have reached the anchor case of the recursive definition of a binary tree, and to complete the traversal algorithm, we must specify how an empty binary tree is to be traversed. But this is easy. We do nothing.

Because traversal of the empty left subtree is thus finished trivially, we turn to traversing the right subtree. We visit its root and then must traverse its left subtree followed by its right subtree:

(III)

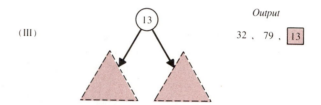

Output

32 , 79 , 13

As both subtrees are empty, no action is required to traverse them. Consequently, traversal of the binary tree in Diagram III is complete, and since this was the right subtree of the tree in Diagram II, traversal of this tree is also complete.

This means that we have finished traversing the left subtree of the root in the original binary tree in Diagram I, and we finally are ready to begin traversing the right subtree. This traversal proceeds in a similar manner. We first visit its root, displaying the value 42 stored in it, then traverse its left subtree, and then its right subtree:

(IV)

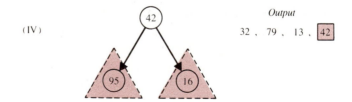

Output

32 , 79 , 13 , 42

The left subtree consists of a single node with empty left and right subtrees and is traversed as described earlier for a one-node binary tree:

(V)

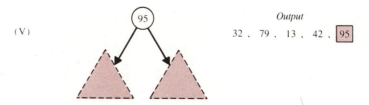

Output

32 , 79 , 13 , 42 , 95

Traversal of the right subtree is carried out in the same way:

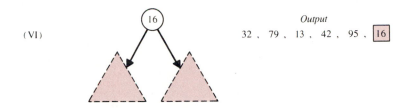

(VI)

Output

32 , 79 , 13 , 42 , 95 , 16

This completes the traversal of the binary tree in Diagram IV and thus completes the traversal of the original tree in Diagram I.

As this example demonstrates, traversing a binary tree recursively requires three basic steps, which we shall denote *N, L,* and *R*:

N: Visit a node.
L: Traverse the left subtree of a node.
R: Traverse the right subtree of a node.

We performed these steps in the order listed here, but in fact, there are six different orders in which they can be carried out:

LNR
NLR
LRN
NRL
RNL
RLN

For example, the ordering LNR corresponds to the following traversal algorithm:

If the binary tree is empty then	(∗ anchor ∗)
Do nothing.	
Else do the following:	(∗ inductive step ∗)
L: Traverse the left subtree.	
N: Visit the root.	
R: Traverse the right subtree.	

For the preceding binary tree, this LNR traversal visits the nodes in the order 79, 13, 32, 95, 42, 16.

The first three orders, in which the left subtree is traversed before the right, are the most important of the six traversals and are commonly called by other names:

LNR ↔ Inorder
NLR ↔ Preorder
LRN ↔ Postorder

To see why these names are appropriate, consider the following ***expression tree***, a binary tree used to represent the arithmetic expression

$$A - B * C + D$$

by representing each operand as a child of a parent node representing the corresponding operator:

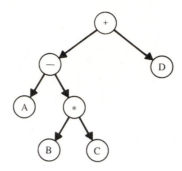

An *inorder* traversal of this expression tree produces the *infix* expression

$$A - B * C + D$$

A *preorder* traversal gives the *prefix* expression (see Exercise 6 in Section 4.3):

$$+ - A * B C D$$

And a *postorder* traversal yields the *postfix* (RPN) expression (see Section 4.3):

$$A B C * - D +$$

A recursive procedure to implement any of these traversal algorithms is very easy. One need only attempt to write a correct nonrecursive version to appreciate the simple elegance of a procedure like the following:

PROCEDURE *Inorder* (*Root* : *BinaryTree*);

    (* Procedure for an inorder traversal of a binary tree with root
       pointed to by *Root*. *)

   BEGIN
      IF *Root* # NIL THEN
         Inorder (*Root*↑.*LChild*);   (* L operation *)
         (* Insert statements here to   (* N operation *)
            process *Root*↑.*Data* *)
         Inorder (*Root*↑.*RChild*)   (* R operation *)
      END (* IF *)
      (* else
         do nothing *)
   END *Inorder*;

Procedures for any of the other traversals are obtained by simply changing the order of the statements representing the L, N, and R operations. The following table traces the action of *Inorder* as it traverses the binary tree:

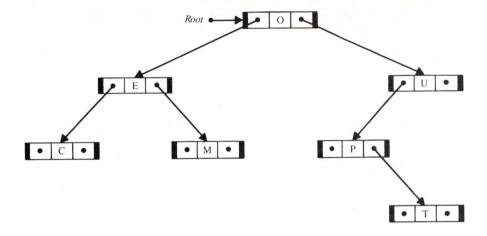

Contents of Current Node	Level in the Tree	Action	Output
O	1	Call *Inorder* with pointer to root (E) of left subtree.	
E	2	Call *Inorder* with pointer to root (C) of left subtree.	
C	3	Call *Inorder* with pointer (nil) to root of left subtree.	
none	4	None; return to parent node.	
C	3	Display contents of node.	C
C	3	Call *Inorder* with pointer (nil) to root of right subtree.	
none	4	None; return to parent node.	
C	3	Return to parent node.	
E	2	Display contents of node.	E
E	2	Call *Inorder* with pointer to root (M) of right subtree.	
M	3	Call *Inorder* with pointer (nil) to root of left subtree.	
none	4	None; return to parent node.	
M	3	Display contents of node.	M
M	3	Call *Inorder* with pointer (nil) to root of right subtree.	
none	4	None; return to parent node.	
M	3	Return to parent node.	
E	2	Return to parent node.	

Contents of Current Node	Level in the Tree	Action	Output
O	1	Display contents of node.	O
O	1	Call *Inorder* with pointer to root (U) of right subtree.	
U	2	Call *Inorder* with pointer to root (P) of left subtree.	
P	3	Call *Inorder* with pointer (nil) to root of left subtree.	
none	4	None; return to parent node.	
P	3	Display contents of node.	P
P	3	Call *Inorder* with pointer to root (T) of right subtree.	
T	4	Call *Inorder* with pointer (nil) to root of left subtree.	
none	5	None; return to parent node.	
T	4	Display contents of node.	T
T	4	Call *Inorder* with pointer (nil) to root of right subtree.	
none	5	None; return to parent node.	
T	4	Return to parent node.	
P	3	Return to parent node.	
U	2	Display contents of node.	U
U	2	Call *Inorder* with pointer (nil) to root of right subtree.	
none	3	None; return to parent node.	
U	2	Return to parent node.	
O	1	Terminate procedure; traversal complete.	

Notice that for this tree, an inorder traversal visits the nodes in alphabetical order,

C, E, M, O, P, T, U

The reason is that this binary tree is, in fact, a binary search tree, so that for each node, the value in the left child is less than the value in that node, which, in turn, is less than the value in the right child. This means that for each node, all of the values in the left subtree are smaller than the value in this node, which is less than all values in its right subtree. Because an inorder traversal is an LNR traversal, it follows that it must visit the nodes in ascending order.

This suggests still another internal sorting scheme in addition to those considered in Chapter 10. We simply insert the list elements into a BST, initially empty, and then use an inorder traversal to copy them back into the list. The following algorithm uses this technique to sort a list stored in an array:

TREESORT ALGORITHM

(* Algorithm that uses a BST to sort a list of *n* items stored in an array *X* so that they are in ascending order. *)

1. Initialize an empty BST.
2. For *i* ranging from 1 to *n*:
   Insert *X*[*i*] into the BST.
3. Initialize an index *i* to 0.
4. Perform an inorder traversal of the BST, in which visiting a node consists of the following two steps:
   a. Increment *i* by 1.
   b. Set *X*[*i*] equal to the data item in the current node.

When we considered BSTs in Chapter 9, we wrote iterative procedures to process them. Now that we have viewed binary trees, and BSTs in particular, as recursive data structures and have seen how easily traversal can be implemented by recursive procedures, we should reexamine the search and insert procedures considered earlier. Recall that to search a BST we begin at the root. If it is the desired item, the search is done; if the item we wish to find is less than the value in the root, we move down to the left subtree and search it; and if it is greater, we descend to the right subtree and search it. If the subtree we select is empty, we conclude that the item is not in the tree; otherwise, we search this subtree *in exactly the same manner* as we did the original tree. This means, therefore, that although we formulated our search procedure iteratively, we were, in fact, thinking recursively and could also have developed a recursive procedure like the following:

PROCEDURE *RecBSTSearch*(*Root* : *BinaryTree*; *Item* : *KeyType*;
                          VAR *Found* : BOOLEAN;
                          VAR *LocPtr* : *TreePointer*);

   (* Recursive procedure to search the BST with the specified *Root*
   for *Item*. *Found* is returned as TRUE, and *LocPtr* points to a
   node containing *Item* in the key field of its data part if the search
   is successful; otherwise, *Found* is returned as FALSE. *)

```
BEGIN
    IF Root = NIL THEN                  (* empty tree *)
        Found := FALSE
        RETURN
    END (* IF *);
    (* else there is a nonempty tree to search *)
    IF Item < Root↑.Data.Key            (* search left subtree *)
        RecBSTSearch(Root↑.LChild, Item, Found, LocPtr)
    ELSIF Item > Root↑.Data.Key         (* search right subtree *)
        RecBSTSearch(Root↑.RChild, Item, Found, LocPtr)
    ELSE
        Found := TRUE                   (* Item found *)
    END (* IF *)
END RecBSTSearch;
```

Because this procedure is not really any simpler or more understandable than the iterative version given in Chapter 9, however, in accord with the guidelines for choosing between a recursive and an interative algorithm, we opt for the nonrecursive version.

A recursive procedure for the insertion operation is, however, a bit easier than the iterative version. The obvious anchor is an empty BST, and we must specify how to insert an item into such a tree; otherwise, we can proceed recursively by inserting an item into the left subtree or the right subtree of the current node, according to whether the item is less than or greater than the value in this node.

```
PROCEDURE RecBSTInsert(VAR Root : BinaryTree;
                           Element : ElementType);

    (* Recursive procedure to insert Element into the BST
       with the specified Root. *)

BEGIN
    IF Root = NIL THEN         (* insert into empty tree *)
        ALLOCATE(Root, SIZE(TreeNode));
        Root↑.Data := Element;
        Root↑.LChild := NIL;
        Root↑.RChild := NIL;
        RETURN
    END (* IF *);
    (* else tree is nonempty — insert into *)
    IF Element.Data.Key < Root↑.Data.Key              (* left subtree *)
        RecBSTInsert(Root↑.LChild, Element)
    ELSIF Element.Data.Key > Root↑.Data.Key           (* right subtree *)
        RecBSTInsert(Root↑.RChild, Element)
    ELSE                                     (* Element already in BST *)
        WriteString('Element already in the tree');
        WriteLn
    END (* IF *)
END RecBSTInsert;
```

In our earlier discussion of binary search trees, we did not consider the operation of deletion because the theme running through Chapter 9 was the problem of searching a collection of data. We assumed that once we had constructed the BST (by repeatedly calling *BSTInsert* or *RecBSTInsert*, beginning with an empty tree), we were interested only in searching it as a static structure. In many other applications, however, the binary trees are dynamic and change because of both insertions and deletions.

To delete a node x from a BST, we consider three cases:

1. x is a leaf.
2. x has one child.
3. x has two children.

The first case is very easy. We simply set the appropriate pointer in x's parent to nil; this is the left or right pointer according to whether x is the left or right child of its parent. For example, to delete the leaf node containing D in the following BST:

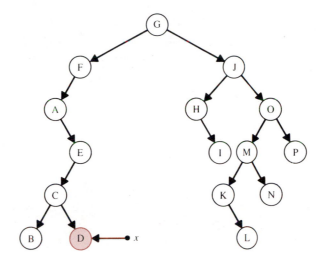

we can simply set the right pointer in its parent C to nil and then dispose of x:

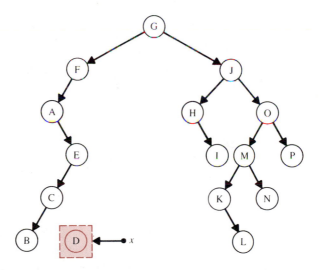

The second case, in which the node x has exactly one child, is just as easy. In this case we need only set the appropriate pointer in x's parent to point to this child. For example, we can delete the node containing E in the BST of our example by simply setting the right pointer of its parent A to point to the node containing C and then dispose of x:

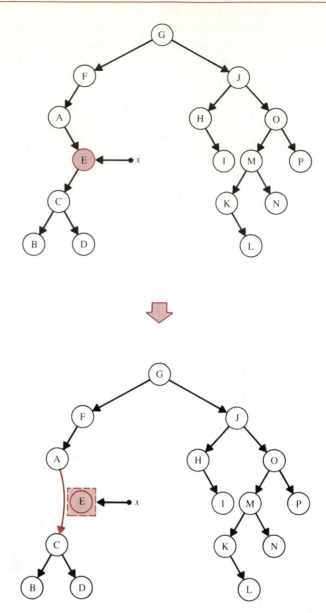

These two cases can, in fact, be combined into one case in which x has at most one nonempty subtree. If the left pointer of x is nil, we set the appropriate pointer of x's parent to point to the right subtree of x (which may be empty—Case 1); otherwise, we set it to point to the left subtree of x. The following statements handle both cases:

```
Subtree := x↑.LChild;          (* pointer to a subtree of x *)
IF Subtree = NIL THEN
    Subtree := x↑.RChild
END (* IF *);
IF Parent = NIL THEN           (* root being deleted *)
    Root := Subtree
```

ELSIF *Parent↑.LChild* = *x* THEN
    Parent↑.LChild := *Subtree*
ELSE
    Parent↑.RChild := *Subtree*
END (∗ IF ∗)

The third case, in which *x* has two children, can be reduced to one of the first two cases if we replace the value stored in node *x* by its inorder successor (or precedessor) and then delete this successor (predecessor). The inorder successor (predecessor) of the value stored in a given node of a BST is its successor (predecessor) in an inorder traversal of the BST.

To illustrate this case, consider again the following binary search tree, and suppose we wish to delete the node containing J:

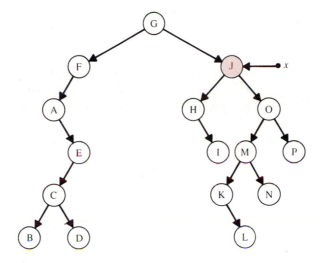

We can locate its inorder successor by starting at the right child of *x* and then descending left as far as possible. In our example, this inorder successor is the node containing K:

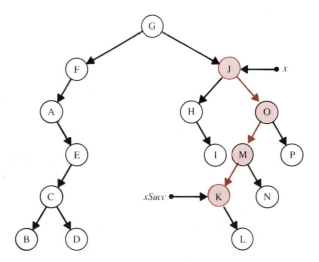

Now suppose we replace the contents of *x* with this inorder successor:

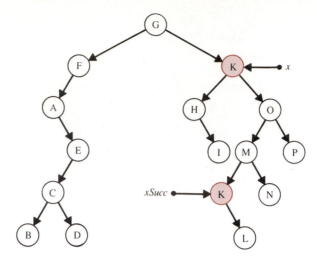

Now we need only delete the node pointed to by *xSucc*, and we do this as described for Cases 1 and 2, since this node will always have an empty left subtree (and perhaps an empty right subtree as well):

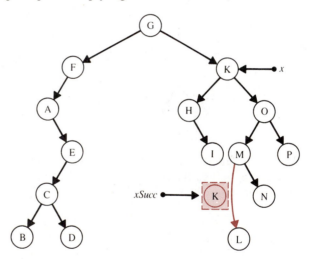

The following procedure implements the deletion operation for all cases, reducing Case 3 to one of the first two cases, when necessary, in the manner we have just illustrated:

PROCEDURE *BSTDelete*(VAR *Root* : *BinaryTree*; *Item* : *KeyType*);

    (∗ Procedure to find a node containing *Item* in the key field of
      its data part and delete it from the BST with the specified
      Root. ∗)

    VAR
       x,   (∗ points to node containing *Item* ∗)

Parent,   (* parent of *x* or *xSucc* *)
xSucc,   (* *x*'s inorder successor *)
Subtree : TreePointer;   (* pointer to subtree of *x* *)
Found : BOOLEAN;   (* TRUE if *Item* is in BST *)

```
BEGIN
    BSTSearch2(Root, Item, Found, x, Parent);
    IF NOT Found THEN
        WriteString('Item not in the binary search tree');
        WriteLn;
        RETURN
    END (* IF *);

    (* Else proceed to delete the node containing Item *)

    IF (x↑.LChild # NIL) AND (x↑.RChild # NIL) THEN
        (* Node has two children; find the inorder
            successor and its parent *)
        xSucc := x↑.RChild;
        Parent := x;
        WHILE xSucc↑.LChild # NIL DO        (* descend left *)
            Parent := xSucc;
            xSucc := xSucc↑.LChild
        END (* WHILE *);

        (* Move contents of xSucc to x and change x to
            point to its successor, which will be deleted *)
        x↑.Data := xSucc↑.Data;
        x := xSucc
    END (* IF node has 2 children *);

    (* Now proceed with case where node has 0 or 1 child *)

    Subtree := x↑.LChild;
    IF Subtree = NIL THEN
        Subtree := x↑.RChild
    END (* IF *);
    IF Parent = NIL THEN
        Root := Subtree              (* root being deleted *)
    ELSIF Parent↑.LChild = x THEN
        Parent↑.LChild := Subtree    (* left child of parent *)
    ELSE
        Parent↑.RChild := Subtree    (* right child of parent *)
    END (* IF *);
    DEALLOCATE(x, SIZE(TreeNode))
END BSTDelete;
```

This procedure uses the following modified form of the search procedure *BSTSearch* given in Chapter 9 to locate the node containing the item to be deleted and its parent:

```
PROCEDURE BSTSearch2(       Root : BinaryTree; Item : KeyType;
                       VAR Found : BOOLEAN;
                       VAR LocPtr, Parent : TreePointer);
```

(* Procedure to search the BST with the specified *Root* for *Item*.
Found is returned as TRUE and *LocPtr* points to a node
containing *Item* in the key field of its data part if the search is
successful; otherwise, *Found* is returned as FALSE. If the search
is successful, *Parent* points to the parent of the node containing
Item or is nil if *Item* is in the root. *)

```
BEGIN
    Parent := NIL;                               (* begin at the root *)
    LocPtr := Root;
    Found := FALSE;
    WHILE NOT Found AND (LocPtr # NIL) DO
        IF Item < LocPtr↑.Data.Key THEN          (* search left subtree *)
            Parent := LocPtr;
            LocPtr := LocPtr↑.LChild
        ELSIF Item > LocPtr↑.Data.Key THEN
            Parent := LocPtr;                    (* search right subtree *)
            LocPtr := LocPtr↑.RChild
        ELSE                                     (* Item found *)
            Found := TRUE
        END (* IF *)
    END (* WHILE *)
END BSTSearch2;
```

It is also possible to design a recursive procedure to delete from a binary
search tree. In this case, the necessary searching can be incorporated into the
deletion procedure. It might be noted, however, that in the case that the node
to be deleted has two children, two descents into the tree are made, the first to
find the node and the second to delete its successor node. (See Exercise 13.)

```
PROCEDURE RecBSTDelete(VAR Root : BinaryTree; Item : KeyType);
```

(* Recursive procedure to find a node containing *Item* in the key
field of its data part and delete it from the BST with the specified
Root. *)

```
VAR
    TempPtr : TreePointer;                       (* auxiliary pointer *)
BEGIN
    IF Root = NIL THEN    (* empty BST—item not found *)
        WriteString('Item not in the binary search tree');
        WriteLn;
        RETURN
    END (* IF *);
```

(* Else recursively search for the node containing *Item* and
delete it from *)

IF *Item* < *Root*↑.*Data.Key* THEN   (* left subtree *)
    RecBSTDelete(*Root*↑.*LChild*, *Item*)
ELSIF *Item* > *Root*↑.*Data.Key* THEN   (* right subtree *)
    RecBSTDelete(*Root*↑.*RChild*, *Item*)
ELSE   (* *Item* found—delete node *)
    IF *Root*↑.*Data.LChild* = NIL THEN
        TempPtr := *Root*↑.*RChild*;   (* no left child *)
        DEALLOCATE(*Root*, SIZE(*TreeNode*));
        Root := *TempPtr*
    ELSIF *Root*↑.*Data.RChild* = NIL THEN
        TempPtr := *Root*↑.*LChild*;   (* left child, but no right *)
        DEALLOCATE(*Root*, SIZE(*TreeNode*));
        Root := *TempPtr*
    ELSE   (* two children *)
        (* find inorder successor *)
        TempPtr := *Root*↑.*RChild*;
        WHILE *TempPtr*↑.*LChild* # NIL DO
            TempPtr := *TempPtr*↑.*LChild*
        END (* WHILE *);

        (* Move contents of successor to the root of the subtree
            being examined and delete the successor node *)
        Root↑.*Data* := *TempPtr*↑.*Data*;
        RecBSTDelete(*Root*↑.*RChild*, *TempPtr*↑.*Data.Key*)
    END (* IF *Item* found *)
    END (* IF searching for *Item* *)
END *RecBSTDelete*;

Exercises

1. Complete the binary tree for Morse code that was begun in this section.

2. For each of the following lists of Modula-2 reserved words,

    (a) Draw the binary search tree that is constructed when the words are inserted in the order given.
    (b) Perform inorder, preorder, and postorder traversals of the tree and show the sequence of words that results in each case:

        (i) PROCEDURE, CONST, TYPE, IMPORT, MODULE, BEGIN, END
        (ii) ARRAY, OF, RECORD, BITSET, CASE, SET, END
        (iii) DIV, MOD, NOT, AND, OR, IN
        (iv) OR, NOT, MOD, IN, DIV, AND
        (v) BEGIN, END, IF, THEN, ELSIF, ELSE, CASE, WHILE, DO, REPEAT, UNTIL, FOR, TO, BY, LOOP, EXIT, WITH
        (vi) END, BEGIN

3. For each of the following, begin with the given binary search tree, and show the BST that results after the operation or sequence of operations is performed:

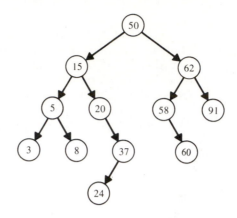

(a) Insert 7.
(b) Insert 7, 1, 55, 29, and 19.
(c) Delete 8.
(d) Delete 8, 37, and 62.
(e) Insert 7, delete 8, insert 59, delete 60, insert 92, delete 50.

4. For the BST in Exercise 3, display the output produced by
(a) an inorder traversal.
(b) a preorder traversal.
(c) a postorder traversal.

5. For each of the following arithmetic expressions, draw a binary tree that represents the expression, and then use tree traversals to find the equivalent prefix and postfix expressions:

(a) $(A - B) - C$
(b) $A - (B - C)$
(c) $A / (B - (C - (D - (E - F))))$
(d) $((((A - B) - C) - D) - E) / F$
(e) $((A * (B + C)) / (D - (E + F))) * (G / (H / (I * J)))$

6. Assuming the array-based implementation of binary search trees described in this section, show the contents of an array used to store the BST in Exercise 3.

7. Repeat Exercise 6, but for the BSTs in Exercise 2.

8. Repeat Exercise 6, but for the binary trees in Exercise 5.

9. (a) Preorder traversal of a certain binary tree produced

A D F G H K L P Q R W Z

and inorder traversal produced

G F H K D L A W R Q P Z

Draw the binary tree.

(b) Postorder traversal of a certain binary tree produced

F G H D A L P Q R Z W K

and inorder traversal gave the same results as in (a). Draw the binary tree.

(c) Show by example that knowing the results of a preorder traversal and a postorder traversal does not uniquely determine the binary tree; that is, give an example of two different binary trees for which a preorder traversal of each gives the same result, and so does a postorder traversal.

10. Write a recursive function procedure to count the leaves in a binary tree. (*Hint*: How is the number of leaves in the entire tree related to the number of leaves in the left and right subtrees of the root?)

11. Write a nonrecursive procedure to perform inorder traversal. (Use a stack of pointers to eliminate the recursion.)

12. Write a procedure to carry out a level-by-level traversal of a binary tree; that is, first visit the root, then all nodes on level 1 (children of the root), then all nodes on level 2, and so on. Nodes on the same level should be visited in order from left to right. (*Hint*: Write a nonrecursive procedure and use a queue of pointers.)

13. Trace the execution of the procedure *RecBSTDelete* for the tree in Exercise 3 as it deletes the following nodes. For each, start with the original tree and draw the subtree that is being processed on each recursive call to *RecBSTDelete*.

(a) 24   **(b)** 58   **(c)** 37   **(d)** 15   **(e)** 5

14. Write a program to process a BST whose nodes contain characters. The user should be allowed to select from the following menu of options:

I followed by a character: To insert a character
S followed by a character: To search for a character
TI: for inorder traversal
TP: for preorder traversal
TR: for postorder traversal
QU: to quit

15. Write a procedure to implement the treesort algorithm for sorting a list of items stored in (a) an array and (b) a linked list. You may assume that procedures *InOrder* and *BSTInsert* or *RecBSTInsert* are available.

16. Use the procedure of Exercise 15 in a program that reads a collection of student numbers and names and then uses the treesort procedure to sort them so that the student numbers are in ascending order.

17. Write a *spell-checker*, that is, a program that reads the words in a piece of text and looks each of them up in a *dictionary* to check its spelling. Use a BST to store this dictionary, reading the list of words from a file. While checking the spelling of words in a piece of text, the program should print a list of all words not found in the dictionary.

18. (Project) For a certain company, the method by which the pay for each employee is computed depends on whether that employee is classified as an *Office* employee, a *Factory* employee, or a *SalesRep*. Suppose that a file of employee records is maintained in which each record is a variant record containing the following information for each employee:

> Name (string)
> Id number (cardinal number)
> Age (cardinal number)
> Number of dependents (cardinal number)
> Employee code (character O, F, S, representing *Office*, *Factory*, and *SalesRep*, respectively)
> Hourly rate if employee is *Factory*
> Annual salary if employee is *Office*
> A base pay (real) and a commission percentage (real) if employee is *SalesRep*

Write a menu-driven program that allows at least the following options to be selected by the user of the program:

GET: Get the records from the employee file and store them in a binary search tree, sorted so that the names are in alphabetical order.
INS: Insert the record for a new employee into the BST.
UPD: Update the record of an employee already in the tree.
RET: Retrieve and display the record for a specified employee (by name or by id number)
LIS: List the records (or perhaps selected items in the records) in order. This option should allow suboptions
> ALL—to list for all employees
> OFF—to list for only *Office* employees
> FAC—to list for only *Factory* employees
> SAL—to list for only *SalesRep* employees
SAV: Copy the records from the BST into a permanent file.
DEL: Delete the record of an employee from the BST.

19. (Project) In Section 11.4 we described how to use an *index* of key values of records in a direct access file to locate these records in the file, and we used an array to store this index. In Exercise 7 of that section we noted that for files for which frequent insertions and deletions take place, it is better to use an index that stores not only the key value of a record but also the number of that record. That exercise asked you to use this indexing scheme in a menu-driven program for managing a database of records in *InventoryFile* (see Appendix E). Now write a similar program, but use a binary search tree for the index and support only the following options:

(0) Display the menu.
(1) Insert a new record into the (possibly empty) database.
(2) Search the database for an item with a given number, and retrieve information about that item.
(3) Search the database for an item with a given number, and change the information (not the item number) in the record for that item.
(4) Quit.

20. (Project) Extend the program in Exercise 19 to allow the additional options:

(4) Search the database to delete the record for an item with a given number.
(5) Print a list of records for all items for which the number in stock has fallen below the minimum inventory level.
(6) Update all records in *InventoryFile* with the information in the file *InventoryUpdate*.
(7) Quit.

12.2 Tree Balancing; AVL Trees

As we observed in Section 9.2, the order in which items are inserted into a binary search tree determines the shape of the tree and how efficiently this tree can be searched. For example, the BST that results when the abbreviations of states NY, IL, GA, RI, MA, PA, DE, IN, VT, TX, OH, and WY are inserted into an empty tree in this order is

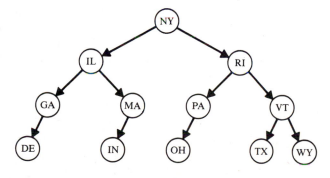

For such nicely balanced trees, the search time is $O(\log_2 n)$ where n is the number of nodes in the tree. If the abbreviations are inserted in the order DE, GA, IL, IN, MA, MI, NY, OH, PA, RI, TX, VT, WY, however, the BST degenerates into a linked list for which the search time is $O(n)$:

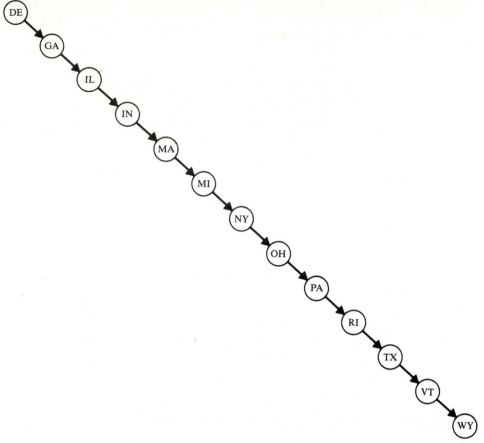

In this section we describe a technique developed in the 1960s by the two Russian mathematicians Georgii Maksimovich Adel′son-Vel′skii and Evgenii Mikhailovich Landis for keeping a binary search tree balanced as items are inserted into it. The trees that result are commonly called *AVL trees*, in their honor.

In a binary tree, the ***balance factor*** of a node x is defined as the height of the left subtree of x minus the height of x's right subtree. Recall that the height of a tree is the number of levels in it. A binary search tree is said to be an ***AVL*** or ***height-balanced tree*** if the balance factor of each node is 0, 1, or -1. For example, the following are AVL trees, and the balance factor of each node is shown in the node:

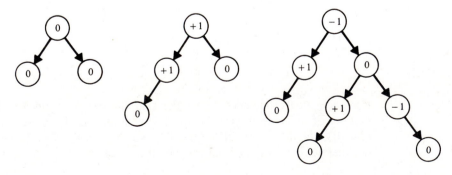

The following are not AVL trees, and the nodes whose balance factors are different from 0, 1, or −1 are highlighted:

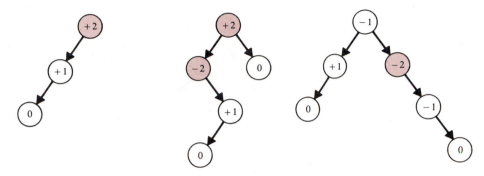

To illustrate the technique for constructing an AVL tree, we consider again the example of a BST containing state abbreviations. Suppose that we begin with an empty tree into which the first abbreviation inserted is RI, giving the following balanced tree:

(1)

In this one node tree, both the state abbreviation and the balance factor are shown in the node. If the next abbreviation inserted is PA, the result is still a balanced tree:

(2)

If DE is inserted next, an unbalanced tree results:

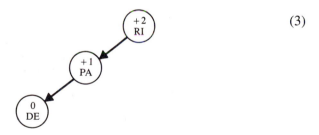

(3)

A *right rotation* of the subtree rooted at the node RI yields the balanced tree

(4)

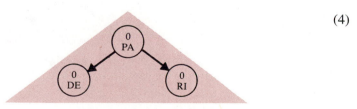

Inserting GA next does not unbalance the tree:

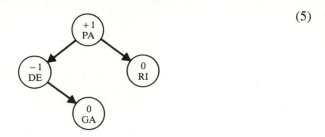

(5)

But an unbalanced tree results if OH is inserted next:

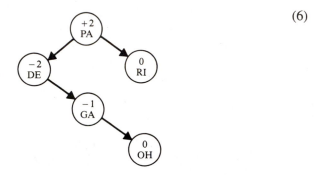

(6)

Performing a *left rotation* of the nodes in the subtree rooted at DE rebalances the tree:

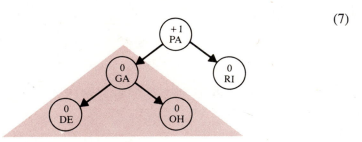

(7)

Inserting MA next produces another unbalanced tree:

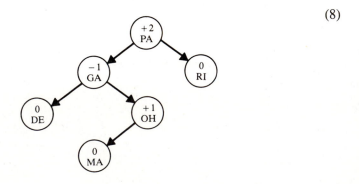

(8)

Rebalancing this tree requires a double *left-right rotation*. We first perform a left rotation of the nodes in the left subtree of PA,

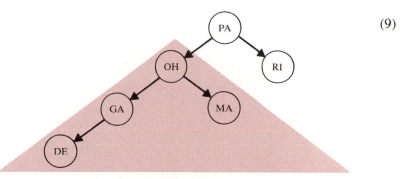

(9)

and follow this with a right rotation of the tree rooted at PA:

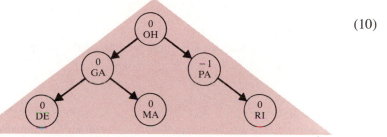

(10)

Inserting IL and then MI does not unbalance the tree,

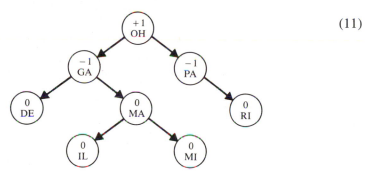

(11)

but inserting IN does:

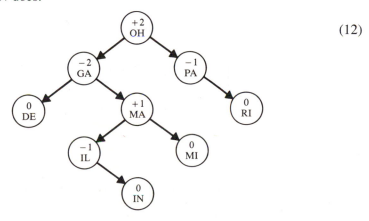

(12)

In this case, a double *right-left rotation* rebalances the tree. We first perform a right rotation of the nodes in the right subtree of GA,

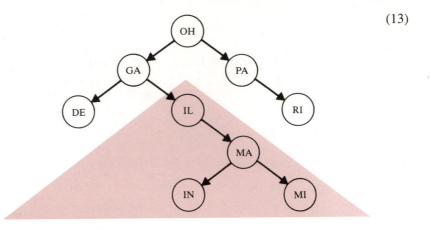

(13)

and follow this with a left rotation of the subtree rooted at GA:

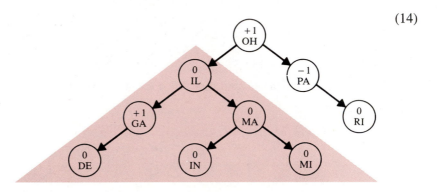

(14)

Inserting NY produces an unbalanced tree,

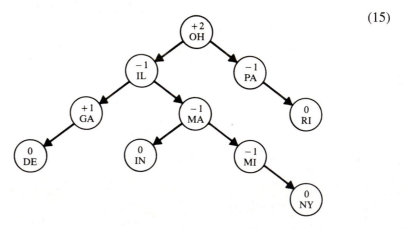

(15)

which requires a double left-right rotation for rebalancing, first a left rotation of the nodes in the left subtree of OH,

(16)

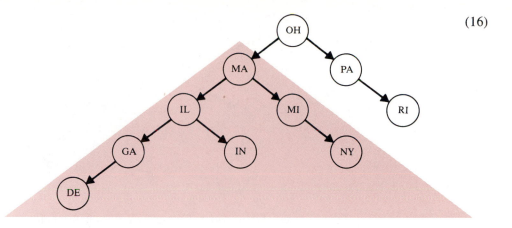

followed by a right rotation of the nodes in the subtree rooted at OH

(17)

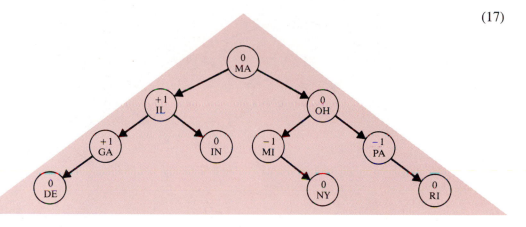

Inserting VT next causes an imbalance,

(18)

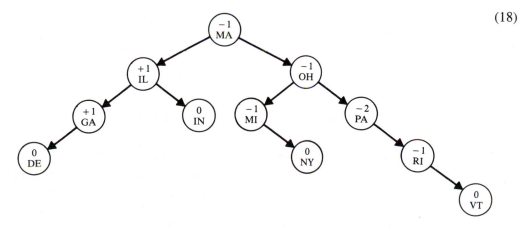

but this tree is easily rebalanced by a simple left rotation of the subtree rooted at PA:

(19)

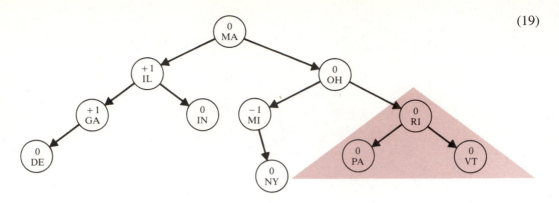

Insertion of the last two abbreviations TX and WY does not unbalance the tree, and the final AVL tree obtained is

(20)

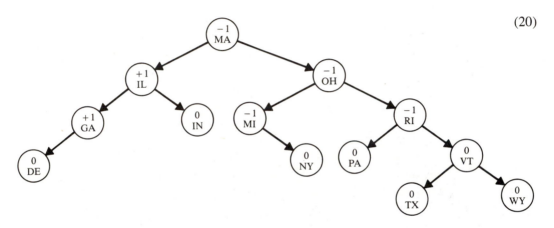

As this example demonstrates, when a new item is inserted into a balanced binary tree, the resulting tree may become unbalanced. It also demonstrates that the tree can be rebalanced by transforming the subtree rooted at the node that is the nearest ancestor of the new node having balance factor ± 2. This transformation can be carried out using one of four types of rotations:

1. *Simple right rotation*: This rotation is used when the new item is inserted in the left subtree of the left child B of the nearest ancestor A with balance factor $+2$.
2. *Simple left rotation*: This rotation is used when the new item is inserted in the right subtree of the right child B of the nearest ancestor A with balance factor -2.
3. *Left-right rotation*: This rotation is used when the new item is inserted in the right subtree of the left child B of the nearest ancestor A with balance factor $+2$.
4. *Right-left rotation*: This rotation is used when the new item is inserted in the left subtree of the right child B of the nearest ancestor A with balance factor -2.

Each of these rotations can be carried out by simply resetting some of the links. For example, consider a simple right rotation, which is used when the item is inserted in the left subtree of the left child B of the nearest ancestor A with balance factor $+2$. A simple right rotation can be accomplished by simply resetting three links:

1. Reset the link from the parent of A to B.
2. Set the left link of A equal to the right link of B.
3. Set the right link of B to point to A.

The following sequence of diagrams illustrates:

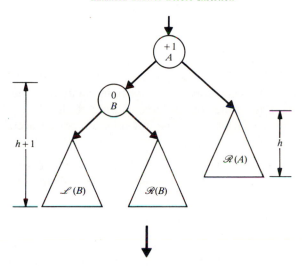

Balanced Subtree Before Insertion

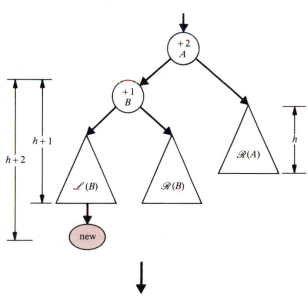

Unbalanced Subtree After Insertion

Rebalanced Subtree After Simple Right Rotation

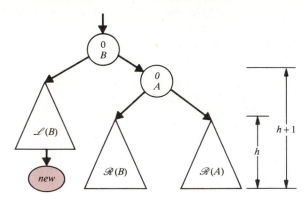

The corresponding simple left rotation can also be carried out by resetting three links and is left as an exercise.

The double rotations can be carried out with at most five link changes. For example, consider a left-right rotation, which is used when the item is inserted in the right subtree of the left child B of the nearest ancestor A with balance factor $+2$. The left rotation can be accomplished by resetting three links:

1. Set the left link of A to point to the root C of the right subtree of B.
2. Set the right link of B equal to the left link of C.
3. Set the left link of C to point to B.

and the right rotation by resetting three links:

4. Reset the link from the parent of A to point to C.
5. Set the left link of A equal to the right link of C.
6. Set the right link of C to point to A.

Note that link change in Step 5 cancels that in Step 1, so that in fact only five links must be reset.

The following diagrams illustrate this left-right rotation in the three possible cases: (1) B has no right child before the new node is inserted, and the new node becomes the right child C of B; (2) B has a right child C, and the new node is inserted in the left subtree of C; (3) B has a right child C, and the new node is inserted in the right subtree of C.

Case 1:

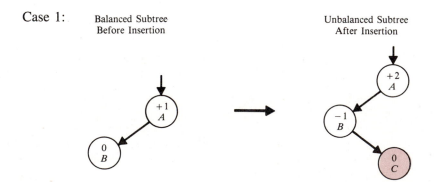

Balanced Subtree After Left-Right Rotation

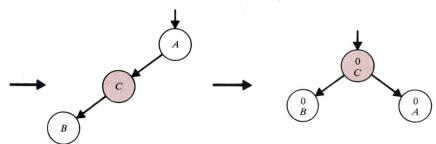

Case 2:

Balanced Subtree Before Insertion

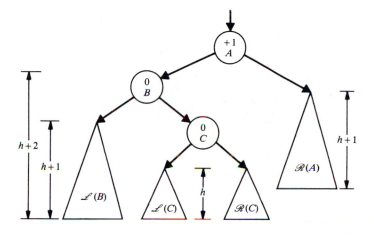

Unbalanced Subtree After Insertion

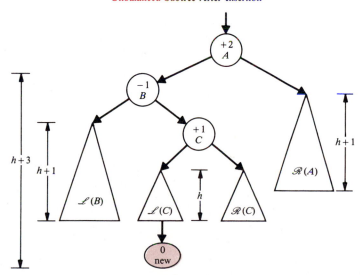

Balanced Subtree After Left-Right Rotation

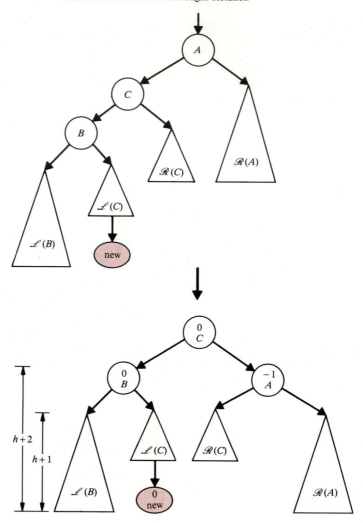

Case 3:

Balanced Subtree Before Insertion

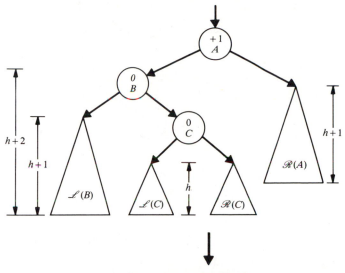

Unbalanced Subtree After Insertion

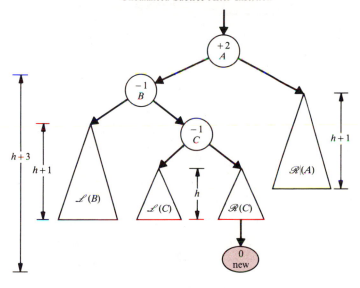

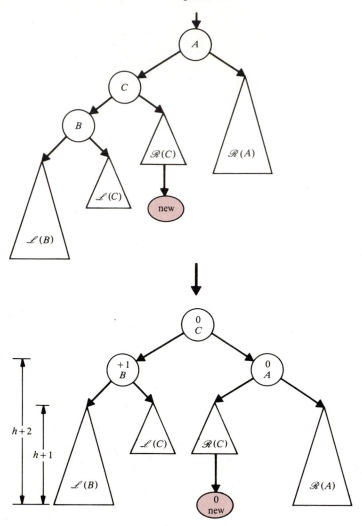

Balanced Subtree After Left-Right Rotation

The corresponding right-left rotations can also be accomplished with at most five link changes and are left as exercises.

Empirical studies have indicated that on the average, rebalancing is required for approximately 45 percent of the insertions. Roughly one-half of these require simple rotations to rebalance the tree, and one-half require double rotations.

Using an AVL tree to store data items rather than allowing the binary tree to grow haphazardly when new items are inserted guarantees that the search time will be $O(\log_2 n)$. There is obviously some overhead involved in rebalancing, but if the number of search operations is sufficiently greater than the number of insertions, the faster searches will compensate for the slower insertions.

Exercises

1. For each of the following, trace the construction of the AVL tree that results from inserting the Modula-2 reserved words in the given order. Show the tree and balance factors for each node before and after each rebalancing.

   (a) MODULE, CONST, TYPE, ARRAY, PROCEDURE, BEGIN, END
   (b) ARRAY, OF, RECORD, SET, WITH, CASE, END, SET
   (c) DIV, MOD, NOT, AND, OR, IN, NIL
   (d) OR, NOT, MOD, IN, DIV, AND
   (e) BEGIN, END, IF, THEN, ELSE, CASE, WHILE, DO, REPEAT, UNTIL, FOR, TO, BY, WITH

2. Proceed as in Exercise 1, but for the following collections of numbers:

   (a) 22, 44, 88, 66, 55, 11, 99, 77, 33
   (b) 11, 22, 33, 44, 55, 66, 77, 88, 99
   (c) 99, 88, 77, 66, 55, 44, 33, 22, 11
   (d) 55, 33, 77, 22, 11, 44, 88, 66, 99
   (e) 50, 45, 75, 65, 70, 35, 25, 15, 60, 20, 40, 30, 55, 10, 80

3. Draw diagrams for a simple left rotation similar to those in the text for the simple right rotation. Also describe what links must be reset to accomplish this rotation.

4. Draw diagrams for a right-left rotation similar to those in the text for the left-right rotation. Also describe what links must be reset to accomplish this rotation.

12.3 Threaded Binary Search Trees

In the preceding section we described a scheme for keeping a binary search tree balanced as it is being constructed. The objective in tree balancing is to produce a BST that can be searched efficiently. Another important tree operation is traversal, and in Section 12.1 we described recursive procedures for performing inorder, preorder, and postorder traversals. In this section we show how special links called *threads* make simple and efficient nonrecursive traversal algorithms possible.

Each of the leaves in a binary tree has two nil pointers. If a binary tree has n nodes, then the total number of links in the tree is $2n$, and $n - 1$ of these point to nodes; the remaining $n + 1$ links are nil. Thus more than one-half of the links in the tree are not used to point to other nodes. A ***threaded binary search tree*** is obtained when these unused links are used to point to certain other nodes in the tree in such a way that traversals or other tree operations can be done more efficiently.

To illustrate, suppose that we wish to thread a BST like the following in such a way that a simple and efficient iterative algorithm for inorder traversal can be developed:

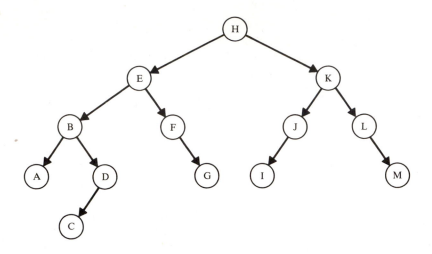

The first node visited in an inorder traversal is the leftmost leaf, that is, the node containing A. Since A has no right child, the next node visited in this traversal is its parent, the node containing B. We can use the right pointer of node A as a thread to its parent to make this backtracking in the tree easy to carry out. This thread is shown as the dotted line from A to B in the following diagram:

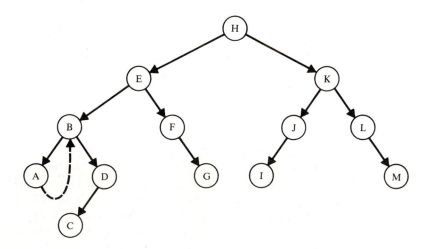

The next node visited is C, and since its right pointer is nil, it also can be used as a thread to its parent D:

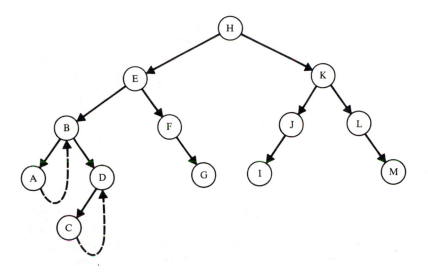

Since the right pointer in node D is again nil, it can be used as a thread to its successor, which in this case is the node containing E:

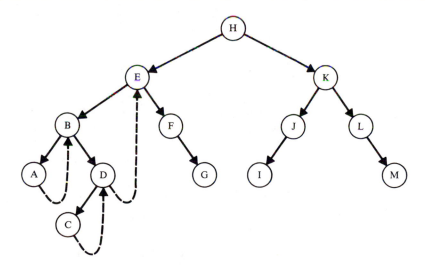

The next nodes visited are E, F, and G, and since G has a nil right pointer, we replace it with a thread to its successor, the node containing H:

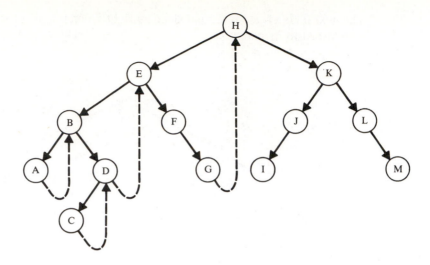

We next visit node H and then node I. And since the right pointer of I is nil, we replace it with a thread to its parent J. We visit J and, since its right link is nil, replace this link with a thread to its parent K. Since no other nodes except the last one visited (M) have nil right pointers, we obtain the final ***right-threaded BST***:

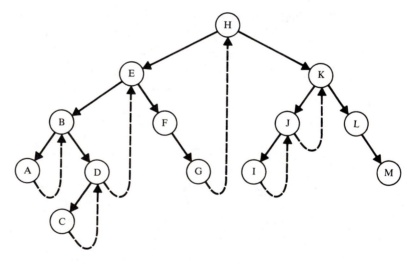

The following algorithm summarizes this process of right-threading a binary search tree:

ALGORITHM TO RIGHT-THREAD A BST

(∗ Algorithm to right-thread a binary search tree. Each thread links a node to its inorder successor ∗)

Perform an inorder traversal of the BST. Whenever a node x with a nil right pointer is encountered, replace this right link with a thread to the inorder successor of x. The inorder successor of such a node x is its parent if x is a left child of its parent; otherwise, it is the nearest ancestor of x that contains x in its left subtree.

An iterative algorithm for traversing a right-threaded binary search tree is now straightforward:

ALGORITHM FOR INORDER TRAVERSAL OF A RIGHT-THREADED BST

(∗ Algorithm to carry out an inorder traversal of a right-threaded BST in which each thread connects a node and its inorder successor. *LLink*(p) and *RLink*(p) denote the left and right links in the node pointed to by p. ∗)

1. Initialize a pointer p to the root of the tree.
2. While p is not nil do the following:
   a. While *LLink*(p) is not nil,
      Replace p by *LLink*(p).
   b. Visit the node pointed to by p.
   c. While *RLink*(p) is a thread do the following:
      i. Replace p by *RLink*(p).
      ii. Visit the node pointed to by p.
   d. Replace p by *RLink*(p)

Note that this algorithm requires being able to distinguish between right links that are threads and those that are actual pointers to right children. This suggests adding a boolean field *RightThread* in the record declarations like those in Section 12.1 for nodes of a BST. While the tree is being threaded, *RightThread* will be set to TRUE if the right link of a node is a thread and will be set to FALSE otherwise. Declarations like the following are thus appropriate for threaded binary search trees:

```
TYPE
     ElementType = . . .;   (* type of data items in the nodes *)
     ThreadedTreePointer = POINTER TO ThreadedTreeNode;
     ThreadedTreeNode = RECORD
                              Data : ElementType;
                              LLink, RLink : ThreadedTreePointer;
                              RightThread : BOOLEAN
                        END;
     ThreadedBST = ThreadedTreePointer;
```

Procedures to implement the algorithms given in this section for threading a BST and traversing a threaded BST are quite straightforward and are left as exercises.

Exercises

1. Show the threaded BST that results from right-threading the following binary search trees:

   (a) The BST in Exercise 3 of Section 12.1.
   (b) The first BST containing state abbreviations in Section 12.2.
   (c) The final AVL tree containing state abbreviations in Section 12.2.
   (d) The BST obtained by inserting the following Modula-2 reserved words in the order given: CARDINAL, REAL, BOOLEAN, ARRAY, BITSET, SET, RECORD, INTEGER, CHAR.
   (e) The BST obtained by inserting the following Modula-2 reserved words in the order given: ARRAY, BITSET, BOOLEAN, CARDINAL, CHAR, INTEGER, REAL, RECORD, SET.
   (f) The BST obtained by inserting the following Modula-2 reserved words in the order given: SET, RECORD, REAL, INTEGER, CHAR, CARDINAL, BOOLEAN, BITSET, ARRAY.
   (g) The BST obtained by inserting the following Modula-2 reserved words in the order given: END, BEGIN, IF, ELSIF, THEN, CASE, ELSE, WHILE, DO, REPEAT, UNTIL, FOR, BY, TO.

2. Write a procedure to implement the inorder traversal algorithm for a right-threaded BST given in the text.

3. Write a procedure to implement the right-threading algorithm for a BST given in the text.

4. (a) Give an algorithm similar to that in the text for threading a binary tree, but to facilitate preorder traversal.
   (b) For each of the binary trees in Exercise 1, show the binary tree threaded as described in part (a).

5. Give an algorithm for carrying out a preorder traversal of a binary tree threaded as described in Exercise 2.

6. Consider a binary tree that is threaded to facilitate inorder traversal. Give an algorithm for finding the preorder successor of a given node in such an inorder-threaded binary tree. Do *not* rethread the tree to facilitate preorder traversal as described in Exercise 4.

7. Proceeding as in Exercise 6, give an algorithm for carrying out a preorder traversal of an inorder-threaded binary tree.

8. The right-threading algorithm given in the text right-threads an existing BST. It is also possible to construct a right-threaded BST by inserting an item into a right-threaded BST (beginning with an empty BST) in such a way that the resulting BST is right-threaded.

   (a) Give such an insertion algorithm.
   (b) Trace the algorithm with the Modula-2 reserved words given in

Exercise 1-(d), showing the right-threaded BST after each word is inserted.

(c) Repeat part (b) for the words in Exercise 1-(g).

9. Give an algorithm to delete a node from a right-threaded BST so that the resulting BST is also right-threaded.

10. A *fully-threaded* BST replaces not only nil right links with threads to inorder successors as described in the text but also nil left links with threads to inorder predecessors. Show the fully-threaded BST for each of the BSTs in Exercise 1.

11. (a) Give an algorithm to fully thread a BST as described in Exercise 10.
    (b) Write an algorithm to insert a node into a fully-threaded BST so that the resulting BST is also fully threaded.
    (c) Write an algorithm to find the parent of a given node in a fully-threaded BST.

12. Write a program that uses the techniques of Section 12.1 to construct a BST, threads it using the procedure of Exercise 3, and then traverses it using the procedure of Exercise 2.

13. Proceed as in Exercise 12, but implement the insertion algorithm of Exercise 8 and use this to construct the threaded BST.

12.4 Application of Binary Trees: Huffman Codes

In Section 12.1 we indicated how a binary tree can be used in various encoding and decoding problems. In particular we showed part of a binary tree for the Morse code, which represents each character by a sequence of dots and dashes. Unlike ASCII and EBCDIC coding schemes, in which the length of the code is the same for all characters, Morse code uses variable-length sequences. In this section we consider another coding scheme that uses variable-length codes.

The basic idea in these variable-length coding schemes is to use shorter codes for those characters that occur more frequently than for those used less frequently. For example, 'E' is encoded in Morse code as a single dot, whereas 'Z' is represented as $- - \cdot \cdot$. The objective is to minimize the expected length of the code for a character.

To state the problem more precisely, suppose that some character set $\{C_1, C_2, \ldots, C_n\}$ is given and certain *weights* $w_1, w_2, \ldots, w_n$ are associated with these characters; w_i is the weight attached to character C_i and is some measure (e.g., probability or relative frequency) of how frequently this character occurs in messages to be encoded. If $l_1, l_2, \ldots, l_n$ are the lengths of the codes for characters $C_1, C_2, \ldots, C_n$, respectively, then the *expected length* of the code for any one of these characters is given by

$$\text{expected length} = w_1 l_1 + w_2 l_2 + \cdots + w_n l_n = \sum_{i=1}^{n} w_i l_i$$

As a simple example, consider the five characters A, B, C, D, and E, and suppose they occur with the following weights (probabilities):

character	A	B	C	D	E
weight	0.2	0.1	0.1	0.15	0.45

In Morse code with a dot replaced by 0 and a dash by 1, these characters are encoded as follows:

Character	Code
A	01
B	1000
C	1010
D	100
E	0

Thus the expected length of the code for each of these five letters in this scheme is

$$0.2 \times 2 + 0.1 \times 4 + 0.1 \times 4 + 0.15 \times 3 + 0.45 \times 1 = 2.1$$

Another useful property of some coding schemes is that they are **immediately decodable**. This means that no sequence of bits that represents a character is a prefix of a longer sequence for some other character. Consequently, when a sequence of bits is received that is the code for a character, it can be decoded as that character immediately, without our waiting to see if subsequent bits change it into a longer code for some other character. Note that the preceding Morse code scheme is not immediately decodable because, for example, the code for E (0) is a prefix of the code for A (01), and the code for D (100) is a prefix of the code for B (1000). (For decoding, Morse code uses a third ''bit,'' a pause, to separate letters.) A coding scheme for which the code lengths are the same as in the preceding scheme and that is immediately decodable is as follows:

Character	Code
A	01
B	0000
C	0001
D	001
E	1

The following algorithm, given by D. A. Huffman in 1952, can be used to construct coding schemes that are immediately decodable and for which each character has a minimal expected code length:

HUFFMAN'S ALGORITHM

(∗ Algorithm to construct a binary code for a given set of characters for which the expected length of the bit string for a given character is minimal. ∗)

1. Initialize a list of one-node binary trees containing the weights w_1, $w_2, \ldots, w_n$, one for each of the characters $C_1, C_2, \ldots, C_n$.
2. Do the following $n - 1$ times:
    a. Find two trees T' and T'' in this list with roots of minimal weights w' and w''.
    b. Replace these two trees with a binary tree whose root is $w' + w''$, whose subtrees are T' and T'', and label the pointers to these subtrees 0 and 1, respectively:

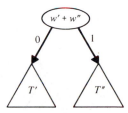

3. The code for character C_i is the bit string labeling a path from the root in the final binary tree to the leaf for C_i.

As an illustration of Huffman's algorithm, consider again the characters A, B, C, D, and E with the weights given earlier. We begin by constructing a list of one-node binary trees, one for each character:

The first two trees to be selected are those corresponding to letters B and C, since they have the smallest weights, and these are combined to produce a tree having weight $0.1 + 0.1 = 0.2$ and having these two trees as subtrees:

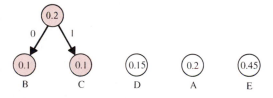

From this list of four binary trees, we again select two of minimal weights, the first and the second (or the second and the third), and replace them with another tree having weight $0.2 + 0.15 = 0.35$ and having these two trees as subtrees:

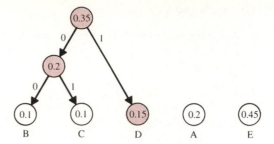

From this list of three binary trees, the first two have minimal weights and are combined to produce a binary tree having weight $0.35 + 0.2 = 0.55$ and having these trees as subtrees:

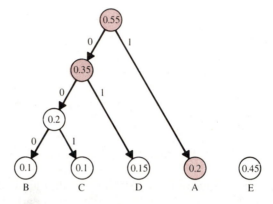

The resulting binary tree is then combined with the one-node tree representing E to give the final Huffman tree:

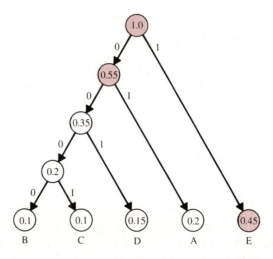

The Huffman codes obtained from this tree are as follows:

Character	Huffman Code
A	01
B	0000
C	0001
D	001
E	1

As we calculated earlier, the expected length of the code for each of these characters is 2.1.

A different assignment of codes to these characters for which the expected length is also 2.1 is possible because at the second stage we had two choices for trees of minimal weight:

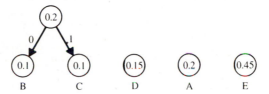

We selected the first and second trees from this list, but we could have used the second and third:

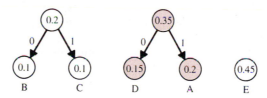

At the next stage, the resulting list of two binary trees would have been

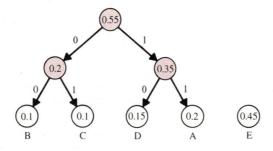

and the final Huffman tree

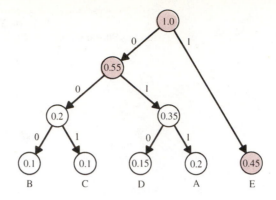

The assignment of codes corresponding to this tree is

Character	Huffman Code
A	011
B	000
C	001
D	010
E	1

The immediate decodability property of Huffman codes is clear. Each character is associated with a leaf node in the Huffman tree, and there is a unique path from the root of a tree to each leaf. Consequently, no sequence of bits comprising the code for some character can be a prefix of a longer sequence of bits for some other character.

Because of this property of immediate decodability, a decoding algorithm is easy:

HUFFMAN DECODING ALGORITHM

(∗ Algorithm to decode messages that were encoded using a Huffman tree ∗)

1. Initialize pointer p to the root of the Huffman tree.
2. While the end of the message string has not been reached, do the following:
   a. Let x be the next bit in the string.
   b. If $x = 0$ then
       Set p equal to its left child pointer.
   Else
       Set p equal to its right child pointer.
   c. If p points to a leaf then:
       i. Display the character associated with that leaf.
       ii. Reset p to the root of the Huffman tree.

As an illustration, suppose that the message string

0 1 0 1 0 1 1 0 1 0

is received and that this message was encoded using the second Huffman tree constructed earlier. The pointer follows the path labeled 010 from the root of this tree to the letter D and is then reset to the root:

0 1 0 1 0 1 1 0 1 0
D

The next bit, 1, leads immediately to the letter E:

0 1 0 1 0 1 1 0 1 0
D   E

The pointer p next follows the path 011 to the letter A,

0 1 0 1 0 1 1 0 1 0
D   E   A

and finally the path 010 to the letter D again:

0 1 0 1 0 1 1 0 1 0
D   E   A   D

The program in Figure 12.1 implements this decoding algorithm. The procedure *BuildDecodingTree* initializes a tree consisting of a single node and then reads letters and their codes from a code file and constructs the decoding tree. For each letter in the file, it calls procedure *AddToTree* to follow a path determined by the code of the character, creating nodes as necessary. When the end of the code string is reached, the character is inserted in the last (leaf) node created on this path. The procedure *Decode* is then called to read a message string of bits from *MessageFile* and to decode it using the decoding tree. Procedure *PrintTree* is included in this program simply to give an idea of what the tree looks like. It is basically nothing more than an *RNL* traversal of the tree. It prints the tree "on its side" without the directed arcs and 0/1 labels. We leave it to the reader to draw these in and then rotate it 90 degrees so it has its usual orientation.

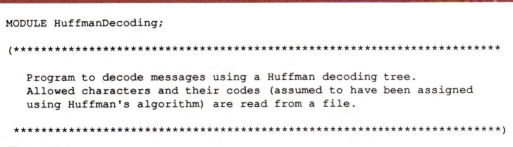

```
MODULE HuffmanDecoding;

(************************************************************************

    Program to decode messages using a Huffman decoding tree.
    Allowed characters and their codes (assumed to have been assigned
    using Huffman's algorithm) are read from a file.

 ************************************************************************)
```

Figure 12.1

Figure 12.1 (cont.)

```
FROM InOut IMPORT Write, WriteString, WriteLn, Read, ReadString,
                  OpenInput, OpenOutput, CloseInput, CloseOutput,
                  Done, EOL;
FROM Storage IMPORT ALLOCATE, DEALLOCATE;

CONST
    StringLimit = 10;   (* limit on number of bits in a bit string *)

TYPE
    String = ARRAY[0..StringLimit] OF CHAR;
    BitString = String;
    ElementType = CHAR;
    TreePointer = POINTER TO TreeNode;
    TreeNode = RECORD
                    Data : ElementType;
                    LChild, RChild : TreePointer;
               END;
    BinaryTree = TreePointer;

VAR
    Root : BinaryTree;    (* pointer to root of decoding tree *)

PROCEDURE BuildDecodingTree(VAR Root : BinaryTree);

    (*************************************************************

        Procedure to read characters and their codes (assumed to be
        found using Huffman's algorithm) from a code file and
        construct the Huffman decoding tree and return a pointer
        to its Root.

    *************************************************************)

    VAR
        Ch : CHAR;            (* character read from  code file *)
        Code : BitString;     (* Huffman code for Ch *)
        CodeLen : CARDINAL;   (* length of Code *)

    PROCEDURE AddToTree(Ch : CHAR; Code : BitString; Root : BinaryTree);

        (*********************************************************

            Procedure to create and add a leaf node to the Huffman
            decoding tree for character Ch with the given Code.

        *********************************************************)

        CONST
            EOS = 0C;            (* end-of-string mark *)

        VAR
            i : CARDINAL;        (* index in Code *)
            TempPtr,             (* pointer to new node(s) *)
            p : TreePointer;     (* pointer to nodes in path labeled by Code *)
```

Figure 12.1   (cont.)

```
        BEGIN
            i := 0;
            p := Root;
            WHILE (i <= StringLimit) AND (Code[i] # EOS) DO
                IF Code[i] = '0' THEN          (* descend left *)
                    IF p^.LChild = NIL THEN     (* create node along path *)
                        ALLOCATE(TempPtr, SIZE(TreeNode));
                        TempPtr^.Data := '*';
                        TempPtr^.LChild := NIL;
                        TempPtr^.RChild := NIL;
                        p^.LChild := TempPtr
                    END (* IF *);
                    INC(i);
                    p := p^.LChild

                ELSIF Code[i] = '1' THEN        (* descend right *)
                    IF p^.RChild = NIL THEN      (* create node along path *)
                        ALLOCATE(TempPtr, SIZE(TreeNode));
                        TempPtr^.Data := '*';
                        TempPtr^.LChild := NIL;
                        TempPtr^.RChild := NIL;
                        p^.RChild := TempPtr
                    END (* IF *);
                    INC(i);
                    p := p^.RChild
                END (* IF *)
            END (* WHILE *);

            p^.Data := Ch
        END AddToTree;

    BEGIN (* BuildDecodingTree *)
        ALLOCATE(Root, SIZE(TreeNode));
        Root^.Data := '*';
        Root^.LChild := NIL;
        Root^.RChild := NIL;
        WriteLn;
        WriteString('Enter name of file containing codes'); WriteLn;
        OpenInput('');
        Read(Ch);
        WHILE Done DO
            ReadString(Code);
            AddToTree(Ch, Code, Root);
            Read(Ch);
        END (* WHILE *);
        CloseInput
    END BuildDecodingTree;

PROCEDURE PrintTree(Root : BinaryTree; Indent : CARDINAL);

(***************************************************************

    Recursive procedure to display a binary tree.   The tree
    is displayed "on its side" with no arcs drawn in.

    ***************************************************************)
```

Figure 12.1 (cont.)

```
        VAR
            i : CARDINAL;    (* index *)

        BEGIN (* PrintTree *)
            IF Root <> NIL THEN
                PrintTree(Root^.RChild, Indent + 8);
                FOR i := 1 TO Indent - 1 DO
                    Write(' ')
                END (* FOR *);
                Write(Root^.Data);
                WriteLn;
                PrintTree(Root^.LChild, Indent + 8)
            END (* IF *)
        END PrintTree;

    PROCEDURE Decode(Root : BinaryTree);

        (**************************************************************

            Procedure to read a message (string of bits) from a file and
            decode it using the Huffman decoding tree with given Root.

            **********************************************************)

        VAR
            Bit : CHAR;            (* next message bit *)
            p : TreePointer;       (* pointer to trace path in decoding tree *)

        BEGIN
            WriteLn;
            WriteString('Enter name of file containing coded message');
            WriteLn;
            OpenInput('');
            WriteLn;
            Read(Bit);
            WHILE Done DO
                p := Root;
                WHILE (p^.LChild <> NIL) OR (p^.RChild <> NIL) DO
                    Write(Bit);
                    IF Bit = '0' THEN
                        p := p^.LChild
                    ELSIF Bit = '1' THEN
                        p := p^.RChild
                    ELSE
                        WriteLn;
                        WriteString('Illegal bit:  ');
                        Write(Bit);
                        WriteString(' -- ignored');
                        WriteLn
                    END (* IF *);
                    Read(Bit);
                    IF Bit = EOL THEN      (* discard end-of-line character *)
                        Read(Bit)
                    END (* IF *)
                END (* WHILE *);
```

Figure 12.1 (cont.)

```
                WriteString('--');
                Write(p^.Data);
                WriteLn
          END (* WHILE *);
          CloseInput
       END Decode;

BEGIN (* main program *)
    BuildDecodingTree(Root);
     WriteLn; WriteLn;
    PrintTree(Root, 8);
    WriteLn; WriteLn;
    Decode(Root)
END HuffmanDecoding.
```

Listing of Code File:

```
A 1101
B 001101
C 01100
D 0010
E 101
F 111100
G 001110
H 0100
I 1000
J 11111100
K 11111101
L 01111
M 01101
N 1100
O 1110
P 111101
Q 111111100
R 1001
S 0101
T 000
U 01110
V 001100
W 001111
X 111111101
Y 111110
Z 11111111
```

Listing of MessageFile:

```
00001001011001101010
01100111011010000101
11011001101011001110011011000110001110
```

Sample run:

```
Enter name of file containing codes
in> CODES
```

Figure 12.1   (cont.)

Figure 12.1 (cont.)

```
Enter name of file containing coded message
in> MESSAGE

000--T
0100--H
101--E
1001--R
101--E
0010--D
01100--C
1110--O
1101--A
000--T
0101--S
1101--A
1001--R
101--E
01100--C
1110--O
01101--M
1000--I
1100--N
001110--G
```

Exercises

1. Demonstrate that Morse code is not immediately decodable by showing that the bit string 100001100 can be decoded in more than one way.

2. Using the first Huffman code given in this section (A = 01, B = 0000, C = 0001, D = 001, E = 1), decode the following bit strings:

   (a) 000001001
   (b) 001101001
   (c) 000101001
   (d) 00001010011001

3. Construct the Huffman code for the Modula-2 reserved words and weights given in the following table:

Words	Weight
BEGIN	.30
END	.30
FOR	.05
IF	.20
WHILE	.15

4. Repeat Exercise 3 for the following table of letters and weights:

Character	Weight
a	.20
b	.10
c	.08
d	.08
e	.40
f	.05
g	.05
h	.04

5. Using the Huffman code developed in Exercise 4, encode the following message: "feed a deaf aged hag."

6. Repeat Exercise 3 for the following table of Modula-2 reserved words and weights (frequencies):

Words	Weight
BEGIN	22
CASE	2
DO	20
ELSE	10
ELSIF	6
END	22
FOR	5
IF	20
LOOP	1
REPEAT	4
THEN	20
TO	3
UNTIL	4
WHILE	15
WITH	2

7. Write a procedure that reads a table of letters and their weights and constructs a Huffman code for these letters.

8. Use the procedure of Exercise 7 in a program that encodes a message that is entered by the user.

12.5 Tries, B-Trees, and Other Trees

Until now we have confined our attention to binary trees, those in which each node has at most two children. In many applications, however, allowing more than two children would seem necessary or at least desirable. For example, in a *genealogical tree* such as the following, it is not the case that each person has a maximum of two children:

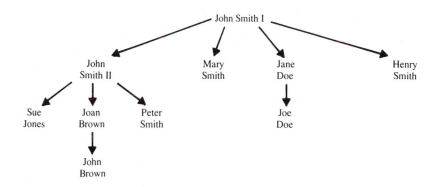

Game trees that are used to analyze games and puzzles usually do not have the binary property. The following tree showing the various configurations possible in the Tower of Hanoi problem with two disks (see Section 5.4) is a simple illustration of such a game tree:

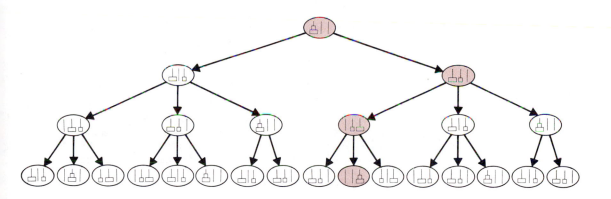

Parse trees constructed during the compilation of a program are used to check the program's syntax. For example, in Section 5.4 we considered the parse tree for the expression 2 * (3 + 4),

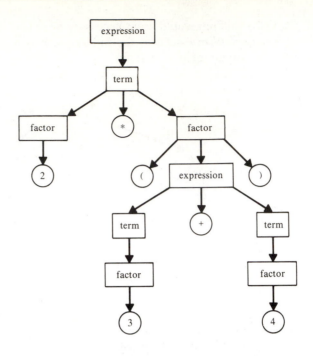

and the following tree could be the parse tree constructed by a Modula-2 compiler for the statement

    IF *x* < 0 THEN
        Flag := 1
    END

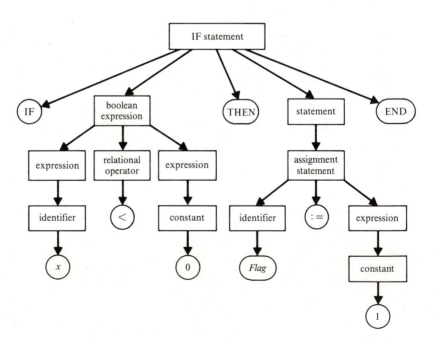

The searching technique used for binary search trees has also been extended to general trees. One method of organizing a general search tree is called a **trie** (derived from the word *retrieval* but pronounced "try"). In the search of a BST for a particular item, the search path descends to the left subtree of a particular node if the item is less than the data value in that node; otherwise, it descends to the right subtree. These are the only two options. A trie is a general tree, however, so that at a given node, there may be several different directions that a search path may follow, and in general, this results in shorter search paths because there are fewer levels in the tree.

To illustrate, suppose we wish to store a collection of words to be used as a dictionary in a spell-checker program. As this program checks a document, it must examine each word and search the dictionary for a match, signaling a possible spelling error if none is found. Because this dictionary must be consulted many times, efficient searching is critical, and thus it is natural to organize the dictionary as a trie.

Each node of the trie stores one letter. The first-level nodes store all first letters of words in the dictionary, those on the second level store all second letters of words in the dictionary, and so on. As a simple illustration, consider a dictionary containing the following words: APE, CAT, COD, COW, DEER, DOE, DOG, DOVE, HORSE, and ZEBRA. This list of words can be stored in the following trie:

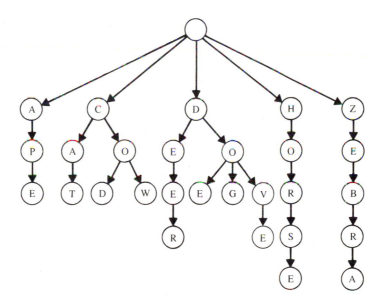

Note that the search time for each word is proportional to the length of that word, and since short words occur more frequently than do long words, this should result in good overall performance for the spell-checker program. One difficulty with this trie is that some words are prefixes of other words. For example, suppose that CATTLE is to be added to this dictionary. If we simply add three nodes with the letters T, L, and E, respectively, to the path of nodes for CAT, then there is no way to check the spelling of the word CAT. One solution is to add a dummy character such as $ to the end of each word so that no word is a prefix of any other word. Thus the trie, with CATTLE added, would be

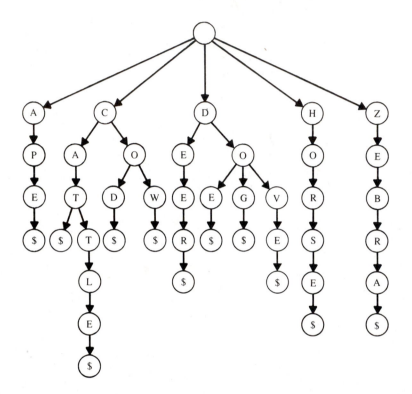

BSTs and tries are data structures used in ***internal searching schemes***, that is, those in which the data set being searched is sufficiently small so that all of it can stored in main memory. A B-tree is one data structure that is useful in ***external searching***, where the data is stored in secondary memory. A ***B-tree of order m*** is a general tree satisfying the properties:

1. All leaves are on the same level.
2. The root has at least two children and at most m children; all other internal (nonleaf) nodes have at least $m/2$ children and at most m children.
3. The number of data items stored in each internal node is one less than the number of children, and these values partition the data items that are stored in the children.

To illustrate, the following is a B-tree of order 5 that stores integers:

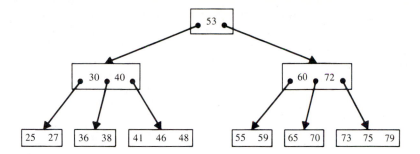

To search this tree for the value 36, we begin at the root and compare 36 with the data items stored in the root. In this B-tree, the single item 53 is stored in the root, and 36 is less than 53, so we next search the left subtree:

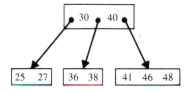

Comparing 36 with the data items 30 and 40 stored in the root of this subtree, we find that 36 is between these values, an indication that 36 is in the middle subtree:

```
36   38
```

Examining the data items in the root of this subtree, we locate the value 36.

The basic step in constructing a B-tree of order m is to begin with a single node and to insert values into this node until it becomes full, that is, until it contains $m - 1$ items. When the next item is inserted, the node is split into two nodes, one storing the items less than the median and one storing those greater than the median. The median itself is stored in a parent having these two nodes as children.

As an illustration, the preceding B-tree of order 5 can be constructed as follows. Suppose the first integers inserted are 25, 40, 41, and 27. These are arranged in ascending order and are stored in the root node of a one-node tree:

```
25   27   40   41
```

Suppose the next item being inserted is 55. Because the root node is full, it must be split into two nodes, one containing 25 and 27, which are less than the median 40, and the other containing the values greater than the median, 41 and 55:

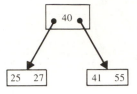

Next 36, 46, and 60 can be inserted into the leaves:

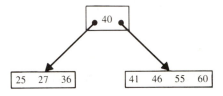

If 53 is inserted, the rightmost leaf must be split:

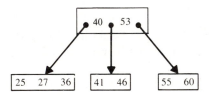

Now 38, 73, 48, and 72 are inserted into leaves; no splitting is necessary:

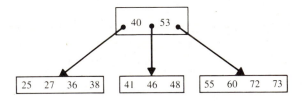

The insertion of 79 forces a splitting of the rightmost leaf:

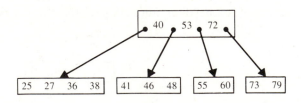

Now 59, 65, and 75 can be inserted into the leaves with no splitting, but the insertion of 30 causes the leftmost leaf to split:

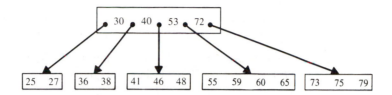

Finally, 70 is inserted into the fourth leaf, causing a split. When the median 60 is inserted into the parent node, which is the root, it also must be split, and the resulting B-tree is

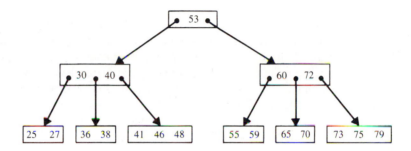

As noted earlier, B-trees are useful for organizing data sets stored in secondary memory, such as files and databases stored on a magnetic disk. In such applications, nodes in the B-tree typically store one file block, the maximum amount of information that can be retrieved in one access. This maximizes the number of data items stored in each node and the number of children. This, in turn, minimizes the depth of the B-tree and hence the length of a search path. Because one disk access is required at each level along the search path, the number of data transfers from the disk also is minimized.

In practice, when the data items are large records, modified B-trees in which only the leaves store complete records are used; internal nodes store certain key values in these records because only the key values are used in searching. Also, the leaves may be linked together to reduce still further the number of disk accesses required.

Because general trees arise in a variety of applications, we must consider what structures might be used to implement them. One implementation is a natural extension of the implementation for binary trees using a multiply linked structure. A node in such a structure representing a general tree has several linked fields rather than just two,

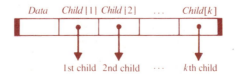

where k is the maximum number of children that a node may have. Its declaration would thus have the form

CONST
    MaxChildren = . . . ; (* maximum number of children per node *)

TYPE
    ElementType = . . . ;   (* type of data items in nodes *)
    TreePointer = POINTER TO *TreeNode*;
    TreeNode = RECORD
                    Data : *ElementType*;
                    Child : ARRAY [1..*MaxChildren*] OF *TreePointer*
                END;
    Tree = *TreePointer*;

The problem with this linked representation is that each node must have one link field for each possible child, even though most of the nodes will not use all of these links. In fact, the amount of "wasted" space may be quite large. To demonstrate this, suppose that a tree has n nodes with a maximum of 5 children per node. The linked representation will thus require n nodes, each having 5 link fields, for a total of $5n$ links. In such a tree, however, there are only $n - 1$ directed arcs, and thus only $n - 1$ of these link fields are used to connect the nodes. This means that $5n - (n - 1) = 4n + 1$ of the link fields are nil; thus the fraction of unused link fields is

$$\frac{4n + 1}{5n}$$

which is approximately equal to four-fifths; that is, approximately 80 percent of the link fields are nil.

It is possible, however, to represent any tree using nodes that have only two link fields, that is, by a binary tree. We use one of these fields to link siblings together (that is, all the children of a given node) in the order in which they appear in the tree, from left to right. The other link in each node points to the first node in this linked list of its children. For example, the tree

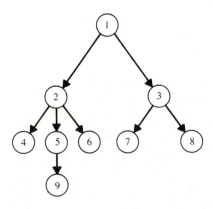

can be represented by the binary tree

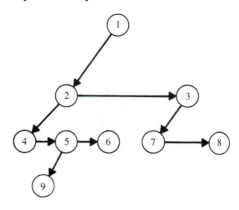

or, if it is drawn in the more customary manner:

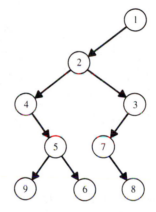

In this binary tree, node x is a left child of node y if x is the leftmost child of y in the given tree, and x is the right child of y if x and y are siblings in the original tree.

When a binary tree is used in this manner to represent a general tree, the right pointer in the root always is nil because the root never has a right child. (Why?) This allows us to use a binary tree to represent not merely a single tree, but an entire *forest*, which is a collection of trees. We simply set the right pointer in the root node of a binary tree used to represent one of these trees to point to the root of the binary tree for the next tree in the forest. For example, the following forest

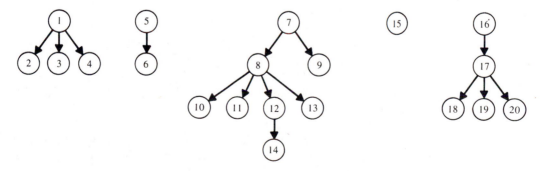

can be represented by the single binary tree:

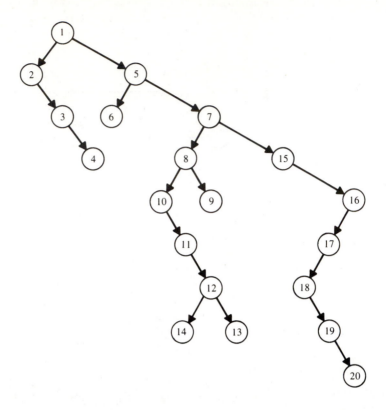

One especially attractive feature of this representation of general trees is that we have studied binary trees in some detail and have developed algorithms for processing them. These algorithms can thus be used to process general trees as described in the exercises; in particular, the traversal algorithms can be used to traverse general trees and forests.

A third representation of general trees is based on the fact that trees are special cases of a more general structure known as a ***directed graph***. Directed graphs are considered in the next chapter, and any of the implementations described there can also be used for trees.

Exercises

1. Draw a trie to store the following set of words: A, AM, AN, AND, BAT, BE, BEEN, BET, BEFORE, BEHIND, BIT, BITE, BUT, BYTE, CAT, COT, CUT.

2. Draw a trie to store the following set of integers: 1, 12, 123, 1234, 12345, 27, 35, 41, 423, 424, 4244, 479.

3. Draw the B-tree of order 3 that results when the following letters are inserted in the order given: C, O, R, N, F, L, A, K, E, S.

4. Construct the B-tree of order 5 that results when the following integers are inserted in the order given: 261, 381, 385, 295, 134, 400, 95, 150, 477, 291, 414, 240, 456, 80, 25, 474, 493, 467, 349, 180, 370, 257.

5. Represent each of the following general trees or forests by binary trees:

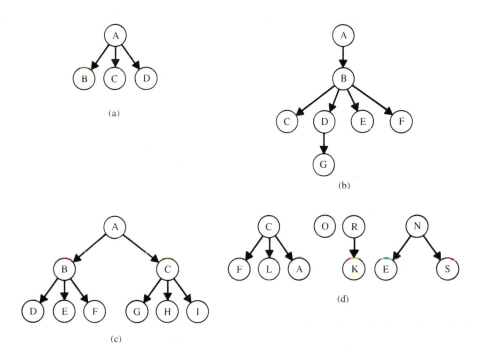

(a)

(b)

(c)

(d)

6. Write a procedure to print in ascending order the data items stored in a trie.

7. Write a program that reads words and constructs a trie to store these words. The program should then allow the user to enter a word and should search the trie for this word.

8. Incorporate the procedure of Exercise 6 into the program of Exercise 7.

9. Write a spell-checker program like that in Exercise 17 of Section 12.1, but use a trie to store the dictionary rather than a BST.

10. Write appropriate declarations for a B-tree.

11. Write a procedure to search a B-tree for a given item.

12. Write a procedure to print in ascending order (of keys) the items stored in a B-tree.

13. Write a program that reads words and constructs a B-tree to store these words. The program should then allow the user to enter a word and should search the B-tree for this word.

14. Incorporate the procedure of Exercise 12 into the program of Exercise 13.

13

Graphs and Digraphs

As we noted in the preceding chapter, a tree is a special case of a more general structure known as a *directed graph*, or simply *digraph*. Directed graphs differ from trees in that they need not have a root node and there may be several (or no) paths from one vertex to another. They are useful therefore in modeling communication networks and other networks in which signals, electrical pulses, and the like flow from one node to another along various paths. In other networks there may be no direction associated with the links, and these can be modeled using *undirected graphs*, or simply *graphs*. In this chapter we consider how both directed and undirected graphs can be represented, as well as algorithms for some of the basic graph operations such as searching and traversal.

13.1 Directed Graphs

A *directed graph*, or *digraph*, like a tree, consists of a finite set of elements called *vertices*, or *nodes*, together with a finite set of directed arcs that connect pairs of vertices. For example, a directed graph having five vertices numbered 1, 2, 3, 4, 5, and seven directed arcs joining vertices 1 to 2, 1 to 4, 1 to 5, 2 to 3, 2 to 4, 3 to itself, 4 to 2, and 4 to 3 might be pictured as

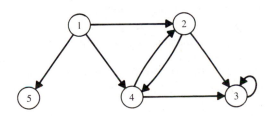

Trees are special kinds of directed graphs and are characterized by the fact that one of their nodes, the root, has no incoming arcs and every other node can be reached from the root by a unique path, that is, by following one and only one sequence of consecutive arcs. The preceding digraph does have a ''rootlike'' node with no incoming arcs, namely, vertex 1, but there are many different paths from vertex 1 to vertex 3, for example:

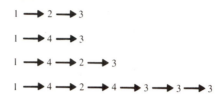

Applications of directed graphs are many and varied. Digraphs are used to analyze electrical circuits, develop project schedules, find shortest routes, analyze social relationships, and construct models for the analysis and solution of many other problems. For example, the following directed graph illustrates how digraphs might be used in planning the activities that must be carried out and the order in which they must be done for a (simplified) construction project:

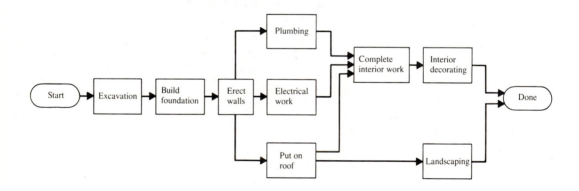

Similarly, flowcharts used to represent algorithms, are directed graphs.

There are several common ways of implementing a directed graph using data structures already known to us. One of these is the **adjacency matrix** of the digraph. To construct it, we first number the vertices of the digraph 1, 2, . . . , n; the adjacency matrix is then the $n \times n$ matrix Adj, in which the entry in row i and column j is 1 (or true) if vertex j is **adjacent** to vertex i (that is, if there is a directed arc from vertex i to vertex j), and is 0 (or false) otherwise. For example, the adjacency matrix for the digraph

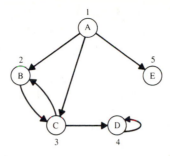

with nodes numbered as shown is

$$Adj = \begin{bmatrix} 0 & 1 & 1 & 0 & 1 \\ 0 & 0 & 1 & 0 & 0 \\ 0 & 1 & 0 & 1 & 0 \\ 0 & 0 & 0 & 1 & 0 \\ 0 & 0 & 0 & 0 & 0 \end{bmatrix}$$

For a **weighted digraph** in which some "cost" or "weight" is associated with each arc (for example, in a digraph modeling a communication network), the cost of the arc from vertex i to vertex j is used instead of 1 in the adjacency matrix.

This matrix representation of a directed graph is straightforward and is useful in a variety of graph problems. For example, with this representation, it is easy to calculate the number of paths of any given length from one vertex to another; the i, j entry of the kth power of Adj indicates the number of paths of length k from vertex i to vertex j. Likewise, it is easy to determine the **in-degree** and **out-degree** of any vertex, that is, the number of edges coming into or emanating from that vertex, respectively. The sum of the entries in row i of the adjacency matrix is obviously the out-degree of the ith vertex, and the sum of the entries in the ith column is its in-degree.

There are, however, some deficiencies in this representation. One is that it does not store the data items in the vertices of the digraph, the letters A, B, C, D, and E in our example. But this difficulty is easily remedied; we need only create an auxiliary array *Data* and store the data item for the ith vertex in *Data[i]*. For our example, therefore, the two arrays

$$Adj = \begin{bmatrix} 0 & 1 & 1 & 0 & 1 \\ 0 & 0 & 1 & 0 & 0 \\ 0 & 1 & 0 & 1 & 0 \\ 0 & 0 & 0 & 1 & 0 \\ 0 & 0 & 0 & 0 & 0 \end{bmatrix} \qquad Data = \begin{bmatrix} A \\ B \\ C \\ D \\ E \end{bmatrix}$$

completely characterize the digraph.

Another deficiency of the adjacency matrix representation is that this matrix is often **sparse**, that is, it has many zero entries, and thus considerable space is "wasted" in storing these zero values. We can alleviate this problem by adapting one of the representations of sparse matrices described in Section 8.7. For example, modifying the representation of a sparse matrix as an array of pointers to linked row-lists gives rise to the **adjacency list representation** for digraphs. The directed graph is represented by an array of pointers $V[1]$, $V[2]$, . . . , $V[n]$, one for each vertex in the digraph. Each array element $V[i]$ points to a head node that stores the data item for that vertex and also contains a pointer to a linked list of ***vertex nodes***, one for each vertex adjacent to node i. Each vertex node has two fields: an integer field, which stores the number of that vertex, and a link field, which points to the next vertex node in this adjacency list.

The adjacency list representation of the digraph

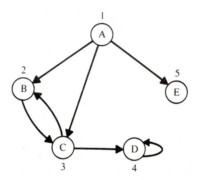

would thus be pictured as follows:

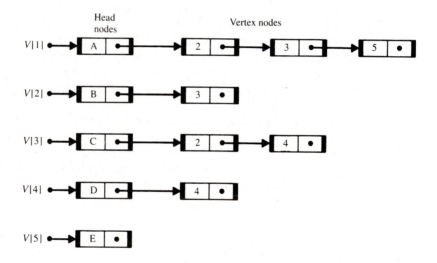

Note that the numbers in these vertex nodes are the numbers of the columns in the adjacency matrix in which 1's appear. These nodes thus play the same role as the nodes in the row lists of the sparse matrix representation considered in Chapter 8.

This adjacency list representation of a digraph can be implemented in Modula-2 with declarations of the following form:

CONST
 MaxVertices = . . . ; (∗ maximum number of vertices in digraph ∗)

TYPE
    ElementType = . . . ;   (* type of data items in vertices *)
    VertexNumber = [1..*MaxVertices*];
    AdjPointer = POINTER TO *VertexNode*;
    VertexNode = RECORD
                Vertex : *VertexNumber*;
                Next : *AdjPointer*
          END;
    HeadNode = RECORD
                Data : *ElementType*;
                Next : *AdjPointer*
         END;
    HeadPointer = POINTER TO *HeadNode*;
    ArrayOfPointers = ARRAY *VertexNumber* OF *HeadPointer*;

VAR
    V : *ArrayOfPointers*;

If we prefer a single declaration for the nodes, we can use a variant record such as

Node = RECORD
       CASE *Tag* : BOOLEAN OF
          TRUE : *Vertex* : *VertexNumber* (* vertex node *)
                |
          FALSE : *Data* : *ElementType*   (* head node *)
       END (* CASE *);
        Next : *AdjPointer*
     END;

To construct these adjacency lists for a digraph, we might proceed as follows:

ALGORITHM TO CONSTRUCT ADJACENCY LIST REPRESENTATION

For *i* ranging from 1 to the number of vertices do:

1. Obtain a head node pointed to by *V*[*i*] and initialize its *Next* field to nil.
2. Read the data item to be stored in this vertex into the data field *V*[*i*]↑.*Data* of this head node.
3. For each vertex adjacent to vertex *i* do:
   a. Read the number of that vertex.
   b. Insert this number into a linked list of vertex nodes pointed to by *V*[*i*]↑.*Next* using one of the insertion algorithms in Chapter 7.

In the next section we use this adjacency list representation in a program to find the shortest path joining two specified nodes in a directed graph. The procedure *MakeDigraph* in the program in Figure 13.1 implements the preceding algorithm for constructing such a representation.

13.2   Searching and Traversing Digraphs

One of the basic operations we considered for trees was traversal, visiting each node exactly once, and we described three standard orders: inorder, preorder, and postorder. Traversal of a tree is always possible if we begin at the root, because every other node is **reachable** from this root via a sequence of consecutive arcs. In a general directed graph, however, there may not be a vertex from which every other vertex can be reached, and thus it may not be possible to traverse the entire digraph, regardless of the start vertex. Consequently, we must first consider the problem of determining which nodes in a digraph are reachable from a given node. Two standard methods of searching for such vertices are **depth-first search** and **breadth-first search**. We illustrate these methods first for trees, as these terms are more descriptive in this special case.

To illustrate depth-first search, consider the following tree:

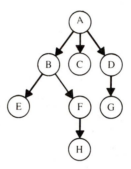

If we begin at the root, we first visit it and then select one of its children, say B, and then visit it. Before visiting the other children of A, however, we visit the descendants of B in a depth-first manner. Thus we select one of its children, say E, and visit it:

A, B, E

Again, before visiting the other child of B, we must visit the descendants of E. Because there are none, we backtrack to B and visit its other child F and then visit the descendants of F:

A, B, E, F, H

Because all of B's descendants have now been visited, we can now backtrack to A and begin visiting the rest of its descendants. We might select C and its descendants (of which there are none),

A, B, E, F, H, C

and finally, visit D and its descendants:

A, B, E, F, H, C, D, G

A breadth-first search of this tree, beginning at the root, first visits the root and each of its children, say, from left to right:

A, B, C, D

The children of these first-level nodes are then visited,

A, B, C, D, E, F, G

and finally, the children of the second-level nodes E, F, and G are visited:

A, B, C, D, E, F, G, H

A depth-first search of a general directed graph from a given start vertex is similar to that for trees. We visit the start vertex and then follow directed arcs as "deeply" as possible to visit the vertices reachable from it that have not already been visited, backtracking when necessary. For example, a depth-first search of the digraph

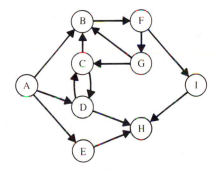

beginning at vertex A might first visit vertices A, B, F, I, and H. We then backtrack to F and from there visit G, from which we can reach vertices C and D (and H, but it has already been visited). Finally, we backtrack to A, from which we can reach the last unvisited vertex E, thus visiting the vertices in the order

A, B, F, I, H, G, C, D, E

A depth-first search starting at B can visit the vertices

B, F, I, H, G, C, D

but we cannot reach vertices A and E.

This description should suggest a recursive algorithm for depth-first search because at each stage, after visiting a vertex, we select some unvisited vertex adjacent to it (if there are any) and use it as the start vertex for a depth-first search. Such an algorithm is

DEPTH-FIRST SEARCH ALGORITHM

(* Algorithm to perform a depth-first search of a digraph to visit all vertices reachable from a given start vertex *v*. *)

1. Visit the start vertex *v*.
2. For each vertex *w* adjacent to *v* do the following:

> If *w* has not been visited, then apply the depth-first search algorithm with *w* as the start vertex.

Assuming the declarations for the adjacency list representation of a digraph given earlier, we can implement this algorithm with the following procedure:

```
PROCEDURE DepthFirstSearch (      V : ArrayOfPointers;
                              VAR Unvisited : SetOfVertices;
                                  Start : VertexNumber);
```

(* Procedure to perform a depth-first search of a digraph represented by adjacency lists, beginning at vertex *Start*. The set *Unvisited* contains the numbers of all vertices not yet visited. *)

```
VAR
    CurrPtr : AdjPointer;      (* pointer to node in an adjacency list *)
    NewStart : VertexNumber;   (* start vertex for next depth-first
                                  search *)

BEGIN
    (* Insert statements here to process V[Start]↑.Data *)
    EXCL(Unvisited, Start);

    (* Traverse its adjacency list, performing depth-first searches
       from each unvisited node in it *)
    CurrPtr := V[Start]↑.Next;
    WHILE CurrPtr # NIL DO
        NewStart := CurrPtr↑.Vertex;
        IF NewStart IN Unvisited THEN
            DepthFirstSearch(V, Unvisited, NewStart)
        END (* IF *);
        CurrPtr := CurrPtr↑.Next
    END (* WHILE *)
END DepthFirstSearch;
```

Here *Unvisited* is a set of type *SetOfVertices* = BITSET or *SetOfVertices* = SET OF *VertexNumber* which is initialized to contain all the vertices before procedure *DepthFirstSearch* is called.

In a breadth-first search of the preceding directed graph

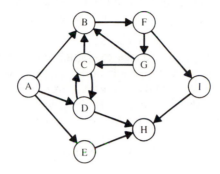

beginning at A, we visit A and then all those vertices adjacent to A:

A, B, D, E

We then visit all vertices adjacent to B, D, and E:

A, B, D, E, F, C, H

Continuing, we visit nodes adjacent to F, C, and H. G and I are adjacent to F, so we visit them:

A, B, D, E, F, C, H, G, I

A, B, and D are adjacent to C, but these vertices have already been visited, and no vertices are adjacent to H. Since all of the vertices have been visited, the search terminates.

A breadth-first search beginning at B could first visit B and F, then G and I, followed by H and C, and finally D:

B, F, G, I, H, C, D

Since A and E are not reachable from B, the search terminates.

In a depth-first search, we follow a path from the start vertex until we reach a vertex all of whose adjacent vertices have already been visited. We then backtrack to the last previously visited vertex along this path so that vertices adjacent to it can be visited. Storing the nodes along this path in a stack makes this backtracking possible. In the recursive procedure *Depth-FirstSearch*, this stack is automatically maintained as described in Section 5.5.

In a breadth-first search, however, we visit the vertices level by level, and while visiting each vertex on some level, we must store it so we can return to it after completing this level so that the vertices adjacent to it may be visited. Because the first vertex visited on this level should be the first one we return to, a queue is an appropriate data structure to use to store the vertices. The following algorithm for breadth-first search uses a queue in this manner.

BREADTH-FIRST SEARCH ALGORITHM

(∗ Algorithm to perform a breadth-first search of a digraph to visit all
   vertices reachable from a given start vertex. ∗)

1. Visit the start vertex.
2. Initialize a queue to contain only the start vertex.
3. While the queue is not empty do the following:
   a. Remove a vertex *v* from the queue.
   b. For all vertices *w* adjacent to *v* do the following:
      If *w* has not been visited then:
      i. Visit *w*.
      ii. Add *w* to the queue.

Search algorithms like those for depth-first and breadth-first searches are
basic to many other algorithms for processing directed graphs. For example,
to traverse a digraph, we can repeatedly apply one of these searches, selecting
new start vertices when necessary, until all of the vertices have been visited.
Thus one possible traversal algorithm is

DIGRAPH TRAVERSAL ALGORITHM

(∗ Algorithm to traverse a digraph, visiting each vertex exactly once.
   A depth-first search is the basis of the traversal. ∗)

1. Initialize a set *Unvisited* to contain the numbers of all the vertices in
   the digraph.
2. While *Unvisited* is not empty do the following:
   a. Select a start vertex from this set *Unvisited*.
   b. Use the depth-first search algorithm to visit all vertices
      reachable from this start vertex.

Another class of problems for which we can design algorithms using one
of the search algorithms consists of **routing problems**. For example, consider
a directed graph that models an airline network in which the vertices represent
cities and directed arcs represent flights connecting these cities. We may be
interested in determining the most direct route between two cities, that is, the
route with the fewest number of intermediate stops. In terms of a digraph
modeling such a network, we must determine the length of a shortest path, one
composed of a minimum number of arcs, from some start vertex to a destination
vertex. An algorithm for determining such a shortest path is an easy modification of the breadth-first search algorithm:

SHORTEST PATH ALGORITHM

(∗ Algorithm to find a shortest path from a given *Start* vertex to a given
   Destination vertex in a digraph. ∗)

1. Visit *Start* and label it with 0.
2. Initialize *Distance* to 0.

3. Initialize a queue to contain only *Start*.
4. While *Destination* has not been visited and the queue is not empty, do the following:
    a. Remove a vertex *v* from the queue.
    b. If the label of *v* is greater than *Distance*, increment *Distance* by 1.
    c. For each vertex *w* adjacent to *v* do:
        If *w* has not been visited, then
            i. Visit *w* and label it with *Distance* + 1.
            ii. Add *w* to the queue.
5. If *Destination* has not been visited then
    Display 'Destination not reachable from start vertex'.
    Else find the vertices *P*[0], . . . , *P*[*Distance*] on the shortest path as follows:
    a. Initialize *P*[*Distance*] to *Destination*.
    b. For each value of *k* ranging from *Distance* − 1 down to 0:
        Find a vertex *P*[*k*] adjacent to *P*[*k* + 1] with label *k*.

The program in Figure 13.1 uses this algorithm to solve the airline network problem just described. The procedure *MakeDigraph* constructs the adjacency list representation of the network using the algorithm given earlier, reading the necessary information from *NetworkFile*. Each city is identified by both number and name, and the *i*th line of the file contains the name of the *i*th city followed by the numbers of all vertices adjacent to the *i*th vertex. The user then enters the name of a start city and the name of a destination, and procedure *FindPath* is called to find the shortest path from the start vertex to the destination vertex if there is one. The queue used in the breadth-first search on which the shortest path algorithm is based is declared using the type *QueueType* and processed using the procedures *CreateQ*, *EmptyQ*, *AddQ*, and *RemoveQ*, all of which are imported from a library module *CardinalQueues* (see Section 6.2).

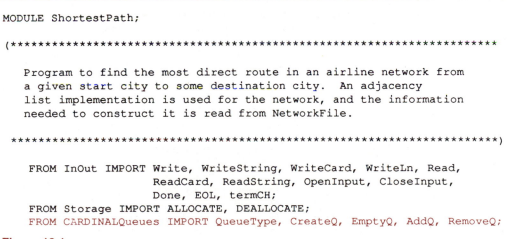

```
MODULE ShortestPath;

(*********************************************************************

   Program to find the most direct route in an airline network from
   a given start city to some destination city.  An adjacency
   list implementation is used for the network, and the information
   needed to construct it is read from NetworkFile.

*********************************************************************)

   FROM InOut IMPORT Write, WriteString, WriteCard, WriteLn, Read,
                  ReadCard, ReadString, OpenInput, CloseInput,
                  Done, EOL, termCH;
   FROM Storage IMPORT ALLOCATE, DEALLOCATE;
   FROM CARDINALQueues IMPORT QueueType, CreateQ, EmptyQ, AddQ, RemoveQ;
```

Figure 13.1

Figure 13.1   (cont.)

```
CONST
    MaxVertices = 25;        (* maximum number of vertices in digraph *)
    StringLimit = 15;        (* limit on number of characters in strings *)

TYPE
    String = ARRAY[0..StringLimit] OF CHAR;
    ElementType = String;
    VertexNumber = [0..MaxVertices];
    AdjPointer = POINTER TO VertexNode;
    VertexNode = RECORD
                      Vertex : VertexNumber;
                      Next : AdjPointer
                 END;
    HeadNode = RECORD
                      Data : ElementType;
                      Next : AdjPointer
                 END;
    HeadPointer = POINTER TO HeadNode;
    ArrayOfPointers = ARRAY VertexNumber OF HeadPointer;
    Path = ARRAY VertexNumber OF VertexNumber;

VAR
    V : ArrayOfPointers;          (* array of pointers to adjacency lists *)
    NumVertices,                  (* number of vertices in digraph *)
    k,                            (* index *)
    Start,                        (* number of start city *)
    Destination : VertexNumber;   (* number of destination city *)
    Distance : INTEGER;           (* length of shortest path P *)
    P : Path;                     (* shortest path from Start to Destination *)
    Response : CHAR;              (* user response *)

PROCEDURE MakeDigraph(VAR V : ArrayOfPointers;
                      VAR NumVertices : VertexNumber;
                          MaxVertices : CARDINAL);

    (***************************************************************

    Procedure to construct adjacency list representation of a
    network stored in NetworkFile.  It returns the array V of
    NumVertices pointers to these adjacency lists.  The ith line
    of the file contains the data item to be stored in the head
    node followed by a list of the numbers of all vertices
    adjacent to vertex #i.

    ***************************************************************)

    CONST
        EOF = '*';                (* end-of-file mark *)

    VAR
        Name : String;            (* name stored in a vertex *)
        i : CARDINAL;             (* index *)
        HeadPtr : HeadPointer;    (* pointer to head node *)
        VertPtr : AdjPointer;     (* pointer to vertex node *)
```

Figure 13.1 (cont.)

```
BEGIN
    WriteString('Enter name of network file');
    WriteLn;
    OpenInput('');
    NumVertices := 0;
    ReadString(Name);
    WHILE Name[0] # EOF DO
        ALLOCATE(HeadPtr, SIZE(HeadNode));
        HeadPtr^.Data := Name;
        HeadPtr^.Next := NIL;
        WHILE termCH # EOL DO
            ALLOCATE(VertPtr, SIZE(VertexNode));
            ReadCard(VertPtr^.Vertex);
            VertPtr^.Next := HeadPtr^.Next;
            HeadPtr^.Next := VertPtr
        END (* WHILE *);
        INC(NumVertices);
        V[NumVertices] := HeadPtr;
        ReadString(Name)
    END (* WHILE *);
    CloseInput
END MakeDigraph;

PROCEDURE FindPath(    V : ArrayOfPointers;
                       MaxVertices, NumVertices,
                       Start, Destination : CARDINAL;
                   VAR P : Path;
                   VAR Distance : INTEGER);

(***************************************************************

    Procedure to find the shortest path from vertex Start to
    vertex Destination in the digraph represented by adjacency
    lists pointed to by V[i], i = 1, ...., NumVertices.

    ***************************************************************)

VAR
    Vert,                   (* one of the vertices *)
    k : VertexNumber;       (* index *)
    DistLabel : ARRAY VertexNumber OF INTEGER;
                            (* distance labels for vertices *)
    PredLabel : Path;       (* predecessor labels for vertices *)
    Queue : QueueType;      (* queue of vertices *)
    ptr : AdjPointer;       (* pointer to run through adjacency list *)

BEGIN
    (* Initialize all vertices as unvisited (DistLabel = -1) *)
    FOR k := 1 TO MaxVertices DO
        DistLabel[k] := -1
    END (* FOR *);

    (* Perform breadth first search from Start to find Destination,
       labeling vertices with distances from Start as we go *)
```

Figure 13.1   (cont.)

```
          DistLabel[Start] := 0;
          Distance := 0;
          CreateQ(Queue);
          AddQ(Queue, Start);
          WHILE (DistLabel[Destination] < 0) AND NOT EmptyQ(Queue) DO
              RemoveQ (Queue, Vert);
              IF DistLabel[Vert] > Distance THEN
                  INC(Distance)
              END (* IF *);
              ptr := V[Vert]^.Next;
              WHILE ptr # NIL DO
                  IF DistLabel[ptr^.Vertex] < 0 THEN
                      DistLabel[ptr^.Vertex] := Distance + 1;
                      PredLabel[ptr^.Vertex] := Vert;
                      AddQ(Queue, ptr^.Vertex)
                  END (* IF *);
                  ptr := ptr^.Next
              END (* WHILE *)
          END (* WHILE *);
          INC(Distance);

          (* Now reconstruct the shortest path if there is one *)

          IF DistLabel[Destination] < 0 THEN
              WriteLn;
              WriteString('Destination not reachable from start vertex')
          ELSE
              P[Distance] := Destination;
              FOR k := Distance - 1 TO 0 BY -1 DO
                  P[k] := PredLabel[P[k + 1]]
              END (* FOR *)
          END (* IF *)
      END FindPath;

BEGIN (* main program *)
    MakeDigraph(V, NumVertices, MaxVertices);
    REPEAT
        WriteLn;
        WriteString('Number of start city?    ');
        ReadCard(Start);
        WriteLn;
        WriteString('Number of destination?   ');
        ReadCard(Destination);
        IF Start = Destination THEN
            WriteLn;
            WriteString('Shortest path is trivial -- distance is 0')
        ELSE
            FindPath(V, MaxVertices, NumVertices, Start, Destination,
                     P, Distance);
```

Figure 13.1 (cont.)

```
            WriteLn;
            WriteString('Shortest path is:');
            FOR k := 0 TO VAL(CARDINAL, Distance - 1) DO
                WriteLn;
                WriteCard(P[k], 3);
                Write(' ');
                WriteString(V[P[k]]^.Data);
                WriteLn;
                WriteString('        |');
                WriteLn;
                WriteString('        v')
            END (* FOR *);
            WriteLn;
            WriteCard(Destination, 3);
            Write(' ');
            WriteString(V[Destination]^.Data)
        END (* IF *);
        WriteLn; WriteLn;
        WriteString('More (Y or N)?  ');
        Read(Response)
    UNTIL CAP(Response) #'Y'
END ShortestPath.
```

Listing of NetworkFile:

```
LOS_ANGELES     3 4 6
SAN_FRANCISCO   1 3 4
DENVER          1 2 3
CHICAGO         3 8
BOSTON          4 6
NEW_YORK        4 7 8
MIAMI           8 3 5
NEW_ORLEANS     1 7
*
```

Sample run:

```
Number of start city?    5
Number of destination?   1
Shortest path is:
  5 BOSTON
     |
     v
  6 NEW YORK
     |
     v
  8 NEW ORLEANS
     |
     v
  1 LOS ANGELES

More (Y or N)?  N
```

A classic routing problem that is of both practical and theoretical interest is the ***traveling salesman problem***. In this problem, a weighted digraph with vertices representing cities and the cost of an arc representing the distance between the cities must be traversed using a path of minimal total cost. The practical importance of this problem should be obvious. It is also an important problem in theoretical computer science because the only known algorithms for solving it have worst-case computing time $O(2^n)$, and as we noted in Section 5.1, such exponential computing times are practical only for very small values of n (the number of cities). In fact, the traveling salesman problem belongs to the large class of problems known as ***NP-complete problems***, for which no algorithms with worst-case polynomial computing times have been found. These problems are equivalent problems in that if a polynomial time algorithm could be found for *any one* of the problems in this class, then the existence of polynomial time algorithms for *all* of the other problems would be guaranteed!

Exercises

1. For each of the following, find the adjacency matrix *Adj* and the data matrix *Data* for the given digraph:

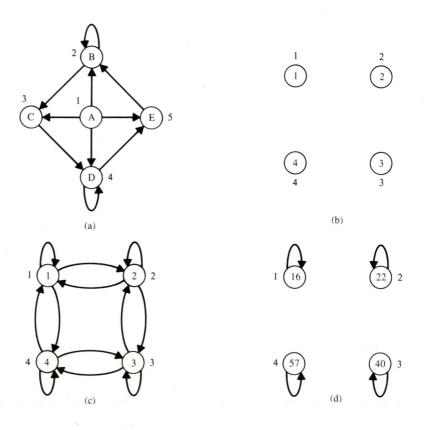

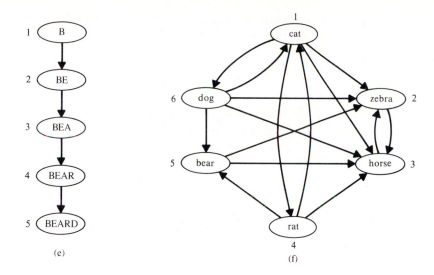

(e)

(f)

2. A simple alternative to the adjacency list representation for a directed graph is to use a linked list of head nodes containing data items and pointers to the adjacency lists rather than an array of pointers to these head nodes. Write an algorithm to construct this *linked adjacency list representation*.

3. For each of the following, find the directed graph represented by the given adjacency matrix *Adj* and the data matrix *Data*:

(a) $Adj = \begin{bmatrix} 0 & 1 & 0 & 1 & 0 \\ 1 & 1 & 1 & 0 & 0 \\ 0 & 0 & 0 & 0 & 1 \\ 0 & 1 & 0 & 0 & 1 \\ 0 & 0 & 0 & 0 & 0 \end{bmatrix}$, $Data = \begin{bmatrix} A \\ B \\ C \\ D \\ E \end{bmatrix}$

(b) $Adj = \begin{bmatrix} 0 & 1 & 1 & 1 \\ 0 & 0 & 1 & 1 \\ 0 & 0 & 0 & 1 \\ 0 & 0 & 0 & 0 \end{bmatrix}$, $Data = \begin{bmatrix} CAT \\ RAT \\ BAT \\ DOG \end{bmatrix}$

(c) $Adj = \begin{bmatrix} 1 & 1 & 1 \\ 1 & 1 & 1 \\ 1 & 1 & 1 \end{bmatrix}$, $Data = \begin{bmatrix} 111 \\ 222 \\ 333 \end{bmatrix}$

(9) $Adj = \begin{bmatrix} 1 & 0 & 1 & 0 & 0 & 0 & 1 \\ 0 & 0 & 1 & 1 & 1 & 0 & 0 \\ 0 & 0 & 1 & 1 & 0 & 0 & 1 \\ 1 & 1 & 1 & 1 & 1 & 1 & 1 \\ 0 & 0 & 0 & 0 & 0 & 0 & 0 \\ 0 & 0 & 1 & 1 & 0 & 0 & 1 \\ 1 & 0 & 0 & 0 & 0 & 1 & 0 \end{bmatrix}$, $Data = \begin{bmatrix} Alpha \\ Beta \\ Gamma \\ Delta \\ Mu \\ Pi \\ Rho \end{bmatrix}$

4. For each of the directed graphs in Exercise 1, give its adjacency list representation.

5. For each of the directed graphs in Exercise 3, give its adjacency list representation.

6. For each of the directed graphs in Exercise 1, give its linked adjacency list representation (see Exercise 2).

7. For each of the following adjacency lists, draw the directed graph represented.

(a)
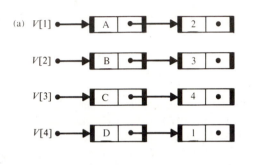

(b)
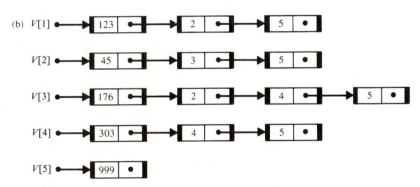

(c)
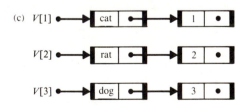

(d)
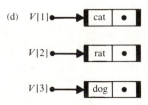

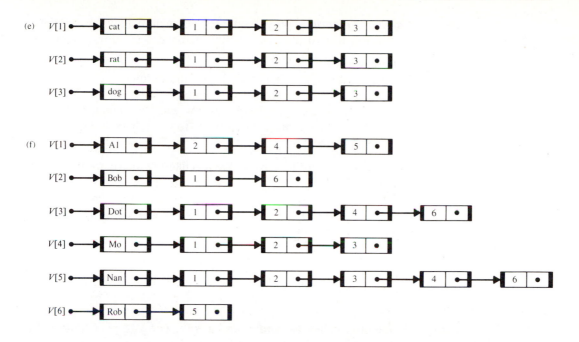

8. Write a program that traverses a directed graph using both a depth-first search and a breadth-first search where the directed graph is represented by its adjacency matrix.

9. Proceed as in Exercise 8, but use the adjacency list representation for the directed graph.

10. Rewrite the program *ShortestPath* in Figure 13.1, but use the adjacency matrix representation for the digraph.

11. If A is an $n \times n$ adjacency matrix for a directed graph G, then the entry in the ith row and jth column of A^k is equal to the number of paths of length k from the ith vertex to the jth vertex in this digraph. The **reachability matrix** R of G is the $n \times n$ matrix defined by

$$R = I + A + A^2 + \cdots + A^{n-1}$$

where I is the $n \times n$ identity matrix having 1's on the diagonal and 0's off. In G, there is a path from vertex i to vertex j if and only if the entry in row i and column j of R is nonzero. Write a program to find the reachability matrix for a directed graph.

12. An alternative to the method of Exercise 11 for determining reachability is to use "boolean multiplication and addition," that is, AND and OR operations, in carrying out the matrix computations (0 = FALSE, 1 = TRUE). Rewrite the program in Exercise 11 to find this form of the reachability matrix.

13. *Warshall's algorithm* provides a more efficient method for calculating the boolean form of the reachability matrix described in Exercise 11:

1. Initialize R to A and k to 1.
2. While $k \leq n$ and R is not all 1's do the following:
    a. For i ranging from 1 to n with $i \neq k$ do:
        If the entry in the ith row and kth column of R is 1, then replace row i with (row i) OR (row k).
    b. Increment k by 1.

Use Warshall's algorithm to find the reachability matrix for the digraph on page 583.

14. Write a program to find the reachability matrix of a digraph using Warshall's algorithm.

13.3 Graphs

A *graph*, sometimes called an *undirected graph*, consists of a finite set of elements called *vertices*, or *nodes*, together with a finite set of *edges*, which connect pairs of distinct vertices. Thus, a graph differs from a digraph in that no direction is associated with the edges, and since the vertices connected by an edge must be distinct, no loops joining a vertex to itself are allowed. For example, the following diagram shows a graph having five vertices with edges joining vertices 1 and 2, 1 and 4, 1 and 5, 2 and 4, 3 and 4, and 4 and 5:

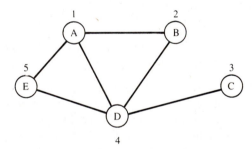

Such graphs are useful in modeling electrical circuits, structures of chemical compounds, communication systems, and many other networks in which no direction is associated with the links.

Like digraphs, graphs may be represented by either adjacency matrices or adjacency lists. For example, the adjacency matrix for the preceding graph is

$$Adj = \begin{bmatrix} 0 & 1 & 0 & 1 & 1 \\ 1 & 0 & 0 & 1 & 0 \\ 0 & 0 & 0 & 1 & 0 \\ 1 & 1 & 1 & 0 & 1 \\ 1 & 0 & 0 & 1 & 0 \end{bmatrix}$$

where a 1 in row i and column j indicates the existence of an edge joining the
ith and jth vertices. Because these edges are undirected, there also is a 1 in
row j and column i; thus the adjacency matrix for an undirected graph is always
symmetric. This means that the entries on one side of the diagonal (from the
upper left corner to the lower right corner) are redundant. Also, since undirected
graphs have no loops, all entries on the diagonal of the adjacency matrix are
0. Consequently, the adjacency matrix is not a very efficient representation of
an undirected graph.

The adjacency list representation for the preceding graph is

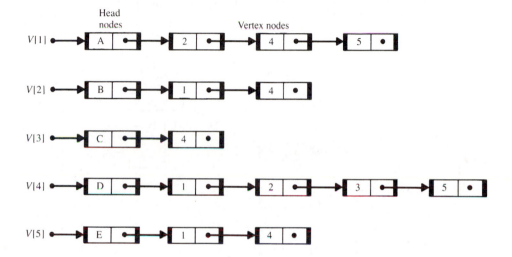

Like the adjacency matrix, this representation is also not very efficient because
redundant information is stored. If an edge joins vertices i and j, then a vertex
node containing vertex i appears in the adjacency list for vertex j, and a vertex
node containing vertex j appears in the adjacency list for vertex i.

A more efficient representation of a graph uses ***edge lists***. Each ***edge node***
in one of these lists represents one edge in the graph and has the form

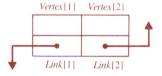

where *Vertex*[1] and *Vertex*[2] are vertices connected by an edge, *Link*[1] points
to another edge node having *Vertex*[1] as one endpoint, and *Link*[2] points to
another edge node having *Vertex*[2] as an endpoint. An array V of pointers to
head nodes storing the data items in the vertices is also used; the head node
pointed to by $V[i]$ also contains a link field that points to an edge node having
the ith vertex as one of its endpoints. The edge list representation for the
preceding graph,

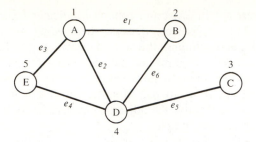

where we have labeled the edges $e_1, e_2, \ldots, e_6$, as indicated, might thus be pictured as follows:

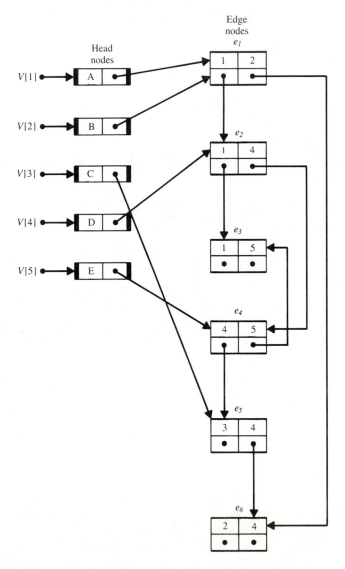

Depth-first search, breadth-first search, traversal, and other algorithms for processing graphs are similar to those for digraphs. For example, the program in Figure 13.2 uses a depth-first search to determine if a graph is ***connected,*** that is, whether there is a path from each vertex to every other vertex. Procedure *BuildGraph* constructs the edge-list representation of the graph, and procedure *DepthFirstSearch* marks those vertices that are reachable from vertex 1. Other algorithms for processing graphs are left as exercises.

```
MODULE Connectedness;

(***********************************************************************

    Program to determine if a graph is connected.  The edge-list
    implementation is used for the graph.

 **********************************************************************)

    FROM InOut IMPORT Write, WriteString, WriteCard, WriteLn,
                      ReadString, ReadCard;
    FROM Storage IMPORT ALLOCATE, DEALLOCATE;

    CONST
        MaxVertices = 15;       (* maximum number of vertices in graph *)
        StringLimit = 15;       (* limit on number of characters in strings *)

    TYPE
        String = ARRAY [0..MaxString] OF CHAR;
        VertexNumber = [1..MaxVertices];
        EdgePointer = POINTER TO EdgeNode;
        EdgeNode = RECORD
                        Vertex : ARRAY [1..2] OF VertexNumber;
                        Link : ARRAY [1..2] OF EdgePointer
                   END;
        ElementType = String;
        HeadNode = RECORD
                        Data : ElementType;
                        Next : EdgePointer
                   END;
        HeadPointer = POINTER TO HeadNode;
        ArrayOfPointer = ARRAY VertexNumber OF HeadPointer;
        VertexSet = SET OF VertexNumber;

    VAR
        i,                          (* index *)
        NumVertices : VertexNumber; (* number of vertices *)
        NumEdges : CARDINAL;        (* number of edges *)
        V : ArrayOfPointer;         (* pointers to edge lists *)
        Unvisited : VertexSet;      (* set of unvisited vertices *)

    PROCEDURE BuildGraph(VAR V : ArrayOfPointer;
                         VAR NumVertices : VertexNumber;
                             MaxVertices : CARDINAL);
```

Figure 13.2

Figure 13.2   (cont.)

```
(******************************************************************

    Procedure to construct edge-list representation of a graph

    ****************************************************************)

VAR
    i, j,                          (* indices *)
    EndPt : VertexNumber;          (* endpoint of an edge *)
    EdgePtr : EdgePointer;         (* pointer to edge node *)

BEGIN
    WriteLn;
    WriteString('Enter # of vertices:  ');
    ReadCard(NumVertices);
    IF NumVertices > MaxVertices THEN
        WriteString('*** Too many vertices ***');
        HALT
    ELSE
        (* create head nodes *)
        WriteLn;
        WriteString('Enter labels of vertices, 1 per line:');
        FOR i := 1 TO NumVertices DO
            ALLOCATE(V[i], SIZE(HeadNode));
            V[i]^.Next := NIL;
            WriteLn;
            WriteString('Vertex #');
            WriteCard(i, 1);
            WriteString(':  ');
            ReadString(V[i]^.Data);
            V[i]^.Next := NIL
        END (* FOR *);

        (* create edge lists *)
        WriteLn;
        WriteString('Enter # of edges:      ');
        ReadCard(NumEdges);
        FOR i := 1 TO NumEdges DO
            ALLOCATE(EdgePtr, SIZE(EdgeNode));
            WriteLn;
            WriteString('Endpoints of edge #');
            WriteCard(i, 1);
            WriteString(':  ');
            FOR j := 1 TO 2 DO
                ReadCard(EndPt);
                (* insert new edge node at beginning
                    of edge list for EndPt *)
                EdgePtr^.Vertex[j] := EndPt;
                EdgePtr^.Link[j] := V[EndPt]^.Next;
                V[EndPt]^.Next := EdgePtr
            END (* FOR j *);
        END (* FOR i *);
    END (* IF *)
END BuildGraph;
```

Figure 13.2   (cont.)

```
PROCEDURE DepthFirstSearch(     V : ArrayOfPointer;
                                Start : VertexNumber;
                            VAR Unvisited : VertexSet);

    (***************************************************************

        Procedure to depth first search a graph represented by edge
        lists and visit all vertices in Unvisited that are reachable
        from vertex Start.  V is an array of pointers to these edge
        lists.

    ***************************************************************)

    VAR
        Ptr : EdgePointer;          (* pointer to run through edge list *)
        StartEnd,                   (* one endpoint of an edge *)
        OtherEnd,                   (* other endpoint of edge *)
        NewStart : VertexNumber;    (* new starting vertex for
                                        DepthFirstSearch *)

    BEGIN
        EXCL(Unvisited, Start);
        Ptr := V[Start]^.Next;
        WHILE (Unvisited # VertexSet{}) AND (Ptr # NIL) DO
            StartEnd := 1;
            OtherEnd := 2;
            IF Ptr^.Vertex[1] # Start THEN
                StartEnd := 2;
                OtherEnd := 1
            END (* IF *);
            NewStart := Ptr^.Vertex[OtherEnd];
            IF NewStart IN Unvisited THEN
                DepthFirstSearch(V, NewStart, Unvisited)
            END (* IF *);
            Ptr := Ptr^.Link[StartEnd]
        END (* WHILE *)
    END DepthFirstSearch;

BEGIN (* main program *)
    BuildGraph(V, NumVertices, MaxVertices);
    Unvisited := VertexSet{};
    FOR i := 1 TO NumVertices DO
        INCL(Unvisited, i)
    END (* FOR *);
```

Figure 13.2 (cont.)

```
    DepthFirstSearch(V, 1, Unvisited);
    WriteLn;
    WriteString('Graph is');
    IF Unvisited = VertexSet{} THEN
        WriteString(' connected')
    ELSE
        WriteString(' not connected;   vertices not reachable from');
        WriteLn;
        WriteString(V[1]^.Data);
        WriteString(' are:  ');
        FOR i := 1 TO NumVertices DO
            IF i IN Unvisited THEN
                WriteString(V[i]^.Data);
                WriteString('  ')
            END (* IF *)
        END (* FOR *);
        WriteLn
    END (* IF *)
END Connectedness.

Sample runs:

Enter # of vertices:  5
Enter labels of vertices, 1 per line:
Vertex #1:   A
Vertex #2:   B
Vertex #3:   C
Vertex #4:   D
Vertex #5:   E
Enter # of edges:     6
Endpoints of edge #1:  1 2
Endpoints of edge #2:  1 4
Endpoints of edge #3:  1 5
Endpoints of edge #4:  2 4
Endpoints of edge #5:  3 4
Endpoints of edge #6:  4 5
Graph is connected


Enter # of vertices:  5
Enter labels of vertices, 1 per line:
Vertex #1:   A
Vertex #2:   B
Vertex #3:   C
Vertex #4:   D
Vertex #5:   E
Enter # of edges:     2
Endpoints of edge #1:  1 4
Endpoints of edge #2:  5 4
Graph is not connected;   vertices not reachable from
A are:  B   C
```

Exercises

1. For each of the following graphs, give its
    (i) adjacency matrix representation.
    (ii) adjacency list representation.
    (iii) edge-list representation.

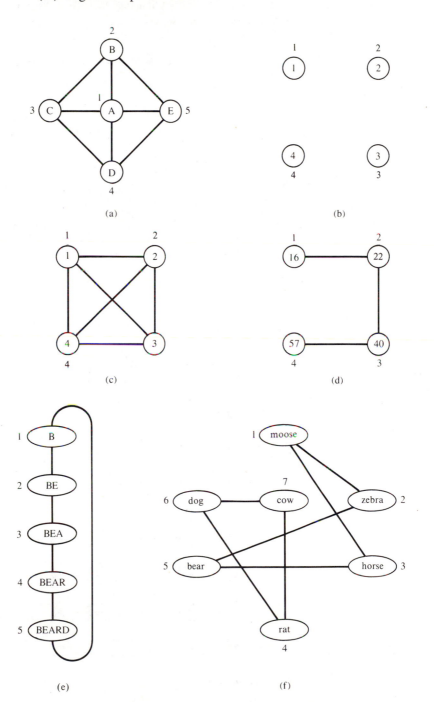

(a)

(b)

(c)

(d)

(e)

(f)

2. The linked adjacency list representation for directed graphs described in Exercise 2 of Section 13.2 can also be used for undirected graphs. Write an algorithm to construct such a linked adjacency list representation.

3. Give the linked adjacency list representation for each of the graphs in Exercise 1 (see Exercise 2).

4. For each of the following adjacency matrices, draw the graph represented:

(a) $Adj = \begin{bmatrix} 0 & 1 & 0 & 1 & 0 \\ 1 & 0 & 1 & 0 & 0 \\ 0 & 1 & 0 & 0 & 1 \\ 1 & 0 & 0 & 0 & 1 \\ 0 & 0 & 1 & 1 & 0 \end{bmatrix}$ **(b)** $Adj = \begin{bmatrix} 0 & 1 & 1 & 1 \\ 1 & 0 & 1 & 1 \\ 1 & 1 & 0 & 1 \\ 1 & 1 & 1 & 0 \end{bmatrix}$

(c) $Adj = \begin{bmatrix} 0 & 0 & 0 \\ 0 & 0 & 0 \\ 0 & 0 & 0 \end{bmatrix}$ **(d)** $Adj = \begin{bmatrix} 0 & 0 & 1 & 0 & 0 & 0 & 1 \\ 0 & 0 & 1 & 1 & 1 & 0 & 0 \\ 1 & 1 & 0 & 1 & 0 & 0 & 1 \\ 0 & 1 & 1 & 0 & 1 & 1 & 1 \\ 0 & 1 & 0 & 1 & 0 & 0 & 0 \\ 0 & 0 & 0 & 1 & 0 & 0 & 1 \\ 1 & 0 & 1 & 1 & 0 & 1 & 0 \end{bmatrix}$

5. For each of the following adjacency lists, draw the graph represented:

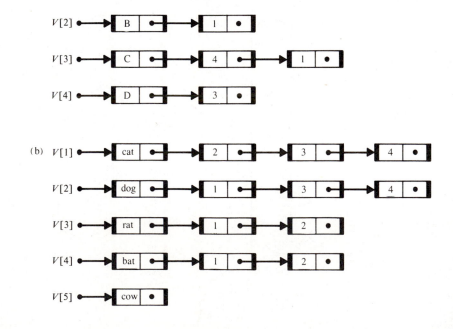

(c)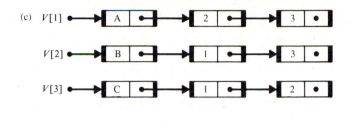

(d)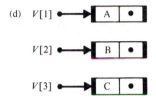

(e)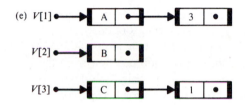

(f)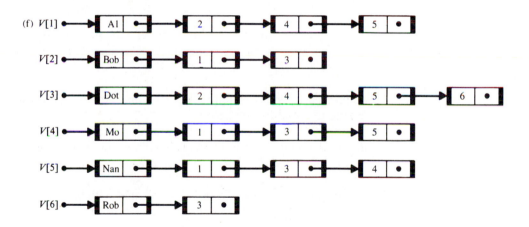

6. Give the edge-list representation for each of the graphs whose adjacency lists are given in Exercise 5.

7. Rewrite the program *Connectedness* in Figure 13.2 using the adjacency matrix representation for the graph.

8. Proceed as in Exercise 7, but use the adjacency list representation.

9. Proceed as in Exercise 7, but use the linked adjacency list representation described in Exercise 2.

10. Consider the following operations to be performed on a graph:

    (a) Insert a new vertex, given a specification of all vertices adjacent to it.

    (b) Search a graph for a vertex that stores a given data item, and retrieve information about that item and/or update the information.

    (c) Delete a vertex containing a given data item and all edges incident to it.

    (d) Find all vertices adjacent to a given vertex.

Using one of the representations for graphs described in this section, including that in Exercise 2, or devising one of your own, give algorithms that implement these operations.

11. Write a program that reads and stores the names of persons and the names of job positions in the vertices of a graph. Two vertices will be connected if one of them represents a person and the other a job position for which that person is qualified. The program should allow the user to specify one of the following options:

    (1) Insert (a) a new applicant or (b) a new job position into the graph.

    (2) Delete (a) an applicant or (b) a job position from the graph.

    (3) List all persons qualified for a specified job position.

    (4) List all job positions for which a specified person is qualified.

Use the algorithms developed in Exercise 10 to implement these operations.

12. Write a program to determine if a graph contains a *cycle*, that is, a path connecting some vertex to itself. Use an adjacency matrix to represent the graph.

13. Modify the program in Exercise 12 so that an adjacency list representation is used for the graph.

14. Modify the program in Exercise 12 so that an edge-list representation is used for the graph.

15. Modify the program in Exercise 12 so that a linked adjacency list representation is used for the graph (see Exercise 2).

16. A *spanning tree* T for a graph G is a subgraph of G containing all the vertices of G but containing no cycles. (A *subgraph* of a graph G has a vertex set and an edge set, which are subsets of the vertex set and the edge set of G, respectively.) The following algorithm can be used to find a spanning tree T for a graph G:

    1. Initialize the vertex set V_T of T equal to the vertex set V_G of G and the edge set of T, E_T, to the empty set.

    2. While there is an edge e in the edge set E_G of G such that $E_T \cup \{e\}$ forms no cycle in T, add e to E_T.

Write a program to find a spanning tree for a graph.

17. *Kruskal's algorithm* finds the spanning tree of minimal cost in a weighted graph. It is a simple modification of the algorithm in Exercise 16; in Step 2, add the edge e of minimal cost that does not create a cycle. Write a program that implements Kruskal's algorithm.

14

Introduction to Concurrent Programming

Up to now, we have assumed for the most part that programs, procedures, and modules are executed one at a time; that is, if a program unit is being executed at a particular time, then it is the only one being executed at that time. In Chapter 6 we did mention, however, that one of the applications of queues is the design of input/output buffers that hold data values begin transferred to and from secondary memory. In a system that supports multiprogramming, that is, a system in which several programs can be in memory simultaneously, the CPU is used to execute some other program unit while this transfer between the buffer and secondary memory takes place. These two activities are thus taking place *concurrently*.

There are many similar examples of concurrent processing in everyday life. Multiple checkout lines in supermarkets process customers concurrently; some activities such as installing plumbing and electrical work in a construction project like that described in Section 13.1 can be performed simultaneously; and persons work on an assembly line concurrently. In applications like the first two, the activities are generally carried out independently of one another, whereas in others like the last one, the concurrent activities must be synchronized.

Computers that provide multiprogramming can be classified according to the multiplicity of their processors. They may have several identical processors, and separate tasks can be assigned to each processer and executed; this is sometimes referred to as *genuine* or *real concurrency*. More commonly, a computer system has a single processor that is shared among programs. The processor works on one program for a specified period of time, then switches to another and executes it for a time, then switches to another, and so on. Although such processing may appear to be concurrent, it is not truly concurrent and is therefore referred to as *quasi-concurrency*.

Modula-2 is one of the few languages that provides concurrent programming constructs, and in this chapter we give a brief introduction to them (as described in Wirth's *Programming in Modula-2*). But a detailed study of concurrent programming techniques is beyond the level of this text and so is left to more advanced studies in algorithm and program design.

14.1   Coroutines

Most programming languages provide subprogram structures that make it possible to develop a program in a modular fashion, with each subprogram performing a particular task. In Modula-2, procedures play this role. When a procedure is called, execution always starts at the beginning of the statement part of the procedure. When execution of the procedure is completed, the local variables of the procedure become undefined and control is returned to the program unit that called the procedure:

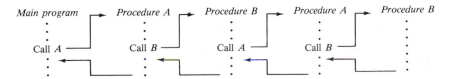

Coroutines are similar to procedures in that they contain statements to perform certain tasks and may have local variables. They differ from procedures, however, in that the values of local variables in a coroutine are retained when control is transferred out of it. Also, control may be transferred into and out of a coroutine several times, and each time such a transfer into the coroutine takes place, execution is resumed at the statement that follows the one that caused the preceding transfer of control out of the coroutine.

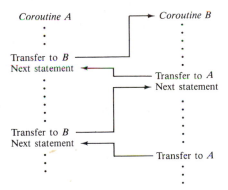

As an illustration of the use of coroutines, we consider a variation of the bubblesort algorithm described in Section 10.1. In the bubblesort scheme, several passes are made over the list of items to be sorted, and on each pass, consecutive items are compared and interchanged if they are out of order. In each scan, the largest item (assuming that the list is being sorted into ascending order) "sinks" to the end of the sublist being scanned, and perhaps some others do as well. Meanwhile, the interchanges also cause some of the smaller items to "bubble up" toward the beginning of the list.

A variation of this inefficient sorting method is a ***two-way bubblesort*** in which scans are made in both directions. A scan to the right causes the largest item to sink to the end of the sublist being scanned, and each scan to the left causes the smallest item to rise to the beginning of the sublist. Although this does nothing to improve the overall performance of bubblesort, we describe it here because it provides a simple illustration of the use of coroutines.

To illustrate the two-way bubblesort scheme, suppose that we wish to sort the following list of numbers into ascending order:

3, 1, 7, 5, 12, 4, 2, 8, 6, 11, 9, 10

We scan the list from the beginning, interchanging consecutive numbers if they are out of order and keeping track of where the last such interchange occurred:

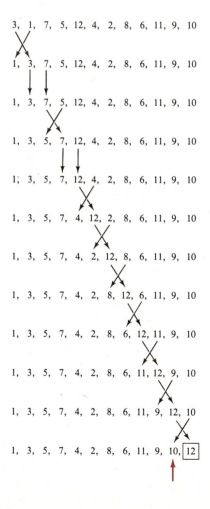

As this sequence of diagrams indicates, the largest number, 12, has sunk to the end of the list, and smaller numbers have started bubbling toward the beginning of the list.

Now we reverse the scan and move from right to left, beginning at the position where the last interchange occurred on the left-to-right scan:

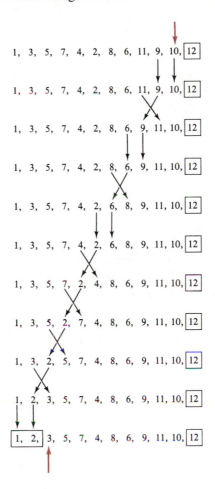

On this right-to-left scan we are assured that the smallest number has bubbled to the front of the list. In fact, in this particular example, since the last interchange involved the second and third elements, we know that the first two numbers are in their proper positions.

We now do another left-to-right scan, but only of the sublist indicated by the colored arrows in the preceding diagram; these arrows point to the two elements involved in the last interchanges. This scan produces the following arrangement:

$$1, \ 2, \ 3, \ 5, \ 4, \ 7, \ 6, \ 8, \ 9, \ 10, \ 11, \ 12$$

where the arrow again indicates the last number involved in an interchange. We know that the numbers to the right of it are in their proper positions. A right-to-left scan of this sublist, beginning with the number 10, gives

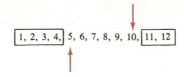

and we know that only those elements in the sublist indicated by the arrows might be out of order. When we perform a left-to-right scan of this sublist, there are no interchanges, which indicates that the entire list is in order.

The following algorithm summarizes this sorting technique:

ALGORITHM FOR TWO-WAY BUBBLESORT

(* Algorithm to sort a list of items $X_1, X_2, \ldots, X_n$ into ascending order using the two-way bubble sort algorithm. *)

1. Initialize *LeftLastSwap* to 1, *RightLastSwap* to n.
2. Repeat the following:
   a. Set *Sorted* to true.
   b. For i ranging from *LeftLastSwap* to *RightLastSwap* $-$ 1 do the following:
      If $X_i > X_{i+1}$ then:
         i. Interchange X_i and X_{i+1}.
         ii. Set *RightLastSwap* to i.
         iii. Set *Sorted* to false.
   c. If not *Sorted* then
      i. Set *Sorted* to true.
      ii. For j ranging from *RightLastSwap* down to *LeftLastSwap* $+$ 1 do the following:
         If $X_{j-1} > X_j$ then:
            (1) Interchange X_j and X_{j-1}.
            (2) Set *LeftLastSwap* to j.
            (3) Set *Sorted* to false.
   Until *Sorted*.
3. The list is now sorted and can be processed in whatever way is required.

The structure of this algorithm does not indicate as clearly as it could the alternating between the left-to-right scans and the right-to-left scans. An alternative approach is to view these two scans as coroutines:

ALGORITHM FOR TWO-WAY BUBBLESORT—
USING COROUTINES

(* Algorithm to sort a list of items $X_1, X_2, \ldots, X_n$ into ascending order using one coroutine to carry out the left-to-right scans and the other for the right-to-left scans of the two-way bubblesort algorithm. *)

1. Initialize *LeftLastSwap* to 1, *RightLastSwap* to n.
2. Transfer to coroutine *ScanLeftToRight*.

3. The list is now sorted and can be processed in whatever way is required.

Coroutine *ScanLeftToRight*

(∗ Coroutine to scan the sublist $X_{LeftLastSwap}, \ldots, X_{RightLastSwap-1}$ from left to right, interchanging consecutive elements that are out of order. ∗)

1. Repeat the following:
   a. Set *Sorted* to true.
   b. For *i* ranging from *LeftLastSwap* to *RightLastSwap* − 1 do the following:
      If $X_i > X_{i+1}$ then:
         i. Interchange X_i and X_{i+1}.
         ii. Set *RightLastSwap* to *i*.
         iii. Set *Sorted* to false.
   c. If not *Sorted*,
      transfer to coroutine *ScanRightToLeft*.
   Until *Sorted*.
2. Transfer back to main algorithm.

Coroutine *ScanRightToLeft*

(∗ Coroutine to scan the sublist $X_{LeftLastSwap+1}, \ldots, X_{RightLastSwap}$ from right to left, interchanging consecutive elements that are out of order. ∗)

1. Repeat the following:
   a. Set *Sorted* to true.
   b. For *j* ranging from *RightLastSwap* down to *LeftLastSwap* + 1 do the following:
      If $X_{j-1} > X_j$ then:
         i. Interchange X_j and X_{j-1}.
         ii. Set *LeftLastSwap* to *j*.
         iii. Set *Sorted* to false.
   c. If not *Sorted*,
      transfer to coroutine *ScanLeftToRight*.
   Until *Sorted*.
2. Transfer back to main algorithm.

The first step in implementing a coroutine in Modula-2 is to create a **workspace** for it. This workspace is a section of memory where the coroutine's local variables, the stack of activation records (see Section 5.5), and other information that describes the current state of the coroutine can be stored when control is transferred out of the coroutine. These items are used later to restore the coroutine to this state when control is transferred back to it. Declarations like the following can be used to create such a workspace[1]:

---

[1] Some Modula-2 systems use a procedure with a name like *InitCoroutines* to create this workspace. This procedure may be part of a special library module for handling coroutines.

```
CONST
    WorkSpaceSize = 1000;
TYPE
    WorkSpaceArray = ARRAY[1..WorkSpaceSize] OF WORD;
VAR
    WorkSpace : WorkSpaceArray;
```

Recall that the type WORD must be imported from the standard library module SYSTEM (see Section 11.1). These declarations create a workspace composed of 1000 memory words. Although the size of the workspace required depends on how much the coroutine requires and varies from one system to another, typical sizes are in the range from 100 to 1000 words.

A variable of type ADDRESS is needed to refer to the coroutine when control is transferred to it:

```
VAR
    coroutine : ADDRESS;
```

The type ADDRESS must also be imported from the library module SYSTEM.[2]

A coroutine is also referred to as a **process** in Modula-2 and is *created* from a procedure within a program by using the procedure **NEWPROCESS** provided in the module SYSTEM.[3] This procedure is called with a statement of the form

```
NEWPROCESS(procedure-name, workspace-address,
           workspace-size, coroutine)
```

where the types of the parameters and their functions are as follows:

procedure-name:	The name of the procedure within the program from which the coroutine is to be created; it is of type PROC. This procedure may not be a function procedure and may not have parameters. Also, it may not be a local procedure within another procedure.
workspace-address:	The address of the workspace; it is of type ADDRESS.
workspace-size:	The size of the workspace; it is of type CARDINAL.
coroutine:	The address used to refer to the coroutine; it is of type ADDRESS (but see Footnote 2). Procedure NEWPROCESS returns the value for this parameter.

---

[2] The second edition of *Programming in Modula-2* specifies that the type of coroutine variables must be PROCESS, and in the third edition, this was changed to ADDRESS. The standard library module SYSTEM in some older Modula-2 systems thus exports the type PROCESS for coroutines. Others use a type *Coroutine*.

[3] In systems that provide a special module for handling coroutines this procedure may have a different name such as *NewCoroutine* and may use different parameters.

Two functions provided in the module SYSTEM that are useful in specifying the address and the size of the workspace for a coroutine are **ADR** and **SIZE**. A reference to the function ADR has the form

ADR(*workspace*)

where *workspace* is an array of type WORD as described earlier. This function returns the address of the specified workspace. The function SIZE returns the size of the workspace, and a reference to it has the form

SIZE(*workspace*)

Thus a typical reference to procedure NEWPROCESS has the form

NEWPROCESS (*procedure-name*, ADR(*workspace*),
      SIZE(*workspace*), *coroutine*)

Control is transferred to a coroutine by using the procedure **TRANSFER**, also provided in the library module SYSTEM.[4] A reference to this procedure has the form

TRANSFER(*from-coroutine*, *to-coroutine*)

where *from-coroutine* and *to-coroutine* are of type ADDRESS. When this procedure is called, execution of the current coroutine *from-coroutine* is suspended, and control is transferred to *to-coroutine*, which then resumes execution. To activate a coroutine for the first time, a call to TRANSFER of the form

TRANSFER(*main*, *coroutine*)

can be used, where *main* is a variable of type ADDRESS declared in the main program. This causes execution of the main program to be suspended while the specified coroutine is executed. It remains suspended unless and until control is transferred back to the main program with a call to TRANSFER of the form

TRANSFER(*coroutine*, *main*)

The program in Figure 14.1 illustrates the use of coroutines. It uses the two-way bubblesort algorithm to sort a list of integers. Since coroutines must be created from parameterless procedures, which cannot be nested within other procedures, we have encapsulated these procedures within a local module where they can share items without making them accessible to the rest of the program.

---

[4] In some Modula-2 systems, this procedure is named *Transfer* and is provided in a special coroutine-handling library module.

```
MODULE SortWithCoroutines;

(*********************************************************************

   Program to sort a list of items into ascending order using
   coroutines to carry out the left-to-right and the right-to-left
   scans of two-way bubblesort.

 *********************************************************************)

   FROM InOut IMPORT Write, WriteString, WriteCard, WriteLn,
                     ReadCard, Done;
   IMPORT SYSTEM;

   CONST
       ListLimit = 50;                 (* limit on size of list *)

   TYPE
       ListOfNumbers = ARRAY [1..ListLimit] OF CARDINAL;

   VAR
       NumElements : CARDINAL;         (* number of elements in list *)
       X : ListOfNumbers;              (* list to be sorted *)

   PROCEDURE ReadCardList(VAR CardList : ARRAY OF CARDINAL;
                          VAR NumElements : CARDINAL);

       (*********************************************************************

          Procedure to read and return an array CardList of NumElements
          cardinal numbers.

        *********************************************************************)

       VAR
           NextNum : CARDINAL;                 (* next number in the list *)

       BEGIN
           WriteString('Enter list of numbers (any nondigit to stop):');
           WriteLn;
           NumElements := 0;
           ReadCard(NextNum);
           WHILE Done DO
               CardList[NumElements] := NextNum;
               INC(NumElements);
               ReadCard(NextNum)
           END (* WHILE *)
       END ReadCardList;
```

Figure 14.1

Figure 14.1 (cont.)

```
MODULE TwoWayBubbleSort;

    (****************************************************************

        Module that exports the procedure Sort which performs
        a two-way bubblesort of a list of items.

        ***********************************************************)

    FROM SYSTEM IMPORT WORD, ADDRESS, ADR, SIZE, NEWPROCESS, TRANSFER;
    IMPORT X, NumElements;

    EXPORT SortCardList;

    CONST
        WorkSpaceSize = 1000;      (* size of work space for coroutines *)

    TYPE
        WorkSpaceArray = ARRAY [1..WorkSpaceSize] OF WORD;

    VAR
        LRWorkSpace,                    (* work space for ScanLeftToRight, *)
        RLWorkSpace : WorkSpaceArray; (* and ScanRightToLeft coroutines *)
        Sorted : BOOLEAN;               (* signals sorting is completed *)
        Sorter,                         (* "main" coroutine *)
        ScanLeftToRight,                (* coroutine to scan left to right *)
        ScanRightToLeft : ADDRESS;      (* coroutine to scan right to left *)
        LeftLastSwap,                   (* last items involved in swaps *)
        RightLastSwap: CARDINAL;        (* on left-right, right-left scans *)

    PROCEDURE Swap(VAR Num1, Num2 : CARDINAL);

        (************************************************************

            Procedure to interchange cardinal numbers Num1 and Num2

            *******************************************************)

        VAR
            Temp : CARDINAL;   (* used to interchange numbers *)

        BEGIN
            Temp := Num1;
            Num1 := Num2;
            Num2 := Temp
        END Swap;

    PROCEDURE ScanLToR;

        (***********************************************************

            Procedure to carry out the left-to-right scans of the
            two-way bubblesort.

            ******************************************************)
```

Figure 14.1 (cont.)

```
    VAR
        LastLRPair,          (* last pair to check on L-to-R scan *)
        i : CARDINAL;        (* index *)

    BEGIN
        REPEAT
            Sorted := TRUE;
            LastLRPair := RightLastSwap - 1;
            i := LeftLastSwap;
            WHILE i <= LastLRPair DO
                IF X[i] > X[i + 1] THEN
                    Swap(X[i], X[i + 1]);
                    RightLastSwap := i;
                    Sorted := FALSE
                END (* IF *);
                INC(i)
            END (* WHILE *);
            IF NOT Sorted THEN
                TRANSFER(ScanLeftToRight, ScanRightToLeft)
            END (* IF *)
        UNTIL Sorted;
        TRANSFER(ScanLeftToRight, Sorter)
    END ScanLToR;

PROCEDURE ScanRToL;

    (*************************************************************

        Procedure to carry out the right-to-left scans of the
        two-way bubblesort.

    *************************************************************)

    VAR
        LastRLPair,              (* last pair to check on R-to-L scan *)
        j : CARDINAL;        (* index *)

    BEGIN
        REPEAT
            Sorted := TRUE;
            LastRLPair := LeftLastSwap + 1;
            j := RightLastSwap;
            WHILE j >= LastRLPair DO
                IF X[j - 1] > X[j] THEN
                    Swap(X[j - 1], X[j]);
                    LeftLastSwap := j;
                    Sorted := FALSE
                END (* IF *);
                DEC(j)
            END (* WHILE *);
            IF NOT Sorted THEN
                TRANSFER(ScanRightToLeft, ScanLeftToRight)
            END (* IF *)
        UNTIL Sorted;
        TRANSFER(ScanRightToLef', Sorter)
    END ScanRToL;
```

Figure 14.1   (cont.)

```
PROCEDURE SortCardList;

    (*****************************************************

        Procedure to sort a list of cardinal numbers using the
        two-way bubblesort scheme.

     ****************************************************)

    BEGIN
        NEWPROCESS(ScanLToR, ADR(LRWorkSpace),
                   WorkSpaceSize, ScanLeftToRight);
        NEWPROCESS(ScanRToL, ADR(RLWorkSpace),
                   WorkSpaceSize, ScanRightToLeft);
        LeftLastSwap := 1;
        RightLastSwap := NumElements;
        TRANSFER(Sorter, ScanLeftToRight)
    END SortCardList;

END TwoWayBubbleSort;

PROCEDURE PrintCardList(VAR CardList : ARRAY OF CARDINAL;
                            NumElements : CARDINAL);

    (*****************************************************

            Procedure to display a list of cardinal numbers.

     ****************************************************)

    VAR
        i : CARDINAL;              (* index *)

    BEGIN
        WriteLn;
        WriteString('Sorted list of numbers:');
        WriteLn;
        FOR i := 0 TO NumElements - 1 DO
            WriteCard(CardList[i], 1);
            WriteLn
        END (* FOR *)
    END PrintCardList;

BEGIN (* main program *)
    ReadCardList(X, NumElements);
    SortCardList;
    PrintCardList(X, NumElements)
END SortWithCoroutines.
```

Figure 14.1 (cont.)

```
Sample run:

Enter list of numbers (any nondigit to stop):
55 33 88 11 44 99 22 77 66
X

Sorted list of numbers:
11
22
33
44
55
66
77
88
99
```

14.2 Concurrent Programming

Programs were entered into the first electronic computers developed in the late 1930s and early 1940s by setting switches and dials, plugging wires, and so on. Modifying a program or executing a different program thus meant rewiring and resetting these switches and dials. In the mid- and late 1940s, several pioneers in the development of computers were studying the feasibility of storing the program in the machine itself. One of the more prominent individuals studying this *stored program concept* was the mathematician John von Neumann, and the model he developed, which describes most of the computer systems used today, is called the ***von Neumann model***. In these systems, a single program, procedure, or module is executed by a single processor. Execution consists of repeatedly carrying out the following ***fetch-execute cycle***:

Repeatedly do the following:

1. Fetch the next machine instruction from memory.
2. Decode the instruction to obtain the op code and the address of the operand.
3. Fetch the operand from the memory location having this address.
4. Apply the operation to the operand.

This kind of processing is usually referred to as ***serial*** or ***sequential processing***.

Because of the high cost of processors in these early machines, ***multiprogramming*** was developed so that these expensive components could be shared among several users. In multiprogrammed systems, several programs reside in memory simultaneously. The CPU is shared by having it execute one program for a short period of time; then it suspends execution of the current program and resumes or begins execution of another program; after this program is executed for a time, it is suspended; and so on. Although this is in fact serial processing, it appears to the users that each of them has the use of a dedicated (but slower) processor, that is, that the programs are being executed concurrently. This kind of processing is commonly referred to as *quasi-concurrent processing*.

More recently, *multiprocessor computers* have been developed, which make it possible for several tasks or parts of tasks to be executed at the same time by different processors. This simultaneous execution of several tasks or subtasks is referred to as *parallel processing*, and so instead of quasi-concurrency, we speak of *real concurrency*. The term *concurrent programming* refers to the techniques of designing programs in such a way that various parts of the program can be processed concurrently, either in a multiprocessor system where parallel processing can be done (real concurrency) or in a single-processor system in which the the various tasks and subtasks share the same CPU (quasi-concurrency).

To illustrate these different kinds of processing, consider the problem of finding the smallest number in a list of numbers. A serial algorithm is straightforward:

SERIAL ALGORITHM FOR FINDING A MINIMAL ELEMENT

(* Algorithm to find the minimal element *MinElement* and its *Location* in a list $X_1, X_2, \ldots, X_n$ of size n. *)

1. Set *MinElement* equal to X_1 and *Location* equal to 1.
2. For i ranging from 2 to n do the following:
   If $X_i <$ *MinElement* then
   a. Set *MinElement* equal to X_i.
   b. Set *Location* equal to i.

To illustrate this algorithm, consider the following list of eight numbers:

Following the algorithm, we initialize *MinElement* to 26 and *Location* to 1:

MinElement is then compared with the second element, and since this element is smaller, the values of *Location* and *MinElement* are updated:

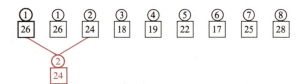

Now *MinElement* is compared with the third element, which is smaller, and so *MinElement* and *Location* are updated again:

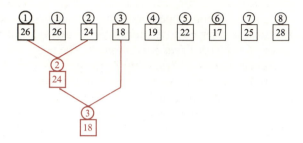

MinElement is smaller than the fourth and fifth elements, and so comparison with these list elements does not change its value. However, the sixth number is smaller and thus causes the values of *Location* and *MinElement* to be updated:

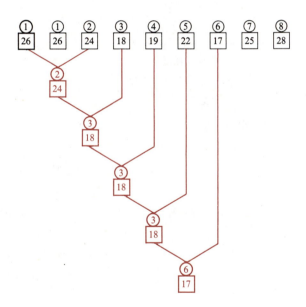

Comparison of *MinElement* with the last two numbers in the list leaves its value unchanged:

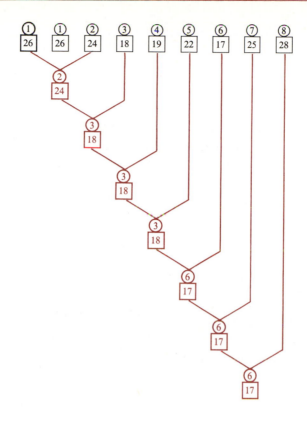

In this example, we see that seven comparisons are required to find the smallest number and its position, one less than the number of elements. This is clearly true in general, since each element of the list except the first must be compared with *MinElement*. The computing time for this algorithm is therefore O(n).

Now suppose that many processors are available. In particular, suppose that there are $n/2$ processors, and consider the same list of numbers:

We assign one processor to the first pair, another to the second pair, another to the third pair, and another to the fourth pair, and have each processor determine the smaller of the two numbers to which it is assigned and the position of this number:

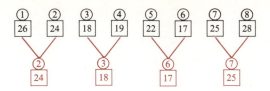

We now repeat this process for the resulting list of four elements, using one processor to find the smaller of the two numbers in the first pair and another to find the smaller number in the second pair:

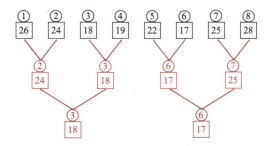

Now we use a single processor to find the smaller of the numbers in this last pair, and this is the smallest value in the original list:

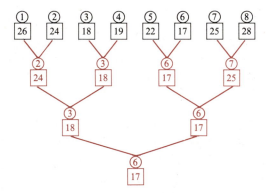

Like the serial algorithm, this procedure uses seven comparisons to find the smallest number and its location. However, the first four comparisons are done concurrently, as are the next two. Thus, the number of comparisons is not a good measure for the computing time of this parallel algorithm; rather, it should be based on the number of levels in the binary tree used to trace execution of the algorithm. In general, because the number of nodes at each level is half that at the preceding level (plus 1, if the number of nodes at the preceding level is odd), we see that the computing time for this parallel algorithm is $O(\log_2 n)$.

Although we cannot achieve such a dramatic improvement in the computing time of an algorithm if only a few processors are available, we nevertheless can often improve it. For example, suppose that only two processors are available. We can use the serial algorithm on one processor to find the smallest number and its position in the first half of the list and concurrently use the other processor to find the smallest number and its position in the second half of the list, and then use one of the processors to compare these two values to find the smallest value and its position in the entire list:

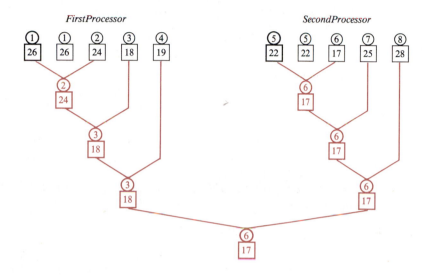

We see that for a list of n elements, the number of levels in this binary tree is $1 + (n - 1)/2$, so that although the computing time is still $O(n)$, it is approximately one-half of the computing time for the algorithm implemented on a single processor.

In this example of concurrent processing, the tasks being performed by the different processors are independent of each other. For example, the processors examining the two halves of the list in the preceding example can proceed independently of each other. They need not carry out their tasks at the same rate, and no communication between the two processors is necessary. After both have done their work, one of these processors or perhaps a different one can find the smaller of the two numbers produced. In many problems, however, the processors cannot work independently. Instead, each processor must communicate with one or more others to ensure that certain tasks that must be finished before this processor can continue have in fact been completed.

To illustrate, consider a list of student records arranged in alphabetical order, each containing a student's name, identification number, and four scores:

Alexander,T.Great	4087	87	92	75	88
Augusta,Ada	1199	99	100	92	84
Babbage,Chuck	1056	56	45	55	62
Boole,Jawge	2122	58	68	77	70

Suppose we wish to calculate the average of the four scores for each student and display these in order of increasing id numbers. Two main tasks are required to solve this problem:

1. Sort the list so that the id numbers are in ascending order.
2. For each record in this sorted list, calculate the average of the four scores.

Developing a serial program to do this is straightforward; we use a sorting scheme like selection sort to do Task 1. After Task 1 is completed, we traverse the sorted list and perform Task 2.

A natural question that arises is: If two processors are available, is it possible to carry out the two tasks concurrently? Since the second task requires that there be records in the sorted list for which averages can be computed, these two tasks cannot be done independently, but with the right kind of synchronization, they can be done concurrently. The second task does not require that the entire list has been sorted, only that the next record to be processed has already been properly positioned by the first task. That is, before the second task can "consume" the next record, this record must already have been "produced" by the first task. This problem is therefore an example of the classic **producer–consumer problem**; and a concurrent algorithm for its solution is as follows:

CONCURRENT ALGORITHM FOR THE PRODUCER–CONSUMER PROBLEM OF SORTING AND AVERAGING SCORES

(∗ Concurrent algorithm for calculating the average of scores in a list of student records and displaying them in the order of increasing student identification numbers. The boolean variable *StillProducing* is true while sorting is being carried out and is set to false when sorting is completed. ∗)

Main Algorithm

1. Read the list of student records.
2. Initialize the boolean variable *StillProducing* to true.
3. Start up the *Consumer* process and initialize its signal *Finished*.
4. Start up the *Producer* process and initialize its signal *RecordReady*.
5. Wait for the signal *Finished* from *Consumer*.
6. Print the list of averages.

Producer

(∗ Algorithm to sort a list of *NumRecords* student records so that student id numbers are in ascending order. The selection sort algorithm is used for this with the modification that each time another record is correctly positioned, a signal *RecordReady* is sent to notify *Consumer* of this event. *StillProducing* is set to false after sorting is completed. ∗)

1. For an index *i* ranging from 1 to *NumRecords* do the following:

a. Find the position of the record in the sublist of records in positions *i* through *NumRecords* that has the smallest id-number and interchange it with the record in position *i*.
b. Send the signal *RecordReady*.
2. Send the signal *RecordReady* and set *StillProducing* to false.

Consumer

(∗ Algorithm to compute the average of the four test scores in each record in the sorted list of records produced by *Producer* and to display this average. The signal *Finished* is sent when the processing of records has been completed ∗)

1. For an index *Count* ranging from 1 to *NumRecords* do the following:
   a. If *StillProducing*,
        wait for the signal *RecordReady* to be sent by *Producer*.
   b. Calculate the average of the four scores in the record in location *Count*.
2. Send the signal *Finished* to indicate that processing has been completed.

In *Programming in Modula-2*, Wirth describes a library module *Processes* that can be used to create processes and to synchronize them by means of signals. The definition part of this module is

DEFINITION MODULE *Processes*;

  TYPE SIGNAL;

  PROCEDURE *StartProcess*(P : PROC; n : CARDINAL);

    (∗ Procedure to start a concurrent process from procedure *P* and with a workspace of size *n*. ∗)

  PROCEDURE *SEND*(VAR s : SIGNAL);

    (∗ Procedure to send signal *s*, allowing execution of a suspended process waiting for *s* to resume. ∗)

  PROCEDURE *WAIT*(VAR s : SIGNAL);

    (∗ Procedure to suspend execution of a process, causing it to wait for some other process to send the signal *s*. ∗)

  PROCEDURE *Awaited*(VAR s : SIGNAL) : BOOLEAN;

    (∗ Returns true if at least one process is waiting for the signal *s*, false otherwise. ∗)

  PROCEDURE *Init*(VAR s : SIGNAL);

    (∗ Procedure to initialize signal *s*; it must be called to initialize every signal. ∗)

END *Processes*.

Although this description of *Processes* does not specify whether the processes will be executed in a real- or a quasi-concurrent environment, Wirth does present an implementation module using coroutines on a machine with a single processor and thus providing quasi-concurrency.

The program in Figure 14.2 uses the type SIGNAL and procedures *StartProcess*, *Init*, *SEND*, and *WAIT* to implement the algorithm for the producer–consumer problem of sorting student records and calculating and displaying the averages of the scores in these records. It uses two signals, *RecordReady*, which is sent by process *Producer* when it has correctly positioned another record, and *Finished*, which is sent by process *Consumer* when it has finished processing the records. The main program initializes these signals using procedure *Init*, calls procedure *StartProcess* to get the two processes started, and then waits for the signal *Finished* to be sent by *Consumer*, at which time it can display the list averages and terminate execution.

```
MODULE ProducerConsumer;

(************************************************************************

    Program that uses concurrent processes to solve an example of
    the producer-consumer problem in which the producer sorts a
    list of student-records so id-numbers are in ascending order
    using the selection sort method, and the consumer calculates
    the averages of the scores in these records.

 ************************************************************************)

    FROM InOut IMPORT Write, WriteString, WriteCard, WriteLn,
                    ReadCard, ReadString, Done, OpenInput, CloseInput;
    FROM Processes IMPORT SIGNAL, StartProcess, SEND, WAIT, Init;

    CONST
        NumberOfScores = 4;         (* number of scores in each record *)
        MaxString = 20;             (* limit on length of student names *)
        ListLimit = 50;             (* limit on size of list *)
        WorkSpaceSize = 1000;       (* size of workspace for processes *)

    TYPE
        String = ARRAY [0..MaxString] OF CHAR;
        StudentRecord = RECORD
                            Name : String;
                            IdNumber : CARDINAL;
                            Score : ARRAY [1..NumberOfScores] OF CARDINAL;
                            Average : CARDINAL;
                        END;
        ListOfRecords = ARRAY [1..ListLimit] OF StudentRecord;

    VAR
        NumRecs : CARDINAL;         (* number of records in list *)
        StuRec : ListOfRecords;     (* list to be processed *)
        StillProducing : BOOLEAN;   (* true if producer still producing *)
        RecordReady,                (* signal when producer produces *)
        Finished : Signal;          (* signal when consumer finished *)
```

Figure 14.2

Figure 14.2 (cont.)

```
PROCEDURE ReadRecords(VAR StuRec : ARRAY OF StudentRecord;
                      VAR NumRecs : CARDINAL);

   (*******************************************************************

        Procedure to read and return the array StuRec of NumRecs
        student records.

    ******************************************************************)

   CONST
       EOF = '*';               (* end-of-file mark *)

   VAR
       StuName : String;        (* a student name *)
       i : CARDINAL;            (* index *)

   BEGIN
       WriteString('Enter name of file containing records.');
       WriteLn;
       OpenInput('');
       NumRecs := 0;
       ReadString(StuName);
       WHILE StuName[0] # EOF DO
           WITH StuRec[NumRecs] DO
               Name := StuName;
               ReadCard(IdNumber);
               FOR i := 1 TO NumberOfScores DO
                   ReadCard(Score[i])
               END (* FOR *);
               INC(NumRecs);
               ReadString(StuName)
           END (* WITH *)
       END (* WHILE *)
   END ReadRecords;

PROCEDURE PrintAverages(VAR StuRec : ARRAY OF StudentRecord;
                        NumRecs : CARDINAL);

   (*******************************************************************

        Procedure to print the id-numbers, names, and averages in
        the array StuRec of NumRecs student records.

    ******************************************************************)

   VAR
       i : CARDINAL;            (* index *)
```

Figure 14.2   (cont.)

```
    BEGIN
        WriteLn; WriteLn;
        FOR i := 0 TO NumRecs - 1 DO
            WITH StuRec[i] DO
                WriteCard(IdNumber, 5);
                WriteString('--');
                WriteString(Name);
                WriteString('--average:');
                WriteCard(Average, 3);
                WriteLn
            END (* WITH *)
        END (* FOR *)
    END PrintAverages;

PROCEDURE Producer;

    (****************************************************************

        Procedure to sort a list StuRec of NumRecords student records
        so that student id-numbers are in ascending order.  It uses
        the selection sort algorithm with the modification that each
        time another record is correctly positioned, the signal
        RecordReady is sent to notify Consumer of this event.
        StillProducing is set to false after sorting is completed.

    ****************************************************************)

    VAR
        i, j,                      (* indices *)
        Position,                  (* location of record with smallest id *)
        SmallestId : CARDINAL;     (* smallest id seen thus far *)
        Temp : StudentRecord;      (* used to interchange records *)

    BEGIN
        FOR i := 1 TO NumRecs DO
            SmallestId := StuRec[i].IdNumber;
            Position := i;
            FOR j := i + 1 TO NumRecs DO
                WITH StuRec[j] DO
                    IF IdNumber < SmallestId THEN
                        SmallestId := IdNumber;
                        Position := j
                    END (* IF *)
                END (* FOR *)
            END (* WITH *);
            Temp := StuRec[Position];
            StuRec[Position] := StuRec[i];
            StuRec[i] := Temp;
            Send(RecordReady)
        END (* FOR *);
        Send(RecordReady);
        StillProducing := FALSE
    END Producer;
```

Figure 14.2   (cont.)

```
    PROCEDURE Consumer;

        (*************************************************************

            Procedure to compute the average of the four test scores
            in the sorted list of records produced by Producer.
            Signal Finish is sent when this processing of records has
            been completed.

        *************************************************************)

        VAR
            Count, k : CARDINAL;                (* indices *)
            Sum : CARDINAL;                     (* sum of test scores *)

        BEGIN
            FOR Count := 1 TO NumRecs DO
                IF StillProducing THEN
                    Wait(RecordReady)
                END (* IF *);
                WITH StuRec[Count] DO
                    Sum := 0;
                    FOR k := 1 TO NumberOfScores DO
                        INC(Sum, Score[k])
                    END (* FOR *);
                    Average := Sum DIV NumberOfScores
                END (* WITH *)
            END (* FOR *);
            Send(Finished)
        END Consumer;

BEGIN (* main program *)
    ReadRecords(StuRec, NumRecs);
    StillProducing := TRUE;
    Init(RecordReady);
    Init(Finished);
    StartProcess(Consumer, WorkSpaceSize);
    StartProcess(Producer, WorkSpaceSize);
    WAIT(Finished);
    PrintAverages(StuRec, NumRecs)
END ProducerConsumer.
```

Listing of file used in sample run:

```
Alexander,T.Great      4087    87   92   75   88
Augusta,Ada            1199    99  100   92   84
Babbage,Chuck          1056    56   45   55   62
Boole,Jawge            2122    58   68   77   70
FORTRAN,Fred            123    77   77   77   77
Pascal,Blaze           3602    88   99   94   97
Zzyzk,Zelda            2555    53   90   42   72
*****
```

Figure 14.2 (cont.)

```
Sample run:

Enter name of file containing records.
in> FILE14.2

  123--FORTRAN,Fred--average: 77
 1056--Babbage,Chuck--average: 54
 1199--Augusta,Ada--average: 93
 2122--Boole,Jawge--average: 68
 2555--Zzyzk,Zelda--average: 64
 3602--Pascal,Blaze--average: 94
 4087--Alexander,T.Great--average: 85
```

The type SIGNAL and the procedures provided in the library module *Processes* are more primitive and thus are considerably weaker than other constructs commonly used in concurrent programming. One of their major weaknesses is that when a process sends a signal to indicate that some event has occurred, this signal is lost if no other process happens to be waiting for that signal at that time. In quasi-concurrent processing that is implemented using coroutines as described by Wirth, this is not a serious problem, but in other types of concurrent processing, it is.

The *semaphore*, introduced by the Dutch computer scientist Edsger Dijkstra in 1965, is a more powerful construct for synchronizing concurrent processes. A semaphore is a record containing one integer field and a queue of suspended processes. The *SEND* and *WAIT* operations are replaced by the *P* and *V* operations. (These are the first letters of the Dutch words *proberen* and *verhogen* used by Dijkstra for these basic operations). These operations are commonly defined as follows:

$P(s)$: 1. Decrement the integer field of semaphore s.
     2. If this integer value is negative, then:
        Suspend execution of the current process and add it to
        the queue of suspended processes for this semaphore s.

$V(s)$: 1. Increment the integer field of semaphore s.
     2. If this integer value is not positive then:
        Remove a process from the queue of processes suspended
        on semaphore s.

In addition to these basic operations, a procedure is needed to initialize a semaphore by setting its integer field to some specified value and creating an empty queue for its second field.

Semaphores can be used to solve the *mutual exclusion problem*. In this problem, two (or more) processes are executing concurrently and processing some common data. However, each process has a *critical section* in which the shared data is being accessed, and while a process is in its critical section, it must have exclusive access to the shared data; that is, all other processes must be blocked from accessing this data.

As an illustration, suppose that we had solved the producer–consumer problem by letting each have access to a common array *Buffer* in which the sorted records are stored. The producer increments a variable *Count* each time it deposits another record in *Buffer*, and the consumer decrements *Count* each time it removes a record and processes it. Here the depositing of a record in the buffer is a critical section of the producer, and the removal of a record is a critical section of the consumer.

To illustrate why mutual exclusion is necessary, consider the operations of incrementing *Count* in the producer and decrementing *Count* in the consumer. The machine instructions required to carry out these operations might be the following:

Producer	Consumer
LOAD *Count*	LOAD *Count*
ADD 1	SUBTRACT 1
STORE *Count*	STORE *Count*

Now suppose that *Count* is initially 0 and that each of the producer and consumer processes executes these instructions three times. One might expect the final value of *Count* to be 0, but the following scenario shows that it need not be:

Time	Producer Instruction Executed	Consumer Instruction Executed	Contents of Accumulator	Value of *Count*
0			0	0
1	LOAD *Count*		0	0
2	ADD 1		1	0
3	STORE *Count*		1	1
4		LOAD *Count*	1	1
5		SUBTRACT 1	0	1
6	LOAD *Count*		1	1
7	ADD 1		2	2
8		STORE *Count*	2	2
9	STORE *Count*		2	2
10		LOAD *Count*	2	2
11		SUBTRACT 1	1	2
12	LOAD *Count*		2	2
13	ADD 1		3	3
14		STORE *Count*	3	3
15		LOAD *Count*	3	3
16	STORE *Count*		3	3
17		SUBTRACT 1	2	2
18		STORE *Count*	2	2

The mutual exclusion of critical sections is easy to enforce by using semaphores. For example, suppose that processes *A* and *B* each have a critical section. We initialize a semaphore *s* to 1 and simply cause each of *A* and *B* to wait on *s* before entering their critical sections and to signal on *s* after exiting:

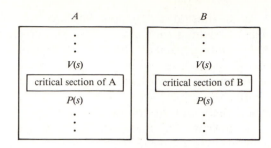

Semaphores and the mutual exclusion problem are described in a bit more detail in the exercises. However, a complete treatment of them together with still more powerful structures such as *monitors* is beyond the level of this text and is left to more advanced courses in the study of operating systems, algorithms, and data structures.

Exercises

1. Trace the execution of the two-way bubblesort algorithm on each of the following lists of numbers:

(a) 15, 5, 10, 20, 40, 25, 50, 35, 30, 45, 55, 60
(b) 15, 5, 10, 20, 50, 40, 45, 35, 30, 25, 60, 55
(c) 60, 5, 10, 15, 20, 25, 30, 35, 40, 45, 50, 55
(d) 10, 5, 20, 15, 30, 25, 40, 35, 50, 45, 60, 55
(e) 5, 10, 15, 20, 25, 30, 35, 40, 45, 50, 55, 60
(f) 60, 55, 50, 45, 40, 35, 30, 25, 20, 15, 10, 5

2. Consider the following program skeleton:

MODULE *Exercise2*;

    (* Appropriate import, constant, type, and variable declarations from part (a) *)

PROCEDURE *One*;
  BEGIN
      WriteString('1'); *WriteLn*;
      TRANSFER(*CoOne*, *CoTwo*);
      WriteString('11'); *WriteLn*;
      TRANSFER(*CoOne*, *CoTwo*);
      WriteString('111'); *WriteLn*;
      TRANSFER(*CoOne*, *Main*)
  END *One*;

PROCEDURE *Two*;
  BEGIN
      WriteString('2'); *WriteLn*;
      TRANSFER(*CoTwo*, *CoOne*);
      WriteString('22'); *WriteLn*;
      TRANSFER(*CoTwo*, *CoOne*)
  END *Two*;

```
BEGIN (* main program *)
    (* Appropriate statements from part (b) *)
    TRANSFER (Main, CoOne);
    WriteString('*** Done processing ***');
    WriteLn
END Exercise2.
```

(a) Write the missing import, constant, type, and variable declarations in this program.

(b) Provide the missing statements in the statement part of this program.

(c) Trace the execution of this program, and describe the output produced.

3. Consider the following program skeleton:

```
MODULE Exercise3;

    (* Appropriate import, constant, type, and variable
       declarations from part (a) *)

PROCEDURE One;
    BEGIN
        WriteString('1'); WriteLn;
        TRANSFER(CoOne, CoTwo);
        WriteString('11'); WriteLn;
        TRANSFER(CoOne, CoThree);
        WriteString('111'); WriteLn;
        TRANSFER(CoOne, Main)
    END One;

PROCEDURE Two;
    BEGIN
        WriteString('2'); WriteLn;
        TRANSFER(CoTwo, CoThree);
        WriteString('22'); WriteLn;
        TRANSFER(CoTwo, CoOne);
        WriteString('222'); WriteLn;
        TRANSFER(CoTwo, Main)
    END Two;

PROCEDURE Three;
    BEGIN
        WriteString('3'); WriteLn;
        TRANSFER(CoThree, CoOne);
        WriteString('33'); WriteLn;
        TRANSFER(CoThree, CoTwo);
        WriteString('333'); WriteLn;
        TRANSFER(CoThree, Main)
    END Three;
```

```
        BEGIN (* main program *)
           (* Appropriate statements from part (b) *)
           TRANSFER(Main, CoOne);
           WriteString('*** Done processing ***');
           WriteLn
        END Exercise3.
```

(a) Write the missing import, constant, type, and variable declarations in this program.

(b) Provide the missing statements in the statement part of this program.

(c) Trace the execution of this program, and describe the output produced.

(d) Repeat part (c), but replace the call to procedure *TRANSFER* in the statement part of the main program by

$$TRANSFER(Main, CoTwo);$$

(e) Repeat part (c), but replace the call to procedure *TRANSFER* in the statement part of the main program by

$$TRANSFER(Main, CoThree);$$

4. Write a program that processes a sequence of consecutive cardinal numbers in the range *FirstNum* through *LastNum*, using one coroutine to print the word "Even" if the number is even and another to print the word "Odd" if it is odd.

5. An **alternating series** is an infinite series $a_1, a_2, \ldots$, in which the terms are alternately positive and negative, for example,

$$1, -\tfrac{1}{2}, \tfrac{1}{3}, -\tfrac{1}{4}, \tfrac{1}{5}, -\tfrac{1}{6} \ldots$$

Write a program that displays successive terms in such an alternative series, using one coroutine to display the positive terms and another to display the negative terms.

6. Proceed as in Exercise 5, but rather than displaying the terms in the series, display the prefix sums, where the *n*-th *prefix sum* is the sum of the first *n* terms.

7. The sequence of Fibonacci numbers

$$1, 1, 2, 3, 5, 8, 13, 21, 34, 55, 89, \ldots$$

which was described in Section 5.2, begins with two 1's, and each number thereafter is the sum of the two preceding numbers. Write a program that uses one coroutine to find the third, fifth, seventh, . . . Fibonacci numbers by adding the two preceding Fibonacci numbers and that uses another coroutine to find the fourth, sixth, eighth . . . numbers in the same way.

8. We might call the sequence

$$1, 1, 1, 3, 5, 9, 17, 31, 57, 105, 193, \ldots$$

which begins with three 1's and in which each number thereafter is the sum of the three preceding numbers, the sequence of "Tribonacci numbers." Write a program that uses three coroutines similar to those described in Exercise 7. That is, one coroutine finds the fourth, seventh, tenth, . . . Tribonacci numbers; another finds the fifth, eighth, eleventh, . . . , Tribonacci numbers; and a third one finds the sixth, ninth, twelfth, . . . Tribonacci numbers.

9. Write a program that uses one coroutine to generate Fibonacci numbers and another to compute successive approximations to the **golden ratio** $\dfrac{\sqrt{5} + 1}{2}$ by dividing each Fibonacci number by its predecessor.

10. Proceed as in Exercise 9, but use three coroutines: two to generate Fibonacci numbers as described in Exercise 7 and a third to compute approximations to the golden ratio.

11. Write a program that uses coroutines to carry out a **two-way linear search** of a list stored in an array. One coroutine should search from left to right and the other from right to left.

12. Proceed as in Exercise 11, but use a symmetrically-linked list.

13. Write a program that uses coroutines to carry out a **two-way insertion sort** of a list stored in an array. One coroutine should work from left to right in inserting numbers, and the other should work from right to left.

14. Proceed as in Exercise 13, but use a symmetrically-linked list.

15. Describe how the mean of a list of n numbers can be calculated most efficiently using parallel processing if

   (a) at least $n/2$ processors are available.
   (b) two processors are available.

   Determine the computing time of each algorithm.

16. Describe an efficient concurrent algorithm for carrying out a linear search of an array of n numbers if

   (a) at least n processors are available.
   (b) two processors are available.

   Determine the computing time of each algorithm.

17. Describe an efficient concurrent algorithm for adding two $n \times n$ matrices using parallel processing if

    (a) at least n^2 processors are available.
    (b) n processors are available.

    Determine the computing time of each algorithm.

18. Describe an $O(\log_2 n)$ algorithm for determining the first n prefix sums of a sequence using parallel processing if at least $n - 1$ processors are available (see Exercise 6).

19. Write a program to solve the producer–consumer problem in which the producer is producing Fibonacci numbers and the consumer is computing successive approximations to the golden ratio (see Exercise 9).

20. Binomial coefficients were defined in Exercise 11 of Section 5.3 and can be calculated as

    $$\binom{n}{k} = \frac{n \times (n - 1) \times \cdots \times (n - k + 1)}{1 \times 2 \times \cdots \times k}$$

    where $0 < k < n$. Write a concurrent program to calculate binomial coefficients, using one process to calculate the numerator, and the other the denominator.

21. *Conway's problem*: Write a concurrent program that reads lines of 80 characters from a text file; replaces each end-of-line character by a blank and all strings of two or more blanks by a single blank; and formats them in lines, each of which contains exactly 60 characters. This is an example of a composition of two producer–consumer problems and can be solved quite nicely by using three concurrent processes. Process 1 simply reads individual characters from the file, replacing each end-of-line character by a blank, and writes these characters into a buffer that it shares with the second process. Process 2 reads characters from this buffer, looking for consecutive blanks, and writes the modified stream of characters into a buffer that it shares with the third process. Process 3 prints the characters from this buffer on 60-character lines.

22. Construct a scenario for the producer–consumer example in the text used to demonstrate the need for mutual exclusion in which the final value of *Count* is

    (a) 0   (b) 1   (c) -2 (d) 3

Epilogue

The Ubiquity of Data Structures

In this text we have noted some of the applications of data structures in computer science, but there are many more. One need only read course descriptions in computer science curricula such as those published by the Association of Computing Machinery (ACM) or look at textbooks for such courses. A course in *numerical analysis* makes extensive use of arrays and perhaps linked lists in numerical computations involving polynomials and matrices. The address translation schemes used to implement arrays are usually one of the topics in a *machine/assembly language* course. Some programming languages, such as *LISP* (*LISt Processing*), require familiarity with linked structures if one is to understand the structure of the language. *Operating systems* texts describe schemes for maintaining the ready queue, the wait queue, the suspended queue, a stack of activation records, a run-time heap, and linked lists for dynamic allocation and deallocation of memory. The design of *databases* makes extensive use of trees and digraphs, as do many areas of *artificial intelligence*. Books dealing with *compiler design* discuss the use of strings, sets, and arrays in the design of lexical analyzers, parse trees generated by the parser, the maintenance of a symbol table as a hash table, flow of control graphs, and code optimization digraphs. The "big Oh" notation is used to measure the efficiency of algorithms in *algorithm analysis* courses, and advanced *data structures* courses expand on our presentation of data structures and introduce new ones.

This small sample of the applications of data structures in computer science, not to mention the many applications in other areas, should serve to demonstrate their importance and their multitude of uses. Although we have considered a fairly large number of data structures, together with their implementations and applications, it must be emphasized that this has been only an introduction; we have barely scratched the surface.

ASCII and EBCDIC

ASCII and EBCDIC codes of printable characters

Decimal	Binary	Octal	Hexadecimal	ASCII	EBCDIC
32	00100000	040	20	SP (Space)	
33	00100001	041	21	!	
34	00100010	042	22	''	
35	00100011	043	23	#	
36	00100100	044	24	$	
37	00100101	045	25	%	
38	00100110	046	26	&	
39	00100111	047	27	' (Single quote)	
40	00101000	050	28	(	
41	00101001	051	29	)	
42	00101010	052	2A	*	
43	00101011	053	2B	+	
44	00101100	054	2C	, (Comma)	
45	00101101	055	2D	- (Hyphen)	
46	00101110	056	2E	. (Period)	
47	00101111	057	2F	/	
48	00110000	060	30	0	
49	00110001	061	31	1	
50	00110010	062	32	2	
51	00110011	063	33	3	
52	00110100	064	34	4	
53	00110101	065	35	5	
54	00110110	066	36	6	
55	00110111	067	37	7	
56	00111000	070	38	8	
57	00111001	071	39	9	
58	00111010	072	3A	:	
59	00111011	073	3B	;	
60	00111100	074	3C	<	
61	00111101	075	3D	=	
62	00111110	076	3E	>	
63	00111111	077	3F	?	

ASCII and EBCDIC codes of printable characters

Decimal	Binary	Octal	Hexadecimal	ASCII	EBCDIC
64	01000000	100	40	@	SP (Space)
65	01000001	101	41	A	
66	01000010	102	42	B	
67	01000011	103	43	C	
68	01000100	104	44	D	
69	01000101	105	45	E	
70	01000110	106	46	F	
71	01000111	107	47	G	
72	01001000	110	48	H	
73	01001001	111	49	I	
74	01001010	112	4A	J	¢
75	01001011	113	4B	K	. (Period)
76	01001100	114	4C	L	<
77	01001101	115	4D	M	(
78	01001110	116	4E	N	+
79	01001111	117	4F	O	|
80	01010000	120	50	P	&
81	01010001	121	51	Q	
82	01010010	122	52	R	
83	01010011	123	53	S	
84	01010100	124	54	T	
85	01010101	125	55	U	
86	01010110	126	56	V	
87	01010111	127	57	W	
88	01011000	130	58	X	
89	01011101	131	59	Y	
90	01011010	132	5A	Z	!
91	01011011	133	5B	[	$
92	01011100	134	5C	\	*
93	01011101	135	5D	|	)
94	01011110	136	5E	∧	;
95	01011111	137	5F	_ (Underscore)	¬ (Negation)
96	01100000	140	60	`	- (Hyphen)
97	01100001	141	61	a	/
98	01100010	142	62	b	
99	01100011	143	63	c	
100	01100100	144	64	d	
101	01100101	145	65	e	
102	01100110	146	66	f	
103	01100111	147	67	g	
104	01101000	150	68	h	
105	01101001	151	69	i	
106	01101010	152	6A	j	∧
107	01101011	153	6B	k	, (Comma)
108	01101100	154	6C	l	%
109	01101101	155	6D	m	_ (Underscore)
110	01101110	156	6E	n	>
111	01101111	157	6F	o	?
112	01110000	160	70	p	
113	01110001	161	71	q	
114	01110010	162	72	r	
115	01110011	163	73	s	
116	01110100	164	74	t	
117	01110101	165	75	u	
118	01110110	166	76	v	

ASCII and EBCDIC codes of printable characters

Decimal	Binary	Octal	Hexadecimal	ASCII	EBCDIC
119	01110111	167	77	w	
120	01111000	170	78	x	
121	01111001	171	79	y	
122	01111010	172	7A	z	:
123	01111011	173	7B	{	#
124	01111100	174	7C	|	@
125	01111101	175	7D	}	' (Single quote)
126	01111110	176	7E	~	=
127	01111111	177	7F		''
128	10000000	200	80		
129	10000001	201	81		a
130	10000010	202	82		b
131	10000011	203	83		c
132	10000100	204	84		d
133	10000101	205	85		e
134	10000110	206	86		f
135	10000111	207	87		g
136	10001000	210	88		h
137	10001001	211	89		i
.	.	.	.		.
.	.	.	.		.
.	.	.	.		.
145	10010001	221	91		j
146	10010010	222	92		k
147	10010011	223	93		l
148	10010100	224	94		m
149	10010101	225	95		n
150	10010110	226	96		o
151	10010111	227	97		p
152	10011000	230	98		q
153	10011001	231	99		r
.	.	.	.		.
.	.	.	.		.
162	10100010	242	A2		s
163	10100011	243	A3		t
164	10100100	244	A4		u
165	10100101	245	A5		v
166	10100110	246	A6		w
167	10100111	247	A7		x
168	10101000	250	A8		y
169	10101001	251	A9		z
.	.	.	.		.
.	.	.	.		.
192	11000000	300	C0		}
193	11000001	301	C1		A
194	11000010	302	C2		B
195	11000011	303	C3		C
196	11000100	304	C4		D
197	11000101	305	C5		E
198	11000110	306	C6		F
199	11000111	307	C7		G
200	11001000	310	C8		H
201	11001001	311	C9		I

ASCII and EBCDIC codes of printable characters

Decimal	Binary	Octal	Hexadecimal	ASCII	EBCDIC
.	.	.	.		.
.		.	.		.
.		.	.		.
208	11010000	320	D0		}
209	11010001	321	D1		J
210	11010010	322	D2		K
211	11010011	323	D3		L
212	11010100	324	D4		M
213	11010101	325	D5		N
214	11010110	326	D6		O
215	11010111	327	D7		P
216	11011000	330	D8		Q
217	11011001	331	D9		R
.	.	.	.		.
.		.	.		.
.	.	.	.		.
224	11100000	340	E0		\
225	11100001	341	E1		
226	11100010	342	E2		S
227	11100011	343	E3		T
228	11100100	344	E4		U
229	11100101	345	E5		V
230	11100110	346	E6		W
231	11100111	347	E7		X
232	11101000	350	E8		Y
233	11101001	351	E9		Z
.	.	.	.		.
.	.	.	.		.
.	.	.	.		.
240	11110000	360	F0		0
241	11110001	361	F1		1
242	11110010	362	F2		2
243	11110011	363	F3		3
244	11110100	364	F4		4
245	11110101	365	F5		5
246	11110110	366	F6		6
247	11110111	367	F7		7
248	11111000	370	F8		8
249	11111001	371	F9		9
.	.	.	.		
.	.	.	.		
.	.	.	.		
255	11111111	377	FF		

ASCII codes of control characters

Decimal	Binary	Octal	Hexadecimal	Character
0	00000000	000	00	NUL (Null)
1	00000001	001	01	SOH (Start of heading)
2	00000010	002	02	STX (End of heading and start of text)
3	00000011	003	03	ETX (End of text)
4	00000100	004	04	EOT (End of transmission)
5	00000101	005	05	ENQ (Enquiry—to request identification)
6	00000110	006	06	ACK (Acknowledge)
7	00000111	007	07	BEL (Ring bell)
8	00001000	010	08	BS (Backspace)
9	00001001	011	09	HT (Horizontal tab)
10	00001010	012	0A	LF (Line feed)
11	00001011	013	0B	VT (Vertical tab)
12	00001100	014	0C	FF (Form feed)
13	00001101	015	0D	CR (Carriage return)
14	00001110	016	0E	SO (Shift out—begin non-ASCII bit string)
15	00001111	017	0F	SI (Shift in—end non-ASCII bit string)
16	00010000	020	10	DLE (Data link escape—controls data transmission)
17	00010001	021	11	DC1 (Device control 1)
18	00010010	022	12	DC2 (Device control 2)
19	00010011	023	13	DC3 (Device control 3)
20	00010100	024	14	DC4 (Device control 4)
21	00010101	025	15	NAK (Negative acknowledge)
22	00010110	026	16	SYN (Synchronous idle)
23	00010111	027	17	ETB (End of transmission block)
24	00011000	030	18	CAN (Cancel—ignore previous transmission)
25	00011001	031	19	EM (End of medium)
26	00011010	032	1A	SUB (Substitute a character for another)
27	00011011	033	1B	ESC (Escape)
28	00011100	034	1C	FS (File separator)
29	00011101	035	1D	GS (Group separator)
30	00011110	036	1E	RS (Record separator)
31	00011111	037	1F	US (Unit separator)

EBCDIC codes of control characters

Decimal	Binary	Octal	Hexadecimal	Character
0	00000000	000	00	NUL (Null)
1	00000001	001	01	SOH (Start of heading)
2	00000010	002	02	STX (End of heading and start of text)
3	00000011	003	03	ETX (End of text)
4	00000100	004	04	PF (Punch off)
5	00000101	005	05	HT (Horizontal tab)
6	00000110	006	06	LC (Lower case)
7	00000111	007	07	DEL (Delete)
10	00001010	012	0A	SMM (Repeat)
11	00001011	013	0B	VT (Vertical tab)
12	00001100	014	0C	FF (Form feed)
13	00001101	015	0D	CR (Carriage return)
14	00001110	016	0E	SO (Shift out—begin non-ASCII bit string)
15	00001111	017	0F	SI (Shift in—end non-ASCII bit string)
16	00010000	020	10	DLE (Data link escape—controls data transmission)
17	00010001	021	11	DC1 (Device control 1)
18	00010010	022	12	DC2 (Device control 2)
19	00010011	023	13	DC3 (Device control 3)
20	00010100	024	14	RES (Restore)
21	00010101	025	15	NL (Newline)
22	00010110	026	16	BS (Backspace)
23	00010111	027	17	IL (Idle)
24	00011000	030	18	CAN (Cancel—ignore previous transmission)
25	00011001	031	19	EM (End of medium)
26	00011010	032	1A	CC (Unit backspace)
28	00011100	034	1C	IFS (Interchange file separator)
29	00011101	035	1D	IGS (Interchange group separator)
30	00011110	036	1E	IRS (Interchange record separator)
31	00011111	037	1F	IUS (Interchange unit separator)
32	00100000	040	20	DS (Digit select)
33	00100001	041	21	SOS (Start of significance)
34	00100010	042	22	FS (File separator)
36	00100100	044	24	BYP (Bypass)
37	00100101	045	25	LF (Line feed)
38	00100110	046	26	ETB (End of transmission block)
39	00100111	047	27	ESC (Escape)
42	00101010	052	2A	SM (Start message)
45	00101101	055	2D	ENQ (Enquiry—to request identification)
46	00101110	056	2E	ACK (Acknowledge)
47	00101111	057	2F	BEL (Ring bell)
50	00110010	062	32	SYN (Synchronous idle)
52	00110100	064	34	PN (Punch on)
53	00110101	065	35	RS (Record separator)
54	00110110	066	36	UC (Upper case)
55	00110111	067	37	EOT (End of transmission)
60	00111100	074	3C	DC4 (Device control 4)
61	00111101	075	3D	NAK (Negative acknowledge)
63	00111111	077	3F	SUB (Substitute a character for another)

B

Modula-2 Reserved Words, Standard Identifiers, Operators

Reserved Words

AND	ELSIF	LOOP	REPEAT
ARRAY	END	MOD	RETURN
BEGIN	EXIT	MODULE	SET
BY	EXPORT	NOT	THEN
CASE	FOR	OF	TO
CONST	FROM	OR	TYPE
DEFINITION	IF	POINTER	UNTIL
DIV	IMPLEMENTATION	PROCEDURE	VAR
DO	IMPORT	QUALIFIED	WHILE
ELSE	IN	RECORD	WITH

Standard Constants

FALSE	TRUE	NIL

Predefined Types

BITSET	CARDINAL	INTEGER	LONGINT	PROC
BOOLEAN	CHAR	LONGCARD	LONGREAL	REAL

Predefined Function Procedures

ABS	FLOAT	MIN	SIZE
CAP	HIGH	ODD	TRUNC
CHR	MAX	ORD	VAL

Predefined Proper Procedures

DEC	HALT	INCL
EXCL	INC	

Operators

Operator	Operation
+	unary plus, addition, set union
−	unary minus, subtraction, set difference
*	multiplication, set intersection
/	real division, symmetric set difference
DIV	integer division
MOD	modulus (remainder)
=	equal
<> or #	not equal
<	less than
>	greater than
<=	less than or equal to
>=	greater than or equal to
AND or &	conjunction
NOT or ~	negation
OR	disjunction
IN	set membership
:=	assignment
↑	dereference a pointer

C

Modula-2 Language Syntax Diagrams

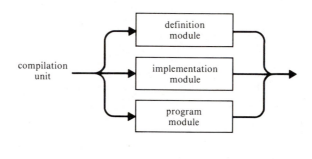

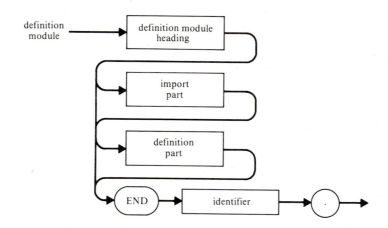

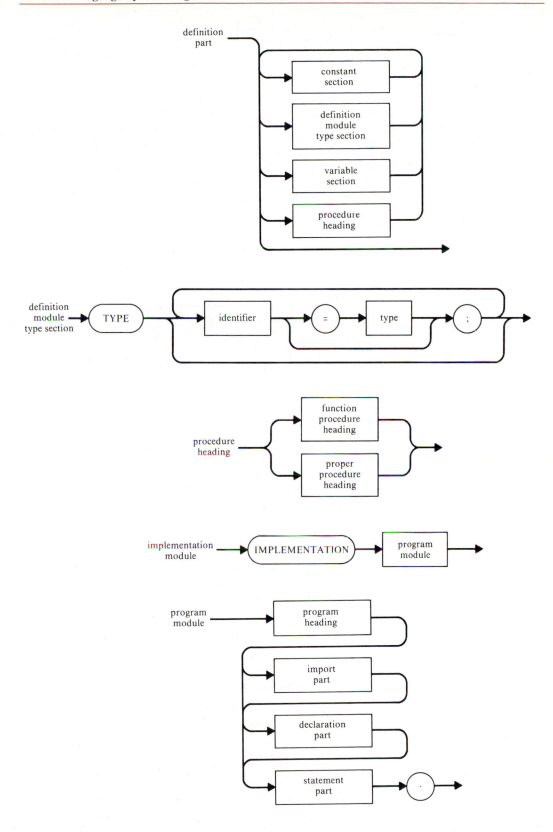

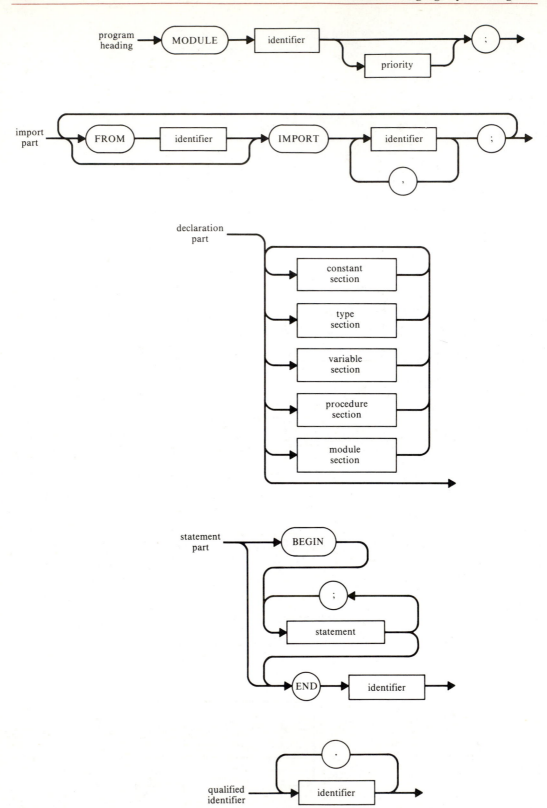

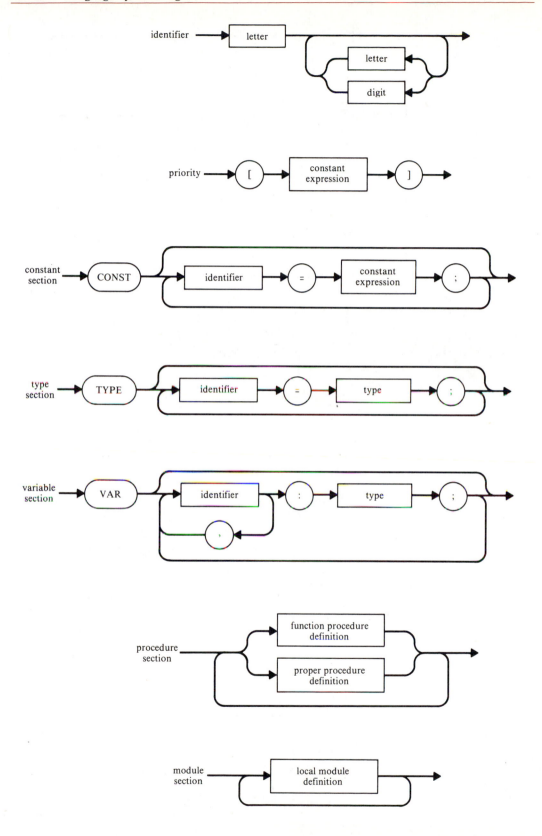

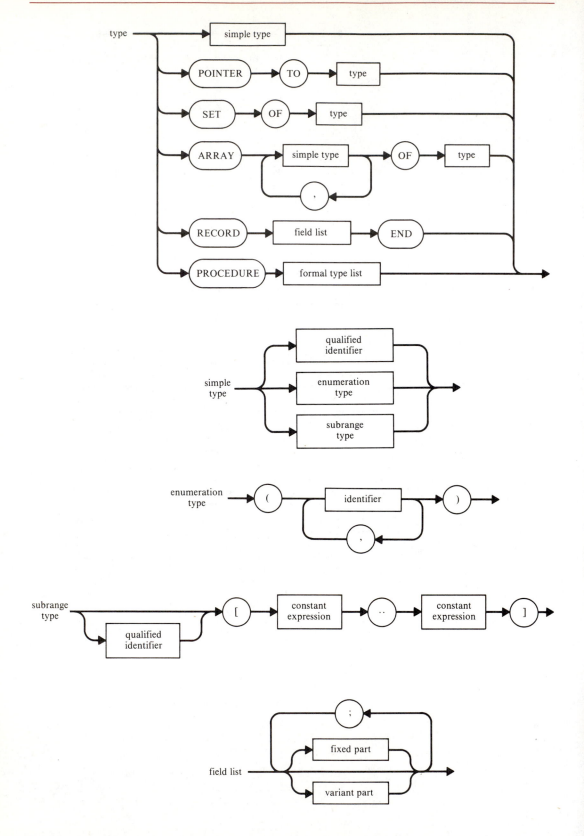

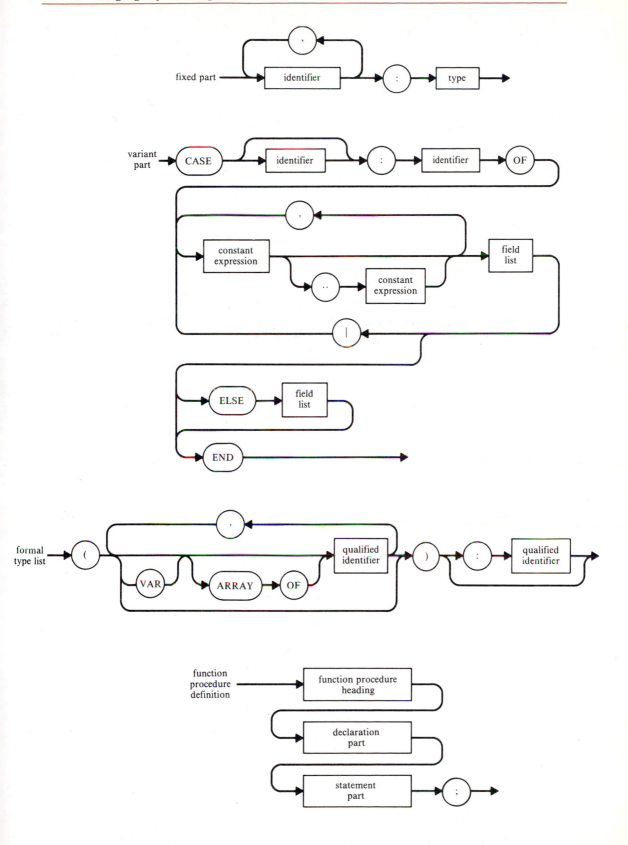

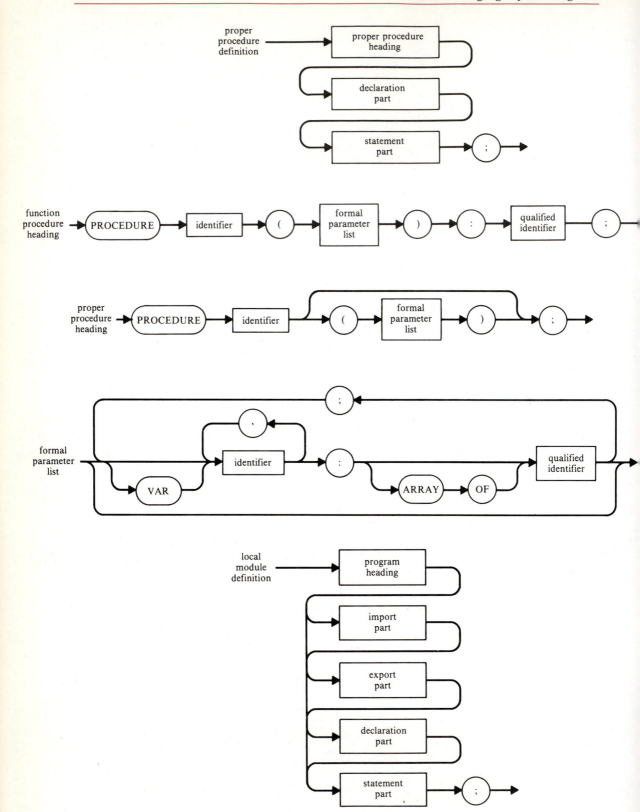

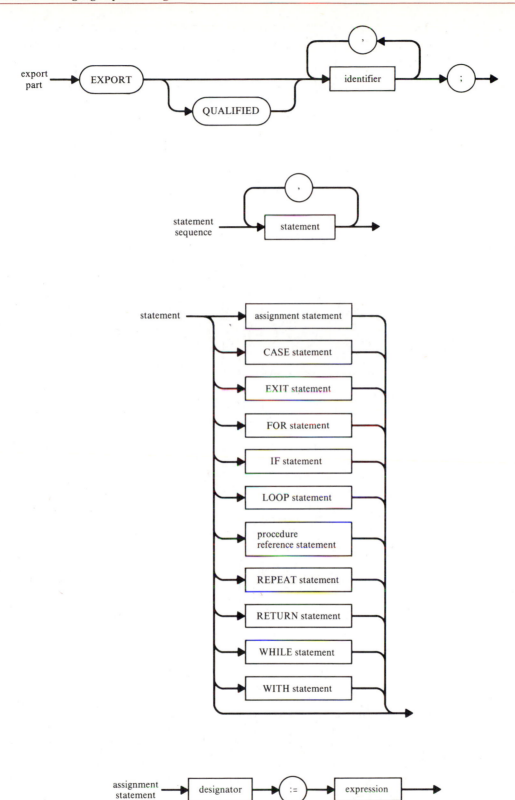

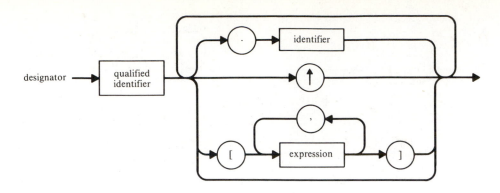

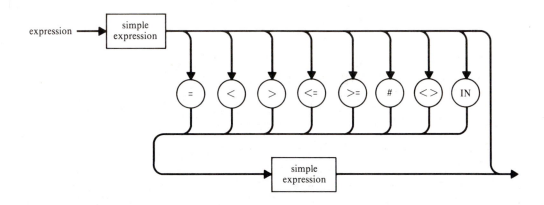

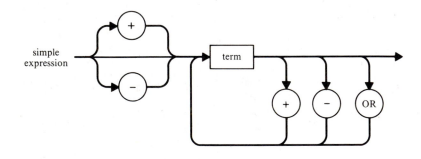

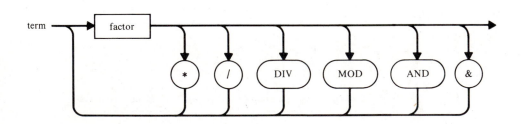

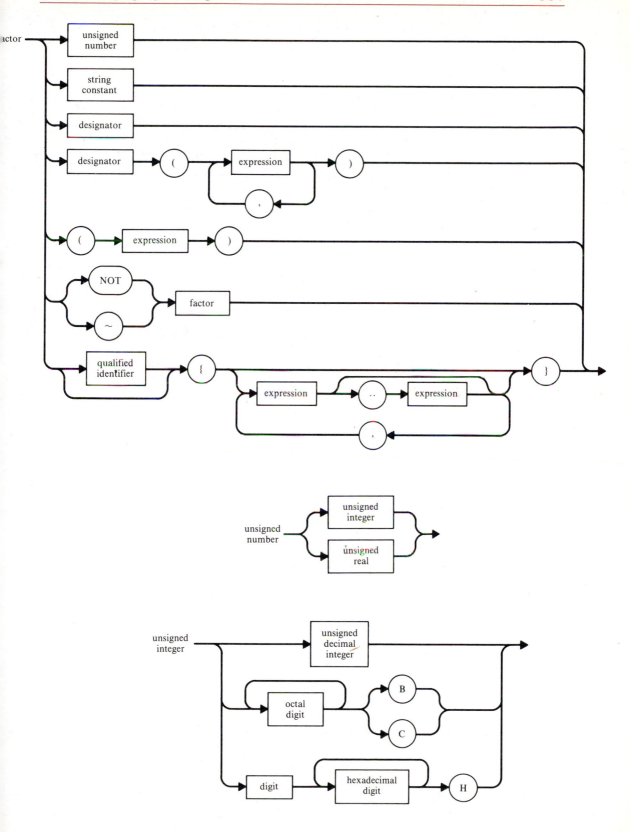

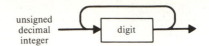

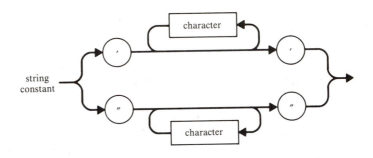

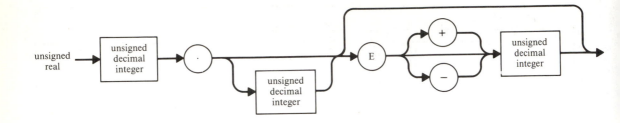

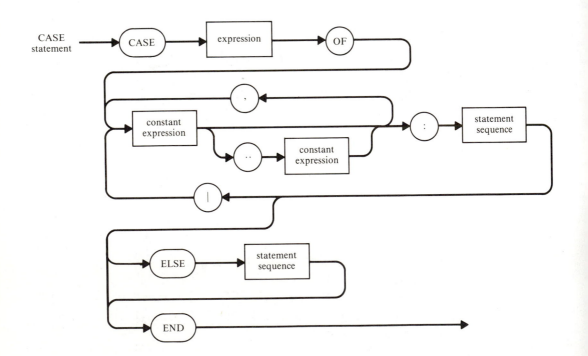

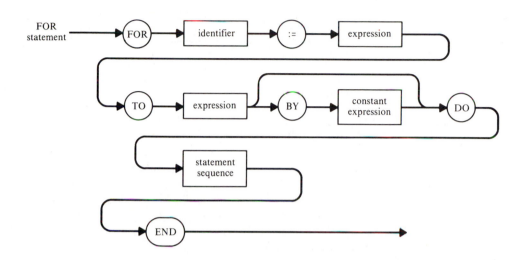

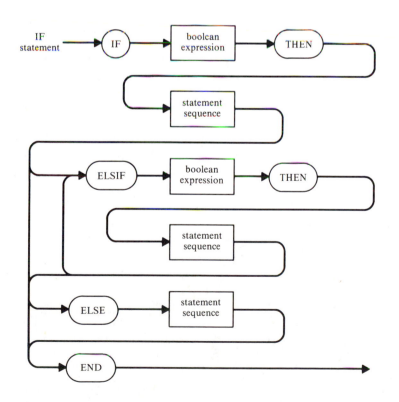

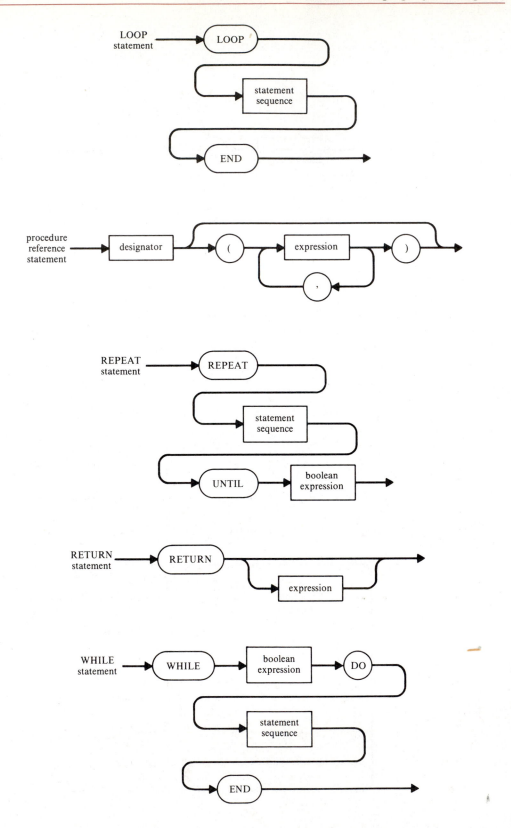

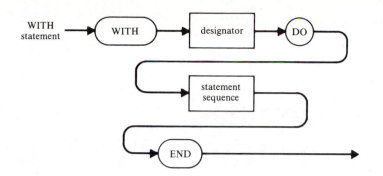

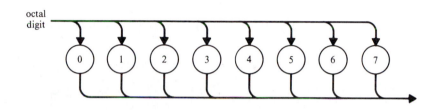

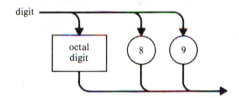

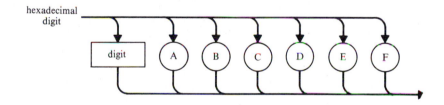

D

Modula-2 Predefined Procedures

Predefined Function Procedures

Procedure	Description	Type of Parameter	Type of Value
ABS(x)	absolute value of x	any numeric type	same as parameter
CAP(ch)	the uppercase letter corresponding to ch, if ch is a lowercase letter; ch, if ch is uppercase.	CHAR	CHAR
CHR(x)	character whose ordinal number is x	CARDINAL	CHAR
FLOAT(x)	real number equivalent to x	CARDINAL	REAL
HIGH(a)	maximum index (in first dimension) of a	any open array type	CARDINAL
MAX(T)	maximum value of type T	any type identifier	T
MIN(T)	minimum value of type T	any type identifier	T
ODD(x)	TRUE if x is odd, FALSE otherwise	CARDINAL or INTEGER	BOOLEAN
ORD(x)	ordinal number of x	CARDINAL, INTEGER, CHAR, or enumeration type	CARDINAL
SIZE(T)	size of variable T or size of a variable of type T	any type identifier or any variable	CARDINAL
TRUNC(r)	integer part of r	REAL	CARDINAL
VAL(T, c)	the value of type T whose ordinal number is c	T is any type identifier, c is of type CARDINAL	T

Predefined Function Procedures

Procedure	Description	Type of Parameter
DEC(x)	decrement x by 1; replace x by its predecessor	CARDINAL, INTEGER, CHAR, or enumeration type.
DEC(x, c)	decrement x by c; replace x by its cth predecessor	CARDINAL, INTEGER, CHAR, or enumeration type.
EXCL(S, x)	remove x from set S	S is a set of some type T (or BITSET); x is of type T
HALT	terminate execution	none
INC(x)	increment x by 1; replace x by its successor	CARDINAL, INTEGER, CHAR, or enumeration type.
INC(x, c)	increment x by c; replace x by its cth successor	CARDINAL, INTEGER, CHAR, or enumeration type.
INCL(S, x)	add x to set S	S is a set of some type T (or BITSET); x is of type T

Sample Data Files

Several exercises in the text use the files *InventoryFile*, *InventoryUpdate*, *LeastSquaresFile*, *StudentFile*, *StudentUpdate*, and *UsersFile*. This appendix describes the contents of these files and gives a sample listing for each.

InventoryFile
Item number: a four-digit cardinal number
Number currently in stock: a cardinal number in the range 0 through 999
Unit price: a real value
Minimum inventory level: a cardinal number in the range 0 through 999
Item name: a string with at most 25 characters

File is sorted so that item numbers are in increasing order.

Sample InventoryFile:

```
1011  20   54.95   15 TELEPHOTO POCKET CAMERA
1012  12   24.95   15 MINI POCKET CAMERA
1021  20   49.95   10 POL. ONE-STEP CAMERA
1022  13  189.95   12 SONAR 1-STEP CAMERA
1023  15   74.95    5 PRONTO CAMERA
1031   9  279.99   10 8MM ZOOM MOVIE CAMERA
1032  15  310.55   10 SOUND/ZOOM 8MM CAMERA
1041  10  389.00   12 35MM SLR XG-7 MINO. CAM.
1042  11  349.95   12 35MM SLR AE-1 PENT. CAM.
1043  20  319.90   12 35MM SLR ME CAN. CAM.
1044  13  119.95   12 35MM HI-MATIC CAMERA
1045  20   89.99   12 35MM COMPACT CAMERA
1511   7  129.95    5 ZOOM MOVIE PROJECTOR
1512   9  239.99    5 ZOOM-SOUND PROJECTOR
1521  10  219.99    5 AUTO CAROUSEL PROJECTOR
1522   4  114.95    5 CAR. SLIDE PROJECTOR
2011   4   14.95    5 POCKET STROBE
2012  12   48.55   10 STROBE SX-10
2013  10   28.99   15 ELEC.FLASH SX-10
3011  13   32.99   15 TELE CONVERTER
3012  14   97.99   15 28MM WIDE-ANGLE LENS
3013  13   87.95   15 135MM TELEPHOTO LENS
3014   8  267.95    5 35-105 MM ZOOM LENS
3015   7  257.95    5 80-200 MM ZOOM LENS
3111   4   67.50    5 HEAVY-DUTY TRIPOD
3112  10   19.95    5 LIGHTWEIGHT TRIPOD
3511  10  159.99    5 35MM ENLARGER KIT
4011   4   35.98    5 40X40 DELUXE SCREEN
4012  10   44.98    5 50X50 DELUXE SCREEN
5011  17    4.29   25 120-SLIDE TRAY
5012  33    2.95   25 100-SLIDE TRAY
5021  12    6.25   15 SLIDE VIEWER
5031  12   55.95   10 MOVIE EDITOR
6011  10   59.95    5 CONDENSER MICROPHONE
6111  80    0.89  100 AA ALKALINE BATTERY
7011  19   19.79   20 GADGET BAG
8011  45    1.49   50 135-24 COLOR FILM
8021  60    0.99   50 110-12 COLOR FILM
8022  42    1.45   50 110-24 COLOR FILM
8023  37    0.59   25 110-12 B/W FILM
8024  43    0.95   25 110-24 B/W FILM
8031  44    0.89   50 126-12 COLOR FILM
8032  27    0.59   25 126-12 B/W FILM
8041  39    6.89   50 8MM FILM CASSETTE
8042  25   11.89   20 16MM FILM CASSETTE
9111  10  959.99   12 COMBINATION CAMERA KIT
```

InventoryUpdate

Order number: three letters followed by four digits

Item number: a four-digit cardinal number (same as those in *InventoryFile*)

Transaction code: a character (S = sold, R = returned)

Number of items sold or returned: a cardinal number in the range 0 through 999

File is sorted so that item numbers are in increasing order. (Some items in *InventoryFile* may not have update records; others may have more than one.)

Sample InventoryUpdate:

CCI7543	1012	S	2		BTP5396	3013	S	1
LTB3429	1012	S	7		GFL4913	3013	S	8
DJS6762	1021	S	9		EHQ7510	3013	S	7
NQT1850	1022	S	1		QQL6472	3013	S	5
WYP6425	1023	S	4		SVC6511	3014	S	4
YOK2210	1023	R	2		XJQ9391	3014	S	4
QGM3144	1023	S	1		ONO5251	3111	S	3
NPQ8685	1031	S	5		CXC7780	3111	S	1
MAP8102	1031	S	13		VGT8169	3112	S	8
JRJ6335	1031	S	1		IMK5861	3511	S	2
UWR9386	1032	S	3		QHR1944	3511	S	1
TJY1913	1032	S	11		ZPK6211	4011	S	2
YHA9464	1041	S	5		VDZ2970	4012	S	6
SYT7493	1041	S	3		BOJ9069	5011	S	9
FHJ1657	1042	S	7		MNL7029	5011	S	9
OJQ2215	1043	S	8		MRG8703	5021	S	10
UOX7714	1043	S	2		DEM9289	5021	S	1
ERZ2147	1043	S	7		BXL1651	5031	S	2
MYW2540	1044	S	1		VAF8733	6111	S	65
UKS3587	1045	S	2		UYI0368	7011	S	2
AAN3759	1045	S	2		VIZ6879	8011	S	16
WZT4171	1045	S	12		GXX9093	8011	S	19
TYR9475	1511	S	1		HHO5605	8021	S	41
FRQ4184	1511	S	1		BOL2324	8021	S	49
TAV3604	1512	S	2		PAG9289	8023	S	15
DCW9363	1522	S	1		MDF5557	8023	S	17
EXN3964	1522	R	1		IQK3388	8024	S	12
OIN5524	1522	S	1		OTB1341	8024	S	28
EOJ8218	1522	S	1		SVF5674	8031	S	24
YFK0683	2011	S	2		ZDP9484	8031	S	15
PPX4743	2012	S	4		OSY8177	8032	S	15
DBR1709	2013	S	4		GJQ0185	8032	S	8
JOM5408	2013	S	3		VHW0189	8041	S	20
PKN0671	2013	S	1		WEU9225	8041	S	6
LBD8391	3011	S	9		YJO3755	8041	S	8
DNL6326	3012	S	9					

LeastSquaresFile

This is a text file in which each line contains a pair of real numbers representing the *x* coordinate and the *y* coordinate of a point.

Sample LeastSquaresFile:

2.18	1.06		7.5	12.32
7.46	12.04		7.49	11.74
5.75	8.68		7.62	12.07
3.62	4.18		7.39	12.17
3.59	3.87		1.88	0.58

(cont.)

6.31	10.09	9.59	15.82
2.53	2.04	1.81	0.45
5.44	8.25	0.99	−0.71
1.21	−0.76	4.82	6.91
9.07	15.5	9.68	16.24
3.95	5.0	1.21	−0.22
9.63	17.01	4.54	5.64
9.75	16.91	1.48	0.3
9.99	16.67	6.58	9.8
3.61	4.69	3.05	3.56
9.06	15.0	6.19	9.62
5.03	6.62	6.47	9.83
4.45	6.12	8.13	10.75
4.54	5.89	7.31	11.73
0.92	−1.02	0.33	−1.93
0.82	−1.5	5.12	7.41
2.62	2.1	5.23	7.73
5.66	8.53	7.14	11.02
8.05	13.05	1.27	−0.21
8.99	14.85	2.51	1.59
5.12	7.03	5.26	7.86
3.85	4.43	4.74	6.19
6.08	9.21	2.1	2.12
1.42	0	5.27	7.73
2.58	2.38	2.85	2.63
5.99	9.42	1.99	1.09
0.63	−1.63	8.91	15.03
9.98	17.25	2.19	1.21
5.63	8.58	1.6	−0.05
8.94	15.27	8.93	15.12
7.34	11.48	3.19	3.56
6.55	9.92	3.37	3.64
4.89	7.07		

StudentFile
Student number: a cardinal number
Student's last name: a string with at most 15 characters
Student's first name: a string with at most 10 characters
Student's middle initial: a character
Hometown: a string with at most 25 characters
Phone number: a string with 7 characters
Sex: a character (M or F)
Class level: a one-digit cardinal number (1, 2, 3, 4, or 5 for special)
Major: a string with at most 4 characters
Total credits earned to date: a cardinal number
Cumulative GPA: a real value

File is arranged so that student numbers are in increasing order.

Sample StudentFile:

```
10103 JOHNSON JAMES L
WAUPUN, WISCONSIN 7345229 M 1 ENGR 15 3.15
10104 ANDREWS PETER J
GRAND RAPIDS, MICHIGAN 9493301 M 2 CPSC 42 2.78
10110 PETERS ANDREW J
LYNDEN, WASHINGTON 3239550 M 5 ART 63 2.05
10113 VANDENVANDER VANESSA V
FREMONT, MICHIGAN 5509237 F 4 HIST 110 3.74
10126 ARISTOTLE ALICE A
CHINO, CALIFORNIA 3330861 F 3 PHIL 78 3.10
10144 LUCKY LUCY L
GRANDVILLE, MICHIGAN 7745424 F 5 HIST 66 2.29
10179 EULER LENNIE L
THREE RIVERS, MICHIGAN 6290017 M 1 MATH 15 3.83
10191 NAKAMURA TOKY O
CHICAGO, ILLINOIS 4249665 F 1 SOCI 12 1.95
10226 FREUD FRED E
LYNDEN, WASHINGTON 8340115 M 1 PSYC 15 1.85
10272 SPEARSHAKE WILLIAM W
GRAND RAPIDS, MICHIGAN 2410744 M 5 ENGL 102 2.95
10274 TCHAIKOVSKY WOLFGANG A
BYRON CENTER, MICHIGAN 8845115 M 3 MUSC 79 2.75
10284 ORANGE DUTCH V
GRAAFSCHAAP, MICHIGAN 3141660 M 2 ENGR 42 2.98
10297 CAESAR JULIE S
DENVER, COLORADO 4470338 F 4 HIST 117 3.25
10298 PSYCHO PRUNELLA E
DE MOTTE, INDIANA 5384609 F 4 PSYC 120 2.99
10301 BULL SITTING U
GALLUP, NEW MEXICO 6632997 M 1 EDUC 14 2.95
10302 CUSTER, GENERAL G
BADLANDS, SOUTH DAKOTA 5552995 M 3 HIST 40 1.95
10303 FAHRENHEIT FELICIA O
SHEBOYGAN, WISCONSIN 5154997 F 2 CHEM 40 3.85
10304 DEUTSCH SPRECHEN Z
SPARTA, MICHIGAN 8861201 F 5 GERM 14 3.05
10307 MENDELSSOHN MOZART W
PEORIA, ILLINOIS 2410747 M 3 MUSC 76 2.87
10310 AUGUSTA ADA B
LAKEWOOD, CALIFORNIA 7172339 F 2 CPSC 46 3.83
10319 GAUSS CARL F
YORKTOWN, PENNSYLVANIA 3385494 M 2 MATH 41 4.00
10323 KRONECKER LEO P
TRAVERSE CITY, MICHIGAN 6763991 M 3 MATH 77 2.75
10330 ISSACSON JACOB A
SILVER SPRINGS, MD 4847932 M 5 RELI 25 2.99
10331 ISSACSON ESAU B
SILVER SPRINGS, MD 4847932 M 5 RELI 25 2.98
10339 DEWEY JOHANNA A
SALT LAKE CITY, UTAH 6841129 F 2 EDUC 41 3.83
10348 VIRUS VERA W
SAGINAW, MICHIGAN 6634401 F 4 CPSC 115 3.25
10355 ZYLSTRA ZELDA A
DOWNS, KANSAS 7514008 F 1 ENGL 16 1.95
10377 PORGY BESS N
COLUMBUS, OHIO 4841771 F 2 MUSI 44 2.78
```

(cont.)

```
10389 NEWMANN ALFRED E
CHEYENNE, WYOMING 7712399 M 4 EDUC 115 0.99
10395 MEDES ARCHIE L
WHITINSVILLE, MA 9294401 M 3 ENGR 80 3.10
10406 MACDONALD RONALD B
SEATTLE, WASHINGTON 5582911 F 1 CPSC 15 2.99
10415 AARDVARK ANTHONY A
GRANDVILLE, MICHIGAN 5325912 M 2 ENGR 43 2.79
10422 GESTALT GLORIA G
WHEATON, ILLINOIS 6631212 F 2 PSYC 42 2.48
10431 GOTODIJKSTRA EDGAR G
CAWKER CITY, KANSAS 6349971 M 1 CPSC 15 4.00
10448 REMBRANDT ROBERTA E
SIOUX CENTER, IOWA 2408113 F 1 ART 77 2.20
10458 SHOEMAKER IMELDA M
HONOLULU, HAWAII 9193001 F 1 POLS 15 3.15
10467 MARX KARL Z
HAWTHORNE, NEW JERSEY 5513915 M 3 ECON 78 2.75
10470 SCROOGE EBENEZER T
TROY, MICHIGAN 8134001 M 4 SOCI 118 3.25
10482 NIGHTINGALE FLORENCE K
ROCHESTER, NEW YORK 7175118 F 1 NURS 15 3.15
10490 GAZELLE GWENDOLYN D
CHINO, CALIFORNIA 3132446 F 2 PE 43 2.78
10501 PASTEUR LOUISE A
WINDOW ROCK, ARIZONA 4245170 F 1 BIOL 16 3.10
10519 ELBA ABLE M
BOZEMAN, MONTANA 8183226 M 3 SPEE 77 3.40
10511 LEWIS CLARK N
NEW ERA, MICHIGAN 6461125 M 4 GEOG 114 3.37
10515 MOUSE MICHAEL E
BOISE, IDAHO 5132771 F 5 EDUC 87 1.99
10523 PAVLOV TIFFANY T
FARMINGTON, MICHIGAN 9421753 F 1 BIOL 13 1.77
10530 CHICITA JUANITA A
OKLAHOMA CITY, OK 3714377 F 5 ENGL 95 2.66
10538 BUSCH ARCH E
ST LOUIS, MISSOURI 8354112 M 3 ENGR 74 2.75
10547 FAULT PAIGE D
PETOSKEY, MICHIGAN 4543116 F 5 CPSC 55 2.95
10553 SANTAMARIA NINA P
PLYMOUTH, MASSACHUSETTS 2351181 F 1 HIST 15 1.77
10560 SHYSTER SAMUEL D
EVERGLADES, FLORIDA 4421885 M 1 SOCI 13 1.95
10582 YEWLISS CAL C
RUDYARD, MICHIGAN 3451220 M 3 MATH 76 2.99
10590 ATANASOFF ENIAC C
SPRINGFIELD, ILLINOIS 6142449 F 1 CPSC 14 1.88
10597 ROCKNE ROCKY K
NEWY YORK, NEW YORK  4631744 M 4 PE 116 1.98
10610 ROOSEVELT ROSE Y
SPRING LAKE, MICHIGAN 9491221 F 5 POLS 135 2.95
10623 XERXES ART I
CINCINATTI, OHIO 3701228 M 4 GREE 119 3.25
10629 LEIBNIZ GOTTFRIED W
BOULDER, COLORADO 5140228 M 1 MATH 13 1.95
10633 VESPUCCI VERA D
RIPON, CALIFORNIA 4341883 F 5 GEOG 89 2.29
```

(cont.)

```
10648 PRINCIPAL PAMELA P
ALBANY, NEW YORK 7145513 F 1 EDUC 14 1.75
10652 CICERO MARSHA
RAPID CITY, SD 3335910 F 3 LATI 77 2.87
10657 WEERD DEWEY L
DETROIT, MICHIGAN 4841962 M 4 PHIL 115 2.99
10663 HOCHSCHULE HORTENSE C
LINCOLN, NEBRASKA 7120111 F 5 EDUC 100 2.70
10668 EINSTEIN ALFRED M
NEWARK, NEW JERSEY 3710225 M 2 ENGR 41 2.78
10675 FIBONACCI LEONARD O
NASHVILLE, TENNESSEE 4921107 M 4 MATH 115 3.25
10682 ANGELO MIKE L
AUSTIN, TEXAS 5132201 M 4 ART 117 3.74
10688 PASCAL BLAZE R
BROOKLYN, NEW YORK 7412993 M 1 CPSC 15 1.98
```

StudentUpdate

Student number: a cardinal number (same as those used in *StudentFile*)
For each of five courses:

Course name: a string with at most 7 characters (e.g., CPSC131)
Letter grade: a string with at most 2 characters (e.g., A−, B+, C∅)
Course credit: a cardinal number

The file is sorted so that student numbers are in increasing order. There is one update record for each student in *StudentFile*.

Sample StudentUpdate:

```
10103 ENGL176 C   4 EDUC268 B   4 EDUC330 B+ 3 PE281    C  3 ENGR317 D   4
10104 CPSC271 D+  4 ESCI208 D-  3 PHIL340 B+ 2 CPSC146 D+ 4 ENGL432 D+  4
10110 ART 520 D   3 ESCI259 F   1 ENGL151 D+ 4 MUSC257 B  4 PSYC486 C   4
10113 HIST498 F   3 PE  317 C+  4 MUSC139 B- 3 PHIL165 D  3 GEOG222 C   3
10126 PHIL367 C-  4 EDUC420 C-  3 EDUC473 C  3 EDUC224 D- 3 GERM257 F   4
10144 HIST559 C+  3 MATH357 D   3 CPSC323 C- 2 PE246    D- 4 MUSC379 D+  4
10179 MATH169 C-  4 CHEM163 C+  4 MUSC436 A- 3 MATH366 D- 2 BIOL213 A-  4
10191 SOCI177 F   4 POLS106 A   4 EDUC495 A- 3 ENGR418 B+ 2 ENGR355 A   4
10226 PSYC116 B   3 GERM323 B-  4 ART350   A  4 HIST269 B+ 4 EDUC214 C+  3
10272 ENGL558 A-  4 EDUC169 D+  3 PSYC483 B+ 4 ENGR335 B+ 2 BIOL228 B   4
10274 MUSC351 B   4 PSYC209 C-  4 ENGR400 F  1 ESCI392 A  4 SOCI394 B-  3
10284 ENGR292 D   4 PSYC172 C   4 EDUC140 B  4 MATH274 F  4 MUSC101 D+  4
10297 HIST464 F   1 HIST205 F   1 ENGR444 F  1 MATH269 F  1 EDUC163 F   1
10298 PSYC452 B   3 MATH170 C+  4 EDUC344 C- 2 GREE138 C- 2 SPEE303 A-  3
10301 EDUC197 A   4 PE372    B   3 ENGR218 D  4 MATH309 C  4 ESCI405 C-  4
10302 CHEM283 F   1 PE440    A   2 MATH399 A- 3 HIST455 C- 4 MATH387 C-  3
10303 HIST111 D-  3 ART151   C+  3 ENGL100 C- 3 PSYC151 D+ 3 PE104    A-  1
10304 GERM526 C-  2 CHEM243 C   4 POLS331 B- 4 EDUC398 A  3 ENGR479 D+  4
10307 MUSC323 B+  3 MATH485 C   4 HIST232 B+ 4 EDUC180 A  3 ENGL130 B+  4
10310 CPSC264 B   2 POLS227 D+  3 ENGR467 D- 3 MATH494 D- 4 ART420   C+  4
10319 MATH276 B   2 ESCI434 A   3 HIST197 B- 4 GERM489 B- 2 ART137   C-  3
10323 MATH377 D-  4 EDUC210 D   4 MATH385 D- 4 ENGR433 C  2 HIST338 A-  4
10330 HIST546 C+  3 ESCI440 B+  3 GREE472 C+ 3 BIOL186 B  4 GEOG434 C+  2
```

(cont.)

```
10331 HIST546 C   3 ESCI440 B+ 3 GREE472 C   3 BIOL186 B+ 4 GEOG434 C+ 2
10339 EDUC283 B   3 CPSC150 B   3 ENGR120 D   4 CPSC122 F   4 ART216  B   4
10348 CPSC411 C-  3 HIST480 C+ 4 PSYC459 B   4 BIOL299 B+ 4 ECON276 B+ 3
10355 ENGL130 C-  3 CPSC282 C+ 4 CPSC181 A-  4 CPSC146 C-  4 SOCI113 F   1
10377 SOCI213 D+  3 PSYC158 D   4 MUSC188 C   3 PSYC281 D-  4 ENGR339 B+ 4
10389 EDUC414 D+  4 PSYC115 C-  2 PSYC152 D-  4 ART366  D-  3 ENGR366 F   4
10395 ENGR396 B   4 HIST102F    3 ENGL111 A   4 PSYC210 D-  2 GREE128 A   4
10406 CPSC160 C+  4 CPSC233 C   1 LATI494 C+  3 ENGL115 C-  3 MATH181 A   3
10415 ENGR287 C   4 EDUC166 B-  4 EDUC106 A-  3 PE190   F   3 MATH171 B-  3
10422 PSYC275 A-  4 MATH497 A   4 EDUC340 F   1 GERM403 C-  4 MATH245 D+ 4
10431 CPSC187 D-  4 CPSC426 F   4 ENGR476 B-  4 BIOL148 B+ 3 CPSC220 F   3
10448 ART171  D+  3 CPSC239 C-  3 SOCI499 B-  4 HIST113 D+ 3 PSYC116 C   4
10458 POLS171 F   1 CPSC187 C+ 4 CHEM150 B   2 PHIL438 D-  4 PHIL254 D   4
10467 ECON335 D-  3 ESCI471 B+ 4 MATH457 C+ 3 MATH207 C   2 BIOL429 D   4
10470 MUSC415 C+  3 POLS177 C   3 CPSC480 A   4 PSYC437 B   3 SOCI276 D   4
10482 ENGL158 D-  4 EDUC475 B   3 HIST172 B-  2 PE316   F   4 ENGR294 A-  3
10490 PE239   F   4 ENGL348 F   3 LATI246 F   4 CPSC350 F   4 MATH114 F   1
10501 BIOL125 F   4 CPSC412 F   3 ESCI279 F   4 ENGR153 F   2 ART293  F   1
10519 SPEE386 B+  4 HIST479 C   4 PSYC249 B-  2 GREE204 B-  4 PE421   A   1
10511 ESCI416 B   3 MATH316 D-  4 MATH287 C   2 MATH499 A-  4 ESCI288 D   3
10515 EDUC563 D+  3 PHIL373 D-  3 ART318  B   4 HIST451 F   1 ART476  C+ 3
10523 BIOL183 D-  2 HIST296 D+ 4 HIST380 B+ 4 ENGR216 C   4 MATH412 B-  2
10530 ENGL559 F   1 EDUC457 D+ 4 CPSC306 A   3 ENGR171 B+ 1 CPSC380 A   4
10538 ENGR328 A-  4 ENGR336 C   3 EDUC418 D+ 3 PHIL437 B+ 4 CPSC475 D   4
10547 CPSC537 A-  4 ART386  D   4 HIST292 D-  4 ENGR467 A-  4 PE464   B+ 4
10553 HIST170 A-  4 SOCI496 D-  3 PHIL136 B+ 4 CPSC371 D-  4 CPSC160 A-  1
10560 SOCI153 D+  3 MATH438 D+ 4 CPSC378 C   4 BIOL266 F   3 EDUC278 D+ 3
10582 MATH388 A-  3 PE311   B   3 ECON143 D   4 MATH304 C+ 3 PE428   C+ 4
10590 CPSC134 B-  3 ESCI114 B+ 3 CPSC492 C   4 ENGL121 C   4 ENGR403 A-  4
10597 PE423   A-  3 BIOL189 D+ 3 PHIL122 D-  4 ENGL194 C-  4 SOCI113 D+ 3
10610 ESCI594 C-  3 PHIL344 F   4 CPSC189 B+ 2 ENGR411 D-  3 MATH241 A   4
10623 GREE412 B-  4 ENGL415 D   4 ENGL234 D-  4 MATH275 F   1 SOCI124 B+ 3
10629 MATH137 D   2 MATH481 F   3 ESCI445 F   1 MATH339 D   4 ART219  B+ 4
10633 GEOG573 B   4 ENGL149 C+ 4 EDUC113 B+ 4 ENGR458 C-  2 HIST446 D+ 4
10648 EDUC132 D+  4 MUSC103 D-  4 ENGL263 C   4 ENGL134 B+ 4 ESCI392 A   3
10652 LATI363 F   3 BIOL425 F   1 CPSC267 C   4 EDUC127 C+ 3 MATH338 B   4
10657 PHIL429 F   1 ART412  D-  4 MUSC473 B-  4 SOCI447 C-  4 MATH237 D+ 2
10663 EDUC580 B-  4 ENGR351 B+ 4 SOCI283 D   4 ART340  C   4 PSYC133 D+ 3
10668 ENGR274 B+  4 SOCI438 C   1 PE327   C   4 BIOL158 A   4 EDUC457 A-  4
10675 MATH457 A   4 ENGR114 C   4 CPSC218 C   3 ESCI433 C-  3 PSYC243 C+ 1
10682 ART483  D+  3 GERM432 C   3 ENGL103 B+ 4 MUSC169 C-  3 SOCI381 C-  2
10688 CPSC182 F   1 HIST371 C+ 4 PSYC408 F   1 MUSC214 B+ 4 MATH151 C   3
```

UsersFile
Identification number: a cardinal number
User's name: a string with at most 30 characters in the form Last Name,
   First Name
Password: a string with at most 5 characters
Resource limit (in dollars): a cardinal number with up to four digits
Resources used to date: a real value

This file is arranged so that identification numbers are in increasing order.

Sample UsersFile:

```
10101 MILTGEN,JOSEPH    MOE          10129 ABNER,LIL    DAISY
  750 380.81                           950 89.57
10102 SMALL,ISAAC    LARGE           10130 TRACY,DICK    CRIME
  650 598.84                           550 392.00
10103 SNYDER,SAMUEL    R2-D2         10131 MCGEE,FIBBER    MOLLY
  250 193.74                           750 332.12
10104 EDMUNDSEN,EDMUND    ABCDE      10132 BELL,ALEXANDER    PHONE
  250 177.93                           850 337.43
10105 BRAUNSCHWEIGER,CHRISTOPHER    BROWN   20101 COBB,TYRUS    TIGER
  850 191.91                            50 32.81
10106 PIZZULA,NORMA    PIZZA         20102 GEORGE,RUTH    BABE
  350 223.95                           350 269.93
10107 VANDERVAN,HENRY    VAN         20103 DESCARTES,RONALD    HORSE
  750 168.59                           250 109.34
10108 FREELOADER,FREDDIE    RED      20104 EUCLID,IAN    GREEK
  450 76.61                            350 63.63
10109 ALEXANDER,ALVIN    GREAT       20105 DANIELS,EZEKIEL    LIONS
  650 405.04                           350 128.69
10110 MOUSE,MICHAEL    EARS          20106 TARZAN,JANE    APES
   50 42.57                            150 100.31
10111 LUKASEWICZ,ZZYZK    RPN        20107 HABBAKUK,JONAH    WHALE
  350 73.50                            950 183.93
10112 CHRISTMAS,MARY    NOEL         20108 COLUMBUS,CHRIS    PINTA
  850 33.28                            850 202.24
10113 SINKEY,CJ    TRAIN            20109 BYRD,RICHARD    NORTH
  750 327.53                           550 168.49
10114 NIJHOFF,LARAN    KKID          20110 BUNYAN,PAUL    BABE
  550 382.03                           550 333.47
10115 LIESTMA,STAN    SAAB           20111 CHAUCER,JEFF    POEM
  650 38.36                            950 37.02
10116 ZWIER,APOLLOS    PJ            20112 STOTLE,ARI    LOGIC
  350 249.48                           750 337.74
10117 JAEGER,TIM    BIKE            20113 HARRISON,BEN    PRES
  250 246.73                           550 262.97
10118 VANZWALBERG,JORGE    EGYPT     20114 JAMES,JESSE    GUNS
  850 466.95                           250 58.81
10119 JESTER,COURTNEY    JOKER       20115 SCOTT,FRANCINE    FLAG
  450 281.16                           350 168.11
10120 MCDONALD,RONALD    FRIES       20116 PHILLIPS,PHYLLIS    GAS66
  250 35.00                            650 322.22
10121 NEDERLANDER,BENAUT    DUTCH    20117 DOLL,BARBARA    KEN
  550 28.82                            350 26.34
10122 HAYBAILER,HOMER    FARM        20118 FINN,HUCK    TOM
  850 37.32                            350 22.86
10123 SPEAR,WILLIAM    SHAKE         20119 SAWYER,TOM    HUCK
  450 337.01                           950 460.30
10124 ROMEO,JULIET    XOXOX          20120 NEWMANN,ALFRED    MAD
  150 100.19                           450 116.00
10125 GREEK,JIMMY    WAGER           20121 SIMPLE,SIMON    SAYS
  250 0.03                             550 486.05
10126 VIRUS,VERA    WORM             20122 SCHMIDT,MESSER    PLANE
  750 67.35                            250 35.31
10127 BEECH,ROCKY    BOAT            20124 LUTHER,CALVIN    REF
  950 256.18                           777 666.66
10128 ENGEL,ANGEL    WINGS           20125 YALE,HARVARD    IVY
  150 16.39                            150 127.70
```

Library Modules

This appendix describes the contents of the library modules *InOut, RealInOut, MathLib0, FileSystem,* and *SpecialInOut*. The items in the first modules are those described by Niklaus Wirth in *Programming in Modula-2*, Third Corrected Edition. The library module *SpecialInOut* is used in the text, beginning in Section 7.1. The definition part and a possible implementation part are given for it.

InOut

DEFINITION MODULE *InOut*;

  CONST
    EOL = 36C; (∗ assuming ASCII ∗)

  VAR
    Done : BOOLEAN;
    termCH : CHAR;

  PROCEDURE *Read*(VAR *Ch* : CHAR);

    (∗ This procedure reads and assigns the next character to *Ch*. *Done* is set to
    true unless an end-of-file condition occurs. ∗)

  PROCEDURE *ReadString* (VAR *s* : ARRAY OF CHAR);

    (∗ This procedure reads a string not containing blanks or control characters
    and assigns it to string variable *s*. Leading blanks are ignored and input is
    terminated by a blank or by some control character (any character preceding
    a blank in the collating sequence); backspacing can be used to erase
    characters during input. The termination character is assigned to the variable
    termCh. ∗)

  PROCEDURE *ReadCard*(VAR x : INTEGER);

    (∗ This procedure reads a string of characters terminated by a blank or some
    control character, converts it to a cardinal number, and assigns it to *x*.

Leading blanks are ignored and backspacing can be used to erase characters during input. *Done* is set to TRUE if a cardinal number is read successfully, FALSE otherwise. *)

PROCEDURE *ReadInt*(VAR *x* : INTEGER);

(* This procedure reads a string of characters terminated by a blank or some control character, converts it to an integer, and assigns it to *x*. Leading blanks are ignored and backspacing can be used to erase characters during input. *Done* is set to TRUE if an integer is read successfully, FALSE otherwise. *)

PROCEDURE *Write*(*Ch* : CHAR);

(* This procedure writes the character *Ch*. *)

PROCEDURE *WriteLn*;

(* This procedure terminates the current output line. *)

PROCEDURE *WriteString*(*s* : ARRAY OF CHAR);

(* This procedure writes the string *s*. *)

PROCEDURE *WriteInt* (*x* : INTEGER, *n* : CARDINAL);

(* This procedure writes integer *x* in a field of width *n*. If *n* is smaller than the number of digits (and sign), the field is enlarged; if *n* is larger than necessary, blanks are added preceding the number. *)

PROCEDURE *WriteCard*(*x, n* : CARDINAL);

PROCEDURE *WriteOct*(*x, n* : CARDINAL);

PROCEDURE *WriteHex*(*x, n* : CARDINAL);

(* These procedures write cardinal number *x* in a field of width *n* in a decimal, octal, or hexadecimal format, respectively. If *n* is smaller than the number of digits, the field is enlarged; if *n* is larger than necessary, blanks are added preceding the number. *)

PROCEDURE *OpenInput*(*extension* : ARRAY OF CHAR);

(* This procedure requests a file name from the user; if this name ends with a period, *extension* is appended to it. *Done* is set to TRUE if the file is opened successfully, FALSE otherwise. If opened successfully, all subsequent input is read from this file. *)

PROCEDURE *OpenOutput*(*extension* : ARRAY OF CHAR);

(* This procedure requests a file name from the user; if this name ends with a period, *extension* is appended to it. *Done* is set to TRUE if the file is opened successfully, FALSE otherwise. If opened successfully, all subsequent output is written to this file. *)

PROCEDURE *CloseInput*;

(* This procedure closes the input file and returns input to the standard input device, normally the keyboard. *)

PROCEDURE *CloseOutput*;

(* This procedure closes the output file and returns output to the standard output device, normally the screen. *)

END *InOut*.

RealInOut

DEFINITION MODULE *RealInOut*;

VAR
  Done : BOOLEAN;

PROCEDURE *ReadReal*(VAR *x* : REAL);

(∗ This procedure reads a string of characters terminated by a blank or some control character, converts it to a real number, and assigns it to *x*. Leading blanks are ignored and backspacing can be used to erase characters during input. This value may be entered in either decimal or scientific form. *Done* is set to TRUE if a real number is read successfully, FALSE otherwise. ∗)

PROCEDURE *WriteReal* (*x* : REAL, *n* : CARDINAL);

(∗ This procedure writes real number *x* in a field of width *n*. If *n* is smaller than the number of characters needed to display the value, the field is enlarged; if *n* is larger than necessary, blanks are added preceding the number. ∗)

PROCEDURE *WriteRealOct*(*x* : REAL; *n* : CARDINAL);

(∗ Like procedure *WriteReal*, this procedure writes the real number *x* in a field of width *n*, but it displays it in an octal format. ∗)

END *RealInOut*.

MathLib0

DEFINITION MODULE *MathLib0*;

PROCEDURE *sqrt*(*x* : REAL) : REAL;

(∗ Returns the square root of *x* ∗)

PROCEDURE *exp*(*x* : REAL) : REAL;

(∗ Returns e^x ∗)

PROCEDURE *ln*(*x* : REAL) : REAL;

(∗ Returns the natural logarithm of *x* ∗)

PROCEDURE *sin*(*x* : REAL) : REAL;

(∗ Returns the sine of *x* ∗)

PROCEDURE *cos*(*x* : REAL) : REAL;

(∗ Returns the cosine of *x* ∗)

PROCEDURE *arctan*(*x* : REAL) : REAL;

(∗ Returns the inverse tangent of *x* ∗)

PROCEDURE *real*(*x* : INTEGER) : REAL;

(∗ Returns the real number corresponding to integer *x* ∗)

PROCEDURE *entier*(*x* : REAL) : INTEGER;

(∗ Returns the truncated value of *x* ∗)

END *MathLib0*.

FileSystem

DEFINITION MODULE FileSystem;

FROM SYSTEM IMPORT ADDRESS, WORD;

TYPE *Response* = (*done, notdone, notsupported, callerror, unknownmedium, unknownfile, paramerror, toomanyfiles, eom, deviceoff, softparityerror, softprotected, softerror, hardparityerror, hardprotected, timeout, harderror*);

Command = (*create, open, close, lookup, rename, setread, setwrite, setmodify, setopen, doio, setpos, getpos, length, setprotect, getprotect, setpermanent, getpermanent, getinternal*);

Flag = (*er, ef, rd, wr, ag, bytemode*);

FlagSet = SET OF *Flag*;

File = RECORD
        res : *Response*;
        bufa, ela, ina, topa : ADDRESS;
        eoldd, inodd, eof : BOOLEAN;
        flags : FLAGSET;
        CASE *com* : *Command* OF
          create, open, getinternal :
                fileno, versionno : CARDINAL |
          lookup:
                new : BOOLEAN |
          setpos, getpos, length :
                highpos, lowpos : CARDINAL |
          setprotect, getprotect:
                wrprotect : BOOLEAN |
          setpermanent, getpermanent :
                on : BOOLEAN
        END (* CASE *)
      END (* RECORD *);

PROCEDURE *Lookup*(VAR *FileVar* : *File*;
                     FileName : ARRAY OF CHAR;
                     New : BOOLEAN);

(* Searches for a file with the specified name *FileName*. If it is found, the file is associated with the specified file variable *FileVar*. If it is not found and the value of *New* is TRUE, a new (empty) file having this name will be created. *)

PROCEDURE *Create*(VAR *FileVar* : *File*;
                    MediumName : ARRAY OF CHAR);

(* Creates a temporary (nameless) file on the device specified by *MediumName* and associates it with the specified file variable *FileVar*. *)

PROCEDURE *Close*(VAR *FileVar* : *File*);

(* Terminates the association between the specified file variable *FileVar* and the permanent or temporary file associated with it. If the file is temporary, it is deleted from the system. *)

PROCEDURE *Rename*(VAR *FileVar* : *File*;
                     FileName : ARRAY OF CHAR);

(* Changes the name of the file associated with the specified file variable *FileVar* to the name given by *FileName*. If the value of *FileName* is the empty string, the file is deleted from the system. *)

PROCEDURE *SetRead*(VAR *FileVar* : *File*);

(* Places the file associated with the specified file variable *FileVar* in read mode. *)

PROCEDURE *SetWrite*(VAR *FileVar* : *File*);

(* Places the file associated with the specified file variable *FileVar* in write mode. *)

PROCEDURE *SetModify*(VAR *FileVar* : *File*);

(* Places the file associated with the specified file variable *FileVar* in modify mode. *)

PROCEDURE *SetOpen*(VAR *FileVar* : *File*);

(* Terminates any i/o operations on the file associated with the specified file variable *FileVar* and places the file in open mode. *)

PROCEDURE *Reset*(VAR *FileVar* : *File*);

(* Returns the file associated with the specified file variable *FileVar* to its initial mode. It repositions it to its beginning and places it in open mode. *)

PROCEDURE *ReadChar*(VAR *FileVar* : *File*;
                    VAR *Ch* : CHAR);

(* Reads the next character from the text file associated with the specified file variable *FileVar* and assigns it to *Ch*. *)

PROCEDURE *WriteChar*(VAR *FileVar* : *File*;
                     Ch : CHAR);

(* Appends the value of *Ch* to the text file associated with the specified file variable *FileVar*. *)

PROCEDURE *ReadWord*(VAR *FileVar* : *File*;
                    VAR *W* : WORD);

(* Reads the next word from the binary file associated with the specified file variable *FileVar* and assigns it to *W*. *)

PROCEDURE *WriteWord*(VAR *FileVar* : *File*;
                     W : WORD);

(* Appends the value of *W* to the binary file associated with the specified file variable *FileVar*. *)

PROCEDURE *SetPos*(VAR *File Var* : *File*;
                  HighPos, LowPos : CARDINAL);

(* Sets the current position of the file associated with the specified file variable *FileVar* to byte $2^{16} * HighPos + LowPos$. *)

PROCEDURE *GetPos*(VAR *FileVar* : *File*;
                  VAR *HighPos, LowPos* : CARDINAL);

(* Determines the current position of the file associated with the specified file variable *FileVar*; the actual position is given by byte $2^{16} * HighPos + LowPos$. *)

PROCEDURE *Length*(VAR *FileVar* : *File*;
                  VAR *HighPos, LowPos* : CARDINAL);

(* Returns the length (in bytes) of the file associated with the specified file variable *FileVar*; the actual length is given by $2^{16} * HighPos + LowPos$. *)

PROCEDURE *Doio*(VAR *FileVar* : *File*);

    (∗ If the file associated with the specified file variable *FileVar* is in read mode,
the buffer associated with it is loaded from the file, starting at the current
position. If *FileVar* is in write mode, the contents of the buffer are written to
the file at the current position and the file is advanced to the new position. If
it is in modify mode, the contents of the buffer are written to the file at
the current position and the buffer is then loaded, beginning at the new
position. ∗)

END *FileSystem*.

SpecialInOut

DEFINITION MODULE *SpecialInOut*;

    (∗ Library module containing special input/output procedures to supplement those
in *InOut* and *RealInOut*. ∗)

FROM *FileSystem* IMPORT *File*;
FROM SYSTEM IMPORT WORD;

VAR
    ReadOkay : BOOLEAN;

PROCEDURE *FWriteReal* (*RealNumber* : REAL;
                         FieldWidth, DecimalPlaces : CARDINAL);

    (∗ Procedure to display a real value in decimal format; *FieldWidth* is the
number of spaces to be used in displaying this value; it is rounded to the
specified number of *DecimalPlaces*. ∗)

PROCEDURE *ReadBoole*(VAR *BooleVar* : BOOLEAN);

    (∗ Procedure to read the character string 'TRUE' or 'FALSE' and return the
corresponding boolean value TRUE or FALSE for the boolean variable
BooleVar. *ReadOkay* is set to TRUE if the read operation was successful,
FALSE otherwise. ∗)

PROCEDURE *WriteBoole*(*BooleVar* : BOOLEAN);

    (∗ Procedure to write the character string 'TRUE' or 'FALSE' corresponding to
the boolean value TRUE or FALSE of the boolean variable *BooleVar*. ∗)

PROCEDURE *ReadAString* (VAR *Str* : ARRAY OF CHAR);

    (∗ Procedure to read characters into string variable *Str* until an end of line is
encountered or the array is filled. If the array is not filled with input
characters, the null character 0C is stored in the array after the last character
read and serves as an end-of-string character. *ReadOkay* is set to TRUE if a
string was read successfully, FALSE otherwise. ∗)

PROCEDURE *ReadBLock*(*InFile* : *File*; VAR *Block* : ARRAY OF WORD);

    (∗ Procedure to read a *Block* of words from *InFile* ∗)

PROCEDURE *WriteBlock*(*OutFile* : *File*; *Block* : ARRAY OF WORD);

    (∗ Procedure to write a *Block* of words at the end of *OutFile* ∗)

END *SpecialInOut*.

IMPLEMENTATION MODULE *SpecialInOut*;

    (∗ Library module containing special input/output procedures to supplement those
in *InOut* and *RealInOut*. ∗)

```
FROM RealInOut IMPORT WriteReal;
FROM InOut IMPORT Read, ReadString, Write, WriteString,
                    WriteLn, WriteCard, EOL;
FROM SYSTEM IMPORT WORD;
FROM FileSystem IMPORT File, ReadWord, WriteWord;

CONST EOS = 0C;

PROCEDURE FWRiteReal(RealNumber : REAL;
                     FieldWidth, DecimalPlaces : CARDINAL);

    (* Procedure to display a real value in decimal format; FieldWidth is the
       number of spaces to be used in displaying this value; it is rounded to the
       specified number of DecimalPlaces. *)

    CONST                           (* maximum number of significant digits
        Precision = 10;                - system-dependent *)

    VAR
        RNum,                       (* the real number to be displayed *)
        RoundingIncrement : REAL;   (* added to the number to round it *)
        I,                          (* index *)
        Sign,                       (* 1 if number is negative, else 0 *)
        LeftDigits,                 (* number digits to the left of the decimal
                                       point *)
        Digit,                      (* one of the digits *)
        NumPositions : CARDINAL;    (* number of positions required *)

    BEGIN
        (* Display minus sign if number is negative *)
        RNum := RealNumber;
        IF RNum < 0.0 THEN
            RNum := - RNum;
            Sign := 1
        ELSE
            Sign := 0
        END (* IF *);

        (* Round the value to DecimalPlaces *)

        RoundingIncrement := 0.5;
        FOR i := 1 TO DecimalPlaces DO
            RoundingIncrement := RoundIncrement / 10.0
        END (* FOR *);
        RNum := RNum + RoundingIncrement;

        (* Normalize the number *)
        LeftDigits := 1;
        WHILE RNum >= 10.0 DO
            INC(LeftDigits);
            RNum := RNum / 10.0
        END (* WHILE *);

        (* If too many digits specified, display a message and display the value using
            WriteReal from RealInOut *)
        NumPositions := LeftDigits + DecimalPlaces;
        IF (NumPositions > Precision THEN
            WriteString('*** Too many places specified for ');
            WriteReal(RealNumber, Precision);
            RETURN
        END (* IF *);
```

```
                    (* Print leading blanks so value is right-justified *)
                    NumPositions := NumPositions + Sign + 1;
                    FOR i := NumPositions + 1 TO FieldWidth DO
                       Write(' ')
                    END (* FOR *);

                    (* Print individual digits to the left of the decimal point *)
                    If Sign = 1 THEN
                       Write ('−')
                    END (* IF *);
                    FOR i = 1 TO LeftDigits DO
                          Digit := TRUNC(RNum);
                          WriteCard(Digit, 1);
                          RNum := 10.0 * (RNum − FLOAT(Digit))
                    END (* FOR *);

                    (* Display the decimal point *)
                    Write('.');

                    (* Display digits to the right of decimal point *)
                    FOR i := 1 TO DecimalPlaces DO
                          Digit := TRUNC(RNum);
                          WriteCard(Digit, 1);
                          RNum := 10.0 * (RNum − FLOAT(Digit))
                    END (* FOR *)
                 END FWriteReal;

         PROCEDURE ReadBoole(VAR BooleVar : BOOLEAN);
```

(* Procedure to read the character string 'TRUE' or 'FALSE' and return the corresponding boolean value TRUE or FALSE for the boolean variable *BooleVar*. *ReadOkay* is set to TRUE if the read operation was successful, FALSE otherwise. *)

```
         VAR
             BooleStr : ARRAY [0..4] OF CHAR; (* character string read *)

         BEGIN
             ReadString(BooleStr);
             ReadOkay := Done;
             IF (BooleStr[0] = 'T') AND (BooleStr[1] = 'R') AND
                (BooleStr[2] = 'U') AND (BooleStr[3] = 'E') AND
                (BooleStr[4] = EOS) THEN
                BooleVar := TRUE
             ELSIF (BooleStr[0] = 'F') AND (BooleStr[1] = 'A') AND
                (BooleStr[2] = 'L') AND (BooleStr[3] = 'S') AND
                (BooleStr[4] = 'E') THEN
                BooleVar := FALSE
             ELSE
                WriteString(''*** Bad input -- not 'TRUE' or 'FALSE' ***'');
                WriteLn;
                ReadOkay := FALSE
             END (* IF *)
         END ReadBoole;

  PROCEDURE WriteBoole(BooleVar : BOOLEAN);
```

(* Procedure to write the character string 'TRUE' or 'FALSE' corresponding to the boolean value TRUE or FALSE of the boolean variable *BooleVar*. *)

```
BEGIN
  IF BooleVar THEN
    WriteString('TRUE')
  ELSE
    WriteString('FALSE')
  END (* IF *)
END WriteBoole;
```

PROCEDURE *ReadAString* (VAR *Str* : ARRAY OF CHAR);

(* Procedure to read characters into string variable *Str* until an end of line
is encountered or the array is filled. If the array is not filled with input
characters, the null character 0C is stored in the array after the last character
read and serves as an end-of-string character. *ReadOkay* is set to TRUE if a
string was read successfully, FALSE otherwise. *)

```
VAR
  MaxIndex,        (* Maximum index in array Str *)
  i : CARDINAL; (* index *)
  Ch : CHAR;       (* current input character *)
BEGIN
  i := 0;
  MaxIndex := HIGH(Str);
  Read(Ch);
  WHILE Ch # EOL DO
    IF i <= MaxIndex THEN
      Str[i] := Ch;
      INC(i)
    END (* IF *);
    Read(Ch)
  END (* WHILE *);
  ReadOkay := Done;
  IF i < MaxIndex THEN
    Str[i] := 0C
  END (* IF *)
END ReadAString;
```

PROCEDURE *ReadBlock(InFile* : *File*; VAR *Block* : ARRAY OF WORD);

(* Procedure to read a *Block* of words from *InFile* *)

```
VAR
  i : CARDINAL; (* index *)
BEGIN
  FOR i := 0 TO HIGH(Block) DO
    ReadWord(InFile, Block[i])
  END (* FOR *)
END ReadBlock;
```

PROCEDURE *WriteBlock(OutFile* : *File*; *Block* : ARRAY OF WORD);

(* Procedure to write a *Block* of words at the end of *OutFile* *)

```
VAR
  i : CARDINAL; (* index *)
BEGIN
  FOR i := 0 TO HIGH(Block) DO
    WriteWord(OutFile, Block[i])
  END (* FOR *)
END WriteBlock;
```

END *SpecialInOut*.

StringsLib

DEFINITION MODULE *StringsLib*;

(* Library module of string processing procedures. If a string variable intended to store the result of a string operation is not large enough, the rightmost characters are truncated. *)

PROCEDURE *Length*(*Str* : ARRAY OF CHAR) : CARDINAL;

(* This function procedure returns the number of characters in string *Str* excluding the end-of-string character 0C if it is present. *)

PROCEDURE *Concat*(*Str1, Str2* : ARRAY OF CHAR;
                    VAR *Str* : ARRAY OF CHAR);

(* Returns the string *Str* obtained by concatenating *Str2* onto the end of *Str1*. *)

PROCEDURE *Copy*(*Str* : ARRAY OF CHAR;
                   Index, Size : CARDINAL;
               VAR *Substr* : ARRAY OF CHAR);

(* Returns the substring *Substr* of the specified *Size* from string *Str*, beginning at position *Index*. *)

PROCEDURE *Position*(*Str1, Str2* : ARRAY OF CHAR) : CARDINAL;

(* Returns the position of the first character of the first occurrence of string *Str1* within the string *Str2* or 1 + HIGH(*Str2*) if *Str1* is not found in *Str2*. *)

PROCEDURE *Insert*(*Str1* : ARRAY OF CHAR;
                    Index : CARDINAL;
                VAR *Str2* : ARRAY OF CHAR);

(* Modifies string *Str2* by inserting the string *Str1* at position *Index*. *)

PROCEDURE *Delete*(VAR *Str1* : ARRAY OF CHAR;
                   Index, Size : CARDINAL);

(* Modifies string *Str2* by removing a substring of the specified *Size,* starting at position *Index*. *)

PROCEDURE *Assign*(*Str1* : ARRAY OF CHAR;
                    VAR *Str2* : ARRAY OF CHAR);

(* Assigns *Str1* to *Str2*; i.e., implements *Str2* := *Str1* *)

PROCEDURE *Compare*(*Str1, Str2* : ARRAY OF CHAR) : INTEGER;

(* Returns −1, 0, or 1 according to whether *Str1* is less than *Str2*, *Str1* is equal to *Str2*, or *Str1* is greater than *Str2*. *)

END *StringsLib*.

IMPLEMENTATION MODULE *StringsLib*;

(* Library module of string processing procedures. If a string variable intended to store the result of a string operation is not large enough, the rightmost characters are truncated. *)

FROM *InOut* IMPORT *WriteString, WriteLn*;

PROCEDURE *Length*(*Str* : ARRAY OF CHAR) : CARDINAL;

(* This function procedure returns the number of characters in string *Str* excluding the end-of-string character 0C if it is present. *)

CONST
  EOS = 0C;   (* end-of-string character *)

```
VAR
  MaxIndex,              (* maximum index in Str *)
  i : CARDINAL;          (* index *)

BEGIN
  i := 0;
  MaxIndex := HIGH(Str);
  WHILE (i <= MaxIndex) AND (Str[i] # EOS) DO
    INC(i)
  END (* WHILE *);
  RETURN i
END Length;

PROCEDURE Concat(     Str1, Str2 : ARRAY OF CHAR;
                  VAR Str : ARRAY OF CHAR);
```

(* Returns the string *Str* obtained by concatenating *Str2* onto the end of *Str1*. *)

```
CONST
  EOS = 0C;             (* end-of-string mark *)

VAR
  Max1, Max2, Max,      (* maximum indices in Str1, Str2, Str *)
  i, j : CARDINAL;      (* indices *)

BEGIN
  Max1 := HIGH(Str1);
  Max2 := HIGH(Str2);
  Max := HIGH(Str);
  (* Copy Str1 to Str *)
  i := 0;
  WHILE (i <= Max1) AND (i <= Max) AND (Str1[i] # EOS) DO
    Str[i] := Str1[i];
    INC(i)
  END (* WHILE *);
```

(* Copy as many characters of *Str2* into the last positions of *Str* as will fit *)

```
  j := 0;
  WHILE (j <= Max2) AND (i <= Max) AND (Str2[j] # EOS) DO
    Str[i] := Str2[j];
    INC(j);
    INC(i)
  END (* WHILE *);
```

(* Add end-of-string mark to *Str* if there is room *)

```
  IF i <= Max THEN
    Str[i] := EOS
  END (* IF *)
END Concat;

PROCEDURE Copy(     Str : ARRAY OF CHAR;
                    Index, Size : CARDINAL;
                VAR Substr : ARRAY OF CHAR);
```

(* Returns the substring *Substr* of the specified *Size* from string *Str*, beginning at position *Index*. *)

```
CONST
  EOS = 0C;

VAR
  Last,                 (* position of last character to copy *)
  i : CARDINAL;         (* index *)
```

```
BEGIN
  IF Size = 0 THEN        (* empty substring *)
    SubStr[0] := 0C;
    RETURN
  ELSE
    Last := Index + Size − 1
    IF Last <= HIGH(Str) THEN
      FOR i := 0 TO Last DO
        Substr[i] := Str[Index + i]
      END (* FOR *)
    ELSE
      WriteString('*** Index out of range ***'); WriteLn;
      RETURN
    END (* IF *);
    IF Last < HIGH(Str) THEN
      Substr[Last + 1] := EOS
    END (* IF *)
  END (* IF *)
END Copy;

PROCEDURE Position(Str1, Str2 : ARRAY OF CHAR) : CARDINAL;
```

(* Returns the position of the first character of the first occurrence of string *Str1*
within the string *Str2* or 1 + HIGH(*Str2*) if *Str1* is not found in *Str2*. *)

```
VAR
  Len1,                  (* length of Str1 *)
  Len2,                  (* length of Str2 *)
  i, j,                  (* indices running through Str1, Str2 *)
  Index : CARDINAL;      (* index of Str1 in Str2 *)

BEGIN
  Len1 := Length(Str1);
  Len2 := Length(Str2);
  (* First take care of special case *)
  If Len1 > Len2 THEN (* Str1 longer than Str2 *)
    RETURN 1 + HIGH(Str2)
  END (* IF *);

  (* Otherwise, use brute-force approach to find the index *)
  i := 0;
  j := 0;
  Index := 0;
  WHILE (i < Len1) AND (j < Len2) DO
    IF (Str1[i] = Str2[j]) THEN   (* continue searching *)
      INC(i);
      INC(j)
    ELSE       (* backtrack and start over at next position in Str2 *)
      INC(Index);
      j := Index;
      i := 0
    END (* IF *)
  END (* WHILE *);
  IF (Len1 = 0) OR (i = Len1) THEN   (* Str1 found in Str1 *)
    RETURN Index
  ELSE
    RETURN 1 + HIGH(Str2)
  END (* IF *)
END Position;
```

```
PROCEDURE Insert(      Str1 : ARRAY OF CHAR;
                       Index : CARDINAL;
                   VAR Str2 : ARRAY OF CHAR);
```

(* Modifies string *Str2* by inserting the string *Str1* at position *Index*. *)

```
CONST
  EOS = 0C;

VAR
  Temp : ARRAY[0..255] OF CHAR;    (* temporary string *)
  i,                               (* index *)
  Len : CARDINAL;                  (* length of Str2 *)

BEGIN
  Len := Length(Str2);
  Copy(Str2, Index, Len − Index, Temp);
  Str2[Index] := 0C;
  Concat(Str2, Str1, Str1);
  Concat(Str1, Temp, Str2)
END Insert;
```

```
PROCEDURE Delete(VAR Str : ARRAY OF CHAR;
                     Index, Size : CARDINAL);
```

(* Modifies string *Str* by removing a substring of the specified *Size*, starting at position *Index*. *)

```
VAR
  i : CARDINAL;

BEGIN
  FOR i := Index TO Length(Str) DO
    Str[i] := Str[i + Size]
  END (* FOR *)
END Delete;
```

```
PROCEDURE Assign(      Str1 : ARRAY OF CHAR;
                   VAR Str2 : ARRAY OF CHAR);
```

(* Assigns *Str1* to *Str2*; i.e., implements *Str2* := *Str1* *)

```
  BEGIN
    Copy(Str1, 0, Length(Str2), Str2)
  END Assign;
```

```
PROCEDURE Compare(Str1, Str2 : ARRAY OF CHAR) : INTEGER;
```

(* Returns −1, 0, or 1 according to whether *Str1* is less than *Str2*, *Str1* is equal to *Str2*, or *Str1* is greater than *Str2*. *)

```
CONST
  EOS = 0C;                  (* end-of-string character *)

VAR
  MaxIndex1,                 (* maximum index for Str1 *)
  MaxIndex2,                 (* maximum index for Str2 *)
  i : CARDINAL;              (* index *)
  Ch1,                       (* character from Str1 *)
  Ch2 : CHAR;                (* character from Str2 *)
```

```
BEGIN
    MaxIndex1 := HIGH(Str1);
    MaxIndex2 := HIGH(Str2);
    i := 0;

    REPEAT
        (* Get next character from Str1 *)
        IF i > MaxIndex1 THEN
            Ch1 := EOS
        ELSE
            Ch1 := Str[i]
        END (* IF *);

        (* Get next character from Str2 *)
        IF i > MaxIndex2 THEN
            Ch2 := EOS
        ELSE
            Ch2 := Str2[i]
        END (* IF *);

        INC(i)
    UNTIL (Ch1 # Ch2) OR (Ch1 = EOS);

    IF Ch1 < Ch2 THEN
        RETURN -1
    ELSIF Ch1 > Ch2 THEN
        RETURN 1
    ELSE
        RETURN 0
    END (* IF *)
END Compare;

END StringsLib.
```

G

Answers to Selected Exercises

Section 0.7 (P. 37)

1. (a) CARDINAL, INTEGER
   (c) REAL
   (e) non (string type)
   (g) REAL
   (i) not a valid constant
   (k) not a valid constant
   (m) not a valid constant
   (o) not a valid constant
   (q) not a valid constant
   (s) not a valid constant
   (u) not a valid constant
   (w) not a valid constant
   (y) not a valid constant

2. (a) legal   (c) not legal
   (e) legal   (g) legal
   (i) not legal   (k) legal
   (m) legal   (o) legal

3. VAR
       Alpha, Beta : CARDINAL;
       Gamma : INTEGER;
       Code : CHAR;
       Root : REAL;
       RootExists : BOOLEAN;

4. (a) *WriteCard(Card1, 2);*
       WriteCard(Card2, 2);
       WriteInt(Num1, 3);
       WriteLn;
       Write(Ch);
       WriteInt(− Num2, 2);
       WriteLn;

   (c) *WriteString('Numbers are');*
       WriteInt(Num2, 4);

```
                    WriteString('and');
                    WriteInt(Num1, 4);
                    WriteLn;
```

5. (a) *ReadCard(Card1)*;
       ReadInt(Num1);
       ReadReal(RNum1);
       Read(Ch1);

       Input;
       12 567 1.234 E

   (c) *Read(Ch1)*;
       Read(Ch2);
       ReadReal(RNum1);
       ReadReal(RNum2);
       ReadInt(Num1);
       ReadInt(Num2);

       Input:
       E*1.234 5.6789 567 −89

6. MODULE *FinancialReport*;

   FROM *InOut* IMPORT *WriteString, ReadCard, WriteCard, WriteInt, WriteLn*;
   FROM *RealInOut* IMPORT *WriteReal*;

   CONST
       Year = 1990;
       InterestRate = 0.18;
       BankName = = ''People's Bank'';

   VAR
       AccountNumber,
       TransCode : CARDINAL;
       GainOrLoss : INTEGER;
       Transaction,
       Interest,
       Balance : REAL;

7. (a) *May*   (c) *Jul*   (e) *Dec*   (g) 5
   (i) *Jun*   (k) 3   (m) *Jul*   (o) 5

9. (a) IF *Distance* <= 100 THEN
           Cost := 5.00
       ELSIF (*Distance* <= 500) THEN
           Cost := 8.00
       ELSIF (*Distance* < 1000) THEN
           Cost := 10.00
       ELSE
           Cost := 12.00
       END (* IF *)

(b) CASE *Distance* OF

   0..100 : *Cost* := 5.00

      |

   101..500 : *Cost* := 8.00

       |

   501..999 : *Cost* := 10.00

    ELSE

      Cost := 12.00

  END (* CASE *)

10. (a) 0 0 0

    1 1 3

    2 2 6

    3 3 9

    12

 (c) 5 1 2 3###

    3 1###

    1***

11. PROCEDURE *GPA*(*Grade* : CHAR) : REAL;

  (* Returns the numeric equivalent of the letter *Grade* *)

  BEGIN

   CASE *Grade* OF

    'A' : RETURN 4.0

     |

    'B' : RETURN 3.0

     |

    'C' : RETURN 2.0

     |

    'D' : RETURN 1.0

     |

    'F' : RETURN 0.0

    ELSE

     WriteString('Illegal letter grade -- returning -1.0');

     RETURN -1.0

   END (* CASE *)

  END *GPA*;

Section 1.6 (P. 79)

13. *Row* := 0;

 Found := FALSE;

 WHILE NOT *Found* AND (*Row* < *n*) DO

  INC(*Row*);

  Col := 0;

```
WHILE NOT Found AND (Col < n) DO
   INC(Col);
   IF Mat[Row, Col] = Item THEN
      Found := TRUE
   END (* IF *)
 END (* WHILE *)
END (* WHILE *);
IF Found THEN
   WriteString('Item found');
   WriteLn
END (* IF *);
```

19. *I*: The input consists of a nonnegative integer *n*.

O: The procedure terminates and when it does, the value returned for the function *Factorial* is *n*!.

Anchor Step: If $n = 0$, then RETURN 1 is executed, and $0! = n! = 1$, so *O* is satisfied.

Induction Step: Now assume that for some cardinal number *k*, the procedure terminates for $n = k$ and returns the correct value *k*!. If $n = k + 1$, then the statement RETURN $n * Factorial(n - 1)$ is executed. So, the value returned for $Factorial(k + 1)$ is $(k + 1) * Factorial(k)$. By the induction hypothesis, the reference $Factorial(k)$ terminates and returns the value *k*!. Thus, $Factorial(k + 1) = (k + 1) * Factorial(k) = (k + 1) * k! = (k + 1)! = n!$, so *O* holds for $n = k + 1$.

Section 2.2 (P. 95)

1. (a) 128   (d) 1934   (g) 32769
2. (a) 16448   (d) -16385
3. (a) 16448   (d) -16383
4. (a) 4040   (d) Cannot be interpreted as a BCD integer.
5. (a) -16320 (d) 16385

6. (a) $0.501953125 * 2^{-16} \simeq -0.000007659$
   (d) $-0.5 * 2^{-15} \simeq -0.000015259$

7. (a) (i) true   (ii) FTFFFFFFFTFFFFFF
   (d) (i) true   (ii) TTFFFFFFFFFFFFFFT

8. (a) (i) @@   (ii) (blank blank)

9. (a) 209   (d) 4095

10. (a) 69   (d) 4095

11. (a) 11010001   (d) 111111111111

12. (a) 1000101   (d) 111111111111

13. (a) 52   (d) 777777

14. (a) 2A   (d) 3FFFF

15. (a) (i) 1100011   (ii) 143   (iii) 63

16. (a) (i) 0.1   (ii) 0.4   (iii) 0.8

17. (a) (i) $0.\overline{1001}$ (ii) $0.4\overline{631}$ (iii) $0.\overline{9}$

18. (a) 0000000001100011   (d) 1111111100000001

19. (a) (i) 0101000000010000   (d) (i) 0100000000001011
     (ii) same   (ii) same

20. (a)   B   E
     0100001001000101

   (d)   M   r   blank   D   o   e
     0100110101110010 0010111000100000 0100010001101111 01100101

Section 2.3 (P. 110)

1. (a) $A[4]$ is stored in words 106 and 107.   (c) $A[4]$ is stored in byte 1 of word 102.

2. (a) $A[i]$ is stored in words $b + 2*(i - 1)$ and $b + 2*(i - 1) + 1$.

3. (a) $M[0,9]$ is stored in words 116 and 117.   (c) $M['F',1]$ is stored in words 150 and 151.

4. (a) $M[0,9]$ is stored in words 164 and 165.   (c) $M['F',1]$ is stored in words 110 and 111.

6. $M[i, j] = \text{Base}(M) + [(i - l_1) + (j - l_2) n]\, w$,
   where $n = u_1 - l_1 + 1$.

10. $M[i, j] = b + [((i - 1)i/2) + (j - 1)]\, w$

12. $M[i, j] = \text{base}(M) + 2i + j - 3$.

Section 2.4 (P. 132)

1. (b) *NameString* = ARRAY [0..20] OF CHAR;
     NumberString = ARRAY [0..11] OF CHAR;
     Color = (*blue, brown, green, other*);
     MaritalStatus = (*Married, Single*);
     Date = RECORD
              Month : [1..12];
              Day : [1..31];
              Year : [1900..2000]
        END;
     PersonalInfo = RECORD
              Name : *NameString*;
              Birthday : *Date*;
              Age : CARDINAL;
              Sex : CHAR;
              SocSecNumber : *NumberString*;
              Height, Weight : CARDINAL;
              EyeColor : *Color*;

```
                    CASE MarStat : MaritalStatus OF
                       Married : NumChildren : CARDINAL
                                    |
                          Single :
                       END (* CASE *)
                    END;

(d)  DateRecord = RECORD
                       Month : [1..12];
                       Day : [1..31];
                       Year : [1900..2000]
                    END;
        String = ARRAY [0..20] OF CHAR;
        Conditions = (Clear, PartlyCloudy, Cloudy, Stormy);
        StormType = (Snow, Rain, Hail);
        CloudType = (Cumulus, Stratus, Nimbus, Cirrus);
        WeatherRecord =
          RECORD
            Date : DateRecord;
            City, State, Country : String;
            CASE WeatherCond : Conditions OF
                    Clear : (* no info stored *)
                               |
                    Cloudy : CloudLevel : REAL;
                             Clouds : CloudType
                               |
            PartlyCloudy : PercentClouds : REAL
                               |
                Stormy : CASE Storm : StormType OF
                            Snow : Depth : REAL
                               |
                            Rain : Amount : REAL
                               |
                            Hail : Size : REAL
                         END (* CASE *)
            END (* CASE *)
          END;
```

4. (b)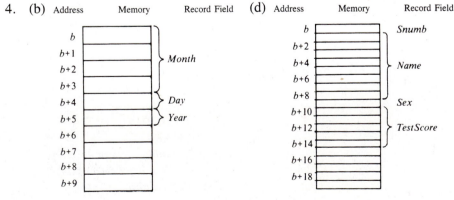

Section 2.5 (P. 147)

1. (a) {2, 4..7, 11}   (d) {8}   (g) {2, 4, 9, 11}
   (j) {9}   (m) { }   (p) {1..9, 11, 12}
   (s) {5, 7}   (v) {2, 4, 6, 11}   (y) { }

2. (a) TYPE
   SmallNumbers = [1..9];
   SmallIntegers = SET OF *SmallNumbers*;

3. (a) Declarations:

   CONST
   N = ...;

   TYPE
   SetOfNumbers = SET OF [1..N];

   VAR
   Evens, Odd : *SetOfNumbers*;
   Number : CARDINAL;

   Statements:

   Evens := *SetOfNumbers*{ };
   FOR *Number* := 2 TO N BY 2 DO
       INCL(*Evens, Number*)
   END (* FOR *);
   Odd := *SetOfNumbers*{1..N} − *Evens*;

   (d) Declarations:

   CONST
   N = . . .;

   TYPE
   SetOfNumbers = SET OF [1..N];

   VAR
   LargeEvenPrimes : *SetOfNumbers*;

   Statements:

   LargeEvenPrimes := *SetOfNumbers*{ };

17. (a) 0101010101010101
    (d) 0111010101010101
    (g) 0000000000000000

18. (a) 100001100000
    (d) 111111111111

Section 2.6 (P. 162)

7. (a) One method of representation is to let $S[0]$ correspond to 0.0, $S[1]$ to
   0.1, . . . , $S[10]$ to 1.0, . . . , $S[100]$ to 10.0. Then set $S[30]$,
   $S[31]$, . . . , $S[40]$ to TRUE, all others to FALSE.

Section 3.2 (P. 183)

1. (a) PROCEDURE *Length*(*Str* : *String*) : CARDINAL;

    VAR
       i : INTEGER;

    BEGIN
       i := *StringLimit*;
       WHILE (*i* >= 0) AND (*Str*[*i*] = ' ') DO
          DEC(*i*)
       END (* WHILE *);
       RETURN *i* + 1
    END *Length*;

    (b) PROCEDURE *ReadAString*(VAR *Str* : *String*;
                                          StringLimit : CARDINAL);

    VAR
       i : CARDINAL;
       NextChar : CHAR;

    BEGIN
       Read(*NextChar*);
       FOR *i* := 0 TO *StringLimit* DO
          IF *NextChar* # EOL THEN
             Str[*i*] := *NextChar*;
             Read(*NextChar*)
          ELSE
             Str[*i*] := ' '
          END (* IF *)
       END (* FOR *)
    END *ReadAString*;

2. (a) PROCEDURE *Length*(*Str* : *String*) : CARDINAL;

    BEGIN
       RETURN ORD(*Str*[0])
    END *Length*;

    (b) PROCEDURE *ReadAString*(VAR *Str* : *String*;
                                          StringLimit : CARDINAL);

```
        VAR
          i : CARDINAL;
          NextChar : CHAR;

        BEGIN
          Read(NextChar);
          i := 0;
          WHILE (i < StringLimit) AND (NextChar # EOL) DO
            INC(i);
            Str[i] := NextChar;
            Read(NextChar)
          END (* WHILE *);
          Str[0] := CHR(i)
        END ReadAString;
```

9. (a) PROCEDURE *PrintString*(*S* : *String*);

```
        VAR
          i : CARDINAL;

        BEGIN
          FOR i := S.Start TO S.Start + S.Length − 1 DO
            Write(Storage[i])
          END (* FOR *)
        END PrintString;
```

Section 3.3 (P. 195)

3. (a) 0554 1486 2112
5. 0295.

Section 3.4 (P. 205)

1. (a) 0 1 1 0 2 0 2 0 1 1 0   (f) 0 1 0 1 3 0 2

2. (a)

Instruction	k	j	Next Value Computed
Initially	-1	0	$Next[0] = -1$
2a	-1	0	
2b	0	1	
2c	0	1	$Next[1] = 0$
2a	-1	1	
2b	0	2	
2c	0	2	$Next[2] = 0$
2a	-1	2	
2b	0	3	
2c	0	3	$Next[3] = -1$
2a	0	3	
2b	1	4	
2c	1	4	$Next[4] = 1$
2a	-1	4	
2b	0	5	
2c	0	5	$Next[5] = -1$
2a	0	5	
2b	1	6	
2c	1	6	$Next[6] = 1$
2a	-1	6	
2b	0	7	
2c	0	7	$Next[7] = -1$
2a	0	7	
2b	1	8	
2c	1	8	$Next[8] = 0$
2a	1	8	
2b	2	9	
2c	2	9	$Next[9] = 0$
2a	2	9	
2b	3	10	
2c	3	10	$Next[10] = -1$

Section 4.2 (P. 218)

1. (b) PROCEDURE *DumpStack*(VAR *Stack* : *StackType*;
                              VAR *Item* : *ElementType*);

   ```
   BEGIN
       WHILE NOT Empty(Stack) DO
           Pop(Stack, Item)
       END (* WHILE *)
   END DumpStack;
   ```

2. (a) 123, 132, 213, 231, and 321 are possible; 312 is not.

9. (a) The maze can be represented by a two-dimensional array of boolean elements, where a true element signifies a doorway and a false element signifies a wall.

Section 4.3 (P. 230)

1. (a) $-7.\overline{3}$ (d) 12.0   (g) 12.0   (j) 8.0

2. (a) $A \; B * C + D -$ (d) $A \; B \; C \; D + / +$
     (g) $A \; B - C - D - E -$

3. (a) $(A - (B + C)) * D$ (d) $((A + B) - C)/(D * E)$
     (g) $A/((B/C)/D)$

4. (a) (i) $- 15$ (iv) 15
     (b) (i) $A \; B \; C \sim + *$ (iii) $A \sim B \sim *$

5. (a) $A \; B$ AND C OR   (e) $A \; B = C \; D =$ OR

6. (a) $- + * A \; B \; C \; D$ (e) $/ + A \; B + C \; D$
                              (g) $- - - - A \; B \; C \; D \; E$

7. (a) -24.5 (d) -2.0 (g) 55.0

8. (a) $(A + B) * (C - D)$ (d) $A - (B - C) - D$
     (g) $(A * B + C) / (D - E)$

Section 5.1 (P. 241)

1. (a) $O(n^3)$

4. (a) $O(n)$ (d) $O(n^2)$

Section 5.3 (P. 258)

1. (b) $n * x$
2. (b) PROCEDURE $F(x :$ REAL$; n :$ CARDINAL$) :$ REAL;

       BEGIN
         RETURN FLOAT$(n) * x$
       END F;

3. (b) *I*: The input consists of real number x and cardinal number n.
     O: The procedure terminates and the value returned is $n * x$.

     Anchor: If $n = 0$, the statement RETURN 0 is executed and the pro-
     cedure thus terminates and returns the value for F of $0 = 0 * x =$
     $n * x$, for all x.

     Inductive Step: Now, assume for some $n = k$, the procedure terminates
     and returns the value $k * x$. Then, if $n = k + 1$, the statement
     RETURN $x + F(x, n - 1)$ is executed. The value of $n - 1$ is k,
     so by the induction hypothesis, the reference $F(x, n - 1)$ terminates

and returns the value $k * x$. Thus, F terminates and returns the value
$x + k * x = (k + 1) * x = n * x$. Thus, we have established that
$I \Rightarrow O$.

Section 5.4 (P. 272)

4. (a) $A * B$ (d) $(A * B) * C$

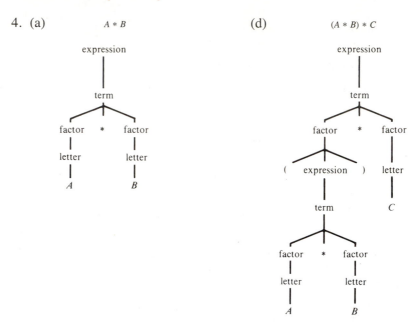

Active Procedure	Symbol	Pos	Valid	Action
Main program		0		Call *CheckForExpression*
CheckForExpression		0		Call *CheckForTerm*
CheckForTerm		0		Call *CheckForFactor*
CheckForFactor		0		Call *GetChar* to get next symbol
	A	1		*GetChar* increments *Pos* and returns
	A	1	TRUE	*Valid* set to true; return to *CheckForTerm*
CheckForTerm	A	1	TRUE	Call *GetChar* to get next symbol
	*	2		*GetChar* increments *Pos* and returns
	*	2	TRUE	Call *CheckForFactor*
CheckForFactor	*	2	TRUE	Call *GetChar* to get next symbol
	B	3		*GetChar* increments *Pos* and returns
	B	3	TRUE	*Valid* set to true; return to *CheckForExpression*
CheckForExpression	B	3	TRUE	Call *GetChar* to get next symbol
	$	4		*GetChar* increments *Pos* and returns
	$	3	TRUE	''Unget'' a character
Main program		3		

Section 6.2 (P. 286)

2. (a) PROCEDURE *DumpQueue*(VAR *Queue* : *QueueType*;
VAR *Item* : *ElementType*);

```
BEGIN
    WHILE NOT EmptyQ(Queue) DO
        RemoveQ(Queue, Item)
    END (* WHILE *)
END DumpQueue;
```

4. (a) 123, 132, 231, and 312 are possible; 321 is not.

5. (a) PROCEDURE *AddQ*(VAR *Queue* : *QueueType*;
Item : *ElementType*);

```
BEGIN
    WITH Queue DO
        IF Count = MaxSize THEN
            WriteString ('*** Attempt to insert in a full queue ***');
            HALT
        ELSE
            Element[Rear] := Item;
            Rear := (Rear + 1) MOD MaxSize;
            INC(Count)
        END (* IF *)
    END (* WITH *)
END AddQ;
```

(b) PROCEDURE *RemoveQ*(VAR *Queue* : *QueueType*;
Item : *ElementType*);

```
BEGIN
    IF EmptyQ(Queue) THEN
        WriteString ('*** Attempt to delete from an empty queue ***');
        HALT
    ELSE
        WITH Queue DO
            Item := Element[Front];
            Front := (Front + 1) MOD MaxSize;
            DEC(Count)
        END (* IF *)
    END (* WITH *)
END RemoveQ;
```

Section 7.1 (P. 301)

2. (a) PROCEDURE *Mean*(*List* : *ListType*; *NoValue* : *ElementType*) : REAL;

```
VAR
    Sum : REAL;
    Num : CARDINAL;
```

```
                    BEGIN
                      Sum := 0.0;
                      Num := 0;
                      FOR i := 1 TO MaxSize DO
                        IF List.Element[i] # NoValue THEN
                          INC(Num);
                          Sum := Sum + List.Element[i]
                        END (* IF *)
                      END (* FOR *);
                      IF Num # 0 THEN
                        RETURN Sum / FLOAT(Num)
                      ELSE
                        RETURN 0.0
                      END (* IF *)
                    END Mean;
```

3. (a) *PolyRec* = RECORD
                       Degree : CARDINAL;
                       Coeff : ARRAY[0..*MaxDegree*] OF *CoeffType*
                    END;

   (b) PROCEDURE *ReadInfo*(VAR *Poly* : *PolyRec*);

       VAR
          i : CARDINAL;

       BEGIN
          WriteString('Enter degree of this polynomial: ');
          WITH *Poly* DO
            ReadCard(*Degree*);
            WriteLn;
            WriteString('Enter the coefficients in ascending order: ');
            FOR *i* := 0 TO *Degree* DO
              WriteLn;
              WriteString('Enter coefficient of x$^{\wedge}$');
              WriteCard(*i*, 1);
              WriteString(': ');
              ReadReal(*Coeff*[*i*])   (* assuming real coefficients *)
            END (* FOR *)
          END (* WITH *)
       END *ReadInfo*;

Section 7.2 (P. 308)

1. Algorithm to count the nodes in a linked list:

   1. Set *Count* = 0 and *Ptr* = *List*.
   2. While *Ptr* <> nil, do the following:
      (a) Increment *Count*.
      (b) Set *Ptr* = *Next*(*Ptr*).

5. The complexity of the algorithm in Exercise 1 is $O(n)$ where n is the length of the list.

Section 7.3 (P. 317)

2.

Array Index	Data	Next
1	J	4
Free → 2	Z	7
3	C	6
4	P	0
List → 5	B	3
6	F	1
7	K	8
8	Q	9
9	?	10
10	?	0

6. (a) PROCEDURE *Length*(*List* : *LinkedList*) : CARDINAL;

  VAR
   Count : CARDINAL;
   Ptr : *ListPointer*;

  BEGIN
   Count := 0;
   Ptr := *List*;
   WHILE *Ptr* # 0 DO
    INC(*Count*);
    Ptr := *Node*[*Ptr*].*Next*
   END (* WHILE *);
   RETURN *Count*
  END *Length*;

(b) PROCEDURE *Length*(*List* : *LinkedList*) : CARDINAL;

  BEGIN
   IF *List* = 0 THEN
    RETURN 0
   ELSE
    RETURN 1 + *Length*(*Node*[*List*].*Next*)
  END *Length*;

Section 7.5 (P. 328)

1. (a) Values of pointer variables cannot be displayed.
 (c) Error: *P1* and *Q1* are not bound to the same type.

2. (a) 123 456
 (d) 12 34 34

3. (a)

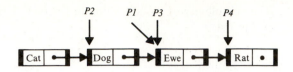

(d) Error occurs—$P4\uparrow.Next\uparrow.Data$ is undefined.

4. (a) PROCEDURE *Length*(*List* : *LinkedList*) : CARDINAL;

> VAR
> > *Count* : CARDINAL;
> > *Ptr* : *ListPointer*;
>
> BEGIN
> > *Count* := 0;
> > *Ptr* := *List*;
> > WHILE *Ptr* # NIL DO
> > > INC(*Count*);
> > > *Ptr* := *Ptr*↑.*Next*
> > END (* WHILE *);
> > RETURN *Count*
> END *Length*;

(c) PROCEDURE *Length*(*List* : *LinkedList*) : CARDINAL;

> BEGIN
> > IF *List* = NIL THEN
> > > RETURN 0
> > ELSE
> > > RETURN 1 + *Length*(*List*↑.*Next*)
> > END *Length*;

Section 8.2 (P. 362)

3. PROCEDURE *CreateQ*(VAR *Queue* : *QueueType*);

> BEGIN
> > *Queue.FrontPtr* := NIL;
> > *Queue.RearPtr* := NIL
> END *CreateQ*;

PROCEDURE *EmptyQ*(VAR *Queue* : *QueueType*) : BOOLEAN;

> BEGIN
> > RETURN *Queue.FrontPtr* = NIL
> END *EmptyQ*;

10. PROCEDURE *Create*(VAR *Clist* : *CircLinkedList*);

> BEGIN
> > ALLOCATE(*CList*, SIZE(*ListNode*));
> > *CList.Next* := *CList*
> END *Create*;

```
PROCEDURE Insert(VAR Clist : CircLinkedList;
                     PredPtr : ListPointer;
                     Item : ElementType);

    VAR
      TempPtr : ListPointer;

    BEGIN
      ALLOCATE(TempPtr, SIZE(ListNode));
      TempPtr↑.Data := Item;
      TempPtr↑.Next := PredPtr↑.Next;
      PredPtr↑.Next := TempPtr
    END Insert;
```

12.
```
    PROCEDURE AddQ(VAR CQueue : QueueType;
                       Item : ElementType);

    VAR
      TempPtr : QueuePointer;

    BEGIN
      ALLOCATE(TempPtr, SIZE(ListNode));
      TempPtr↑.Data := Item;
      IF CQueue = NIL THEN
        TempPtr↑.Next := TempPtr
      ELSE
        TempPtr↑.Next := CQueue↑.Next;
        CQueue↑.Next := TempPtr
      END (* IF *);
      CQueue := TempPtr
    END AddQ;
```

Section 8.3 (P. 370)

1. O(mn)

5.
```
    PROCEDURE CardinalNumber(A : SetType) : CARDINAL;

    VAR
      Count : CARDINAL;
      PtrA : SetPointer;

    BEGIN
      PtrA := A↑.Next;
      Count := 0;
      WHILE PtrA # NIL DO
        INC(Count);
        PtrA := PtrA↑.Next
      END (* WHILE *);
      RETURN Count
    END CardinalNumber;
```

Section 8.4 (P. 379)

2. (a) PROCEDURE *Length*(*S* : *String*) : CARDINAL;

    BEGIN
      RETURN *S.Length*
    END *Length*;

5. (a) PROCEDURE *Length*(*S* : *String*) : CARDINAL;

    VAR
      Ptr : *StringPointer*;
      Count : CARDINAL;

    BEGIN
      IF *S* = NIL THEN
        RETURN 0
      ELSE
        Ptr := *S↑.Next*;
        Count := 1;
        WHILE *Ptr* # *S* DO
          INC(*Count*);
          Ptr := *Ptr↑.Next*
        END (* WHILE *)
      END (* IF *)
      RETURN *Count*
    END *Length*;

Section 8.6 (P. 398)

1. (a) I   (e) *P1*

2. (b) *Ptr* := *P1*;
    Ptr↑.BLink↑.Data := 'M';
    Ptr↑.FLink↑.Data := 'S';

3. (b) Change first line in the answer for 2 to: *Ptr* := *P2↑.BLink↑.BLink*;

4. (a) B   (e) *P1*

5. (b) *Ptr* := *P1*;
    ALLOCATE (*TempPtr*, SIZE (*NodeType*));
    TempPtr↑.Data := 'L';
    TempPtr↑.BLink := *Ptr*;
    TempPtr↑.FLink := *Ptr↑.FLink*;
    Ptr↑.FLink := *TempPtr*;
    TempPtr↑.FLink↑.BLink := *TempPtr*;
    Ptr↑.FLink↑.FLink↑.Data := 'A';

6. (b) Change first line in the answer for 5 to: *Ptr* := *P2↑.FLink↑.FLink*;

Section 8.7 (P. 407)

2. (a)

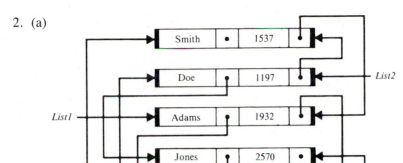

(b)

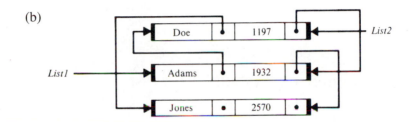

9. (a) TYPE
        ElementType = INTEGER;
        NodePointer = ↑*NodeType*;
        NodeType = RECORD
                        Col : CARDINAL;
                        Data : *ElementType*;
                        Next : *NodePointer*
                    END;
        RowArray = ARRAY [1..*MaxRows*] OF *NodePointer*;

   VAR
       A : *RowArray*;

16. (a)

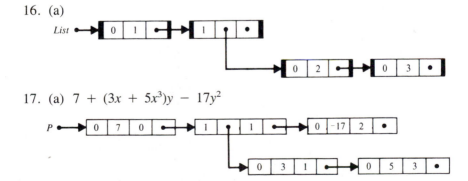

17. (a) $7 + (3x + 5x^3)y - 17y^2$

Section 9.1 (P. 414)

1. PROCEDURE *LinearSearch*(VAR *X* : *ListType*; *n* : CARDINAL;
                                             Item : *ElementType*;
                                             VAR *Found* : BOOLEAN;
                                             VAR *Loc* : CARDINAL);
     BEGIN
        Loc := 1;
        X[*n* + 1] := *Item*;
        WHILE *X*[*Loc*] # *Item* DO
           INC(*Loc*)
           END (* WHILE *);
           Found := (*Loc* <= *n*)
     END *LinearSearch*;

Section 9.2 (P. 426)

1. (a)   (b)

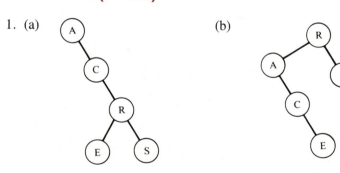

Section 9.3 (P. 438)

1. (a)

	Table
0	44
1	12
2	80
3	36
4	26
5	5
6	92
7	59
8	40
9	42
10	60

Section 10.2 (P. 459)

1. (c)

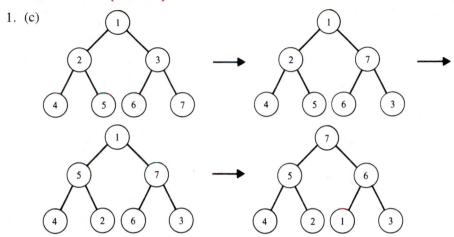

Section 10.3 (P. 467)

1. (b)

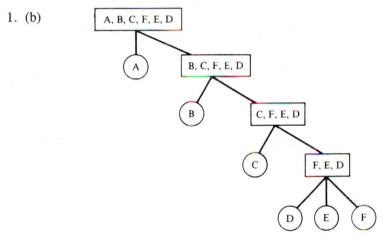

4. PROCEDURE *QuickSort* (VAR *X* : *List*; *Low, High* : CARDINAL);
   VAR
      Mid; CARDINAL;

   BEGIN
      Split (*X, Low, High, Mid*);
      IF *Mid* − *Low* < *LBound* THEN
         InsertionSort(*X, Low, Mid* − 1)
      ELSE
         QuickSort(*X, Low, Mid* − 1)
      END (* IF *);
      IF *High* − *Mid* < *LBound* THEN
         InsertionSort (*X, Mid* + 1, *High*)
      ELSE
         QuickSort (*X, Mid* + 1, *High*)
      END (* IF *)
   END *QuickSort*;

Section 11.3 (P. 499)

1. (a)

F	13 57 39 85 70 22 64 48

F1	13	39	70	64
F2	57	85	22	48

F	13 57 39 85 22 70 48 64

F1	13 57	22 70
F2	39 85	48 64

F	13 39 57 85 22 48 64 70

F1	13 39 57 85
F2	22 48 64 70

F	13 22 39 48 57 64 70 85

2. (a)

F	13 57 39 85 70 22 64 48

F1	13 57	70	48
F2	39 85	22 64

F	13 39 57 85 22 48 64 70

F1	13 57 70	48
F2	39 85	22 64

F	13 39 57 70 85 22 48 65

F1	13 39 57 70 85

F2	22 48 64

F	13 22 39 48 57 64 70 85

7. (a) Not stable.
    (e) Not stable.

Section 12.1 (P. 531)

2. (a) (i)

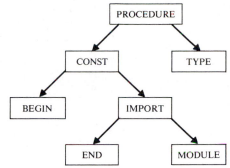

(b) Inorder: BEGIN, CONST, END, IMPORT, MODULE, PROCE-DURE, TYPE
Preorder: PROCEDURE, CONST, BEGIN, IMPORT, END, MOD-ULE, TYPE
Postorder: BEGIN, END, MODULE, IMPORT, CONST, TYPE, PROCEDURE

3. (a)

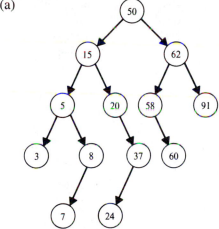

4. (a) 3, 5, 8, 15, 20, 24, 37, 50, 58, 60, 62, 91

5. (a) Preorder: $-$ $-$ A B C
Postorder: A B $-$ C $-$

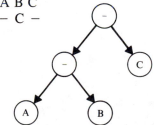

7. (i)

1	PROCEDURE
2	CONST
3	TYPE
4	BEGIN
5	IMPORT
6	
7	
8	
9	
10	END
11	MODULE
12	

8. (a)

1	–
2	–
3	C
4	A
5	B

Section 12.2 (P. 549)

1. (c)

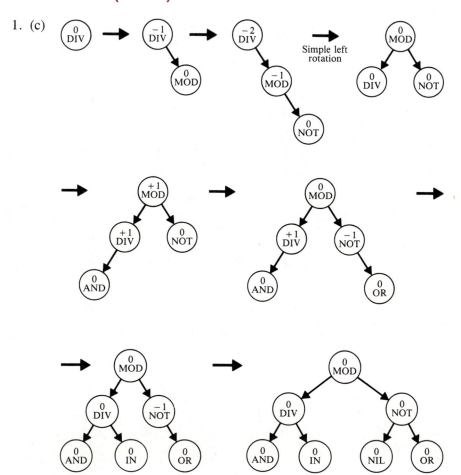

2. (a) The final AVL tree is:

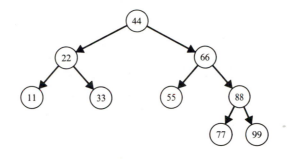

Section 12.3 (P. 554)

1. (b)

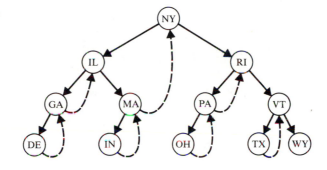

2. (b)

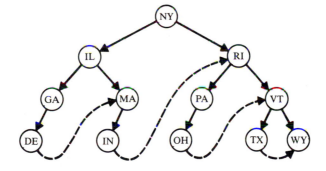

10. (b)

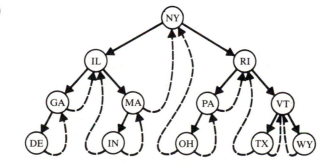

Section 12.4 (P. 567)

2. (a) BAD   (c) CAD

3. Note: other answers than the one given here are possible.

BEGIN	10
END	11
FOR	000
IF	01
WHILE	001

Section 12.5 (P. 578)

2.

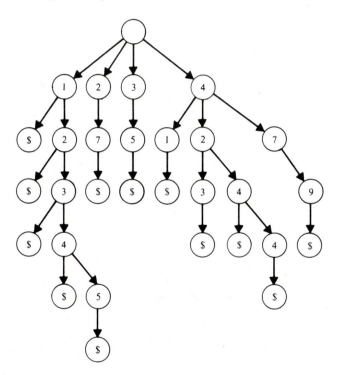

5. (a)

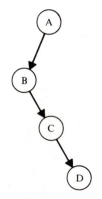

Section 13.2 (P. 596)

1. (a)

$$Adj. \begin{bmatrix} 0 & 1 & 1 & 1 & 1 \\ 0 & 1 & 1 & 0 & 0 \\ 0 & 0 & 0 & 1 & 0 \\ 0 & 0 & 0 & 1 & 1 \\ 0 & 1 & 0 & 0 & 0 \end{bmatrix} \; Data: \begin{bmatrix} A \\ B \\ C \\ D \\ E \end{bmatrix}$$

3. (a)

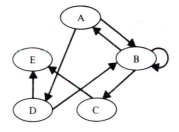

4. (a)

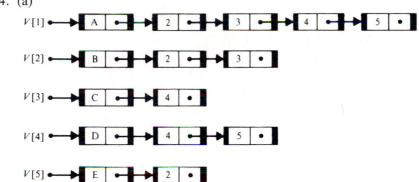

6. (a)

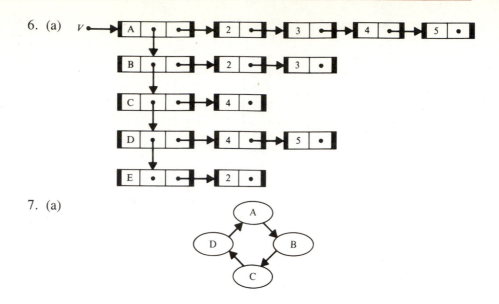

7. (a)

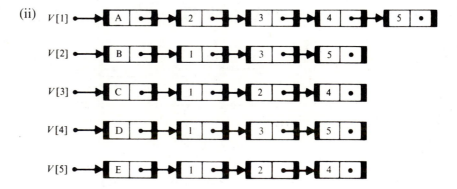

Section 13.3 (P. 607)

1. (a) (i)

$$
Adj: \begin{bmatrix} 0 & 1 & 1 & 1 & 1 \\ 1 & 0 & 1 & 0 & 1 \\ 1 & 1 & 0 & 1 & 0 \\ 1 & 0 & 1 & 0 & 1 \\ 1 & 1 & 0 & 1 & 0 \end{bmatrix} \quad Data: \begin{bmatrix} A \\ B \\ C \\ D \\ E \end{bmatrix}
$$

(ii)

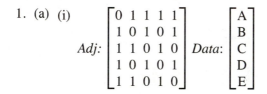

(iii)

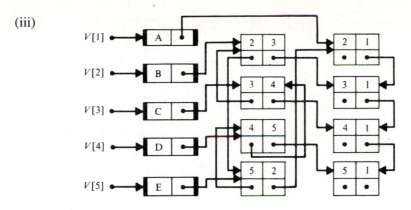

3. (a)

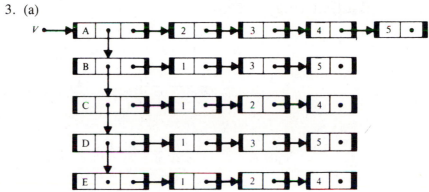

4. (a)

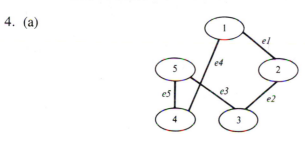

5. (a)

6. (a)

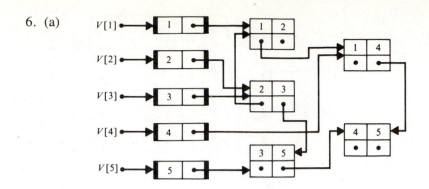

Section 14.2 (P. 638)

1. (a)

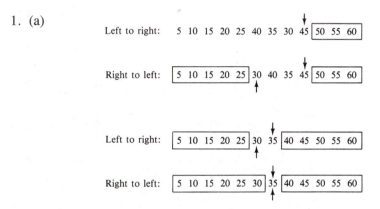

2. (c) Output:

```
     1
     2
    11
    22
   111
*** Done processing ***
```

INDEX